REVOLUTIONS AESTHETIC

Stanford Studies *in* Middle Eastern *and* Islamic Societies *and* Cultures

REVOLUTIONS AESTHETIC

A Cultural History of Baʿthist Syria

Max Weiss

STANFORD UNIVERSITY PRESS
Stanford, California

Stanford University Press
Stanford, California

Printed in the United States of America on acid-free, archival-quality paper

Library of Congress Cataloging-in-Publication Data

Names: Weiss, Max, 1977- author.
Title: Revolutions aesthetic : a cultural history of Ba'thist Syria / Max Weiss.
Other titles: Stanford studies in Middle Eastern and Islamic societies and cultures.
Description: Stanford, California : Stanford University Press, [2022] | Series: Stanford Studies in Middle Eastern and Islamic societies and cultures | Includes bibliographical references and index.
Identifiers: LCCN 2022004392 (print) | LCCN 2022004393 (ebook) | ISBN 9781503630581 (cloth) | ISBN 9781503631953 (paperback) | ISBN 9781503631960 (ebook)
Subjects: LCSH: Politics and culture—Syria—History. | Syria—Cultural policy. | Syria—Intellectual life—20th century. | Syria—Intellectual life—21st century. | Syria—Politics and government—1971-2000. | Syria—Politics and government—2000-
Classification: LCC DS94.6 .W447 2022 (print) | LCC DS94.6 (ebook) | DDC 956.9104/2—dc23/eng/20220217
LC record available at https://lccn.loc.gov/2022004392
LC ebook record available at https://lccn.loc.gov/2022004393

Cover design: Angela Moody
Cover image: Nihad Al Turk, *Sacred Tree*, 120cm X 140 cm. Acrylic on canvas, 2013.
Typeset by Newgen in Brill Roman 10.5/14.4

For Mom and Dad

Contents

Note on Transliteration and Translation ix

Introduction: Aesthetics and Politics in Contemporary Syria 1

1 Baʿthist Cultural Revolution 40

2 Men of Commitment 84

3 The Funny Thing About Dictatorship 134

4 Reading Writing Mukhabarat 181

5 The Slow Witness 227

6 Faces of Death 268

Conclusion: The Art of the Real 314

Acknowledgments 343

Notes 349

Index 417

Note on Transliteration and Translation

Arabic terms have been transliterated primarily in accordance with *International Journal of Middle East Studies* (*IJMES*) guidelines. However, I have opted to retain all diacritical markings throughout, including for some proper names and places. Names of individuals are spelled according to their preferred or commonly used English or French version (e.g., Hafiz al-Asad, not Ḥāfiẓ al-Asad, Bashar al-Asad, not Bashshār al-Asad).

All translations are my own, unless otherwise indicated.

REVOLUTIONS AESTHETIC

Introduction

AESTHETICS AND POLITICS IN CONTEMPORARY SYRIA

The revolution works in the new stage for the formation of a culture that aims at facilitating the mission of the revolution in construction, establishing the progressive national outlook among the ranks of the people and helping all other people in their struggle against backwardness and imperialism. . . . In doing this the state takes recourse to various means of spreading forms of culture, such as writing, translation, the theatre and cinemas, and all other arts.

—Regional Congress of the Arab Baath Socialist Party, *Program of the March 8th Revolution* (1965)[1]

It almost seems that the word "revolution" itself possesses such revolutionary power that it continually broadens itself to include every last element on our globe. . . . What is there in the world that could not be revolutionized—and what is there in our time that is not open to revolutionary effects?

—Reinhart Koselleck, "Historical Criteria of the Modern Concept of Revolution"[2]

the word "freedom" in my language
takes the shape of an electric chair.

—Muhammad al-Maghut, "After Long Thinking"[3]

REVOLUTIONS AESTHETIC IS A CRITICAL-HISTORICAL STUDY OF aesthetics, politics, and cultural production in Syria during the late twentieth and early twenty-first centuries, one that places literature and cinema at the center of the story. Historical scholarship dealing with this period tends to focus on politics, war, and socioeconomic transformation. By contrast, this book draws on rich sources that have gone neglected or underappreciated by historians and other scholars—novels, films, and cultural periodicals—in order to throw new light on the historical evolution of Syrian state, society, and culture. Some of these materials were produced under state auspices; others were made independently. Either way, Syrian art and culture have had a complicated relationship with the state and the political. *Revolutions Aesthetic* takes as its object certain dimensions of the cultural universe of the Baʿthist regime, nominally in power in Syria since March 8, 1963 and then fundamentally transformed with the coming to power of Hafiz al-Asad (1930–2000) through the November 1970 "corrective movement" (*al-ḥaraka al-taṣḥīḥiyya*). In addition to launching myriad economic, social, political, and military initiatives, this regime also embarked on a project I refer to as *Asadist-Baʿthist cultural revolution*, which ought to be apprehended as a "problematic and therefore potentially productive concept."[4] In my use of the term, Asadist-Baʿthist cultural revolution entailed the conceptualization, dissemination, and (often haphazard) implementation of a new aesthetic ideology, one that drew on existing modes of artistic engagement while also charting new directions for Syrian, pan-Arab, and Third Worldist cultural and intellectual life. State institutions and regime elites were enlisted to reshape Syrian culture through an aesthetics of power that hinged on communicative languages that I characterize as *speaking-to* and *speaking-for*. Despite the substantial efforts dedicated to state- and nation-building, the Syrian regime could never completely capture the cultural and intellectual fields. Competing artistic visions, comprehensible in terms of the aesthetics of resistance and the aesthetics of solidarity, were articulated respectively through what I term *speaking-against* and *speaking-with* and therefore coexisted with regime power and state culture in uneasy but sometimes unexpectedly untroubled ways. I elaborate on these concepts and categories at greater length here.

The title of the book—*Revolutions Aesthetic*—rhymes, imperfectly, with other concepts: "revolutionary aesthetics," "revolution's aesthetic," "aesthetic revolutions." While I am interested in all of them, none precisely captures or conveys the range of interpretive possibilities for understanding the relationship between aesthetics and politics in contemporary Syria. *Revolutions Aesthetic* sees works of literature and film as sites of agonistic struggle over aesthetic ideology. Thereby, I hope, it fundamentally recasts the cultural and intellectual history of contemporary Syria. The tangled histories of state power, ideological refashioning, technocratic reform, and social transformation can be understood through this evolving, dialectical relationship between aesthetics and politics. If the aesthetic ideology of Asadist-Baʿthist cultural revolution supported the wider aims of a revolutionary Arab nationalist agenda—the struggle to liberate the peoples of the Arabic-speaking world from Zionism, imperialism, economic "backwardness," and cultural malaise—its exponents seemed untroubled by the consolidation of a cult of personality around Hafiz al-Asad and the concomitant solidification of an authoritarian security state under his rule and that of his son Bashar, who succeeded him in 2000 as a consensus replacement acceptable to the most influential elements in the ruling apparatus. Despite gestures toward the conceptual foundations of Baʿthist Arab nationalism—the ongoing and comprehensive reordering of society as part of Arab nationalist "resurrection" (*al-baʿth*) and nods to the venerable slogan "Liberty, [Arab] Unity, Socialism" (*ḥurriyya, waḥda, ishtirākiyya*)—the aesthetic ideology of Asadist-Baʿthist cultural revolution during the late twentieth century entailed, however implicitly, the disavowal of early Baʿthists, including most importantly Michel ʿAflaq (1910–1989), cofounder of the Baʿth Party during the early 1930s. This ideological and personal falling out with ʿAflaq and all that he stood for was defined as much by the political-economic orientation of the new regime in its sputtering progress toward liberalization and détente with the capitalist West as it was by internal party factionalism. In place of that vanguardist pan-Arab nationalism with its Marxist or Marxisant tinges, the Asadist-Baʿthist cultural revolution was oriented otherwise: promoting Syrian nationalism as an iteration of pan-Arab nationalism; foregrounding the inspirational powers of a heroic leader and muscular leadership generally; and constructing an aesthetics of power that resonated with the signature style of al-Asad's political rule. Salah al-Din al-Bitar (1912–1980), cofounder with ʿAflaq of the Baʿth Party, adhered more stringently to a left political project typically identified with the so-called Neo-Baʿth that seized power in February 1966, even though he served multiple terms as prime minister between 1963 and 1966. And while al-Bitar clashed with the program of the Asadist-Baʿthists associated with the corrective movement—he was shot to death in Paris in July 1980 in an assassination reported to have been ordered by the Syrian regime—he shared their views that revolution in Syria should not be exclusively political or political-economic in nature. "In the Baathist system," wrote al-Bitar, "the Arab revolution is not only a social, economic and even national revolution, but a total revolution; or, to employ a modern term, a 'cultural' revolution, in which the first aim is to restore Arab unity and personality."[5]

The revamped aesthetics of power attributable to the Asadist-Baʿthist cultural revolution promoted specific visions of heroism, masculinity, virtuous leadership, pan-Arab unity, state sovereignty, cultural patriotism, and political commitment. State-affiliated institutions such as the National Film Organization (al-Muʾassasa al-ʿĀmma li-l-Sīnamā, NFO) and the Arab Writers' Union (Ittiḥād al-Kuttāb al-ʿArab, AWU) were authorized to advocate for robust literary, cinematic, and cultural engagement at a time of regional military antagonism, domestic and international sectarian conflict, and economic crisis. The intellectual shift from what I have elsewhere called the "ʿAflaqism" of the mid-twentieth century to what can be thought of as the "Asadism" of the late twentieth century therefore constituted a sort of epistemic cultural revolution in its own right.[6] Over the course of this period, the Baʿth Party—along with the military, the domestic security services, and the government bureaucracy—was instrumentalized in reshaping the institutional and political landscape of the country in a way that also transformed Baʿthism itself. Once a vanguardist Arab nationalist party with aspirations of becoming a mass political movement, the Baʿth hardened into one core component of a corporatist state anchored by pragmatic bargains with delineated sectors of national society rather than a revolutionary leadership pursuing more idealistic commitments. Given the parallels and overlaps between the political and aesthetic dimensions of this transformation, Syrian cultural and intellectual history can be profitably interwoven with scholarship on politics, military affairs, and social dynamics. I stage this encounter through, for example, a discussion of the intellectual dimensions of Syrian military history in the 1960s through the 1980s (Chapter 1); and a cultural analysis of the security state as reflected in literature and film produced during the early 2000s (Chapter 4).

Strictly speaking, there has not yet been a concerted effort to write concept histories of "revolution" in Syria or the broader Arab world. Nevertheless, a historical-linguistic analysis of "revolution"—through the *Begriffsgeschichte* associated with Reinhart Koselleck—might be a fruitful avenue for inquiry by intellectual historians of the modern Middle East.[7] To the extent that "revolution" animated and addled Syrian intellectuals, artists, and bureaucrats—from Asadist-Baʿthist cultural revolutionaries of the 1970s and 1980s and subsequent keepers of the regime's "revolutionary" flame during the 1990s and early 2000s to activists and artists who took up an altogether different revolutionary project to topple the Syrian regime in 2011—these discursive formations were articulated in the midst of a historical struggle around aesthetic ideology, one that I argue needs to be understood in relation to both political and cultural analysis. *Revolutions Aesthetic* draws these threads together in a cultural and intellectual history of literature and film in Baʿthist Syria that speaks across distinct fields of scholarly inquiry rarely placed within the same frame. The sections that follow address conceptual and methodological challenges for these three corners of Syrian studies—political science, modern Middle East cultural and intellectual history, and aesthetic theory—while the remainder of the Introduction is given to a thumbnail sketch of modern Syrian history.

THE TYRANNY OF THE POLITICAL

Political scientists and historians have offered various explanations as to how crucial clientelist power sharing predicated on kinship bonds, sectarian affiliation, and other loyalties was to the al-Asad regime's consolidation of a robust authoritarian-populist rule. The struggle around aesthetic ideology in Syria can therefore also be read against the backdrop of a persistent scholarly debate in which some have argued that the autocratic government that developed over the course of the late twentieth century in Syria amounted to totalitarianism. In this view, the totalizing power of the ruling military clique—often misrepresented simply as a sectarian "ʿAlawī regime"—coalesced into a seamless military, institutional, and ideological unity.[8] Political theorist Michael Walzer, for example, adheres to a hard line of muscular liberalism by arguing that the distinction between authoritarianism and totalitarianism "is hard to draw . . . and to insist upon its central importance doesn't serve any useful political or moral purpose. More accurately, that insistence serves a repugnant purpose: it provides an apologia for authoritarian politics."[9] In other words, if one wishes to stage a comparison of authoritarianism and totalitarianism—no matter how subtle or nuanced—one automatically becomes an apologist for both. This is more polemic than scholarly reasoning. Slavoj Žižek rejects the impoverished thinking of Walzer, the ideologue Paul Berman, and their ilk, dispatching the idea of totalitarianism, which,

> far from being an effective theoretical concept, is a kind of *stopgap*: instead of enabling us to think, forcing us to acquire a new insight into the historical reality it describes, it relieves us of the duty to think, or even actively *prevents* us from thinking.[10]

Scholars must be rigorous in their consideration of the totalitarian and careful not to casually apply the label to every historical context where freedom is restricted, surveillance is widespread, and room for maneuvering in political and cultural terms is limited—all of which are apt descriptions of life in Ba'thist Syria. We need not look any further than Hannah Arendt, the signature theorist of totalitarianism, to find intellectual resources that help dispel the notion that the Syrian dictatorship that grew up during the post-1970 period should be described in such terms. For Arendt, the "most conspicuous external characteristic" of totalitarian movements

> is their demand for total, unrestricted, unconditional, and unalterable loyalty of the individual member. This demand is made by the leaders of totalitarian movements even before they seize power. It usually precedes the total organization of the country under their actual rule and it follows from the claim of their ideologies that their organization will encompass, in due course, the entire human race.[11]

Even the pervasive cult of personality surrounding the leader would not seem to rise to Arendt's conceptualization of the phenomenon. Ironically, the sacralization of Hafiz al-Asad in cultish discourse suggests that he did not depend so much on the "will" of the masses as on their adoration and worship in light of his divine or superhuman attributes, a phenomenon discernible not only in political and public life but also in the world of culture and ideas. This is a theme I take up at greater length in Chapter 1.

In her study of the General Union of Syrian Women (created in 1967), an instructive example of the regime's corporatist approach to managing society, Esther Meininghaus describes Syria under the Ba'th as an iteration of "*imperfect totalitarianism*." Despite her often compelling interpretation of political rule,

Meininghaus perhaps unwittingly points up the limitations of totalitarianism as a category of analysis in this context.[12] Baʿthist ideology is totalitarian, she says, because it "represents a more or less elaborated set of utopian ideas that is original and serves as a source of legitimisation for the ruling individual or group" and the regime itself is totalitarian "in the sense that it claims to create a new society, thus not only reforming the system but also re-educating all those living within this system."[13] Rather than quibble over the lineaments of some imagined totalitarianism that might qualify as *perfect*, however, it might be more useful to learn from Anson Rabinbach that "more often than not over the years historical precision was sacrificed to the political gains of invoking the word [totalitarianism]."[14] More concretely, political scientist Volker Perthes may have put it best in his succinct description of the Syrian regime on the eve of Hafiz al-Asad's death in 2000: "while not regulating all spheres of life—the regime [was] authoritarian not totalitarian—it [had] deeply penetrated society, effectively monopolized the means of organized violence, and largely succeeded in making the Syrian nation-state the accepted frame of politics."[15]

Leading figures in Syrian studies demonstrate that the Syrian regime since the 1970 corrective movement is best understood as decentralized.[16] For example, as political scientist Joshua Stacher notes, "the description of the Syrian state as built solely on personalized institutions is problematic."[17] Pushing back against the notion of a "strong" Syrian state embodied in the leader, his tribe, or his sect, decentralization permits Stacher to bring elites and other nonstate actors into the conversation, one that is not only about regime durability but also about political transformation. Neoinstitutionalists, then, may also recognize the signal role played by ideology in the Syrian state, society, and culture during the late twentieth century. As Stacher puts it, Baʿthist ideology "became enmeshed in the state."[18] Nevertheless, one might caution that it is equally problematic to broaden scholarly analysis beyond the president and "his cronies" only to take into account elites, a political system characterized by "heterogeneity," and a society characterized as a "diverse mosaic."[19] Here is an inherent limitation collaring neoinstitutionalist approaches to political rule in Baʿthist Syria, in part because of their failure to wrestle with the ways in which (aesthetic) ideology travels beyond the purview of the state itself.

My interest here is neither to issue a normative judgment on the system of rule in Syria since the 1970s nor to render a political verdict on the Asadist-Baʿthist state and its aesthetic ideology. Rather, *Revolutions Aesthetic* describes and analyzes state power, authority, and ideology as they constitute and are reflected in cultural production. Beyond those who would convert the study of politics in Baʿthist Syria into a referendum on authoritarian (or totalitarian) rule and those who prefer (neo)institutionalist, social movement theory, or network analysis approaches, one can identify a scholarly current that incorporates critical theories of ideology into the study of the political. Writing the cultural and intellectual history of literature, film, and other kinds of art in Baʿthist Syria requires engagement with the problem of ideology and disciplinary power. I will return to aesthetic theory as it pertains to the political in Baʿthist Syria, with specific reference to the Marxist and Marxian modes of Ideologiekritik, but first a word about ideology itself. Like that of many, my understanding is indebted to the interpretation of Louis Althusser. For Althusser, "while there is *one* (Repressive) State Apparatus, there is a *plurality* of Ideological State Apparatuses," all of which function in their own way to interpellate (or hail) subjects as volitional actors while simultaneously rendering them objects, holding out the possibility, utopian as it may be, of a consummate Hegelian sublation (*Aufhebung*) of subject and object.[20] Althusser thereby builds on but also departs from Marx's underdeveloped theory of ideology—"an imaginary assemblage (bricolage), a pure dream, empty and vain" that consequently has no history[21]—because of his dissatisfaction with that notion of "the system of the ideas and representations which dominate the mind of a man or a social group."[22] In contrast to ideology—in the singular—Althusser advocates for a more expansive understanding of disciplinary power in its historical forms by way of what he terms Ideological State Apparatuses (ISAs). One of the most compelling moments in Althusser's argument is his injunction to understand the *materialization* or *concretization* of ideology as an institutional(ized) form of coercive rule. Furthermore, ISAs—in stark contradistinction to ideology in its various Marxist iterations—*have* a history that can be reconstituted both theoretically and empirically through "the history of social formations, and thus of the modes of production combined in social formations, and of the class struggles which develop in them."[23] From this vantage point, and even though my analysis does not hew to the conventions of class analysis as such, the history of state-sanctioned and state-driven Asadist-Baʿthist ideology may be disentangled into a skein of ISAs functioning autonomously but also in relation to the "master narrative" of the regime. For example, the ubiquitous mantra "A Single Arab Nation with an Eternal Message" (*umma ʿarabiyya wāḥida dhāt risāla khālida*) would seem to overlap with the figure of the "Eternal Leader" (*al-qāʾid ilā al-abad*). This personalization of political ideology—instantiated in both the all too real leader Hafiz al-Asad (*al-raʾīs*) and in the metaphorical and somewhat ethereal or even spectral leader figure (*al-qāʾid*) discussed in Chapter 1—may become legible, by turns, in the cultural production under study throughout *Revolutions Aesthetic*. Be that as it may, and even though such maxims increasingly seemed hollow and even distasteful to some, it cannot be argued that these were mere slogans or purely ideological window dressing. Rather, the enunciative claims repeated ad nauseum through certain Syrian ISAs—mass media, cultural production in its myriad varieties, schools, prisons, everyday vernacular, and so on—must be understood, adapting Althusser, as material manifestations of a historically conditioned and discursively fungible form of aesthetic ideology.

It is relevant to question whether notions of the political implicit throughout Syrian studies are usefully compared with the aestheticized politics that critics of ideology decry in the language and practice of other illiberal regimes during the twentieth and early twenty-first centuries.[24] These characterizations seem specious, unfounded, and typically based on normative political accusations against the regime's corruption, violence, and repression in a way that mirrors the frivolous claims made about Baʿthist totalitarianism introduced earlier. A more satisfying approach to these phenomena, I would argue, can be found in a capacious understanding of Asadism itself: a clientelist system revolving around Hafiz al-Asad, his family, and his supporters, extending into politics, the economy, and war making, *but also* an aspirational ideological project forwarded by means of a "cultural revolution" promoting its revolutionary aims through language, literature, and the arts. The enduring relevance of certain aspects of political Asadism (which, I argue later, is dissociable from the interrelated phenomenon that is cultural Asadism) into the post-2000 period demonstrates the declining significance of pan-Arab nationalism and the rising centrality of Syrian nationalist discourse, often articulated through the figure of the president and Asadist-Baʿthist state- and nation-building projects. As the book moves forward chronologically, recognition of the complex and multifaceted nature of the transition from al-Asad père to his son Bashar need not be straightjacketed by tendentious arguments about personalist rule or totalitarianism. Instead, scholars may fruitfully turn to historical analysis of the disciplinary power of Asadist-Baʿthist ideology as it permeates malleable discursive landscapes.

Revolutions Aesthetic consequently addresses ongoing debates around how to write the history of the Middle East during the post–World War II period, a time characterized by endemic military conflict, authoritarian entrenchment and retrenchment, and restrictions on the life of the mind. While the book is not concerned with the problems and promise of decolonization per se, it does offer some perspective on how one might rethink and profitably recuperate archives both "material and ideational," in the elegant framing of intellectual historian Omnia El Shakry, that have escaped the attention and excavational energies of historians and other scholars. In this regard, I follow El Shakry's inspiring lead, taking seriously the argument that we ought to view the making of the post–World War II Middle East as a "history without documents":

> Rather than search for the root causes of a present postcolonial melancholia, as tempting as that might be, we might be better served by the reconstruction of the disparate "horizons of expectation" and "indeterminate futures" that decolonization, as a complex series of both historical experiences and ongoing events, offers up.[25]

The crushing defeat of Arab armies by Israel during the Six-Day War in 1967 was a cataclysmic rupture in regional political, military, and cultural life, as devastating as—and in some senses more so than—the collapse of the colonial order and the achievement of national independence after the Second World War. This resulted in widespread malaise, that is, until the "victory" (*al-intiṣār*) of the October 1973 War. But lachrymose histories of the post-1967 Middle East focus excessively on the politics and culture of despair and insufficiently on the creative responses to those transformative events.[26] Historians of the modern Middle East might blanch at the notion that Asadist-Baʿthist Syria could be a fruitful site for plumbing "horizons of expectation" and "indeterminate futures," given what is (even when only implicitly) taken to be the seemingly inexorable closing of the Syrian mind over the course of the late twentieth century. Moreover, some would argue that Syrian cultural and intellectual milieux were fundamentally thin for not engaging with ideas and art at a level worthy of serious study.[27] *Revolutions Aesthetic* argues instead that Syrian intellectuals, artists, writers, filmmakers, and even regime officials and supporters—however differently positioned in political, ideological, and cultural terms—did not suffer from ignorance, false consciousness, or bad faith when they embraced and perhaps actually believed in a distinctive politics of possibility for Syria.[28] Consciousness and critique were reflected widely in Syrian cultural production, sometimes in explicit terms, as in the plays of Saʿdallah Wannous, the early poetry and poetic prose of Adonis, the political thought of Sadiq Jalal al-ʿAzm and Yasin al-Hafiz, and the fiction of Haydar Haydar and Hanna Mina (Chapter 2). Sometimes 1967 was an oblique reference in a work of art, as in *Nights of the Jackal* (*Layālī Ibn Awā*), the 1989 narrative feature film by ʿAbd al-Latif ʿAbd al-Hamid (Chapter 2); sometimes there was hardly any explicit reference to local or regional political circumstances at all, as in Mamdouh Azzam's 1989 novel *Ascension to Death* (*Miʿrāj al-Mawt*) and in Riyad Shayya's 1995 film adaptation *Al-Lajāt* (Chapter 2). Across the political spectrum, then, and regardless of the extent to which these artistic endeavors were definitively linked to any concrete social reality, there was a widespread commitment to politicizing art and culture in ways that (re)animated the struggle around aesthetic ideology, and not always or exclusively in ways governed by the state. This story cannot be neatly delineated or easily understood in binary terms of power and resistance or of hopefulness and despair. Neither can the kind of history I have in mind be written exclusively from one disciplinary vantage point: the methods of political science, aesthetic criticism, and history are all essential instruments in *Revolutions Aesthetic*.

CULTURAL HISTORY AND/AS INTELLECTUAL HISTORY

One corollary stemming from my argument that there are disqualifying limits to thinking of totalitarianism as an analytical category appropriate for Asadist-Baʿthist Syria is that this historical context has only ever been capable of producing "political" art. To accept this unconvincing claim would mean that truly antitotalitarian practice must aspire to produce *nonpolitical* or *antipolitical* art—art for art's sake, one might say. But it is worth remembering, to take a cue from Andrew Hewitt, that "the popular notion of an ideologically unencumbered art is itself radically political."[29] In other words, rather than debating whether literary works and other forms of cultural production are political, it might make more sense to consider how aesthetic ideology shapes the conditions of possibility for certain kinds of art to become salient, meaningful, and sometimes political in specific historical contexts in the first place. This approach would only gain strength from a double-barreled form of cultural history and/as intellectual history.

Peter Gordon lays out a relevant typology of intellectual history, splitting it into four segments: philosophy, political theory, sociology, and culture. "The line between intellectual history and cultural history is not always easily discerned," Gordon writes.

> The difference is chiefly methodological: whereas an intellectual historian may investigate a given idea for its own sake, a cultural historian is more likely to examine the cultural circulation of that idea, its diffusion beyond the confines of an intellectual elite and into the wider sphere of society. . . . Cultural historians tend to be less interested in the finer points of concepts alone and more interested in what happens to such concepts when they are taken up within the realm of public discourse.

Gordon extends this line of reasoning through an elegant metaphor: "When an idea gets taken up within the larger circuit of culture, it rarely manages to retain its original shape; it sheds its conceptual substance to become instead something diffuse, atmospheric." Here he seems to harbor a subtle yet discernible predilection for the history of philosophy and political theory, though, where ideas possess an "original shape" that may become "diffuse, atmospheric" recapitulations elsewhere, in the circuitry of culture.[30] My aim throughout *Revolutions Aesthetic* is to demonstrate some of the ways in which ideas about politics and aesthetics—foundational concepts such as revolution, nationalism, imagination, death, truth, commitment—were instantiated in literature, film, and intellectual culture sometimes but not always in "diffuse, atmospheric" ways, often in ways that articulated with the concrete political and social struggles at the core of the making of modern and contemporary Syria. Writers, filmmakers, directors, and actors, *as well as* government officials, state bureaucrats, and others who typically might not be acknowledged as intellectuals, critics, and idea producers in their own right have played those roles in important and often unexpected ways.

Intellectual history and cultural history fit together best when historians push back against the anticontextualism endemic to certain strains of intellectual history and literary critique, but at the same time resist the countervailing impulse to reduce cultural production to social text. Throughout *Revolutions Aesthetic*, I am mindful of Zeina Halabi's insightful caution that scholars of literature and culture face a pressing "danger of collapsing the visual, the cinematic and the artistic to the textual."[31] Halabi's argument is an important corrective to scholarship that overemphasizes political and social factors at the expense of aesthetic criteria. If there is a danger in collapsing the visual, the cinematic, and the artistic to social text, it is in the potential for undervaluing textual or narrative aspects of a work by viewing them exclusively as unmediated reflections of social and political reality. On the one hand, then, scholars of literature and culture should take care not to allow the subject of narrative to overshadow other potential objects of critical-cultural analysis. On the other hand, cultural and intellectual historians surely can be less fixated on the social ramifications and political significance of cultural production without swinging too far in the direction of decontextualization. Simply put, aesthetic criticism in Syrian cultural studies should address formal and generic issues as well as political and historical questions.

Revolutions Aesthetic aims for a balance between historicized claims about the significance of particular writers and filmmakers and their works and aesthetic criticism of the formal aspects of these works. Scholarship on modern and contemporary Syria might move in new directions by taking up these challenges of cultural and intellectual history in tandem, not as a replacement for the crucial analysis of geopolitics, political economy, and social science but as a way to enhance the library of Syrian studies and consequently Middle East intellectual and cultural history. As with any inquiry into art, aesthetics, and cultural production, though, scholars of Syria need to reckon with the autonomy of art while also doing the recuperative work of cultural history as a means of discerning, decoding, and deducing the ideas and intellectual commitments that shine throughout those specific iterations of cultural production.

Throughout the book, I interrogate cultural production in terms of how literature and film reflect social and political realities while also attending to various aesthetic and formal qualities of these works. *Revolutions Aesthetic* introduces a wide range of Syrian Arabic-language novels, films, and cultural periodicals to an Anglophone audience for the first time; many of them are underappreciated by scholars and critics working in other languages—including Arabic—as well. The effects of state power on the cultural field need to be isolated and disentangled in relation to how cultural producers have managed to refashion, confront, or sidestep the aesthetic ideology of Asadist-Ba'thist cultural revolution. Yasmeen Hanoosh's related point about Ba'thist Iraq is instructive here, as it was similarly the case in Syria that the state "was never able to achieve full cultural hegemony." Writers, filmmakers, and intellectuals, moreover, were never "able to fully assume the role of the 'organic intellectual' in the face of the dictates of state agenda."[32] The extent to which the aesthetic ideology of Asadist-Ba'thist cultural revolution—its aesthetics of power—successfully achieved cultural hegemony remains an open question subject to further debate. Whatever the case, there was a robust attempt by state institutions to craft a coherent aesthetic ideology in Asadist-Ba'thist Syria, an aesthetics of power articulated through languages I refer to as *speaking-to* and *speaking-for*. State-sponsored artistic initiatives achieved incomplete cultural hegemony at best, to follow Hanoosh, securing only relative uniformity of thought and successfully cementing only a delimited range of mass taste. At the same time, as we will see, other works of literature and cinema responded to or coexisted with state cultural discourse through the articulation and embrace of other modes of address—*speaking-against* and *speaking-with*, most importantly—under the sign of an aesthetics of resistance but also an aesthetics of solidarity. These alternative and oppositional artistic practices change over time. Consequently, it remains unclear, in an inversion an aesthetics of power in Asadist-Ba'thist aesthetic ideology, whether "dissident" or "oppositional" artists, writers, and filmmakers can be said to have served as vectors of an identifiable and intentional set of counter-hegemonic discourses.

Films produced by the NFO and literature produced with and against the literary establishment represent another rich, untapped source of material for writing Syrian cultural and intellectual history. What Patricia A. Herminghouse notes about the significance of cultural production in the German Democratic Republic could also be said about the case of Asadist-Ba'thist Syria:

> An eminent GDR social scientist, Jürgen Kuczynski, asserted that future historians would, in fact, find more useful information in the fiction of the GDR than in its social science studies or its newspaper, constrained as they were to report only positive aspects. Such perceptions of the "truthfulness" of literary accounts owed less to any particular commitment on the part of authors to

> writing "realistically" than to their strategic location outside the sphere of mass media, such as television and the press, where content and language were known to be subject to more direct party control.[33]

There is no clear and permanent dividing line between authors and other artists who inhabit a "strategic location outside the sphere of mass media" and those who are hopelessly "subject to more direct party control." Nevertheless, the struggle to create a new subject, political rationality, and state strategy inside what was often described in regime discourse as the budding "beating heart of Arabism" or the "Hanoi of the Middle East"—signature phrases of the Asadist-Baʿthist "revolution"—also extended to cultural production. There was ample ideological latitude through which writers, filmmakers, artists, and intellectuals could maneuver to challenge but also, counterintuitively at times, help reconstitute state power. In this regard, the agonistic struggle around aesthetic ideology in Syrian literature, film, and cultural production in the age of Asadist-Baʿthist rule can help us better understand and ultimately transcend the outmoded binary parameters that set an idealist cultural/intellectual history against and apart from a materialist social/political history.

THE IDEOLOGY OF THE (ASADIST-BAʿTHIST) AESTHETIC

The struggle over aesthetic ideology in Syria can also be understood from a comparative literary-critical perspective. *Revolutions Aesthetic* draws on the study of aesthetics and aesthetic theory in other world-historical contexts, departing from the rise of modern aesthetic theory among European philosophers Immanuel Kant and Edmund Burke in the eighteenth century and continuing through contemporary theorists and critics such as Jacques Rancière and Sianne Ngai.[34] Further efforts to integrate cultural and intellectual histories of Syria into this body of scholarship might go some way toward deprovincializing Syrian studies.[35] The articulation of Asadist-Baʿthist aesthetic ideology—from cultural revolution from above (1970–2000) through the ostensibly guided reformism of Bashar al-Asad's first decade in power (2000–2011), continuing into the uprising of 2011 and the ensuing horrors and dislocations of the Syria War and beyond—coincided with ongoing efforts by the state to aestheticize politics alongside parallel and competing attempts to politicize aesthetics. In this regard, Rancière provides a useful and oft-cited point of departure for thinking about "the politics of aesthetics" in general terms: "the way in which the aesthetic experience—as a refiguration of the forms of visibility and intelligibility of artistic practice and reception—intervenes in the distribution of the sensible."[36] For Rancière, the dialectical tension between the autonomy and the heteronomy of art generates a kind of "metapolitics": a "way of producing its own politics, proposing to politics rearrangements of its space, reconfiguring art as a political issue, or asserting itself as true politics."[37] While discussions of cultural production throughout this book consistently return to representations of and struggles over the political in Syrian literature and film, they remain incomplete without substantive attention to the formal, narratological, visual, and conceptual dimensions of art.

Early Marxist scholars of aesthetics struggled to reconcile their belief in the universal potential of reflective judgment characteristic of European Enlightenment philosophy—namely the universalist conception of aesthetic experience—with their political commitment to transcend the subjective idealism of Kantian aesthetics in order to drive criticism beyond the luxurious preserve of the bourgeois political subject. In his preface to the 1951 German edition of Hegel's *Aesthetics*, a crucial steppingstone in the intellectual-historical genealogy of Marxist aesthetics, Georg Lukács—a touchstone for Syrian writers, artists, and critics throughout the twentieth century (as we will see in Chapter 1 and elsewhere)—critiques the Janus face of Hegelian aesthetic theory. "As an objective idealist," Lukács writes,

> Hegel struggles very energetically—against Kant and the empiricists—for the recognition of the objective, absolute truth of the aesthetic categories. As a dialectician, however, Hegel connects this absolute essence of the categories with the historical, relative character of their concrete appearance.[38]

Subsequently, Marxist critics of ideology and aesthetics, including Lukács, critical theorists from the Frankfurt School (Theodor Adorno, Herbert Marcuse, and Walter Benjamin, to name the most influential), Louis Althusser, Terry Eagleton, and others have tried to further concretize and particularize Hegel's insightful identification of the historical unfolding of artistic genres and aesthetic categories. In this view, the dialectical tension between subject and object, subjective experience and objective reality, content and form, cannot so easily be quenched, sublated, or transcended. Literary critic Terry Eagleton is one of the most eloquent exponents of this materialist mode of aesthetic critique. "If politics and aesthetics are deeply at one," Eagleton points out,

> it is because pleasurable conduct is the true index of successful social hegemony, self-delight the very mark of social submission. What matters in aesthetics is not art but this whole project of reconstructing the human subject from the inside, informing its subtlest affections and bodily responses with this law which is not a law.[39]

Mike Wayne suggests another avenue along which to push the potential of Kant's conception of aesthetic experience, as articulated in the *Critique of Judgment*, beyond conventional interpretations of "the sublime" and "delight." He tethers Kantian visions of beauty to agonistic forms of cultural engagement and social struggle: "To say that the aesthetic can be a vehicle for ideology goes without saying, but to say that the aesthetic is inherently ideological because it unites abstraction with the perceptible/sensual . . . really closes off an important resource," namely, "a crucial pedagogic resource."[40] Instead of viewing the aesthetic as purely ideological or merely formal, therefore, *Revolutions Aesthetic* resituates the struggle for Syria during the late twentieth and early twenty-first centuries as, in part, a struggle over the aesthetic itself.

Conventional approaches to aesthetic theory tend to scrutinize artistic expression of and engagement with the ineffable or the sublime.[41] My analysis of the Syrian cultural field under Baʿthist rule, by contrast, is premised on the notion that an agonistic and dialectical tension emerged between a predominantly state-supported aesthetics of power—predicated on an authoritarian artistic language characterized as *speaking-to* or *speaking-for*—and alternative conceptions of creative expression. These challenges to the aesthetics of power are interrelated but not always coextensive: the first, an aesthetics of resistance, is a more straightforward form of oppositional art that seeks to directly challenge the hegemonic aspirations of state culture by *speaking-back* or *speaking-against*; the second, an aesthetics of solidarity, is a subtle variation that is nonhegemonic (as distinguished from counter-hegemonic) and therefore opens up the possibility of *speaking-against* but also generates a language of *speaking-with*. For my purposes, the bridge between an aesthetics of resistance and an aesthetics of solidarity is that both rely on the linguistic capacity—whether through text, image, or any other aesthetic form—of *speaking-with* and *speaking-against* instead of reproducing the doctrinaire and domineering style of *speaking-to* or *speaking-for*. By framing the agonistic struggle around aesthetic ideology in these terms, I contend that dialectical understandings of the relationship between power and resistance can remain in place, without going unchallenged. Crucially, the state's attempts at cultural hegemony may also be reinforced even as new or contentious forms of creative expression find new ways of evading or exiting the stranglehold of power/resistance altogether.

While scholars of Syria have not proposed this sort of agonistic aesthetic theory exactly for understanding the political, ideological, and institutional dimensions of Asadist-Baʿthist Syria, the scholarly literature on spectacle, dictatorship, and authoritarian power hints at the value inherent in such a schema. Lisa Wedeen crucially identifies the spectacular as well as the subtle forms of domination, compliance, and symbolism at work in this world. "Systems of domination are never total," she teaches us, "and everyday forms of resistance suggest the partial, less-than-optimal ways in which power is exemplified and produced in Syria."[42] All too often, though, this aesthetics of power is simplistically opposed to an aesthetics of resistance, as many presume the latter is emblematic of a struggle to establish counter-hegemony in reaction to state power and its aspirant cultural hegemony. Yaseen Noorani offers a helpful alternative way of thinking through this relation, encouraging us instead

> to recognize resistance is constitutive of hegemony rather than an element fundamentally alien to the hegemonic order and disruptive of it. This is particularly apparent in the case of artistic practices, which frequently contain countercultural, parodic and transgressive dimensions apparently tolerated by the ruling order.[43]

In this light, my alternative framing of cultural production draws attention to an aesthetics of solidarity that is not entirely reducible to the aesthetics of resistance, although the two may overlap and reinforce one another in some instances. My point is neither that the aesthetics of solidarity only ever amounts to posturing, public relations, or image management nor that the aesthetics of solidarity is guaranteed to circumvent or disrupt the circuit of power/resistance. On the contrary, certain works of art examined in this book adorn an alternative space of cultural production grounded in the ethics, politics, and aesthetics of solidarity, neither always nor exclusively for the purposes of resisting state power and regime violence. Whether in the context of Asadist-Ba'thist authoritarian rule prior to 2011 or during the Syrian uprising and the Syria War, literature and film served as mechanisms not only for the generation of new forms of creative expression but also for building local, national, and global senses of community from the bottom up.[44]

Revolutions Aesthetic tracks the struggle around aesthetic ideology in literature and film. The book is an exercise in describing, analyzing, and understanding how crucial aesthetic ideology was to the constitution of a state-driven Ba'thist-Asadist cultural revolution; how this "revolution from above" was refashioned into a "reformism from above" under the regime of Bashar al-Asad after 2000 that was subsequently challenged by writers, filmmakers, and artists during the first decade of the twenty-first century; and how the myriad responses to this cultural production "from above" could encompass outright resistance, subtle adaptation, evasive maneuver, or obedience to official norms and cultural parameters. While there never was a single Syrian aesthetic promulgated or uniformly imposed by the regime, cultural agents of the modernizing, centralizing Ba'thist security state under Hafiz al-Asad sought to unify and standardize the aesthetic-ideological and cultural fields. "While certain artists manage to carve out some [independent] spaces (*se ménager des espaces*), they are relatively isolated," Alexis Tadié wrote in the French Catholic journal *Esprit* during the early 2000s, when Syria was in the midst of what appeared to be a meaningful cultural opening after the accession to power of Bashar al-Asad.

> They are rarely able to live off of their art. The political system, outside of the Ministry of Culture, has stifled all collective discourse, every unifying public reflection, all divergent voices. Apart from the forms surveilled by the State, taking a position is forbidden for Syrian artists and intellectuals on principle. But—and this is not the least paradoxical aspect—these artists manage all the same, inside of the system, inside of their country, to blaze a trail, to pursue their own itinerary, to open up a debate.[45]

This assessment nicely identifies the bind in which Syrian artists and intellectuals found themselves both before and after the death of Hafiz al-Asad. Rather than reinscribing an understanding of "proregime" and "dissident" or "oppositional" or even "revolutionary" cultural politics, however, it would be more worthwhile to explore the ways in which state cultural institutions were sites—and not the only ones—of struggle over aesthetic ideology. There is a widespread misunderstanding (one that is prevalent in scholarly, journalistic, and popular understandings of Syria) that runs the risk of oversimplifying the analysis of art and politics in Syria by accepting prima facie the opposition between binary aesthetic categories such as "state" art on the one hand and "independent" or "autonomous" art on the other hand.

Novels and films sponsored, released, published, and distributed by state-affiliated agencies such as the AWU or the NFO restricted but did not fully tie the hands of writers and filmmakers. On the other hand, novels that were self-published or published abroad and films made with private support could be incorporated into the national cultural field, whether or not they were even made, circulated, and consumed in Syria. While I have argued against the facile representation of the Asadist-Baʿthist regime as totalitarian or fascistic, there are analytical lessons to be drawn from work on aesthetics and politics in other illiberal political contexts. Susan Buck-Morss brilliantly reads the critique of fascist aesthetics in Walter Benjamin's "The Work of Art in the Age of Its Technological Reproducibility," for example, in order to reframe the call typically identified with Benjamin to resist the national-socialist aestheticization of politics by politicizing aesthetics instead.[46] Benjamin's scathing critique of Leni Riefenstahl's *Triumph of the Will* is predicated on his rejection of "the militarization of society for the teleology of making war." Buck-Morss identifies another crucial dimension of cultural production in the service of state power or other such projects of ideological imposition, namely that "aesthetics allows an *an*anesthetization of reception."[47] In contrast, Buck-Morss argues that the true "antidote to fascism" not only would be a "political response"—the classical understanding of politicized aesthetics—but also would be a shift to "describe the [aesthetic] field" within which such a response could be imagined and articulated in the first place.[48] To be clear, I unequivocally reject the simplistic notion that Asadist-Baʿthist cultural revolution and its aesthetic ideology are characterizable as purely fascist in nature or that the Syrian state was ever capable of capturing the cultural field in a manner that would allow the regime to uniformly indoctrinate, brainwash, or control its population. Again, I must reiterate here that my point throughout this book is neither to support nor substantiate state and non-state discourse on/of Asadist-Baʿthist cultural revolution. One of the central claims of *Revolutions Aesthetic*, however, is that a more nuanced historical investigation of the Syrian cultural field under Baʿthist rule can reveal the political nature of an agonistic struggle around aesthetic ideology. This, to my mind, is a more plausible and convincing argument about aesthetics and politics, one that accounts for historical contingency in the creation, circulation, and reception of works of art but also attends to the shifting construction of the ideological and epistemological grounds on which the aesthetic field has been established and refashioned in contemporary Syria. Such an interpretation avoids reinscribing stale tropes of Baʿthist totalitarianism or the monopolization of cultural production by state institutions; it can also complicate reductive narratives of (state) power versus (popular) resistance.

Since the advent of the corrective movement, the Syrian state has endeavored to instrumentalize art as a way of dominating the cultural field. That project needs to be situated in relation to analogous efforts by the state to co-opt social and economic life through strategies of clientelism, coercion, and violent repression. How the Asadist-Baʿthist cultural revolution promulgated its own aesthetic ideology but was also challenged by certain voices will be addressed in Chapter 1 through a panoramic reading of literary, cinematic, philosophical, and intellectual periodicals. The voices of leading cultural commissars such as the long-serving minister of culture Najah al-ʿAttar will stand out but other writers, critics, artists, and filmmakers—some of whom have achieved international recognition but many others who are barely known—will also be given voice as they debated a whole host of aesthetic, political, and cultural issues. No doubt, the wooden sloganeering and constraining aesthetic ideology promulgated by the regime had an impact on cultural production during this period. But in attending to the complicated nature and construction of the Syrian cultural field, one finds good reason to consider a *contrapuntal* reading of Syrian cultural history, one that tracks how the aesthetic-ideological conformity demanded by cultural Asadism was sometimes enforced while at other times it was adapted or even subverted. This means taking seriously what film historian and critic Cécile Boëx calls "work that reflected the political and social progress of the Arab world and, implicitly, transmitted and promoted the discourse of state power and the Baʿath Party."[49]

The Asadist-Baʿthist cultural revolution was intercalated with the political objectives of promoting the collective liberation of the Arab peoples, unifying the Arab world in the face of colonialism, imperialism, and Zionism, and leading a socialist transformation on a national scale in Syria. Anticolonial nationalism and the doctrine of socialist realism produced an aesthetic ideology rooted in the practice of commitment literature—or committed cultural production more broadly—that would not only communicate the spirit of a political moment but also speak in a language that was accessible to and satisfied the taste of the masses. One instructive example of where the theoretical rubber of these commitments by Asadist-Baʿthist cultural revolutionaries meets the road of the cultural field (explored more fully in Chapter 1) was an aversion to the mass popularity of melodrama in Arab cinema, which circulated primarily through the powerful Egyptian film industry. This institutional and ideological culture industry signified to cultural revolutionaries an impoverishment of the aesthetic imagination, making melodrama a genre (or even an ideological formation) that was to be condemned and avoided. Debates raged over undesirable bourgeois or romantic works of literature, whether those appeared as allegories or stories without a doctrinal remit. As in Southern Cone countries under military dictatorship, allegory in Syrian cultural production (discernible in Ossama Mohammed's 2002 film *Sacrifices* [*Ṣundūq al-Dunyā*] discussed in Chapter 2; Nihad Sirees's 2004 novel *The Silence and the Roar* [*al-Ṣamt wa-l-Ṣakhab*], in Chapter 4; and Mazin ʿArafa's 2017 novel *The Cranes* [*al-Gharānīq*], in Chapter 6) likewise

> can be conceived as a function of the virtual crisis of representation engendered by authoritarian discursive practices. Under dictatorship, the sphere of public communication and the media became the property of an elite few (the military and its supporters) who attempt to manipulate them to their own ends, thus making truth more and more difficult to know and turning the production of meaning into the exclusive domain of the authoritarian regime.[50]

Melodrama, satire, and allegory were among the devices used by writers, filmmakers, television producers, and others as they attempted to create appealing art that would both communicate emotional, cultural, *and* political themes under conditions of restricted freedom while also finding spaces to circulate within a monitored media landscape. Rather than argue over the sufficiency and limitations of allegory (national or otherwise) in the context of what was once called Third World literature, therefore, it seems more sensible to apprehend allegory along a spectrum of cultural representation.[51] Scholars of Syrian literature and film should be more concerned with what Mary Beth Tierney-Tello calls "the ethical function of allegory," not as the exclusive mode of representation amid a "crisis" or realism or a debasement of meaning, but rather as one mode of creative expression among others.[52]

If allegory, satire, and melodrama are not always convincingly read as allusive or obfuscatory genres, there have also been explicitly political forms of cultural production on display in Asadist-Baʿthist Syria. The manufacture of compliance and the performance of obedience in this context relies on the widespread understanding that, for the most part, it is not relevant whether citizens sincerely believe in the truth-effects of regime ideology or its system of domination.[53] Wedeen's deconstructive reading of authoritarian state culture under Hafiz al-Asad (introduced above) is an important overture to my reading of the aesthetics of power, the aesthetics of solidarity, and the aesthetics of resistance. A complementary spin on the relation between aesthetics and politics under conditions of authoritarian domination is to be found in the notion of "subversive affirmation," a term that emerged with the rise of Russian conceptualism. "Subversive affirmation," write Inke Arns and Sylvia Sasse,

> is an artistic/political tactic that allows artists/activists to take part in certain social, political, or economic discourses and to affirm, appropriate, or consume them while simultaneously undermining them. It is characterised precisely by the fact that with affirmation there is simultaneously taking place a distancing from, or revelation of what is being affirmed. In subversive affirmation there is always a surplus which destabilises affirmation and turns it into its opposite.[54]

In this formulation, subversive affirmation requires a kind of "overidentification" with the aesthetic project by the viewer, reader, or listener. In tandem, these concepts—subversive affirmation and overidentification—"allow artists to take part in certain social, ideological, political, or economic discourses, and affirm, appropriate, or consume them while simultaneously undermining them."[55] This subtle form of critique, not only "acting 'as if'" in public and private social settings but also subversively affirming the aesthetic ideology of Asadist-Baʿthist cultural revolution, can be discerned, for example, in *Stars in Broad Daylight* (*Nujūm al-Nahār*), the 1988 film by Ossama Mohammed (Chapters 2 and 4); *The Empire of Ghawar* (*Imbrāṭūriyyat Ghawār*), the 1982 film by Durayd Lahham (Chapter 3); and *The Extras* (*al-Kūmbārs*), the 1993 film from Nabil Maleh (Chapter 4). These works have been singled out for their daring criticism of state repression, surveillance, and even the figure of the president himself. If the Asadist-Baʿthist cultural revolution has a history, as I have been arguing, it needs to be understood in relation to the making of modern Syria, a schematic version of which I offer in what remains of this introduction.

A VERY BRIEF HISTORY OF POSTCOLONIAL SYRIA

One might say that the specter of revolution haunts modern Syrian history. From the earliest calls for the overthrow of the imperial order during the early twentieth century after nearly four centuries of Ottoman rule over the lands of Greater Syria (*Bilād al-Shām*) (1516–1918); successive rebellions against French Mandate colonial rule (1920–1946) that gave rise to nationalist leadership and grassroots movements that would inspire, guide, and govern Syria in its transition to independence into the middle of the twentieth century; military coups d'êtat during early independence that threatened to overturn Syria's fragile postcolonial parliamentary democracy; late twentieth-century Baʿthist military dictatorships that ruled the country from 1963 to the present; various forces that challenged or directly resisted the quasi-hegemonic order of Asadist-Baʿthist rule—be they Islamist, leftist, liberal, secular, or nondoctrinal; and, finally, an unprecedented uprising in early 2011 that was powerless to prevent the country from sliding towards war and humanitarian catastrophe. Revolutions and revolutionary movements have punctuated the making of modern and contemporary Syria. As I have argued throughout this introduction, while historians recognize the centrality of politics to modern Syrian history, less scholarly energy has been devoted to understanding the intellectual- and cultural-historical dimensions of this story—including ideas of revolution, theories of aesthetics, and the cultural politics of literature and film.

Despite the repressive and reactionary political rule under the Asadist-Baʿthist regime over the past fifty years, the rhetoric of revolution—at the level of state, society, and various sectors of everyday life—remains an underappreciated aspect of Syria's contemporary intellectual and cultural history. The study of "revolution" as a concept in modern Arabic political discourse has its own checkered past. Orientalists have long shoehorned the Arabic lexicon into a cartoonish Islamic conceptual universe. For example, Ami Ayalon semantically analyzed the relevant Arabic-language terms under the rubric of moral judgment, which is to say whether certain words hold a positive or a negative connotation. Relying on hidebound tropes derived from classical Orientalism, Ayalon makes sweeping claims about obedience to authority in "the Islamic Middle East": "Revolt was the antithesis of obedience—a strongly recommended principle, even a strict duty, of every Muslim." Logic thereby dictated the inappropriateness or even the unthinkability of such opposition during the postclassical period. "If revolt was unwelcome," from the vantage point of the political sovereign, then "revolution was inconceivable."[56] Whether or not revolutions must be conceivable by a political authority—or preconceived by those who take up the cause—in order to take place is less a moral, semantic, or philosophical question, though, than a historical one. Matters were said to have changed considerably in the transition to modernity, which Ayalon identifies with the Napoleonic invasion of Egypt in 1798, citing ʿAbd al-Rahman al-Jabarti and Rifʿat Rafiʿ al-Tahtawi, for example, who continued to use the term *fitna* to indicate "all that was objectionable in an act of rebellion against the government: it meant sedition, civil strife, the disruption of political and religious order, and a grave menace to the social fabric of the community."[57] If *fitna* was "harshly denunciatory," *ʿiṣyān* and *ʿaṣāwa*—insubordination, insurrection, disobedience—were "still unmistakably negative."[58] Meanwhile, *inqilāb*—upheaval, toppling, or overturning; the term would come to mean both "coup" and "revolution" in Syria and elsewhere in the Arabic-speaking world—"usually denoted a change of fortune, status or circumstance. Of all the words used for revolution *inqilāb* was etymologically the closest to its European counterpart; both were associated with a cyclical concept."[59] Ayalon thinks with moral categories in order to understand revolt, rebellion, uprising, and revolution in "the Islamic Middle East" because "civic freedom and individual political rights" were "alien to Middle Eastern Islamic tradition, in which the reverse of tyranny was not freedom but justice."[60]

This outlook is distinguishable from that of Hannah Arendt, who connects revolution to the claims of freedom and necessity, which might be understood as aspirational revolutions and inevitable revolutions, respectively. Arendt provides a historical framework for thinking conceptually about revolution—its causes, its champions, and its consequences. In her widely read work on the subject, she opposes a voluntarist model for the emergence of revolutionary situations, favoring one that approximates a kind of revolutionary destiny.[61] Given how enamored Arendt is of the example of the American Revolution over and above all others (with the possible exception of the French Revolution), scholars informed by postcolonial theory have rightly called her out for belittling non-Western revolutionary situations and refusing to recognize the historical lessons that might be learned from them.[62] Ayalon argues stridently against the possibility of "non-Western revolution" when he characterizes the Arabic term *thawra* as "an outburst of fury against a foreign presence and control by foreigners . . . a struggle for national independence rather than a quest for civic and political freedom."[63] During the postcolonial age, Ayalon claims, the term *thawra* was deemed more forceful than *inqilāb*, which "became a pejorative for a vain pretense to change: *inqilāb* was, in a sense, a frustrated *thawra*."[64] But such a moral distinction between *inqilāb* and other terms that describe rebellion, resistance, and opposition to unjust rule as well as the bizarre differentiation of these terms according to the amount of force employed in order to (or attempt to) bring about some desired political transformation fails to account for other aspects of the social, political, military, and cultural struggles in play; they also obstruct almost any attention to historical contingency.[65]

In the aftermath of the First Word War, the recently constituted League of Nations authorized French quasi-colonial rule over Lebanon and Syria in the form of Mandate states, carving new national entities out of a wider world long known as Greater Syria, which had been ruled as provincial territories of the Ottoman Empire since the early sixteenth century. There were numerous attempts—through popular action, elite political activity, and international diplomacy—to justify or rectify the loss of territory (including Syria's painful cession of the province of Alexandretta/Hatay to Turkey in 1936–1939) even as the Mandate state profoundly shaped the emergence of new government institutions, national identities, and social movements. In Syria under the Mandate, social and political forces coalesced around an anticolonial nationalist platform steered but never monopolized by bourgeois elites—primarily the large landowning families in the provinces and urban notables in the major cities. Popular forms of nationalism sprang up in the countryside that often challenged but could also bolster the entrenched sway of the elites. By the time Syria won its hard-fought independence from the French in April 1946, the political field was populated by bourgeois nationalists affiliated with mainstream political factions (most importantly the National Bloc [*al-Kutla al-Waṭaniyya*] and the People's Party [*Ḥizb al-Shaʿb*]) that represented elite families who had dominated the politics of the major cities—Damascus, Aleppo, Homs, Hama—and their agricultural hinterlands. During the 1930s and 1940s, those forces were increasingly challenged by radical political currents that represented different social strata that were primarily young, educated, and urban. The political parties emerging around this time, from the Syrian Social Nationalist Party (SSNP) of Antun Sa'ada to the Ba'th Party of Michel 'Aflaq and Salah al-Din al-Bitar, began to call for more vigorous opposition to colonialism and imperialism as well as a redistributive political-economic agenda that could challenge the entrenched power of the notables. Religious organizations such as the Muslim Brothers, which established a Syrian branch in the 1930s, added an emergent Islamist dimension to the political sphere. With the advent of independence, fragile alliances within the anticolonial struggle ebbed and flowed as these political and social forces came together in the fight against imperialism across the region and the Zionist colonization of Palestine.[66]

If the problem of foreign occupation and international meddling in Syrian affairs became a defining feature of legal, political, and social life under the Mandate, the advantages and challenges of parliamentary rule would come to the fore during the postindependence period. After the French were expelled from Syria, the country entered a period of marked political instability. Syria oscillated wildly between moments of stability—the so-called golden age of parliamentary democracy (1954–1958)—to moments of instability and rapid-fire coups d'état (1949, 1949, 1949, 1951, 1958, 1961, 1963, 1966, and 1970). The charismatic masculinity and strong statism consonant with the Asadist-Ba'thist regime had antecedents in military strongmen such as Husni al-Za'im and Adib al-Shishakli, who had sought to govern Syria during the fractious period of the late 1940s and early 1950s. Kevin Martin brilliantly describes the vital flourishing of cultural and intellectual life during the early years of Syria's independence,[67] but not all scholars saw this period in such sunny terms. In his 1965 dissertation, for example, Saïd M. Ajami described Syria during its first two decades of independence as "the sad Eastern laboratory of Western democracy."[68] Intellectual, political, and social struggles against colonial rule were largely replaced by power politics and factionalism as "the struggle for Syria" squarely placed the country at the intersection of Cold War politics, regional intra-Arab debates, the Arab-Israeli conflict, and global Third World liberation movements. The ongoing conflict with the State of Israel, formally established in May 1948 but unrecognized until today by the Syrian government, would remain an essential threat to Syrian attempts to pursue state-building, development, and regional integration. Instability effectively became a way of life in mid-twentieth century Syria, though it needs to be understood in light of regional and international forces that militated against the stabilization or normalization of national politics, society, and culture.

Despite the existence of a functioning parliamentary democracy throughout the 1950s, there was a growing perception by young people, military officers, and government bureaucrats, especially from minority communities in provincial regions, that their needs were not being met by the elites, notables, and bourgeois politicians who dominated all spheres. This rising dissatisfaction was articulated by radicalized Arab nationalists and rising political Islamists.[69] Vicious internecine battles among Baʿthists, Communists, Nasserists, varieties of Marxists, Islamists, and other Syrian nationalists augured fiercer political struggles to come. Widespread affinities for Arab nationalist solutions to regional and international problems also opened the door to an unlikely political project, that of Syria's fusion with Gamal Abdel Nasser's Egypt in the form of the United Arab Republic (1958–1961).[70] Nasser's self-aggrandizing style of rule was seen by many in Syria as grounds for ending this experimental alliance, as Egypt dominated Syria—"the northern province"— through, for example, the creation of a fearsome security apparatus under the watchful eye of intelligence chief ʿAbd al-Hamid al-Sarraj. Syrian nationalist opposition to the Nasserist domination of the UAR led to a "secessionist" (*infiṣālī*) movement that seized power in September 1961.

The coup that brought the Baʿth Party to power in Syria for the first time in March 1963 ushered in a distinctively new era in the history of modern Syria. Raymond Hinnebusch describes the Baʿthist seizure of power and the party's early policies as a "revolution from above" that resulted in the consolidation of a Bonapartist state. Inspired in part by a Baʿthist coup that took place in Baghdad in February, the Baʿth Party took power in Damascus on March 8 in an action that was styled and memorialized by its supporters as a "glorious revolution." The party had evolved significantly since its inception as an intellectual current among teachers and professionals in Damascus and other Syrian cities during the 1930s and 1940s, eventually growing into a mass-based political party after fusing with the Arab Socialist Party of Hama-based lawyer and organizer Akram al-Hawrani in 1952–1953. Intellectual historians are beginning to reconsider the genealogies of Baʿthism to more carefully tease out the relationship between the foundations of Ba'thist thought and subsequent Syrian (and Iraqi) political formations.[71] Inasmuch as its foundational philosophy of Arab/ic nationalist resurrection became tethered to a social and political program, Ba'thists increasingly found themselves divided over personal factional disputes as well as more complicated political disagreements regarding tactics, strategy, and ideology. Moreover, the successes of the more radical nationalist forces in Syria during the mid-twentieth century were predicated, in part, on the activation and activism of elements drawn from ethnic, religious, and sectarian minoritarian backgrounds. Given the trenchant criticisms of the UAR over the trampling of Syrian sovereignty under the command of the Egyptian state, the rising *Syrian* nationalism that accompanied the arrival of the Ba'thists to power was somewhat contradictory: Syrian nationalist sensibilities that had been disrespected in the experience of *actually existing* Arab unity with Egypt would have to be avenged and celebrated through the pan-Arab unifying aspirations of the Ba'th as it took command of Syria alone (to say nothing of the perpetual friction and factionalism that would complicate Syrian-Iraqi relations amid discussions of a potentially comparable union between the two in the years to come). This came to a head in a left-wing or "Neo-Ba'th" coup that took place on February 23, 1966, led by a faction affiliated with Salah al-Din al-Bitar, Salah Jadid, and Amin al-Hafiz, among others. The country swung toward more radical redistributive policies, land reform, and an expansion of social rights at the same time that Communists and left-leaning Ba'thists were permitted to become more active participants in political life. During this period, state-led development was pursued under the sign of a "socialist transformation" of the national economy, which was still overwhelmingly agricultural. Modernization of the Syrian countryside proceeded alongside the steady growth of the cities and their aggressive embrace of industrialization.[72] Michel Seurat argues that the two-pronged strategy of planners who animated the socialist transformations of the 1960s and 1970s was aimed at smashing the power of the traditional, landed elites—the small number of notable families who had dominated Syrian politics throughout the twentieth century—on the one hand and securing the material and ideological loyalty of the peasantry on the other.[73]

But the ideological pendulum swung back the other way when a coup—dubbed the corrective movement or rectification—was carried out by then defense minister Hafiz al-Asad and his supporters in November 1970, halting the momentum of the Neo-Ba'th project. In addition to consolidating rule by sidelining its political rivals within the party, the army, and the bureaucracy, this new regime embarked on an unprecedented project of state-building and development, seizing command of the "revolution from above" and tightening the state's grip on political-economic and infrastructural affairs. The calls for a more comprehensive transformation of the Syrian political economy through the late 1970s can be explained largely by the fact that Syria remained a thoroughly agrarian society, a country in which some three-quarters of the population were still rural.[74] Relying on government statistics, Fred Lawson points out that in 1970 about half of "the country's labor force was engaged in agriculture" but that this figure would drop to 31.8 percent in 1979.[75]

On the heels of the myriad failures of bourgeois nationalists to live up to the promise of postcolonial state-building (1946–1958), the dashed aspirations of Arab nationalist revolutionary ambition through the United Arab Republic (1958–1961), and the crushing defeat of the entire Arab world in the 1967 Six-Day War, it could be argued that Syrian society was ready to embrace a new kind of politics, a new form of leadership, and new forms of aesthetic ideology in order to enter the future more hopefully. To the extent that Ba'thist ideology presented a novel and evolving set of philosophical principles and political prescriptions, though, this discursive formation deformed and devolved over the course of the mid-twentieth century. "The Ba'th could have spread its ideas and won over many people," according to Salah al-Din al-Bitar; they "did not come to power by a popular revolution. The revolution was made from on high. The military officers made it. They didn't have any program—neither a social program nor a national program."[76]

The construction of one-party rule required the institutionalization and renegotiation of what Steven Heydemann called a "corporatist state," Raymond Hinnebusch called a "Bonapartist state," and Nazih Ayubi called a "fierce state."[77] The ferocity of this state was nowhere on plainer display than in the regime's ongoing conflict with its political rivals. Any discussion of this period in Syrian history must wrestle with overt, at times violent opposition to Asadist-Ba'thist authoritarian rule. Minor challenges to the regime from the Communist and non-Communist left were co-opted or outflanked by the Progressive National Front (*al-Jabha al-Waṭaniyya al-Taqaddumiyya*, created in 1972) and other state-administered entities. The more serious threat came from political Islamist forces, though, including the Syrian Muslim Brothers as well as more extreme expressions of Islamic politics such as the Islamic Front and the Fighting Vanguard, organizations identified with figures like ʿIsam al-ʿAttar (brother of long-serving minster of culture Najah al-ʿAttar, discussed in Chapter 1), ʿAdnan Saʿd al-Din, and Saʿid Hawwa. As the spaces for legitimate political opposition were progressively shut down by the regime, activists in Hama, Aleppo, and elsewhere engaged in direct action, including violence and terrorism such as the brazen assault on the Aleppo Military Academy in June 1979, the attempted assassination of Hafiz al-Asad in June 1980, and the armed uprising that subsequently spread throughout Hama, Aleppo, Tadmor (Palmyra), Idlib, and even parts of the northwest coastal region around Latakia. As Thomas Mayer puts it, "the great majority of the Syrian people, in spite of considerable dissatisfaction with the Asad regime, were disinclined to participate in an Islamic revolution."[78] Moreover, a sectarianist interpretation of these events is of limited analytical value, given that "the Islamic revolutionaries did not enjoy the support of the entire Sunni community."[79] Irrespective of these sociological realities, the regime responded with collective punishment and pulverizing force. Reprisals included the coordinated massacring of political prisoners in notorious prison complexes such as Tadmor (Palmyra) and Sednaya. Furthermore, the regime mobilized the so-called Defense Brigades (*Sarāyā al-Difāʿ*) under the command of Rifʿat al-Asad, Hafiz's brother, waging an unprecedented war by the Syrian government against its own cities, focusing on Hama, where the entire metropolis was bombarded to the ground in February 1982 and upward of an estimated 20,000 people lost their lives. This era in modern Syrian history has received some attention from social scientists and scholars of Islamic politics. The significance of Hama and "the events" of 1979–1982 have yet to be fully established in Syrian cultural memory or integrated into the cultural and intellectual history of the country, though. This is an issue to which I will return in the book's Conclusion.

The al-Asad regime carried out related campaigns in the economic sphere. Both Heydemann and Hinnebusch call the trajectory of Syrian political-economic development during the 1980s "selective liberalization."[80] Hinnebusch argues that economic liberalization, which took place with the formation of a new government in 1985 and the passage of new investment laws in 1986 and 1991, did not automatically result in political liberalization.[81] Among the consequences of this incomplete liberalization in economic affairs under the umbrella of a postpopulist authoritarian state was the rising significance of new merchant classes and minority communities that could serve as counterweights to the regime but, more often than not, as instruments of its power.[82] Furthermore, the redistributionist policies of the 1970s and 1980s gradually gave way to a platform of austerity. The authoritarian dictatorship that crystallized over the course of these thirty years radically transformed Syria, co-opting or coercing a substantial share of support from the national population. In Chapter 1, I will return to the ways in which the state's "revolution from above," to adapt Hinnebusch's term, entailed *Asadist-Ba'thist cultural revolution*, a reflection of cultural Asadism that promoted an aesthetic ideology—the aesthetics of power—consonant with the broader principles of single-party rule. This was not a static cultural formation but rather one that would evolve over time, both in relation to political transformation inside the country and in tandem with global developments.

REVOLUTION—REFORM—REVOLUTION'

While the Eternal Leader may have been represented as—and perhaps believed by some to be truly—immortal, Hafiz al-Asad did, in fact, die. The concept of the Eternal Leader—the embodiment of Ba'thist political notions of eternity and historical destiny—did not perish, though it was dramatically transformed upon this monumental turning point. After his death in June 2000, Hafiz was succeeded by his son, Bashar al-Asad, a British-educated ophthalmologist who had been groomed as a potential heir ever since the tragic and dramatic demise of his older brother Basil in a freak automobile accident in 1994. Although most analysts agree that the institutional foundations of the regime remained relatively unchanged during this transition, there is debate regarding the relative extent of ideological, material, and public relations recalibration. Regardless of where one comes down on this question, substantive social, political, and cultural reforms did take place. For example, one finds the acceleration of certain privatization efforts, the reinforced hegemony of the military (mainly 'Alawī and other minoritarian officers), the enhanced position and influence of urban merchants (primarily Sunnis from the urban centers), and increased talk about the liberalization of the political field toward "pluralism" in a manner that might give comfort to minorities even if this softened rhetoric did not extend to Sunni Muslim political parties.[83]

"Syria's succession in 2000," Joshua Stacher argues, "resulted from a clear consensus by the top elites from the military, intelligence services, and ruling party."[84] The new regime primarily comprised loyalists who had been in their positions for many years but paid lip service to a multipronged strategy of reformism from above, often discussed in the language of reform within limits or with restrictions. As Bassam Haddad notes, the populist-authoritarianism of the early Asadist-Ba'thist regime underwent a "dilution" or "unraveling" during the late twentieth century as the corporatist arrangements linking state and society as well as state and business interests began "to give way to populist demobilization and alliance shuffling" in favor of previously excluded political and economic actors.[85] Be that as it may, this early transitional period was characterized by a widespread sense of possibility as new political and cultural demands were placed on the government. Suzanne Kassab contrasts the "Sisyphean struggle" of intellectuals against the dictatorship of Hafiz al-Asad to the "Promethean moment" of Bashar's infant presidency.[86] The "Damascus Spring" of 2000–2001 encompassed public demands made and actions taken by Syrian writers, artists, and intellectuals for the cause of more robust liberalization in politics, the economy, and society as well as cultural and intellectual opening. One of the signature documents of this era was the Statement of 99, released on September 27, 2000, which called for an end to the national state of emergency, the release of political prisoners, and greater freedoms of speech, public assembly, and movement. Interestingly, the first draft of the statement was written by documentary filmmaker Omar Amiralay (discussed in the Conclusion) and revised with the assistance of filmmaker Ossama Mohammed (Chapters 2 and 4) and political activist Muwaffaq Nayrabia. Notable signatories included novelist Mamdouh Azzam (Chapter 2), filmmaker 'Abd al-Latif 'Abd al-Hamid (Chapter 2), and philosopher Tayyib Tizini (Chapter 1).

Meaningful steps were taken in the direction of a holistic transformation of the country: a crackdown on corruption was launched, the mixed economic system that would come to be known as the "Social Market Economy" platform was introduced in 2005, and some restrictions on the circulation of ideas were lifted.[87] The introduction of privately financed and internationally produced media also signaled an opening that many pundits understood as a start down the road of real reform. For many Syrians, however, reformism from above scarcely amounted to more than window dressing, a continuation of the same old song in a new key. This efflorescence of public discussion and political optimism did not immediately result in the substantive transformation demanded by intellectuals, artists, filmmakers, writers, and ordinary people. The regime managed to reconstitute itself through a kind of "authoritarian upgrading" that ultimately resulted in an ideological and political system that Lisa Wedeen aptly labels "neoliberal autocracy": a package of reforms that set the country on a path of technocratic improvement that privileged tourism, heritage preservation, conspicuous consumption, and other fantasies of the good life.[88] The northern capital of Aleppo was named the Islamic capital of culture in 2006, for example, and urban rehabilitation and revitalization projects popped up around the country, auguring mass tourism for the first time in the country's history. Meanwhile, Syria's foreign policy remained steeped in the language of Arab nationalism and anti-imperialism even if militarily and strategically there was little action to back it up. The regime's decision to support (or at least stand back during) the US invasion and occupation of Iraq in 2003 illustrated an aversion to regional or international conflict. Meanwhile, despite Syria's alliance with Iran and its ongoing support for Hizballah in its struggle against Israel, the withdrawal of Syrian forces from Lebanon in 2005 demonstrated the waning appetite among the Syrian political elite for regional military adventurism. Despite regular Israeli violations of Lebanese and Syrian airspace as well as the continuing Israeli occupation of the Syrian Golan Heights, the regime remained more inclined to expend its military capabilities domestically rather than regionally or internationally.

Economic, political, and, to a lesser extent, security liberalization during the first decade of Bashar al-Asad's rule coincided with relaxation of restrictions on intellectual life, too. With the coming to power of Bashar, older, ideologically encrusted forms of literature and film that had been embedded in Asadist-Ba'thist modes of thought and organs of cultural production were increasingly challenged, criticized, or even dismissed. If the cultural and intellectual fields under Hafiz al-Asad had come to be institutionalized in a way that remained faithful to a nationalist aesthetic ideology of cultural revolution, part and parcel of Hinnebusch's "revolution from above," the cultural transformation of the country in the wake of al-Asad père's death can be analogously understood in terms of reformism from above. The Asadist-Ba'thist cultural revolution of the

1970s and 1980s receded and new forms of creative expression emerged during the 1990s and early 2000s that were less doctrinaire, more reflective of a coalescing zeitgeist of intellectual openness and cultural experimentation. In the formulation of Volker Perthes, Bashar's regime "retains all the instruments of authoritarianism, and uses them where it deems necessary. However, repression has become much more selective than it used to be, and is even cloaked in a semblance of rule-of-law and institutional procedure." Even if this resulted in a political environment that was "more pluralistic," Perthes says, the security state remained well in place: "People fear it less, but the *mukhabarat* is still an essential means of control."[89] At the same time, surveillance itself would come to be objectified with unprecedented verve in literature and film during the early 2000s. In Chapter 4, I will analyze several novels—by Nihad Sirees, Rosa Yaseen Hasan, and Samar Yazbek—that exemplify both the potential and the limitations of this tentative opening in the cultural field through their direct engagement with psychological and literary reflections of authoritarian rule and state surveillance.

There is no simple historical line of causality that can be traced between these forms of literary and cultural critique and political transformation during the first decade of Bashar al-Asad's rule. Historians and other scholars of contemporary Syria continue to debate the complicated relationship between political liberalization and cultural liberalization. Nevertheless, the regime proved exceptionally adept at managing, muffling, and ultimately absorbing political, social, and cultural opposition. In an interview with the *Wall Street Journal* in late January 2011, Bashar al-Asad discussed the challenges confronting the Syrian regime. In response to questions about the sluggish pace of "reform," he identified "internal" refurbishments that were of particular importance. "These are the changes that we need," he said.

> But at the same time you have to upgrade the society and this does not mean to upgrade it technically by upgrading qualifications. It means to open up the minds. . . . You cannot reform your society or institution without opening your mind. So the core issue is how to open the mind, the whole society, and this means everybody in society including everyone. I am not talking about the state or average or common people. I am talking about everybody; because when you close your mind as an official you cannot upgrade and vice versa.[90]

Al-Asad and his advisers would seem to have been reading the current scholarly literature on authoritarianism. Although his cagy response did not directly address the persistence of brutal techniques employed to perpetuate the status quo, al-Asad suggested that "successful" regimes must keep all practical reformist options on the table, especially when state authority is questioned or challenged in more forceful ways. Neoliberal reform pursued during the early 2000s may have generated financial and cultural benefits for Syria's technocratic elite, but the majority of the population could find little hope for their economic future. By no means was it obvious to historians or anyone else, however, that this period of reformism from above would intersect with a national and regional conjuncture of ecological crisis, economic precarity, cultural ferment, and political uprising on the order of the so-called Arab Spring that erupted in Tunisia in 2010 and in Egypt in 2011.

Even in the midst of mounting opposition and widespread dissatisfaction with the course of reformism from above, hardly anyone predicted a spontaneous, nonviolent uprising against corruption and political repression breaking out in Syria. If the mass uprising of 2011 was mostly unanticipated, neither could it have been known in advance that fulsome expressions of antiregime sentiment would be concentrated, at first, in provincial cities and towns long consigned to the periphery of state-led reform and modernization. Popular mobilization boiled over in February and March 2011, initially as sporadic demonstrations that sprang up around poor and working-class districts of Damascus but soon evolving into expressions of outrage against the unconscionable horror that took place in the southern city of Dar'a in March. After a handful of teenage boys scrawled graffiti critical of the regime in public, reprisals against protestors turned swift and severe. Thirteen-year-old Hamza al-Khatib became an iconic and galvanizing figure at this moment, as he was among scores of activists and ordinary people who went out to protest corruption and regime repression elsewhere throughout the Dar'a Governorate a month later. Al-Khatib was detained in April and mutilated and murdered by state security forces, who unceremoniously returned his body to his family in May. When members of the family and their supporters protested, as one version of the events has it, the governor spitefully told them to bring their wives over and they would help them make more children. At this point, demonstrations exploded all over the country, capped by regular mass protests every Friday, part of a cycle of activism that electrified the nation, mobilizing Syrians who had little to no experience in political organizing.[91] Reinoud Leenders reminds us of "an alternative view" regarding the early mobilization, namely "that it was not perceived weaknesses of the state or negligence of the regime's main constituencies that were primarily responsible for the Syrian uprising but a widely shared perception of the strength of the opposition."[92] Environmental factors also played a role, though their impact is open to debate—in Syrian cities and towns where migrants from the eastern desert had fled and in poorly performing agricultural regions such as Dar'a, Homs, and Idlib, which together became a tinderbox for potential social unrest.[93] Uprisings around the Arab world also helped deliver the message that there was a real possibility of political transformation, that perhaps even the overthrow of the political order—exemplified by the ubiquitous slogan "The People Want the Fall of the Regime"—was not such an outlandish or far-fetched idea.[94] Expressions of frustration from broad segments of the Syrian working and middle classes, moreover, shredded the mantle of ideological progressivism that had cloaked the state for so long even as the regime immediately tarred its opponents as fanatical jihadis or foreign wreckers.

Despite accusations hurled against intellectuals during the early days of the revolution for not being involved enough in the political upsurge, writers, filmmakers, and many artists played a crucial role in defining, supporting, and reflecting the aspirations of the Syrian people.[95] The eruption of popular protest against authoritarian rule in this incipient revolution calling for life, liberty, and dignity refashioned the struggle around aesthetic ideology in dramatic ways that are still playing out, both within Syria and across the global Syrian diaspora. Literature and film produced during the post-2011 period have drawn attention to political and epistemological anxieties forged in the crucible of the Syrian revolution and the Syria War. As part of my explanation regarding how writers and filmmakers—especially, albeit not exclusively, those in exile—attempted to bear witness not only to the excitement but also to the danger of this moment, in Chapter 5 I will introduce the "the slow witness" and slow witnessing, which have been articulated not exclusively through an aesthetics of slowness per se but also through attempts to isolate and perhaps step outside of the demands of a historical moment characterized by the manic acceleration of time. In this moment of uncertainty and danger, narrator-witnesses and filmmaker-witnesses were animated by a *documentary imperative*: a collective narration device that entailed *mitsprechen*, or, *speaking-with* a range of Syrian voices that simultaneously introduced a contemporary aesthetics of solidarity and enabled writers and other artists to clarify and manage the distinction between the aesthetics of power and the aesthetics of resistance. In addition to the work of Maha Hasan, Khalil Suwaylih, Ossama Mohammed, and Wiam Simav Bedirxan examined in Chapter 5, that of other writers, filmmakers, and artists helped to generate a critical archive for this period that remains invaluable for thinking about the revolution and the war in both aesthetic and historical terms. If the slow witness held out hope of an alternative imaginative horizon for the Syrian revolution, the lived experiences and consequences of the Syria War have been much darker and bloodier. The uprising tragically devolved (or was hijacked depending on one's viewpoint) into a bloody civil war layered with multiple proxy conflicts, a geopolitical struggle for Syria that remains unresolved. In Chapter 6, I will confront the visceral brutality of this war by looking at how the appearance of death and dead bodies in cultural production—iterations of Syria War necroaesthetics, as I put it—represents a morbid reckoning with the causes and consequences of violence. While there is no single experience or unified understanding of death and dying in Syria War culture, a deeper engagement with literary and cinematic representations of death—by Khaled Khalifa, Sawsan Jamil Hasan, Mazin ʿArafa, and Soudade Kaadan—enables alternative perspectives from which to consider the history, present, and possible futures of war-torn Syria.

My modest scholarly contribution in *Revolutions Aesthetic* pales in significance compared with the scale of human suffering and loss that is the true tragedy of the Syria War: over a half million dead and nearly half of the Syrian population internally displaced, made into international refugees, or otherwise forced into exile. If the Syrian revolution and the war that followed have attracted substantial international attention in terms of geostrategic military analysis and humanitarian concern for the shocking displacement, destruction, and human suffering that has ensued, the cultural consequences of the revolution and the aesthetic dimensions of cultural production in the time of the war have attracted less attention. The destruction and persistent inaccessibility of archives and other historical materials in Syria will continue to complicate the research agenda of both Syrian and non-Syrian scholars. By gathering a range of literature and film into a single chronological narrative, *Revolutions Aesthetic* provides a glimpse into underappreciated perspectives on contemporary Syrian history which deserve to be studied and celebrated in their own right but also, crucially, might become part of the foundation for imagining different futures for the country. Because of the relatively ahistorical cultural analysis of this period hitherto, what has not yet been adequately appreciated is the extent to which the aesthetic ideology of Asadist-Ba'thist cultural revolution as well as the ensemble of competing aesthetic ideologies that occasionally challenged and sometimes affirmed state cultural production described in Chapters 1 through 4 left its mark on the conditions of possibility for writers, artists, and filmmakers to generate new kinds of cultural production in the time of the Syria War, discussed in Chapters 5 and 6 and the Conclusion. This entailed, among other things, attempts at unlearning statist cultural ideology and struggling to revolutionize culture in new ways, to re-revolutionize a cultural field that had already been staked out and incompletely captured by the rhetoric of revolution so pervasive in Asadist-Ba'thist Syria. The repurposing of "revolution" after the aesthetic-ideological field had been structured and surveilled by the security state for forty years was a monumental challenge for writers, filmmakers, artists, and intellectuals during this moment of possibility and danger. While my focus is not the military or political history of the Syrian revolution or the Syria War, extensive discussion in the pages that follow shows how crucial the Syrian revolution and the Syria War have been to the renewed flourishing of and sharpened contestation within the literary and cinematic domains. *Revolutions Aesthetic* showcases how the struggle over aesthetic ideology in Asadist-Ba'thist Syria became all too relevant once again, in ways both old and new, in the time of the Syria War, with repercussions that are still being felt and consequences yet to be understood.

Chapter 1

BAʿTHIST CULTURAL REVOLUTION

There rests on all of your shoulders . . . the burden of responsibility to lead the battle in one of its most dangerous domains, that of language, and with the language of truth you stand shoulder to shoulder with the armed forces as well as the popular masses in battling imperialism and the untruths of our enemies. Your part is an extremely important contribution to the work of rallying the troops, mobilizing the forces, and assembling the masses both morally and psychologically in order to confront and defeat the enemy.

— Hafiz al-Asad[1]

Find in any country the Ablest Man that exists there; raise *him* to the supreme place, and loyally reverence him: you have a perfect government for that country; no ballot-box, parliamentary eloquence, voting, constitution-building, or other machinery whatsoever can improve it a whit. It is in the perfect state; an ideal country. The Ablest Man; he means also the truest-hearted, justest, the Noblest Man: what he *tells us to do* must be precisely the wisest, fittest, that we could anywhere or anyhow learn.

— Thomas Carlyle, *On Heroes, Hero-Worship, & the Heroic in History*[2]

It is possible that a distinct reactionary and a repressive authoritarian can produce authentic literature. The question is: under what historical conditions?

— Herbert Marcuse, "On 'The Aesthetic Dimension'"[3]

UPON THE DEATH OF PRESIDENT HAFIZ AL-ASAD IN JUNE 2000, THE Syrian minister of culture Maha Qannut (b. 1953) penned a flowery elegy to the dearly departed leader that was published in *al-Maʿrifa*, the country's signature state-run intellectual-cultural journal, under the title "Saddle the Horse for its Final Journey." Her tribute figures the departure of the leader as a horseman preparing his steed for a last ride into the unknown. Qannut, who earned a doctorate in Arabic literature at Damascus University and would serve a strikingly short term as minister of culture (2000–2001), lamented the fact that "words [have] suddenly fallen from my hands . . . as I continue to search for the right expression . . . without finding it."[4] Al-Asad was mourned in a torrent of florid, even maudlin, verse: "the guardian of the dream of Arabism"; the "teacher" who had flung open the gates of Arab nationalism (*al-qawmiyya*); the "great knight [who] has dismounted his horse"; "the hero of all the heroic epics"; "the prosody around which all of the poets concentrated their meter, like a sword that has accumulated marks of heroism on both sides of the blade"; the metaphor great writers struggle to articulate; "the mountains that protected our plains from wolves and the biting icy wind." In what would likely come across as darkly ironic to Syrians critical of al-Asad's repressive regime and its enforced

FIGURE 1. October War Panorama Mural, Damascus

ideological and political conformity, Qannut concludes by equating al-Asad with "a guard standing alone in the face of the storm . . . repelling tyranny [*al-ṭāghūt*] wherever it may be."[5] If the minister of culture was driven to vivid eulogizing here, she was also left with vexing, seemingly unanswerable questions: "After today for whom shall I thread my rhymes . . . to whom [shall I send] laurel bouquets and garlands of flowers?"[6] "O beacon of the Arabs," she rhapsodized, "how can it be that you have left the lighthouse?" Qannut could not accept that al-Asad's departure from his post was a dereliction of duty, though. Rather, she addressed the "Eternal Leader" directly, "certain that if the choice were in your hands, you would decide to remain our trustworthy guardian in the icy-cold night . . . you would choose fifty [more] years of struggle."[7]

By no means was this the only—or the lengthiest—ode to al-Asad written in the wake of his passing. Nor was it the first time Syrian government officials, public intellectuals, and ordinary people offered sycophantic praise of their heroic president.[8] Over the course of the 1970s and 1980s, Syrian intellectuals produced a noteworthy body of writing that amounted to a library of obsequiousness in praise of the leader, a president who had seized power in a military putsch dubbed the "corrective movement" (*al-ḥaraka al-taṣḥīḥiyya*) in November 1970. This cadre of devout loyalists to the Syrian regime did not need to wait for his death in order to pay their awestruck respects. Aphorisms and insights of the Eternal Leader and his intellectual genius were published by "committed" publishers and publishing houses.[9] Pseudo-scholarly works by public intellectuals such as Safwan Qudsi—historian, literary critic, and long-time editor of *al-Maʿrifa*—flourished like mushrooms, and some of this work was published by al-Asad's consigliere and defense minister, Mustafa Tlas.[10]

Hafiz al-Asad ruled Syria for thirty years (1970–2000) with an admixture of cunning and ruthlessness, leaving a legacy that has continued to shape the country over the two decades since his death. Despite the political, economic, and social legacies of that defining period in Syria's modern history, the intellectual and cultural dimensions of his era have received strikingly little attention from historians. Studies of modern and contemporary Syria have generally failed to account for the wide-ranging contributions made by writers, intellectuals, political theorists, and other artists in shaping the cultural and intellectual fields. Building on but also moving beyond the social scientific literature on the consolidation of one-party rule, the evolution of foreign policy and national strategy, and the transformation of Syria's political economy, *Revolutions Aesthetic* thus presents a fresh cultural and intellectual history of Baʿthist Syria, paying specific attention to the literary and cinematic realms. This chapter presents a historical reassessment of what Lisa Wedeen calls "the nationalist aesthetics and bombastic prose of the 1970s–80s Baʿthism."[11] We find in literary, intellectual, cinema, and even military journals of the period complicated engagements with the agonistic struggle around aesthetic ideology that defined cultural politics in Syria, the tensions between cultural Asadism and those who resisted it or sought alternatives to its logic, between what I describe as the aesthetics of power and the aesthetics of resistance or the aesthetics of solidarity. The crucial significance of culture (*thaqāfa*) in Syria and the Arabic-speaking world at large was not discovered in the 1970s, of course.[12] But new ideological reference points and key words for cultural production were introduced during this period. This transformation entailed a turning away from the doctrinaire theoretical language of the early Baʿth and a leaning toward more militantly pragmatic Arab nationalist conceptions of Syria's place in the Middle East, the Third World, and beyond. Whether this agenda was worthy of the name, regime figureheads, bureaucrats, and supporters envisioned what I call Asadist-Baʿthist cultural revolution, although the term was rarely used as one of art. The aim of this chapter is not to issue a verdict on the aptness of this notion of cultural revolution; instead, I establish some of the aesthetic ideological grounds on which the cultural field became a site of agonistic struggle among writers, filmmakers, and critics.

The "corrective movement" of November 1970 was nothing short of an internal coup. The left-leaning Neo-Baʿth who had seized power in February 1966 from the Baʿthist forces who themselves had declared their "revolution" on March 8, 1963, were trounced by supporters of then defense minister Hafiz al-Asad, who in turn charted a new course for Syrian political, political-economic, and military strategy. Less often remarked on are the ideological and cultural dimensions of the corrective movement. This chapter explores publications and journals that pushed for a new conception of "the hero" and "the intellectual leader," one that situated the rural and uneducated Hafiz al-Asad (1930–2000) as an avatar of Baʿthist erudition and commitment. Here I stage a historical reading of leading cultural periodicals of the 1970s and 1980s in order to situate literary and visual cultural production during this period within the Syrian intellectual and public spheres. These are hardly transparent sources even if the editors and writers who filled the pages of *Cinema Life* (*al-Ḥayā al-Sīnamā'iyya*), *Military Thought* (*al-Fikr al-'Askarī*), *Knowledge* (*al-Ma'rifa*), and *Literary Standpoint* (*al-Mawqif al-Adabī*) often telegraphed their political and ideological aims. By the same token, it would be facile to understand Ba'thism as the sole animating principle guiding the production of culture during this period. Be that as it may, what I am calling Ba'thist aesthetic ideology is to be found not only in the theoretical writings of the founders—Michel 'Aflaq (1910–1989), Salah al-Din al-Bitar (1912–1980), Zaki al-Arsuzi (1899–1968)—the directives of the party, or the speeches of the leader. Rather, the cultural and intellectual spheres in Ba'thist Syria accommodated a range of perspectives on literature, film, theater, television, and art. The Asadist-Ba'thist regime sought to promote a new discursive and ideological agenda for Syrian writers, filmmakers, and intellectuals that was articulated in the militant language of an aesthetic ideology of cultural revolution. This chapter demonstrates that there was a widely held or at least convincingly performed belief that the corrective movement would transform and even revitalize the cultural sphere. Cultural policy and practice were conditioned and transformed in an attempt by the state to promulgate its own aesthetic ideology through Asadist-Ba'thist cultural revolution. In order to flesh out my argument more fully, I present close readings of these literary, intellectual, and cinema journals published by the state during this period. This refinement in our understanding of the complicated relationship between aesthetics and politics in the making of the Syrian cultural and intellectual fields sets the stage for the substantive chapters to follow.

CULTURAL ASADISM

Alongside the fundamental transformation of Syria through state- and nation-building—what has been called political Asadism—there was a concomitant, affiliated, but substantively distinct, set of practices constituting what I term *cultural Asadism*. Political scientist Volker Perthes was among the first to use the term:

> Asadism, so to speak, depoliticizes: it implies that Syria's future is guaranteed as long as Asad is at the helm, and that neither the party, nor government, parliament or civil society should worry about or deal with the country's high policies as long as the leader does so.[13]

The term would be used both analytically and vernacularly, in Arabic at least, although for the most part *al-Asadiyya* (Asadism) connotes the system of clientelist rule institutionalized through the cultivation of patronage networks based on tribe, kin, and personal interest. In other words, what has typically been called Asadism refers more strictly to political Asadism.[14] Perthes's related argument about the relative weakness of state ideology (he is skeptical of the term being used at all) is bolstered by Wedeen's clarifying note that "the effects of Asad's cult, although powerful, are also ambiguous, indeterminate, and limited."[15] However "ambiguous, indeterminate, and limited" these effects may have been, political Asadism was accompanied by consonant policies and practices that I identify as cultural Asadism. State-driven Asadist-Baʿthist cultural revolution, an attempt to institutionalize and promulgate a hegemonic aesthetic ideology and its leader cult through cultural means, is legible in periodicals, public culture, and cultural production. This aesthetic ideology could be adapted, challenged, and evaded by Syrian artists, writers, filmmakers, and intellectuals. The struggle for aesthetic power, value, and taste is a crucial dynamic at the heart of the cultural history of Baʿthist Syria.

Najah al-ʿAttar (b. 1933), who preceded Maha Qannut as minister of culture, was the longest-serving representative in that position in Syrian history (1976–2000). Always ready to heap praise on the leader for his vanguardist role in the cultural sphere at any public event or in any of the state's cultural organs, al-ʿAttar published a fulsome expression of this position in *al-Maʿrifa*, Syria's premier literary-intellectual journal in 1979. "Do I deserve to speak in the name of the intellectuals?" she asked rhetorically, no doubt certain that her position as minister of culture granted her license to do so. In order to avoid answering the question, she chose instead to "speak in the name of culture . . . and in its name I raise a salute to its Leader." The leader of culture in Syria was, of course, the leader of all things and was characterized not only by cultural knowledge and intelligence but also by heroic qualities recognized all over Syria and well beyond. "If politics has a leader [*qāʾid*], and if the economy has a leader, and if war has a leader," al-ʿAttar wrote, "then culture also has a leader." Al-Asad was this leader, of course, but he was also "an eagle who spreads his wings, and in soaring high above he doesn't fail to watch and to notice the most precise details on earth. In fact, he is sustenance for the people."[16] These descriptions are entirely consonant with the role Hafiz al-Asad promoted for himself, as when he announced to the late British journalist and historian Patrick Seale on March 18, 1988, "I am the head of the country, not of the government."[17] Even if the power of al-Asad's rule rested on a hand-picked elite that included intellectuals, writers, and artists—all of whom were nourished in part by his strength, heroism, and benevolence—al-'Attar concluded her lionization of the president with reference to the theory of the hero articulated by Scottish philosopher and historian Thomas Carlyle (1795–1881). From Carlyle al-'Attar understood "the great man" to be great not by virtue of his "personal characteristics alone . . . but rather because he is endowed with qualities that make him more qualified than others to understand the needs and problems of his age." What stands out here—what distinguishes the cultural politics of Asadism from other forms of aesthetic ideology in modern Syrian history—is the combination of secular political concepts drawn from Ba'thism, other varieties of Arab nationalism, and anti-imperialism on the one hand and what might be called the divine right of leadership imputed to Hafiz al-Asad on the other. Not only was al-Asad "a great Arab leader and a great Arab hope, the Leader of this nation [*umma*] that has lost [Gamal] Abdel Nasser, but [also a leader] granted by the heavens."[18] The sacralization of al-Asad in this manner indicates an unrecognized yet crucial aspect of incipient Asadism, which needs to be understood in cultural and not only political terms.[19] It is also important to remember that sectarian identity is not ideological destiny in Syria. After all, Najah al-'Attar was the sister of 'Isam al-'Attar, who in 1961 became the second person to hold the position of superintendent-general (*al-murāqib al-'āmm*) of the Syrian Muslim Brothers three years before the death of founding figure Mustafa al-Siba'i. After fleeing to Lebanon during the antigovernment uprisings that followed the March 8, 1963, Ba'thist coup, al-'Attar wound up in exile in Aachen, Germany. From that point forward, though, he would represent a relatively marginal constituency in the Syrian Islamist political arena, outshone by more radical voices both on the ground in Syria and elsewhere, including Marwan Hadid, Sa'id Hawwa, and 'Adnan Sa'd al-Din. Thomas Mayer notes that Sa'd al-Din and others accused al-'Attar of abdicating his leadership role, softening his rhetoric, and blunting his actions because of his sister's position in the regime, though this rancor subsided somewhat and the Muslim Brothers' ranks would close somewhat around a more radical program of resistance to the regime after the death of al-'Attar's wife in 1981.[20]

Leader worship was translated into servile intellectual speak that circulated throughout the cultural sphere. The aesthetic ideology of cultural Asadism was marked by a broad conceptualization of heroism, one that found expression in literature and film throughout this period. In a special issue on the state of Syrian Arabic literature in *al-Mawqif al-Adabī* (*Literary Standpoint*), the monthly journal published by the Arab Writers' Union (Ittiḥād Kuttāb al-ʿArab, AWU), which prided itself on retaining institutional autonomy and intellectual independence despite its ties to the state cultural apparatus, critic and writer Hanna ʿAbbud attempts to historicize the representation of "the hero" in European philosophy while drawing links to Syrian prose writing. In the first part of the essay, ʿAbbud catalogs various meanings of the hero and heroism in historical contexts.[21] "Heroism individualizes," he writes, in the most abstract terms,

> in the arena of life or in the arena of the novel. No heroism without individuality. And individuality is no stranger to the broad range and specific character of humanity. This can take a variety of forms, including an outsized personality, with both positive and negative characteristics.

He then turns to the literary significance of the hero: "The realist hero [*al-baṭal al-wāqʿī*] must be entirely positive, in the minds of his supporters, at least."[22] This does not mean that the heroic individual exists in a vacuum, however, because "in his individuality," this figure is "a human role model," one that every individual strives to emulate. Thus the hero can never be fully reduced to an individual or separated from "the social." There is a sort of contradiction between "a hero made of flesh and blood" and "a hero made of paper."[23] If the writer cannot establish a firm bond between the literary hero (paper) and the reader with respect to an actual real-life hero (flesh and blood), then the "positive" effects of heroism cannot be fully realized in literature.

Heroism, in other words, is at its most potent when the author relies on idealism.[24] But idealism is a set of philosophical principles that does not come without risks, and the ideologies such as Marxism, Freudianism, and fascism that ʿAbbud identifies—however tendentiously—as idealist converge in their valorization of a staunchly masculine form of heroism. In Marxism, the hero "is the true protector of the interests of mankind, which marches behind him." For Freud, heroism is epitomized by an archetype or symbol (*ramz*) of the father, who must be either a "sadist" to others in defense of his family or a masochist as he sacrifices himself on their behalf. Either way, the centerpiece of this ideological system is the patriarch. The cultural reflections of heroism in the

FIGURE 2. "Yes to the Leader-Symbol," *al-Maʿrifa*, No. 339 (December 1991)

representation of patriarchy and the patriarch will become clearer in the discussion of masculinity and power in the literature and film of the 1970s–1990s in Chapter 2. Hafiz al-Asad portrayed as a "leader-symbol" (Figure 2) nicely expresses this argument. Meanwhile, the dialectical entanglement of sadism and masochism in the leader's exercise of his guardianship points to the place of violence in this conceptualization of heroism on display in Nihad Sirees's 2004 novel *The Silence and the Roar* (*al-Ṣamt wa-l-Ṣakhab*; Chapter 4) and Mazin ʿArafa's 2017 novel *The Cranes* (*al-Gharānīq*; Chapter 6). When human beings become aware of their weaknesses, they search for causes, including "the father," who must, in a form of psychological compensation, be characterized by heroic features: "generous, brave, bold, loyal, self-sacrificing [*mutafān*]." These prime virtues of heroism touted by Asadist-Baʿthist cultural revolutionaries could be as easily discerned through experience as narrative, leading ʿAbbud to a political definition that would not seem unfamiliar to Syrians of the time: "The hero, therefore, is the true guardian of the interests of the human group that marches behind him."[25] The relationship between the hero and the guardian is analogous to the relationship between heroism and leadership.

"History is for heroes," ʿAbbud crows, inserting his own interpretation of Nietzsche's übermensch. For Hitler, by contrast, who ʿAbbud arrives at not long after his discussion of nineteenth-century European Romantic philosophy, the hero is the one who embodies the aspirations of the nation (*al-umma*), which may be a glib interpretation of the national-socialist leader and his genocidal ambitions but may also be one that raises discomfiting questions, with implications for the type of heroism ʿAbbud extols here as well as that articulated by al-ʿAttar and other state officials in different venues. ʿAbbud concludes his survey of the intellectual history of heroism with the existentialist hero, who differs entirely from previous examples as "a protest against existence itself. The [existentialist] hero is the offspring of existence, and yet at the same time he struggles against this existence because it is an absurd one."[26] ʿAbbud is broad-minded and flexible about the variety of hero characters that are available for the critic and the intellectual to think with. In what appears to be a passing yet telling comment, however, he directly equates heroism (*al-buṭūla*) with leadership (*al-zaʿāma*)—instead of other virtues he has already introduced such as bravery, loyalty, and self-sacrifice, syllogistically relating the deeds and position of the leader figure to the historical function of the hero.[27] And while there is no mention made of the Syrian president himself as the "Eternal Leader" or "Hero," it is not a far stretch to conclude that this conception of heroism and the hero "in flesh and blood" and "on paper" would resonate well beyond the mind of one literary critic and into the Syrian body politic, indicating that representations of heroes and heroism in narrative should be carefully constructed in light of their capacity to reflect the virtues and characteristics of the Eternal Leader, the one true hero "in flesh and blood." By this point, the concept of heroism has been unmoored from any material foundations. The leader qua hero is tautologically defined as a heroic leader. Regardless of what he does (always a he, of course), his heroism is ensured by his leadership. Any other attributes of the hero become less important than his political and ideological commitments. One is reminded of Hannah Arendt's observation about dictatorial systems: "The Leader is irreplaceable because the whole complicated structure of the movement would lose its *raison d'être* without his commands."[28] For ʿAbbud, the aesthetic significance of the hero in different kinds of art must be apprehended in relation to the outsized importance of the heroes of contemporary Syria, starting first and foremost with Hafiz al-Asad and then state officials themselves. Before turning to look in greater detail at what aesthetic ideology and cultural

FIGURE 3. "Greetings to our Air Force on the Commemoration of Their Founding—16 November—," *Jaysh al-Sha'b* N° 954 (October 13/20, 1970)

revolution in Baʿthist Syria looked like, I first establish the institutional grounds on which this new regime articulated its own significance.

MILITARY STRATEGY AND INTELLECTUAL HISTORY

The so-called corrective movement was a crucial turning point in the history of modern Syria and had consequences that would be felt in political, military, ideological, and cultural terms. The declining significance of party ideology was counterintuitively accompanied by and expanded the scope for the party itself, the "committed" military, and the security apparatus. "By the time of Asad's ascension to power," political scientist Steven Heydemann notes,

> the competing visions of the Syrian state that had emerged with the coming of independence—visions that were centrally implicated in post-independence political struggles—had been suppressed in favor of a single, dominant image of Syria's political identity as a radically populist regime.[29]

The foundations of Syria's authoritarian populism would be expanded and transformed under al-Asad's rule. Raymond Hinnebusch identifies the army, the Baʿth Party apparatus, and the state bureaucracy as the fundamental building blocks of the post-1970 regime.[30] In 1972 this new order established the Progressive National Front, an umbrella political organization that officially licensed and defanged specific leftist parties, thus co-opting a substantial segment of the oppositionist political field. Similar initiatives—Heydemann calls them "social pacts"—were employed to both empower and manage the country's social and economic forces in a corporatist fashion. "Exceptional" executive powers were asserted by the central committee of the Baʿth Party, made manifest, for example, in the declaration of a renewed state of emergency. Syria had been under martial law technically since 1948, but new legal and constitutional reforms were passed, including promulgation of a Permanent Constitution of the Syrian Arab Republic in 1973. Right away the country saw a substantial shift of national defense spending away from the army and other pillars of national defense and toward the security services and paramilitary organizations. Loyalty to the leader and the regime was secured through preferential and nepotistic appointments, gradually transforming the social character of regime institutions. Military spending rose dramatically during the postindependence period but never so sharply as in the boost following the corrective movement.[31] Drawing on 1978 figures, Michel Seurat and Jim Paul identify a more than fivefold increase in military expenditures between 1955 and 1970 ($71 million in 1955 compared with $384 million in 1970). This was dwarfed by a subsequent spike from $384 million in 1970 to nearly ten times that, $3 billion, by the early 1980s.[32] Citing more modest statistics, Fadia Kiwan finds a comparable magnitude of growth in military spending, noting that the Syrian defense budget ballooned from about $220 million in 1970 to $2.036 billion in 1980.[33] National military resources were being put to use domestically to combat the raging Islamic insurgency as well as internationally in both the ongoing conflict along the southern border with Israel and the military's deployment to Lebanon in 1976 to prevent, unsuccessfully, an unspooling thread of civil conflict.[34] Whereas Syria is a majority Sunni Muslim country, and the military and state bureaucracy reflected this demographic reality through the 1970s, by the time of the Syrian uprising in March 2011, scholars were estimating that nearly 70 percent of soldiers in active military service and some 80 percent of the military leadership were members of the 'Alawī community. Although ethnic or sectarian ties, to borrow Alasdair Drysdale's phrasing, "lubricated the Ba'th's climb to power," it would be superficial and inaccurate to characterize the 1963, 1966, and 1970 coups d'état (or, for that matter, the 2011 uprising and subsequent war) as sectarian transformations pure and simple.[35]

"Asad's rise marked the victory of the military over the radical intelligentsia," as Hinnebusch aptly notes. "Asad's aim was to consolidate the unstable Ba'th state and mobilize Syria for a war to recover the lost territories. In the process, he turned the Ba'th state from an instrument of class revolution into a machinery of power in the service of raison d'état."[36] But it is also worth remembering that Michel 'Aflaq himself—the ideological founder of the Ba'th Party who remained marginal to Syrian political life and would have a much more public political persona in Saddam Hussein's Iraq after his exile from Syria—had also advocated for a greater role of the military in political life. At a certain point, he too wished to see the army and other national institutions acquire a more "popular" (*sha'bī*) character. To be sure, the al-Asad regime oversaw an even more radical reorientation of the armed forces and security services, dedicating resources to reinforcing domestic stability at the expense of waging conflicts abroad. In a sense, however, 'Aflaq had already been calling for the "correction" of the relationship between the military and civilian sectors in Syria during the 1960s. "Comrades," he wrote in 1966:

> A number of our military fellow comrades have slipped into blocs, domination over the party and the people and to opportunism and selfishness. This almost destroyed the revolution. We are not denying the struggle that those comrades had undertaken, nor are we denying their role in the revolution. But it is not right or fair that we should sacrifice the party and the revolution just because these comrades had rendered services to the party and the revolution. There are many questions being asked today. How can we correct the situation inside the army? How can we stop the army from interfering in politics? Responsibility of this interference is borne by a few military men—but the majority of our military fellow comrades are innocent of this combination. When we say that the army must be kept out of politics this does not mean we are trying to create barriers between the army and the party or between the army and political action. In fact, we want to increase the link of the army with the party and the party with the army. . . . We seek to correct the function of the army in socialist society, which is led by the party. The army is a popular army, and it includes strugglers directly linked with the interests of the masses and with the interests of the party.[37]

There would be other points of disagreement between the Asadists and the ʿAflaqists—the pragmatists and the ideologues, to be simplistic about the distinction—that would lead to ferocious internecine purges within the Syrian Baʿth, but on the role of the army in Syrian life—at least during the 1960s—there does not seem to have been much ideological disagreement. This was an era of unprecedented state-building and regime consolidation in Syria, premised on ideological and cultural as well as material bases in the army, party, bureaucracy, and security services. On military affairs, moreover, the discourse was not always or exclusively expressed in terms of grand strategy or foreign policy; it was also grounded in rhetorical strategies and cultural dispositions on clear display in military journals and public pronouncements. The role of the military in society would expand beyond even where it had been during the tumultuous era of military coups and shifting regional alliances during the first two decades following national independence. In Fadia Kiwan's phrasing, rather than "a politicization of the military," this period witnessed "a militarization of society and politics."[38] Hinnebusch's point about the launch of a "revolution from above" under Hafiz al-Asad can be expanded to account for how the consolidation of power also transformed cultural and intellectual life. The growing power and influence of the state in Syrian life had important cultural consequences. In this regard, a cultural history of militarism in Syria has yet to be written.

"The political and ideological indoctrination of the army is no less important than military training," according to the October 1963 Baʿth Party *Munṭalaqāt* (*Principles of Departure*).[39] The ethos of this authoritarian Baʿthist state was predicated on the inculcation of new modes of affect and ideology, as can be gleaned, for example, from the language of the military-political leadership itself. Mustafa Tlas, longtime Syrian minister of defense and aide-de-camp to Hafiz al-Asad, spelled out the significance of doctrine for the Syrian armed forces and the nation at large in the pages of the military periodical *Jaysh al-Shaʿb* (*The People's Army*) in March 1972. Tlas waxed bombastic as he attempted to communicate directly with the ordinary man on the street as well as the new recruit in the barracks: "The doctrinal army is the army that believes in the doctrine of the people. . . . [As] for our Syrian Arab Army this doctrine is . . . the doctrine of the socialist Arab Baʿth Party. And nothing else."[40] Al-Asad himself used identical language in insisting that the Syrian army

> is neither a partisan army nor a political party; rather, it is a doctrinal army that believes in the doctrine of the socialist Arab Baʿth party and works to implement what the leadership of the armed forces strategizes for the common good of the people.[41]

Tlas illuminates the grandeur and the promise of such a fighting force with the light of history, identifying "the army of the Islamic revolution founded by the Arab Prophet" Muhammad as "the first doctrinal army in history." Not only is the Syrian doctrinal army thus imbued with sacred importance, but it is a more effective army than its rivals. According to Tlas, "the doctrinal soldier in my opinion is much better than the ordinary soldier or the mercenary soldier."[42] Tlas seems particularly attuned to those who might decry this ideological refashioning by the new regime as the imposition of one-party dictatorship. In turn, he offers a subtle if flimsy justification for the new ideology of military unity under the banner of the Baʿth Party:

> Some people may find that the Syrian Arab army has become a partisan army. Far from it . . . it has only become a *doctrinal army* . . . because not all of the officers and the second-class soldiers and individuals of the Syrian Arab army belong to the socialist Arab Ba'th party, but they are all believers in the principles and doctrine of the Party.

Tlas acknowledges those who do not believe in the principles of the Ba'th, but reduces them to "a minority that almost doesn't deserve to be mentioned." In a sense, this is a fairly explicit statement of the politics of "as if" skewered by Lisa Wedeen, in which it hardly matters whether ordinary Syrians accept party ideology because one way or another they must demonstrate that they are "believers"—regardless of whether they actually are—or else they do not "deserve to be mentioned."[43] In order to burnish the credibility of the new regime, Tlas lambastes the "rightists" in the nationalist leadership (*al-qiyāda al-qawmiyya*) for trying to unite with General Amin al-Hafiz, who served as president until the Neo-Ba'th coup of February 23, 1966. He layers a different metaphor on top of this critique of al-Hafiz and his allies, arguing that their faith in the virtue of the party is tantamount to the belief of Abu Sufyan—one who doubted the divine message of the Prophet Muhammad and, not incidentally, one who was brought around through the use of force. This invocation of Islamic history in his political discourse is not the only kinship one can find here to Michel 'Aflaq, as al-Hafiz would also wind up in Iraqi exile. Unlike 'Aflaq, though, who died and was buried in Baghdad, al-Hafiz would eventually return to Syria, where he passed away in 2009.

More important than this biographical footnote is the historical analogy Tlas employs in order to celebrate Comrade Hafiz al-Asad taking the reins of the armed forces and manning the helm of the national leadership (*al-qiyāda al-quṭriyya*), through which he acquires an allegorical significance as redeemer or messenger. Tlas elaborates some of the overarching principles of the corrective movement: supporting the armed forces and the military officers; infusing fighters with the principles of the Arab Socialist Ba'th Party; instructing the nation to fight in the spirit of loyalty to the Arab nation. In addition to these patriotic-nationalist themes, one also finds the seeds of an inchoate military dictatorship emerging in this incipient discourse of instruction: "Inculcating in the soldiers both obedience and loyalty to the Leader of our march Comrade Hafiz al-Asad,

General Secretary of the Arab Socialist Baʿth Party."[44] Tlas's adulation of al-Asad was emblematic of the former's own political pragmatism: "Power [*al-quwwa*] is the cornerstone of strategy, without power there is no strategy."[45] This rhetorical move may have marked a turning point in Baʿthist military theory; it also reconfigured the ideological relationship between the armed forces and the leader as well as "ordinary" people. From the 1960s onward, the Syrian Arab Army would be transformed into a doctrinal army, albeit one that did not precisely map onto ʿAflaq's vision of such an institution. Hafiz al-Asad used similar language in likening the Syrian army to "a model of the patriotic nationalist school," which

> always has been and always shall remain the vanguard of the sacrificing struggle on behalf of the cause of the people and the nation [*umma*]. It always has been a sacrificing vanguard and it always shall continue to be that vanguard. The cause of this army is the cause of the toilers. There is absolutely no discussion on this matter whatsoever.[46]

Amos Perlmutter presents a different interpretation of the expansion of such militaristic discourse into everyday life:

> The army no longer acts as an arbitrator of nationalist and progressive forces. It has been persuaded of its unique historical destiny and special political role as the "savior" of society from the "corrupt" politician. It has assumed the "role of hero" and considers itself the key and the *only* hope for honest politics, stability, order, and progress. These expectations and aspirations, now claimed exclusively by the army, have been supported in the last two decades by the civilian politicians, by the progressive forces, by the intellectuals, and the modernizers.[47]

Such a transformation in the social content and political orientation of the Syrian army reflects and would be reflected in Syrian national culture as well as the shifting ideological positions among elites and other sectors of society. Stock phrases such as "the cause of the toilers" were part of the discursive repertoire advanced by al-Asad, Tlas, their military-security advisers, and others as national institutions—especially but not exclusively the military—were refashioned into doctrinal and ideological instruments.

French sociologist Michel Seurat identifies a growing "ideological void" in the ranks of the Syrian armed forces. Even as the discourse of a doctrinal army was gaining currency in the inner circle of Baʿthist elites and regime players, Seurat argues that, by 1970,

> political life in the army had totally disappeared, and loyalty to the "Revolution" was nowhere more in evidence than at the highest levels of the military hierarchy. In fact, this ideological void was the direct consequence of the eradication by the Baʿth of a large national movement that had shaken the country during the 1950s, and then the eradication of the Baʿth itself inside of the army by the bureaucratic military apparatus.[48]

Contrary to the ideal propagated by Tlas, al-Asad, and others within the regime, then, Seurat sees the doctrinal army as little more than an ideological smokescreen and "an enormous repressive machine."[49] Elizabeth Picard similarly notes the evacuation of ideology from the institutions of Baʿthist rule. In her estimation, both the Neo-Baʿthists who held power from 1966–1970 and the Syrian regime that took control in 1970 were responsible for an overinflation of the party, which reduced it to little more than "an empty shell." This leads Picard to the provocative claim that it might be "preferable to avoid using the term 'Baʿth'" at all when discussing the country's leadership.[50]

The massive expansion of the security services under the ever tightening control of the ruling clique was just as important as the transformation of the Syrian military into a doctrinal army during this period. Consolidation of the Syrian national security state was accomplished in part through "coup-proofing," an institutional process by which the regime and the armed forces were rendered impermeable to the chaos and instability characteristic of Syria and other nations in the Arab world during the 1950s and 1960s. As Yezid Sayigh helpfully clarifies, coup-proofing throughout the Arab Middle East

> from the 1970s onward resulted in a proliferation of additional intelligence agencies entrusted with monitoring one another. Whether attached to the military or under the direct control of ruling parties, presidential offices, or royal courts, almost all engage in policing their own populations. And all are tasked with regime security, even when in implicit or open competition with each other.[51]

The Syrian regime maintained itself as coup-proof through the use of robust force and violence, cornerstones of its domestic security strategy.[52] But there was also a noticeable amount of what might be called intellectual and cultural coup-proofing accomplished in part by the expansion of an ideological infrastructure that promoted Asadist-Baʿthist cultural revolution through its own aesthetic ideology.

Hafiz al-Asad, it is often said, was a strategist, a man who had the shrewdest political sensibility. "From the beginning Asad projected a different level of seriousness in state-building from anyone who had gone before," as Patrick Seale writes in his indispensable biography. "Syrian Baʿthist rule as Asad developed it was a hybrid animal. . . . His ambition was, above all, to establish his rule on a firm footing."[53] Many have noted how overly sanguine and credulous Seale is in the treatment of his subject. However, writing at about the same point during the 1980s, political sociologist Elizabeth Picard similarly argues that al-Asad's main goals during this period were, first, "to advance and broaden the foundations of the regime through a policy of economic liberalization and democratic dialogue" and, second, to pursue a policy of "realism" in various ways: "state-building, legitimizing the regime in the eyes of the national community, downplaying relations with neighboring countries, and reorienting the Syrian alliances and interventions according to the regional interests of the country."[54] One of the ironies of Asadist-Baʿthist state-building and cultural revolution was the extent to which Syrian nationalism after 1961—that is, following the dissolution of the United Arab Republic experiment with Egypt—simultaneously articulated Syrian nation-state nationalism and pan-Arab nationalist sentiment, breeding a kind of ambiguity that generated new kinds of politics and publics while obscuring the specific concern and contributions of Syrian intellectuals, writers, and artists. In Syrian state and public discourse, "the country" (*al-quṭr*)—an Arabic term of art in the Baʿthist lexicon that can mean "section" or "region" or "division" in both geometrical and geographical terms—whether in military matters, political affairs, or cultural life, was both discursively linked to and ideologically autonomous from the struggling vanguard of the all-encompassing "Arab nation" (*al-qawm*).[55] The corrective moment was launched in November 1970, around the time of the Baʿth Party's Tenth Extraordinary Regional Congress, at which point al-Asad and a substantial part of the army expelled the remnants of the Neo-Baʿth. Then General al-Asad installed a People's Council of 173 members that began drafting a constitution on February 16, 1971, which was ratified as the Permanent Constitution of the

Syrian Arab Republic on March 12, 1973. Two years earlier, on March 12, 1971, al-Asad was the only candidate for president and was elected with an improbable 99.2 percent of the vote.[56]

"State building is one of those tasks that requires assembly," Steven Heydemann playfully argues, "and instructions do not come printed on the side of a box."[57] The commitments of Asadist-Baʿthist state-building coursed through the spheres of culture, aesthetics, and politics. The statist agenda of the new regime was reflected and pursued in the cultural sphere in contradictory ways as literary, intellectual, and film journals maintained their connections to international styles and celebrated internationalism while also cultivating and promoting Syrian national culture, which was marked by traces of the Asadist-Baʿthist cultural revolution's aesthetic ideology. In remarks to the eighth conference of Arab writers in Damascus in October 1971, al-Asad intoned that Syria and the greater Arab world were involved in an epic struggle, "an economic, political, cultural, and scientific battle as much as a military one"[58]:

> We will work to provide the writer with the appropriate and free environment within which to write and to compose, comfortable and at peace with their present and their future, without any censorship [*raqāba*] other than the censorship of conscience and that which is required by commitment to the principles of our nation [*umma*] and our grand causes.[59]

Al-Asad and his closest allies and advisers imagined him as an intellectual at the vanguard of Syrian thought, representing him as a "struggler" and the Eternal Leader but also as a thinker (*mufakkir*) and an intellectual (*muthaqqaf*). In this light, the cultural-intellectual field—including journals published by the state—is crucial to an understanding of aesthetic ideology during this period. The remainder of this chapter is concerned with how the aesthetic ideology of Asadist-Baʿthist cultural revolution was articulated and contested in literary, intellectual, and cinema journals as well as other writing by intellectuals and artists who populated these discursive spaces.

MAPPING SYRIAN LITERATURE AND CULTURE

There was a striking resonance between the envisioned expansion of military strategy and planning into broader spheres of national life and the ideological refashioning of public intellectual life. Al-Asad, Tlas, and their allies believed that doctrinal commitment to the political cause of Arab nationalism in general and Baʿthism in particular needed to extend beyond the barracks and across the cultural and intellectual fields. From its inception, the corrective movement—often synonymized with revolution by regime supporters—sought to transcend politics in order to energize Syrian society in cultural and intellectual terms as well. A suite of intellectuals invented slogans about the need for engagement with the patriotic struggle in service to the Syrian people, the Arab homeland, and the Third World masses as part of their collective struggle against imperialism and Zionist aggression.

The Asadist-Baʿthist cultural revolution entailed "revolutionizing culture" in a manner that comes through quite distinctly in the writings of Syrian Marxist philosopher Tayyib Tizini. Tizini (1934–2019) was born in Homs, earned a doctorate in history in East Germany, and later became a professor of philosophy at Damascus University. Although his politics would change over time,[60] in one of his earliest books, on the problems of culture and revolution in the Third World, Tizini defined the role of intellectuals and culture in forwarding a revolutionary socialist agenda in a place like Syria. "Scientific cultural revolution," Tizini wrote, is asserting itself in more and more profound ways. "Our country [Syria], which desires, along with other Arab countries, to overcome the stage of transition from a backward capitalist feudalist society—in a total way—into an advanced Arab socialist society, must set its sights on the goal of revolutionizing culture [*tathwīr al-thaqāfa*]."[61] In pursuit of this goal, Tizini found no fault with the integration of so-called revolutionary intellectuals into the state apparatus. Syrian intellectuals and cultural producers were no different from artists and critics around the world who participated in debates that tended to pit those who advocated "art for art's sake" against those who pushed for avant-gardist approaches to cultural production. Tizini predicted that the former was doomed to extinction.

> The reactionary, unscientific theories about apolitical "culture for culture's sake" will find their death in our country [Syria] and the larger Arab world through the strengthening of this deep and constructive dialectical relationship between intellectuals and the state [*al-sulṭa*], and between the state and the intellectuals and the masses.[62]

With state-sponsored and regime-supporting intellectuals now claiming the vanguardist mantle, cultural production became politically supercharged.

The acclaimed short story writer Zakariya Tamir promoted vanguardist literary criticism in an interview published in *al-Maʿrifa* in August 1972. The absence of "serious works of criticism" in Syria could be attributed primarily to "intellectual laziness" manifest in a form of "criticism [that] lacks its vanguardist role."[63] The task of criticism, he said, is to "play the educational role of enlightening readers while cultivating and developing the taste for modern literature."[64] Criticism was a contact sport in the minds of those advocating cultural revolution during this period. In a manner echoed by Hanna Mina and Najah al-ʿAttar in their work on war literature (Chapter 3), Tamir calls for

> a courageous, rigorous critic, one who does not compromise, who won't capitulate to terrorism, a critic who considers silence a shame as well as a betrayal of both thought and literature, a critic who recognizes their crucial responsibility, a critic who refuses to be incorporated into the hordes that look at literary life as positions that must be occupied by any means necessary.

Tamir's ideal critic was a pugilist, in other words, one "skilled in combat [who] carries a big stick, and chases their prey."[65] Thus, there would be no logical contradiction in rejecting oppositional art in Syria as reactionary a priori—art for art's sake being just one name for that—in contradistinction to the revolutionary artistic raison d'être of the regime and its exponents. As Hal Foster teaches us,

> the politics of representation is a strictly contextualist affair: what seems radical in SoHo may be counterrevolutionary in Nicaragua. To rethink the political, then, is not to rule out any representational mode but rather to question specific uses and material effects.[66]

Of course, the proliferation of these understandings of cultural revolution in Syria under Hafiz al-Asad could not magically transform state-supported culture into revolutionary art.[67] Be that as it may, state-sanctioned periodicals and other media became a space for the state to promote a new kind of aesthetic ideology, one that aspired to be hegemonic, national-popular, and faithful to creative expression that would articulate such notions of cultural revolution.

"Freedom that is not exercised has no meaning," Hafiz al-Asad said, simultaneously expressing an aversion to political theory as well as saluting the practical dimensions of the struggle for postcolonial liberation. Such unconverted liberatory potential energy, according to al-Asad, would ultimately amount to little more than "nonexistent freedom."[68] Perhaps harboring an implicit desire to reject those idealist conceptions of politics so prevalent in the 'Aflaqist-Ba'thist lexicon that prevailed prior to his rise to power—liberty, unity, and socialism, most notably—al-Asad gestured instead toward a pragmatic theory of liberation (if his thinking is indeed worthy of such grandiose language) while also stipulating that freedom cannot be truly put into practice or harnessed to institutions without being made available by some kind of authority. Here the spirit of Ba'thism was transformed into the ideological superstructure of a corporatist authoritarian state that became increasingly bloated, repressive, and even incoherent.[69] In the late 1990s, Naomi Saqr pointed out that "words such as"'freedom'—and others such as 'liberalization' and even 'pluralism'—are used by those in Syria but rarely with their internationally recognized meaning."[70] Once Asadist-Ba'thism took command, "freedom" would be bestowed from on high and then put into practice in the name of the Syrian citizen just as "the people" and "the masses" were transformed into instruments in service to the state. Or, in the words of the ever-irascible poet Muhammad al-Maghut, "the word 'freedom' in my language / takes the shape of an electric chair."[71]

Around the time that Tlas and al-Asad were extolling the virtues of the doctrinal army and its role in many sectors of national life, Syrian writers and intellectuals were enjoined to embrace a new cultural orientation, one that would inform and inspire literary writing and other kinds of cultural production. "Intellectuals occupy an important place in the constellation of power" in Syria, Michel Seurat and Jim Paul argue, "even if they are clearly secondary to the military. . . . They are responsible for reproducing the regime's Arab nationalist and anti-imperialist ideology."[72] Al-Asad and his advisers were unequivocal in their conception of a total struggle, one in which the various sectors of society would work in unison toward the nationalist-patriotic goal. "Our battle is fought in many fields," al-Asad said, and "the military sphere is not the only one, and we must wage [the battle] in every domain in absolute lockstep."[73] Literature did not exist only within the minds and imaginations of writers and readers; in postcolonial Syria, it was a battlefield. The stakes of struggle had been put forward in a militantly Arab nationalist idiom earlier in the twentieth century in Shihada Khuri's 1950 *al-Adab fī al-Maydān* (*Literature in the Field*).[74] Literary and cultural concerns were also discussed throughout the Syrian armed forces. The leading military journals—*al-Jundī* (*The Soldier*), *Jaysh al-Sha'b* (*The People's*

Army), and *al-Fikr al-ʿAskarī* (*Military Thought*)—were packed with pieces by writers and literary critics. For example, in 1967 the acclaimed Syrian writer Hani al-Rahib, in *Jaysh al-Shaʿb*, wrote about the role of literature in Syrian and Arab society: "Literature is an operation like giving birth [*ʿamaliyyat makhāḍ*], like revolution, and it cannot give birth through pressure on the womb but rather by spontaneous outpouring."[75] Syrian intellectual culture and literary life would be subject to the institutional and political monitoring of such high-flown principles. As for publishing and broadcasting, so-called freedom of thought, conscience, and expression was enshrined in law but subject to ideological contestation.[76]

Syrian writers and intellectuals had begun to band together into associations as early as the 1950s. The Syrian Writers' Collective (Rābiṭat al-Kuttāb al-Sūriyyīn) was founded in 1951 and was then transformed into the AWU in 1954. Formally incorporated only in 1969, it was meant to function as an independent body but over time became bound to the ideological strictures and political influence of the state. Alexa Firat argues that during the 1960s—and even more so after ignominious defeat in the 1967 Six-Day War—Syrian writers, readers, and intellectuals constructed an autonomous field within which literature, film, and other forms of cultural production could gain symbolic and institutional power, with specialized journals, venues for discussion and debate, and modes of marking distinction.[77] Syrian writers were experimenting with the novel as a literary form during the first half of the twentieth century. The history of Syrian novels stretches as far back as the earliest works of Shakib al-Jabiri, starting with *Naham* (*Hunger*), in 1937.[78] Faris Zarzur, Walid Ikhlasi, ʿAbd al-Salam al-ʿUjayli, Hani al-Rahib, Nabil Sulayman, and Khayri al-Dhahabi, among many others, laid the foundations for the modern Syrian novel. Mid- to late twentieth century Syrian writing evinced a particular focus on the alienation of the intellectual; the fundamental transformations in society and the economy spanning industrialization, urbanization, and rural-urban migration; the spread and radicalization of various ideologies; changing mores in Syrian society; and the ethics of political commitment and engagement. Most of the scant scholarship dealing with literature in contemporary Syria focuses on the "generation of the sixties," on prison literature and commitment literature, on the rise and fall of Arab nationalism, and on the broader renovation of Arab intellectual culture in the wake of the 1967 war. In 1974 Nabil Sulayman and Bu

ʿAli Yasin presented a diagnostic anthology of key writers and critics in Syria who showcased the diversity of voices and viewpoints represented in Syrian letters in the period between the 1967 defeat (*al-hazīma*) and the 1973 victory (*al-intiṣār*).[79] In *al-Aydiyūlūjīyā wa-l-Adab fī Sūriya, 1967–1973* (*Ideology and Literature in Syria, 1967–1973*), they were more interested in establishing the parameters of appropriately committed literary writing than, say, providing a framework for thinking about the relationship between aesthetics and politics. Sulayman and Yasin were not the only critics to tackle what was perceived as backwardness and stagnation. ʿAdnan Bin Dhurayl, for example, writing in *al-Maʿrifa* in April 1974, identified both literary and intellectual malaise. For him, Syrian literature and culture needed to come out of its "shells of backwardness" (*qawāqiʿ takhallufihā*).[80] Similar arguments would rage in published works on the state of literary criticism and prose writing in Syria throughout the following decades.[81]

The two leading journals of literary criticism in Baʿthist Syria were *al-Maʿrifa*, published by the Ministry of Culture and National Guidance starting in 1962/1963, and *al-Mawqif al-Adabī*, published by the state-administered AWU beginning in 1971. *Al-Mawqif al-Adabī* was embroiled in the Arab nationalist politics of the time and committed to a socialist-realist agenda. While expectations were placed on writers to adhere to the conventions of socialist realism as both a style and a mode of political engagement, aesthetic ideological conformity was never achieved. By contrast, *al-Maʿrifa* followed a political line that would be renegotiated in the wake of the corrective movement. This journal was the gold standard for intellectual periodicals in Baʿthist Syria. As recently as the early 2000s, the literature scholar Hassan Abbas would note that *al-Maʿrifa* "is considered the most prestigious journal in Syria."[82] Launched by the Ministry of Culture in 1962, it hewed ever closer to state-sanctioned intellectual currents after the Baʿthist coup in 1963 and the corrective movement of 1970, although it managed to carve out a measure of independence from state control. It was not until December 1973 that *al-Maʿrifa* was iconographically integrated into the ideological ambit of the al-Asad regime; this issue was the first time a color portrait of Hafiz al-Asad served as the frontispiece, accompanied by a quotation from Arab nationalist thinker Najib ʿAzuri. While this might be viewed as a relatively minor development in the intellectual history of modern Syria, the inclusion of the portrait signified the interpenetration of political symbols and nationalist messages into the cultural sphere. And it was a phenomenon that was by no means limited to *al-Maʿrifa*, as we will see below.

Al-Maʿrifa had been around for over a decade when its editors declared that their mission needed rejuvenation in a manner strikingly similar to the *Kulturkampf* endorsed by the new regime. Its lead editorial of August 1974, for example, called for an "Arabic Cultural Revival [*baʿth*]."[83] The piece departed from the premise that the Arab world lacked "nationalist culture" (*thaqāfa qawmiyya*) as a consequence of the legacies of colonialism and Zionism, rejecting the notion that the Arab world was little more than a hodgepodge of "local cultures . . . only bound together by a common language, i.e. Arabic."[84] One connotation of this claim—even when deployed in a soi-disant nationalist and anti-imperialist idiom—was that "Arabic literatures" (*ādāb ʿarabiyya*) were comprehensible not as a diversification of "Arabic literature" (*al-adab al-ʿarabī*) but instead as "the literatures of peoples with different sects and races and environments."[85] The rallying cry was therefore that "the Arabs" needed to mobilize collectively in order to confront a "civilizational challenge," one that could "transform the Arabs into a new kind of American Indian suitable for being displayed in museums."[86] In a discourse of indigeneity and authenticity, the editors championed Arab nationalist identity and rallied for its defense via culture. In turn, the outward-facing cultural revolution against imperialism on a regional scale would be refashioned as resistance to cultural-genocidal influences coming from abroad, as a vital defense of literary unity in the face of imperialism. A successful Arab nationalist agenda—spearheaded by the Baʿth in Damascus, the "Hanoi of the Middle East," as the city was often metaphorized by regime supporters—required the diminution of national differences in language and cultural production across the Arab world as well as a more robust assertion of Syria's role as the vanguard of Arab solidarity. The very possibility of formal and ideological diversity in literature and culture, across different Arabics or Arabic literatures or Arab cinemas, was anathema to the spirit of Asadist-Baʿthist cultural revolution.[87]

If *al-Maʿrifa* was concerned with intellectual and cultural matters broadly, the AWU began publishing its own journal in 1971 with a much more specific emphasis on literary affairs. *Al-Mawqif al-Adabī* (*Literary Standpoint*) harbored in its title the doctrinaire orientation of taking a stand through and with literature. Its editorial board—Sidqi Ismaʿil (the founding editor-in-chief), Ghassan al-Rifaʿi, Zakariya Tamir, and Muhi al-Din Subhi—represented the state-sanctioned intellectual elite of the time. Jurj Sidqi succeeded Ismaʿil as editor-in-chief in late 1972 after the latter passed away. Editors regularly moved between the boards of *Al-Mawqif al-Adabī* and *al-Maʿrifa*, however, and many writers contributed to both. Subsequent *Al-Mawqif al-Adabī* editorial board members included Sulayman al-ʿIsa, Hanna Mina, Khaldun al-Shamʿa, Antun Maqdisi, Saʿdallah Wannous, and ʿAbd al-ʿAziz Hilal. The first issue appeared in May 1971 and contained an editorial by Sidqi Ismaʿil, interviews, poetry, original artwork, a short story by Colette Khoury, pieces about the relationship between literature and cinema, notices about new publications (e.g., Zakariya Tamir, Haydar Haydar), as well as a listing of events held by the AWU. In its editorial, the union affirmed that it

> is still in its preliminary phases of creating a progressive cultural environment that affords Arab intellectuals, scholars, writers, and poets the space to secure the firm bond between intellectual, literary, and artistic labor and issues of contemporary Arab life.

For the editors, "cultural liberation" was intimately bound up with "the experiences of the masses" in their quest for "building the unified Arab future." In this connection, the AWU sought to "fill the cultural void in the Syrian Arab region": to provide writers with

> an environment that will pave a way for them to renew their cultural production, their freedom of debate about criticism and aesthetic value [*al-naqd wa-l-taqyīm*], their ability for the broadest possible connection with the masses.[88]

More specifically, the editors of the journal expressed their commitment to a number of causes:

> To build in this country [*quṭr*] new vanguardist guidelines that endeavor to make out of literary work a creative effort, not a hobby or a means of self-aggrandizement, in order to open up a space protected by material and moral restrictions on the writer: authentic literature shall be his primary cause in life, his truthful words shall participate with others in their human suffering along the path of renewal and struggle, in the name of freedom.[89]

In some sense, the editors seemed to want to have their cake and eat it too when it came to the age-old debate between art for art's sake and engaged cultural production or *littérature engagée.*

> Insofar as it is true that every literary product must be literature before all else, containing within itself the elements of the mature work of art, it is no less appropriate to state that every cultural product must be a true expression of the Arab person, in terms of their circumstances and tribulations. But the avant-garde cultural product cannot rise to the level of conscious responsibility unless it emanates from the belief in freedom of expression [*ḥurriyyat al-kalima*] and plays an active role in the struggle for the liberation of the contemporary Arab person as well as the building of his new life.[90]

In his first piece for the journal, editor-in-chief Sidqi Isma'il wrote about "Mass Sentiment and the Lung of Arabic Criticism."[91] Isma'il was born in Antakya in 1934 and had studied philosophy in Damascus before going on to teach in Aleppo and Damascus until 1968, at which point he was appointed member of the Supreme Council of Arts, Literature, and Social Sciences (al-Majlis al-Aʿlā li-l-Funūn wa-l-Adāb wa-l-ʿUlūm al-Ijtimāʿiyya). Subsequently, he participated in the founding of the AWU and in 1971 became the founding editor-in-chief of *al-Mawqif al-Adabī*, a position he occupied until his untimely death the following year.[92] Isma'il opened his article with a statement from Søren Kierkegaard about the isolation of the individual in modernity and followed with an unabashed critique of the elitism of Arabic criticism since the days of the Nahda, "when the taste of the masses for literary works was neglected." This was reflective of larger gaps between elite opinion and the tastes of the masses. Isma'il went on to laud "the ordinary reader," by which he meant "the Arab person who began to liberate himself from the concept of literature and art in the Age of Decline [*'aṣr al-inḥiṭāṭ*] and to recognize the fundamental role the writer or the artist can play in everyday life in general." Writers, artists, and critics needed to come down from their lofty heights and play a greater role in everyday life. Critics were to blame for "crowning" those poets and writers most tightly connected to global trends in literature and the arts.

> The misguidance that is practiced by literary criticism in this regard imposes upon mass taste [*al-dhawq al-jamāhīrī*] a derogatory impression of superstition.

> In superstition—as is well known—a higher power is hegemonic, above the power of humans and factors of reality, over the minds of the people, making them feel as though human achievements, whether in the fields of literature, art, or political and civilizational development . . . etc., only arise from a supernatural force that cannot be understood.[93]

Not unlike the strong language from Zakariya Tamir introduced earlier, Isma'il held critics responsible for creating out of a "traditional generation" of poets and writers a particular vision of "an imaginary artistic personality" or "an imaginary reader" that were not familiar to Arab audiences and readers.[94] If critics did not give the audience enough credit, it was because "the Arab audience—despite all the reasons for cultural backwardness it suffers—retained a kind of spontaneous response to the Arab message," leading to a rejection of incorrect interpretations by Orientalist scholars and others regarding Arabic and the "anaesthetization of language" (*takhdīr al-kalimāt*). But while one might have expected a radical Arab nationalist and cultural vanguardist to call for the creation of radically new forms of art, Isma'il modestly concluded with a call for recognition of a singular historical truth, namely that Arab society was distinguished by its ability to hold onto and guard their literary tradition and affiliated human values. Such forms of tradition needed to be nurtured as a feature of modern Arab life in the twentieth century.[95] And if this sounded like a rebuttal to Orientalist claims about Arab cultural backwardness, the argument also echoed the riposte to claims about art for art's sake from modernists who sought to disrupt traditional form and leave tradition behind altogether.

In a subsequent issue, Isma'il expanded on the role of the vanguard in political transformation. After a cursory reference to the works of Paul Valéry, Andre Gide, and Leo Tolstoy, who was highlighted for representing the tension between "romanticism" and "avant-gardism" (*al-ṭalī'iyya*), he ended with Bertolt Brecht and Georg Lukács, who, according to Isma'il, put the concept of "commitment" (*al-iltizām*) into practice in the form of the avant-garde (*al-ṭalī'a*). As I elaborate subsequently, Lukács was a literary-critical touchstone for many critics and writers in Syria. Mention was also made of Che Guevara, Frantz Fanon, and the cultural revolution in China as intellectual resources that would enable readers and writers to move past the bourgeois conception of modernity toward the goal of "popular consciousness."[96] Sidqi set his sights on the previous generation of Nahdawi intellectuals, dismissing as a "delusion" the idea that the banner of the Nahda was responsible for the making of "the modern Arab intellectual." In Sidqi's estimation, the Nahda was indubitably a turning point in terms of "artistic" consciousness and cultural opening, but early Nahdawi figures "were nothing more than a continuation of the derivative literary traditions of classical Arab society."[97] What was needed at this historical conjuncture was the opposite of bourgeois Nahdawi intellectuals: a true avant-garde, one that "creates the climate of revolution and carries the desire for change."[98] Despite Ismaʿil's attempt to identify commitment literature and art as avant-garde, it is worth keeping in mind Peter Bürger's provocative claim that "engaged art is defined only formally, not in its substance."[99]

Lukács was a rich resource for Syrian writers and critics thinking about committed literature that would at once appease the political exigencies of the new aesthetic ideology of Asadist-Baʿthist cultural revolution, which turned on a so-called avant-gardism while also adhering to the totalizing impulses of socialist realism. Take, for example, the statement of literary critic Husam al-Khatib, writing in *al-Mawqif al-Adabī* in 1972:

> [There] is something new in criticism. The critic is no longer a passive "intermediary" trying to reliably explain the content and the form [*maḍāmīn wa-īḥāʾāt*] of a literary work from the vantage point of the author's intentions but, rather, the critic has become a "re-creator" [*yuʿīd khalq*] of the work of art, adding a great deal to it from his own knowledge, personal viewpoint, and taste. Perhaps he even presents this as something relatively new.[100]

Literature was both the grounds for and the medium of a broader ideological struggle. The parameters and criteria for literary judgment were to be determined through an engaged battle. In modernity, the critic should not only be capable of evaluating cultural production but also be conscripted into "creating taste" and "shaping taste."[101] In these pursuits, al-Khatib said, Lukács was one central inspiration. Frederic Jameson's reading of Lukács is illuminating for those who wish to understand the role Lukács played in the making of Syrian (and Arab/ic) prose writing and literary criticism during this period, especially in light of my earlier discussion of the centrality of the hero in the aesthetic ideology of Asadist-Ba'thist cultural revolution. For Lukács, according to Jameson, "the hero of the novel is always a solitary subjectivity . . . he must always stand in opposition to his setting, to nature or society, inasmuch as it is precisely his relationship to them, his integration into them, which is the issue at hand."[102] At the same time, here introducing the dialectical punch of Lukács's theory of the novel, "realistic characters" are distinguished

> by their *typicality*: they stand, in other words, for something larger and more meaningful than themselves, than their own isolated individual destinies. They are concrete individualities and yet at the same time maintain a relationship with some more general or collective human substance.[103]

This tension between political position taking and national(ist) specificity—one might call it concreteness in a nod to Lukács—of "realistic characters" and the universal(izing) message of their particular experience is a hallmark of Syrian literary discourse.

Given the extent of engagement with the problem of form and content, taste and judgment, ideology and cultural production throughout the cultural journals of this period, the absence of Syrian academic or philosophical writing on aesthetics is striking. Rather, the bulk of literary-critical work on Syria has been focused on the pragmatic and ideological dimensions of aesthetic criticism. One important exception can be found in 'Ali Najib Ibrahim's early 1990s study of aesthetics in the Syrian realist novel, which deals with seven novels, including those by Hanna Mina, Hani al-Rahib, 'Abd al-Salam al-'Ujayli, and Faris Zarzur.[104] Ibrahim explores representations of "the heroic" (*al-buṭūlī*) and "the sublime" (*al-sāmī*; *al-jalīl*). Although not a work of aesthetic theory per se, the book is among the few that look at contemporary Syrian criticism to engage with the technical language of aesthetics. Here aesthetics (*'ilm al-jamāl*) is understood as "the study of aesthetic relations between the human being and reality," which focuses on aesthetic statements (*maqūlāt*) that are expressive of the aesthetic relations between human beings and the world.[105] Ibrahim's conception of the novel as well owes a debt—however implicit—to Lukács's theory of the novel:

> The problems of the novel form are here the mirror-image of a world gone out of joint . . . reality no longer constitutes a favourable soil for art; that is why the central problem of the novel is that that art has to write off the closed and total

> forms which stem from a rounded totality of being—that art has nothing more to do with any world of forms that is immanently complete in itself.[106]

In this sense, Ibrahim presents a mainstream conception of the aesthetics of the novel: Syrian prose fiction describes and diagnoses the alienation of human beings in a time of imperialism, Zionist aggression, and postcolonial malaise.

Robert Campbell observes that literary-critical discourse in Syria during this period was split between "the so-called right (art for art's sake, or an emphasis on form) and the so-called left (art in the service of the masses, or an emphasis on subject matter)." This distinction is betrayed, however, as Campbell notes, by the extent to which both sides harbored ambivalence and even contradictions concerning the meaning of these concepts and such terms as *aesthetics*, *art*, and *style*.[107] Ideological differences would endure throughout the late twentieth and early twenty-first centuries. As Alexa Firat points out, after the fierce ideological debates of the 1950s and 1960s in Syria, "literary discourse would rediscover its dialectical relationship to both aesthetics and social realism" over the course of the 1970s.[108] Similar debates over how the aesthetic ideology of Asadist-Baʿthist cultural revolution would be defined, applied, and adapted were also staged in the realm of cinema.

TOWARD ALTERNATIVE CINEMA

The conceptualization, institutionalization, and production of "revolutionary culture" in Asadist-Baʿthist Syria extended beyond literature into film, television, and other forms of artistic creation. Cinema was by no means new in 1970s Syria, of course, but it would receive unprecedented attention during this period. The first Syrian film ever made, *al-Muttaham al-Barīʾ* (*The Innocent Accused*), was a privately funded thirty-minute work, directed by Ayyub Badri and released in 1928.[109] Other films were made with private capital over the next four decades, but it was not until the 1963 Baʿthist coup that cinema would receive state funding. Law 258 of November 12, 1963, officially created the National Film Organization (al-Muʾassasa al-ʿĀmma li-l-Sīnamā, l'Organisme général du cinéma), or NFO, which came into existence the following year. Although the NFO was an administrative body with national status, the pace of production remained modest during the 1960s and into the 1970s, with rarely more than a handful of films released annually, not all of them receiving national, let alone international,

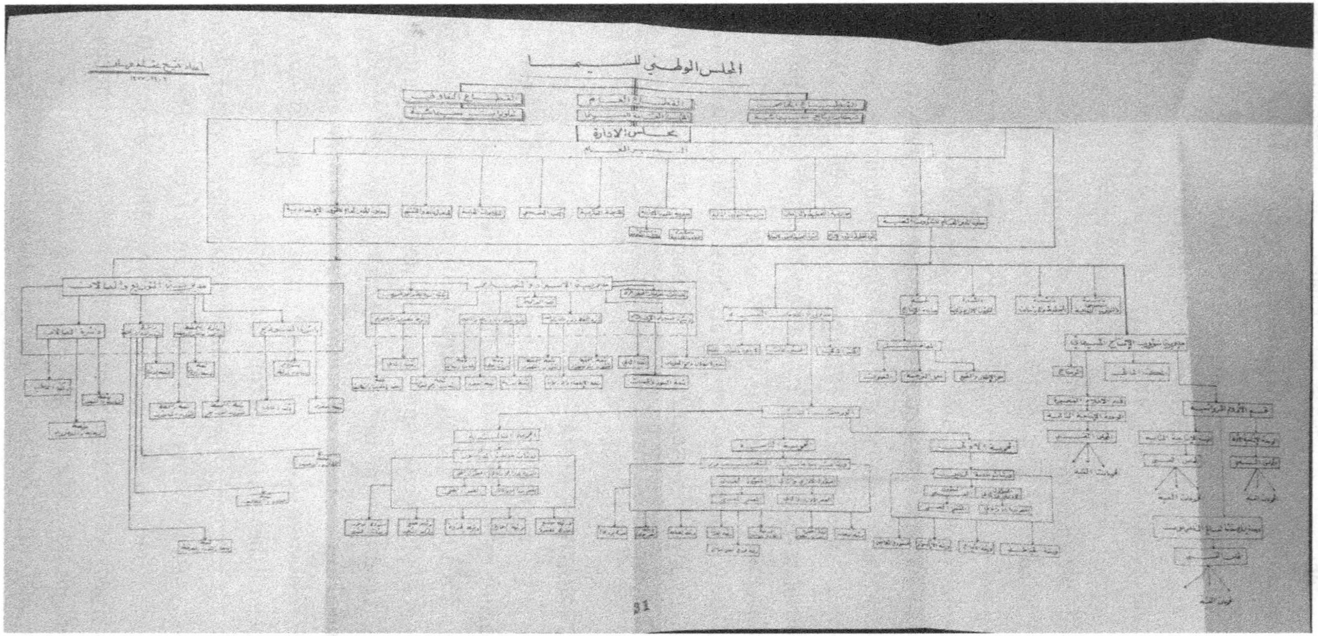

FIGURE 4. Fatih ʿUqla ʿArsan, *Wāqiʿ al-Sīnamā al-Sūriyya wa-Āfāq Taṭawwuruhā* (Damascus: Manshūrāt Wizārat al-Thaqāfa wa-l-Irshād al-Qawmī, 1978), appendix.

distribution. Alongside the rise of state-sponsored cinema, magazines, and other outlets with little apparent connection to public culture addressed topics related to film. In February 1967, for example, Subhi al-Shaykh wrote an article in the magazine *al-Jundī* (*The Soldier*), which was not exclusively dedicated to military affairs, entitled "The National Film Organization in the Syrian Arab Region Upholds Its Obligation Completely." al-Shaykh lauded the NFO and the Ministry of Culture and conducted an interview with the filmmaker and critic Salah Duhni, the NFO's "creative director." [110]

Over the course of the 1970s, the state further expanded its commitment to cultural production. In fall 1978, the first and only Syrian film journal, *Cinema Life* (*al-Ḥayā al-Sīnamā'iyya*), was launched cooperatively by the Ministry of Culture and National Guidance and the NFO. The journal continues to be published today. Even with an expanding space for discussions of cinema and film criticism, however, Syrian filmmakers and filmgoers remained unsatisfied with the state of the field of both filmmaking and film criticism. Six years after the journal's launch, and alongside the release of his acclaimed film *The Border* (*al-Ḥudūd*) (1984), one of the most successful Syrian film comedies every made (Chapter 3), comedic actor, director, and cultural icon Durayd Lahham identified a fundamental paradox in the Syrian cinematic domain. "We do not have a Syrian cinema that I can say has fallen backwards or advanced . . . a film or two every year is not enough to judge. . . . We don't have cinema and yet we publish a cinema journal. . . . Why?"[111] There were certainly others who felt the same way. Yet a reconsideration of *Cinema Life* and its aesthetic ideology is necessary in order to more deeply understand the history of film and cultural politics in Baʿthist Syria.

The founding editorial board of *Cinema Life* included Muhammad Shahin, Salah Duhni, Fatih ʿUqla ʿArsan, and Bandar ʿAbd al-Hamid. The first issue included articles about the Damascus International Film Festival held in October 1979, the first such event in over a decade; the NFO itself and its official mission; Sergei Eisenstein; and Charlie Chaplin. Subsequent issues addressed a wide-range of topics: Japanese cinema, film festivals around the world, Jean Cocteau, Nabil Maleh's *The Leopard* (*al-Fahd*) (based on the 1977 Haydar Haydar novel), and regular coverage of developments in Syrian, Arab, and international cinemas. The launch of *Cinema Life* was timed to coincide with "the golden jubilee" of Syrian cinema. The inaugural editorial hailed the first issue for helping to commemorate an important moment in "our country" (*quṭrinā*), namely the release of the first Syrian film, *The Innocent Accused* (*al-Muttaham al-Barī'*, 1928). Sadly, that film is lost, yet it remains a touchstone for Syrian cultural memory of a film tradition going back to the early twentieth century. The first generation of critics and filmmakers was educated primarily in Syria, the Soviet Union, or the Eastern Bloc. Syria's most influential filmmakers were products of the "revolutionary school" of the All-Union State Institute of Cinematography in Moscow (VGIK).[112] For example, Riyad Shayya (Chapter 2), Ossama Mohammad (Chapters 2 and 4), and Mohammad Malas all studied in Moscow. And while others may have gained experience elsewhere—Nabil Maleh (Chapter 4) studied in Czechoslovakia; Omar Amiralay (Conclusion) went to Paris—the language of Syrian cinema on the whole was marked by the symbolist and abstract style of filmmaking taught at VGIK. It was not simply "silent cinema"—as argued in *Un Cinéma muet*, Mayyar Al-Roumi's 2001 short documentary illuminating the lives and work of Syrian filmmakers—although some Syrian film does speak through silences and whispers.[113] For the editors of *Cinema Life*, Syrian film took as its subject a figure in search of liberation, a theme that mirrored the literary aesthetic ideology of Asadist-Ba'thist cultural revolution I discussed previously.

The editors of *Cinema Life* hoped that the journal would fulfill "a persistent need in the Arab artistic press," expressing their gratitude directly to the minister of culture Najah al-'Attar.[114] It was certainly not coincidental, then, that the first piece in the magazine was written by Dr. al-'Attar herself, who said that the journal was one among several "cultural channels" in the country, part of a national network distributing "the nectar of knowledge" that would allow readers and viewers alike to engage with culture in terms of authenticity and modernity while also contributing to the development of national consciousness and the identity of "the Arab person."[115] The speeches (transcribed from public addresses) and writings of Dr. al-'Attar appeared in all state cultural periodicals over her nearly twenty-five years in office. Here the Ministry of Culture recognized cinema as one vehicle for inculcating audiences with Syrian national culture while also propagating the aesthetic ideological principles emergent in the Asadist-Ba'thist cultural field. Al-'Attar situated *Cinema Life* in relation to other Ministry publications and periodicals, *al-Ma'rifa* most notably, through which "we aim to spread nationalist, humanist, progressive, struggling [*niḍālī*] thought, and to call for Arab unity, the most noble goal of our Arab nation, the

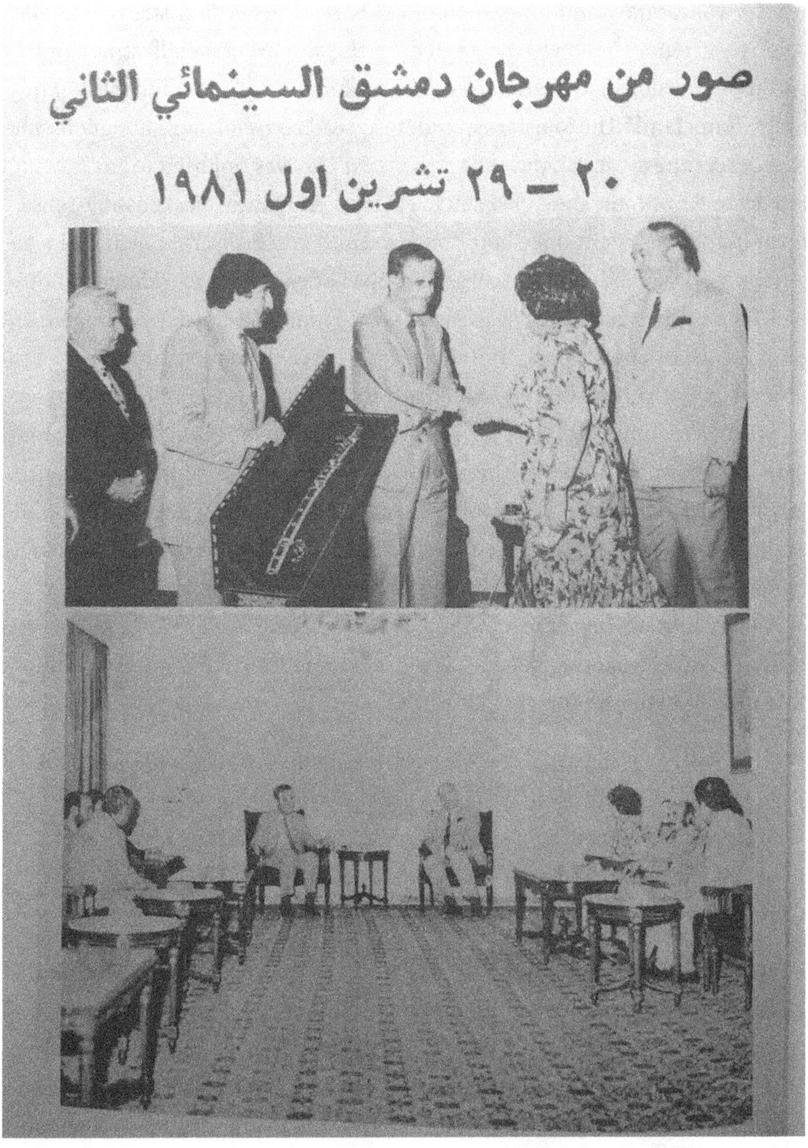
صور من مهرجان دمشق السينمائي الثاني
٢٠ – ٢٩ تشرين اول ١٩٨١

FIGURE 5. "Photos from the Second Damascus Film Festival," 20-29 October 1981," *al-Ḥayā al-Sīnamā'iyya*, No. 11 (Fall 1981).

most revolutionary and fundamental." This was part of "our struggle [*kifāḥ*] against surrender" and was presented "in the service of steadfastness in the battles for freedom and liberation and the reclamation of rights and the building of the homeland." The journal aspired "to spread consciousness about cinema that serves these aims." And though *Cinema Life* was opposed to "narrowing intellectual freedom," she called cinema "a mass art in the widest possible sense," meaning that it was at once both "outsized and crucial."[116] That being said, al-ʿAttar emphasized that cinema was part of a wider project to promote culture endorsed by the state, which was, in her words, nationalist, patriotic, humanist, progressive, earnest (*jādda*), and intentional, all of which must be opposed to other forms of culture that she called nonnationalist, unpatriotic, nonhumanist, superficial, nihilistic (*ʿābitha*), and dissociated (*mutaḥallala*). Any work that gave a platform to "imperialist and reactionary culture" enabled indifference, laziness, despair, criminality, and disappointment.[117] One would have trouble finding a better enumerated (or more prolix) lexicon of the aesthetic ideology of Asadist-Baʿthist cultural revolution.

In their discussion of the 1979 Damascus Film Festival, the editors of *Cinema Life* highlighted what they deemed significant dimensions of cultural revolution as it pertained to cinema.

> Our Syrian Arab nation [*quṭr*]—which has been and will remain the leading and struggling vanguard of our people [*ummatinā*]—is distinguished now as ever for bearing the standard of struggle and progressive liberation of our people and all the peoples of the world who struggle in the path of liberation, progress, and flourishing.

They praised this event as the festival "of all the Arabs" and celebrated all the cultural, intellectual, and artistic initiatives under the purview of the Ministry of Culture and National Guidance's agenda.[118] In a subsequent issue, film critic and filmmaker Muhammad Shahin (1931–2004) disrupted the message of Arab unity somewhat by calling for resistance to Egyptian cultural hegemony in film. Arab cinema, which ought to be understood as part and parcel of a rising Third World cinema, according to Shahin, had been dominated by the Egyptian film industry, underwritten by a capitalist political economy that was reflected in a bourgeois system of cultural production. Consequently, the Arab world lacked a vanguardist cinema that would better present the revolutionary cultural orientation of Arab film to the world.[119] Shahin was one of the most active and influential *Cinema Life* board members during the journal's early years and beyond. He was also an actor, artistic director of the NFO, and co-director of the 1970 NFO adaptation of Ghassan Kanafani's novella *Men in the Sun* (*Rijāl fī al-Shams*).[120] Shahin had long been an advocate for what he called committed cinema and elaborated a new vision of "alternative cinema." Shahin lamented that the Arab viewer had been "besieged" by a system of filmmaking that produced a "numbing cinema" (*al-sīnamā al-takhdīriyya*)—evocative of Sidqi Ismaʿil's anesthetized language discussed earlier—which depended on a "bourgeois economic system" only interested in producing "sentimental melodrama." This debased mode of filmmaking—a not so veiled attack on the Egyptian studio system—relied on a technical approach that jammed shots together in seemingly illogical ways. Characters might appear in waking dreams or in an artificial and constructed world that created what Shahin called a false vision of justice and equal opportunity by way of "metaphysical or coincidental solutions," leading the viewer to the conclusion that a person "cannot do anything to change their negative condition or build a better future. This is the true danger that lurks in such films." If the form of these films was risible for its superficiality, there was a comparable danger of the work dissolving into "degenerate content" (*al-maḍmūn al-marīḍ*), an infelicitous usage given the history of art criticism and aestheticized politics around the question of "degenerate art" in the European context.[121] In his preferred aesthetic, form would represent "the truthful frame" through which the viewer could identify the "sick" (*marīḍ*) reality depicted in the film. Again with an implicit dig at Egyptian cinema, Shahin argued that this only started to change in the 1960s when the "revolutionary" regimes in Syria, Iraq, and Algeria began to produce new films that were capable of challenging those entrenched modes of filmmaking.[122] Shahin viewed a political-cultural alliance among these countries as the best way for otherwise weak film markets to cover the expenses of production while also "expanding the technical and artistic humanist principles on which film relies." Here Shahin began to develop his concept of "alternative film" (*al-film al-badīl*), which would contribute to cinema that would provide "a truthful reflection of the conscience of the Arab nation."[123]

Shahin further elaborated this argument in his essay "The Cinema We Want," returning to the topic of alternative cinema (*al-sīnamā al-badīl*), which he counterposed to traditional film.[124] Traditional film did not offer "Arab audiences" anything but "negative qualities" along with "intellectual and politically backward concepts." Those films were vulgar and distant from reality; they were hamstrung by sentimentalism and even a "contrived style" (*al-uslūb al-tarkībī*) that aimed to establish "emotion and consciousness" as cornerstones of the narrative structure. Even more problematic than this formal aspect was that the style required all plot points and events to revolve around "the individual hero," also referred to as "this distinguished character," thereby relegating the true content to the background. This resulted in the creation of a star, an "ideal character," meant to attract the largest possible number of viewers by "misrepresenting reality and filming it the way they wish to see it." In this sense, the hero lived out the audience's "dreams and hopes and ideas": "Rarely do traditional films force the viewer to confront the film in order to find himself ultimately arriving at the exercise of judgment that would cause him to take a position in the end." For Shahin, cinema should force viewers to contemplate the ideas presented in film in such a way that enables them to rethink their own viewpoints, not to leave them unchallenged.[125]

Shahin elaborated a theory of "alternative" or "mass-based" cinema that fell in line fairly neatly with the aesthetic ideology of Asadist-Baʿthist cultural revolution. "In my view cinema is a mass-based [*jamāhīrī*] artform and it cannot be only for the elite." Improbably, given the level of ideological commitment in play here, Shahin did not want to promote film as a programmatic or as simple "artistic acrobatics" that spin ideas out in all directions. "Cinema can only thrive in the soil of collaboration, between the subject and the self," Shahin argued, "between reality and the creative producer [*al-mubdiʿ*]." This alternative cinema would articulate an aesthetic of "simplicity, clarity, and respect for the ordinary viewer." Shahin was not advocating radical experimentalism or avant-garde posturing, insisting instead that "humanistic film" (*al-film al-insānī*) fundamentally depends on a "human story" (*qiṣṣa insāniyya*). Shahin did not call for a cinema so simple that it insulted the audience's intelligence: "I also believe that it is extremely possible for a successful film to put the viewer into conflict with it without causing him to run away." This type of film "offers him intellectual pleasure and forces him to stand by himself"; this viewer "is capable of judging matter and not accepting everything as given, the way it is presented in traditional film."[126] Therefore, in the final analysis alternative cinema was to serve the masses as well as inculcate the values of revolutionary culture into their everyday lives. "The main sources of power in any work of art are to be found in how quickly it can arrive at the life lived by the masses." Here the implication was that "difficult" cinematic work was to be avoided lest its message be obscured from the audience. How ironic, then, that auteurist style would come to dominate the cinematic field in Baʿthist Syria, or at least be healthily represented among the films produced by the NFO during the 1970s and 1980s.[127] Shahin failed to recognize that flimsy aesthetic categories such as simplicity, clarity, and artistic enjoyment (*al-imtāʿ al-fannī*) might be mistaken for the bourgeois pursuit of aesthetic pleasure. Ultimately, for Shahin, the cinematic realm ought to be understood as a space for aesthetic engagement with political and social matters. "The camera should be the means and the loyal instrument for transmitting the issues, concerns, and hopes of our Arab person [*insānunā al-ʿarabī*]. The human being should not be a means for showcasing the technical capacities of the camera."[128]

These proposals for a new aesthetic and political approach to cinema in Syria and the Arab world generated stimulating questions and left certain contradictions unaddressed. Was this a rejection of the socialist-realist hero who literally embodied the aspirations of the people, or its reinscription? What was the status of "the hero" and representations of heroism in alternative cinema? How would Shahin's theory of alternative cinema make sense of comedic films such as those made by Durayd Lahham (Chapter 3), which tried to thread the needle between commercial appeal and principled politics? Were the neighborhood residents in *The Empire of Ghawar* (Chapter 3), for example, represented as autonomous subjects, an embodiment of the collective desires of the masses, or were they relegated to a supporting role for Ghawar the hero? Was this representation of a heroic character rising above the masses a justification for or a lampooning of the notion of a heroic leader standing apart from the people, like so many of the intellectual justifications offered to support al-Asad's ostensibly necessary leadership? To what extent was there a struggle between art for art's sake and politically committed avant-garde art in the pages of *Cinema Life*? Was the goal of alternative cinema to motivate the individual against the backdrop of the collective or, by contrast, was the individual assumed to dissolve into the flow of mass politics? Did the denigration of psychological realism or "inner consciousness" in the cinematic realm differ from or overlap with analogous discourses of literary criticism during this period?

The discussion of Syrian films in the light of Asadist-Baʿthist cultural revolution and the struggle over aesthetic ideology in Baʿthist Syria offers no easy answers to these questions. Filmmakers recognized the importance of responding to these and other questions. "The contemporary world consumes a large and never-ending number of images," the Czech-educated Syrian filmmaker Nabil Maleh wrote in *al-Maʿrifa* in January 1973. "It's possible for one to expect that the character of the world of the future will be based on this consumption, and if the world is unable to evaluate this phenomenon, it won't be capable of evaluating itself. It will live without consciousness."[129] As the following chapters of this book demonstrate, Syrian filmmakers, writers, and artists were capable of working within fairly rigid ideological parameters at certain times while subverting such homogenizing political restrictions through innovative experimentation with both form and content at other times. The Syrian cultural-intellectual field under Baʿthist rule was characterized by an underappreciated degree of contradiction, diversity of opinion, and breadth of debate in a moment of Syria's modern history that has all too often been understood, unjustly, as hopelessly hamstrung by authoritarian or even totalitarian repression and insurmountable limitations on speech.

CONCLUSION

Over the thirty years during which Hafiz al-Asad held power, Syrian intellectuals, artists, writers, and filmmakers innovated distinctive styles of film, literature, and other modes of cultural production. Even though Syrian literary and cinematic discourse rarely thematized the philosophy of aesthetics, struggles around the stakes and modalities of creative expression would redefine aesthetic boundaries in practice while rendering certain aesthetic theories legible and usable in the first place. If "commitment" (*iltizām*) remained the guiding moral and political imperative for mid-twentieth century art, both literature and cinema began to move in new directions from the 1970s onward. Like other strains of Arab nationalist ideology, the rhetoric of Asadist-Baʿthist cultural revolution was progressivist, modernizationist, and revolutionary. The philosophy of Baʿthism's earliest theorists and architects aimed at the fundamental transformation of society. Inspired by French social thought and German idealism, Baʿthism aimed at a total renovation of society by cultivating a broad culture of renaissance and resurrection (two acceptable translations of the term *Baʿth*).

Although the idea was to build an entirely new society around the trinity of Arab unity, liberty, and socialism, the spread and absorption of Baʿthist ideology was uneven and took different forms in the political, military, cultural, and intellectual spheres.

In the wake of the corrective movement, Asadist-Baʿthist cultural revolution entailed the state-driven attempt to promote a new aesthetic ideology, an aesthetics of power. Still concerned with "commitment" in the sense of politically engaged intellectual and cultural labor, the terms of this political orientation were adjustable to suit the interests of the coalescing Asadist-Baʿthist regime. Within this discursive universe, the struggle over aesthetic ideology was never finally resolved. The cultural field was caught between the centripetal forces of state-driven standardization on the one hand and agonistic disagreement leading to contradictions and unevenness in Syrian culture on the other. The cultural and intellectual fields in Baʿthist Syria were never fully dominated by the state and its affiliated institutions. Hafiz al-Asad's regime endeavored to construct revolutionary Arab nationalism in one country, to paraphrase the language of Soviet communism. In the words of culture minister Najah al-ʿAttar, the Syrian state fantasy of making Damascus the Hanoi of the Arabs can be understood as part of a broader, regional struggle. No matter whether there was "pride for Damascus" in this comparison to Hanoi, though, there was "pride for every Arab capital" in such a reference to a Middle Eastern Vietnam, "a point of pride [*maʿazza*] for Syria as well as for every Arab country."[130]

As Asadist-Baʿthist cultural revolutionaries sought to define their project in ways that would be a source of pride and affection for both Syrian nationalists and Arab nationalists, they also cultivated a new terrain for struggle over aesthetics—an aesthetic ideology for Syria that would also be relevant to the entire Arab world. Unlike the culture of modernist and experimental writing that developed in Lebanon and Egypt, say, the state in Syria expected writers, filmmakers, and other artists to hew to certain Arab nationalist conventions—dialogue written in formal instead of colloquial Arabic, for example; cultural production in service to the national mission—that would become a distinguishing feature of Asadist-Baʿthist aesthetic ideology. This would hinge on adherence to various ideological commitments as well as a deeply—sometimes slavishly—submissive orientation to state power and military authority. In what was perhaps the first (and only) invocation of Baʿthist aesthetics, in the Iraqi context, though, Fatima Mohsen identifies "a cultural code of its own: Ba'thist literature, Ba'thist aesthetics, and a Ba'thist notion of history centred on the role of the absolute leader as a saviour with whom the destiny of the nation is identified."[131] While there are important differences between the Syrian and Iraqi contexts during this period—a topic worthy of further research—there is an important insight here as regards the Syrian context. Some of the language, symbolism, and spirit of Ba'thist ideology survived in the cultural production of the Hafiz al-Asad period and after, but by the mid-1980s these concepts and slogans began to ring hollow to many filmmakers, writers, cultural critics, and intellectuals. Syrian cultural production was inspired less and less by an older, doctrinal conception of Ba'thism than by the pragmatic precepts of cultural Asadism, the lodestar around which other ideological engagements would increasingly gravitate. And while genuflection to the absolute leader as savior or hero would become standard in some quarters, Ba'thist aesthetics in Syria were not always so straightforward, reductive, or restrained. The normative aesthetics of power embodied in public spectacle, iconography, and everyday life was reflected in cultural production but was also subject to critique, defiance, or evasion.

The establishment of Asadist-Ba'thist rule turned on new conceptions of cultural revolution, authenticity, and "the national-popular" to invoke some Gramscian categories of cultural analysis, even if Syrian intellectuals, activists, or politicians did not always use such language during this period.[132] Nevertheless, Gramsci seems relevant in various ways with his concept of a "governing party," which no longer has any substantial political rivals, as in the case of single-party rule. In such circumstances,

> the functions of such a party are no longer directly political, but merely technical ones of propaganda and public order, and oral and cultural influence. The political function is indirect. . . . In such parties cultural functions predominate, which means that political language becomes jargon. In other words, political questions are disguised as cultural ones, and as such become insoluble.[133]

In this conjuncture, the relationship between aesthetics and politics was remade to serve the doctrinal message of the state, but aesthetic power was adapted and repurposed by writers, filmmakers, and artists in contingent and unpredictable ways. A similar process of cultural revolutionizing was at work in the Soviet

Union during the 1930s. "Socialist realism," Katerina Clark notes, referencing the dominant narrative style, "was not just about heroes building power stations or even about the wisdom of Party decrees. Aesthetic value and political value were closely linked" by way of a "critical vocabulary" and "discursive repertoire." The rising Asadist-Baʿthist aesthetic ideology of cultural revolution—its aesthetics of power—suffused a range of Syrian literature, film, and intellectual culture. In a fashion similar to the Soviet context Clark analyzes, Asadist-Baʿthist cultural revolution "identified the 'hero' as an example of anthropological ideality."[134]

This chapter has documented overtures to the heroism of the leader that valorized not only the hero himself but also heroism as a conceptual national virtue. While he was editor-in-chief of *al-Maʿrifa* in the early 1980s, Safwan Qudsi wrote *al-Baṭal wa-l-Tārīkh* (*The Hero and History*), a book-length tribute to the "political thought" of Hafiz al-Asad, as if the latter were a political theorist. Qudsi identified the hero as the product of historical becoming that unfolds over time: "History does not produce its heroes in the absence of consciousness."[135] Across vast stretches of time, Qudsi argued, history makes certain demands of people and the hero-leader responds with historic vision and strength. In the final analysis, the dialectic between the hero and history is bolstered by the bonds between "the struggler Hafiz al-Asad" and "the masses of *his* people."[136] This attribution of the people directly to Hafiz al-Asad is instructive for its allusion to the sycophantic culture of heroism that permeated the intellectual and cultural spaces of Asadist-Baʿthist Syria. Attending to the entanglement of heroism and history in this regard explains the politics of culture in contemporary Syria in general and the aesthetic ideology of Asadist-Baʿthist cultural revolution in particular. In the chapters that follow, I will present a panorama of Syrian cultural production from the 1970s through the time of the Syria War which have reflected the interests and concerns of many writers, artists, filmmakers, and intellectuals who have been engaged in the struggle around aesthetic ideology. The next chapter explores how filmmakers and writers have transformed these atmospheric conceptions of heroism into concrete engagements with the problematic of gender and power, primarily in their representations of masculinity.

Chapter 2

MEN OF COMMITMENT

'Abd al-Halim al-Murr swore he would divorce his wife Nabila if she dared to leave the house alone without his permission, and Nabila was sure to leave the house every day after his oath, and he got upset, and he swore he would divorce her if she dared to walk down the street without covering up, and Nabila took off her black wrap and used it as a dust rag on the ground, and he got upset, and he swore he would divorce her if he ever found out that she had spoken with a man other than him. One afternoon he came home unannounced and found her in bed talking to a man he had never seen before, and he got upset, and he swore he would divorce her if it came to pass that this unknown man was the reason for her bloated stomach, and Nabila just laughed, saying that fatty foods were making her as gassy as a balloon, and months later she gave birth to a daughter, and 'Abd al-Halim al-Murr got upset, and he swore he would divorce Nabila if it ever occurred to her to have another daughter, but he divorced her a few weeks after that as punishment for forgetting to put enough salt in his food.

— Zakariya Tamir, "Men"[1]

Women are depicted in a quite different way from men—not because the feminine is different from the masculine—but because the "ideal" spectator is always assumed to be male and the image of the woman is designed to flatter him.

— John Berger, *Ways of Seeing*[2]

> The male subject's identification with power and privilege is threatened from many directions.
>
> — Kaja Silverman, *Male Subjectivity at the Margins*[3]

IN LATE TWENTIETH-CENTURY SYRIA, THE CULTURAL FIELD WAS a site of struggle around the contours and content of aesthetic ideology in ways that were transformative and comparable to—if categorically distinct from—the political and military challenges the country experienced. The glorification of the leader, the valorization of heroism, the committed adherence to nationalist causes, and the championing of Arab unity were among the prime virtues in Asadist-Baʿthist aesthetic ideology, reflections of a state-centric aesthetics of power. Even if advocates of "committed" culture were ambivalent about the status of "the individual hero"—a heroic avatar of a larger cause but also an individualistic riposte to the power of the collective will—the paradigmatic character in Syrian literature and film would remain dedicated to the causes of Syrian patriotism, Arab unity, anti-imperialism, Third Worldist solidarity, and

FIGURE 6. Ossama Mohammed, *Ṣundūq al-Dunyā* (*Sacrifices*) (National Film Organization, 2002)

anti-Zionism, just to name the most salient. Chapter 1 introduced concepts and keywords of Asadist-Ba'thist cultural revolution that were first proposed, circulated, and debated during the 1970s and 1980s. But what tends to go unremarked in the scholarly literature on Ba'thist Syria is the simple but profound fact that the ideal subject expected to conform to these ideological principles and social norms was *a man*. While the political symbolism of Syrian Ba'thist patriotism, commitment, and loyalty were certainly embraced—and often ignored—by men and women alike, the hero remained a gendered figure, one predominantly marked as male. To a similar extent, even "antiheroes" who appeared in Syrian literature and film were men, especially when it came to works written or directed by a man. Even more important is the set of attributes that characterized the cultural definitions of manhood and masculinity in Syrian literature and film.[4]

How did men in particular frame, stage, and represent masculinity in novels and films during the time of Hafiz al-Asad? If John Berger is correct in noting, as cited previously, that "the 'ideal' spectator is always assumed to be male and the image of the woman is designed to flatter him," then what is the image of the man supposed to do to the "ideal" (male) spectator, perhaps also flatter him? Scholarship on the Arabic novel and film during the mid- to late-twentieth century contended with the problems of realism and ideology, describing both the power of the socialist-realist hero and the loss of his fire after the ignominious defeat of 1967. This death of the hero over the course of the late-twentieth century was also a function of challenges to the virility, masculinity, and patriarchy of Arab society and culture.[5] Even as the power of the patriarch, the husband, and the state were reinforced in some Syrian cultural production from this period, critical representations of the father might be launched from the same epistemological grounds as the critique of state power. While the library of Middle East masculinity studies is growing, more work can still be done on discourses of masculinity with specific reference to cultural production.[6] In her pathbreaking book on masculinity in the post-1967 Arabic novel, Samira Aghacy identifies the myriad forms and meanings of masculine identity in modern Arabic fiction: "the virile macho, the romantic idealist, the tyrannical father, the domineering husband, the daring freedom fighter, the committed intellectual, the ruthless militiaman, the persecuted prisoner, and the soft and effeminate subaltern, to name but a few."[7]

The novels and films investigated in this chapter engage issues of gender in ways that foreground and skewer patriarchy, masculinism, and men's experience. By no means should this focus be taken to suggest the insignificance of women and girls in these works; on the contrary, female characters in the films and novels discussed here as well as the stakes and representations of girlhood, womanhood, and femininity demand attention. My interest here, though, is to reframe the study of gender in modern and contemporary Syrian literature and film in a way that draws attention to the centrality of masculinity *alongside and in relation to* femininity, which is only part of a comprehensive gender analysis. Furthermore, a targeted investigation of tropes and ideologies of masculinity opens up a new line of scholarly argument about the relationship of gender and power in the making of modern Syria. By attending to the reflections of Syrian state discourses on leadership, heroism, and virtue in cultural production, a new understanding of men, manliness, and masculinity emerges. This chapter begins with a close reading of two novels that speak to the relationship between patriarchy and violence in the Syrian countryside: *Nihāyat Rajul Shujāʿ* (*End of a Brave Man*) (1989) by Hanna Mina and *Miʿrāj al-Mawt* (*Ascension to Death*) (1989) by Mamdouh Azzam. Both works have had second lives in Syrian visual culture, the former in a television serial; the latter, in an acclaimed film. Then I look at three films: *Al-Lajāt* (1995), Riyad Shayya's film adaptation of Azzam's *Ascension to Death* (cowritten with Azzam and, regrettably, Shayya's only film); *Layālī Ibn Awā* (*Nights of the Jackal*) (1989) by ʿAbd al-Latif ʿAbd al-Hamid; and *Ṣundūq al-Dunyā* (*Sacrifices*) (2002), the second film by Ossama Mohammed. I also briefly comment on Mohammed's first feature, *Nujūm al-Nahār* (*Stars in Broad Daylight*) (1988). All of these narrative films employ striking visual language to address—however directly or obliquely—the interrelated problems of violence, power, and masculinity. The aesthetic ideology of cultural revolution in Asadist-Baʿthist Syria—its aesthetics of power—expressed through the language of the state and its affiliated cultural institutions needs to be seen in relation to other literary and cinematic engagement with discourses of heroism, masculinity, and violence. Despite the state's attempt to make its discourse of cultural revolution hegemonic, aesthetic ideology was appropriated and resignified in unexpected and sometimes inspiring ways, whether through an aesthetics of solidarity or through an aesthetics of resistance. The Syrian cultural field was characterized by an ongoing agonistic dialectic between this aesthetics of power and the various aesthetic projects that challenged it, one that comes into sharp relief in relation to discourses of masculinity.

EMBODIED MASCULINITY: HANNA MINA'S *END OF A BRAVE MAN* (*NIHAYAT RAJUL SHUJA'*)

Despite the centrality of Hanna Mina (1924–2018) in twentieth-century Syrian letters—he might be considered the paradigmatic postwar Syrian writer—there has been relatively scant scholarly engagement with his work. Born in Latakia in 1924, Mina grew up in the province of Alexandretta (Iskandarūn) and then moved back to Latakia with his family, where he worked as, among other things, a porter, a barber, and a sailor. After writing actively for the Lebanese and Syrian press, Mina became a founding member of the Syrian Writers' Collective (Rābiṭat al-Kuttāb al-Sūriyyīn) in 1951, which in 1954 became the Arab Writers' Union (Ittiḥād al-Kuttāb al-ʿArab, AWU).[8] Across dozens of popular novels, Mina's plots highlight individual moral dilemmas, social drama, and political struggle. Scholars of Arabic literature in Syria generally agree that Mina's 1954 novel *al-Maṣābīḥ al-Zurq* (*The Blue Lanterns*) marked a meaningful shift away from romantic prose and toward social realism and committed literature.[9] These works celebrate everyday life and ordinary people in Syria, with specific attention to the trials and travails of the working class and the peasantry. His novels are neither dogmatic nor doctrinaire—although the main characters typically espouse right-thinking "committed" positions—but relatively uncomplicated, straightforward, and quick reads. "As a literary figure," literary historian Alexa Firat notes, "Mīnah is credited with a gift for authenticity that most writers cannot begin to match by literally embodying the virtues of socialist realism on the simple basis of his birth and upbringing."[10] This gift for authenticity resulted in his being immortalized as the name for the most prestigious literary prize in the country. Mina remained on good terms with successive Syrian governments throughout his life.

Mina also needs to be situated against the intellectual- and political-historical backdrop of his time. He came of age in the Syrian Marxisant-Arab nationalist milieu of the 1960s and 1970s. In an article published in the socialist journal *al-Ṭarīq* in 1970 which was based on a lecture he gave at the Soviet Cultural Center in Damascus celebrating the centenary of Lenin's birth, Mina expounded on his views of literature broadly. "Literature, as you know," he wrote,

> is the squadron leader [*kawkaba*] of the vanguard in the retinue of thought, coming first in the procession of this universe, the caravan of those who are thirsty in the desert, to quench their thirst and to guide them, like Solomon's woodpecker, to awaken them and call upon those who are slumbering to rise up, then to illuminate the path of revolt, like ants in a row, and to fashion out of whispered complaints an anthem of rage.[11]

This sentiment, articulated through flowery description and militant metaphor, squarely locates Mina in the midst of mid-twentieth-century committed Arabic literature and its politics of engagement. During the 1950s and 1960s, an age of postcolonial tumult in Syria, this position could be oppositional, calling out repressive military regimes around the Arab world while also adhering to the hegemonic literary and cultural norms of leftist and Arab nationalist social movements. With the institutionalization of Asadist-Ba'thist cultural revolution during the 1970s, Mina would be folded into an institutional apparatus of cultural production. In 1979 he coauthored *Adab al-Ḥarb* (*War Literature*) with minister of culture Najah al-'Attar. The authors noted that Syria and the Arab world faced a dangerous situation in the shadow of Israeli hegemony and US imperialism, and that literature was paramount in the struggle against foreign aggression. "The question before us: So long as the enemy surrounds us, and we are threatened on more than one side, and war still looms over our country," Mina and al-'Attar asked, "why is it that some of our literature before October [1973] was cocooned in on itself, far removed from the battle?" In other words, why did literature not take a more direct approach to the question of war and "struggle"?[12] Their diagnosis was that intellectuals, writers, and other cultural producers had insufficient cultural awareness and political engagement. In other words, even the committed literature of the mid-twentieth century had not gone far enough to promote revolutionary consciousness through writing. In a sense, then, the Asadist-Ba'thist cultural revolution envisioned by Tayyib Tizini, Zakariya Tamir, Muhammad Shahin, and others (Chapter 1) was portrayed as a viable solution in the incomplete project of revolutionizing Arab consciousness through culture. It was high time that writers and artists took up their places in the cultural vanguard that would lead the nation to glory.

End of a Brave Man (*Nihāyat Rajul Shujā'*) (1989) is a bildungsroman that narrates the story of Mufid, a young man who grows up in a rural hinterland

FIGURE 7. Hanna Mina, *Nihāyat Rajul Shujāʿ: Riwāya* (Beirut: Dār al-Ādāb, 1989).

outside of the northwestern city of Banyas. The novel opens with Mufid describing how at the age of twelve he cut off the tail of a donkey that belonged to an old man in the village. First-person voice was not an altogether uncommon in the mid-twentieth century Arabic novel even though it was often disfavored by "committed" writers who preferred free indirect discourse, which allowed smooth movement between third-person omniscient narrative and the interior thoughts of characters. Mufid's mischievous act symbolizes his rambunctiousness and malaise, garnering him the nickname "Mufīd al-Waḥsh" (Mufid the Beast), a moniker that recurs throughout the novel. He struggles against the authority of his parents—especially his overbearing, violent father—his schooling, his community, and the pressures bearing down on him in the realms of the economy, society, and politics. In a gesture toward his earliest conception of manhood, he describes his father as having "the frame of a camel, the head of a sheep, the strength of an ox, and I inherited his gigantic stature, the strength in my forearms."[13] Like much of Mina's fiction, the novel is set during the French Mandate (1920–1946), which literary historians argue can be understood as enabling the expression of the writer's anticolonial politics but also serving as a literary device through which the writer can avoid sticky entanglements with mimetic representations of the contemporary regime.

Mufid drops out of school and runs away from his home village, eventually finding his way to Banyas, where he is imprisoned for clandestine anticolonial activities—assaulting a French officer at one point—before moving to Latakia and falling in love with a woman named Labiba. He takes on a number of odd jobs—a baker's helper, a sailor, a porter—but is perpetually in and out of work. Mufid strives to remain a virtuous person even as he is pulled into the city's criminal underworld. Through his relationship with ʿAbdush, a young man from the same village, Mufid learns about life in the port city while struggling to become a man. "I don't want to be a thug (*balṭajiyyan*)," he says. "I'd prefer to earn an honest living."[14] This turns out to be easier said than done. Goaded into fighting as part of ʿAbdush's crew, Mufid reckons with his options: "I had no choice. I'm a young man and I want to seem like a man. It's true that I'm a man without any experience but I have the strength of a stallion, so what am I afraid of?"[15] Throughout the novel, the metaphor of "stallion-hood" (*fuḥūla*) as virility is code for true manhood. Fighting against the French occupiers or standing up to rival gangs becomes an index of Mufid's worth, a hallmark of his character. There are also sexual implications of Mufid's budding manhood, depicted in part around his relationship with Labiba. Mufid finds that consorting with ʿAbdush "had transformed me from a young man into a mature man."[16] When he first meets Labiba, she comments on his masculine virtues.

> "I saw you before and after [the fight]. . . . Something drew me to you."
> "What's that?"
> "Admiration. You're a real man. You're my [kind of] man."
> "But I'm a wanted man."
> "Doesn't matter."
> "I could be jailed tomorrow."
> "Doesn't matter either."[17]

Mufid is carted off to prison for a couple of years, first held by the French in Latakia and then transferred to Aleppo. Mufid's prison experience is an education, not unlike other prison narratives—whether fictional and factual—in the history of Arabic literature.[18] ʿAbd al-Jalil, a man he encounters in prison who happens to be a friend of his mother's cousin Ibrahim al-Shankal—the man who helped to orient him when he first arrived in Latakia—advises him on how to live:

> "Be honorable and understanding. . . . Don't fritter away your life, don't waste your energies, always remember that life is struggle, and that the human being is a struggler, that he possesses a mind that guides him. This is what distinguishes a human being from an animal."
> "But I am an animal!" I blurted out.
> "Bite your tongue," he retorted. "You're a human being."[19]

These binary distinctions between man and woman and between human and animal cut through the novel. When matters turn existential, the nature of Mufid's humanity—as opposed to his animality—is called into question. Mufid consistently refers to himself as a "beast" (*waḥsh*), but recall that the defining act of his childhood was to slice off the tail off a donkey, which both established his command over the animal and affirmed his own savage instincts. This traditional conception of manhood and masculinity falls in line with the discourse of Asadist-Baʿthist cultural revolution on heroism discussed in the Chapter 1.

There is a kind of blustering masculinity on display throughout the novel that has eluded analysis by scholars and readers. Whereas the work of Hanna Mina remains understudied, there has been next to no critical analysis of *End of a Brave Man*, as far as I am aware. Samira Aghacy situates another one of Mina's novels, *Journey Towards the Dusk* (*al-Raḥīl ʿind al-Ghurūb*) (1992) in the light of her searing feminist critique of patriarchal culture and masculinist discourse. Aghacy speculates that "Mina's novels are predominantly set during the French Mandate, in the past rather than in the present, most probably for fear of state reprisals."[20] The voices of male characters in *End of a Brave Man* are equivocal and their "true" or "brave" masculinity is sometimes confirmed and sometimes undermined. Given that Mina is one of the most important Syrian writers of the twentieth century, Aghacy's claim that Mina's "fantasy tale" about "personal valor and muscular feats" is an overcompensation for his "marginal position in the public sphere" seems overstated.[21] If Mina's representation of masculinity relies on a traditional conception of male virtue—strength, commitment, sexual potency—there is also recognition that those attributes are forged in struggle and multifarious life experiences. Mina's normative conception of masculinity is contrasted to archetypal conceptions of women, including a reductive depiction of the sea as a woman expressed in Mufid's voice when he elaborates on his vow to give up the sailing life:

> I'm going to leave the sea behind, leave it forever. But did I ever actually leave it behind? No. I lied. The sea is a woman. Is it possible to leave a woman behind and never come back? A monk does so but the monk is emasculated, whereas I'm a stallion. I'll spend my life in the service of a woman, and I'll spend it in the service of the sea, which makes me a slave, and the only thing that can release me from the slavery of women and the sea is death, that whore who shows up precisely when you don't want her to.[22]

Rendering death as a whore and women as the boundless, watery depths of the ocean is the kind of salty language one might expect from a working-class sailor such as Mufid. On the other hand, there is an aesthetic entwinement of "woman" and "sea" that hinges on retrograde binary conceptions of gender in which women are soft, fluid, and unknowable while men are firm, committed, and conscious. But this swaggering masculinity, puffed up with bravado, also betrays Mufid's craving for recognition in the eyes of friends, family, employers, political representatives, and perhaps even God.

When Mufid is released from prison in the middle of World War II, he returns to Latakia to look for work. Reclaiming his job at the port, he gets mixed up with other hoodlums and takes part in a raid on a barge off the coast, which becomes a cause celèbre among the authorities and the "sharks" in the criminal underworld. Even as rival gangs—Abu Dahir and his boys, Shaykh Rida and his—struggle to figure out what is going on in the local port economy, Mufid and his associates ʿAbdush and Halish are never caught. Mufid is now adrift, occasionally meditating on the kind of person he is and may yet become.

> I'm confident in myself. Confident in my arms. I have strong arms, a strong heart, a head as large as a bull, even more solid. I know this head, and I know that if I hit something, or butted the wall with it, there would be a gaping hole left behind. This head was created for head-butting. It's a good thing it doesn't have two horns, I wouldn't like to have two horns. That would give me a bad reputation. Horns on a bull aren't the same as horns on a human head. Horns on a bull are weapons against another bull, against any beast. They are the adornment of a bull, its weapons, the symbol of its virility, but this would not be so in the case of human beings. Horns would be appropriate for a pimp, and I don't believe that a man, in the fullness of his masculinity, is the same thing as a pimp. Pimps aren't real men [*al-qawwādūn mukhannathūn*]. Tfu! Curse all the pimps in the world.[23]

Mufid has all the physical attributes of an animal, yet he fears his masculinity could be undermined if his animality grows too pronounced. If stallion-hood is a desirable quality in a real man, the virility of a beast embodied in a bull's horns transforms a man into a pimp, which, it turns out, is not a more robust man for his power over women but a violently emasculated one; the term *mukhannath* has connotations of effeminacy, bisexuality, and even hermaphroditism. While he dreams of reuniting with Labiba, Mufid continues to look for work.

Mufid struggles to walk the straight and narrow path, buffeted by economic pressures and personal challenges. "I tried to walk a different path, other than the one I have walked until now: the path of a brave man, one who commands a modicum of respect, the respect of a man, who once and for all removes the garb of a thief, the shame of stealing, and the vileness of dishonorable deeds, which have forced me to hide out in this hovel."[24] Mufid expresses a similar sentiment about his aspirationally virtuous masculinity: "I just wanted to say one thing: that I respect myself!"[25] Self-respect means not being bullied by anyone, holding his own in the port, on the water, throughout his life.

> Without hesitation I said to myself: "I'm a man! Mufid, you are a man." But what does it mean to be a man? It means that you put your blood in your hands, that you leave the house in the morning without knowing if you're going to make it home in the evening.[26]

While Mufid manages to reconnect with his old friends ʿAbdush and Halish and a number of employers along the dock, one influential figure he cannot seem to get right with is Muʿallim Yusuf al-Bathish, whose gang ultimately contributes to Mufid's downfall. When Mufid reconnects with Labiba, she confesses she had not been sure she would recognize him. He tells her that he is the same person she once knew. "But you've become a man!" she shouts. Improbably, they get married the very next day.[27] Not only is Mufid trapped between warring gangs in the port but he is also caught up amid clamoring demands from the port workers for a union, which pits them against local employers as well as the sovereign power of the French Mandate authorities.

After a brawl, Mufid is imprisoned for five years in Latakia. By the time he is released here, he has been diagnosed with diabetes by the prison doctor but has received no treatment. A more serious diagnosis is provided by a doctor on the outside: one of his toes will have to be amputated. Back with Labiba, he despairs over assimilating into normal life now that he has been forbidden alcohol, coffee, tobacco, and sugar. Harping on the same conception of his own animality, Mufid insists to Labiba that he truly is "beastly" (*waḥshī*):

> Beast! That's the word. Don't call me by my name, the word "beast" is enough, it's perfect, appropriate for the situation, in the past and the present, in the future as well. I'm a real beast. I'm more of a jackass than that jackass whose tail I cut off.[28]

Mufid is at his wit's end as he reflects on the life he left behind and where he now finds himself after getting out of prison. His rejection of medical expertise and his embrace of his own nature represents the victory of animality, "his beastliness," in the face of a version of humanity—venal, managed, power-hungry—that he can no longer tolerate. Mufid's suffering is the quintessential struggle in a world characterized by injustice, a clarion call for a return to a more natural, animalistic kind of humanity. When his leg is amputated above the knee—rather than just a toe—Mufid careens toward self-annihilation. He drinks and smokes and does everything proscribed by the doctor, refusing to let life devour him and proclaiming that he will be the one to devour life. Labiba alternately shames and coaxes him about his drinking and smoking, insisting that for her to call him "beast" would be "incorrect. You're a bashful little boy." This is met with a soliloquy:

> I found my bravery in all of these hardships. My shirt and my manhood were made from its material, and tomorrow, when I die, I'll die at peace because I was brave. Disease has come for me. It's come for me and that's the end of that. I have nothing left, and I'm not sorry for anything. But no creature in the world can deny that I was brave, and I'll remain brave. When I look into the eyes of death, I'm not afraid.[29]

The narrative voice switches unexpectedly in the novel's concluding moment:

> I'm Labiba al-Shaqraq. I'll tell you what happened next, I'll say a few, simple words, with the simplicity and spare language of Mufid . . . words that are wet with my tears, but it isn't sadness, because Mufid accustomed me, ever since we met, not to be sad about anything, not about him or about myself.[30]

The moral of being a committed, struggling individual, to rise to the challenge of life, perhaps to embody heroic qualities—to be a brave man—is to have no fear. When Zurayyik the customs officer tries to break into the house to search for contraband, Mufid whips out a gun and pulls the trigger, which sends the men running and puts a slug in Zurayyik's chest, leaving him on the floor as blood drips from his mouth. At that instant, as Labiba calls out to him, Mufid turns the gun toward his own temple and blows his brains out.[31] This is when the narrative unravels and must be drawn to a close. Mufid's suicidal act can be read as the inevitable end for a frustrated hero struggling just to survive in a time of injustice and violence. To foreshadow a discussion in Chapter 6 about death and dying in the Syria War novel, the dead most definitely and definitively die in socialist-realist and existentialist fiction, whereas they may live on in the literature of the ongoing war. In this case, however, the reader is asked not to tarry with Mufid's suicide, with the dead, but rather to understand that death at one's own hand may be the appropriate end of a brave man.

End of a Brave Man was made into a popular television serial drama for the 1994 Ramadan season, directed by Najdat Isma'il Anzur. The adaptation fit into the styles of melodramatic nostalgia and historical fiction characteristic of a growing television drama market.[32] Also, it was shot with a single camera, a sign of what has been called the "cinematic turn" in Syrian television. The script was developed by Hasan M. Yousef. The show ran for twenty-seven episodes and is widely available on YouTube. Media anthropologist Christa Salamandra argues that the series was noteworthy for being set outside of Damascus and depicting life "in a village thought to be 'Alawi." Because the private production company that made the series was owned by the son of Syrian vice president 'Abd al-Halim Khaddam, Salamandra concludes that its "link to the regime was obvious."[33] Rebecca Joubin comes to a different conclusion in her analysis of the series.[34] While recognizing the formal connection to the regime through the production company, Sharikat Sham al-Duwwaliyya, Joubin states that the series "does not propagate official dogma. On the contrary, it complements the movement of transferring viewers into another time in order to critique the current Ba'th party regime."[35] The theme of masculinity looms large in the series, although the original narrative of the novel is modified. Mufid's most laudable televised virtues are those of a true "*qabaday*—decisive, strong, honorable, and heroic." These qualities are to be contrasted with those of a "betrayer" with a "compromised conscience [that] leads to his inferior masculinity."[36] On more than one occasion, Joubin equates masculinity with "conscience" (*ḍamīr*), a trait that is malleable enough to fit within most ideological vocabularies of mid- to late twentieth century Syria. Joubin also identifies a domineering and violent boss at the Latakia port, where Mufid finds employment after getting out of prison, as a stand-in for Hafiz al-Asad, alternately "a direct reference to Hafiz al-Asad" and "a not-so-subtle depiction of Hafiz al-Asad."[37] The ending of the television serial is quite different from that of the novel, where Mufid reaches his tragic end by shooting himself in the head after wounding the customs officer in the chest. In the televised version, which is pitched to a broader audience in Syria and beyond, the heroic sacrifice in the climax instead involves Mufid's response to Zurayyik coming one last time to shake him down for money. They are on a bluff overlooking the sea, Mufid in a wheelchair and Zurayyik resting against a bamboo fence. Suddenly Mufid grabs Zurayyik, strangles him, and releases his wheelchair, sending both of them careening over the edge, presumably tumbling to their dramatic deaths in the sea. This is certainly a more daring end to the story than the shootout in the novel. Joubin finds that this "story depicts a brave and defiant masculinity, a secular outlook on a manhood constantly under threat. Political marginalization is pervasive, but a *qabaday* must confront the authority and not be subdued."[38]

While it might appear that Salamandra and Joubin disagree about the status of masculinity and power in the series, I argue that in the end they both reinforce the interpretive stance that cultural production can be categorized as either pro- or antiregime. The truth of the matter is that the novels of Hanna Mina and the television adaptation of *End of A Brave Man*, the films of ʿAbd al-Latif ʿAbd al-Hamid, and those of Ossama Mohammed (discussed below) are more nuanced. Joubin's discussion of the *qabaḍāy* (strong man) prefigures some of my discussion in Chapter 3 about Durayd Lahham and the aesthetics of power exemplified by his character Ghawar al-Tushi, particularly in the 1982 film *The Empire of Ghawar* (*Imbraṭūriyyat Ghawār*). As in that film, the masculinist virtues of *qabaḍāy'iyya*, of *qabaḍāy*-ness, of being "decisive, strong, honorable, heroic" are emblematic of Asadist-Baʿthist cultural revolution. But even if certain characters or works of art are indicative of this aesthetics of power, which would suggest some degree of kinship with regime ideology, this does not mean that the same work cannot contain contradictions or multiple messages, in ways that might reflect an aesthetics of solidarity or an aesthetics of resistance, which presumably justifies classification of the work as antiregime. Asadist-Baʿthist cultural revolutionary heroism was inscribed in the bedrock of Syrian literature and film. Syrians (especially men) might seek to emulate the ostensible virtues on display in the literary analysis of Hanna ʿAbbud (Chapter 1), the novels of Hanna Mina discussed here, and the plays and films of Durayd Lahham (Chapter 3), knowing full well that only the Eternal Leader is capable of truly embodying them. Even in the midst of a valiant and virtuous anticolonial nationalist struggle against the French, and amid his questing to transcend his provincial and patriarchal upbringing, the "conditions of life" can ultimately wear down a brave man such as Mufid, perilously leading him toward his demise. If the end for this brave man is suicide by a bullet to the head, it remains undecidable whether his bravery comes to an end *because of* his decision to kill himself or he is brave until the very end, through and despite his bold decision to end his life.

WOUNDS OF MASCULINITY: MAMDOUH AZZAM'S *ASCENSION TO DEATH* (*MIʿRĀJ AL-MAWT*)

Representations of masculinity in Syrian cultural production reflect a range of anxieties, desires, and contradictions. In *End of a Brave Man*, masculinity is debated and defended vehemently. But patriarchal society in provincial Syria does not always rise to the level of such explicitly thematized discourse. Mamdouh Azzam's caustic first novel, *Ascension to Death* (*Miʿrāj al-Mawt*), originally published in 1989, is a striking example of how literature can obliquely address political repression while also drawing attention to patriarchal authority and violence.[39] Azzam (b. 1950) is from Suwayda in southern Syria and has published several novels, although *Ascension to Death* is his most popular and influential.[40] Told from multiple perspectives—albeit consistently voiced by the same third-person omniscient narrator—it is an austere, fractured, tragic love story tracking the heartbreaking demise of Salma, a peasant girl from the southern Druze region of Syria. When we meet her, Salma is married to a man named Saeed, whom she does not love. Her marriage is characterized by coercion and loveless sex: "There was nothing more Salma could do other than surrender to her husband in bed without even bothering to take off her clothes. It was better for her just to passively receive his manhood so that he would fall asleep satisfied."[41] Salma never fully accepts her domestic situation, however. "She didn't hate him but she didn't love him either."[42]

A couple of years after their wedding, Saeed leaves the country in search of work. Salma falls head over heels in love with Abd al-Kareem, a young man from the village whom Salma's family had not allowed her to marry. Salma grows increasingly despondent but also committed to finding a way to live out her dreams of romantic love, to subvert both male and female gender roles in her conservative rural society.

> She resented the life she had lived up until that point, the dark stream of difficulties, that strange amalgam of frustration and obedience. She was determined to raise her fist and chart a new course. She resolved to get there, to think for herself, to find strength in all the things that could be found on a path leading

> to him, unfettered by hidebound tradition that required a man to take the first step.[43]

How Salma and Abd al-Kareem met and fell in love is not introduced until the final, fifth chapter of the novella, which adds to the disorientation of the plot and to a sense of the inevitability of Salma's downfall. Abd al-Kareem adheres to the courtship norms of chaste romantic love.

> He couldn't think of any other way to prove his love to her. The Platonic ideal of love that inspired him was exemplified by his unwavering commitment not to bring sex into the relationship at this stage. It wasn't an act. His resolve was so strong and so true that she was able to draw strength from his desire. He believed that not holding back from sex would be a mistake that might destroy their love. Even though he was rock solid in his commitment to this decision, to the point of piety, the power of love compelled him to kiss Salma again and again without any sexual connotations.[44]

Unlike the interiorized evolution of Mufid's desire for Labiba in *End of a Brave Man*, Abd al-Kareem articulates an innocent, romantic version of heterosexual love. His shyness, hesitation, and respect for Salma—as an individual and as a woman enmeshed in complicated social and familial circumstances—reflects an altogether different way of inhabiting and performing masculinity. Abd al-Kareem musters up the courage to ask Salma to come with him:

> "Let's run away together, Salma. We'll just run away."
> "And live together forever?"
> "That's right."
> "And I'll have your son?"
> "A daughter, like you."
> "A son would be better."

Even with an apparently egalitarian relationship brewing between the two illicit lovers, Salma reminds us that no matter how deeply a man and a woman may love one another, a boy "would be better" in this society. Salma commits herself to being with Abd al-Kareem, asking for a divorce from Saeed, but this never comes to pass. The lovers decide to elope instead, staying in the rural guesthouse of a sympathetic man named Abu Nayef.

Even though Saeed had abandoned her and left the country, Salma's family conspires to punish her for pursuing an immoral relationship. The police chief attempts to persuade her uncle Sayyah not to take revenge. Sayyah snarls that he is "going to kill her with my own two hands,"[45] that he is "going to kill her even if all the prophets are on her side!"[46] Consequently, and this is how the novel opens, Salma is locked in a shed where her female relatives treat her like a common criminal, provisioning her with food and basic necessities but keeping her under constant surveillance. Abd al-Kareem struggles to find any trace of Salma:

> It was as if Abd al-Kareem's devastated soul was now being covered in hard and muddy sorrow. He couldn't do anything. Every moment of Salma's disappearance deepened his sadness. . . . With all the disrespect that people were showing him, there was little more for him to do than fade away. He became a ghost, condensed into a cloud.[47]

Whereas the men of Salma's family assert themselves with confidence, pride, and violence, Abd al-Kareem's innocence and impotence are reflective of a man incapable of satisfying his own desires, saving his beloved from danger, and defending both her honor and his own. With Salma missing, this weakened man has to be cared for by his tender mother. The psychological and physical scars of a repressive patriarchal society are legible not only on the incarcerated body of Salma, who is denied the right to love and happiness but also on the vanquished heart of her frail, demoralized, and passive male lover.

The Zeeb clan colludes to carry out Salma's lethal punishment. Sayyah Zeeb, the patriarch, used to enjoy his position of power and "once took pleasure in that automatic acquiescence, the obedience laced with respect and reverence that he received from siblings and relatives alike."[48] But his power is dwindling, not unlike the fortunes of many notable families.

> The fate of his family was slipping through his fingers like water: the famines of the fifties, exile and migration, prophesied news of an impending apocalypse. All of this disoriented him, especially as he was unable to shake off those fantasies of authority that he had concocted from his longstanding thirst for power.[49]

After having proved his mettle on the battlefield in Palestine in 1948, Sayyah now believes he will wield his charismatic authority in perpetuity.

> He had become a hero, unfortunately. He was stunned by the welcome, confounded by the ordinary feelings and humdrum emotion that . . . he thought could be attributed to the thanklessness of being a *za'im* at a time when the regime could install anyone they wished in that position. That night he was made even more miserable when his wife refused to sleep in the same bed with him because she had her period. Her condition was more powerful than his burning desire to sleep with her, and he had no choice but to give in. And so, because of all that, he started to become pessimistic.[50]

Here is one of the few moments in which historical circumstances are referenced. As we will see later in ʿAbd al-Latif ʿAbd al-Hamid's 1989 film *Nights of the Jackal* (*Layālī Ibn Awā*) and in Ossama Mohammed's 2002 film *Sacrifices* (*Ṣundūq al-Dunyā*), a man's demonstrated bravery, success, and authority on the battlefield or in public do not easily transfer into the domestic sphere. Sayyah occasionally betrays his insecurity.

> On more than one occasion he thought about sending someone to threaten her so that she'd keep her mouth shut. The plan emerged from his desire to erect some kind of barrier, whether imaginary or real, in the face of anyone who would try to ferret out his tortured soul by brandishing the spectre of that murdered girl. He was in dangerous territory, threatened by worldly scandal and divine retribution. He inhabited the bloody wound that was his decision, the scar of an anxious and disheveled mind.[51]

When Salma first dares to speak for herself, asserting her right to be with the man she loves, he finds it disturbing.

> Sayyah was horrified at the new woman she had become. He was accustomed to having girls and women panic whenever they encountered him. He could tell from the way their legs shook or the way their tongues froze in their mouths. His power was thunderous. He was puffed up by the sense of being in charge, even though his behaviour had created a rift between him and all the women around him, one that time could never bridge. His house was overflowing with women whose only concern was to attend to his family line.[52]

Even if Sayyah has the power and authority to control the behavior and fate of the women and girls in his family, he remains subject to doubt, misgivings, and ultimately the risk of incompetence and failure. His pompous commitment to tradition, lineage, male power, and family discipline is undermined at every turn, whether by his wife's aversion to sleeping with him, Salma's outright defiance, or his own occasional hesitation.

Male characters in *Ascension to Death* seem afflicted by their masculinity. Sayyah's manhood is overgrown power, dominating those he purports to love, punishing anyone who threatens conventional propriety. Abd al-Kareem, by contrast, is beaten down by patriarchal violence, wounded by his inability to change his own fate or protect Salma. He has a brief and meaningless tryst with a married woman named Umm Samer, who is "pained by his weakness and his frailty, believing that she could empower him just by being with him, that she could repair his troubled soul and his shattered body."[53] When Abd al-Kareem first meets Salma, he is nearly obliterated by his feelings of love.

> There was no power in the universe strong enough to prevent what happened a few minutes later. His heart nearly burst, blood rushed to his face, his scalp was on fire as warm sweat oozed, thick and sticky, all over his body: he loved the possessor of those reflecting eyes, now and forever.[54]

During their first, awkward romantic encounter, he stumbles over his words.

> He felt like an idiot when he recalled his inability to utter even a single word that might convey the feelings their encounter had inspired in him. He remembered all too well how he had to struggle against his dimwittedness, his inadequate, tortoise-like thinking. He blamed himself for the lukewarm way in which she had greeted him.[55]

Abd al-Kareem is left dumbstruck by his feelings. His love for Salma verges on fairytale. Their impossible relationship, crushed under the bootheel of the tyrannical Sayyah, is reminiscent of star-crossed lovers denied the opportunity to be together, opening up a potentially allegorical reading of the novel.

Ironically, it is in death that Salma exercises the most agency.

> All alone now, she could no longer put up any kind of fight. Her energy had been sapped during this losing battle. Bad timing. She felt as though she were disappearing even as she watched herself drift into that terrifying darkness. She started to shiver, overcome momentarily, her body bathed in an icy sweat.

When she finally snapped out of it she had become a new woman. She wouldn't surrender—this was her decision. There was no going back, from that moment until her death, murdered in the horse shed, with Jamil Zeeb's delirious shouting ringing in her ears:

Die!

Die!

Die![56]

In *End of a Brave Man*, frustrated masculinity reaches an impasse that results in the death of the hero. In *Ascension to Death*, the bold embrace of romantic love by two young people in the countryside elicits patriarchal revenge against them both, although it is Salma who must perish as a sacrifice for their transgression. Her death is perforce not a voluntary one, reflecting the pulverizing violence of patriarchal tradition. In her final seconds, she finds a momentary composure as a kinsman, Jamil Zeeb, is whipped into a murderous frenzy, perhaps the unavoidable outcome of a social system predicated on the domination of women and men by male violence. Abd al-Kareem is humiliated and has no means of exercising his own masculinity—not finding the strength to defend either himself or Salma—despite the fact that other men are willing to help him. What kind of man is he if he is unwilling or unable to fight for his own dignity or for the very life of his beloved? What does it say about the possibility of nonhegemonic masculinity if the only coherent male behavior is the brute exercise of lethal force in order to quash any challenge to its power and potency? The violence of patriarchy conjures opposing forces of resistance but mostly results in the destruction of dreams, love, and life.

SHADOWS OF PATRIARCHY: RIYAD SHAYYA'S *AL-LAJĀT*

Riyad Shayya's film adaptation of *Ascension to Death*, *Al-Lajāt* (1995), which Shayya co-wrote with Mamdouh Azzam, is even more minimalist and elliptical than the novel, which is ironically one of the ways it is most faithful to the book. Shayya was also born in Suwayda, in 1954, and, like fellow filmmakers 'Abd al-Latif 'Abd al-Hamid and Ossama Mohammed (discussed later), he studied cinema at the All-Union State Institute of Cinematography in Moscow (VGIK). Shayya passed away in 2016 after a battle with throat cancer.[57] His film was produced and released with the support of the National Film Organization (NFO); Ossama Mohammed is credited as artistic adviser.

If one has not read the novel, it can be difficult to puzzle out exactly what is going on in the film. There is scant narrative exposition, relatively vague character development, and a striking absence of dialogue. Furthermore, none of the patriarchal violence that leads to Salma's death takes place on camera; there are only oblique references to her confinement and physical punishment, as in the moment when she is ripped away from her beloved Abd al-Kareem and forced back into isolation. *Al-Lajāt* absorbs the viewer in the world of a Syrian village where the desires of both men and women are circumscribed and repressed.[58] Perhaps the most distinguishing features of the film are its melancholic mood, its lusciously dark color palette, and its unhurried pacing. Like the films of Ossama Mohammed, who was a collaborator, close friend, and stalwart supporter of Shayya, *Al-Lajāt* is patiently meticulous. There are fleeting moments of staggering beauty as the landscape emerges triumphant, framed reverently in each "shot" (*al-laqṭa*), a rather quotidian term elevated into a veritable photographic aesthetic roughly equivalent to the long takes in Shayya's work and championed by Mohammed (Chapter 4). The pace of everyday life in this rural community is unhurried. *Al-Lajāt* is perhaps best understood as "slow cinema." For film scholar Emre Çaglayan, "slow films are minimalistic by design: they retard narrative pace and elide causality." In an argument that sheds light on the allusive visual language and convoluted narrative structure of *Al-Lajāt*, Çaglayan makes an insightful point:

> [Slow] films' aesthetic features include a mannered use of the long take and a resolute emphasis on dead time: devices that foster a mode of narration that initially appears baffling, cryptic, and incomprehensible, but offers, above all, an extended experience of duration on screen.[59]

The "extended experience of duration" in *Al-Lajāt* permits the spectator to fully inhabit the physical space of the narrative and the indeterminate subjectivities of its characters. What makes it striking and perhaps even aesthetically revolutionary is not only its pacing, color palette, and technical sophistication, however, but also, like its literary inspiration, its progressive depictions of gender. I have been arguing that gender and power are crucial to an adequate understanding of cultural production in Syria during the 1980s and 1990s, even if the most influential work during this period—especially in cinema—was produced by men and therefore beholden to the male gaze. Through the creative manipulation of mirrors, screens, doors and other passageways, Shayya (like Mohammed) scrambles the optics of power characteristic of the male cinematic gaze in order to disrupt the boundaries between domination and resistance, outside versus inside, public versus domestic, and masculine versus feminine.

Claustrophobia haunts *Al-Lajāt*. Cloistered spaces limit physical and emotional movement, severely restricting the exercise of personal freedom even as the spectacular natural landscape stretches out in all directions. In the opening scene, white-scarved women glide through ancient stone buildings in funereal movement, reminiscent of herded animals. This may foreshadow a sheep marked for death later in the film, branded with a circle on the left side of its face in a long slow take. In another moment of prevision, Salma (Hanan Shqeir) hears her aunt's story about being banned by her family from entering the main house after falling in love with a man named Salim in al-Lajat village, forbidden from being with him in much the same way Salma is denied her own romantic desires. As Salma is surveilled by an older woman, the camera faces out of her prison shed (Figure 8, top-left image). Life proceeds at an unhurried pace, with little plot other than successive scenes of everyday life: women baking bread and washing clothes, men striding around slaughtering sheep and supervising, in a setting reminiscent of a medieval walled city. The film's color palette is uniformly dark: this mood suffuses the film, interrupted by moments of hope and possibility like Salma's initial encounter with a kindly man named Saeed by the water well. As if in a dream sequence, the reflection of Saeed's face gradually resolves in the rushing water as romantic music swells in the background, and Salma looks up at him with a smile on her face. This is the first time we see her in such a state. Saeed then appears before her in a doorway, dressed in a formal coat and gazing directly into her eyes, smiling unrestrainedly as she balances a metal water jug on her shoulder, struggling to smile back at him, clearly fighting against her instinct to remain dour and demure. A hard cut to her returning home with the water raises the possibility that she has confabulated the whole thing, but we later find Salma sitting beside Saeed next to a window (Figure 8, center-right image), explaining to him (and the viewer) that after her mother died she was taken to live with her uncle Sayyah, which made her feel as though she had been thrown into prison, and that nobody except for her aunt Nassiba would speak with her. Despite the affection that Salma and Saeed clearly have for one another, their relationship is cut short when he disappears. Although this remains unexplained, from the plot of *Ascension to Death* we understand he has left the country.

Not long after, Salma bumps into Abd al-Kareem at the well. With her face alone in the frame fetching water, a man off camera asks her if she is tired and she says she has gotten used to it. "Do you know me?" she asks him in astonishment. "You're Salma," he responds. Salma is positively beaming at him as Abd al-Kareem smiles back. This is followed by a sharp cut to Salma gazing in on a schoolhouse with a group of schoolgirls smiling out at her (Figure 8, bottom-left image). This scene is perhaps an externalized representation of her sudden flush of childlike joy and romance. Unlike Saeed, who appeared and then disappeared before disappearing for good, Abd al-Kareem inspires pure and innocent feelings in Salma, suggesting that she has forged a deep and originary bond with him already, that he could spend the rest of his life with her. Salma's disorientation and difficulty in finding her footing in life is reflected in the cinematography of openings (doors and windows), mirrors, and other mechanisms of trompe l'oeil. One example is her initial encounter with Saeed as he is inverted and reflected in the water (Figure 8, center-left image). The fact that Salma meets both Saeed and Abd al-Kareem while fetching water is significant; as Khalil Suwaylih points out, water "carries fundamental meanings in the events of the film."[60]

Salma seems to be at peace and even happy when she is with Abd al-Kareem. Here is a striking similarity in the relationship between romantic intimacy and confined spaces in *Al-Lajāt* and *Stars in Broad Daylight* (discussed later). In *Stars in Broad Daylight*, when Sana' briefly enjoys a respite of romantic courtship with a kind teacher in Latakia, their intimacy is reflected through the same technical frame shots but also in moments of calm repose (Figure 8, bottom-right image). Shayya's lens reflects the capacity of cinema to frame and reframe even the most everyday moments and spaces, much like the narrative films of Mohammed. Given Salma's restricted movement throughout *Ascension to Death*, it is somewhat aesthetically disorienting to see multiple shots of Salma and others *from inside*. Salma has been imprisoned by her family physically in the shed and socially through an arranged marriage; she is shot outside, though, in spaces where she appears to enjoy greater freedom. One way to interpret the camera being confined to these tight spaces would be as reflecting Shayya's desire to communicate to the audience a sense of enclosure or claustrophobia. This formal practice—shots framed from inside out and outside in— reinscribes

FIGURE 8. Riyad Shayya, *Al-Lajāt* (National Film Organization, 1995), five stills. Ossama Mohammed, *Nujūm al-Nahār* (*Stars in Broad Daylight*) (National Film Organization, 1988)

and subverts the public/private divide, demonstrating the power of cinema to escape confinement and transcend masculinist power exercised in the domestic patriarchy as well as in the repressive atmosphere of public life. By the same token, though, the camera's view of life on the outside suggests a potential source of uplift for the audience trapped inside its own constraints. The calm and satisfied gaze that Sana' directs toward the camera in *Stars in Broad Daylight* and the nurturing exhibited by Salma toward playful and innocent schoolchildren in *Al-Lajāt* suggests a different kind of visual communication and perhaps another vision of political community grounded in the affective lives of these characters.

Al-Lajāt follows Salma and Abd al-Kareem's attempted elopement, first into the wilderness outside al-Lajat and then into the refuge of Abu Nayef's home in the countryside. The couple are guided by Abd al-Kareem's loyal friend Halim and his trusty dog, both of whom bark at the sky in abandon. As they tramp through the otherworldly rock formations, Salma remembers how her mother used to say that rain can turn everything white, and thinks that she has never seen black stone like those they are seeing and that the rain can cleanse the earth of drought or dryness, which she compares to "the heart of a tyrant" (*qalb al-ẓālim*). Interestingly, since there are far fewer structures capable of framing their movement in the way doors and windows do at her uncle Sayyah's house, when Abd al-Kareem asks Salma what she most wants as a trousseau for their imagined marriage, she responds by asking for a mirror, of all things (see the discussion below of mirrors in Ossama Mohammed's *Stars in Broad Daylight* [*Nujūm al-Nahār*]).[61] Adding to their romantic hopefulness, Abd al-Kareem asks if Salma is afraid, and when she says that she is not, the rain inexplicably ceases. "Tomorrow everything's going to be fine," she declares. "What, did we destroy the whole world or something?" Abu Nayef offers them shelter, protection, and his promise that every problem has a workable solution. Torn between running away again and returning to beg her family for mercy and forgiveness, Salma grows despondent. Abu Nayef attempts to act as mediator, walking out of Salma's family home utterly defeated. In a symbolic statement of closure, the attendants secure all the doors and windows, blocking entry and exit but also cutting off any means of dialogue. The interior of the home is dark, lit only by a bubbling cauldron and some candles, as sounds of women praying and reciting incantations fill the space, a visual ensemble reminiscent of the home in Ossama Mohammed's *Sacrifices* (*Ṣundūq al-Dunyā*) (see below). Even more ominous, an interior courtyard of the house is filled with sheep, one of which is pulled aside and branded with a circle on the left side of its face. Despite the protestations of Salma's older female relatives, who spit in the face of Uncle Sayyah (and are spat on in return), Uncle Sayyah and his men assault Abu Nayef's house the next day with support from local police. Salma is dragged out of the house amid the wailing of one of the girls who had helped to protect her and Abd al-Kareem. Salma gazes up at the camera with tears streaming down her face; this is followed by a shot from below of Abu Nayef, also crying, that wordlessly announces the end of Salma's dream. A funereal air descends upon the compound as Salma is returned to her cell and Abd al-Kareem sits there in the middle of a darkened room, alone, a husk of his former self.

Syrian responses to the film were decidedly mixed. *Al-Lajāt* received honorable mention at the Ninth Damascus International Film Festival and won

FIGURE 9. *"Al-Lajāt," al-Ḥayā al-Sīnamā'iyya*, No. 45 (Summer 1996)

several awards at the Alexandria Film Festival. Critic and novelist Khalil Suwaylih [whose 2014 novel, *Barbarians' Paradise* (*Jannat al-Barābira*), is discussed in Chapter 5)] dubbed it "meditative cinema" (*al-sīnamā al-ta'ammuliyya*) because "every shot . . . is an independent aesthetic composition in itself."[62] This composition consists of natural elements: earth, fire, and water. If it is true that through cinema "the making of images no longer shares an anthropocentric, utilitarian purpose," as André Bazin puts it, then Shayya's craft guides the viewer towards "a larger concept, the creation of an ideal world in the likeness of the real, with its own temporal destiny."[63] For Suwaylih, Al-Lajat is not only the village where Salma lives but the territory on the outskirts where she flees near the end of the film; we might expand this observation further still and see al-Lajat as the emotional, psychological, and even philosophical ground on which the aesthetics of the film are launched. This spatializes Salma's journey around the patriarchal oppression she endures on her quest to exercise free will, to experience the fullness of romantic love, and to find some measure of happiness. When she retreats to Al-Lajat, this is a "desolate land that is full of secrets where the stones give voice to the secrets of the exiled alongside the howling of the jackals that protect them." Even in her rebellion, when she breaks out of her monitored existence at home, she finds nothing but "loneliness and isolation" that reflect and reveal "the spiritual ruin" in her soul and at the heart of the community.[64] *Al-Lajāt* "proved that cinematic innovation enriches the film thematically, rather than undermining it," Diana Jabbour writes approvingly, "and brings to light nuances of meaning that would otherwise be inaccessible."[65] Mayyar Al-Roumi and Dorothée Schmid argue that Shayya "uses the benefits of silent cinema, in order to suggest, in a succession of extremely aestheticized steps, a fundamental critique of the Baʿthist political system."[66] Shayya himself "considered the form, sometimes and possibly all of the time, to be richer than the content," as he stated in a conversation with Salwa Naʿimi. This in turn allowed him to experiment with "how it would be possible . . . to present cinema without words." In a discussion of Nihad Sirees's 2004 novel *The Silence and the Roar* (*al-Ṣamt wa-l-Ṣakhab*) in Chapter 4, I will return to this question of how silence may be represented in literature as a critique of autocracy that is as powerful as speech or sound, but here is evidence of a unique and formally daring experiment in a "cinema without words" that may offer an alternative to the prolix discourse of Asadist-Baʿthist cultural revolution, an aesthetics of solidarity, perhaps, against an aesthetics of power or a restricted countervailing aesthetics of resistance.

Shayya does not advocate any explicit social or political agenda in the film that would enable critics to assimilate its aesthetic qualities into oppositional or antiregime cultural production. If there is such critique here—a possibility worth considering seriously—it is more subtle than a specific political or ideological position. "A whisper, a glance, a sigh, a smile: all of this has the right to exist [in cinema], and could exist without a single word being uttered," Shayya explained in an interview with Salwa Na'imi. "That's what I like, the image in which meaning can be seen, and which expresses what words cannot say."[67] There is nothing inherently or obviously political about Shayya's defense of gesture, nor does the formal embrace of visible meaning—signification beyond the verbal—axiomatically encode any specific kind of politics. One might argue that the retreat into silence or the embrace of wordlessness can be interpreted as a shying away from politics or political responsibility.[68] Be that as it may, rather than responding to the logorrhea of an ideologically bloviating regime—its aesthetics of power that assertively speaks-to or barks-at its spectators, that claims to speak-for its imagined audience—perhaps this vision of cinema can withstand or even approximate a powerful roar with silence, an aesthetics of solidarity that seeks to speak-with instead, speaking-with men and women alike, human and animal, culture and nature. Salma seeks paths where she can feel loved and supported, where she can speak with her aunt Nassiba, her departed lover Saeed, her impossible love Abd al-Kareem. A strange aesthetic power is at work in this rather obscure film we well as the original novel, *Ascension to Death*, perhaps two more examples of the "dark aesthetic" in Ba'thist Syria cogently identified by Christa Salamandra.[69] The reception of both the novel and the film by Syrian readers and audiences suggests something compelling and perhaps even true about these flawed male characters and a strong female lead like Salma. Even the simplest stories, of jilted love and patriarchal repression—when told with creative flair and new modes of narration—can leave readers and viewers spellbound.

Unfortunately, *Al-Lajāt* is the only work from Shayya that we have the privilege of seeing. It hardly seems necessary or appropriate to subject Shayya's film to some kind of ideological litmus test that would locate it on the side of the state-sponsored NFO or in the oppositional politics of Syrian auteur cinema. After all, the hardy rural dwellers depicted in the film and the novel could be said to represent a trope of the Syrian countryside in Syrian cinema and literature as well as in regime discourse. Their struggle for a better life would not seem out of place, moreover, in a statist modernizationist narrative of revolutionary transformation, one in which the backwardness of rural society and the underdeveloped countryside cries out for state intervention. In that sense, the film's ambiguity opens up a myriad of interpretive readings, aesthetic and political, emotional and sociological. Beyond its formal experimentalism, the film evinces a specific craft that resists political categorization while also presenting a searing indictment of patriarchy. The long shots, hopeless landscape, and moribund society on display in *Al-Lajāt* provoke the viewer to reckon with the darker side of everyday life while reminding us of the potentially redemptive power of cinema, especially when expressed through unusual aesthetic idioms. By foregrounding Salma's deep and sometimes ineffable human yearning, her ultimately fruitless struggle, *Al-Lajāt* refuses to aestheticize politics. There is no trace in the film of the aesthetic ideology of masculinist heroism that we have seen was so crucial to Asadist-Baʿthist cultural revolution. Suwaylih identifies "a new vision" (*mashhadiyya jadīda*) in Shayya's work, one that leads "towards a different path in Syrian cinema."[70] By way of conclusion, I would stress that this path does not automatically or inevitably lead to any particular aesthetic or political outcome; the film's style may have been a dead end, and not only because, tragically, this was the only film that Shayya was able to make before his passing. Without resorting to melodrama, Shayya imbues a stillborn heterosexual romantic relationship predicated on the aspirational exercise of free will and mutual respect with affecting power. If Salma and Abd al-Kareem are ultimately annihilated by social forces beyond their control, their romance remains stubbornly embedded in the film as a reminder of latent challenges—and patient alternatives—to the power of patriarchal violence as well as the masculinist heroism of Asadist-Baʿthist aesthetic ideology.

WOEBEGONE MASCULINITY: ʿABD AL-LATIF ʿABD AL-HAMID'S *NIGHTS OF THE JACKAL* (*LAYĀLĪ IBN AWĀ*)

Riyad Shayya reworked the romantic allegory of *Ascension to Death* in *Al-Lajāt* in ways that retain the complicated representations of gender. His contemporaries Ossama Mohammed and ʿAbd al-Latif ʿAbd al-Hamid also addressed their films to the overdetermined relationship between masculinity and power, albeit in distinct aesthetic languages. *Nights of the Jackal* (*Layālī Ibn Awā*) (1989) by ʿAbd al-Hamid (b. 1954) is one of the most acclaimed Syrian films by one of the country's best-known directors. If the inability of Abd al-Kareem and Abu Nayef to assert their independent manhood in the face of the hegemonic masculinity of Uncle Sayyah and his alliance with other forces of political authority in *Al-Lajāt*, *Nights of the Jackal* tracks a proud country father's slide into impotence, a rural Syrian everyman on the ropes. Like Mohamad Malas, Riyad Shayya, Ossama Mohammed, and many others, ʿAbd al-Hamid studied at the VGIK, completing his studies there in 1981. After collaborating with Malas and Mohammed on their first films, ʿAbd al-Hamid worked with the NFO throughout his career, from *Nights of the Jackal*, his first feature, through later works such as *Rasāʾil Shafahiyya* (*Verbal Letters*) (NFO, 1991) and *Khārij al-Taghṭiyya* (*Outside of Service*) (NFO, 2006). Perhaps his defining work, *Nights of the Jackal* is at once a cinematic treasure and a powerful indictment of provincial ignorance and patriarchal power. The male violence deployed by and embodied in the protagonist Abu Kamal (Assad Feddah) showcases the rapaciousness with which force can be exercised in a family and throughout a society. If these manifestations of masculine power are critiqued or lampooned at certain points, the demands of family and national-patriotic obligation remain fundamentally unchallenged, even reinforced by the end of the film, as evinced by loyalty to the cause of Arab unity and national liberation which Abu Kamal fervently demonstrates in the face of Israeli aggression at the time of the 1967 war.

The film both opens and closes against the backdrop of nighttime silence in a Syrian village somewhere in the mountainous hinterland of the coastal city of Latakia. Howls of jackals nearby are progressively driving Abu Kamal insane as he finds it impossible to sleep. The incessant noise hounds him, and he cannot quiet the creatures himself, although his wife Mutiʿa/Umm Kamal (Najah Abdullah) can, with a single well-timed whistle. Primarily a well-paced social drama, there are also long, beautiful shots of the countryside as well as the city that grant the viewer an opportunity to properly inhabit the setting. In a creative sequence that follows the opening credits, a long horizontal pan introduces the viewer to the layout of the family farm as well as to the entire cast of characters, offering a brief snapshot of each one: Abu Kamal doing jumping jacks, Talal (Bassam Kousa) surreptitiously urinating against the wall, women churning butter or sweeping.

The rhythms of everyday life—farming, cleaning, cooking—are interrupted by the arrival and departure of family members and friends and by news reports on the radio, the only technological portal for communication with the outside world. Watching Abu Kamal bumble his way through life at home and in other social interactions provides comic relief against the background of this grueling rural existence. Early in the film, for example, he injures his foot, which he immediately blames on his wife before pelting her with tomatoes in feigned outrage. The family's harvest of tomatoes will become a weapon later in the film, when the eldest son Kamal (Muhsen Ghazi) returns home to visit the family while they are deep in the work of gathering the tomato crop. Word has just come in on the radio that the state-mandated price for tomatoes is much lower than anticipated, so Abu Kamal is on edge. Kamal is dressed to the nines and has a bit of a swagger. Abu Kamal resents his son for living it up in the city rather than contributing to the hard labor of the family. Kamal throws himself at him, but he is pinned to the ground by his father, who smashes tomatoes in his face. Instead of retaliating, Kamal simply pulls himself up and flees the scene.

Abu Kamal had been primed to explode at Kamal after visiting Latakia to check up on him. When Kamal first moved to the city to pursue his university studies, his father set him up with an apartment and an allowance to make life easier for him. Abu Kamal stops in at Abu Ghazi's shop to settle the family accounts, where he learns that Kamal has racked up a sizable debt, profligately spending money on cologne, soap, shoes, and clothes, all of which reflect his new urban lifestyle. Abu Kamal heads over to the apartment, which he finds is a run-down shambles: pornographic posters on the walls, scattered women's underwear, and rotting fruit. As soon as Abu Kamal returns home from this maddening visit, the jackals are there to torment him once again, throwing fuel on his simmering emotional fire, reminding him of his weakness and even dread before the natural world and his own family.

The struggle between father and son is just one axis in this volatile family dynamic. Umm Kamal has already had her role and station defined—to behave as a reliable mother, to remain obedient (the very meaning of her unsubtly chosen name, *muṭīʿa*) to her husband, and to loyally meet the demands of the family. When a suitor comes seeking permission to marry their daughter Rima, the man's masculinity is described in terms of both physical prowess and financial status. The engagement is celebrated by the whole family except for Rima herself, who departs on a horse with a look of nausea on her face. Similar disappointment is in store for the younger sister Dalal (Tulay Haroun), who is courted by a feckless man named Ali. After having unsatisfying sex with him in the woods one day, Dalal cries as they eat from the abundant apple trees surrounding them. She winds up pregnant and, after consulting with her mother, decides to run away in order to avoid social censure and perhaps even worse punishment.

In addition to the power struggle with his oldest son, Kamal, and the ongoing drama surrounding his daughters, Abu Kamal has an ambivalent relationship with his youngest son, Bassam. Young enough to retain an innocent attachment to this father, Bassam is starting to understand that being a man in the family means standing up for yourself, with force if necessary. After he finally manages to get the bicycle he has always wanted, his father becomes enraged at him for not playing a more active role in household chores. Bassam fires back that he gets in trouble at school for falling asleep, which is "all because of you." The patriarch is disrespected by everyone in the film, especially members of his own family, even the youngest.

Abu Kamal regains some self-respect when soldiers come to inform him that he is being called up for military service. As patriotic music blares in the background, the radio announces that the Zionist enemy must be repulsed, transmitting both information and misinformation, however, as when Abu Kamal receives the false impression that Palestine has been liberated. Set in the time of the 1967 war, the film can be understood—like much Syrian cultural production of the time—to take refuge in an earlier period of clear geopolitical danger and unmistakable ideological unity rather than risk direct engagement with contemporary political realities. Abu Kamal instructs his family and everyone around him to dig trenches now that there is a war on, but nobody seems to understand what he is raving about or have any sense of what they can do now that the Israelis have taken Quneitra and are making their way north. What are people supposed to do, they wonder? Switch off the lights? Get down on the ground? Abu Kamal's son Sulayman thinks they need to torch the fields. Before long Abu Kamal is dismissed from the army just in time for the jackals to come roaring back to life, unsilenced.

Talal's maturation and emergent sexuality are portrayed as more dangerous than his older brother Kamal's. Talal still lives and works at home. Walking down to the riverbed one day, he encounters Hayat, a woman who lives alone with her baby. She allows him to get close to her and even fondle her breasts. Abu Kamal happens to witness this encounter and punishes Talal with extremely draconian discipline: burying him in the ground up to his neck, shaving his head, and slathering his bald pate with honey, which attracts a swarm of aggressive flies as he remains immobilized, defenseless, and humiliated. This is an iconic shot in Syrian cinema (see Figure 10), but the question of motive and meaning is also crucial. Rebecca Joubin points out that forced head shaving is a "traditional punishment in the Syrian military, although it is not restricted to the army." Furthermore, she argues that this figural moment, among others in Syrian film and television drama, is "a form of emasculation, a gendered punishment."[71] It is also an unmistakable act of torture, which calls to mind not only the violence of the father or the leader but also the cruelty and arbitrariness of a repressive political regime, gesturing toward the lengths to which such authorities and authoritarians will go to ensure compliance broadly as well as concrete acts of obedience. Talal's sexual immorality has besmirched the good name of the family and subverted his father's authority. The punishment here can be understood, in part, as a performance of authoritarian politics, a spectacle intended both to hurt Talal and to serve as a warning to those who see his mutilated head. At the same time, from the vantage point of the filmmaker, the spectator is conscripted into regarding the brutal consequences of unbridled patriarchal authority, opening up a margin for oblique criticism of the violence of hegemonic masculinity. But the motive and the cause are not necessarily congruent here. The irony of the film is that the unrestricted power of the patriarch is offset, undermined, and perhaps destroyed by the lack of respect he suffers and by his own self-doubt, his inability to care for himself, whether that means cooking, providing for his family, successfully disciplining his children, keeping the jackals at bay, or gloriously fighting a war for his country. The tragedy of this punishment is that Talal will later die and his funeral will be a moment of grief-stricken communal release for the family, including Abu Kamal. Despite the brute force and rash vengeance unleashed on his children, the father cannot stop Kamal and Dalal from running away, cannot prevent Talal's death, and cannot fully connect with his youngest, Bassam. In the closing shot, Abu Kamal struggles in vain against the elements—the incessant rain—and the surrounding biological world—the ceaseless baying of the jackals—and dramatically recedes into impenetrable darkness.

While it is not a conventional comedy, *Nights of the Jackal* has its funny moments, inviting a discussion of the kind of humor that might be at play in Syrian social drama. In her consideration of a range of Syrian films, Diana

FIGURE 10. ʿAbd al-Latif ʿAbd al-Hamid, *Layālī Ibn Awā* (*Nights of the Jackal*) (National Film Organization, 1989)

Jabbour speculates about the films of ʿAbd al-Latif ʿAbd al-Hamid: "The reasons for the films' popularity were not clear; was the audience laughing at the dialogue and [coastal] accent of the characters in the film, or because that accent was identified with officials whom the public could not joke with and who had power over them?"[72] The language of the characters (a reference to the northwestern dialect typically identified with the ʿAlawī community) is only part of the humor in the film. There are well-timed gags, humorous gestures, and even moments of slapstick that pepper the plot. In an interview he gave to *Cinema Life* in 1989, ʿAbd al-Hamid confessed to being "inclined towards sarcasm and laughter" even though in this film he also wished to present an "honest" look at Syrian society.[73] Unlike other filmmakers who prefer not to simplify interpretations of their work—specifically Ossama Mohammed, as discussed in the next section—ʿAbd al-Hamid responded to a question about whether ordinary people would be able to understand his film:

> I rely upon simplicity in presenting ideas, even in terms of cinematic style. I hate hidden symbols very much, what matters to me is for the ideas to reach everyone on the same level. I think that I'm simple by nature, in my daily life, but my attempt to connect with people doesn't mean giving up on the requirements of art.[74]

The purpose of art is to entertain by speaking to the condition of the common person. Questions of patriarchal authority and authoritarian power are addressed in the idiom of social realist drama. Even in this understanding of the filmmaker and his relationship to his films, ʿAbd al-Hamid sees himself as part of the auteur tradition that grew up under the supervision of the NFO. His oblique engagement with an aesthetics of power makes it difficult to locate the film along the Syrian aesthetic-ideological spectrum: although adhering to the formal and narrative conventions of "alternative cinema," *Nights of the Jackal* presents a distinctive craft that is more reflective of auteur cinema. In other words, the range of films made under the sign of Asadist-Baʿthist cultural revolution constituted a broader canvas of cinematic expression than historians have tended to recognize.

THE DANGERS OF BECOMING A MAN: OSSAMA MOHAMMED'S *SACRIFICES* (*ṢUNDŪQ AL-DUNYĀ*)

Syrian cinema during the late twentieth century was strongly defined by social realism. But the style championed by Asadist-Baʿthist cultural revolutionaries—the "alternative cinema" envisioned by Muhammad Shahin and others—was subject to adaptation and challenge, evolving over the course of the 1980s and 1990s. *Al-Lajāt* employed a symbolic cinematic language in order to convey the loss, grief, and impossible longing of the star-crossed lovers in *Ascension to Death* while eschewing conventional emplotment and narration. A similarly dense and elusive visual language was paired with a much more political statement in Ossama Mohammed's second feature film, *Sacrifices* (*Ṣundūq al-Dunyā*) (2002), which he had been conceptualizing and preparing to make ever since completing his first narrative feature, *Stars in Broad Daylight* (*Nujūm al-Nahār*) (1988). Formally *Stars in Broad Daylight* is distinguished for its reliance on mirrors and frames, tightly composed shots, and trompe l'oeil. The patriarch of an ʿAlawī family in the Syrian northwest struggles to maintain his family's distinction through marriage, business deals, and negotiations with state authorities. I will return to this film in my discussion of surveillance and the politics of vision in Syrian literature and cinema in Chapter 4, but here I would like to highlight how the virility of male characters relates to their power and social status. The patriarch of the family, Khalil (played by none other than ʿAbd al-Latif ʿAbd al-Hamid, who, it is often noted, bears a striking resemblance to Hafiz al-Asad), wields power in both subtle and explicit ways. When the dual wedding staged as the opening scene of the film falls apart, his daughter Sana' (who was going to be married at the same time as her deaf-mute brother Kasir) finds herself in a difficult situation: she has rebelled against her father's authority and disrupted this ceremony, but she is later subjected to a new family plan, for her to marry a wealthy man who has recently returned from East Germany, even though he is vile, violent, and disrespectful. His face is pockmarked and strangely disfigured. His virile manhood is on display when he rides around Latakia on a motorcycle, struts through the city, and later chases Sana' through the woods while they are on a walk and violently forces himself on her. Both of them collapse in a muddy ravine, where a young girl and a cow witness a rape that is not portrayed on screen but is no less shocking for its lack of graphicness (Figure 11). Other scenes in which characters have sex are caricatured, with women moaning loudly, even comically, as men fall all over their bodies. At the end of the day, this execrable predator is venerated through a group portrait taken in downtown Latakia (see

FIGURE 11. Ossama Mohammed, *Nujūm al-Nahār* (*Stars in Broad Daylight*) (National Film Organization, 1988)

FIGURE 12. *"Nujūm al-Nahār (Stars in Broad Daylight)," al-Ḥayā al-Sīnamā'iyya*, No. 37 (Spring 1990)

Figure 12), one that I might add, indulgently, bears a family resemblance to the staged photo of Wes Anderson's *The Royal Tenenbaums* (2001).

There is a cryptic relationship between creative expression and the censorious exercise of state power in Asadist-Baʿthist Syria. Many struggle to explain how *Stars in Broad Daylight* was even approved in the first place; some claim that the symbolic language of the film duped the representatives of the NFO or the Ministry of Culture. As Ossama Mohammed told me, decisions about approval, production, distribution, and screening were taken by boards that consisted of both filmmakers and government bureaucrats, an unstable cultural infrastructure enabling discussions and debates in state institutions about the production of Syrian cinema. At the same time, the savviness of the filmmaker and the subtlety of the film need to be taken into account. Consider, for example, the elliptical response Mohammed offered during an interview with *Cinema Life* on the eve of the film's premiere, when asked why he was making this film:

> How can I answer that question after seven or eight years of waiting to make this film? . . . Most questions about the film or about cinema are difficult for me, and to answer them is extremely complicated and cannot be reduced to a single dimension or to great simplification. You make a film first and foremost because you, in one form or another, you are it, the film is you, it is your world when you are inclined to get involved with the cinema of other worlds, to lean in this direction, and when a film is from the worlds of the person who makes it then this answers most of your question. Why should you tire yourself explaining your world to others?[75]

In the same interview, Mohammed criticized the premise of a question suggesting that participating in international film festivals was somehow "highbrow" or "bourgeois" or even "unpatriotic."[76] (Note the irony in the celebration of the film on the cover of *Cinema Life* after its glitzy rollout at European film festivals.) Bandar 'Abd al-Hamid (1950–2000), a film critic, poet, and member of the editorial board of *Cinema Life*, interviewed Mohammed after the film had been shown around the world.

> You seem sarcastic and bitter, but sweet at the same time. Do you suffer from a personal issue? Did someone mistreat you during your childhood or more recently? How are feelings of bitterness and sarcasm reflected in your artistic work?

Mohammed stood his ground, reprising his snarky persona and insisting that he had no interest in playing the part of a "positive role model" (*baṭal ījābī*); it does seem noteworthy and not entirely coincidental that Mohammed chooses to use the word hero (*baṭal*) here. "In sarcasm there is a vision, imagination,

اخيها الكبير لانها تراه شيئا عظيما .. وترى الاستاذ كذلك
اعظم من اخيها . انها تقهر ذاتها لترضي الآخرين .

FIGURE 13. Photograph of Ossama Mohammed, *al-Ḥayā al-Sīnamā'iyya*, No. 33-34 (Summer 1988)

meditation, a special sketching of the relationship between form and content, an advanced view of reality." Sarcasm is capable of peeling away layers, of allowing things to be seen as they really are. "Do I suffer from personal problems?" With impish humor, Mohammed shoots back that answering the question "would require a doctor."[77]

If Mohammed's sensibility and insouciance are on abundant display in *Stars in Broad Daylight*, they are reinforced and expanded in *Sacrifices*. The film is a symbolic tone poem: hermetic, strange, and surreal. *Sacrifices* is a meditation on the (im)possibility of redemption in a fallen world; it is also about gender politics, the dangers of masculinity, and the ubiquity of violence in human history. In the opening shot, an eye is covered in mud as a spare stringed instrument is bowed in a screeching, haunting phrase that recurs throughout the film. The visual landscape is elemental: chicken, egg, eye, tree. As in both *Stars in Broad Daylight* and *Silvered Water, Syria Self-Portrait* (Chapter 5), Mohammed addresses morality and human nature by reference to creation, the original paradox of the chicken and the egg. On a hillside with a gorgeous view of the northwestern Syrian mountains sits a mysterious structure, a yurt with circular windows, and through the camera's concave lens small children and babies gaze out at the viewer. The film begins with a collective gathering inside a mud house, where an old man appears to be on the brink of death, though the growing crowd is preparing offerings for a visitor whose arrival seems to be imminent. A red-haired orphan girl named Firouzeh is running around playfully. The dying man implores those around him to "open up" for the one who is arriving, who turns out to be a baby or, rather, two babies. The old man speaks with a dove that has flown into his room, as if to negotiate the fate of these children. Two women are in the process of giving birth side by side, endlessly repeating, "Woe is me! Woe is me!" When they pass their newborn babies to the old man, no names are given.

Now the plot focuses on three boys—all of them called Mahmoud (Figure 14)—who are part of a group of elementary school-aged children, including Firouzeh, the only girl among them. As these children spread out across the stunning rural landscape, their youthful activities—running, racing, sparring with one another—are perpetually threatened by the risk of violence. A striking image of one of the village boys standing stock-still, his head tilted to the right as he falls backward off the edge of a cliff, carries both religious gravitas

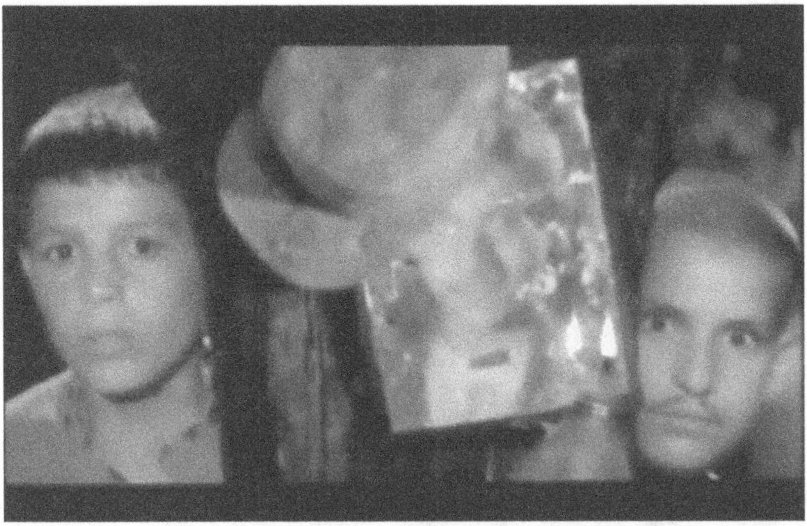

FIGURE 14. Ossama Mohammed, *Ṣundūq al-Dunyā* (*Sacrifices*) (National Film Organization, 2002)

and psychological grief. The image-action recurs several times. The narrative time of the film is rarely linear in any simple sense. Meanwhile, sweet Mahmoud (as I refer to him to distinguish him from the others) has fallen in love with Firouzeh, and his showing off for her becomes a source of comic relief, as when the children climb a massive, ancient tree and their teacher orders them to recite Qur'an in unison. Later, in one of the most visually stunning sequences in the film, he and Firouzeh are passing through a forest and crossing a stream, with Firouzeh riding a donkey. They find themselves with butterflies on their faces. When Firouzeh blows on Mahmoud, some of her freckles are transferred onto his face and he miraculously sprouts a mustache. Mahmoud magically becomes a man in this beautifully intimate scene without an explicit sexual act (Figure 15, top-left image).

When another Mahmoud asks his mother about his father, she tells him he went to fight at the front. When he insists on knowing why, she replies, "Injustice, my son." This is a militaristic tradition that extends back in time, as his mother's father also went off to war: "There was injustice, and he stood against it." Even if there is no justice in the event, this Mahmoud is hurt when he falls out of a tree and undergoes a strange transformation. Whether due to physical injury,

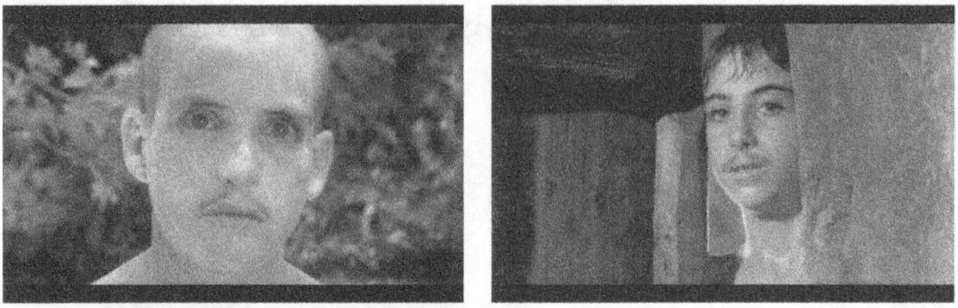

FIGURE 15. Ossama Mohammed, *Ṣundūq al-Dunyā* (*Sacrifices*) (National Film Organization, 2002)

abandonment by his father who goes off to war, his crazy mother, or insuperable human nature, he is steadily overtaken by a primal, destructive force. He sleeps on a treehouse-like platform with his parents until one night his sheets spontaneously ignite, completing his cryptic metamorphosis, and he is transformed into an increasingly powerful figure. This new incarnation, whom I call evil Mahmoud, has an insatiable desire for eggs, other food, power, and sex; the emphasis here on eggs can be read as a return to Mohammed's fascination with them in the constitution of power and violence. Evil Mahmoud wears a jacket that is too large for him. He begins sadistically harming creatures all around him, including a bull, which he tortures by throwing a rock at its testicles; at another point, he drinks directly from a cow's udder, grabs an egg, and storms out of the house. But his power and virility are put to the test when he is encouraged to slaughter one of the cows, which he does, splattering his friends with blood in a dramatic shot, drenching Firouzeh as well in a manner at once gory and sexual. When evil Mahmoud's mustache appears, there is a subtle suggestion that one might become a man through sex or violence or both. Evil Mahmoud is ravenously hungry and lusty, descending into a primitive state of need, growling, "I want!" without ever stipulating what it is that he wants exactly. The family and the community conclude that the boy must be in heat, that perhaps he wants to be with Firouzeh. When he is unable to have her, though, evil Mahmoud stands under a sheet and masturbates while thinking about her.

The talismanic relationship of the egg to power and potency is reinforced as evil Mahmoud's mother descends into furious madness. She appears in the treehouse, looking up toward the camera, allowing the viewer to see a nest full of eggs by her side, which suggests a permeable boundary between humans and nonhuman animals while also foregrounding the central yet fragile location of eggs and life. The relationship between humans and nonhumans becomes more vexed later, when a frustrated evil Mahmoud creates a kind of wicked menagerie in the treehouse, stuffing all kinds of birds into vessels of various shapes and sizes. It is unclear what this grotesque display is meant to symbolize, but there is a sickening sadism and barely restrained violence here. Evil Mahmoud cuts one of the chickens, which gawks at the camera with an eye of horror. The nondiegetic sound of warplanes overhead interrupts the scene and signals a transition back to a more conventional narrative time (Figure 15, bottom-left image). After their father returns from the front as a war hero, bloody and covered in mud, there is a signature composition of Mohammed's in which the boys gaze at him in the reflection of several mirrors captured in the same frame. As the father begins to relate his wartime experiences—the dirt and noise during the three days he spent underground—he says that he felt as though he was dead. "Where is the sacred nation? Who is responsible" for what he and his comrades went through? After uttering these probing questions, he insults the men who stayed home and did nothing for the cause. "What are we?" he asks about collective and national identity. "Our father is the Arab homeland [*al-waṭan al-ʿarabī*]! The Mother? The Arab nation [*al-umma al-ʿarabiyya*]! Where is the action? Where is it?" At this point, the father stages a coming-of-age ritual for the boys, one that entails drinking castor oil as a show of strength, which they must do or else he will tear off evil Mahmoud's mustache. In the midst of this macabre ritual, a television switches on, broadcasting an eye, then a nuclear blast, then the father himself in military fatigues, maniacal laughter. Evil Mahmoud becomes mesmerized by the television set: on screen he sees himself laughing at Firouzeh as she rubs freckles onto her own shoulders. Sweet Mahmoud announces he does not want to see anymore even as evil Mahmoud plucks an apple out of the screen before climbing inside, disappearing for good. Television screens not only broadcast metaphorical imagery but also interact with characters in surreal ways in *Stars in Broad Daylight* (Chapter 4). In the final scene, sweet Mahmoud is alone in a rainy, muddy field. A door closes, signaling the end of the film, and he climbs into a coffin as if to take shelter from the rain, but just then the lid slams shut and the coffin shoots off the hillside as sweet Mahmoud shouts, "God! Firouzeh!" In a reprise of the mysterious opening image of the film, the viewer sees a human eye looking at the tree outside.

Critical analysis of the film has focused on its opaque visual language, which seems to resist interpretation. For Cécile Boëx, *Sacrifices* remains "inaccessible even to general Syrian audiences" yet can be understood as part of "a particular shift in Syrian cinema toward a complex, metaphorical language—a recurrent recourse to metaphor, the fantastic, the absurd, the comic."[78] Viola Shafik situates it in relation to a broader trend in Syrian filmmaking toward "isolationism and crypticism," which is discernible in this "quasi-mythical story about an archaic family."[79] Film critic and curator Rasha Salti identifies the key technical innovations in Mohammed's work:

> The framing of every shot, the movement of his camera, his skill for visual composition all display a supreme talent. Scenes are almost invariably filmed through a bias; the camera follows characters from within a window or door frame, or films their reflection in a mirror or a puddle of war. This frame within the frame reminds the spectator of the director's self-conscious subjective sensibility. The use of mirrors is particularly powerful, as it re-composes a character from a skewed perspective, as if to reveal another ordering, often in relation to the psychological state of the characters in the scene. . . . Filming from within frames, filming the reflection of illusions and staging archetypal characters allow Mohammad to say what cannot be said and to visualise what cannot be visualised.[80]

Mohammed problematizes the cinematic gaze, too, as his own skilled directorial eye draws attention to the mechanics of the shot itself. This highly technical visual apparatus is harnessed to an older tradition of representation and modes of seeing, not well recognized by film scholars, indicated by the original title of the film, *Ṣundūq al-Dunyā* (literally, "Box of the World"), which can be translated as "coffin" but also refers to an Arabic tradition of storytelling and shadow theater performed inside a small wooden box. The otherworldly structure that appears at the beginning of the film, with young people submerged in water and peering out at the camera, returns as the film ends with the appearance of a single disembodied eye: perhaps bookends of the *ṣundūq al-dunyā* itself. Viola Shafik argues that because the characters in traditional *ṣundūq al-dunyā* performances "cannot make facial expressions or use mimesis, there is little individuality or ambiguity," setting up a premise within which "grotesque characteristics are intensified by their stereotyped, frozen facial expression."[81] Mohammed foregrounds human facial expression, highlighting the power of emotion to shine through allegorical narrative. Meanwhile, by employing the artifice of shadow theater as a framing device for the film, Mohammed populates the ostensible space of allegory with grotesque characters—to borrow Shafik's term—who may be interpreted as ciphers or prototypes that shed light, however obliquely, on the social and cultural constraints of life under conditions of political repression and patriarchal violence. In *Sacrifices*, to a much greater extent than in *Stars in Broad Daylight*, masculinity and what it means to be(come) a man remain mysterious. The origins, purpose, and effects of making men are obscured by ambiguity, danger, and delirium. Conventional understandings of manhood and heroism demand explanation at the very least and, perhaps more radically, rejection or elimination. The frame-within-a-frame aesthetic that is a hallmark of Mohammed's work is deployed to draw attention to the simultaneously obfuscating and clarifying work of ideology as it produces and refashions conceptions of masculinity, power, and identity in Asadist-Ba'thist Syria.

FIGURE 16. Ossama Mohammed, *Ṣundūq al-Dunyā* (*Sacrifices*) (National Film Organization, 2002)

CONCLUSION

In his acid condemnation of political elites, Arab intellectuals, and Islamic culture in the wake of the 1967 defeat, the late Syrian intellectual Sadiq Jalal al-ʿAzm (1934–2016) diagnosed the failure of the postcolonial revolution.[82] The historic defeat in the Six-Day War was called "the setback" (*al-naksa*), implying that the Arab world would reclaim its stolen grandeur by facing down enemies both local and international, first and foremost the colonial forces of Zionism and Western imperialism. Here was an attempt to reassess postcolonial Arab state strategy but also to reconsider cultural identity itself. Arab intellectual culture was plunged into seemingly perpetual crisis during the late twentieth century. For al-ʿAzm, responsibility for myriad failures in the Arab world fell on the retrograde religious elements who remained frozen in the past and the petrified "revolutionary" governments that were constitutionally unable to rise to the challenge of the Arab revolution.[83] One interpretation of the cultural consequences of 1967 is that ideology no longer held out the promise of transformation and inspiration that it had during the 1950s and 1960s. Dreams of pan-Arab unity in service to an anti-imperialist politics that could unite disparate regimes and peoples across the Arab world had been dashed. As Suzanne Kassab points out, anxieties surrounding authenticity, cultural identity, and political impotency became the central issue addressed by leading Arab intellectuals from Egypt to Lebanon and Syria. The promise of refashioning the landscape of political and social life across the Arabic-speaking world soon devolved into a crisis of cultural confidence that took new shape in debates over heritage and authenticity.[84] Intellectuals, artists, and ordinary people struggled to comprehend the sheer magnitude of the defeat. And while this moment has been understood and interpreted in various scholarly idioms, "defeat" in the post-1967 Arab world can also be considered in terms of its effects on masculinity, power, and identity.[85] As many in other world-historical contexts shaped by colonial violence and postcolonial instability, including Caribbean intellectuals described by anthropologist David Scott, Syrian writers, filmmakers, and others in the post-1967 period struggled through "the trough of despondent years" in which "a whole generation has grown up . . . unfazed by the graying narrative of revolutionary heroism."[86]

In "Men," the short story included as an epigraph to this chapter, Zakariya Tamir subtly satirizes the arbitrariness of patriarchal privilege. Alessandro

Columbu rightly notes how male characters in Tamir's stories generally "have internalized obedience, contributing [to] the perpetuation of the brutal practices of the state, which in turn produces complicity with and acceptance of its brutality, exploiting the male's conformity to a system that degrades him."[87] Unlike the heroic subject of Asadist-Ba'thist cultural revolution on display in *End of a Brave Man*, though, Tamir's male protagonists are reminiscent of the constrained masculinities on display in *Al-Lajāt* and *Nights of the Jackal*. In another piece of flash fiction, "Waiting for a Woman," Tamir imagined a man, Faris al-Mawwaz, who "was born without a head." Although his family and the doctors were shocked by this freak of nature, the headless man lived a "long life, in which he couldn't see or hear or speak or complain or work. Many people envied him, saying that he had gained more than he had lost." His deformity could not quell his desire for heteronormative companionship, however, and he "never stopped waiting for a woman to be born without a head so that the two of them could meet and give birth to a new kind of human being."[88] Even when a man is physically disfigured, the norms of hegemonic masculinity, skewered in this story, I would add, prescribe the pursuit of a woman in the image of this new man.

The relationship between masculinity and power was central to the production and reinforcement of a contested aesthetic ideology still grappling with the consequences of defeat and the promise of a new dawn, one that is discernible across the landscape of literature and film in late twentieth and early twenty-first century Syria. Discourses of heroism embedded in the larger project of cultural revolution during Hafiz al-Asad's rule drew on traditional conceptions of manhood and masculinity even as they were recast in the image of a struggling revolutionary vanguard. These tropes—characteristic of Asadist-Ba'thist "hegemonic masculinity"—were subject to adaptation and refashioning by filmmakers, writers, intellectuals, and ordinary people. Hegemonic masculinity

> embodied the currently most honored way of being a man, it required all other men to position themselves in relation to it. . . . Hegemony did not mean violence, although it could be supported by force; it meant ascendancy achieved through culture, institutions, and persuasion.[89]

Throughout the literary texts and films analyzed in this chapter, patriarchy and dictatorial power exist in government and public life as well as in the household, where it can be just at potent yet simultaneously at risk of being challenged and undermined at any moment. "Using family metaphors," Rebecca Joubin points out, Syrian television writers "capture the essence of dictatorship and the breakdown of social relations."[90] This turns out to be true in the domains of literature and film as well. An adequate historical critique of masculinism and patriarchy cannot ignore representations of women and femininity; by no means has the latter received sufficient attention here. In the works under discussion in this chapter, gender plays a complex role in shaping narrative, developing character, and unfolding plot. And while a gender-based analysis is not the only way to think about them, there is much to be learned from the gendered dimensions of Syrian cultural production with respect to the struggle over aesthetic ideology.

The power and potency of the hero, the leader, and the patriarch were established in terms expressed by Asadist-Baʿthist cultural revolution over the course of the 1970s and 1980s. By the time Ossama Mohammed, ʿAbd al-Latif ʿAbd al-Hamid, and Riyad Shayya started making films in the 1980s and 1990s, the crisis of patriarchal authoritarianism was one reference point for representations of flawed and weak male protagonists. Critical depictions of traditional and domineering ways men sought to control the life choices and everyday life of wives, children, and extended families were at times the vector for veiled criticism of masculinist state power. None of the three films discussed here is easily classifiable according to the categories proposed by the NFO or the editors at *Cinema Life*. It remains unclear, for example, whether or not they are "alternative cinema," the form of cinematic address articulated by Muhammad Shahin and others (Chapter 1) as an oppositional discourse to the bourgeois melodrama of the Egyptian studio system, which was underwritten by a capitalistic political economy and culture industry. Although the films do not seem to qualify as cinema for the masses, there is something accessible and appealing about them as social dramas, however abstract or symbolic their form and however modest their spectatorship given poor distribution and anemic infrastructure, among other factors. This chapter explored how heroism was both thematized and called into question, how the prideful male hero could be brought low through Mufid's suicide in *End of a Brave Man*; Abd al-Kareem's inability to prevent Salma's murder at the hands of her patriarchal family in *Ascension to Death* and *Al-Lajāt*; Abu Kamal's insurmountable impotence in *Nights of the*

Jackal; or the multiple Mahmouds' collective inability to fully realize their male birthright in *Sacrifices*. Regardless of how weighty these political and social issues might have been, though, one ought not draw a hard and fast distinction between the aims and pleasures of drama and comedy. The next chapter shifts gears in order to isolate cultural critique deployed in Syrian cinema through the style and vocabulary of comedy, in particular the commercial works of Durayd Lahham and his signature Ghawar character. The staging of satire and farce could potentially undermine the repressive ideological apparatus of art that was predicated on the tenets of Asadist-Ba'thist cultural revolution. As we will see, Syrian film comedy could also lend itself to reinforcing the power of the regime even if and when it challenged some of the state's symbolic authority.

Chapter 3

THE FUNNY THING ABOUT DICTATORSHIP

> Personally, I see political theatre in two forms; it can be the mouthpiece of the regime or it can criticize the regime. If there is another form, I do not know about it.
>
> — Durayd Lahham (1980)[1]

> We had thought that artwork could shock and make change. But no, artwork, at the end of the day, even if it is critical, is entertainment.
>
> — Durayd Lahham (2006)[2]

> He who has laughter on his side has no need of proof.
>
> — Theodor W. Adorno, *Minima Moralia*[3]

IN AN INTERVIEW ON AL-MAYĀDĪN TV ON SEPTEMBER 3, 2018, THE Syrian actor, comedian, and cultural icon Durayd Lahham was asked to reflect on how critical he and his colleagues had actually been during the 1960s and 1970s while creating some of the most popular Syrian plays, television programs, and films. He responded that it was in the very nature of theater and performance to be critical of "corruption" and "repression," though he failed to specify the direct object of such criticism. Lahham was loath to identify a particular regime or call out individuals by name. When the interviewer followed up with a more pointed question about why things had turned out the way they had in Syria in recent years, Lahham argued that the problem had been sectarian fanaticism all along and, it could be inferred quite easily, not authoritarian dictatorship, as so many antigovernment protestors would have asserted. People in Syria had lost touch with true "belief" (*al-imān*), according to Lahham, which had been replaced by what he derisively referred to as "religions" (*adyān*). Rather than touching a third rail of Syrian politics—antipathy toward or challenge to the president—Lahham squeezed out a thin plea for "tolerance" and something like ecumenical thinking even as Syria struggled to move forward through the morass of a grinding and seemingly unresolvable war. Lahham then waxed sentimental and magnanimous about a religious authority figure who had come to seek his counsel, a man Lahham perceived not as one of "the religious" (*rijāl al-dīn*) but as one of "the faithful" (*rijāl al-īmān*). If everyone in Syria believed in the one true God, it would follow logically that there could be no legitimate "sects" (*ṭawā'if*) capable of dividing the country. Consequently, whatever divisions might exist after the advent of the uprising and the metastasis of the Syria War must have been fomented by foreign agents. In effect, a long-beloved cultural icon was caught in the act, doing informal public relations for the avowedly secularist regime, avoiding any discussion of the political aspects of the Syrian uprising since 2011—to say nothing of long-standing demands for justice and transparency, even within the parameters of the Ba'thist regime's ideology, that pre-dated the Syrian revolution—and staying laser-focused on the ubiquitous scourge of

FIGURE 17. Hafiz al-Asad and Durayd Lahham

sectarianism, which he identified as the dominant factor fueling the country's unrest and perduring violence.

Perhaps unsurprisingly, such media appearances contributed to the debasement of Lahham in the eyes of Syrian revolutionaries and more moderate folks who sympathized with demands for liberalization and reform. But this particular television interview was not the only time the comic actor, playwright, screenwriter, and director disappointed Syrian fans because of his politics. During the early years of the revolution, opposition forces vilified Lahham for taking positions deemed out of step with his audience, some of whom even considered themselves devoted fans. These public betrayals were considered profound enough that some began arguing that his work—including the earlier, acclaimed work—should be boycotted, sidelined, and condemned—a kind of Syrian revolutionary cancel culture avant la lettre. One example of this discourse could be found on a website run by the Media Center to Support the Revolutionaries of Homs, which designed a Wanted poster accusing Lahham of having betrayed his people by unstintingly supporting the regime. "Wanted for Justice: On the Charges of Lying [*al-tazwīr*], Media Distortion, and Covering Up Crimes Against Humanity: The Shabbih of Syrian Drama, Hypocrite Durayd Lahham: ENEMY OF THE SYRIAN PEOPLE."

This accusatory language of treason and betrayal suffused the discursive environment around the Syria War. Be that as it may, the cultural field in Syria had long been a space for a war of position between regimists and oppositionists, a site for struggle around aesthetic ideology and other political matters. But this dynamic was less volatile—if also more restricted—during the years of Hafiz al-Asad's rule, when Lahham and his cocreators were at their most active. The first two epigraphs of this chapter reflect contradictory positions that Lahham was caught up on over the course of his career, toggling between a view of the dramatic arts as political engagement and, conversely, as pure entertainment. Throughout the 2000s and 2010s the regime of Bashar al-Asad undertook a cosmetic makeover that embraced neoliberal economic reform and a form of technocratic development that did not fundamentally challenge concomitant processes of autocratic retrenchment. This entailed slick and sophisticated public relations campaigns that retouched the regime and effectively (re)branded Syria.[4] Even as the al-Asad regime itself was being feted during this period of reformism from above, the cultural scene attracted unprecedented attention.[5]

Throughout these transformations, Lahham remained a widely treasured (and state-sanctioned) cultural icon. In a 2006 profile in *The New York Times*, Lahham made it clear that there was scant space for oppositional cultural work.[6] Like other secularist intellectuals and cultural producers—Syrian poet Adonis springs to mind as do Sonallah Ibrahim and Alaa Al-Aswany in Egypt, among others elsewhere—Lahham doubled down on his assertion that art cannot "shock and make change," which meant throwing in his lot with the regime for all intents and purposes. It may very well have been that his celebrity star was falling anyway, as younger, more energetic forces—whether or not affiliated with the Syrian revolution—engaged in new forms of cultural activism and creative experimentation, from the fine arts, theater, dance, and film to more technologically mediated genres of cultural production. Actors and writers and producers and auteurs, including Mai Skaf, Abounaddara, and others, criticized the éminence grise of Syrian stage and screen for his loyalty to the regime and his refusal to take to the streets with the people, or at least express sympathy for and solidarity with those who had sacrificed in the name of life, liberty, and dignity, the lifeblood of the revolution.

None of this would necessarily have come as a surprise to those who had watched Lahham throughout his career, tracking his prerevolution, prewar politics. Lahham expressly articulated his political commitments as yielding and malleable. For example, when he was asked about the role of the artist in society as far back as 1980, in an interview published in English, he replied, "He should be committed to its problems":

> This commitment does not mean saying, I am this or I am that. I am against commitment to a limited political trend because it prevents the artist from thinking and expressing himself outside his party line or ideology. Sometimes it prevents him from seeing what is going on around him.[7]

When Syria's top clown appears on satellite television to chime in with his support for the regime and its avowed principles of secularism, tolerance, and national unity, how should this articulation be located in the history of Syrian cultural production? How might this invocation of Baʿthist principles intersect with contemporary and historical Syrian comedic cultural production? How does Lahham's biography and cultural legacy fit with the political and intellectual history of modern and contemporary Syria? Moreover, what place, if any, has there been for comedy as a genre and a mode of expression—in cinema and literature—in shaping Syrian social, cultural, and political life during the late twentieth and early twenty-first centuries? Here is a moment in the global cultural history of film when consumers of cultural production reserve and exercise the right to critique, refute, and boycott ciphers of national literature, cinema, and television. For many, Durayd Lahham came to "represent" the Syrian regime—both as a symbol *of* state power and as a spokesperson *for* the status quo—and representations of Lahham in the sphere of visual culture therefore also had to be resisted. This, in turn, raises interesting questions from a film studies perspective about the place of power, politics, and aesthetic criticism in the history of Syrian cinema.

This chapter focuses on Durayd Lahham as one of the defining figures of Syrian film comedy, an avatar of Syrian cultural life regionally and internationally. The case of Lahham is doubly important because of Ghawar al-Tushi, Lahham's alter ego in theater, television, and (to a lesser extent) film, whose legacy is the subject of a similarly polarizing debate in Syrian cultural politics. As we will see in this chapter, Ghawar is a lewd, plain-spoken everyman who has bumbled his way across and through a wide range of televisual and cinematic contexts in dozens of films. With the shtick and occasionally the look of Woody Allen but without the sensitivity of Elia Suleiman, the elegance of Charlie Chaplin, or the studied clumsiness of Harpo Marx, I would argue that many of Lahham's characters (other than Ghawar, that is) embodied the aspirations, ambivalent relationship to comedy and power, and aesthetic ideology of Asadist-Ba'thist cultural revolution. Although Ghawar was not the only role Lahham would play in his many films, it would become ever more difficult to separate one from the other. The focus in this chapter will be on three standout films from the 1980s—not exactly a trilogy, as the movies have no explicit connection to one another but rather a series conceived by Lahham in tandem with his interlocutor Muhammad al-Maghut, which lends these works some kind of affinity with one another: *The Empire of Ghawar* (*Imbrāṭūriyyat Ghawār*; directed by Marwan 'Akkawi, 1982), *The Border* (*al-Ḥudūd*; directed by Durayd Lahham, 1984), and *The Report* (*al-Taqrīr*; directed Durayd Lahham, 1986). Each of these films tackles a specific issue in Syrian society: governance, municipal administration and social relations; patriotism, Arab nationalism and the state system; and the problem of bureaucracy and political power. A comprehensive analysis of the films of Durayd Lahham must address not only ideology and representation—which are at the heart of the discussion that follows—but also mood, narrative, and genre, meaning comedy itself. Lahham shows impressive range in his engagement with highbrow themes while also executing gut-level gags. There are cases in which Ghawar/Lahham—and by no means do I mean to suggest that one is reducible to the other in all cases—descended into a stock character, starring in such minor films as *My Hippie Wife* (*Zawjatī min al-Hībīz*; directed by ʿAtef Salem, 1973), *Ghawar James Bond* (directed by Nabil Maleh, 1974), and the Ramadan comeback series *Return of Ghawar: The Friends* (*ʿAwdat Ghawār: al-Aṣdiqāʾ*; directed by Marwan Barakat, 1998).

These films and the Ghawar/Lahham character are essential elements in the struggle around aesthetic ideology in Asadist-Baʿthist Syria. All three directly engage with Arab malaise following the 1967 defeat; the ongoing conflict with Israel, politics and everyday life in a postcolonial context; and the continuing challenges of creative expression in a country hamstrung by war and political repression. There has been a subtle bias in Syrian film studies toward conceptual or "serious" films and away from commercial, popular films. This may be attributable to the persistent interest on the part of Syrian film critics in Muhammad Shahin's "alternative cinema" (Chapter 1) or to the appeal of the auteur cinema of filmmakers such as Riyad Shayya and Ossama Mohammed (Chapters 2 and 4). Through the exploration of Lahham's commercial films and their popular appeal, this chapter shines a different light on the cultural politics of Syrian cinema during Hafiz al-Asad's rule. It might even be argued that these films are among the most highbrow comedies Lahham made during this period. But given the centrality of Durayd Lahham, Nihad al-Qalʿi, and Muhammad al-Maghut to late twentieth-century Syrian cultural history, it is worth plumbing these works for their function in aesthetic terms—in other words, how and why they are funny and not only how and why they speak to the political constraints of the post-1967 Syrian condition. The psychology of a visual character like Ghawar relies on a cultural intimacy with—and overwhelming trust in—the leading man. I will not spend as much time as I could on jokes themselves, their delivery and reception, although that is worth exploring. I am more interested in how slapstick, farce, satire, absurdism, and mockery are deployed in film narratives, how plots and characters are co-implicated in an aesthetic of the comedic, how the comedic itself has been essential in the construction and maintenance of an aesthetic ideology of Asadist-Baʿthist cultural revolution with Ghawar/Lahham often on the prow if not always at the helm of this cultural-nationalist vessel. I view these films not exclusively as social texts but also as cultural products reflecting and inculcating certain values and political objectives. At the same time, there are underappreciated forms of pleasure and desire embedded in their humor.

The elaboration of state-sanctioned cultural revolution under Hafiz al-Asad promoted an aesthetic ideology that was malleable enough to accommodate the dark drama discussed in Chapter 2 as well as the popular comedy discussed here. One should not understand there to be an impermeable boundary between the two, of course, as there are moments of levity and humor even in the most serious dramatic films and the comedies analyzed here are deeply engaged with weighty political matters. Most of the scholarship on Durayd Lahham, his stage plays and films in collaboration with Nihad Qalʿi, and his work with the bilious poet Muhammad al-Maghut views these projects as exercises in *tanfīs*, literally a letting-off of steam, although more a forced exhalation meant to clear the air of any resentment or social tension brought about by political repression. If some of the significance of these films has been situated in relation to political ideology, however, less attention has been paid to how their humor works and how comedy is related to the struggle over aesthetic ideology in Asadist-Baʿthist Syria. Lisa Wedeen explores the significance of Lahham, Qalʿi, and al-Maghut's writing, theater, and films in order to show how "tolerated parodies" tackled the problem of state repression obliquely, without directly confronting the regime.[8] Cécile Boëx sharply reads the corpus of Syrian cinema produced with the financial and technical support of the National Film Organization (NFO), founded in 1964 as part and parcel of the creation of new state-run media. For Boëx, Syrian filmmakers, audiences, and spectators are part of what she calls a "community of experience" conjured by the production, circulation, screening, and viewing of Syrian film. In her fascinating deployment of common sense as an analytical category for thinking through the sociological dimensions of Syrian film production, circulation, and consumption, Boëx is attentive to the "universal" significance of film as well as the "particular" resonance of Syrian filmmaking.[9]

Not all of these films can be said to have been "assembled" with such specific intentions as both Boëx and Wedeen seem to suggest. When filmmakers attempt to communicate a particular message or didactic instruction through these works, whether one that reinforces state power or another that lionizes struggle and resistance against the cultural power of the state, there is always a margin for misfire and contrasting interpretations. The transmission of an ideological message becomes even more convoluted given the irony and improvisation on display in Lahham's work. What the vast majority of Syrian film studies—Middle Eastern film studies more broadly—fail to take seriously is that writers, actors, and films themselves might actually be funny; nor do they consider, at a bare minimum, what it might mean to be funny in Syrian film. Subversion (or subversive affirmation) does not always cleanly follow from a calculated political objective but can also emerge from the vagaries and inaccuracies of performance itself. By the same token, seemingly apolitical or absurdist humor can pack a powerfully critical punch. One should not ignore or shy away from the racist subtext implicit in questions I have received from non-Syrians in the course of my research: *Wait, there are Syrian comedies?* Or, more baldly, *Are Syrians funny?* Here I might like to appropriate those questions in order to recuperate a different understanding of Syrian film, one that does not reduce film criticism to Ideologiekritik or resort to hamstringing Syrian filmmakers and audiences within the confines of national cinema studies. This is not meant to minimize the power of reading film politically, of course; in this chapter I engage such modes of interpretation throughout. My point here is simply that there are multiple systems of signification at work in Syrian film and there is reason to consider how resignification, comedic irony, and play can enhance and even transform our understanding of Syrian film in particular and the cultural politics of comedy more generally.[10] The insights of performance studies permit us to consider the work of filmmakers, producers, technicians, crew, audiences, spectators, publics, and critics in light of myriad intellectual, political, identitarian, and embodied perspectives. For example, Masʿud Hamdan views the collaboration between Lahham and al-Maghut as an expression of satirical carnivalesque, drawing on the canonical work of Mikhail Bakhtin.[11] Hamdan identifies the carnivalesque as the determining form in Lahham and al-Maghut's work, arguing that it is through the topsy-turvy absurd enacted on screen that the reality of the regime can be challenged and that the chaos of an inverted reality leaves reality more or less untouched off screen. Film scholars and critics identify the figure of the clown itself as transgressive by virtue of its capacity to exist outside the state apparatus, the lexicon of power, and even the laws of nature in a given political or social situation. This does not guarantee that the clown is always capable or even interested in undermining power, however. There is no reason the court jester cannot be as amusing to the rabble as to the ruler. Moreover, the clown is capable of drawing attention to state power or other forms of coercive violence while simultaneously reinscribing the ostensible naturalness or immutability of powerful institutions.[12]

Durayd Lahham and his films have been well received all over the Arab world, demonstrating that his comedy is quite broad and not narrowly concerned with local or national matters in Syria.[13] While most of the discussion in this chapter attends to cultural, ideological, and technical dimensions of Lahham's oeuvre, he also needs to be properly contextualized in the cultural and intellectual history of modern Syria. Lahham was born in the al-Amin quarter of the old city of Damascus in 1934. While a schoolboy he worked as an apprentice to an ironworker, in a laundry, and in a tailor shop. After completing his primary education, he enrolled at the University of Damascus, where he studied chemistry, then taught at a government school and occasionally lectured at the university. When Syrian state television launched in 1960, its first director, Sabah Qabbani (brother of the poet Nizar Qabbani), considered Lahham and his college performing troupe as possible collaborators. This was around the time that Lahham befriended Nihad Qal'i, who was then the head of the National Theater.[14] Qal'i and Lahham received attention through their adaptation of stage plays for Syrian state television and would go on to garner national and international fame on both large and small screens. *Ḍay'at Tishrīn* (*October Village*) (1974), *Kasak ya Waṭan* (*Cheers Oh Homeland*) (1979), and other early performance pieces became the foundation Lahham and Qal'i's hugely successful career in Syria and around the Arab world.[15] The first appearance of Ghawar was in *Maqālib Ghawār* (*The Trials and Tribulations of Ghawar*; directed by Khaldun al-Malih, 1967). The manner and affect of Lahham and his alter ego would define Syrian performance for decades to come.

W.J.T. Mitchell invites us to reflect on some of the most fundamental questions concerning spectatorship and the terms of engagement with the image:

> What do the images want from us? Where are they leading us? What is it that they *lack*, that they are inviting us to fill in? What desires have we projected onto them, and what form do those desires take as they are projected back at us, making demands upon us, seducing us to feel and act in specific ways?[16]

Similar questions could be raised about the (moving) image of Ghawar in Syrian cinema. Who is Ghawar, really? What does he want from the spectator? On what terms does he address the Syrian citizen, the Syrian nation, and an even broader Arab public? What are his political motives and aims? What sort of cultural, social, and intellectual universe does he inhabit? How do Ghawar's travails potentially incite, inhibit, or assuage the desires and anxieties of the viewer? The remainder of this chapter focuses on three indispensable Syrian films, perhaps the most important Lahham ever made—*The Empire of Ghawar* (1982), *The Border* (1984), and *The Report* (1986)—in light of Syrian cultural history but also in the global comparative film context. I closely examine their ideological dimensions and their comedic significance. Lahham's costume, deadpan delivery, ability to perform as a fish out of water with such consistent bemusement—all suggest that he might well deserve the rotely repeated moniker "the Arab Charlie Chaplin." Ironically, though, Lahham himself never saw much truth in that comparison. During a 1980 interview with *The Middle East*, he was asked whether he had "any ambition to make Ghawwar into a universal comic character like Chaplin's tramp. . . ." His response was categorical. "Not at all; I am not interested in the Hollywood superstar image. All I care about is being here and dealing with the problems of the Arab world." But the interviewer persisted: "There are times when you approach the tragi-comic in your work, which is of an almost Chaplinesque nature. Was Chaplin an example to you?" Lahham remained unruffled.

> I have not studied Chaplin carefully, though he is an example to all of us. I respect and admire his works, but I would say my comedy springs essentially from the life and everyday experiences of the Arab world. There is certainly enough paradox, absurdity, and tragicomedy in our existence.

Concluding on a doctrinaire note that could be seen as placating censors and regime officials, Lahham declared, "My friend, our play is not a farce. We are not playing the clown. We carry the word."[17] Regardless of these protestations,

Ghawar and his associates—especially Husni Barazan (Nihad Qalʿi) and Abu ʿAntar (Naji Jabr) as well as others in the cast of characters who populate their imaginative landscape—seem to be the closest one can find to a Syrian tradition of slapstick, though there is never quite the sheer revelry and release of the Marx Brothers or even some of the films of Adel Iman in Egypt. The NFO is the largest producer of films in Syria, but it has been primarily focused on dramatic narrative features. Between 1928 and 2011, upward of 150 films were produced, a modest but not insignificant number for such a small country, but only a tiny sliver were comedies. For comparison's sake, this number is dwarfed by the 3,000, or perhaps more, Egyptian films made during the same period. Regardless of the moribund institutional landscape supporting film comedy in Syria, there remain questions about style, mood, genre, and politics that are essential to an understanding of the significance of these films: whether or not Ghawar is a derivative character, whether Lahham is a regime stooge or a critical cultural voice, and whether Syrian cinema adheres to the conventions of state ideology or national(ist) allegory. At the risk of espousing a radical pragmatism, there is also value in simply watching these films for the sheer enjoyment.

HAIL TO THE CLOWN

The Empire of Ghawar (*Imbrāṭuriyyat Ghawār*) (directed by Marwan ʿAkkawi) was meant to be something of a comeback for Lahham after he had spent time behind the scenes in commercial cinema. Although there is no specific reference to the time or place of the film, *Empire* was filmed and set in a popular quarter of Damascus with characters dressed in somewhat vague costumes chronologically speaking, indicating that this could be the late Ottoman Empire, the French Mandate, or early Syrian independence. At a certain level, the specific setting is less important than the events that transpire in the film's narrative. Based on a story by Zakariya Tamir, one of the movie's prevailing themes is the tension between forms of power locally and political authority more broadly. The people of two neighborhoods in this quarter of the city find themselves increasingly embroiled in conflict that stems from the relative power relations between their sectors as well as the relationship between each one and the centralized power structure in the city and beyond. When the film opens, Ghawar al-Tushi (Lahham) is working as a barber and the boy whose hair he is cutting is demonstrably uncomfortable, fidgeting but stayed by Ghawar's stern hand.

This exercise of control can be understood as a foreshadowing of the maneuver Ghawar will attempt to pull off as he reinvents himself into a powerful man capable of caring for but also dominating the masses. Abu ʿAnad, the *zaʿīm* of the Saʿdi neighborhood, is locked in a perpetual struggle with Abu Jamil, *zaʿīm* of the neighboring al-Mirjan neighborhood. Perhaps because there are those who have seen him work with scissors in the barbershop or because people trust Ghawar unquestioningly, he also moonlights as a doctor, and we witness him perform two surgeries, one circumcision on the young boy whose hair he has cut and the other on the ailing Abu ʿAnad. Just before he escorts the boy inside for his "treatment," Ghawar insists that he has the neighborhood's interests at heart but cannot defend it against Abu Jamil if the people do not pay him what they owe him as tribute or protection money (*al-maʿlūm* or *al-maʿlūmiyya*). Ghawar steps in and tries to perform the surgery, but the bungled operation leads to the residents calling the shaykh to pray and to be ready to perform last rites. It turns out that Ghawar has made mistakes, occasionally with lethal consequences, and yet everyone continues to hold him in the highest esteem.

When the thugs working for Abu ʿAnad come by the café to order the people to stand out of respect for his carriage when it passes by, a local teacher announces that he might not stand. Why? Because he is free. And, what, those who do not stand are not free? No. Abu Jamil is celebrating his victory, saying that both neighborhoods are his dominion, a single political unit. And he makes plain that he does not want to be supported with words only, that he is owed money and that all of the neighborhood institutions and individuals need to pay him tribute (*maʿlūmiyya*). Hut, the violent enforcer loyal to Abu Jamil, shows up and begins stirring up trouble with beatings and general intimidation, claiming that Abu Jamil is tough enough to dominate two neighborhoods, invoking the language of the *qabaḍāy*, a local tough or political boss.[18] In addition to threatening ordinary people, Hut assaults a police officer on patrol, telling him that under the leadership of Abu Jamil there is already enough security (*amān*) in place. At around the same time, Ghawar is addressing his friends about the danger they all face amid the rising political tensions when the officer turns up to report that he has just been assaulted by Hut. Although Ghawar had originally been discussing his personal problems, he turns to consider the political situation, telling the people that they will need to rise up against Abu Jamil, that he will be no different from Abu al-ʿAnad, and that the future of the *ḥāra*

FIGURE 18. Marwan ʿAkkawi, *Imbrāṭūriyyat Ghawār* (*The Empire of Ghawar*) commercial poster (National Film Organization, 1982)

(neighborhood) is too important to leave to others. He argues that the new security station (*makhfar*) they intend to set up—the symbol of bureaucratic order and representative democracy but also, crucially, an institution of law and order—is not going to check the power of Abu Jamil and his informal administration. The people will have the same problems they faced before, perhaps even worse. Who can resist the power of authoritarian neighborhood toughs? Ghawar asks. "You, and all of the people of the neighborhood," he answers. And if Abu Jamil and his men come at them with knives, Ghawar announces that his people will bring their own in order to defend their neighborhood. "We all need to become *qabaḍāy*s. *Qabaḍāy*s raise their heads," Ghawar tells them. "They'll be afraid of us, we won't be afraid of them." The message here appears to support what is called democratic socialism in the film, which would be rhetorically consonant with the stated commitments of the Syrian regime during this period, but the concept is transformed to now mean that everyone must embody the swollen masculinity of the *qabaḍāy*. Put otherwise, the inscription of violence on the social milieu of the *ḥāra* is essential, as it becomes incumbent on the masses to exercise their dedication to popular democracy and socialistic solidarity through the use of force. Even with this discursive admonition, the question remains: Who has access to and is licensed to employ violence in Syrian society?

At this point in the plot, Abu Jamil flexes his muscle over both neighborhoods, asserting that the two zones have been incorporated under the banner of his neighborhood. Abu Jamil jokes graphically about eventually slaughtering Ghawar, aiming to impale him and scrub the neighborhood with his corpse. After Ghawar loses his composure and successfully stands up to Abu Jamil, he is praised for being a stallion (*faḥl abū faḥl*) but he refuses any special treatment, emphasizing the collective action they must take and refusing to be a hero, refusing heroism itself. Still, the community needs to figure out what to do next. Abu Jamil and his gang visit the *hammam* to strategize, and he dispatches them, with Hut in the lead, to teach the neighborhood a lesson by getting rid of Ghawar. But Ghawar's allies ambush the gang when they come looking for him at Abu Akram's house. Ghawar is casually chatting with Abu Akram's family as his men tie up Abu Jamil's men. Ghawar relishes the power of this moment, asking what they should do to forward their "revolution" (*inqilāb*), and it is instructive here that Ghawar uses the term *inqilāb* rather than *thawra*, suggesting a kinship with the Baʿthist "revolutions" (*inqilābāt*) of the mid-twentieth century. One of his men chimes in: "The best thing would be to hang them by their eyelashes." But Ghawar stays focused, insisting that if they do not smash the big boss, it is all for nothing. And here is the moment when the political valence of this allegory becomes deeply troubling. When they bring the captives out into the street, the men begin chanting: "Ghawar! Ghawar!" It becomes unclear whether there is a way past the heroization of Ghawar, of Ghawar as the essential hero. Ghawar claims to be of the people and for the people, but so does the Syrian regime throughout this period. Is this a reproduction of authoritarian power, reinscribing the political authority of the leader, of *a* leader, in the face of organized gangs and other forms of unregulated violence? Is there no other way to politically organize society in such a state of nature? The film offers no easy answers, but there is certainly a strong indication that the key message is that a strongman is required to keep all the other strongmen at bay, even if that struggle is conducted in the name of revolution or the people or even democratic socialism.

The situation on the street is getting more heated, headed toward climax. Everyone has weapons, and Ghawar begins to dance with his sword drawn, prepared for battle with Abu Jamil. "Brothers!" he shouts when his men seize Abu Jamil, telling them that they have rid the neighborhood of the thugs (*balṭajiyyeh*) and the scofflaws (*zaʿrān*). A leading merchant praises Ghawar and claims that there is nobody better suited to protect and lead and guide the two neighborhoods. At first, Ghawar demurs, but the people convince him that popular sentiment (*shuʿūr al-nās*) is with him. After this cajoling, including their telling him that he is meant to be *qabaḍāy*, to protect the neighborhood, he finally agrees but only under certain conditions so that the people will not find him unjust. This means that he will need to have total authority, that leadership will be his responsibility entirely, which will entail a monthly wage and spending money. Ghawar also insists that he will need a place to live and that he should pay no rent, and then tells the elites (*effendiyya*) of the neighborhood that he will provide protection in exchange for their providing him with freedom, by which he means total freedom to act as he sees fit. Finally, he says that he will need their full support. This strikes me as a key ideological inversion in the meaning of freedom in such a way that passes as endearing or humorous behavior by Ghawar but ultimately shores up the unchecked power of the leader, paving the way for a conception of freedom that appears to be commonsensical but is actually quite radical in an antidemocratic sense. One might ask if is this depiction of the arrogation of powers by a local leader is meant to be understood as critical of "reactionary" Arab leaders, of course, or is there something going on here that signifies the reactionary nature of freedom itself in the Ba'thist lexicon? It is worth considering how Hafiz al-Asad himself spoke of freedom in one instance: "When we speak of freedom, we realize that freedom cannot be provided to the individual as long as freedom has not been provided to the nation [*al-umma*] to which this individual belongs."[19] The freedom of the ordinary individual is thus held hostage to the liberation of the country. As national (here, with Ghawar, the local plausibly standing in for the national) leadership falls into the hands of an unchecked authority, freedom appears to be held hostage. Ghawar's seizure of power is blunted somewhat, however, by his unserious affect and slapstick behavior. It is precisely at this moment that he is placed in the carriage once used by Abu Jamil, and as it sets off Ghawar falls backward, tries to stand up, then falls once again. Perhaps the idea is that this

FIGURE 19. Marwan 'Akkawi, *Imbrāṭūriyyat Ghawār* (*The Empire of Ghawar*) (National Film Organization, 1982)

is a leader who can barely live up to the position, that he is harmless because he is clumsy and funny, that he does not know how to be a boss or a leader. And yet he continues to occupy a position of charismatic authority, always capable of exercising his absolute control.

Now that he occupies his position of increasingly unquestioned authority, Ghawar demonstrates to his followers how a leader behaves, or perhaps communicates to the audience how the leader ought to behave. When he wakes up the morning after becoming the neighborhood *zaʿīm*, his servant has dutifully brought him coffee, telling him it is time for his first meeting, at which point the two men reminisce about the celebration the day before, and his servant hoists him up on his shoulders in the bedroom. Ghawar responds to an errant comment by hitting and kicking him, a habit he will repeat, establishing that power is accompanied by the free use of violence against those weaker than he or subservient to him, and that the correct response to such actions is laughter and submissive avoidance (Figure 21). When he gets dressed, his first time dressing as a *zaʿīm*, he chooses a ridiculous suit, perhaps transforming the *zaʿīm* into a clown: one cannot help but wonder whether this is a clown *of* the people or someone clowning the people. His first order of business is to determine what to do with Abu Jamil's men who have been locked up in this transition to power. Should they be put on trial? Shamed publicly? Left in prison? Ghawar wants to decide how to proceed, though his men express some uncertainty, but he says he needs to pursue his own plans, though the men begin to question whether he should enjoy "unlimited powers" (*ḥurriyyat al-taṣarruf bidūn ḥudūd*).

By this point, Ghawar proudly struts around town with an entourage, dressed in garish colors, performing an exaggerated caricature of what he deems to be an appropriate persona for a leader. But many in the neighborhood are beginning to tire of his leadership, convinced that he has done more to aggrandize himself than to benefit the people. Consequently, Ghawar becomes suspicious of his own men and sends thugs to check on them. He considers it necessary to have his men call him by his proper title: savior (*munqidh* or *munajjī*). His self-confidence and power are inflated to a state of unfettered bombast and aspirational grandeur. In a pep talk to some of his supporters that sounds eerily like that of the former occupant of the White House in the United States, he claims to have been "born to be great" and that his greatness was passed down to him "from grandfather to father" before him. His work as a barber, when the

FIGURE 20. Marwan ʿAkkawi, *Imbrāṭūriyyat Ghawār* (*The Empire of Ghawar*) (National Film Organization, 1982)

viewer first meets him, was merely temporary. In political terms, anyone who opposes his leadership should be "smashed," as he puts it, but democratically, which seems again to soften the violence of his authoritarian tendencies while also scoffing at the very notion of democratic practices. He then riles up a crowd by performing a call and response with the words "democracy!" and "law!" There remains some ambiguity here in how such lampooning of democracy and law ought to be understood. Is this a satire of democracy and law as empty concepts in the absence of a well-established principle of popular sovereignty? Or is this a more fundamental rejection of liberal values such as democracy and the rule of law? Viewers are left to struggle on their own in order to conclude whether *The Empire of Ghawar* is a realm where autocracy is subject to comedic critique or one where authoritarian rule is justified through the back door, with a wink and a smile.

The end of the film suggests that there is risk in well-ordered political life. The rebellion that is brewing against Ghawar is led by those who wish to see the completion of the police station (*makhfar*) that will protect the neighborhood from Ghawar. When one of Ghawar's supporters threatens to tear the *makhfar* down, he interrupts and says, "No, let it remain up. We'll show them that we're more democratic than they are." Ghawar's "democracy," an imperial democracy it begins to seem, is performed at the film's end with Ghawar dressed in military regalia and accompanied by a marching band as he walks through the neighborhood in order to inaugurate the *makhfar*. The concluding scene shows Ghawar arriving in the middle of the neighborhood, dressed in what can be described as a mashup of Hitler, Mussolini, and Haile Selassie. The way he is distinguished from Arab dictators is a hat reminiscent of Ottoman military personnel. The film ends with someone announcing the opening of the *makhfar* with the honorific line "In the name of justice . . . " But even if such a democratic institution is being opened, it is a punitive arm of the state, and the film confirms that, alongside such bureaucratic institutions of punishment and control, the leader remains unavoidable, necessary, perhaps indispensable. Or perhaps the message is that power corrupts and Ghawar is nothing more than a temporary vessel for its transmission. In the final shot, the *makhfar* is under assault, stormed by the crowd with Ghawar at its head. The freeze-frame ending is one that characterizes all three of the films under discussion in this chapter.

It would be sensible to interpret the film comedies of Durayd Lahham the way Masʿud Hamdan treats his stage plays, as a carnivalesque space for the critique of state power, authoritarianism, and patriarchy, with *The Empire of Ghawar* being no exception. The extent to which these films directly tackle such sensitive and even volatile social and political matters demands our attention be directed to the contradictory nature of cultural production in Baʿthist Syria: on the one hand the seemingly unavoidably political nature of narrative film in the first place and on the other the fraught enterprise of engaging with the political in relation to heroism, masculinity, leadership, and authority. Even armed with a more generous understanding of the critical nature of the films, one cannot help but also conclude that the Ghawar/Lahham films cleverly shore up not only the authority but perhaps also the *necessity* of a strong regime, of authoritarian power as such. If the empire of Ghawar is ruled by an emperor, it stands to reason that this beloved figure stands in for "The Leader," here a cinematic, sanitized, and universally endorsed authoritarian populist—an organic dictator, to coin a phrase. Emperor Ghawar thereby emerges "from the people" as a democratically sanctioned leader; he plays by his own rules, but he always rules, by definition, in the name of the people. Ghawar's sentimental commitments to democratic rights and popular sovereignty are belied by the alacrity with which he resorts to violence. To be sure, there are violent dimensions to democratic politics, but the regularity with which comedic bits are performed through the use of violence, whether with the specific intention of cowing his opponents or because of his hapless ascent to a position of increasing influence suggests the co-implication of violence, humor, and political authority, a point to which I will return in Chapter 4 with respect to Nihad Sirees's 2004 novel *The Silence and the Roar* (*al-Ṣamt wa-l-Ṣakhab*).

But there are divergent philosophical opinions on the power of laughter. Hannah Arendt, for example, was optimistic on this score: "The greatest enemy of authority, therefore, is contempt, and the surest way to undermine it is laughter."[20] Other thinkers are less sanguine about the subversive potential of satirical modes of critique. "He who has laughter on his side has no need of proof," Theodor Adorno writes in *Minima Moralia*. "Historically, therefore, satire has for thousands of years, up to Voltaire's age, preferred to side with the stronger party which could be relied on, with authority."[21] Georges Bataille is even more strident in his locating of laughter on the side of power: "To laugh it is necessary that one not risk losing one's position of dominance."[22] The authority on display in *The Empire of Ghawar* is both strong and masculinist. As with the earlier stage plays for a television audience, critical analysis of these later commercial films suffers from relative inattention to the politics of gender. As Rebecca Joubin rightly points out, the earlier work of Lahham, Qalʿi, and al-Maghut constituted "a strong critique of government bureaucracy and corruption in society and politics told entirely through a masculine perspective, with women solely existing to actualize the male characters."[23] In most of the Ghawar/Lahham films, including *The Empire of Ghawar* (and, as we will see, *The Border* and *The Report*) there are musical interludes in which seductive women—often Bedouin women in Syrian cases—perform in front of leering male audiences, whether in private or public settings.

Finally, it cannot be ignored that *The Empire of Ghawar* was released the same year as the horrific massacre of tens of thousands of people by regime forces—including the *Sarāyā al-Difāʿ* (Defense Brigades), the elite strike force commanded by Hafiz al-Asad's brother Rifʿat—in the central Syrian city of Hama. Alasdair Drysdale points out that defense and internal security accounted for approximately 58.5 percent of government expenditures in 1982.[24] While there is no necessary or direct correspondence between those horrifying events and the plot or characters of *The Empire of Ghawar*, there are ideological lessons to be learned from a film like this in terms of the message that there are potential pitfalls and even danger in overthrowing an autocratic order that is being communicated to a wide Syrian audience. The suspension of any resolution to the conflict in the film perhaps speaks to the suspended judgment of the ongoing conflict in Syria during that period. Furthermore, the recourse to slapstick and roughhouse gags suggests an attempt on the part of the writers, producers, director, and even the actors themselves to caricature such acts of individual, collective, and state violence. As opposed to other instances of this comedic form—Charlie Chaplin is the most obvious—Ghawar does not indulge in these violent practices in order to transgress the social structure of the film (or its mimetic counterparts in reality) but rather to harness it to his own advantage or to soften the blow of such force. Film scholar Noël Carroll emphasizes "the theme of imagination" in Chaplin's slapstick: "It is an essential feature of his character that he can see things differently from others, that is to say, imaginatively."[25] Ghawar, by contrast, conforms strictly to the reality of the film as it is, operating within the parameters of social life as designated by the rules of the setting and the plot. Rightly capturing the rather modest scope of the character, Edward Ziter notes, "Ghawar was something of a clever fool whose seeming confusion masked wry observations, a lowly laborer who often got the better of his superiors."[26] Markedly different from the Chaplin described by Carroll, Ghawar is capable of bending the rules in a manner that approximates regime rationality and precisely *not* in a manner that is oriented toward upending convention or challenging institutional power, lest that kind of action lead to his being cast out of this status quo. Rather, Ghawar remains impervious to the force of law as well as to the potential power of the people. *The Empire of Ghawar*, we might say, functions in the state of exception, a setting in which power exists everywhere and nowhere at the same time, one in which slogans and marches and other trappings of the political may appear—and even

FIGURE 21. Marwan ʿAkkawi, *Imbrāṭūriyyat Ghawār* (*The Empire of Ghawar*) (National Film Organization, 1982)

motivate and inspire people—but have precious little effect on the structural and institutional forms of rule, all of which remain safely in place.

In a 1984 interview with *al-Ḥayā al-Sīnamā'iyya* (*Cinema Life*), Lahham boasted that the script for *The Empire of Ghawar* was "fantastic," but ruefully concluded that "the cinematic treatment wasn't adequate to the level of the script." This is an odd formulation in light of the fact that Lahham then goes on to criticize the very premise of the film as faulty for including "two *zaʿīms* to be in charge of the people . . . the masses represented in *The Empire of Ghawar* don't care about the struggle *between* two *zaʿīms* . . . they care about their struggle with one."[27] It may well be the case the Lahham was carefully considering how the relative success of the screenplay differed from its practical execution in the finished film product. At the very least, one simple conclusion that can be drawn is that there can only be one leading political authority against which the people may define themselves, whether in support or in opposition. Having two leaders or two political parties simply cannot make sense in the aesthetic ideology of Asadist-Baʿthist cultural revolution. In that regard, the message of *The Empire of Ghawar* is one *spoken-to* the audience, enacting an aesthetics of power rather than an aesthetics of solidarity or an aesthetics of resistance. An irony that appeared to be lost on Lahham here but reflected well the aesthetic ideology of Asadist-Baʿthist cultural revolution, from which Ghawar/Lahham may be inseparable at times, is that Ghawar ascends to the status of untouchable *zaʿīm* in what is (occasionally sardonically) portrayed as heroic fashion even as he continues to thunder in the name of the national-popular, in a manner that is strikingly reminiscent of the leader himself. While authoritarian power is softly lampooned, *The Empire of Ghawar* also makes clear to the audience that the leader is—perhaps axiomatically—an everyman, a man of the people, an authentic reflection of national culture, perhaps an organic intellectual but at the very least a broadly relatable personality. "The aura of the dictator," as Andrew Hewitt notes, "consists in the recognition of a certain arbitrariness: in the awareness that he could be anyone."[28] Again, while such comedic portrayals of the dictator figure can be understood as eroding the perceived power of the leader, another effect of this narrative is the seemingly unavoidable reinscription of leadership—in both conceptual and institutional terms—in an authoritarian idiom. In turn, the clown dictator figure functionally reinforces the political status quo. Moreover, the absence of a happy ending, namely the incomplete struggle to establish representative democracy, is telling of the film's message that the narrative of political development cannot be tied up so easily. The image of Ghawar attacking the *makhfar* communicates that there remains an indispensable role to be played by the heroic leader. Again, the freeze-frame ending, a suspended conclusion—a structural similarity that unites all three Lahham films under discussion in this chapter—hints at an opening to an untold future of political transformation, an undecidable moment of aesthetic ideology, a promise of possibility without a plan of action. To return to the Chaplin analogy, we can learn from film theorist André Bazin, who points out that Chaplin, "is never at a loss in any situation. There is a solution for everything even though the world (and especially things in it rather than the people) is not made for him."[29] This is what permits Charlie to consistently evade his circumstances, "imaginatively," as Carroll teaches us. But it seems to me that the world *is* made for Ghawar. Like Chaplin, he, too, will no doubt return in the future—we must believe this—but he is frozen in place at the end of this film. In the case of *The Empire of Ghawar*, one finds it difficult to definitively conclude whether this is an abdication of moral responsibility by the filmmaker, a move that ultimately reinforces the status quo, or a revolutionary statement of radical contingency. In other words, Ghawar's politics remain stubbornly undefined.

CLOWNING ON THE BORDERLINE

By the time Lahham's next major picture was released in 1984, he had reestablished himself on the cultural scene. Cowritten with his longtime collaborator

Muhammad al-Maghut, Lahham saw *al-Ḥudūd* (*The Border*) as an opportunity to make a splash, returning to the center of Syrian cultural politics as both movie star and film director. *The Border* would tackle issues more politically complex than *The Empire of Ghawar*, in a cinematic style more technically sophisticated and with a language aspiring to the universal. *The Border* highlights the predicament of an Arab everyman caught between competing nation-state nationalisms, a kind of allegory of national unity pitched to the entirety of the Arab world rather than fixated on any geographical or political engagement with Syria per se, however vague that engagement may be in *The Empire of Ghawar* and *The Report*. It should again be emphasized that one effect of this expression of pan-Arab ideology in the cultural production of the period was to shore up contemporary Syrian regime discourse, which effectively disavowed any distinction between Syrian national identity and pan-Arab nationalist sentiment.

Al-Ḥudūd appropriately begins and ends at a checkpoint. In the opening scene, a guard asks a driver, ʿAbd al-Wadud (Lahham), whose name translates to "friendly" and rhymes with "border" in Arabic, where he is headed. ʿAbd al-Wadud announces that his destination is Eastistan (*sharqistān*), adding that he has been touring the divided country, which is physically mapped onto his beat-up yellow Studebaker, creating a comic bit when he overdramatically guides the guard around all the places he has been and how he came to where he now finds himself. Once past this checkpoint, he picks up a hitchhiker, a woman in Bedouin dress named Sudfeh (played by Raghda), who appears to be pregnant. Although the viewer is meant to understand that ʿAbd al-Wadud is a character with his own life and backstory, we never learn about it, which leads to the conclusion, based on his behavior, that he is a Ghawar-type figure. He gives Sudfeh a ride and arranges her passage at the border-crossing office. When he stops later to change a tire, he loses both his and Sudfeh's passport and when they arrive at the entry point to Eastistan, they are unable to enter. ʿAbd al-Wadud expresses the Arab nationalist sympathies of the film's cowriters when he tells Sudfeh, "A single nation shouldn't require passports." A comedy of errors briefly ensues as ʿAbd al-Wadud must convince the guards at one or both of the two country's checkpoints that he is actually who he claims to be, even though he has no identification. When asked about his political affiliation, he declares that he has none. Neither side will budge and he ends up trapped in limbo, suspended in a kind of uncharted no-man's-land. Meanwhile, Sudfeh

FIGURE 22. Durayd Lahham, *al-Ḥudūd* (*The Border*) (National Film Organization, 1984)

(the literal meaning of her name is "chance" or "coincidence") has disappeared into the woods, and ʿAbd al-Wadud comes to realize that he has been giving cover to a smuggler disguised as a pregnant woman in order to avoid detection by the authorities.

ʿAbd al-Wadud tries to make his own way across the border, on foot the way Sudfeh had gone, but he is quickly apprehended by military personnel, literally caught with his pants down in a cheap gag. Then there is a sharp cut to the interior of a bus as ʿAbd al-Wadud leads a gratuitous singalong in Arabic and French, a musical interlude that lasts until armed guards board the bus and demand passports, which ʿAbd al-Wadud cannot produce. He subsequently attempts to cross the border by various means, which include dressing up as a sheep and smuggling himself in the back of an oblivious driver's truck. None of his ruses work. By the time he is released from additional questioning, he has grown a full beard and a cigarette dangles from his mouth. Fed up with his repeated failures, he decides to make a stand, to shelter in place as it were, building a rest stop (*istirāḥat al-musāfir*) in the borderlands. When soldiers discover his encampment, they ask him whom the structure belongs to, and ʿAbd al-Wadud responds, "To the international community" (*hay'at al-umam*). The soldiers ask how he thought he could possibly get away with such a stunt, demanding to know what he will do when they evict him; he offers to simply move to the other side. And if the other side kicks him out? Then he will come back. What if both sides work together against him? ʿAbd al-Wadud is nonplussed, saying that he has never seen the two sides agree on anything. He then goes on a rant about the media and how it had always taught him that the Westistanis and Eastistanis are all part of one country, causing some soldiers to awkwardly look away. Eventually, soldiers from both Westistan and Eastistan begin showing up with food and construction supplies. ʿAbd al-Wadud announces that they are all family (*ahl*) and therefore welcome to stay with him any time. Soldiers from both countries wind up drinking and eating with ʿAbd al-Wadud late into the night, resulting in a friendly, drunken celebration and a stylized dance battle. Their song, which begins on the topic of borders, evolves into a musical joke about who drinks the hardest and then improvised shanties about peace and friendship.

In the midst of this revelry and the apparent thawing of relations between the two countries, ʿAbd al-Wadud becomes increasingly despondent, more comfortable communing with sheep, chickens, and other barnyard creatures than with humans. He has been living beyond conventional geographical boundaries; now he is existing outside of space and increasingly outside of time. When a tourist passing through asks whether he has any newspapers, ʿAbd al-Wadud replies that he has *The Times* from tomorrow and Arabic newspapers from last year. Haven't you got anything more recent? "They all say the same thing," ʿAbd al-Wadud retorts. Seemingly on the brink of bottoming out, he hears gunfire erupting in the night; then Sudfeh shows up. When he asks her if she was involved in that battle, she says it was one that enmeshed "the entire clan." At this point, ʿAbd al-Wadud regains his morale, and when the soldiers come to search his place, they find Sudfeh and a weapon, but he claims she is his friend and that the gun belongs to him. He asks Sudfeh to stay, reasoning with her that she has no family, he has no country—why not live together? The homelessness of Arab citizens in a time of national rivalry and regional weakness is mirrored here by the unpredictable nomadic life of Sudfeh's Bedouin family. The unlikely couple tries to make a life together until a photojournalist turns up asking questions about a man she heard had been living with his pregnant wife in the wooded borderlands. Her editor rebuffs her pitch for a photo essay, telling her that it is not a real story. Who is this guy, he muses, and how could they ever independently verify that the man is who he claims to be, echoing the language of state authorities articulated earlier in the film. When the editor advises against taking on any political stories, the reporter replies that their magazine is called *The Truth.* He snaps back, my name's Mr. Waseem (which means "handsome" in Arabic), so does that make me handsome? And what if the authorities ban the story? Well, then, says the reporter, it will sell better. She follows through on her story, and it becomes a media sensation, galvanizing public opinion: "This is a crime," some say. "How can a citizen from our country not have a country?" Ordinary people are interviewed and respond in various ways: a fusty academic fulminates over the question: What is a passport? A mere collection of papers and stamps!, but then he bombastically revises Cartesian principles in his ruminations on ʿAbd al-Wadud's liminal condition, saying I think therefore I am, certainly. But how can one establish and prove something that does not exist, a passport for example, like an identity altogether? How can one deem something not present when it is right there in front of you? The growing intellectual and political pandemonium around the case of ʿAbd al-Wadud raises more questions than it is able to answer, and his very existence throws the Arab state system—its political legitimacy, its cultural institutions, and its societies—into turmoil. The hapless travails of this unwitting protagonist, have triggered a reckoning with the fundamental demands of contemporary Arab nationalist ideology.

All of this comes to a head when a political rally is organized in ʿAbd al-Wadud's no-man's-land, with spokespeople from Northistan, Centristan, and all the neighboring countries coming to speak about the need for regional unity, declaring there shall be no more borders from that day forward. The film's satire reaches its most pointed when the wooden language of these leaders is belittled by the juxtaposition of their words with a variety of inexplicable activities: a man selling cold drinks; a boy playing with a toy balloon and then being chided; somebody banging on bottles to the tune of a song; chickens lounging in a coop; goats bleating and drowning out the hollow words being uttered on the dais. The last speaker, from Southistan, refuses to speak—by speaking!—about how there should be no festivals, no more conferences, that the true expression of anti-imperialism would be utter refusal to engage whatsoever. He hilariously rails against the microphone for getting in the way of the unity of the people. Pushing the satire into farce, the speaker's words make things fly into the air, and he suddenly leaves the scene in a comic exit.

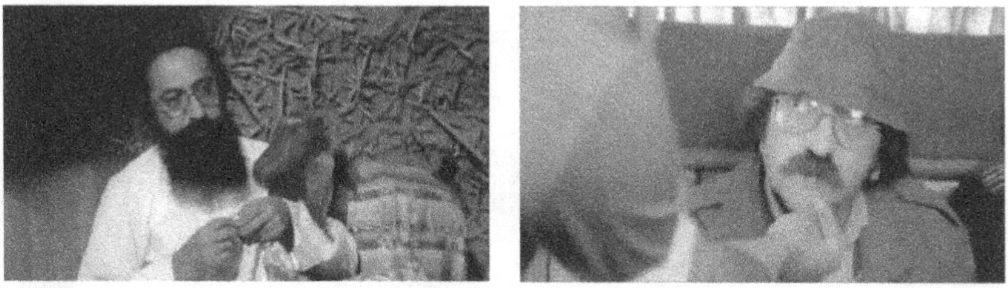

FIGURE 23. Durayd Lahham, *al-Ḥudūd* (*The Border*) (National Film Organization, 1984)

This sequence is perhaps one of the most paradigmatic of Lahham and/as Ghawar's blending of absurdism with social realism. Although politicians declaim confidently about matters of international order and national security; soldiers carry guns, ready for war; media professionals claim to work in the national interest; military personnel, political representatives, and journalists alike are consistently portrayed as out-of-touch, incompetent buffoons, their attention focused all too often on irrelevant intra-Arab disputes and petty matters of everyday life. There is an implicit message here that the ongoing struggle for Arab unity in the face of Zionism and imperialism is being sidelined. When tourists who have just returned from Kenya show up at ʿAbd al-Wadud's rest stop, they complain about security measures at the border, about the ugliness of passport stamps. When asked to explain the significance of his place, ʿAbd al-Wadud jokes that he has requested the United Nations to recognize it as an independent country. His friend Abu Ahmad jokes about "the Republic of Abd al-Wadud"! No, ʿAbd al-Wadud replies, "Solidarity-stan" (*taḍāmunistān*). The sincere attempt to found a political entity in the name of solidarity itself points up the emptiness of "solidarity" when invoked as a rhetorical slogan of Baʿthist pan-Arab nationalism. Nonetheless, the term is resuscitated here as a site for the celebration of universalist sentiment, Arab fellowship, and broad calls for unity. Although reference is made here to the concept of solidarity, the sloganeering without grassroots or mass political action communicates an aesthetics of power, the individual force of will embodied in ʿAbd al-Wadud's struggle to affirm his principles through valiant and dedicated action. Meanwhile, there is never any explicit indication that the setting of the film is Syria or, aside from the use of Arabic and some other symbolic indicators, any other Arab country for that matter. The critique of Arab nationalism's failures remains confined to the realm of ideology, as the violence of the state along the border—and any

FIGURE 24. Durayd Lahham, *al-Ḥudūd* (*The Border*) commercial poster (National Film Organization, 1984)

reference to a conflict with an external enemy, meaning Israel or other forces of imperialism—remains muted.

By the conclusion of their nationalist jamboree, both ʿAbd al-Wadud and Sudfeh have become convinced that they will be able to cross the border as they originally planned. They gather their animals—chickens and goats among others—and engage in the transgressive, potentially revolutionary act of smashing the guardrail and simply racing toward the other side of the border. The film ends at this moment, in freeze frame, the ending undecided, undecidable. Like *The Empire of Ghawar*, Lahham's directorial debut ends in a moment of promise and potential liberation that is by no means guaranteed to circumvent or subvert the authority of the state and, by extension, its hegemonic aesthetic ideology. The people—embodied, or at least reflected, in the Lahham and/as Ghawar everyman—will rebel against the unjust and unfamiliar repression of separation from their neighbors even as the state seeks to police its boundaries with an eye to law and order. Throughout the film, ʿAbd al-Wadud has played nice with the authorities, eventually turning his existence in no-man's-land into an opportunity for merriment, for profit, and even for service to the regimes of both states. It is conceivable that the opening of his third space—"Solidarity-stan"—will benefit the quest for Arab unity, to accomplish the dreams nurtured among generations of anticolonial nationalists by calling attention to the contradictions of the current political moment. While this cosmopolitan message might be understood to have even broader, perhaps universal significance, the film is underwritten by a firm commitment to radical Arab nationalist principles embedded in a Baʿthist ideology that refuses to recognize the *quṭrī* (nation-state nationalist) aspects of Arab identity. Again, this critique of Arab nationalist weakness or fatigue is one that the Syrian regime would regularly articulate in its aspirational leadership of a future, unified Arab world.

THE CLOWN REPORTS FOR DUTY

In *The Border*, the Arab world in its entirety is referred to as "the homeland" or "the country" (*al-waṭan*). This conforms neatly with Syrian Baʿthist discourse in the sense that Syria, the nation-state, is known as a "portion" (*al-quṭr*) of the Arab world or Arab people (*al-qawm*). This near-perfect overlap between the country and the Arab world is an effective cover for broad critique of political corruption in a great deal of the theatrical and cinematic collaboration between

Muhammad al-Maghut and Durayd Lahham. In *The Report* (1986), the third and final film under discussion here, Lahham plays ʿAzmi Bek, a seemingly unremarkable and professional bureaucrat at the High Bureau of Investigation (*maṣlaḥat al-taftīsh al-ʿulyā*), commonly known in the film as the Bureau. A legal expert, ʿAzmi Bek is assisted by Rima (played by Raghda, reprising her role as a pugnacious female foil to Lahham in *The Border*), who is constantly by his side at work as he relentlessly considers (and often rejects) project applications for government approval. ʿAzmi Bek is consumed by his work, and early in the film we watch him arriving at the office and inspecting plants lining the hallway of his office, indicating his commitment to order and propriety. When a restaurateur requests permission to expand his business, Rima and ʿAzmi Bek read the list of supplies: whiskey and wine, all kinds of food, including a "Muslim Fleeing" (*Muslim harbān*) and a "Jew Traveling" (*Yahūdī musāfir*)—"That's not food, that's political cooking," ʿAzmi Bek quips—and caviar, which he insists should have no place in a country as poor as theirs. ʿAzmi Bek's wife Falak (Muna Wassef) and his daughter Amal (Christine Choueiri), love him dearly, but wish he would not work so much.

The *mukhtar* of a village just outside Damascus has brought ʿAzmi Bek a plan for an irrigation system that will support a number of investment schemes. This real estate developer is summarily rejected by ʿAzmi Bek, who insists there must be respect for "the law above all else" (*al-qānūn fawq al-jamīʿ*). Not even the overtures of a lascivious woman—who happens to be ʿAzmi Bek's neighbor—can cause him to budge. The business associates of a businessman named Abu Faris and the *mukhtar* get together and bemoan ʿAzmi Bek, insisting that they are true patriots because of their commitment to economically developing the country, by whatever means necessary. The investors have assembled a gaudy and overproduced ceremony that will mark the opening of their valuable tap (*ḥanafiyya*), and a single waterspout comes to symbolize the entire project, adorning some of the movie's promotional materials as well. A professional troupe of musicians and dancers is trotted out to entertain the patently unimpressed locals even as the *mukhtar* and business elites make hollow speeches—uttered in a wooden language that echoes the political speechifying in both *The Empire of Ghawar* and *The Border*, and comes across as not all that different from regime discourse. Finally, a ceremonial ribbon is

FIGURE 25. Durayd Lahham, *al-Taqrīr* (*The Report*) commercial poster (National Film Organization, 1986)

FIGURE 26. Durayd Lahham, *al-Taqrīr* (*The Report*) (National Film Organization, 1986)

perfunctorily cut so that the illustrious faucet can be thrown open for the first time. Banners strung up behind the officials read "No More Buckets from Now On" and "Thirsty? Come and Drink."

When the *mukhtar* and the performing troupe pay a visit to ʿAzmi Bek, his assistant Rima asks who they are and whether they have an appointment, to which the *mukhtar* replies, "We've been on TV for an hour, and you don't know who we are?" Rima is unimpressed, but the group forces their way into ʿAzmi Bek's office, where they play music and dance, uninvited, until ʿAzmi Bek refuses their request. "So you're against art?" the flutist asks. "Just the opposite," ʿAzmi Bek replies. "Art is civilization," which the applicants misunderstand to mean that their proposal is about to be fast-tracked, causing the *mukhtar* to begin crooning poetically in honor of ʿAzmi Bek, who wryly says, "Welcome to all of you. And goodbye" (Figure 26). From here the business associates escalate matters, climbing the bureaucratic chain of command, reaching as far up as a minister, who reaches out to ʿAzmi Bek's office and tries to persuade him telling Rima that their office is "the beacon [*nibrāsa*] of truth and law" in the country.

Even as Rima warns him against resisting these powerful interests, ʿAzmi Bek is unmoved, telling her, "Girl, I'm like Lebanon in the past. My strength is my weakness," referencing an old adage about Lebanon's divided society and dysfunctional political system being one of its virtues. Rima ominously replies, "I'm afraid you're going to wind up just like it," subtly reinforcing the Syrian regime's narrative that celebrates its unique capacity to provide stability in the face of sectarian division from within and imperialist aggression from without. ʿAzmi Bek returns to dictating a pompous discourse about civilization, science, and order, citing both Oswald Spengler and the classical Arab poet al-Shamaqmaq. When further pressure is put on him by higher-level officials, ʿAzmi Bek tenders his resignation, the gambit being that his principles, his "conscience" (*ḍamīr*) as he puts it—a key word that resonates with the political commitment of Arab nationalist ideology—will sustain and protect him.

When ʿAzmi Bek returns home, his wife Falak is entertaining their flirtatious neighbor, the one who previously had tried to intervene on behalf of the developers. Before he arrives, we see Falak explaining an array of military photos on the wall: the War of 1948, the Suez War, the Yemen War, the Algeria War, the Golan War, and . . . Star Wars, which Falak assures her ʿAzmi Bek would be sure to fight if it ever took place. However, Falak admits that her husband has never served in the military even if he has always wanted to defend something. His resignation over this matter of brazen corruption is the stand he is going to take. "I want to make them understand who ʿAzmi Bek is," he tells his daughter, laying out the conditions under which he would consider returning to his position, assuming that his superiors will eventually beseech him to come back to work. Alas, nobody comes to see him, and there is no mention of his resignation on the radio news. Amal goes out the next day to pick up some newspapers and, finding that nothing has been reported about her father, she visits a printer in order to have a fake news story pressed onto the front page. Then Rima drops by to update ʿAzmi Bek on the situation, informing him that they have accepted his resignation: "The fastest transaction in the history of the agency," she says. When Rima praises ʿAzmi Bek as "an education [*madrasa*] in administration and the law," one immediately thinks of the state discourse during this period about law and order, a trope that persists down to the present, of course. In an interview with the journalist Patrick Seale on March 18, 1988, Hafiz al-Asad said, "I have always been a man of institutions."[30] If the film's irrigation and development projects represent the corruption of the private sector and the perils of arbitrary rule, ʿAzmi Bek now appears to emerge as a budding hero who stands for principled honesty and sound bureaucratic order.

His wife and daughter and his assistant want to take ʿAzmi Bek out for the night so he can forget all his troubles, but he decides to go out alone and visit the development site. "It's either me or it [the irrigation pipe] in this country [*al-waṭan*]," he grumbles. Upon arrival at the site, he initially tries to smash the pipe but is accosted by security guards and brought to a nightclub, which is going to be part of a much larger complex that will eventually expand to include a motel, a bowling alley, and an amusement park. When he demands to know why no local representatives were consulted for the project, he is told, "The people of the village don't enjoy bowling." ʿAzmi Bek is seated at the restaurant/nightclub, and pressured to order more than his initial cup of coffee, so he orders a plate of hummus, at which point he is asked whether he would prefer a male or female singer. "A plate of hummus comes with an orchestra?" he asks, startled. When he refuses to pay the outlandish bill that comes after the performance, ʿAzmi Bek is thrown in jail, where he leads a rousing version of the national anthem, which happens to actually be the Egyptian national anthem, "Bilādī." Here is one simple yet effective and concrete example of how Syrian patriotism can be performed through the symbols and ideology of pan-Arab nationalism, effectively effacing any specific reference to the political conditions of contemporary Syria in the process. Rima and Amal convince the prison guard that he can release ʿAzmi Bek in good conscience because he has not been officially notified of his resignation from the agency and therefore should be released on his own recognizance as a state employee. After voicing his opposition to this special treatment, ʿAzmi Bek announces his intention to write a report about the corruption surrounding the development project—and any other corruption he has ever encountered—and physically hand it to the president. "What should I do?" he asks. "Accept reality as it is?" Now ʿAzmi Bek becomes committed to reporting and even citing any instances of corruption he sees, including street ordinance infractions. With Rima he stops to interrogate a driver illegally parking who identifies himself simply as an importer (*mudīr taṣdīr*); before the driver can explain himself, ʿAzmi Bek tells him to keep quiet so he and Rima can take a photo of his violation (Figure 27). When the scofflaw speeds away, ʿAzmi Bek and Rima hop in a cab and order the cabby to "follow the state!" (*ilḥaq al-dawla*). The driver turns out to be a moonlighting university professor who immediately launches into a monologue about human nature, disorder, and chaos, citing Spengler in a callback to ʿAzmi Bek's earlier monologue. At this point, ʿAzmi Bek tells him to stop the car and then shoves him into the back seat and starts driving, continuing a conversation about teachers and students, learning and wisdom. The professor laments the fact that the faculty now serve the students instead of the other way around, that nobody respects him, that nobody would respect his position even if he were Plato himself. "Where is the failing [*al-khalal*] in our cultural ideology," ʿAzmi Bek asks. "When a kilo of garlic costs forty lira," Rima chimes in, rather reductively connecting the matter of "cultural ideology" to political economy. This leads Rima and ʿAzmi Bek to press the professor in order to know how he can claim to be happy when he must drive a taxi to make ends meet. "Everything will be included in the report," Rima assures him. When ʿAzmi Bek rear-ends a truck, distracted by their deep conversation, he begins shouting at the truck driver, telling him he should respect them because there is a university professor in the cab. Who cares, the man retorts, I'm the president of the university. In this scene,

FIGURE 27. Durayd Lahham, *al-Taqrīr* (*The Report*) (National Film Organization, 1986)

what might be written off as superficial and even absurdist comedy directly implicates state authority in matters of law, education, and political economy.

Meanwhile, ʿAzmi Bek's daughter Amal is threatened by men speeding down the street in a sports car. Lisa Wedeen convincingly argues that these men are meant to be understood as regime thugs, as *shabbīḥa*.[31] When they try to follow her, even driving onto the sidewalk at one point, they run over a young boy in broad daylight as numerous people walk past, oblivious to what has just happened, minding their own business. There is a brief fantasy scene inserted here in which the thugs are placed on trial, a stylized court sequence in which the judges wear white wigs and appear to be on the verge of pronouncing their sentence of three years for the crime of manslaughter. The pronouncement is interrupted by a phone call, which results in the judge reducing the sentence to two years; another phone call leads him to reduce the sentence to just one year. The defendant claims he was not speeding and when asked by the judge where he was going, he boldly asserts that he was going to blow himself up in South Lebanon or the Bekaa Valley, that he was rushing off to fight Israel. The judge now turns the sentencing entirely on its head, claiming that it was the little boy who was at fault because he impeded the so-called criminal from going to wage war on the Zionist enemy; he was "an obstacle in the way of this hero," the judge says. The boy's father is in visible distress, and Rima appears beside him, saying not to worry because they will be including everything in their report. Viola Shafik rightly notes that the fact that this sequence unfolds in a dream state restricts the pursuit of justice to a space of fantasy.[32]

Back home, ʿAzmi Bek and Rima set about writing their multichapter report, tirelessly working to produce a document that will be detailed and convincing to the president. They conduct further field research, observing construction proceeding without permits; they check passports at the airport and refuse to allow well-educated people to travel to Europe and the United States, effectively standing in the way of the slow-motion brain drain they represent. Finally, ʿAzmi Bek returns to the original irrigation and development project that started it all. Here he photo-documents corrupt men showering money on a belly dancer performing at the same restaurant and nightclub that ʿAzmi Bek had visited previously. As his camera captures the ongoing debauchery, the film flashes to images of refugee camps, the 1982 massacres at the Sabra and Shatila refugee camps in Beirut, starving children around the world. ʿAzmi

FIGURE 28. Durayd Lahham, *al-Taqrīr* (*The Report*) (National Film Organization, 1986)

Bek then grabs all the money and doles it out to a bunch of unemployed men gathered outside. He is arrested again, this time for "disturbing the peace," and when Rima, Falak, and Amal show up to take him home, Rima asks how one can disturb the peace of a cabaret. Upon his release, ʿAzmi Bek encounters a man begging for money while smoking a cigarette and wearing a placard around his neck with a Qurʾanic verse celebrating charity. The man tells ʿAzmi Bek he is disabled, "unable to express myself," and ʿAzmi Bek promises to put *that* in the report. Now he seems to be assembling all the information he can possibly find, even arrogating to himself a broad spectrum of surveillance powers, as when he breaks open a public complaint box posted outside the police station.

The report is ready to be delivered. With what might be a subtle reference to the political geography of *The Border* and the maligned divisions between the different parts of the Arab world, ʿAzmi Bek learns that the president is attending a soccer match between "East" and "West." The climactic sequence of the film transforms the delivery of the report into a series of fantasy scenes. Dressed in his fine white suit, ʿAzmi Bek traverses the city on foot waving a stick like an orchestra conductor. Suddenly he is leading an army—one that includes his wife, daughter, Rima, the beggar, musicians and performers, but also, importantly, police officers and other representatives of the state—as they attack multiple faces of corruption in the name of justice. 'Azmi Bek is dressed like Che Guevara as he and his comrades smash up the party at the cabaret that the corrupt businessmen are enjoying, upending tables and destroying the symbolic irrigation pipes. In the next scene, the group rushes into a torture chamber where the businessmen and their supporters have beaten senseless a man who is chained to the ceiling; the beggar hurls an oversized pencil, like a javelin, into the side of the executioner. In the third fantasy 'Azmi Bek is a knight on horseback, evoking Saladin and his band of brave soldiers as they march—with the giant pencil, an *oud*, a hubbly-bubbly, in tow—toward Jerusalem as patriotic music blares in the background. Finally, 'Azmi Bek struts triumphantly into the stadium, alone, and onto the field, wandering into the middle of a football match. He holds the report aloft, clearly believing himself to be a champion of the people in the stands. But he comes across as a fool as the referee gives him a yellow card. He holds the report up in response, recording this illegal infraction in the report itself. 'Azmi Bek falls to the ground as players run over him; he is hit in the head by the ball, and his papers are strewn everywhere. A penalty kick is given, but a fight breaks out between the two teams, between East and West, as the mob tramples 'Azmi Bek, smashing his glasses. He crawls out of the scrum, as if in a rugby match, and is left lying there alone when the match ends. The stands are empty and 'Azmi Bek is lying prostrate, as if dead, his eyes open, cleat marks on his face.

There is much to consider in this engaging allegory of bureaucratic power. The question is whether it is an embrace of the models of heroism or is meant to belittle them or to point up the absurdity of challenging them. Before setting off on his glorious mission, 'Azmi Bek speechifies before Rima and Falak and Amal as practice for his address to the president. He extols the magnificent historical achievements of the Arab people, with swords and horses, citing al-Mutanabbi on the glorious struggle between East and West. He is dressed in a fancy white suit that befits the gravity of his grandiose report. Rejecting any pessimism about his quest, 'Azmi Bek employs grandiloquent language in defense of the principle holding that, if there is even one barefoot or poor citizen, the entire political-economic system is an abysmal failure; even the smallest problems can have the greatest consequences. "I see my country as a bridal gown," he intones, a "blaze of light." He suddenly starts to cough uncontrollably. He insists he is a nobody, "merely transmitting the concerns of the Arab citizen, from the ocean to the sea"—the classical language of pan-Arab unity—criticizing how the "I" (*al-anā*) has become the homeland (*al-waṭan*) of far too many people. ʿAzmi Bek ceremoniously bows before an empty chair, playacting the servile submission of his report to the esteemed leader (Figure 29). In understanding the film, this performance of loyalty to the *idea* of authority—the slavish bow to an empty chair as an articulate metaphorical image—is as important as the ultimate impossibility of directly communicating with the leader. Wedeen reads this performance as an expression of sincere concern for the principles of right conduct and bureaucratic transparency: "By holding the 'responsibles' responsible," she writes, "Lahham can be read as implying that Asad is responsible too."[33] Moreover, this gesture—both the exaggerated bow and the failed delivery of the report itself—is a symbolic statement of hyperbolic loyalty. But it is also a comic gesture, one in which the buffoonish bureaucrat is ultimately an avatar of failure. He is incapable of communicating directly with the president, and that is significant. Furthermore, the broad appeal to some kind of

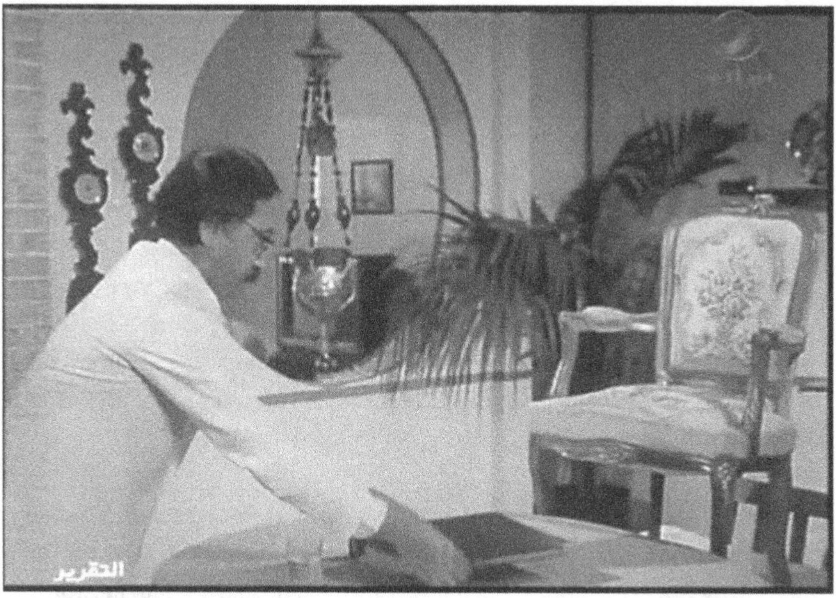

FIGURE 29. Durayd Lahham, *al-Taqrīr* (*The Report*) (National Film Organization, 1986)

social justice, political reform, and Arab unity fits with the pan-Arab sensibility of state-sanctioned aesthetic ideology. In other words, even if the viewer is convinced that the president is the Syrian president, the responsibility he bears is not only to the Syrian nation but also to the masses of the Arab world who long for unity and harmony alongside any kind of reform.

DURAYD LAHHAM, GLOBAL CLOWN

For film scholar and philosopher Robert B. Pippin, "A film . . . can have a mood suffused through it, something not quite the same as a signature style, but an effect of a consistent, controlled style."[34] Throughout this discussion of his work from the 1980s, the most memorable period in terms of his writing, directing, and acting, it may have seemed that Durayd Lahham did not innovate a "signature style," at least not one that is comparable to those Pippin identifies: John Ford's "historical fundamentality," Alfred Hitchcock's "brittle anxiety and eventually dread," Douglas Sirk's "desperate emotional intensity," David Lynch's "perversity."[35] All three Lahham films display elements of melodrama, historical epic, political thriller, musical theater, and psychological intrigue. In each of his sociopolitical dramas, the protagonist—Ghawar/Lahham—is capable of transcending his modest social stature in order to accomplish (or, more importantly, *struggle* to accomplish) something meaningful in the face of substantial obstacles: to establish democratic governance in *The Empire of Ghawar*; to freely move across international borders and help to bring about pan-Arab unity in *The Border*; and to combat corruption by (hypothetically) bending the ear of the president himself in *The Report*. The "mood" that suffuses these films might therefore be called *anxious ambition*. Bureaucratic-institutional realities that dominated the cultural consciousness of Asadist-Ba'thist Syria during the 1980s are on plain display here: government bureaucracy in *The Report*; political leadership and the cult of personality in *The Empire of Ghawar*; and the army, the border, and international relations in *The Border*. All three films end with shots than can be best described as moments of frustration, suspended animation, and undecidability.

Another aspect of the films that distinguishes them from the bulk of Syrian cinema during this period is their commercial nature and broad accessibility, anecdotally evidenced by their regular airing on pan-Arab satellite networks. There is no question that the audience for Ghawar/Lahham films was large at times; the films circulated more widely than, say, the auteur cinema of Ossama Mohammed, Riyad Shayya, and even the relatively accessible movies of ʿAbd al-Latif ʿAbd al-Hamid. In other words, the films of Lahham and al-Maghut can hardly be characterized as "alternative cinema," the epigone of the aesthetic ideology of Asadist-Baʿthist cultural revolution. When it comes to characterization, mood, and political content, they need not be simply understood, following Lahham, as "entertainment" without any relation to the aesthetic ideology of Asadist-Baʿthist Syria. After all, Ghawar typifies the virtues and strengths of the hero more than the antihero, epitomizes the commitments and aspirations of an ideal leader, a man of the people, perhaps, but who is nonetheless set apart and above them. In *The Border* there is neither ideological nor aesthetic disagreement with the regime's avowed commitment to national unity and international solidarity. The relationship between state and citizenry is respectful, familial, and governed not just by the law (*qānūn*) but by precedent (*uṣūl*) as well. Officious and efficient bureaucracy is required for the country to function, as the administrator of Eastistan tells ʿAbd al-Wadud, but it is also the obligation of the committed citizen to bring warring nations together and transcend the border through its very enactment. The language and aesthetics of power on display in the films of Lahham and/as Ghawar are overdetermined. It remains unclear, moreover, what Lahham and/as Ghawar want(s) from his national audience, his Arab audience, and his (potential, however limited) international audience. Lahham and/as Ghawar can manifest a reflection of Syrian society or represent a didactic avatar of a regime that demands conformity and only permits "commissioned criticism," in the words of literary critic miriam cooke.[36] In a different way, I tend to agree with Marilyn Booth's critique of cooke's understanding of cultural expression under the Baʿth when she argues that the term *commissioned criticism* "suggests state intervention in the thematic force of the art work itself."[37] Lisa Wedeen hits closer to the mark in identifying the constellation of critical humor at play in Baʿthist Syria as "tolerated parodies."[38] But whereas Wedeen's work—and that of cooke—is concerned with the passive "toleration" or the active "commission" by the regime and its representatives, I am more interested here in understanding what makes these films funny and how that articulation of comedic voice, gesture, and narrative is shaped, in cinematic form, by the struggle over aesthetic ideology in the Syrian cultural field. Here what is of interest is not only the significance of the narrative discourse or the analytical framework of Syrian cinema but also the specific linguistic, aesthetic, and cultural referents of the work. One of the messages communicated by *The Empire of Ghawar* is that the rabble-rousing man of the people can be transformed through the experience of organizing and beating the *zuʿamāʾ* at their own game, but he may wind up finding himself turned into one of them, no longer entirely of the people he once claimed to represent.

Whether or not in character as Ghawar, there have been persistent attempts to dub Durayd Lahham the Arab Charlie Chaplin. As we saw earlier, Lahham pushed back against this comparison, but in a different interview he saw himself this way, in terms not only of the Ghawar persona but also of his own comedic genius. In an interview with *al-Ḥayā al-Sīnamāʾiyya* in the same year that *The Border* was released, Lahham expressed himself rather boldly:

> The presence of some artistic personalities who are responsible for writing, acting, and directing their own works, such as Woody Allen and Charlie Chaplin and so forth, is internationally well-known. . . . They always need to base their comedy upon a particular sensibility that only the comedian knows, perhaps the average director does not even know the plot of the comedic work too well and does not know how to set up the comedic situation . . . The comedic perspective [*al-mawqif*] is like a hunter's shot: it takes a long time to finish preparing the aim, but when it finally shoots it comes out quick, in a very short period of time. Ordinarily, directors who work with them in cinema are not inclined towards comedy in the first place . . . that is, some of them don't even understand a joke, they're simply someone who films. That's one of the reasons—and it's a main reason—that drove me to direct *The Border*.[39]

Lahham claimed that there were not many film directors with the comedic "perspective" required to envision, shoot, or properly execute his artistic vision. The commercial success of *The Border* demonstrated that Lahham was able to translate his comedic sensibility into cultural power. At the same time, the characters Lahham played in these films were often quite subtle and understated. In a sense, it might be useful to think of Lahham's impish characters as Žižek does, for whom "the stuff of comedy is precisely this repetitive, resourceful popping-up of life—whatever the catastrophe, no matter how dark the predicament, we can be sure that the little fellow will find a way out."[40] But Ghawar and his ilk typically find their way out though some kind of accommodation with power. In other words, his way out may not be an option for the audience, although his fans are expected sympathize with their "little fellow" as he opts in to an alliance of convenience with individuals and institutions of power. Their desires may be projected on screen in their collective aspirations toward government transparency, individual freedom, and international unity, but the moral of these stories might actually be that those objectives will have to remain in the realm of fantasy rather than reality. Whatever the case, Lahham briefly indicated that he might "distance [himself] from cinema forever" after the commercial failure of *The Empire of Ghawar*, but upon returning with *The Border* he found that cinema "became a means to express a specific idea."[41] Even if a filmmaker like 'Abd al-Latif 'Abd al-Hamid would not consider himself chiefly making films of ideas (Chapter 2)—and it may not matter in the end whether or not filmmakers themselves work with that intent—Lahham's comment seems to suggest that Syrian filmmakers, regardless of their politics, inevitably have some relationship with auteur cinema or some kind of cinema of ideas even when the work fits into the genre of popular comedy and reaches a wide commercial audience.[42]

An analysis of the comedic dimensions of the Ghawar films thereby opens up the question of genre, calling into question not only the status of comedy in the films themselves but also the significance of comedy in the history of Syrian film. Some film critics during this period were averse to comedy and/as popular cinema because of the conventional association of such works with melodrama and its perceived crass ideology. According to Ibrahim al-Jaradi, for example, writing in *al-Ḥayā al-Sīnamā'iyya* in the early 1980s, the mainstay of Arab comedy was melodrama, an "affecting" but "low-class" artform, a sign of poor education and the absence of a critical spirit adequate to the political and intellectual demands of cultural production such as cinema and television.[43] Rather than rejecting melodrama out of hand, though, Peter Brooks encourages critics to carefully consider it in relation to other genres such as tragedy. "Tragedy," Brooks writes, "generates meaning ultimately in terms of orders higher than one man's experience, orders invested by the community with holy and synthesizing power." Although Ghawar does function as a cipher for a broader imagined public, his experience—embodied and rational—is the (or, at least, a) locus of the generation of meaning. "Melodrama," Brooks continues, "offers us heroic confrontation, purgation, purification, recognition," but it "cannot figure the birth of a new society—*the role of comedy*—but only the old society reformed."[44] Brooks appears to be slightly extending a Lukácsian perspective on "the great and timeless paradigmatic forms of world literature: epic, tragedy, philosophy."[45] Whereas the novel for Lukács is a pale shadow of the epic in a world shorn of meaning, a cultural product that reflects man's utter alienation in modernity, Brooks sees melodrama as a shadow of classical tragedy and comedy. Comedy is a complex genre, to be sure, but it is worth remembering that it can be a noble pursuit, one concerned with no less than "the birth of a new society." In the aftermath of the socialist realism of the mid-twentieth century Arabic novel, similar questions might be raised about the capacity to represent the aspirations and desires of the people in a specifically Syrian comic idiom. Scholars of Syrian film and filmmakers, therefore, and not only those interested in dramatic narrative films and documentaries, would do well to heed Gilles Deleuze's argument: "It is not sufficient to compare the great directors of the cinema with painters, architects or even musicians. They must also be compared with thinkers."[46]

In his trenchant analysis of fascist modernism, Andrew Hewitt reads Walter Benjamin on the power of aura in cultural production in order to point out an apparent contradiction in the Frankfurt School's critique of cinema. "How can it be that the charismatic dictator and the Hollywood star are produced by precisely that medium that is most inimical to aura? . . . Clearly, it is necessary to rethink the aura of the dictator and the star in this [cinematic] context."[47] This point should not be forgotten in a discussion of the work of Durayd Lahham. In a 2006 *New York Times* profile, Lahham argued that art "never transformed a dictator into a democrat . . . it never did much but entertain."[48] Regardless of whether cinema can channel dissent toward meaningful political change, Lahham's films are profound examples of the reflective power of film, even in authoritarian contexts. The films of Lahham and/as Ghawar are also distinctive in that the work and the characters have managed to survive and even evolve across different periods of modern Syrian history. Lahham and/as Ghawar is a figure with national significance, and his survival into the post-Hafiz al-Asad period is significant. His films can be seen as a bridge between two periods of Syrian cultural history. The next chapter will consider how Syrian novels and films—some from this same period but also those that appeared during the first decade after the death of Hafiz al-Asad, with the coming to power of his son,

FIGURE 30. Durayd Lahham and Bashar al-Asad

Bashar—presented a critique of the political on altogether different grounds from those discussed in this chapter. Novels by Nihad Sirees, Samar Yazbek, and Rosa Yaseen Hasan incorporate the sensory experience of surveillance and authoritarian repression even as the regime ostensibly pursued a path of reformism from above. It may have proved difficult to generate art that directly targeted the mechanics and symbols of authoritarian dictatorship during the rule of Hafiz al-Asad. During the post-2000 period, by contrast, there were new opportunities to lampoon the leader, satirize the security services, and tackle the problem of political tyranny itself.

Chapter 4

READING WRITING MUKHABARAT

I laugh in the dark
I cry and write in the dark
until I can no more distinguish between finger and pen
Whenever a knock resounds
whenever a curtain moves
I cover my papers with my hand
like a prostitute covers herself during a raid.

— Muhammad al-Maghut, "The Tattoo"[1]

In a system of ubiquitous spying, where everybody may be a police agent and each individual feels himself under constant surveillance; under circumstances, moreover, where careers are extremely insecure and where the most spectacular ascents and falls have become everyday occurrences, every word becomes equivocal and subject to retrospective "interpretation."

— Hannah Arendt, *The Origins of Totalitarianism*[2]

Besides locating a text in its original context . . . readers might want to dislocate it, relocate it, and line it up against competing voices . . . to see how it sounds and resounds.

— Wai Chee Dimock, "A Theory of Resonance"[3]

IN NABIL MALEH'S *THE EXTRAS* (*AL-KŪMBĀRS*) (1993), ONE OF THE most critically acclaimed Syrian narrative films, Nada and Salem arrange a romantic tryst in their friend's empty apartment. With the exception of the opening and closing scenes, which feature street and aerial views of Damascus, the entire film takes place in the confines of this living space. Although intended to be unremarkable, everyday scenes, in the aftermath of the Syrian revolution and the Syria War, these external shots are striking visual monuments to an urban landscape now radically reduced to ruin. The social and political world of Ba'thist Syria impinges on their intimate experience even as Nada and Salem struggle to carve out a private sanctuary where they can enjoy being with one another: speaking freely, flirting, improvising theatrical performances. Risky love and paranoid delusions hammer against the protagonists' interior lives as they are subjected to unannounced visits from the state security services as well as friends and neighbors. Unlike most of his peers who studied film in Moscow or Paris, Maleh's training was in Czechoslovakia, a different, perhaps more experimental cinematic culture. His visual style and emotional sensibilities are of a different type when it comes to pacing, mood, and humor.[4]

Salem is a law student who makes ends meet by working part-time as a theater extra and a gas station attendant. Like many young men of his generation, he is politically repressed, financially precarious, and sexually unfulfilled. The only way he can spend time alone with Nada, a widow trying to piece her life back together, is to borrow his friend 'Adel's apartment. Salem doubts he will ever be able to afford his own place or get married. Lisa Wedeen convincingly points out the contradictions between Salem's "fantasies of a heroic response to the security police, while his actual behavior remains fearful and compliant."[5] The "political and sexual impotence" Salem endures here is an important aspect of his character. Wedeen's argument is made more convincing by the fact that Salem speaks with a stutter, which can be interpreted as yet another manifestation of relative powerlessness.

There is another dimension to the shared experience of confinement and surveillance on display in *The Extras*, a somewhat different way in which political reality impinges on everyday life. In a sense, Nada and Salem's unfettered imaginative play inside the apartment and the sheer continuation of romantic dalliances are a sort of triumph, not entirely comprehensible as resistance to state power but perceptible as a kind of personal enjoyment. Moreover, while this behavior may not appear heroic according to the lexicon of Asadist-Ba'thist aesthetic ideology, their cloistered endurance and imaginative paths to pleasure give rise to an alternative subjectivity and perhaps even another experience of heroism. To put this point in terms I have been using throughout the book, Nada and Salem create a universe in which an aesthetics of solidarity can emerge, one in which their combined acts of *speaking-together* (*mitsprechen*) permit the viewer to experience an alternative to the aesthetics of power generated by the state.[6] When a security agent barges in to ask about a neighbor's activities, this before 'Adel has even left, the official justifies his entry by saying, "It's nothing, a simple matter," expressing the quotidian, even banal nature of regime surveillance. It also seems a telling if minor point that Salem's last name is al-Shāhid, "the Witness," resonant with the capacity of ordinary Syrians and Syrian filmmakers to chronicle their experiences in a mode of witnessing or providing testimony even when options for overt political resistance are limited.

Meanwhile, Nada and Salem take comfort in each other and assert their individual agency through laughter—unbridled, unsupervised laughter. Banter sustains them, and their happiness grows with their staging of an impromptu theatrical performance. Their discussion of the multiple roles that actors and citizens play at different moments in their lives distills a critical political riposte to the authoritarian conditions under which they live, a subtle acknowledgment of Wedeen's politics of "as if," if there ever was one.[7] At one point Nada reminds Salem that the role of extras in a theater performance or film is often to say nothing at all. One irony about the silence of extras is that they have such prominent voices throughout this film, and inside their domestic space they become the leading characters. The cinematography adds and removes distorting lenses at different moments, making the light appear translucent or hazy at certain points while creating an impression of swirling vertigo at others. Because they are unable to leave the apartment, doors, windows, and mirrors acquire an electric significance, as physical manifestations of symbolic closure as well as portals to different spheres of the real world outside. The door is a prime site of danger and uncertainty too, as a knock might mean the return of 'Adel and his fiancée, marking the end of Nada and Salem's tryst, or perhaps the arrival of state security agents, which could threaten their relative liberty. Whatever the case, the anxiety of being interrupted causes them to hide whenever the door is opened, "like a prostitute covers herself during a raid," in Muhammad al-Maghut's vivid simile. Meanwhile, the mirror provides a site of refuge and improvisation as Salem finds solace in acting the ham

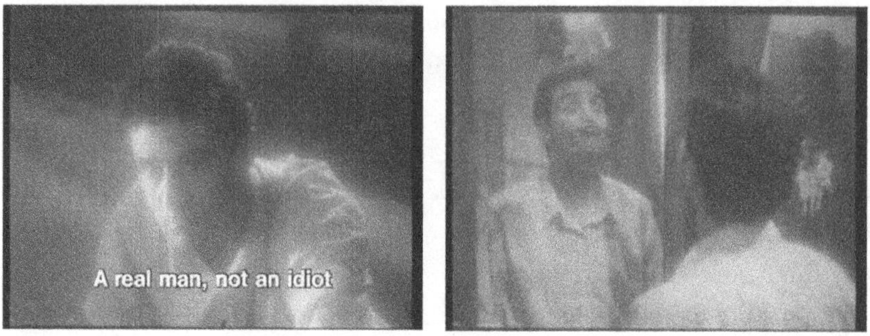

FIGURE 31. Nabil Maleh, *al-Kūmbārs* (*The Extras*) (National Film Organization, 1993)

(Figure 31), at times for his own entertainment or else entering into a space of fantasy, as when he imagines himself in bed with multiple women. Later in this chapter, I discuss how crucially symbolic the mirror has been in some of the most important works of Syrian literature and film, acquiring a new significance during the 2000s.

SIGHT, SOUND, AND SENSES OF SURVEILLANCE

The Extras is a romantic social drama set entirely in a middle-class Damascus apartment that is also an extended meditation on the intimate consequences of state surveillance. The creeping paranoia, the dreaded knock at the door, the seemingly inevitable interruption of private intimacy: these are challenges facing those who struggle to construct some modicum of normalcy in their everyday lives. Chapter 3 considered Durayd Lahham's character Ghawar and film comedy more broadly in relation to state power in Asadist-Baʿthist Syria. In this chapter, I address a different facet of the agonistic relationship between state power and cultural production, specifically how Syrian writers, artists, and filmmakers represent, adapt, and refashion the security apparatus itself. While there are some who encounter the state as a purely repressive instrument that curtails freedom of speech, constrains the possibility for direct political action, and sends Syrians in droves to languish in prison where they may be subjected to inhuman forms of torture, there are others—including those who enjoy an official or bureaucratic relationship with the regime or stand outside of the system and write or make art without state support—who suggest ways around, under, and through the thicket of authoritarian state culture.

This chapter is concerned with what I call the affective politics of surveillance in Syrian literature and film, which was crucial for a number of influential works of cultural production during the period of Asadist-Baʿthist rule, on display in both *The Extras* and Ossama Mohammed's 1988 debut feature film *Nujūm al-Nahār* (*Stars in Broad Daylight*) (discussed later). Literary representations of surveillance and the security state became more robust in the post-2000 period, during which Bashar al-Asad and the new regime oversaw a gradual loosening of certain restrictions in the country while others went relatively unchanged. My discussion here of what I call *mukhābarāt culture* aims to draw attention to the fact that the Syrian state and its surveillance apparatus were not only an ever-present aspect of the everyday lives of Syrians but also a fixture in the imaginative life-worlds created by Syrian writers, filmmakers, and other artists. As I have argued throughout this book, though, the Asadist-Baʿthist regime should not be viewed as totalitarian; rather, it needs to be understood as an authoritarian system exhibiting certain totalitarian tendencies. Of course, the state maintained a stable of informants and intelligence gatherers who populated a system—the various agencies of the *mukhābarāt*—that was comparable to the NKVD, the Stasi, the Securitate, and other national security services. As in those contexts, however, the Syrian security state never successfully stamped out independent thought and creative expression. As Ossama Mohammed remarked about the problem of free expression under authoritarian conditions,

> our cinema is free, but its freedom is like a whisper in a closed room. We too are free, but locked in an enclosure, the historic contingency that weighs over our sky. It is as if we sneaked into that closed room from the keyhole, and we grew inside it. In its turn, it sneaked inside us and grew. And we are stuck in this locked embrace.[8]

Literary engagements with dictatorship, the authoritarian state, and surveillance practices can be understood in relation to historical, political, and aesthetic criteria. Lebanese poet, novelist, and critic ʿAbbas Beydoun proposes the "*mukhābarāt* novel" as an analytical category for texts in which the *mukhābarāt* (state security services) play an integral part in setting, plot, or characterization. The *mukhābarāt* novel, for Beydoun, is concerned with the "stripping bare and exposure" of politics in a manner that "confronts the power inside the regime [*al-sulṭa dākhil al-sulṭa*]." Beydoun provocatively suggests that there are at least two heroes, or protagonists, in the *mukhābarāt* novel: one who is visible—"an intellectual or a politician who has a lover or a spouse and history and roots"—and another that is either the human embodiment of the *mukhābarāt* or the institutions and practices of the *mukhābarāt* itself.[9] But whereas Beydoun suggests that this genre may take the form of "a quasi-police novel but without the structure, techniques, or formula. . . ," there are other works of art—romances, tragedies, psychological fiction—in which the *mukhābarāt* play a leading role.[10] I have briefly elaborated the significance of Maleh's *The Extras*; subsequently I analyze Ossama Mohammed's *Stars in Broad Daylight* in this light. Here I would emphasize that these two films directly address state surveillance in Syria and were made during the time of Hafiz al-Asad, and that they were produced by the National Film Organization (NFO) itself. Given the extent to which the affective politics of the surveillance state appears throughout the Syrian cultural field—as in the films of Maleh and Mohammed—it makes sense to expand Beydoun's essential insight in order to name a broader phenomenon I term *mukhābarāt culture*.

In the subsequent sections of this chapter, I perform a close reading of three novels published during the first ten years of Bashar al-Asad's rule (2000–2011)—the interregnum between the death of Hafiz al-Asad and the beginning of the Syrian uprising—to demonstrate the variety and depth of the *mukhābarāt* novel in Syria. Through an analysis of *al-Ṣamt wa-l-Ṣakhab* (*The Silence and the Roar*) by Nihad Sirees (2004), *Brūfā* (*Rough Draft*) by Rosa Yaseen Hasan (2011), and *Lahā Marāyā* (*In Her Mirrors*) by Samar Yazbek (2010), I argue that the political in late twentieth and early twenty-first century Syrian cultural production was distinguished at least in part by direct engagement with the security state and its practices of surveillance. The Asadist-Ba'thist cultural revolution of the 1970s–1990s, discussed in the first three chapters of this book, relied on slogans and aesthetic conventions that rang increasingly hollow to Syrian writers, filmmakers, and others. The aesthetics of power and conventions of *speaking-to* inherent in it would be challenged, adapted, and even discarded altogether in novels, films, television serials, and other works of art that promoted what I have been calling an aesthetics of solidarity and an affiliated mode of address best described as *speaking-with*. With the advent of the Syrian revolution in 2011, a more robust aesthetics of resistance and a related *speaking-back* or *speaking-against* would come into view. In addition to identifying the influence of authoritarian domination on cultural production, the Syrian *mukhābarāt* novel of the first decade or so of the twenty-first century also suggests some of the ways in which fiction may critique, subvert, or even resist the seemingly durable and invulnerable "truth" of Baʿthist rule.

Modern Arabic literature is littered with figures of authoritarianism. Gamal al-Ghitani's *Waqāʾiʿ Ḥārat al-Zaʿfarānī* (*The Zafarani Files*) details the observations of an unnamed informant, the *baṣṣāṣ* (the one who sees), who monitors the daily life of a popular quarter in Cairo. Al-Ghitani similarly addresses the question of political authority in his landmark *al-Zaynī Barakāt* (*Zayni Barakat*).[11] The novels of Sonallah Ibrahim, such as *Tilka al-Rāʾiḥa* (*That Smell*), *al-Lajna* (*The Committee*), and *Talaṣṣuṣ* (*Stealth*) might be read under this rubric as well.[12] In *Iʿjām* (*Ijaam: An Iraqi Rhapsody*), Sinan Antoon draws attention to the conditions of possibility for self-expression through prose writing in the stultifying atmosphere of Iraq under authoritarian dictatorship.[13] The protagonist in *Iʿjām* is a political prisoner on whom is bestowed the opportunity to continue writing while incarcerated, which he does in creative camouflage, presenting one way in which the novel form enables modes of narration capable of contesting the rationality of the authoritarian state.[14] Seeing and hearing, vision and sound, communication through rumor as well as the stealthy accumulation of evidence or the production of truth, watching and listening, embodiment and performance—these are just some of the tropes recurring throughout Arabic prose writing inside, with, and against the *mukhābarāt*. Political and affective reflections of the security state, its tactics of surveillance, and its techniques of rule index the influence of state power on cultural production in Syria while also highlighting the potential forms of evasion, subversion, and even resistance immanent to narration itself.

A small yet vibrant and growing body of scholarship critically interrogates literature written during the three decades of Baʿth Party rule under Hafiz al-Asad (1970–2000).[15] The Syrian literary field has often been described in terms of generic rigidity and ideological conformity, but it was by no means monolithic. Prose writing—especially prison literature—from the mid- to late twentieth century occasionally addressed questions of literary representation and the matter of state power and surveillance.[16] The three novels discussed in this chapter also push back against a reductive understanding of the totalitarian and the sectarian in Asadist-Baʿthist society and culture. Two of the authors under discussion here, Rosa Yaseen Hasan and Samar Yazbek, belong—in contradictory, unresolved ways—to the Syrian ʿAlawī community. An offshoot of Shīʿī Islam, the ʿAlawīs make up approximately 10 percent of the Syrian population. Although the degree of the community's power, autonomy, and visibility ebbed and flowed over the course of the medieval and early modern periods, it has played an outsized, if controversial, role in the political history of the country since independence in 1946, even more so since the coming to power of the Baʿth Party in March 1963 and especially since the November 1970 "corrective movement" (*al-ḥaraka al-taṣḥīḥiyya*) launched by Hafiz al-Asad.[17]

Syrian writers figure the authoritarian state and its methods of surveillance and repression through characters drawn from the security apparatus itself, situating the *mukhābarāt*—from ordinary secret agents to high-ranking officials—alongside other figures drawn from what I call *Syrian uncivil society*.[18] Literary culture in Syria has changed since 2001, when critic and novelist Mohja Kahf wrote:

> Contemporary Syrian literature is created in the crucible of a tenacious authoritarianism. Manifold silence, evasion, indirect figurative speech, gaps and lacunae are striking features of Syrian writing, habits of thought and wary writerly techniques have developed during an era dominated, in Syria more overwhelmingly than in other Arab countries excepting Iraq and perhaps Libya, by authoritarian governments with heavy-handed censorship policies and stringent punitive measures. . . . Syrian literature today is jittery with what it cannot say, and that is its genius.[19]

From as early as the 1990s, in an era of neoliberal transformation and ongoing repression—but well before the popular nonviolent uprising against the regime that broke out in early 2011—Syrian writers and other culture producers were experimenting with new forms of creative expression, much of which contained overtly political plots and themes.[20] During the 2000s, both political economy and regime ideology were sites of significant experimentation. Immediately following the coming to power of Bashar al-Asad in summer 2000, the so-called Damascus Spring (2000–2001) augured a potentially far-reaching transformation in the relationship between state and society, especially regarding freedom of expression and individual rights. The September 2000 "Statement of 99" called on the regime to implement meaningful political and legal reforms; at the same time, a number of informal social gatherings and intellectual salons sprang up as venues for public deliberation and debate about political matters once deemed taboo. Meanwhile, a system inspired by German economic policy, a social market economy, was proposed at the 2005 Ba'th Party Regional Conference in order to further normalize public-private partnerships in the Syrian economy and gradually advance liberalizing measures that had been haltingly implemented since the 1980s. The regime also continued to make promises of expanded freedoms of political association, speech, and cultural production. The 2005 Damascus Declaration, signed by over 250 individuals and organizations, criticized the Syrian regime for falling short on its promises of reform from above. Meanwhile, the spaces of Syrian literature and culture became capacious enough to accommodate creative expression with a growing and evolving political bite. While the short stories of Zakariya Tamir and the plays of Sa'dallah Wannous had long been recognized as indicators of critical cultural production in Ba'thist Syria, the Syrian novel struggled to find its own way to challenge the hegemonic aesthetic ideology of Asadist-Ba'thist cultural revolution. The death of Hafiz al-Asad allowed for more strident and unabashed political criticism in Syrian literature, which may have become jittery, to repurpose Mohja Kahf's important insights, with what it increasingly *could* say about political matters.[21]

POKING FUN AT THE PARTY: NIHAD SIREES'S *THE SILENCE AND THE ROAR* (*AL-ṢAMT WA-L-ṢAKHAB*)

There is no better starting point for thought than laughter.

— Walter Benjamin, "The Author as Producer"[22]

While Syrian authors have always taken risks when directly engaging with political themes, during the 2000s a different kind of novel emerged in Syria, one that represented a formal as well as an ideological challenge to the hegemonic cultural forms of committed literature, socialist realism, and historical fiction. Novels may confront the obfuscation, the arbitrariness, the sheer violence of the regime—of Syrian life more generally, perhaps—through literary devices ranging from avoidance and detachment to plain talk, pyrotechnic intellectualizing, varieties of irony, and droll humor. Fiction writing in the 2000s extends into new territory the criticism of arbitrary arrest, detention, torture, and the general climate of fear. Recent Syrian novels contain plots that revolve around themes of conspiracy and state control, ultimately purporting to pierce the veil of ideology and obscurity that surrounds the practice of politics, which in recent years has come to be described as the functioning of a "*mukhābarāt* state." All three novels examined in this chapter address the problem of authoritarianism in complicated ways. Constrained between the long-standing dialectic of mimesis—the visceral depiction of reality—and allegory—moral judgments of an existential condition—how might these novels open up a space for interrogating the place and the politics of humor and laughter, of silence and sound, of repression and freedom in contemporary Syria? All of these novels wind up at common sorts of existential conundrums: how one can or ought to revive moral agency under conditions in which it has been evacuated from the modern Syrian subject. In response, some of the burning questions for writers (and their readers) might be, for example, Who gets to have the last laugh? How, when, or why does one get to do so?

The depiction of the leader, dictatorship, the security state, and the social consequences of political repression in *The Silence and the Roar* (*al-Ṣamt wa-l-Ṣakhab*) by Nihad Sirees operates in the domain of allegory and satire, much like the films of Durayd Lahham (Chapter 3).[23] The gradual transformation of Syrian authoritarian culture has allowed the emergence and coalescence of literary forms that take greater liberties in criticizing the regime through irony and other humorous styles. *The Silence and the Roar* is Sirees's most politically charged novel to date. Born in Aleppo in 1950, Sirees traveled abroad to study civil engineering, eventually earning a master's degree in 1976. Although he continued working part-time as a licensed engineer, Sirees wrote television serials including the commercially successful *Thurayyā* (directed by Haitham Haqqi), plays, children's drama, and historical novels set in Aleppo. These include *al-Kūmīdiyā al-Fallāḥiyya* (*The Peasant Comedy*) (1990), *Khān al-Ḥarīr* (*The Silk Market*, 2004, which also appeared as a popular television drama), and *Rīyāḥ al-Shamāl* (*North Winds*) (1989/1993). Sirees lampooned the deployment of party officials and bureaucrats into the countryside to promote developmentalist aims of the state but also to command loyalty to the ruling ideology of the party. Conversely he sent up the unprecedented deluge of rural-urban migrants in Aleppo in the aftermath of these rural modernization campaigns, the fodder for Sirees's social critique in his earlier novels *Ḥālat Shaghaf* (*States of Passion*) (1998) and *al-Kūmīdiyā al-Fallāḥiyya*.[24]

The Silence and the Roar takes up the problem of the individual in a society dominated and disciplined by a dictator, a repressive state apparatus, and "The Party."[25] Its time frame is one twenty-four-hour period in an unnamed city, which bears a striking resemblance to Sirees's native Aleppo, on the occasion of another all too familiar state-sponsored march. This first-person narrative is told from the perspective of Fathi Sheen, a hapless writer and intellectual who is unemployed and down on his luck after straying from the dictates of the cultural establishment, which has resulted in his consignment to oblivion and social death. Following a brief run-in with security agents at the march, when Fathi tries to fight them off a young man they are arbitrarily beating, the agents confiscate his ID and inform him he must now pay a visit to *mukhābarāt* headquarters in order to retrieve it.

Meanwhile, Fathi has been involved with a woman named Lama, whom he has been unable to marry for both personal and financial reasons. Perhaps adding insult to injury, Fathi's widowed mother is romantically pursued by the nefarious party functionary Ha'il 'Ali Hasan, a man who owes his meteoric rise to power to a stroke of dumb luck: at a public event in the small, remote town where he once lived, Ha'il instinctively reached out his hands to protect "the Leader" from falling, earning a spot in the dictator's intimate coterie of advisers. But Ha'il has an ulterior motive for marrying Fathi's mother: to return Fathi back to the ideological fold, to convince him to start writing again in the service of the regime. This meta-narrative of intellectual co-optation by the regime—the literal but also psychosexual union of a regime official with Fathi's mother—is reinforced as Fathi reclaims his ID, his very physical identity, from the *mukhābarāt*. In other words, Fathi needs to figure out the practical matter of how to recover his ID as well as the existential matter of whether to collaborate or resist under the emotional strain of his mother's prospective relationship with Ha'il.

The silence and the roar of the title index Fathi's extreme sensitivity to sound. The roar metonymizes the incoherent blathering of an authoritarian regime with little credibility in the eyes of its citizenry. Some of the most beautiful passages in the novel have to do with how Fathi conceives of both the deeply personal and the potentially political nature of sound itself. "I wished that all the man-made sounds would fall silent, leaving only the soft sounds of nature, like those made by the breeze when it blows through strong, leafy trees."[26] But Fathi is no radical pastoralist. "I'm not talking about absolute silence."

> That's impossible anyway and I'm not asking for it. What I mean instead is the silence that allows for those gentle sounds that are all around us to actually reach our ears. Noise prevents them from doing so; it kills them. . . . I imagined how many beautiful and tender sounds are lost to us because of the noise made by our noble politicians, their vehicles and their ways of exporting the revolution. . . . The most beautiful thing in the entire universe is the silence that allows us to hear soft and distant sounds.[27]

In the end, the dialectic between silence and roar comes to represent the binary logic through which the regime frames the world. Silence becomes a politicized habit, as Lama reminds Fathi during one of their discussions about the ethics of writing on behalf of the regime. Although silence is not always an expedient choice when one's life is at stake, Fathi manages to find room to valorize silence—at least theoretically. Fathi resents the fact that Ha'il has forced him to choose between "the silence of prison" and the "roar of the regime"; he is admonished to be careful lest he find himself confronted with "the silence of the grave." In the end, Fathi subverts this false choice between the silence and the roar by embracing (and perhaps fetishizing) laughter.

Irony is a humorous resource in the discursive repertoire of critics and opponents of autocratic regimes. Syrian writers rely on various deployments of humor in order to poke fun at the party. One recurrent theme is the attribution of political and cultural symbolism to prose and poetry—and the distinction between the two—most often valorizing the former as the purview of freethinking individuals and disparaging the latter as exemplifying the party's simplicity and therefore intellectual bankruptcy. In *al-Mutarjim al-Khā'in* (*The Treasonous Translator*), the 2008 novel by the indefensibly underappreciated Syrian novelist Fawwaz Haddad, for example, the protagonist, Hamid Salim, becomes convinced that a well-known writer, Sharif Husni, is making both real and rhetorical attacks against him for his work as a translator and public intellectual. While trying to come up with a strategy to defend himself, Hamid bumps into a journalist who writes about economics for the newspaper where Husni works and who tells him that Husni is responsible for having sent people to jail and that his could be the same fate:

> "Is [Husni] the one who sent him there?"
>
> "Who else? He wrote a report to the *mukhābarāt* in which he accused him of writing stories filled with anti-government and anti-Party references. Tell me, who would dare to ask about this, the Writer's Union, his friends, his family?!"

> "The Party wouldn't allow that to happen."
> "What do you know about what the Party would or wouldn't allow?"
> "Don't tell me Party members don't read."
> "The Party is mad about poetry, at certain times, on nationalist occasions. But they don't like literature, and if they read it, it's only in order to ban it."[28]

Beyond a jab at the arbitrariness of the party and its censorship regime, here is a critique of the ideological uses of poetry that resonates with several moments in *The Silence and the Roar*. In one moment of foreshadowing, Fathi muses about the relationship between poetry and prose:

> We are a people who love poetry so much that we love things that only resemble poetry. We might even be satisfied with only occasionally rhyming speech, regardless of its content. . . . Prose is oriented toward rational minds and individuals whereas poetry directs and is directed towards the masses. . . . Poetry inspires zealotry and melts away individual personality, whereas prose molds the rational mind, individuality and personality. . . . My works and prose writings are the imaginations of a traitor and a fucking cunt, as the man in khaki was kind enough to remind me a little while ago.[29]

Rather than portraying poetry, say, as the cultural patrimony of the Syrian citizenry, the Arab nation, or the Muslim *umma*, both Haddad and Sirees take an ironic stance toward poetic form.[30] This turns farcical when, at another point in *The Silence and the Roar*, an entire institutional apparatus is literally unearthed beneath party headquarters, where poetry is instrumentalized in the service of state power as an industrious underground hive of cultural workers slave away at sloganeering for the commemoration and reinforcement of party authority, hegemony, and legitimation. One of these workers hopes Fathi will join them, but Fathi prefers to stay on the margins, out of the limelight, to observe the world around him and, in the process, open a window for the reader onto some of the absurd dimensions of these fictionalized Syrian landscapes. In their exchange, Fathi asks:

> "But, I mean, who comes up with the sayings and the slogans that you put on the posters?"
> Pointing toward another room, he said, "There's a special team whose members are specialists in psychology and education. Comrades, intellectuals and poets who work twelve hours a day coming up with slogans or writing poetry for the

> masses to recite at marches, which are then printed on posters or published in the media and online."
>
> "That is very special work."
>
> "Indeed, it's tremendous educational and emotional labor as well because the matter involves affection, that is, the affection the masses have for the Leader. It's never easy work . . . The best poems and slogans are those that somebody can remember after only hearing them once."
>
> "It's an important consideration for choosing slogans."[31]

Fathi feigns indifference at the sight of this literalization of an entity he had earlier theorized, and his deadpan response is one way in which political criticism may be creatively launched through humor. Such depictions of the banality of poetry might be read as a critique of "traditional" forms of Arabic culture as well as a send-up of the cynical packaging and reinvention of the "traditional" by the progressive, secular Baʿthist regime. Even more revealing, here is a wholesale rejection of the perceived artificiality of Asadist-Baʿthist aesthetic ideology, inexpertly produced in underground workshops.

Laughter is portrayed as a discursive as well as political weapon in the arsenal of these fictional characters. "We used to take revenge on our situation through laughter," Fathi declares before equivocating: "But laughter is accursed chattering that only exposes us and gets us into uncomfortable situations."[32] When a party cadre asks for a moment of silence at a ceremony in honor of a recently deceased intellectual, the reader quickly learns that this functionary is also dedicating the event to the recently deceased father of the leader. In response, Lama fails to keep herself from bursting out in laughter. She is clearly responding to the absurdity of an out-of-touch regime. Her laughter might also be read as letting off steam (*tanfīs*). Another moment when what might be considered "laughter out of place" successfully subverting the power of political repression comes when Fathi is thrown into solitary confinement underneath party headquarters for failing to agree to return to work for the regime.

> This was the first time I had even been detained. I had not even been reprimanded once during my military service. I measured the length and width of the cell by my steps to calculate that it was three by six steps. Then I sat down against the wall, taking pleasure in the quiet and adjusting the bandage around my wrist. . . . I tried to figure out whether I was truly happy there or had deceived

> myself into believing I was. Arriving at the conclusion that I was really quite comfortable, I laughed out loud because the tranquility had calmed me down.[33]

This is a far cry from the brave, defiant voice of resistance in some late twentieth-century Arabic literature.[34] Critics might claim that this derisive attitude toward authoritarian power is naive, unconsciously privileged, or even dismissive of suffering in Syrian incarceration. But another view of this type of bonding through laughter and release would be framed in terms of an aesthetics of solidarity, wherein affective ties are strengthened between Fathi and Lama through their *speaking-with*, which in this regard entails laughing-together or laughing-with. Furthermore, this is not unlike the strained romantic relationship between Nada and Salem in *The Extras* as they similarly bond, dissolving their fears and stunted desires in laughter, improvisation, and touch (Figure 32).

The Silence and the Roar concludes with Lama and Fathi falling asleep together at the end of their very long day. The final scene is a dream sequence, suggesting, perhaps, both the irreality and irreconcilability of the situation in which Fathi finds himself. In this dreamscape, Lama and Fathi bear witness to

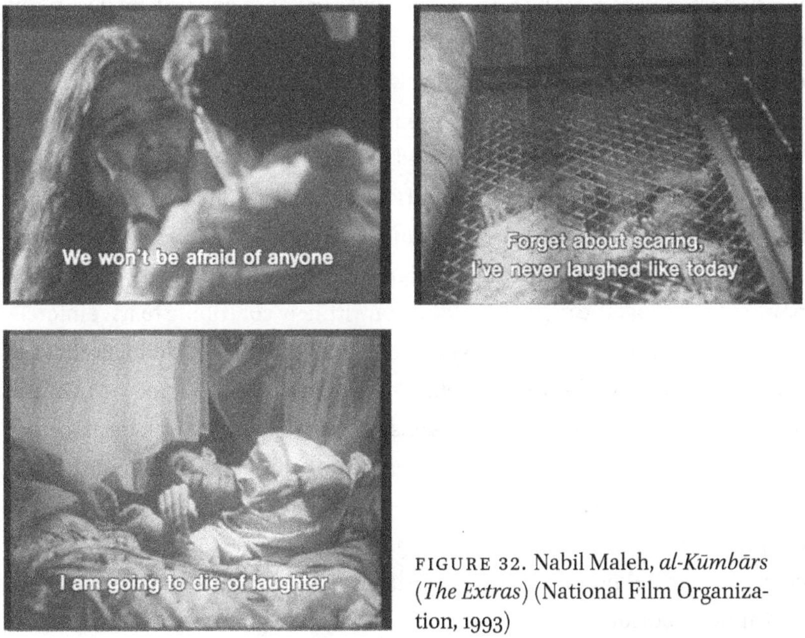

FIGURE 32. Nabil Maleh, *al-Kūmbārs* (*The Extras*) (National Film Organization, 1993)

Fathi's mother and Mr. Ha'il in a violently climactic scene, but in response to that brutality they simply fall down laughing. It is not obvious how to sort through the thorny ethical implications and myriad political effects of this attempt to transform authoritarianism and its violence into a joke or a comedic narrative. The strategic deployment of laughter in *The Silence and the Roar* subverts a false choice between the silence of complicit acquiescence and the roar of violent repression. It is in this sense that Fathi, Lama, and presumably the reader can aspire to have the last laugh, even at the risk of punishment, censorship, or irrelevance. "To this day, whenever we're together," Fathi says of his relationship with Lama, "we still laugh whenever the Party is mentioned."[35] Fathi prefigures a kind of postpartisan (or even postideological) Syrian subjectivity; when it comes to Baʿthism and its obligatory genuflection, he is "over it," it might be said. But the concluding scene, like other moments in the novel, gives the impression that escape from the strictures of this repressive authoritarian society might be accomplished through retreat (or perhaps indulgence) in dreams, fantasies, sexual pleasure, and absurdist derision. Perhaps this is as it should be, though. "In one way or another," Agnes Heller writes, with an insight that offers one potential interpretive key to the end of *The Silence and the Roar*, "one of the main characters of a comic novel always lives in another world; he dwells not in a pragmatic world, but in a dream, an illusion, in his own phantasm or phantasmagoria."[36] Fathi may be a dreamer, but he is not the only one.

An ironic perspective permits political and imaginative acrobatics that would seem implausible in hard-boiled realism. But what are the ethical implications or political effects of literary or discursive transformations of authoritarianism into another sort of sound, into laughter, into a joke? Does this upended representation of authoritarianism in literature actually subvert the power of an autocratic regime, or does it unwittingly contribute to its reinforcement in the cultural universe of writers and readers? Is there a danger that the truth of the regime, the wizard behind the curtain, will be exposed? On the other hand, is it possible that the exercise of imagination in such terms serves to further insulate the regime from legitimate political criticism in the real world? Is the simple naivete of sloganeers and paid bureaucrats supposed to undermine the fearmongering of the regime or ensure that the true working of power remain unknown? In *The Silence and the Roar*, Fathi acquires a surfeit of eyewitness information that leads him to take the regime and its minions less seriously. By transforming the juggernaut of Syrian authoritarianism into sound, Sirees endows his characters with some measure of control over that infernal noise; in satirizing the ostensibly all-powerful regime, characters acquire power that would be more difficult to muster in reality. Fathi literally has the last laugh, even if fundamental questions remain about the relationship between laughter—humor and comedy more broadly—and politics.

Is laughter an adequate response to authoritarianism, censorship, and state repression, though? Slavoj Žižek argues against the "underlying belief in the liberating, antitotalitarian force of laughter, of ironic distance."[37] This is a fair point that needs to be taken seriously without slipping into the trap of instrumentalizing laughter. Theodor Adorno similarly contends that laughter tends to benefit the powerful even when it accompanies satire, which "prefer[s] to side with the stronger party"; irony, by contrast, "convicts its object by presenting it as what it purports to be; and without passing judgment, as if leaving a blank for the observing subject, measures it against its being-in-itself."[38] A nuanced understanding of laughter as psychological, social, and political phenomena can harbor multiple meanings. A different way of apprehending this form of humor is proposed by film and television critic Jerry Palmer. In his view,

> humour is neither essentially liberatory nor conservative, for its nature is such that it always refuses to make any commitment to any 'opinion' about anything (except of course the opinion that levity is appropriate under these circumstances); its very basis is ambivalence.[39]

Furthermore, the ambivalence of humor forged in the encounter between ruler and ruled under authoritarian circumstances is often refracted through a lens of absurdity, a surreal commentary on the deformed social contract between a regime and its people. "The autocrat," for Achille Mbembe, "is thus at once a site, a moment, a time-span, and a multiplicity present and to come. He challenges the very condition of mortality; he is 'for life.'"[40]

Even though characters in *The Silence and the Roar* laugh out loud in the face of party bureaucrats, they might also be understood as contributing to the legitimation of an absurdist regime that depends on the apathetic resignation of its citizenry. And even if throughout the novel there are very real markers of life in contemporary Syria, whether this is an effective challenge to the discourses and practices of Syrian authoritarianism remains undecidable. By the same token, given the psychological and material terrorism deployed by the regime against the everyday lives of the author-narrator and other characters—in a manner strikingly similar to that seen in Mazin ʿArafa's 2017 novel *al-Gharānīq* (*The Cranes*) (Chapter 6)—it remains uncertain whether the novel is capable of exceeding the space of the regime's ideological universe even as it points up the laughable contradictions of its ostensibly popular cultural revolution.

PORTRAIT OF THE *MUKHĀBARĀTĪ* AS A YOUNG MAN: ROSA YASEEN HASAN'S *ROUGH DRAFT* (*BRŪFĀ*)

> Eavesdropping dramatizes a primal human curiosity to know, and to know those aspects of others' lives that we are not supposed to know, those that they wish to keep hidden from us. This desire to know is linked to pleasure, although specific instances of eavesdropping while inducing pleasure for some, create pain for others.
>
> —Ann Elizabeth Gaylin, *Eavesdropping in the Novel from Austen to Proust*[41]

Rosa Yaseen Hasan was born in Damascus in 1974 and studied architecture at Damascus University. She published her first collection of short stories in 2000 and has published four novels since then, including *Abnūs* (*Ebony*) (2004), which won the Hanna Mina literature prize; *Nīghātīf* (*Negative*) (2008), which is what Hasan calls a "documentary novel" that tracks the experiences of female political prisoners in Syria, including Islamists, experimenting with multivocality as a means of narrating a collective story as well as muddying the boundaries between fact and fiction; *Ḥurrās al-Hawāʾ* (*Guardians of Air*); and *Al-Ladhīna Masaḥahum al-Siḥr: Min Shaẓāyā al-Ḥikāyāt* (*Those Touched by Magic: Fragments of Stories*).[42] Hasan was a critical voice in the nonviolent Syrian uprising from the earliest days of the revolt in 2011 when she still lived in Damascus, and has remained a stalwart revolutionary intellectual since fleeing to Germany in 2012.[43] Her 2011 novel *Brūfā* (*Rough Draft*) sheds light on the practice of surveillance and its relationship to politics and everyday life.[44] A daydreaming secret agent with long-standing interests in literature and philosophy languishes in a lonely listening booth in a state security services station (*farʿ*) in the northwestern coastal city of Latakia. It is perhaps a consequence of his grounding in the study of philosophy that this *mukhābarātī* is inclined to question the ethics—even the epistemology—of his role in the state surveillance regime. The rough draft (*brūfā*) of the title is "the novel" itself, his collection of notes and narratives culled from years in the listening booth.[45] Through aural engagement with the individuals he surveils, the *mukhābarātī* attempts to spin out a rough draft of his first novel, which is subject to revision and reconceptualization throughout the text and which he envisions as true to life, based on actual events and feelings he is capable of accessing directly through his recorder. *Rough Draft* swerves from one narrative position to another, often without warning, although each chapter indicates at the outset the voice or range of voices that will be included: third-person omniscient narration (understood to be the voice of the *mukhābarātī* himself), ostensibly verbatim transcripts of phone conversations, the *mukhābarātī*'s diary entries, his tentative reconstructions of events, and even the thought processes of characters. The text is peppered with footnotes, the *mukhābarātī*'s marginalia, notes to self, and proposed revisions or embellishments. There remains something unsettled and unsettling about this unfinished, perhaps even sloppy "rough draft" that has improbably made its way into the reader's hand as a published book.[46] The material constitutes a private space that the reader somehow winds up surveilling. In this sense, the reader's perspective not only parallels the *mukhābarātī*'s view but also suggests a gaze above and beyond his own, one that knows things he (and presumably the reader) does not. The novel in progress he believes he is drafting on the sly has already been captured by a broader web of signification, namely the recording apparatus of the regime itself, even if it gestures toward the wider world represented by the reader's subject position.

Hasan uncovers the mechanics of state control—interrogating the surveillance apparatus as a literary device—through a range of narrative strategies, including three first-person vignettes from the *mukhābarāt* agent himself: one at the beginning, a brief interlude in the middle, and one at the end. His first entry, dated Thursday, January 11, 2005, sets the scene. Sound is striking, synesthetic: the voices he hears have "a color, a mood, and an individuality." In a turn of phrase that might be taken as ironic, he claims that his sense of hearing is his "only weapon."[47] If audition is a weapon, though, the *mukhābarātī* does not intend to use it exclusively in his patriotic service to the state. There is an educational and edifying potential inherent in the surveillance enterprise itself: "Sound is my gateway to knowledge and discovery, [and] since I am the one who listens, I listened, I learned and discovered."[48] The *mukhābarātī* turns out to be more interested in capturing the everyday challenges, aspirations, and life experiences of those he repeatedly calls "my characters" than he is in carrying out orders or doing his duty to protect the homeland. "I was interested in the private lives of these people, and I recorded them for my own good, for my own interest," but he insists that their stories "would not be complete if I didn't complete them."[49] The first-person narration in these sections contrasts with the free indirect discourse articulated by an omniscient third-person narrator elsewhere as the indeterminacy of the *mukhābarātī*'s "I" comes to mirror some aspects of the disembodied surveillance and the regime's invasion of privacy.[50]

The interlude comprises a statement jotted down a few months after the *mukhābarātī* has begun his compulsory service, in which he provides a glimpse of his personal background and family life. Dated August 14, 2004, the entry announces that becoming a surveillance agent has made him feel as though he is being transformed "from an executioner into a victim."[51] One might expect that his position of relative privilege in the security services will insulate him from the dangers associated with living under a brutal authoritarian dictatorship. From this assumed position of victimhood, however, he rails against retrograde positions taken by his father, a man proud of his ʿAlawī heritage who used to go on and on about rampant unpatriotic disloyalty in the country, "about the future of the [the ʿAlawī community] if their rule were to end, about the need for our loyalty to [the ʿAlawī sect] in order to safeguard its existence."[52] There has been a great deal of scholarly and public debate concerning the extent to which the post-1970 Syrian Baʿth regime deserves to be labeled an ʿAlawī regime.[53] It is worth recalling the apt words of Eberhard Kienle: "A monopoly by ʿAlawites [of state power] is not the same thing as saying a monopoly by the ʿAlawites."[54] Still, the *mukhābarātī*'s father is proud to watch his son embark on his military service as a member of the ʿAlawī community, and he is happy because his son ". . . was going to leave behind teaching philosophy once and for all and volunteer in the *mukhābarāt*." The *mukhābarātī* recalls his father posing a rhetorical question to friends at a dinner party: "What do we need with philosophy and philosophizing, all the philosophers are . . . traitors." Philosophy and philosophizing are unjustifiable in this vision of duty and country; his father insists that joining the *mukhābarāt* is "the way for him to truly serve his country, and this is how he's going to participate in protecting it from the devils who want to torch it." His father ends on a scoffing note: "Philosophy, he says, philosophy."[55]

Even as his father inveighs against perceived treason—a trope that recurs in Samar Yazbek's *Lahā Marāyā* (*In Her Mirrors*), discussed later—the *mukhābarātī* steals another moment of reflection, ruing the fact that he has been unfaithful by passively maintaining a sham engagement to his fiancée, Madiha. Meanwhile, he recognizes other infidelities, at one point analogizing treason against the homeland referenced by his father to betrayal of a more diffuse kind:

> In that moment in particular I thought about treason. Not treason in its well-known meanings, but rather betrayal in another sense I had started to feel. The betrayal if I were to reveal the secrets of my characters to the authorities, because for the first time I feel as though there are others, others who have something to live for and to talk about and to feel. For the first time I try to understand what others believe!! Is that because I, for the first time in my life, was forced to listen without being able to talk? In many conversations I had always wanted to scream and cut one of them off or comment on an idea I thought was wrong or to voice my opinion or . . . but after a few seconds of screaming I would discover that the walls of the monitoring room were the only things that could hear me.[56]

It is ironic to contemplate this experience of betrayal even as the *mukhābarātī* is betraying the confidence of "his" characters and the integrity of the security apparatus itself by sharing so much. What would it mean, moreover, psychologically or politically, if state security agents were to believe that the transmission of secrets to the authorities constituted outright betrayal? Who are the authorities if not him? Does this imply that the *mukhābarāt* and the people are joined through bonds of loyalty and solidarity that the regime threatens to (and sometimes does) undermine? Would it logically follow that the *mukhābarātī* is having an affair either with the state or with the people? Or both? This passage might also be read ironically, as the *mukhābarātī*, a listener for the state, purports to be unaware that the reader—and not only the walls of the listening booth—are surveilling his listening. Returning to the relationship between sound and power, the *mukhābarātī* asks, "What is all this that is happening to me? What is this tyranny [*ṭughyān*] that sound practices upon me?"[57] The narrator imbues something as seemingly commonplace as sound with a robust authority generally associated with political tyranny.[58] The contradictory experience of being embodied as a subject of the regime while also serving as its agent—an unseen, all-hearing ear of the unseen, all-knowing state—destabilizes the *mukhābarātī*.

The dysphoric anxiety encountered by this eavesdropping security agent pales in comparison with the difficult lives of "his" characters. For example, Saba 'Abd al-Rahman is a young woman who has had nothing but bad luck in matters of love. After walking out on her abusive husband, bloody and battered, in May 2000—potentially a meaningful date one month before the death of President Hafiz al-Asad and the succession to power by his son Bashar—she attempts to get her life back in order even as she serially deals with men who are no good. Perhaps as a consequence of those abusive relationships, or simply because of her own liberated sexuality, Saba engages in sex and other uninhibited amorous activities. At one point, Mihyar al-Salimi, who is beginning to develop feelings for Saba, invites her over for a romantic dinner of grilled fish and vegetables. Saba arrives bearing vodka, grapefruit juice, and a pornographic video. Mihyar is not aroused, though, and becomes mildly disoriented when she aggressively unzips his pants.[59] Mihyar is studying at the Fine Arts Academy, working part-time as a waiter in a coffee shop. He also has to take care of his mother, Hala al-Sammaqi, who used to work as a secretary in a dentist's office and a clerk in a lingerie shop before she was disabled in a freak accident.[60] Mihyar is hardly a well-adjusted man, as we discover he is prone to using blood from his mother's soiled bandages in some of his paintings.[61] Another character, Hani al-'Abbas, confides in his friend al-Ayham al-Sarim that he has a sexual fetish for mannequins, but only because he is unable to act on, let alone consummate, his undying love for his sister, Lamya al-'Abbas.[62]

Unorthodox social behavior is not expressed only in sexual terms. The characters observed by the *mukhābarātī* are also fascinated by esoteric spiritual pursuits, as when Hala al-Sammaqi puts on seances to communicate with the dead, including her husband who was assassinated—she is convinced—either by the state security forces or by Islamist terrorists; she also regularly asks her son Mihyar to procure books and lectures on tape from the Maharishi Society in India that are available in Beirut. Toward the end of the novel, after the death of his mother, Mihyar refuses to participate in a communal burial ritual, embarking instead on a group pilgrimage to India, a "metaphysical journey" that he believes will demonstrate his "loyalty" to her and her memory.[63]

Through these episodic vignettes that chronicle the lives of the *mukhābarātī*'s" characters, the reader is invited to bear witness to the exercise of state power by a representative of the regime. Saba moves back in with her mother in Latakia, where she manages to recover some stability as well as to reckon with what she perceives as her relative privilege:

> In fact, my existence as the daughter of an army officer made my childhood much easier than that of many of my peers . . . my existence as a daughter of an army officer made the horrible eighties pass us by like years of felicity, and our house was constantly filled with bottles of whiskey and Pepsi cola and sweets and sacks of fresh fish. With time it seemed to me that I wasn't a part of my generation: the generation of the seventies. . . . So while my friends would spend hours waiting in long lines for their turn at the consumer cooperatives in order to get rice or tea or cooking oil, I wouldn't go to school except in Peugeots driven by a handsome driver usually dressed in a military uniform.[64]

For Saba, her generation is damaged and deprived, suffering wide-ranging sexual and social pathologies, subject to strictures placed on Syrian society in the political and economic spheres under Hafiz al-Asad. Here is a matter-of-fact, almost nostalgic description of class privilege and clientelist favoritism in Baʿthist Syria. While this scathing critique of regime injustice might seem to be grounds for further investigation by an agent of the state, the *mukhābarātī* is more interested in how that sentiment may be a key to understanding Saba (taken as a metonym for her generation). The *mukhābarātī* relegates to a footnote the possibility of including a more detailed, "panoramic account of the Syrian political scene during the eighties, a map of alliances and struggles."[65] One wonders whether the *mukhābarātī* has in fact unwittingly completed such a work of social and political mapping, albeit one that remains incomplete, in the form of his rough draft.

A more comprehensive reckoning with Syria during the eighties would also have to grapple with political sectarianism. Not only did the personalized leadership of Hafiz al-Asad secure the consolidation of Baʿthist rule through the army, the party and the bureaucracy; it also engaged in intermittent civil conflict with armed as well as nonviolent opposition from leftists and Islamists, echoes of which reverberate today. The violence of the Syrian regime during this period is nowhere better attested than by the 1982 Hama massacre, in which as many as 20,000 people perished. Several times the *mukhābarātī* reveals his own ʿAlawī background as being essential to his family's pride in the work that he does for the state in defense of the homeland. The nature of ʿAlawī belief, specifically metempsychosis, or the transmigration of souls (*al-taqammuṣ*; *tanāsul al-arwāḥ*)—a theme that also runs through Samar Yazbek's *In Her Mirrors*, as we will see—crops up several times. For example, Hala al-Sammaqi, who, again, suffered paralysis after a domestic accident and now is in need of constant care from her son Mihyar, is convinced that her condition must be punishment for something she had done in a previous life. Mihyar quips that, in order to deserve such a fate, she must bear responsibility for the malevolent (re)incarnations of Hitler, Mussolini, Pinochet, and Genghis Khan. Hala laughs, but insists that Mihyar recognize that "life is much deeper than this form that is visible to us. The non-material body is the foundation."[66] The vagueness of this statement notwithstanding, the sentiment seems to be reflective of an interest on the part of the *mukhābarātī* himself in how "his" characters discuss the relationship between appearance and essence, between illusion and reality, and the capacity to casually joke about ʿAlawī beliefs generally not discussed in public. Beyond this reference to esoteric ʿAlawī cosmology, therefore, the *mukhābarātī* himself operates in a conceptual universe where philosophical problems are not excluded from the discourse and experience of everyday life.

Mihyar does not put much stock in the notion that belonging to the ʿAlawī community necessarily has any advantages in Syria, though. His friend al-Ayham al-Sarim, a medical doctor trained in Libya, claims he was denied entry to a Syrian medical school because he was not a member of the Baʿth Party. Mihyar insists that he knows plenty of people who studied there who are not in the party. "Then they didn't accept me because I'm not from the ruling sect," al-Ayham responds, using a common epithet for the ʿAlawīs. Although Mihyar tries to argue back ("I know a lot of people who aren't . . . "), al-Ayham interrupts him, saying, "Don't fight with me Mihyar . . . they didn't accept me for some reason that has nothing to do with my ability . . . of that I'm certain."[67] Party membership, sectarian affiliation, and bureaucratic necessity are all grounds for corruption and exclusion.

But these political issues that govern his characters are often incidental to the *mukhābarātī*, obscured by his own concern with literary matters. For example, the agent expresses metafictional ambivalence, fundamentally undecided as to whether or not he ought to be a character in the text at all. In one of his placeholding footnotes, the narrator shares:

> I hadn't yet decided whether I would write about myself as a character in the novel, that is, as the narrator or the writer. That's a tired technique anyway. If I do decide that I'm going to be a character in the novel, I can indicate here how I felt the listening device emitting a tingly heat.[68]

This footnote is betrayed by the obvious inclusion of the *mukhābarātī* as a character in the novel. Moreover, the narrator often uses the footnote in particular as a repository for his ambivalence, hinting that he might have chosen not to allow himself to exist immediately alongside the lives of his characters but rather to be kept at the level of the omniscient voice in the frame story. To be sure—and this is one of the most striking aspects of the novel—the *mukhābarātī* has included himself in his notes alongside his characters. He has been a character all along.

After nearly a year spent lurking in the shadows of his characters' lives, the *mukhābarātī* is unable to turn up a shred of evidence of subversive or seditious activity. There are strange moments in which the security agent notices that his subjects of surveillance are aware they are being monitored. For example, Hani al-ʿAbbas, who is in love with his sister and displaces that unrequited affection onto his fetish for mannequins, appears to be approaching a breakdown. "I heard him whisper to Mihyar al-Salimi that he felt that there was someone monitoring his phone calls," the *mukhābarātī* notes, but then Hani continues his conversation, "rid of (the delusion of) his surveillance."[69] Why the security agent describes this surveillance parenthetically as a delusion (*wahm*) is never explained. A clue may be found in the concluding section of the novel, though, in the *mukhābarātī*'s personal reflections dated Friday, January 12, 2005: "Spying on other lives isn't my life!" he exclaims. "It's a funny thing, really, for me to write: the other, the enemy, outside the circle, or whatever that can be called, it's strange for me to write down their memory in my language. As if my ear were transformed from a spying tool into a means of understanding."[70] It would almost seem that the creative aims of the *mukhābarātī*'s surveillance, his interest in becoming a novelist, negates or at least diminishes his understanding of the act of surveillance as an invasion of privacy. Calling his eavesdropping or his social research or his quest for literary inspiration "surveillance" amounts to delusion for the *mukhābarātī*. In the end, however, he vows not to "give a second chance to people who didn't have a second chance," and dutifully reports to his superiors because "I felt that I would betray my job if I hid any information I knew."[71] But there remains a gap between the interests of the regime and the desires of this individual who operates its machinery. "I wasn't interested in general activities of my characters or their political secrets," the *mukhābarātī* writes. "I wasn't interested in their affiliations or their doctrinal debates or what they did against the authorities. What interested me was present and written here in my leather briefcase along with my laptop. That's all that interests me. That's all that interests me in life now."[72] The narrative arc of these lives is less important than the fact that they constitute raw material for the aspiring novelist.[73]

Ultimately, the *mukhābarātī* and, by extension, the Syrian state security apparatus, like the East German security state described by Stephen Brockman, "views writing as a method of control which will make it the lord and master of its flesh and blood characters, rather than a partner in a conversation with them."[74] At the same time, however, the text asks the reader to (re)consider the humanity of agents of the Syrian dictatorship by focusing on their ambivalent position at once inside and outside of the regime. From this vantage point, the *mukhābarātī* is capable of exercising a different sort of agency, one that criticizes the confining project of surveillance even as the he enjoys his ability to use the information he has amassed for his own purposes, to generate (real or imagined) intimate connections between the observer and the observed, the hearer and the heard, perhaps even to imaginatively disrupt the logic underwriting the security state itself.

Hasan dedicates *Rough Draft* to what she calls "her generation," the "generation of the seventies." Everyone caught up in the gears of the regime during this period, even those who would seem to have an enviable sinecure in the *mukhābarāt*, are susceptible to sexual deviance, spiritual aimlessness, generalized anomie, and psychological despair. Critics Dima Wannous and Khalil Suwaylih—both accomplished Syrian novelists in their own right—praise Hasan for her verve in depicting the trials and tribulations of this "disappointed generation."[75] Meanwhile, Nabil Sulayman takes Hasan to task for concocting an implausibly omniscient narrator, ventriloquizing through the *mukhābarātī* in order to ruminate about matters of highbrow intellectual concern.[76] Such criticism of the Arabic novel is nothing new; Stefan G. Meyer faults the modernist experimentation of the 1960s, for example, because "instead of a dialogue between distinct voices, we have merely an authorial voice in dialogue with itself."[77] To be sure, *Rough Draft* repeatedly challenges the reader as it (re)creates this character who believes only the walls are listening. It may seem implausible to some that a secret agent should be so erudite and naive simultaneously. It is reasonable to question the extent to which a "reliable" or compelling narrative from the perspective of the state security services is even possible, but the humanizing of the *mukhābarāt* agent is one of the most striking aspects of *Rough Draft*. The *mukhābarātī* subverts state power in order to pursue dilettantish aims. At the same time, the inclusion of fragmented voices in this polyphonic narrative suggests the anomie of an often depoliticized Syrian populace scraping by under a brutal authoritarian regime. The reader is reminded that ordinary people appear in the "transcript"—are included in the political or historical record— only by virtue of the *mukhābarātī*'s surveillance; the very conditions of possibility for narrative itself to break through the written text are structured by regime surveillance.

Rough Draft may be profitably compared to communist and postcommunist literature and film produced in the Soviet Union and the Eastern Bloc countries.[78] In *The Lives of Others* (*Das Leben der Anderen*), for example, the 2006 Academy Award winner for best foreign-language film by Florian Henckel von Donnersmarck that explored the culture of listening under Stasi rule in the German Democratic Republic, a state security agent eavesdrops on a well-known playwright and his wife, but when he discovers that the minister of culture has romantic intentions toward the wife, the Stasi agent finds himself caught between conflicting professional commitments and protective feelings toward the couple.[79] The *mukhābarāt* novel might be read against what John Griffith Urang calls the "erotics of surveillance" in his discussion of *The Lives of Others* and other East German cultural production, in which the security state is not reducible to impersonal or technologically driven social control but diffuses into the spaces and experiences of intimate life.[80] Conspiracy and conspiracy theories are turned on their heads. A "conspiratorial public sphere" under conditions of "state surveillance also creates the conditions for the 'conspiratorial' mode, that intimate confederacy of writer and reader that raises the stakes, heightens the drama, overdetermines the significance of the communication that passes between them."[81] Although Urang enjoys the benefit of hindsight, namely literary and political perspectives from a postcommunist and reunified

Germany while the Asadist-Baʿthist regime remains well in place (for the moment anyway), this approach might throw different light on the Syrian literature of authoritarianism and the *mukhābarāt* novel itself.

A FRACTURED MIRROR FOR PRINCE(SSE)S: SAMAR YAZBEK'S *IN HER MIRRORS* (*LAHĀ MARĀYĀ*)

> And moving through a mirror clear
> That hangs before her all the year,
> Shadows of the world appear . . .
>
> —Alfred Tennyson, "The Lady of Shalott"[82]

> We trust mirrors just as, under normal conditions, we trust our organs of perception.
>
> — Umberto Eco, "Mirrors"[83]

Samar Yazbek was born in 1970 in the northwestern Syrian coastal city of Jableh and studied literature at university before working as a journalist and a screenwriter. She has published nearly a dozen novels and nonfiction books since her first publication in the early 2000s. Her oeuvre has deeply engaged with the problem of authoritarianism in Baʿthist Syria, the politics of ʿAlawī identity and community, questions of gender, and the experience of the individual confronting the violence of state power. Yazbek has been a vital figure in the Syrian revolution since 2011, and her critique of the state's repression of the Syrian people as well as its manipulation of the hearts and minds of the ʿAlawī community in particular grew more pronounced as the Syrian uprising escalated and the situation descended into sectarian civil war. Her most recent writings lean toward politically committed reportage on and about the Syrian war and the global refugee catastrophe.[84]

If *Rough Draft* directly engages with the politics and poetics of domestic espionage, occasionally wrestling with the relationship between the ʿAlawī community and the Syrian Baʿthist regime, Samar Yazbek brings to bear a much more severe condemnation of the *mukhābarāt* state and its intimate forms of surveillance by way of a romantic reenactment of ʿAlawī history and memory.[85] *Lahā Marāyā* (*In Her Mirrors*) (2010) is a tragic romance that continues to track themes—ʿAlawī identity, patriarchy, friendship, political corruption—central to her previous novel *Ṣalṣāl* (*Clay*) (2005). *In Her Mirrors* is the tale of Layla al-Sawi, a washed-up television and film star, and her tormented love affair with Saʿid Nasir, a fellow ʿAlawī who hails from the same village and is a high-ranking military figure with personal connections to the ruling elite. Despite the fact that her family and community have been trampled by the regime he defends, Layla is unable to overcome her attraction to him. Their tortured love story is a kind of fractured ʿAlawī fairy tale set against the backdrop of history, in which the tragic connection linking these two "soul mates" survives the transmigration of their souls.[86]

In Her Mirrors opens with the death of the president, placing the reader squarely in Syria in the year 2000. Having just heard the breaking news, Saʿid Nasir watches the funeral on national television from his mountain retreat in the coastal northwest. He is disgusted to see the president's body borne along by an ordinary cart rather than held aloft on the people's shoulders as that was "how the president came out, from the people, and that's how he should return!"[87] He is racked with guilt for not having been there to arrange "a funeral adequate to the majesty of the leader, the leader who will never die."[88] In addition to a fulsome statement of obsequiousness before the president's legacy, this too is an allusion to the "eternal leader" (*al-qāʾid ilā al-abad*), a common salute to President Hafiz al-Asad in state and party discourse. The phrase owes something to the intellectual genealogy of Baʿthism itself, which turns on the motto "a single Arab nation with an everlasting message" (*umma ʿarabiyya wāḥida dhāt risāla khālida*).

Still in shock over the president's demise, Saʿid Nasir reminisces about formative political experiences he and the leader shared during their tumultuous adolescence, buffeted by coups and military instability. He recalls having told the future president in a discussion about political responsibility, "Security doesn't mean force alone, it means making the people trust in you and entrust themselves to you." The president responded, "The Party needs intelligent and devoted people like you,"[89] an expression that will come to haunt Layla and her family later on.

Layla was serving jail time for political dissidence. On the inside, she had degenerated into an addict hooked on heroin and hashish. Although disheveled and disoriented on her release, Layla is now dead set on piecing together her shattered life. Arriving on the doorstep of the House of Beauty, her salon and longtime hangout in the city, she ruminates on how different it is to be clean than to be using. When she was high, her "magic needle" would transform her into "a princess, or an invisible creature, a transparent creature, unseen, unseeing."[90] If the aural dimensions of surveillance are central to *Rough Draft*, *In Her Mirrors* highlights the political and personal power associated with vision and ways of seeing. As Layla stumbles across the threshold of the salon, her old confidante and stylist Mary tells her "the world is turned upside down outside. The president is dead."[91] Mary was the only one to visit her in prison—until Saʿid Nasir personally denied her request to have visitors—and Layla shared stories of having her head shaved while incarcerated, of constant degradation and abuse, of being gang-raped.[92] With nowhere else to turn, Layla has crashed with Mary, who still lives with her abusive mother. Layla confides in Mary how her mind constantly returns to Saʿid Nasir even as she rebukes herself for wanting to see him despite the fact that he had left her to rot in prison for so long.

The backstory of Layla's family is stitched into the tapestry of ʿAlawī sacred and secular history. She is the granddaughter of a notable ʿAlawī figure from the northwest, Shaykh ʿAli al-Sawi, whose family had fled persecution, settling in a mud house on the outskirts of their village. His son moved to the capital and saved up enough money to build a nicer house on a mountain. Saʿid Nasir's family and others deride Shaykh ʿAli, describing him as a kook only concerned with preserving his collection of books, a special box he imbued with magical properties and containing some yellowing papers—the physical inheritance of the community. Shaykh ʿAli had fought against the French colonial forces, participating in one of the locally organized rebellions that had broken out against foreign intervention in the aftermath of the First World War. Shaykh ʿAli is described as a contemporary of Shaykh Salih al-ʿAli, an ʿAlawī leader who had organized an uprising that acquired mythical status in ʿAlawī collective memory, but who also has had a complicated relationship with Syrian nationalist historiography.[93]

The history and memory of ʿAlawī persecution by the Ottomans and the French remain important to Layla and her family without overshadowing the political repression suffered by Syrians of all sectarian affiliations in the authoritarian present of the novel. Layla's younger brother ʿAli, a medical student, is jailed for political activity. When Layla discovers that ʿAli had been detained and tortured—and that Saʿid Nasir himself had authorized his arrest—she is devastated. ʿAli's interrogation—narrated in a flashback from the perspective of Saʿid Nasir, who was not only present but supervised the proceedings—brings to the fore the politics of identity and community under Baʿthist authoritarian dictatorship. At first Saʿid Nasir offers kind words about ʿAli's family but then condemns him for consorting with scum (*ḥuthāla*):

> "Tell me, ʿAli, how did you meet those scum and become one of them?"
> "Which scum?"
> Saʿid Nasir suppressed his rage. Was this little boy playing with him? Were they not children of the same village, he would have stomped him right then and there in his office, made them take him down to the cellar, where blood and iron and human flesh are mixed together, but he remained calmly silent, then added:
> "You know which scum I'm talking about."
> "Nobody is scum anymore."

Despite his vulnerability to Saʿid Nasir's unchecked power, ʿAli does not back down.

> "You're right. There are no scum left, and we won't allow there to be any more scum. . . . Don't you agree with me that they're scum, though?"
> "I don't. They weren't scum. They just wanted to express their ideas. And you . . . "
> He cut him off with a sharp and angry tone:
> "What did you say? To express their ideas? Just expression, you say?!"
> "That's right, just expression. And you know what I mean. Just a difference of opinion. And because of that you lock all of us up and . . . "
> "Great. Just great. Now you're speaking in the plural, which means that you're . . . anyway, that's not the point. The important thing is that it pains me to see the grandson of Shaykh al-Sawi among those people. Are you of any use for the homeland? We want you . . . you're a doctor, intelligent, a strong young man . . . we could be proud of you."[94]

Saʿid Nasir, in turn, echoes the intimate language the president once used with him, expresses concern for ʿAli, his life, his reputation and that of his family in what we might call, following Urang, "conspiratorial" mode, how language and communication function in intimate spaces of surveillance and repression.[95] The conspiratorial tone of narration mirrors but also potentially subverts the demands of loyalty, solidarity, and identification with the leader and his power. At times cajoling, at times heartfelt, Saʿid Nasir insists that involvement in an opposition party can only come to a bad end:

> "This world is ruled by power alone. And do you know what power is here? Power is for there to be a strong man who rules us."
> "What do you mean by 'us' . . . who do you mean?" 'Ali replied provocatively, having lost his nerve.
> "I mean us . . . me and you and everyone else." Sa'id Nasir conceals his rage again, gets up from his desk and sits down on a chair on the other side of the room, lighting up a cigarette. "Do you know what kind of torture we went through? Take a good look now at our situation, where we once were, how far we've come."

Following this invocation of power and force, 'Ali remains defiant:

> "You think you can convince me that I have to take shelter behind this slogan of yours in order to feel secure? You know better than most that you don't protect us: you're protected by us. You and I both know that . . . "
> Sa'id's calmness began to subside, and he shouted, "What the hell do you know?!"[96]

At this point, the reader enters 'Ali's thoughts through free indirect discourse. This shift towards third-person omniscient narration might be said to mirror 'Ali's vulnerability and victimization, literally taking away his capacity to narrate the ongoing scene. Even if he admits that he and his friends may be idealistic, 'Ali refuses to let anyone question his integrity by calling him a traitor:

> He always believed that the biggest losers in all that was happening were the people of his sect, which he likened to a parasite burrowing inside his body, dwelling inside his stomach, devouring slowly until nothing but skin remained, to emerge later on as a monstrous creature. He was silent once again. He didn't want to discuss anything. He was in his prison, not knowing when he would be tried for the crime of conspiracy against the public good of the country, perhaps it wouldn't be for years. The security apparatus had long been accustomed to kidnapping and imprisonment and torture. The emergency law allowed them to do that. All he could do was await his release and [hope to] peacefully get on with his life. He decided that, as soon as he got out, he wouldn't ever think about politics; he would re-dedicate himself to studying medicine, or maybe he would leave the capital altogether and go live in his grandfather's house.[97]

Briefly emerging from this reverie, 'Ali feebly attempts to defend himself, but Sa'id Nasir interrupts, scoffing at his weakness even as he confesses that this display of willfulness reminds him of his own youth, when he and his peers were persecuted, "imprisoned and tortured" for their subversive activities. ʿAli continues in defense of himself and his comrades:

> "So why are you doing the same thing to us?"
> "I'm building a homeland."
> "You're destroying one."[98]

Saʿid Nasir smacks ʿAli to the ground and proceeds to beat him further, insulting him all the while,[99] but ʿAli will not submit:

> "You're the one who did this, you're the one beating me, and you're the one who's a traitor to his people, a traitor to the legacy of our ancestors. You're the one who doesn't belong. Wild animals live by the survival instinct and kill in order to live. . . . You take pleasure in the fact that you have all the power. You're a jackal arming himself in order to use his weapons on someone from his own sect who is defenseless. You beat him and torture him and you might even kill him just because he isn't like you. You jail and kill people the way it was done to our ancestors. . . . Who's the traitor? Is it me or is it . . . "

Saʿid Nasir flicks away his cigarette. Unhinged, he leaps up to pulverize ʿAli, smashing his head against the wall, stomping on him, pounding him with a chair, until his colleagues have to step in and restrain him. ʿAli lands in a coma that lasts for days and, left with localized amnesia, he will not remember what happened, not just on that day but on many others as well.[100]

After ʿAli's release, Layla tries to persuade him to abandon his political activities. ʿAli attempts to convince her to move back to the village with him, to get away from Saʿid Nasir. He is shocked to discover that Saʿid Nasir has "bought her a big house, broke all her mirrors, and prevented her from having mirrors in her new house."[101] When ʿAli asks if she is happy, she says she does not know:

> "We're all just dust. My skin is dust. Our bodies are earth and dust. Sometimes I almost don't believe I even exist, except when I see myself on television. . . . Don't you see? There are no mirrors here. Do you remember how you used to disapprove of all the mirrors in my home?"

Slowly realizing that some part of Layla has been destroyed, that television has become her psychological screen, that her connection to reality is growing increasingly tenuous, ʻAli probes further, inquiring about her mirrors. Layla responds:

> "All those mirrors I once had have disappeared. You once said that the mirror is a hideous human invention, but for me it's the only certainty I have that I am alive. I can feel an entire life in every mirror. Don't you see? Now I'm a prisoner without my mirrors."[102]

Layla seems to be articulating a philosophy of life, perhaps even an ontology: "Mirrors are the opposite of what people say about them being the love of the self! They're a place of nothingness . . . a place for you and you alone . . . where there's nothing but the void."[103] ʻAli again pleads with her to return to the village: "Come back with me, Layla . . . or [at least] go back to your mirrors."[104] In the end, ʻAli goes home alone.

The disorientation that results from living in such a kaleidoscopic reality, of striving to see through propaganda, intimate disinformation, and political paranoia, is epitomized by Layla's obsession with mirrors. Layla seems to be stranded in "the mirror stage," the notion popularized by French psychoanalyst Jacques Lacan (1901–1981) in which the developing human subject is alienated from himself or herself but which should also function as a transitional step toward self-identification, even if the subject formation is only ever partial or incomplete.[105] Michel Foucault took those insights further in "Des espaces autres," viewing the mirror as a space both from and toward which a radical politics of presence—one marked on and by the body—may be enacted.[106] Space and the body may be rendered "utopian," but Foucault also suggests that this utopian body (*le corps utopique*) may turn out *not* to be a utopia at all. For Foucault, utopias are nonfictional but also nonexistent: "Utopias in fact come to us as barely audible messages from a future that may never come into being."[107] As long as the nonidentical self appears in the mirror before the developing subject, Foucault notes, there are other spaces, forms of alterity, alternate universes—not all of which are imaginary—toward which the human subject may strive or be inclined: "*hetero*-topias, those spaces that are absolutely other."[108] But heterotopia has its flip side: bodies on this side of the looking glass that are fragile, docile, and, perhaps most important, subject to various kinds of power. If a liberatory politics of the body may be derived in the interstices of Lacan and Foucault, a psychoanalytic reading of *In Her Mirrors* should also attend to the physical and psychological experience of gender in the plot as well as in the construction of narrative itself. One place to start might be the striking resemblance between *In Her Mirrors* and what Carolyn Burke calls, in her illuminating reading of Luce Irigaray,

> the "other side," a conceptual realm beyond the law of the *Logos*, Woman's place . . . beyond the mirror of [men's] languages in a new psychic space . . . an ideological space beyond the psychic economy of patriarchy . . . a realm—at once emotional and intellectual—in which woman is no longer defined in relation to man as his negative, other, or as lack.[109]

In Chapter 2, I argued that gender and power are central to an understanding of cultural production in Syria during the 1980s and 1990s, though it bears remembering that the bulk of this work—especially films—was made by men and should therefore be contextualized in relation to the male gaze. The gendered dimensions of surveillance are not only governed by a relationship of domination and submission. The men caught in this web of power can be rendered just as powerless as the women, while expectations for the appropriate performance of masculinity and femininity differ. Recall, for example, the scene in *Layālī Ibn Awā* (*Nights of the Jackal*) (Chapter 2), when Abu Kamal buries his son Talal up to his neck, shaves his head, and slathers him with honey for his transgressions against the patriarch. Staging and viewing punishment for transgressions against the regime (of the father and the leader) have political and psychological effects that speak to the force of authoritarian and misogynistic violence.

Mirrors and screens are pervasive in *Sacrifices* (*Ṣundūq al-Dunyā*) (2002), Ossama Mohammed's searing critique of patriarchy and dictatorship (Chapter 2). Another kind of light is shone on the intimate politics of gender and surveillance in Mohammad's stunning 1988 debut feature *Stars in Broad Daylight* (*Nujūm al-Nahār*). The arranged double marriage that opens the film is envisioned as the means for a notable landed family in the mountainous hinterland of Latakia to consolidate its economic and social power, but the scheme unravels when the young woman betrothed to the deaf-mute son Kasir calls off the marriage in the middle of the wedding party. Kasir's sister Sana' also spurns her intended husband. The patriarch, Khalil (played by filmmaker 'Abd al-Latif 'Abd al-Hamid, Figure 33), manipulates his personal connections and charismatic authority to secure a new husband for Sana', a thuggish man who

- Hello Damascus?
I want to talk to Abbas.

FIGURE 33. Ossama Mohammed, *Nujūm al-Nahār* (*Stars in Broad Daylight*) (National Film Organization, 1988)

has returned to Syria from abroad. After Sana' resists and tries to flee this man's brutish advances, he rapes her in the woods. Sana' later falls in love with a kind Arabic teacher in Latakia, but when she has the temerity to introduce the man to her aging grandfather, Khalil unleashes some of his goons—including the man who raped Sana'—to assault the happy couple in the market and beat the man within an inch of his life.

Ossama Mohammed's oeuvre is a master class in the cinematic language of "the shot" (*al-laqṭa*), a term he uses to describe his aesthetic vision. Through multiple viewings of his films as well as personal conversations with Mohammed, I came to appreciate how these long, languorous shots can be manipulated to construct an alternative view of identity, community, and the political. The technical aspects of *Stars in Broad Daylight* (1988) are echoed in Riyad Shayya's 1995 film *Al-Lajāt* (Chapter 2); Mohammed affirms that the two filmmakers shared a strikingly similar vision, an unmistakable common interest in doors, frames, windows, and shots within shots. In the films of Ossama Mohammed, surveillance radiates outward from the father, the leader, and the state, represented through a panoply of sensuous perceptions: sight, sound, and embodied supervision.[110] In *The Extras*, which evokes the claustrophobia of living under constant watch, "surveillance has become *the condition of the narration itself*... the formal signature of the film's narration."[111] *Stars in Broad Daylight*, by contrast, directly addresses the themes of surveillance and dictatorship while also engaging with the problem of violence: guns, beatings, rape—these are the unmistakable techniques of patriarchal control as well as dictatorial rule. For example, the ubiquity of technology and surveillance are affirmed through shots of televisions placed around the wedding party (Figure 34, top row and second row left images). But the idea of who is "on screen" shifts when Kasir—an otherwise muted character because of his speech impediment—is shown in a state of awe or confusion when forced into the limelight. In the case of the bombastic poet, booming out Arab nationalist verse in praise of the happy couples, the authority of ideology is on screen, beaming out at a captive audience even as the spectator watches the watchers and the watching.

The use of mirrors and screens creates a dizzying experience for the viewer of lines of sight that move in all directions, an omnidirectional gaze that at once universalizes the power of vision and prevents the viewer from establishing the physical and political location of authority. At the level of plot, these screens and mirrors permit the multiplication of characters in the shot without unduly crowding the scene, in a sense calling onto the set an entirely new cast, perhaps in the process even hailing a different conception of community into being (Figure 34, second row right and bottom two rows images). In this regard, there is much to be learned from philosopher Robert B. Pippin, who convincingly argues that mirrors can be understood

> to suggest the reflective status of the film itself. We see not only the movie world, we see (or we should see) that it is represented in a way, or we see ourselves seeing in such a distinct way (the cinematic irony has the same effect). The technique also opens the question of whether and if so how the characters see not just their world but how they are taking, imagining that world to be.[112]

The way *Stars in Broad Daylight* ends—with Mohammed's brazen decision to film in broad daylight, as it were, on the streets of Damascus, and not to disclose the ultimate fate of the protagonists—is best understood as both a remarkably subtle feat of lampooning an authoritarian dictatorship in real time and a marvelous achievement of guerrilla filmmaking. As Mohammed

FIGURE 34. Ossama Mohammed, *Nujūm al-Nahār* (*Stars in Broad Daylight*) (National Film Organization, 1988)

tells the story, he took advantage of his crew as well as petty officers and cops on the beat to establish an alternative universe in which the iconography of public culture was no longer beholden to the ubiquitous leader Hafiz al-Asad but rather to the celebrity singer in the film. But there is another side to the craft here: the capacity to compose shots that resemble portraits and to use mirrors and screens in a way that approximates camera lenses.

Syria under Baʿthist rule might be well thought of as a house of mirrors. Words such as "liberty, "unity," and "socialism" as well as "women's liberation" and "equality" were evacuated of content and ideologically repurposed in the service of state power. Before her psychological unraveling in *In Her Mirrors*, Layla slept in a room with mirrors hanging from the walls and the ceiling: "When she would lay down on her bed, turning on the small lamp beside it, and looking up into the mirror, she would look like a distant point approaching from an infinite darkness. She would close her eyes and feel safe, as if the reflections spreading all around her were the realization of her very existence."[113] In contrast to clinical conceptions of narcissism as an obsession with the self (without recognizing the object of desire as self, of course) by way of a fixation on the mirror (or reflecting pool in the classical version), Layla insists that self-regard in her own mirrors is a means of annihilating the self. Mirrors function here, somewhat counterintuitively, to anchor Layla in the (ir)reality of her circumstances in authoritarian Syria, to establish the very conditions of possibility for her experience of being. ʿAli had once described his sister and politics as his only connections to the world. There was a "strong rope" tethering him to life, with Layla representing a knot.[114] The rope metaphor comes back to shock Layla after ʿAli moves home to the village, where he becomes increasingly despondent and eventually hangs himself in the family's old mud house.

If *In Her Mirrors* has proceeded in a minor key until this point, the conclusion swells to a dooming crescendo. Layla plummets into a drug-fueled madness as her grip on reality slips. She has, as she puts it, "lost her mirrors,"[115] lost her marbles, her bearings. Unmoored from the country she (thought she) once knew, Layla also no longer has access to the space of retreat embodied by her mirrors. She forgets whatever dreams she had of reviving her acting career: "She forgot everything, thinking how she wanted to write an end to the story between her and Saʿid Nasir so that ʿAli's soul could be at peace."[116] This deeper disruption of her dysphoria sends her hurtling toward collapse.

Meanwhile, Sa'id Nasir loses patience with Layla, telling her that the mourning period (*ḥidād*) for 'Ali's suicide has passed.[117] Still, she persists in demanding to know what happened to him:

> "He brought it upon himself. That brother of yours was crazy, and so are you. . . . Your family is a bunch of crazies. . . . I didn't have anything to do with what happened to 'Ali. . . . I heard from others that he was in jail . . . don't blame me for your brother's mistakes . . . I tried to help him but he refused . . . "
> "How did you try?"
> "That was a long time ago."
> "How did you try?" she insisted.
> "None of your business. It's my job, part of my patriotic duty and responsibilities."
> "Patriotic," she said sarcastically.[118]

Whereas the *mukhābarātī* in *Rough Draft* does not seem to do his "patriotic duty" with much conviction, Sa'id Nasir is a true believer in national loyalty and he will not hesitate to mete out cruelty against dissidents and intimates alike. "The traitor," as Tobias Kelly and Sharika Thiranagama convincingly argue, "lies not so much at the margins or beyond the nation but at its heart."[119] Desperate and distraught over the loss of her brother and the pressure she finds herself under, Layla momentarily attacks Sa'id Nasir before collapsing into a crumpled heap.

Layla relapses into addiction, careening out of control. In a way that might be read as complementing Layla's fractured psyche, the temporality of the novel splits open as successive sections trace Layla and Sa'id Nasir's relationship as a story of star-crossed lovers spanning centuries of Greater Syrian and Anatolian history. In the description of their ancestral village, where 'Alawīs had sought refuge from massacres and persecution, the people were said to have had to "carry their souls in their hands" (*yaḥmilūn arwāḥahum 'alā akuffihim*).[120] This idiomatic expression carries at least two meanings. First, historically speaking, 'Alawīs who were chased from their homes had to take their lives into their own hands. At the same time, when sacred texts were burned and as esoteric beliefs and ritual practices had to be hidden behind *taqiyya* (purposeful dissimulation), the community was steadily denuded of its cultural memory. Wonders once taken for truth were transformed over time into "ancient tales" (*ḥikāyāt mūghila fī al-qidam*) as the "survivors" of the community turned 'Alawī sacred history into "superstitions and myths" that were subsequently forgotten along with the "souls" (*arwāḥ*) lost in those massacres.[121] As Saʿid Nasir plies Layla with hashish and opiates, the discussion of ʿAlawī rites, specifically the belief in reincarnation—metempsychosis or the transmigration of souls—acquires crucial significance. She insists that the two of them had been lovers "for generations," now convinced they had known one another in past lives, one of which ended in the early sixteenth century with their dying in each other's arms as Ottoman Sultan Selim I conquered Aleppo and the city burned. The persecution of the ʿAlawī community in what is referred to as "the white city" (*al-madīna al-bayḍāʾ*) in the novel [as opposed to the more traditional "Aleppo the gray" (*Ḥalab al-shahbāʾ*)] is reconstructed in gory detail.[122] These sections fudge the boundaries between history and myth.[123] The historically minded reader is left with dizzying questions: Should these stories be taken as "real," a lived aspect of ʿAlawī cosmogony in which the transmigration of souls is understood as a social reality? Has Layla gone mad—"lost her mirrors"—in the wake of her traumatic prison experiences? Does her brother's suicide cause her to snap? Is she turned upside down by her conflicting—and self-destructive—feelings for Saʿid Nasir? Has Saʿid Nasir's emotional abuse taken an irreversibly destabilizing psychological toll? Or has drug use twisted her mind, propelling her into a phantasmagorical dream world? If the novel provokes these and other stirring questions, the reader is ultimately left with a sense of undecidability, a text riddled with paradox, a novel overdetermined by politics, history, and warring identities.

Wasting away in a spare garret in the Shaʿlan neighborhood, adrift in her chemically addled state, Layla is broken. Paralleling her all-consuming grief over ʿAli's tragic demise, words have become "like a noose hanging in [her] throat."[124] In the climactic scene, Layla shows up at Saʿid Nasir's house late one night, unhinged, screaming for him to recognize her condition: "Come down here if you're a man!"[125] She demands that Saʿid Nasir admit responsibility for her unraveling and for ʿAli's death, for the moral decay of the community and even the corrosion of the nation. Here is a marked difference between the ambivalence and restricted power of the *mukhābarātī* in *Rough Draft* and the sadism and seemingly limitless authority exercised by Saʿid Nasir. Furthermore, the execrable actions of bumbling security officers and the mishaps of political representatives in *The Silence and the Roar* appear downright toothless and even cartoonish by comparison with the cruelly intimate violence on display in *In Her Mirrors*. After the building guard slaps her, Layla spits in his face and he pistol-whips her, throwing her to the ground before she skulks off into the night. Saʿid Nasir leaves the house with his driver, Abu Mahmud, shortly thereafter; cruising the city aimlessly, they listen to Qur'an recitation, the book of Maryam (Mary) to be precise, which concerns how a barren woman may procreate through divine intervention, which is the Islamic reference to the Virgin Mary. Saʿid Nasir cannot get Layla's voice out of his head.[126] He still feels connected to her, tormented by divergent feelings, unsure whether he "hated her deep in his soul" or "loved her so much he was afraid of getting near her." He is comforted, though, by one of his favorite maxims: "Punishment is one of the most important reasons for man's success, without punishment and fear there is no continuity."[127] Punishment and fear are two governing principles of regime doxa. Saʿid Nasir relishes the fact that Layla will suffer further still. "She'll get her punishment," he grumbles. "'She'll get her punishment . . . ' [even as] it crushed his heart."[128] If the novel starts with a bang, it ends with a whimper: Layla sobbing on the shoulder of an anonymous passenger as their bus crawls toward the northwest coast, the ʿAlawī heartland, a funereal return to her ancestral village where she will never truly feel at home.

This closing image is poignantly cinematic. Nabil Sulayman argues that *In Her Mirrors* succeeds as social commentary but fails as literature.[129] However, Moroccan novelist and critic Muhammad Barrada praises its rich characters and creative imagination.[130] Rasim al-Madhun goes so far as to argue that the novel represents a rupture in the tradition of Syrian prose writing, moving from the "political novel" to "the novel of life."[131] To the extent that a broken mirror still offers the possibility of reflection, and insofar as damaged subjects constituted through *méconnaissance* are still somehow implicated in a politics of (mis) recognition, there is no necessary contradiction in concluding that *In Her Mirrors* turns on a ferocious criticism of the regime and social surveillance as well as an imaginative recombination of history, memory, and myth in the service of a distinctive vision of politics and (ʿAlawī) identity in contemporary Syria.

SEEING (AND LISTENING, AND FEELING) LIKE A STATE (SECURITY AGENT)

> The eyes are the organic prototype of philosophy. Their enigma is that they not only can see but are also able to see themselves seeing. This gives them a prominence among the body's cognitive organs. A good part of philosophical

> thinking is actually only eye reflex, eye dialectic, seeing-oneself-see. For this, reflecting media, mirrors, water surfaces, metals, and other eyes are necessary, through which the seeing of seeing becomes visible.[132]
>
> —Peter Sloterdijk, *Critique of Cynical Reason*

In his short story "A Summary of What Happened to Muhammad al-Mahmudi," Zakariya Tamir satirizes the power of the police state by constructing a world in which a dead man is conscripted into the machinery of surveillance. A lonely single man who never married or had children, Muhammad al-Mahmudi is buried under the café that was once his daily haunt and that he comes to haunt as a ghostly informant. When the police search the café for dissidents, Muhammad is interrogated for his supposed political activities, which he flatly denies. "Me curse the government?" Muhammad responds.

> I seek refuge in God! I'm not one of those people who drinks from the well only then to spit in it. Ask anyone about me. I was a model employee. I followed orders and the law, carrying them out to a tee. Ask anyone about me. I never got drunk. I never harassed a woman. I never harmed anyone. And I . . .

As the police chief at the station presses him further, Muhammad continues to plead his case. "I swear to God I lived my whole life without ever talking about politics, I never cursed anyone, not in my entire life, neither the government nor any of its officials" And here is where the lesson of politics in an authoritarian dictatorship takes a decidely Syrian turn. "Haha . . . You say that you never cursed the government, but what you didn't say is that you ever praised it. Doesn't it deserve praise in your estimation?" From here Muhammad is conscripted into working as a government agent from beneath the café and beyond the grave.[133] Poking fun at this imperative for "responsible" citizens to ostentatiously heap praise on the state and the leader can be read as a riposte to the cultlike behavior of regime supporters in the shadow of the Asadist-Baʿthist aesthetic ideology discussed in Chapter 1. Here, though, Tamir darkly imagines the surveillance apparatus to be capable of monitoring Syrians who have passed on, even conscripting the dead into service, an eerie premonition of the work of the dead in literature and film during the time of the Syria War (Chapter 6).

Literary representations of uncivil society are an important yet underappreciated detail of Syrian fiction from the late twentieth and early twenty-first centuries. Whereas the individual and collective experience of incarceration or the inhuman application of torture against regime opponents animated Syrian writing throughout the 1980s and 1990s, state power in the Syrian *mukhābarāt* novel of the early 2000s is depicted in terms of visual, auditory, and sensual surveillance as well as other modes of affective experience. *Rough Draft* and *In Her Mirrors* illustrate some of the ways in which "the seeing of seeing becomes visible" in Syrian literature, but also how, adapting Sloterdijk, listening to listening becomes audible and how both seeing and listening—the entire gamut of affective experience, really—are essential to giving state power shape, making it comprehensible, perhaps even containable, within the space of the novel. In *The Silence and the Roar*, Sirees draws the reader's attention to the power of pleasure—whether experienced through sex or laughter or both simultaneously—in apprehending, adapting, and even repelling the infringement of state power on everyday life. To be sure, drawing attention to the aesthetic power of the senses would have seemed redundant in an earlier age, for as Susan Buck-Morss reminds us, "*Aisthisis* is the sensory experience of perception" itself.[134] Nevertheless, the thematization of the senses in direct relation to Syrian surveillance society is a meaningful development in the cultural history of Baʿthist Syria.

While it would be tendentious to describe Asadist-Baʿthist Syria as a "socialist society" *senso stricto*, it is fair to argue, in consonance with literary criticism of East German fiction of the 1990s, for example, that Syrian writers in the early 2000s "no longer aspire[d] to change or improve (a no longer extant) socialist society, but rather [sought] to initiate a process of self-understanding, including a search for the author's own fragmented or injured identity and stance toward past and present events."[135] Sirees, Hasan, and Yazbek all imbue the *mukhābarātī* and other individuals in the security apparatus in Baʿthist Syria with varying degrees of depth and complexity. Whereas Yazbek consistently calls attention to the ruthlessness of Saʿid Nasir despite his familial and social connections to the victims of both state and intimate violence, Hasan winds up contextualizing the cruelty and callousness of the regime's minions in terms of their banal experiences and desires. Meanwhile, Sirees transforms the thuggish goons and regime apparatchiks who work for the dreaded security forces as savage instruments of repression into craven seekers of sexual satisfaction, and paltry excuses for creative writers.

Even as a growing body of scholarship situates representations of state power and surveillance in relation to political, social, and cultural practices,[136] additional research into the *mukhābarāt* novel may help to further integrate Syrian cultural studies into the framework of a more robust "case for comparative literary studies of surveillance representations."[137] Even though characters in *The Silence and the Roar* laugh out loud in the face of party bureaucrats, they might also seem to be legitimating an absurdist regime that depends on the apathetic resignation of its citizenry; although there are markers throughout the novel that index life in contemporary Syria, it remains undecidable whether this should be interpreted as an effective challenge to the discourses and practices of Syrian authoritarianism. For Layla in *In Her Mirrors*, the mirror is a site of reprieve, a means of escape, a vehicle to her own private heterotopia; Saʿid Nasir engages in what might be called informal or everyday forms of surveillance and social control. The fact that the listening booth—his very own portal to heterotopia—is where the *mukhābarātī* in *Rough Draft* both practices surveillance and hones his creative faculties suggests another space in what might be called the Syrian security archipelago: sites offering some semblance of mimetic coherence. State and nonstate power—understood here as the politics and erotics of surveillance—are deployed in these texts to achieve social control. But the texts also refigure the ambiguity and undecidability inherent in just existing in such dystopic circumstances, perhaps as a means of destabilizing ideological conformity. All three authors call our attention to the uncertainty that seems to represent the achievement of dictatorial domination but at the same time may open up the possibility of undermining, or at least challenging, authoritarian *raisons d'état*. Moreover, their novels showcase the capacity of literature to complicate and contest metanarratives of power promulgated by the state and other coercive institutions, simultaneously highlighting their artifice and their durability by capturing and celebrating quiet moments of intimacy, vulnerability, and humanity. Lisa Wedeen's subtle insight that transgressive acts performed under conditions of authoritarian dictatorship—including, one might add, shining a light on the exercise of state power and surveillance through fiction—can be meaningful without necessarily being transformative remains particularly resonant.[138]

Both the form and the content of the political in Syrian literature has changed over time. "Syrian culture," Mohja Kahf wrote around the time that

Bashar al-Asad came to power, "has become most associated with the posture of paranoia stemming from a realistic fear of a police state with a vast surveillance apparatus and great demands of public shows of allegiance."[139] Given the level of intimidation and terrorism by the *mukhābarāt*, it is hardly surprising to find a *paranoid style* in Syrian culture. Fictionalized renditions of the *mukhābarāt*—their characterization and caricature, perhaps—can also distance, objectify, and reimagine the brutality of state power. Syrian novels from the 1990s and early 2000s simultaneously narrativize and call into question the fear that many Syrians shed in rebelling against authoritarian dictatorship at the outset of the uprising in 2011. The works discussed in this chapter variously represent the redemptive and productive—and crucially the political—power of literature and cinema. One of the most consequential features of the *mukhābarāt* novel—as well as its analogues in film and elsewhere—may be its capacity to showcase the power inherent in narration itself. If this mode of engagement with the security state and its surveillance apparatus in literature and film extends back to the late twentieth century, to the time of Hafiz al-Asad, the contours of what I call *mukhābarāt* culture have changed over time, like any form of literary and cinematic culture shaped by competing aesthetic ideologies. The persistent tension among what I have called the aesthetics of power, the aesthetics of resistance, and the aesthetics of solidarity would continue to define the Syrian cultural field into the 2010s and beyond. Revolutionary upsurge, grinding war, mass death, physical destruction, and unprecedented human displacement might make some of the political concerns discussed in this chapter seem almost quaint by comparison. But the kind of witnessing and political critique on display in the novels and films explored in this chapter would turn out to be prescient, revelatory even, as the country was to be rocked by revolution and war in the coming years and literature and film were to be dramatically transformed, as detailed in the next two chapters.

Chapter 5

THE SLOW WITNESS

No need to search out the origin of narrative in time—it is time that originates in narrative.

— Tzvetan Todorov, "Narrative-Men"[1]

It is impossible to live with the worst thing there is, so we have no choice but not to take it into account, and in a certain sense to forget it. But this does not mean that, at the same time, we do not know that hell exists. We do not even have to believe in hell, since the most terrible things happen to some people in reality. And the witness, who sees and cannot avoid the worst thing, he who is confronted with it, is horrified.

— Bart Verschaffel, "The Depiction of the Worst Thing"[2]

It is speed that supports the armies' morale.

— Paul Virilio, *Speed and Politics*[3]

IN *A WOMAN IN THE CROSSFIRE: DIARIES OF THE SYRIAN Revolution*, journalist, activist, and novelist Samar Yazbek documents her experiences of crisscrossing Syria during the heyday of the Syrian uprising, March–July 2011, from Damascus to the northwest coast, caught between the regime and the coalescing forces of the uprising. "I was confused," she writes on May 5, 2011, "as dry as a scarecrow. I couldn't find the time to write in my diary and I started feeling there was no use in writing down what was happening to me anyway. But I soon discovered that these diaries were helping me to stay alive."[4] Like other Syrian writers, intellectuals, artists, and filmmakers, Yazbek discovered new voices, identities, and inspiration through writing, speaking, and acting—living on—in the time of the Syrian revolution and subsequent war. While she was recording her diaries Yazbek also managed to collect testimonies and recollections from dozens if not hundreds of ordinary Syrians living through those extraordinary events. In Chapter 4, we encountered Yazbek as a novelist who subjects the ideological and institutional manifestations of the Syrian security state to literary critique. If the prosaic, deceptively private act of keeping a personal diary could help Yazbek stay alive now, as she puts it, perhaps the collective act of witnessing, of speaking in more than one voice, *mitsprechen*, could help an entire community stay alive or at least keep alive the memories of those who had experienced the excitement, danger, and destruction looming over this moment in Syrian history, and those who were lost in the carnage. Some chronicled the stories of groups that ventured into the streets and squares of cities large and small across the country to raise their voices in protest; others smuggled video footage of collective action and regime atrocity; journalists tracking the situation on the ground completed a "first draft" of contemporary history; and an emergent mass of novelists and other writers generated an unprecedented deluge of prose during this period. This mixture of empirical documentation and creative expression had a profound impact on the Syria Warscape. Literary and cinematic stories of collective struggle and artistic experimentation in these unsettled times throw a different light on a broader cultural striving for life, liberty, and dignity, the keywords of the Syrian revolution.

In the face of unpredictable life circumstances and unimaginable violence, Syrian artists, writers, filmmakers, and ordinary people struggled—consciously and not—to find a language adequate to these jarring experiences. In her entry from May 10, 2011, Yazbek writes, "I wake up and touch my skin. I am just an idea, a character in a novel. I drink my coffee and believe that I am only thinking about a woman I'll write about one day. I am a novel."[5] Confusion, the utter collapse of any grounding sense of reality, a conflation of the real and the imaginary, the breakdown of epistemological foundation—these forces all converge in her hypothetical novel, featuring a character with skin that Yazbek can touch and feel while also reflecting the unstable conditions in which millions of Syrians lived during the first few exhilarating months of the uprising.

This disbelief, given literary and visual form through a stuporous gaze, is at the heart of Syrian cultural production in the time of the Syria War, as demonstrated in this chapter and in Chapter 6. Writers, filmmakers, and artists were pushed not only to defend their right to self-expression but also to situate their art in relation to the very conditions of possibility of knowledge itself, oriented toward the themes of time, temporality, and witnessing.

If disbelief became widespread, it was never the only emotional and cultural response to the revolution and the Syria War. For some the revolution managed to clarify aspects of politics, culture, and life itself. Many came to believe—some more fervently than others—that they were part of a process that would bring down a regime that had managed to co-opt its leading intellectuals and keep its population docile for decades. Perhaps the opposite of the disbelief or confoundment articulated in the work of Yazbek and others is not belief as such but the fundamental notion that an individual might yet find some measure of epistemological certainty or foundational truth through immediate and personal experience—what might be called phenomenological politics in the time of the Syria War. In this sense, an emergent cultural politics of witness, wherein witnessing itself—at multiple scales, from the individual to the collective, based on a specifically situated perspective—was perceived and portrayed by writers, readers, and critics as capable of subverting or perhaps even transcending the abject stupefaction that settled over people who were being subjected to overwhelming disinformation and seemingly endless violence.

We have seen how, during the rule of Hafiz al-Asad (1970–2000), in that era of authoritarian domination that left a relatively small margin for creative expression, cultural production could be interpreted as bearing aesthetic witness to history, comprehensible in some instances as social text, literary and otherwise. With the coming to power of Bashar al-Asad in 2000, Syrian writers, artists, filmmakers, and other cultural producers found new ways not only to document the past and present through their work but also to call into question the ideological representation of "Syrian art" promoted through regime mouthpieces and institutions. I have argued throughout *Revolutions Aesthetic* that the wide-ranging experiments and experiences of filmmakers, novelists, critics, and audiences over five decades of Asadist-Baʿthist rule belie the facile notion that Syria had been trapped in some kind of totalitarian cultural malaise. From the novels of Hanna Mina and Mamdouh Azzam and those of

Samar Yazbek and Rosa Yaseen Hasan, to the films of Ossama Mohammed, ʿAbd al-Latif ʿAbd al-Hamid, and Riyad Shayya, there were diverse ways of seeing, writing, and creating. As we saw in Chapter 4, there was a meaningful opening of space for novelists to redefine the parameters structuring critical discourse on the state, surveillance, and political power under the evolving rule of Bashar al-Asad. With the gradual transformation of economic, cultural, and everyday life under this reformism between 2000 and 2011, artists, writers, and filmmakers imagined alternative futures beyond their constrained and regulated horizons of possibility. Political scientists continue to debate the relationship between economic liberalization on the one hand and related processes of political transformation or cultural opening on the other. My discussion of the political in Syrian fiction of the early 2000s does not resolve the issue of whether there is a causal relationship between the reformist steps taken under Bashar al-Asad and the more expansive cultural production of the period. Chapter 4 explored how sensorial experience—the relatively free exercise of the senses in judgment and knowledge production—informed the creative endeavors of writers, journalists, filmmakers, and ordinary Syrians during this era. One did not always have to believe what one was seeing, as Lisa Wedeen taught us, in the time of Hafiz al-Asad. More recently, it might be said, one often yearns to see *in order* to believe or *not* to believe as the case may be.

With the eruption of the Syrian uprising and the onset of the Syria War, the state-administered cultural revolution of Hafiz al-Asad's era and the state-led reformism of Bashar's rule were interrupted by new forms of revolutionary culture. This chapter and Chapter 6 deal with cultural production—staying with novels and films—during the time of the Syrian uprising and the Syria War, showing how the aesthetic ideology of "revolution," no longer monopolized by the regime, could be appropriated, renegotiated, and deployed in new ways by writers, filmmakers, artists, and others. The reappropriation of the watchful gaze of the state surveillance apparatus in literature and cinema reflected a shift from what I have called an aesthetics of power toward an aesthetics of solidarity. If the regime narrative voice is one that *speaks-at* and *speaks-for* the people, cultural production in the time of the Syria War has blown open spaces for artists, writers, and filmmakers to *speak-back* and to collectively *speak-with*. The language of revolution itself was unmoored from any anchors in regime discourse and became a site of aesthetic ideological struggle. One hallmark of this new phase in the cultural history of Syria was an altogether different configuration of the relationships among aesthetic ideology, cultural production, and time itself. Witnessing in the time of the Syria War has been a response not exclusively to what is happening but also to how (quickly) it has taken place.

This chapter focuses on how the Syrian revolution fundamentally transformed the field of cultural politics, with a focus on the novel and, for the first time in this book, documentary film. Between the epistemological uncertainty and phenomenological politics at stake here, cultural production in the time of the Syria War became fixated on the question of truth. "At the beginning of a war, people first devote themselves to activity," Samuel Weber writes in his study of how aesthetics and epistemology become intertwined with war and its metaphors. "But when they have already experienced some disaster, they cling to thought."[6] Between disbelief, therefore—whether artificially constructed or authentically sincere—and a countervailing will to knowledge, a space emerged wherein the Syrian revolution could flourish, however fleetingly, constituting an imaginative horizon just out of reach yet renewably inspiring. In the first part of this chapter, I stage a critical reading of two novels that appeared during the early days of the revolution and civil war—Maha Hasan's *Drums of Love* (*Ṭubūl al-Ḥubb*) (2013) and Khalil Suwaylih's *Barbarians' Paradise* (*Jannat al-Barābira*) (2014). My concerns are twofold. First, both works shed light on how insider/outsider dynamics were at play in the contentious politics of witnessing. The protagonists in these novels at once serve as a window onto contemporary events unfolding in a time of extreme uncertainty and articulate the emotional and literary stakes of inhabiting the subjective space of life in wartime. This alienating experience of distance from ongoing events enables these characters to give an account of the unfolding revolution and war in narrative time. Second, I am interested in how this embattled position of witnessing was shaped in turn by the experience of time itself, more specifically, how grappling with speed—the experience of time in acceleration—was of the essence in order to make sense of this moment. Both novels represent, in a sense, literary efforts to respond to crisis and catastrophe. On the one hand, writing in times of war is an "attempt" (*muḥāwala*), as Rima, the protagonist of *Drums of War*, puts it, to transcend or undermine the alienation and despair many have felt in the time of the Syria War. On the other hand, the recuperative impulse of novel writing might also represent a different kind of attempt, one concerned with documentation, a gesture toward conservation in a moment of rapid and frightening change. Similar concerns animate the experimental documentary *Silvered Water, Syria Self-Portrait* (*Māʾ al-Fiḍḍa*) (2014) by Ossama Mohammed and Wiam Simav Bedirxan, which is the subject of the final part of this chapter. War has been central to visual imaginaries in the modern Middle East.[7] Like *Drums of War* and *Barbarians' Paradise*, *Silvered Water* is concerned with the interconnected problematics of witnessing and representation. However, this film, in a notable departure from Mohammed's narrative features, which as we have seen in Chapters 2 and 4 are distinguished by their auteurist style and opaque visual language, is a cinematic attempt at *mitsprechen*, affirming the collective experience of many Syrians in wartime. Like the novels by Hasan and Suwaylih, *Silvered Water* addresses the questions of insider/outsider dynamics and fragmented subjectivities in wartime as well as the representation of time, temporality, and speed as part of an attempt to track the parameters of the revolution and war, to carve out the conditions of possibility for what I call slow witnessing.

ARTIFACTS OF DISBELIEF

Syria War literature and film should not be seen as emerging in a cultural or historical vacuum. On a regional scale, the aesthetics and politics of war rose to the forefront of Arabic prose writing from the mid-twentieth century, which is unsurprising given the horrific history of the region as it coasted from war to war, conflict to conflict.[8] Syria War writing would seem to have more of a kinship with Iraq War writing since 2003 than, say, with the literature of the Lebanese civil wars (1975–1990). Citing a paradigmatic Lebanese example marked by postmodern style and an unreliable narrator, Emily Drumsta convincingly argues that the "author-narrator" of Elias Khoury's *White Masks* (*al-Wujūh al-Bayḍāʾ*) "is caught in a liminal place between the necessity of bearing witness and the impossibility of doing so through conventional narrative forms."[9] The witness-narrators of *Drums of Love* and *Barbarians' Paradise*, by contrast, express themselves through more conventional first-person narrative. And while these are literary texts that might be read "as a communal, polyvocal act"—Drumsta's analysis has a kinship with my invocation of *mitsprechen* and the aesthetics of solidarity—literary and cinematic accounts in the time of the Syrian revolution and the Syria War unmistakably attempt to construct a firm relationship to "journalistic truth," or what might be called documentary realism with aspirations to literature. In a way that advances and reinforces the argument I have been making about *A Woman in the Crossfire*, all three works discussed in this chapter become spaces for the author-narrators (I will elaborate further on why Ossama Mohammed should be understood as an author-narrator in *Silvered Water*) to express their own voice while also serving as vehicles for speaking-with a collective subject, whether in the name of the people and international conscience or as an instrument for the amplification of other people's voices. "The documentary novel," as Barbara Foley explains,

> is a species of fiction distinctly characterized by its adherence to referential strategies associated with nonfictional modes of discourse but also demanding to be read within a fictional Gestalt familiar to contemporaneous readers. Its dramatically altering strategies of representation do not mean that fictional discourse and nonfictional discourse are indistinguishable; they point instead to the changing terms of the fictional contract in different social formations.[10]

The line between fact and fiction has been blurred in the literature and film of the Syria War. Writers and filmmakers relentlessly seek epistemological certainty in an era of deception, misinformation, and state repression. Perhaps it was the absence of centralized state authority or of common national understandings in the case of the Lebanese civil wars that splintered fiction writing into "a communal, polyvocal act": Syrian writers during the early stages of the war—whether partisans of the Syrian revolution or those more sympathetic to the regime—seemed to speak in a multitude of voices but still attempted to say more or less the same thing. At a moment of concerted disinformation campaigns and propaganda war, novelists were increasingly transformed into writers of political fiction even as they attempted to establish the ontological grounds of the real. Writers during the Syria War fought against distorting polyphony and dispersed subjectivity in a quest for some measure of reliable truth.

From inside the blast zone of this ongoing disaster, prose writing fractured in other ways, confounding conventional boundaries of genre: memoir and fiction, reportage and invention, political advocacy and objective description. New media allowed for documentation, monitoring, and commentary about war in real time with regularity, convenience, and, most important, speed. Meanwhile, the war of words was accompanied by a clash over images—over the politics of the image as such—that had a profound impact on creative expression. One factor that united all of these forms was a burning need to capture what was happening, what I term a documentary imperative in fiction and film. This documentary imperative functions in multiple, sometimes contradictory ways. Broadly considered, it was an attempt to establish epistemological certainty, however minimal and provisional, or perhaps to explore the conditions of possibility for establishing certainty at all. This is most evident stylistically in a kind of hyper-realism marked by a commitment to witnessing, to bearing witness, as activists and cultural producers challenged and rewrote narratives of Syrian history, politics, and culture. In the wobbly handheld mobile phone videos uploaded or smuggled out of the country from the earliest stages of the uprising, the camera wielder or those appearing in the frame would hold up a piece of paper scrawled with the date and place or breathlessly identify their time and location.[11] Similarly, indefatigable activists in Kafranbel demonstrated their determination to resist the politics of uncertainty through pithy slogans and caricatures emblazoned on posters held up by rotating groups of village residents that would then be posted to social media. In fact, a spectrum of visual culture circulated on Twitter and Instagram that injected humor, insight, and humanity into the global discourse on Syria, however fleeting or ineffectual. By the same token, uncertainty about the believability or truth value of images and other visual material could be inflated in order to invalidate the claims of political or military rivals. Be that as it may, the documentary imperative—a will to document—was shaped by the politics and power of the image, conditioned by the desire to visualize and simultaneously contain the juggernaut that has been the Syria War.[12]

In order to make sense of the striking output of novels by Syrian writers—some of whom may be characterized as what literary critic Rob Nixon calls "writer-activists"—in a moment of calamity during the early stages of the revolution, I propose conceiving of the range of visual, digital, and literary practices that emerged in response to this tumultuous media environment as rapid witnessing. In his subtle reading of the ways in which environmental crisis is (re)figured in contemporary postcolonial fiction and reinforces forms of environmental racism and violence against the poor, Nixon refers to ours as "an age that increasingly genuflects to the digital divinity of speed."[13] The power of instantaneous communication—in visual and verbal forms—creates the difficulty and perhaps the impossibility of adequately responding to the insatiable demands of the moment, of keeping up with the speed at which news and other forms of digital content endlessly gush forth. The immediacy of images and the imaginary of the immediate dominate minds and politics, stretching out to occlude other horizons of possibility, alternative speeds of engagement. The acceleration of time and the intensification of destruction are accompanied by a madcap effort to keep pace by documenting every last detail of waking life.

A specter stalks writing and other forms of cultural production in the time of the Syria War: a stumbling, stuporous, slow-moving witness. Critics have struggled to make sense of this figure that can possibly stand for and straddle the manifold contradictions at the heart of experiencing, representing, and understanding the cataclysmic constellation of events from 2011 to 2018. The slow witness that I introduce here can be contrasted to the witness who obeys the imperatives of speed. The slow witness confounds the demands of speed and immediacy—what Lisa Wedeen calls "high-speed eventfulness," or "the sheer velocity with which information is transmitted and apprehended in the internet age,"[14] at times on purpose and at times unwittingly refusing to shy away from ubiquitous monstrosity but ill at ease with dancing to the ever accelerating beat of an eternally vanishing present. At the same time, the aesthetic dimensions of rapid witnessing—documenting, transmitting, and understanding the scale of suffering in Syria in relation to "high-speed eventfulness"—no doubt informs and structures how the slow witness can possibly reflect and make sense of the world otherwise. To be sure, the work of Syrian writers and filmmakers who conjure this slow witness need not evince any interest in such trends as slow reading or slow cinema, although there may be some formal resemblance to these cultural styles. On the contrary, the representational logic of novels and film that narrativize acts of witness and testimony is predicated on an engagement with the perils and plasticity of time and temporality. It is particularly striking in this regard how many Syrian writers have turned to memoir, testimony, and journalistic convention even as writers and cultural producers struggle with and against the breakdown of language itself. The time—but also the word and the image—is out of joint for the slow witness, who is sometimes inspired by the barrage of images and emergency situations but at other times is incapable of making sense of things or even using language as a means to describe, explain, or understand an experience. Again, my conceptualization of a slow witness is not comprehensible exactly in the same way as slow literature or slow cinema (which I discussed in relation to Riyad Shayya's 1995 film *Al-Lajāt* in Chapter 2), although there is a kinship between these, as we will see in the discussion of Ossama Mohammed's *Silvered Water*. The dialectical relationship between Wedeen's high-speed eventfulness and my conceptualization of the slow witness is governed by an emergent documentary imperative, which might be what keeps these two speeds in the same frame.

One feature of slow witnessing, as I conceive of it, is the interdependence of the witness-narrator and the voices of other subjects or characters in a co-construction of narrative. The constellations of documentary realist slow witnessing in literature and film that I take up in this chapter can be understood, borrowing from the Holocaust scholar Michael G. Levine,

> in the sense of *mitsprechen*, in the sense, that is, of voices speaking with and through one another, *at the same time*. . . . To bear witness to the witness in this context is to assume co-responsibility for that which *mitspricht* in the discourse of the witness, for that which remains adrift on its surface as a floating message in a bottle, as a letter in sufferance, as the flotsam and jetsam of unconnected and still unassimilated memory fragments.[15]

Therefore, rather than situating the author or the filmmaker as external to narration, there is a symbiotic and mutually constitutive relationship between these authorial presences.[16] In this regard, to put it somewhat abstractly, the novel in the time of the Syria War has been written in more than one voice, at times in the name of a collective author and audience. In *Regarding the Pain of Others*, Susan Sontag explores the power and limitations of photography as a medium, drawing our attention to the ethical and political implications of viewing death and human suffering from afar. Whereas the shock of the modern in the mid-nineteenth century was in part an experience of compressed and accelerated everyday time, the introduction of photographic images transformed popular understandings of social experience, including war. As Sontag notes, more advanced technological means of disseminating photographic and video material "provides a nonstop feed: as many images of disaster and atrocity as we can make time to look at."[17] The construction and consumption of this nonstop feed are made possible by political, military, and economic realities often impervious to attempts to make time. Making time to view disaster cannot always entail clearing an autonomous mental space from which to engage in the aesthetic criticism of witnessing. But literary critic and media scholar Jan Mieszkowski sees things differently in *Watching War*:

> The modern perception of warfare was distinguished by a conjunction of physical devastation and elusive simulacra long before the invention of photography or film, much less television or the Internet. If we live in an era of hyperreal wars, we have been doing so for a long time, which is why verbal media that make no claim to facilitate unmediated transmissions of information have been and continue to be as central to war spectatorship as visual media, which appear to offer a more direct encounter with the exigencies of being under fire.[18]

Mieszkowski concerns himself with the transformation of war spectatorship in the context of the Napoleonic Wars, emphasizing how essential nonvisual representations of war were to informing lay engagement with armed conflict. He rightly insists that little has changed in the qualitative phenomenological experience of war despite the advent of real-time reporting, embedded witnesses, and accelerationist visual circulation. Those who reside outside of a war zone are also exposed to multiple experiences of war, which are no less phenomenologically meaningful for lying beyond the pale of tangible reality. In this respect, aesthetic engagements with traversing the distance between the "outside" and the "inside" of the Syria Warscape can be usefully considered in relation to comparable visual encounters with war. What outside(r) and inside(r) mean in relation to Syrian literature and film in these times is subject to contestation.

LOVE IN THE TIME OF REVOLUTION: MAHA HASAN'S *DRUMS OF LOVE* (*ṬUBŪL AL-ḤUBB*)

In January 2013, Maha Hasan, who was born in Aleppo in 1966 and later moved to France, published *Ṭubūl al-Ḥubb* (*Drums of Love*), one of the first novels to be set against the backdrop of the Syrian revolution.[19] The author-narrator, Rima Khuri, a Syrian émigré in Paris and professor who has not lived in her homeland for years, becomes inspired to reconnect with Syria in response to the activist energy of the uprising that began in March 2011. Rima starts working on a book about the Syrian revolution, which she envisions as neither fiction nor nonfiction but instead a kind of "literary attempt," as she calls it, a concept that can also be used to describe *Drums of Love* itself as it reflects the kind of narrative realism that has evolved in relation to what I am calling the documentary imperative of Syria War culture. Rima becomes friends online with a man named Yusuf Sulayman, a lawyer and human rights activist in Kafranbel. Rima and Yusuf talk over Messenger, occasionally on the phone, often while getting drunk. For Rima, Yusuf becomes a "bridge" to her homeland, a way of rediscovering Syria, what she calls her "lost paradise."[20] Yusuf—an avatar of the revolution—allows Rima to rediscover the very "idea of homeland," unraveling the alienation and estrangement that had accumulated over her twenty years in exile. This setup may emerge from a kind of romantic nostalgia precipitated by the widespread enthusiasm surrounding the uprising, or perhaps Hasan wishes to draw critical attention to such a response. Whatever the case, Rima returns to Syria, visits family in Damascus and Aleppo, and talks to as many people as she can along the way. Her hope is to reach Homs, capital of the revolution, but she never makes it there.

Rima keeps track of her journey in a travelogue, marking dates but also orienting herself and the reader with casualty reports and body counts, a narrative device that suggests that Syrian history and politics are now defined by death as much as the passage of historical time (a phenomenon discussed in Chapter 6). Rima is beset by nightmares as a consequence of first-hand experience of "the Syrian nightmare" (*al-kābūs al-sūrī*). In this time of personal and collective trauma, dreams surge to the surface as if to filter the ubiquitous horror. One of her recurring dreams is being trapped in a giant bottle with thousands of Syrians as they drown in an ocean of blood. Bodies float all around her, yet they defiantly continue to sing at the top of their lungs "Yalla Irhal Ya Bashar," the rousing anthem by Ibrahim Qashush, the musician who, for singing in support of the revolution, had his throat torn out and his body dumped into the Orontes River, which flows through his native Hama. Throughout the novel, in waking life as well as in dream states, references to real people who played a part in the revolution abound: here the songs of Qashush; elsewhere memoirs by French writer Jonathan Littell and by foreign journalists such as Marie Colvin who disappeared or were killed. The mimetic realism of the novel is confirmed through specific citations. In thinking about these tropes, it bears remembering that Hasan and other writers—all Syrians—had been consumed with journalism, reportage, and other accounts of the war, exposed to a global discourse on Syria, that inform, influence, and, in this case, literally appear in the novel.

The main characters in *Drums of Love* are intellectuals and activists, and while they are lionized they are not spared criticism. Three of Rima's intellectual friends, Husayn, Yusra, and Fu'ad, function as points of entry into a discussion of those who are dismissively called "velvet intellectuals" (*al-muthaqqafūn al-mukhmaliyyūn*). In Aleppo Rima's cousin Radwan introduces her to his friend Rayyan, who confronts her with a barrage of provocative claims about the proper roles for Syrian intellectuals, some of which fly in the face of Rima's doe-eyed optimism. Rayyan has strong opinions about the "true" or "real" intellectual and her responsibilities in and toward society. "The true intellectual has no political loyalties, neither to the regime nor to the opposition," Rayyan says. In another moment, he opposes any attempt on the part of intellectuals to fraternize with the rabble.

> The real intellectual doesn't belong to the mob [*al-ghawghā'*]. These are demagogic revolutions [*thawrāt ghawghā'iyya*]. The intellectual must remain a safe distance from them. The real intellectual is like a scholar or a researcher, working in his private laboratory, studying and analyzing and mastering and discovering and inventing, on behalf of the far-off human future, and not in order to line up with the contemporary moment.

Rayyan grows even more bombastic about the rarefied power of his class: "The intellectual is a prophet of the time-to-come [*al-zaman al-qādim*]" and yet goes on to affirm that "the real intellectual is one who works in the shadows, in silence, in solitude."[21]

One central issue at the heart of the novel is how activists, intellectuals, and ordinary people react to the ubiquity of violence, the ethics of armed struggle against the regime, and the romance of the revolution itself. The uprising in its early days was celebrated for nonviolent resistance; many lamented its subsequent militarization, with all its bloody consequences. Rima's cousin Fadi, another figure with whom she spends time on her journey, is a twenty-something translator, journalist, student, and playwright who has just written a play, "The Trial of the President," which tackles the thorny problems of law and transitional justice. The verdict handed down by this fictional revolutionary tribunal is that the president be sentenced to eternity, where he will be forced to endure the howling torments of unsettled dead souls who perished at the hands of his security apparatus. The slogan *al-qā'id ilā al-abad*—the Eternal Leader, a fixture of Asadist-Ba'thist heroism—is here turned on its head through a kind of revenge therapy. Instead of his leadership and reputation lasting for eternity, timelessness is weaponized in the service of revolutionary justice after decades of authoritarian rule and regime terror. The hegemonic discourse of heroism that defined Syrian cultural production during the 1970s and 1980s no longer elicits subtle satire, as its hollow ideological slogans no longer receive a shred of respect from young Syrian revolutionaries. Claiming the play's novelty, with perhaps a not so subtle nod and wink to what she thinks about her own writing, Rima muses, "I think this is the first artistic text written about the events in Syria and its legendary revolution."[22]

Drums of Love as a finished text exists in tension with Rima's protestation to her mother in Damascus that she has no intention of publishing it. "I'm not a writer," as she puts it (echoing something Khalil Suwaylih's narrator says about his own role in *Barbarians' Paradise*, discussed later). "Even if I've recorded what is happening all around me, it's only for me, for my personal memory, perhaps for those closest to me . . . I have no intention of publishing . . . At least, not right now."[23] In the end, Rima insists that "the novel isn't ready for publication, I haven't settled on a title."[24] But in a footnote Rima explains that the working title for her manuscript is "Intellectuals and the Kalashnikov," indicating that the relationship between Syrian intellectuals and violence is central to the novel's thematic aims. Rima, for her part, finds it more important that Fadi's play be published and performed, vowing to take a copy to the real-life publisher Riyad el-Rayyes in Beirut. Rima's friend Fu'ad wholeheartedly agrees: "[The play] must be put out. Until now, no literature has appeared about the Syrian revolution. These writings must be published."[25] Of course, Maha Hasan's version was published, by Riyad el-Rayyes, with an image of an antiregime demonstration flying the revolutionary Syrian flag juxtaposed with bombed-out buildings in what could be Homs or another flattened Syrian city. This postmodern convention of characterizing the novelist in relation to real-world figures, documentary realism with a side of metafiction, is echoed in Suwaylih's *Barbarians' Paradise* and in a great deal of the literature and memoirs published about the Syrian revolution and the Syria War.

Rima eventually gets a ride to Aleppo, visiting more friends and family along the way, hoping to finally meet Yusuf so that he can take her with him to Homs. In these heady times, Rima's abiding hope remains to reach the center of revolutionary action. On the verge of meeting Yusuf at a demonstration in Aleppo, when they finally see each other across the square even as they continue chatting on the phone with one another, Rima recounts:

> I suddenly found myself speaking to Yusuf like a little girl. I forgot how old I was and everything I'd been through. I clung to him through the phone: "Yusuf, I'm begging you, please, let me go to Baba 'Amro, help me get there. I'm sure you can get me there. I'll kiss your hand, I haven't slept or been able to close my eyes. I must see with my own two eyes what's happening there. Please . . . just let me get to the liberated areas. I'll never forgive you if you don't help me get to Homs."[26]

In the climactic moment, Rima is shot in the head by a sniper and collapses to the ground, conveying a kind of relief and wonder as she drifts into a reverie of blissful martyrdom, perhaps even redemption. As she enters a liminal state between life and death, ascending toward the sky in a celestial chariot as the world fades to purple all around her, Rima can feel "warm liquid" oozing from her bloodied head, hear her mobile phone ringing, and read newspaper headlines, Facebook posts, and conflicting news accounts.[27] "The world is still all purple, I feel a strange kind of comfort, ease washes over me, ecstasy greater than any physical pleasure I've ever felt before . . . I'm flying, the chariot is taking me towards the purple sky . . . "[28]

Rima's fantasy of returning to a liberated Syria comes to a screeching halt in this final moment of violence. As witness to her sentimental education about her own country, the reader has been taken on a high-speed journey around Syria, encountering different facets of the conflict along the way. *Drums of Love* often reads more like breathless reportage than literary text, a documentary-realist narrative of emergency. Rima admits that the situation and the people she has met have transformed her from an academic into a "war reporter": "a creature voraciously gathering information, polling opinions."[29] Rima attempts to travel at the speed of journalism, at the speed of war. But as an exilic intellectual she also confronts a condition of belatedness—too slow, always running after the revolution, never physically connecting with Yusuf, never arriving in Homs, never truly meeting the revolution. Even in her brave attempt to embody the role of witness, Rima cannot keep up with the speed and destructiveness of war.

Drums of Love is written in spare, vernacular, occasionally repetitive prose, "journalistic language" (*al-lugha al-ṣiḥāfiyya*), as Hisham al-Wawi describes voice in some contemporary Syrian fiction, including Khaled Khalifa's 2016 novel *al-Mawt ʿAmal Shāq* (*Dying Is Hard Work*) (Chapter 6).[30] There is a propulsive quality to the story as Rima's search for the revolution inexorably moves toward its denouement. "This revolution has given me the power to write," Rima declares, celebrating the connection she feels with this "legendary people."[31] *Drums of Love* is also a tragedy laced with romance, a failed love story in which the female protagonist is enamored with a man but unable to consummate her desires, as well as a paean to revolutionary optimism. Rima therefore functions as a "reference point," to borrow from Dominic LaCapra, for idealists in the face of defeat, true believers in the Syrian revolution, indicative of what LaCapra describes as the "tendency to transfigure trauma," in this instance the trauma of state violence that crushes the nonviolent revolution and destroys Rima,

> into the sublime . . . where violent, traumatizing action is understood as marking a radical, even total rupture with the past—a kind of creation *ex nihilo*, conversion experience, or primal leap . . . taken to be the necessary condition for a breakthrough into a typically blank or unknowable utopian future.[32]

For LaCapra, reference points may also become "constraining frames of reference" over time. In a sense, the dashed expectations and catastrophic violence irrevocably linked with the difficulties activists faced in supporting democratic transformation in Syria led to the limiting of creative thought around the Syria War within certain constraining frames of reference, structured by both high-speed eventfulness and the documentary imperative. One way to disrupt this anxious agitation between high-speed eventfulness and the documentary imperative might be the figure and the practice of slow witnessing. As the ground shifts beneath millions of Syrians' feet, the will to certainty, the desire for home and homeland, and the submerged experience of the slow witness are refracted in literature through those constraining frames of reference, giving structure to a chaotic, structureless present, voice to the voiceless, hope to the distraught.

INTO THE SYRIAN INFERNO: KHALIL SUWAYLIH'S *BARBARIANS' PARADISE* (*JANNAT AL-BARĀBIRA*)

Rima Khuri naively hopes to connect with her "lost paradise" in *Drums of Love*. Khalil Suwaylih, who was born in al-Hassakah in 1959 and ran the cultural supplement of the state-run *Tishrīn* newspaper for many years, filters stories of suffering and devastation through the eyes of an unnamed first-person narrator who identifies wartime Syria as a *Barbarians' Paradise* (*Jannat al-Barābira*).[33] In the novel, published in 2014 by an Egyptian publishing house, the protagonist records his daily thoughts and activities in Damascus between April 2012 and December 2013, chronicling up and through the first 1,000 days of the Syria War. In the concluding entry, the narrator writes: "On the thousandth day, and the day that followed, the war didn't stop, and so 'my' exhausted Scheherazade had to summon more nights in order to be delivered from total devastation [*halāk*]."[34] The credibility of this narrator is established through his intimate knowledge of Damascus, his erudition demonstrated with citations of writing from and about Syria over the centuries, and his cosmopolitan outlook evinced by deep learning as well as the capacity to travel outside the country and return to it.

The "heaven" or "paradise" of the title stands in unsettled opposition to the "inferno" (*al-jaḥīm*) that the author-narrator runs into at every turn. While the term is a common one for hell, it's also evocative, of course, of Dante's *Inferno*. In the narrator's journey into this hellscape, invocations of the European masterwork are accompanied by references to classical Muslim scholars such as al-Tabari, Ibn Athir, Ibn 'Asakir, Ibn 'Arabi, Ibn Khaldun, and Abu Hayyan al-Tawhidi, as well as to the eighteenth-century barber-chronicler Ahmad al-Budayri al-Hallaq, *nahḍawī* writers 'Abd al-Rahman al-Kawakibi and Fransis Marrash, and more contemporary cultural figures including Omar Amiralay, Mahmoud Darwish, Federico García Lorca, Muhammad Malas, and Yusuf Abdallaki, who make cameo appearances.

Suwaylih's author-narrator guides his readers through the Syrian inferno, exposing them to its various manifestations, which makes it difficult to discern a judgment of the conflict itself. Heroes and villains, evildoers and victims bleed into one another, unlike characters with unbridled enthusiasm for the revolution such as those in *Drums of Love*, even if the latter also express discomfort and distress at the ensuing war. As in Dante's *Inferno*, Suwaylih's author-narrator is an incredulous observer, leisurely wandering the city as a slow witness: through his return to history, his habit of seeking comfort in his neighborhood through repetition, walking familiar streets, frequenting Café Rawda, where he socializes regularly. Here the slow witness as a character in the novel becomes a moral judge of history, armed with traditional literary sources, guided by a sense of the eternal nature of Damascus. Of course, Dante was also engaged with the problematic of eternity in his canvas of suffering: Virgil leads Dante's narrator through "an eternal place"[35] where tortured souls endure unending pain.[36] The eternity of the Syrian regime has been irrevocably called into question; the idea of the Syrian president representing "the leader for all eternity" (*al-qā'id ilā al-abad*) is rejected by many as nothing more than a wooden slogan. The sentencing of the leader to an eternity in hell in Fadi's play in *Drums of Love* is echoed when someone tells Rima that the most important consequence of the revolution is "the fall of the concept of eternity" (*isqāṭ mafhūm al-abad*).[37] The duration of the Syrian inferno that Suwaylih's narrator encounters, however, is indeterminate.

In comparison with Rima Khuri, Suwaylih's author-narrator seems detached. He views the ongoing death and destruction through the eye of a free-floating flaneur. "I'm not a historian," he announces in the opening line, "and I never wished to occupy the role."[38] Be that as it may, he certainly has his own opinions of history and the historical imagination. "In the near future," he says elsewhere, "the calm historian will find himself without work because of contradictory information, the absence of reliable sources, and the fabrication of events."[39] Furthermore, as he assembles a polyvocal historical narrative, the witness-narrator recognizes that this account will remain "incomplete" in the absence of other "storytellers," many of whom have already departed "for unknown graves." In this moment, however, language (*al-balāgha*) cannot express the fright experienced by those people "with the same precision brought by events themselves,"[40] partly because of his belief that the war has contributed to the breakdown of language itself. "The linguistic war is at the heart of the broader conflict. Language (*al-balāgha*) retreats with the stubbornness of a plow ox… Come along, Roland Barthes, to the theater of war, hurry up, deconstruct the codes of what has happened and what is happening."[41] In response to the breakdown of language, then, and the very possibility of linguistic certainty, the narrator turns to semiotics (Roland Barthes) as well as enumeration, the affirmation of specific information—names, dates, and places—even truth and sense more generally:

> 20 months, 80 weeks, 600 days. Hold on, how can we account for the number of the dead and missing and disabled in this war, those sickened by the freedom snatched away from them, the displaced, the thousands of miles of banners and slogans, flags, maps, the transformation of meaning in the interpretation of the country, the varieties of bombs, the names of weapons, accusations of treason, displacement, thuggery [*al-tashbīḥ*], counter-thuggery [*al-tashbīḥ al-muḍād*] checkpoints, massacres, imaginary political parties, human rights organizations, thieves, loves, kidnapped, *fatwa*s and vengeance seekers?[42]

In the face of unsettling instability, the specific dates of successive diary entries may help to orient the reader. But the sense of disorientation is reinforced for the witness-narrator, rendered more challenging by his hallucinatory encounters with dead literary and intellectual figures. Even as he meditates on the deep history of Damascus in trying to go about his everyday life, he must also dodge bombs and other dangers caused by urban warfare. Occasionally the narrator seems on the verge of retreating inside his own mind and into the encyclopedias of tradition as a means of surviving and making sense of the madness all around him. His acts of witnessing are confused and episodic, seeming to call into question the coherent expertise of the *adīb* he embodies, the quintessential man of letters, whose authority—as Maha Hasan suggests—may be of little use in a time of war as intellectuals prove to be ineffectual or get trampled, in some instances quite literally. For example, at one moment in which the narrator witnesses a private library spilling over the edge of a blown-out apartment building, books precariously perched over an unknown fate, he ponders, almost comically, whether books by al-Masʿudi (*Murūj al-Dhahab*) or al-Tabari (*Tārīkh al-Umam wa-l-Mulūk*) or al-Jahiz (*al-Bayān wa-l-Tabyīn*) might be found in that collection.[43] Meanwhile, statues of luminary figures from Arab intellectual history—al-Maʿarri, Abu Tamam—are being smashed all over the country, inspiring similar acts in Egypt, for example, but also elsewhere: an iconoclastic and antihistorical horror show gone global. Mocking the futility of turning to those poets and scholars and artists, the narrator instead needs a "military expert" to explain the endless variety of bombs and missiles that clutter his existence. Fragments of life and memory, learning and experience form kaleidoscopic images that recreate the distorted image of Syria circulating in global culture but also reflect the chaotic reality and realism of those living the conflict. In addition to a poignant image of the mixing of the mundane with the monumental in the depiction of an ongoing war, this is also a visual representation of the death of a historical archive, perhaps the evisceration of cultural memory altogether.

There is something unsettling about this fragmented and inconclusive narrative, one that sometimes fails to make sense. The language and form of the book embody the disruptions and dislocations of war. The punctuation can be rough, rushed, and occasionally incorrect, as if each word or phrase or clause of each sentence were being squeezed out with labored breath. The reader may wonder whether the failure to close quotation marks, for example, is an oversight or purposeful or even a subconscious blending of the voice and consciousness of the narrator with his interlocutors, another iteration of *mitsprechen* as the slow witness patiently assembles collective testimony. The novel slips easily, almost unconsciously, among multiple narrative perspectives:

> This morning you saw a documentary clip about the war in Kosovo, and in a flash the same scene repeats itself: a militiaman opening fire from an opening in the wall, with a subtle difference: that clip was filmed in black and white whereas we're experiencing the war in color, perhaps so that we may see the red color of blood, in the streets and on screen at the same time.[44]

The fluid shift from first-person to second-person address, then to first-person plural and on to the first-person perspective of a peripheral character may suggest the indeterminacy of subjectivity and identity in this time of chaotic upheaval. Of course, it might also be a case of rushed or even bad writing. But what could it mean for the witness-narrator to be explicitly confounded by seeing color on the street and on the screen at the same time? Does the slow witness exist both in the real world and in the virtual world at the same moment? Do they then need to be understood as appearing "inside" or "outside" the literary scene? Perhaps both? Or is this slow witness better understood as "slow" in the developmental sense, incapable of mastering their surroundings, of making sense in language in the first instance? Have they become a transcription machine recording sounds and sights and smells? Does the slow witness fulfill their historical destiny by satisfying the documentary imperative? Is the slow witness in danger of disembodiment, of being reduced to organs without a body, a walking sensorium? It may very well be the case that the acceleration of the Syria War also propels the slow witness toward a horizon of experience that stops making sense, one that suffers from an impoverishment of meaning.[45]

Marking dates and times, places and names, may be one way to punctuate and thereby exercise mastery over the empty time and fragmented spaces of war. These conventions are complicated—if sometimes clarified—by reference to sensory experience. Take smell: "There's someone finishing his coffee, the moment a missile falls, and the smell of cardamom mixes with his blood."[46] Or, in an example of third-person narrative that occasionally interrupts the text: "The smell of war is coming from all directions, he steps out onto his balcony and smells the aroma of wilting basil; it's not that smell alone, though, but the smell of gunpowder, smoldering corpses, gases, trash."[47] The grammatical subject may occasionally be confused but the sense of smell is indispensable:

> Damascus today is a barbarians' paradise, the land and the ruins [*al-arḍ wa-l-khurāb*] the origin of sorrows. Beneath the roots of the apricot and the apple and the walnut trees, in the Ghouta, you'll find tunnels for militiamen, ammunition storehouses, black flags, you'll smell the stench of Sarin gas instead of the aroma of cherry blossoms, and as you cross the street in Jawbar or Daraya or al-Muadamiya, you won't notice the dead bodies that have been neglected for days because the sniper will prevent you from getting near them.[48]

The irruption of fruit trees in the midst of gruesome urban warfare is particularly striking. Over time, senses fail, go numb. The narrator wakes up at one point "to a wilting basil plant on the balcony. It has no scent, the coffee has no taste, cigarettes have no flavor, the body has no pleasure."[49]

The degradation of the senses is accompanied by the destabilization of epistemological certainty:

> With utter certainty, as I watch a film clip on YouTube of a man carrying his little girl who has just perished underneath the rubble, I say to myself: this country is going to hell without a doubt. We can no longer listen to the stories of the dead with the same bafflement that afflicted our senses even a few months ago, thanks to the similarity and the repetition of these events.[50]

Even survivors "cannot describe what happened with precision, since every victim has his own way of narrating what happened."[51] This difficulty in ascertaining truth is exacerbated by the cynical manipulation of events and images: in the hands of Islamist fighters (from Katibat al-Tawhid or Katibat Ahrar al-Sham), for example, who record their "heroism" and "glory" for the purpose of "find[ing] funders for them to carry out even more ruthless deeds, all in exchange for breaking news on the screen."[52] The barbarism on display in the media beggars belief:

> A sociologist will find it difficult to describe, in studying Syrian society, the difference separating the first peaceful demonstration in mid-March 2011 and the sight of a militiaman called Khalid al-Hamad, nicknamed Abu Saffar, from the ʿUmar Faruq brigade, chewing on the heart of a soldier he has just killed, without trial. But hang on, hadn't the regime *shabbīḥa* slit the throat of that singer at the demonstrations in Hama, Ibrahim al-Qashush, torn out his voice box, tossed his ragged body in the Orontes River?[53]

If the horror of events—high-speed eventfulness—has spun the narrator's political compass, the act or process of slow witnessing may work to bring the needle to a halt.

Clips of torture that rebels and soldiers upload to YouTube are unbearable, though: "Utter barbarism from times before the image."[54] Still, the narrator resists this onslaught of images, withstanding the compulsion to view "live images of death that activists broadcast" on YouTube, disgusted by what he sees. "Spectators document the moment of butchery with their mobile phones, less affected by what's happening than they are interested in the angle of the shot, the visibility of the scene, and the capacity to shock, without any apparent regret."[55] The narrator implicitly references the long-standing debate about the aestheticization of violence, evincing a strong aversion to such voyeuristic tendencies in popular media while failing to look away. The narrator continues his criticism of the manipulation of images by noting how the accumulation, volume, and persistence of such visual materials dulls and depletes the human faculty for moral judgment and aesthetic criticism. "Most broadcasted images do not require the deconstruction of their visual system because the incessant accumulation accomplishes their erasure, as in a meat grinder. One image effaces the other like the dissipation of pleasure or the expiration of a food product."[56]

Returning to his interests in history, the narrator conceptualizes this visual mass of inhumanity as a YouTube archive. While some try to "record the specific photographic moment" with "their own personal archive," they are criticized for "traveling hundreds of miles, crossing the Turkish-Syrian border in order to take a picture with the rebels in the 'liberated areas,' then returning immediately with visual discoveries to be circulated on social media." This is all so that the war photographer can join the "hero's camp" and possibly earn a piddling $500 for his labor. Meanwhile, others record a demonstration in a neighborhood some distance away in order to sell the footage to a television station.[57] Scoffing at the amateur eyewitness that has been produced by the "wars of the Arab Spring," the narrator pronounces the end of the era of professional photographers. The lens of the mobile phone is the new strategy of deterrence, regardless of the validity of the image or its capacity to convince. What matters is that truth and meaning are now blended in the same frame, achieving the desired "sensual appeal" (*al-ighrāʾ al-ḥissī*), which can be best understood in the language proposed by Jean Baudrillard: "Things don't happen unless they are seen." Building on this theory of ocular power, the narrator concludes that there is danger in the potential victory of a "fabricated visual" (*al-marʾī al-muzayyaf*) that prevails over the truth, part of a larger "machinery of vision" (*mākinat al-ibṣār*).[58] Perhaps most bluntly: "Hundreds of explosive clips stack up on YouTube, reeking from the stench of hatred and blood and treason-calling [*al-takhwīn*] even as true stories have disappeared."[59] The subtle argument embedded in the narrator's worldview is that there is reason to be suspicious of the torrent of images flooding the digital space in the time of the Syria War. In other words, the slow witness need not remain loyal to one political affiliation or another: the war of images is waged at multiple speeds and with a number of literary devices, pummeling individual sensory experience, undermining the possibility of discovering truth, challenging the powers of literary expression. The force of critical theory and media studies is brought to bear on a local and regional context within which truth is *fabricated* rather than documented by the camera. The author-narrator, now comprehensible as a slow witness par excellence, thus announces himself as a more reliable source of information than images spirited out of the country, propelled by media companies and status seekers in a context of high-speed eventfulness.

Repetitious pondering of these difficult questions propels the narrator toward angry rants about physical and moral dissolution. "A country that is no longer a country, not even on school maps," is what he sees. "Displaced persons and partisans hurl accusations at one another atop the remains of a country sprawled out on an eight-thousand-year-old bed." Monstrous visions dominate his dreams:

> A mythical creature stomping around the ruins. It has swallowed the tablets of Ebla, the pottery of Mari, the alphabet of Ugarit, the monasteries of Maʿalula, the hanging bridge of Dayr al-Zur, and the statue of Ishtar in the National Museum. A beast on four legs, a book of *fatwa*s, torture chambers, ancient vengeances and sacrifices. A voracious beast in the form of a prehistoric creature awakened to the smell of blood, the scent of virgins and wild fruits, a monster who starts fire with his fingers, scorching haystacks and bridges and tires, apricot and eucalyptus and apple trees, electricity poles, heaving corpses from the walls of the Damascus citadel, shaking the grave of Salah al-Din al-Ayyubi, rattling the walls of the Umayyad Mosque, sending the rooftops of the Hamidiyeh *souq* flying.[60]

Here is a terrifying vision of apocalypse on the march, nightmares incarnate, the collapse of ancient, medieval, and modern civilization, sucked into a swirling vortex of total devastation and eternal damnation. The Syrian inferno consumes everything in its path:

> Now, there is no escape from the lexicon of death . . . choose your own death, go to the cemetery, hand over your mangled corpse at the threshold of your own house, or what remains of it, in improvised shrouds. The morgues aren't big enough for the slaughter, and the mass graves have split open the yellow fields of corn and mint and cilantro into parallel lines under the poplar trees . . . only death walks the streets.[61]

In this narrative, death is encountered, observed, witnessed. In the end, though, unlike the representations of death to be discussed in Chapter 6, death, dying, and the dead themselves remain wholly other, beyond the cognitive grasp of the narrator in *Barbarians' Paradise*. In the penultimate entry of the novel, dated November 26, 2013, the narrator recounts traveling to Sidi Bou Said, Tunisia, for a conference, where he marvels at the quiet beauty of Tunis, which is shocking by comparison with Damascus. After strolling the cobblestone streets, Andalusia in white and blue in his experience, he switches on the National Geographic channel in his hotel room in order to escape for a bit longer, but breaking news of fresh attacks and renewed violence in Damascus intervenes. Still, the narrator tries "to brush away the images of the Damascus inferno [*al-jaḥīm al-dimashqī*] from the screen of my thinking."[62]

In an interview with the *al-Ḥayā* daily newspaper in July 2014, Suwaylih elaborates his vision:

> This text is one of many texts that are going to take the Syrian scene by storm in the coming years, which will no longer afford the Syrian writer respites from the nightmare of war, and he will have to spend a long time dismantling all kinds of landmines, through various narrative means. What I tried to do is to document one thousand days of the Syrian inferno [*al-jahīm al-sūrī*], as raw material for engaging with death and violence and freedom. Today every Syrian has his own story, which doesn't resemble anyone else's story, or, rather, they only partially intersect, at the checkpoint, for example, in a destroyed neighborhood, with an incident of rape or some other violation of dignity.[63]

The novel's final entry, on the thousandth day of the conflict, is dated December 9, 2013. On the edge of the mythical 1,001 nights, Suwaylih's narrator does not travel alone into the "Syrian inferno"; all along he has been accompanied by a prehistoric creature, a dinosaur, that "roams around the ruined earth [*al-arḍ al-khurāb*], in search of his ancestors. The dinosaur shares my coffee and my bed and my books with me.[64] Does this suggest Suwaylih himself, the novelist and the narrator, is a metaphorical dinosaur? What about the reader? Is the slow witness, by extension, outmoded, evolutionarily left behind, rendered obsolete in an extinction-level event called the Syria War? At the very least, Suwaylih's narrator coexists or even cohabitates with this beastly figure. In such a situation, "there's nothing you can do but learn to count all over again: one day, two days, one month, a hundred days, five hundred days . . . and the dinosaur is still with us."[65] The barbarism of humanity on display in the Syria War surpasses that of the most terrifying beasts to have ever roamed the earth. In war literature and literature of trauma, enumeration acquires an almost talismanic power, the power of inventory, and the illusion of mastery over uncontrollable and arcane destructive forces in the world. When Suwaylih's narrator says that he lives with the dinosaur, he is communing with an extinct creature, a monster, an entire species that could not keep up with the demands of evolution and progress, destroyed by a cataclysmic event like a meteor or natural disaster... or perhaps a civil war.

SPEAKING-WITH CINEMA: OSSAMA MOHAMMED AND WIAM SIMAV BEDIRXAN'S *SILVERED WATER, SYRIA SELF-PORTRAIT* (*MĀ' AL-FIḌḌA*)

The creative expression that emerged during the early period of the Syrian uprising and emergent civil war wrestled with the problematics of belonging, witnessing and testimony, and temporality and speed. In *A Woman in the Crossfire*, Samar Yazbek produced a hybrid text that might be thought of as a testimonial memoir attempting to bridge the gap between recording collective experience and narrating inner psychological turmoil. In *Drums of Love*, Rima reconnects with her estranged homeland through a tour of Syria toward the beginning of the 2011 uprising, giving voice to her own affective experience while describing the lives and struggles of others. In *Barbarians' Paradise*, Khalil Suwaylih acquaints readers with a witness-narrator who serves as a Virgilian guide through the darkest reaches of the Syria War inferno. Technological transformations in the time of the Syria War generated comparable disorientation and spurred a search for epistemological certainty that is visible in the cinematic realm as well. Those mythical thousand and one nights referenced in *Barbarians' Paradise* were transmogrified into visual material by way of the voices of ordinary Syrians in Ossama Mohammed and Wiam Simav Bedirxan's documentary feature *Silvered Water, Syria Self-Portrait* (*Mā' al-Fiḍḍa*) (2014). In Chapter 2, I considered Mohammed's work in terms of the aesthetics and politics of masculinity in his 2002 film *Sacrifices* (*Ṣundūq al-Dunyā*) as well as through tropes of surveillance and political power in his 1988 feature *Stars in Broad Daylight* (*Nujūm al-Nahār*) in Chapter 4. When he traveled to the Cannes Film Festival in May 2011 to take part in a panel, alongside Costa-Gavras, on cinema in the shadow of the dictator, Mohammed decided not to return to Syria because of credible death threats for his outspoken support of the uprising. The speech he gave at Cannes, which is an extended meditation on a number of short videos of ordinary people being tortured by regime forces, anchored Mohammed as a witness-narrator in his own film, *Silvered Water*, a figure who both assembles a visual language and supporting characters and offers his own emotional and political reactions to events that are still transpiring. Like many observers outside the country—Syrian and non-Syrian alike—Mohammed struggled to break through the propaganda noise that surrounded and obscured what was going on inside of Syria. This attempt to pierce the veil of uncertainty bears fruit in *Silvered Water*, which was made in collaboration with Kurdish-Syrian schoolteacher Wiam Simav Bedirxan, who only started using a camera amid the demonstrations, shelling, and siege of Homs, and "a thousand and one Syrians," as the closing credits announce, individuals who contributed anonymously by way of cell phone footage uploaded to the internet. It is through Mohammed's relationship with Bedirxan, one that evolves over the course of the film, that he (and we, as spectators) are able to experience first-hand the danger and the complexity of the Syria War. *Silvered Water* is not Mohammed's first foray into documentary. His first film, *Step by Step* (*Khaṭwa Khaṭwa*, 1979), a student project at the VGIK in Moscow, is a 23-minute black-and-white short set primarily in the northwestern village of al-Rama in 1976–1977 (with a brief visit to Latakia), with music by 'Abd al-Latif 'Abd al-Hamid. *Step by Step* combines Mohammed's keen eye for beautiful composition with a sociological understanding of rural life in Syria, interweaving candid scenes that include students and teachers, parents and children, farmers and soldiers. The defining principle that governs these ordinary Syrians' experience of home, school, public life, national service, and their very capacity to imagine the future is violence, not only the violence of war and state repression but the highly localized violence of everyday life that seeps into the basic building blocks of family and community, both in the countryside and in the city.

While *Silvered Water* is dedicated to those thousand and one Syrians who contributed to its making, tracking some of the consequences of forty years of life under the pressurized social and political circumstances on display in *Step by Step*, Mohammed also contributes footage from his recent exile in France. In this regard, the tension between polyvocality and an omniscient narrator is foregrounded as Mohammed's voice guides the viewer through the visual and moral wreckage. Shohini Chaudhuri argues that "the figure of the film-maker in exile acts as a proxy for the spectator."[66] *Silvered Water* is described as an interactive film, one in which the filmmaker, the film's subjects, and the audience are co-implicated and even collapsed into a single figural viewer. But the film can also be read in terms of witnessing from a distance, thereby placing it in dialogue with both *Drums of Love* and *Barbarians' Paradise*; *Silvered Water* stands out for its unmistakable technique of *mitsprechen*, of speaking-with those ordinary Syrians who appear throughout the film both behind and in front of the camera. Moreover, *Silvered Water* needs to be distinguished from the literary works examined previously, in part because the cinematic collaboration between crowd-sourced video and edited filmmaking produces a different kind of working-together (*mitarbeiten*), what might be called, to creatively follow the German construction, *visually projecting-together* (*mitprojizieren*) or perhaps more prosaically in English, video sharing. Simply put, Mohammed the filmmaker should not be understood exclusively as a proxy or a spectator but as a witness-narrator himself as well, one who speaks both with and in relation to other Syrians in search of a visual language adequate to the horrors and dislocations of the Syria War.[67] In this regard, *Silvered Water* is a paradigm of what I have been calling the aesthetics of solidarity in Syrian cultural production. Rather than being primarily concerned with drawing attention to regime violence and popular resistance—the aesthetics of power and the aesthetics of resistance—Mohammed and Bedirxan stage a profound meditation on the capacity of ordinary Syrians to pursue social solidarity and political action through the power of the image and its circulation. While the two forms are closely related and often overlapping, the aesthetics of solidarity exceeds the bounds of an aesthetics of resistance to state power and authoritarian rule.

The film's narrative unfolds in chapters divided into unequal increments. After a brief explanation of the tragic events in Dar'a in March 2011 that left several young boys murdered in gruesome fashion by the security services, which were followed immediately by the regime taunting the families of those deceased, the film launches into a section entitled "And Cinema Began," suggesting that a new kind of cinema is being born with the Syrian revolution. In *Silvered Water*, the conjoined metaphor of birth and rebirth—each with its own forms of violence—is visually referenced in the opening shot of a newborn baby being scrubbed clean in a bowl as water is poured over it from a coffee can, jarringly followed by cell phone footage capturing a young man who has been stripped to his underwear and then taunted, beaten, and kicked by state security forces. This opening image is a powerful expression of the cosmic danger to human life in its most vulnerable moments; it also manifests a self-referential homage to Mohammed's other films, which begin with similarly cryptic visual references to the powers and dangers of creation, a recurring fascination with eggs and babies. Then there is the first of many fades to black followed by a smash cut to videos of demonstrations taking place in Syria shot by people who, as this section introduces them, "don't know how to film."

The temporality of regime violence is established early on when images of a demonstrator who has been shot dead by state security forces screeches to a halt, allowing the camera to linger on the dead body, drawing the viewer's attention to the malleability of time in our own perception of such events. Although death and gore do not occupy a substantial proportion of the film, the slowness of these shots, measured and intentional, amplifies their influence, leaving the viewer with the impression that they have seen more of this footage than has actually been screened. In "The First Martyr," a regime helicopter flies toward the camera in slow motion, followed by footage of demonstrations, then a funeral procession. As the procession appears to have been bombed, the scene devolves into blurry images and piercing shrieks. When the scene finally resolves, blood is splattered on the ground and a number of people have been killed. In the ensuing melee, as hundreds run for their lives, intrepid camerapersons return to the streets where dozens have been shot and now lie unmoving on the ground. It is here, in this moment, that Mohammed's voiceover narration draws our attention to the beauty and monstrosity of cinema in the time of the Syria War. Mohammed refers to two varieties of cinema—cinema of the perpetrator and cinema of the victim. In this connection, Mohammed the witness-narrator weighs in on the force but also the challenge of the long shot, his long-standing technique in both narrative and documentary filmmaking, drawing attention again to both the craft of cinema and the embedded ideology of the image. As we saw in previous chapters, Ossama Mohammed, like his kindred spirit Riyad Shayya, is a master of what they both call the shot (*al-laqṭa*). There is a productive tension at the heart of the film inasmuch as Mohammed inserts his own aesthetic vision for cinema while also gesturing toward the collective narration represented by crowd-sourced footage culled from the internet. Whatever the case, it is no coincidence that many of these shots proceed in what seems like slow motion, although some might question whether this sluggish camerawork indulges or even encourages a kind of puerile voyeurism. Mohammed keeps his distance, permitting the viewer to conclude that this problem of insipid viewership is ultimately undecidable. Even with the overwhelming flood of visual material, violence, and uncertainty, Mohammed's craft "exaggerates this tendency toward de-dramatisation, draining emotional distance and narrative obfuscation even further by extending the stretches of *temps mort* and subordinating non-events to extended duration within the shot."[68]

Rather than advancing political analysis or making an emotional appeal, Mohammed the filmmaker remains agnostic, inviting his audience to observe at their own pace the absurd banality of the Syria War, even in its most extreme iterations. After all their marching in support of the regime, and now in their tireless demonstrations against injustice, in the section entitled "Marathon" Mohammed points out how the Syrian people should be acknowledged for an ersatz accomplishment, that of having completed what he calls the strangest marathon in human history. With footage of celebrations in honor of the leader, Mohammed notes that the Syrian people spent forty-two years honoring "the individual" but now find themselves marching in reverse. This is analogized to film vernacular as "shot and counter-shot." In a culture dominated by an iconography and ideology of obedience to the Eternal Leader and his descendants, the problem of heroism and heroes discussed in Chapter 2 with respect to the Asadist-Baʿthist cultural revolution comes to mind. In addition to making the world's longest national march, Syrians have been involved in the making of history's longest funeral. "They filmed the longest funeral in history," Mohammed narrates—"1,001 lives" over one thousand and one days. This is not the only time Mohammed superimposes the lexicon of cinema onto the Syria War. Footage of regime forces beating men handcuffed and on the ground in the street are described as "realist cinema"; bare-chested demonstrators in the road blocking a tank represent "surrealist cinema" (*sīnamā gharāʾibiyya*); footage of a prisoner being shot in the head is Mohammed's "cinema of the perpetrator"; a grieving old woman stars in the "cinema of the victim"; a funeral with an open casket as snow falls all around is "poetic cinema"; wondrous images of men underwater scuba diving with a Syrian revolutionary flag and a sign that reads "The People Want the Fall of the Butcher and the Fish Want the Fall of the Butcher" embody, simply put, "fantasia" (Figure 35). But the amateurish cellphone videos uploaded to the internet and the otherworldliness of this romanticized "fantasia" speak to another possible reading of the ambiguity embodied in such blurry images, which Allen Feldman terms "the apophatic blur of war," in which certain modes of representation "question the very historical possibility of proper focus and depth of field"[69] and, by extension, perhaps

FIGURE 35. Ossama Mohammed and Wiam Simav Bedirxan, *Māʾ al-Fiḍḍa* (*Silvered Water, Syria Self-Portrait*) (Les Films d'ici, Proaction Film, 2014)

the very intelligibility or coherence of the work's aesthetic ideology. The blur, in what Feldman calls photopolitics, "gestures toward a remainder, a surplus, and an excised becoming as the incorporeality that supports, backs, and literally advances the corporeality and objectivity of the photographic real."[70] I have been arguing that Mohammed's cinematic oeuvre is shot through with a photographic aesthetic. Here I would also suggest that an analogous reading of blur and distortion in film—particularly but by no means exclusively in documentary—can be linked to the undecidability of a film like *Silvered Water*. In other words, rather than mindlessly accepting the reductive and binary rubric of proregime versus pro-opposition aesthetic ideology, Mohammed's enduring commitment to the auratic force of the shot has perhaps been irreparably ruptured by the calamity of the Syria War, scrambling and ultimately blurring the form, language, and aesthetic ideology of cinema.

Mohammed's experience of disorientation as both director and witness-narrator is a recurrent theme in *Silvered Water*. Eerie footage shot on a metro train in Paris didactically communicates the confusion of everyday life in exile. First-person shots of soaring through a cloud-filled sky accompany Mohammed the witness-narrator as he introduces himself and explains his departure by plane from Syria in May 2011. Speaking of the morally challenging experience of exile, Mohammed says, "I wanted to be in danger, so that I would be a part of my people. At night, I say tomorrow I'll return. In the morning, I buy a microwave." A single egg rotating inside of a microwave flashes on screen. Eggs are a recurrent metaphor throughout Mohammed's narrative films. His interest in the philosophical problem of which came first, the chicken or the egg, speaks to his elliptical engagement with the problem of historical causality. Never more so than in the 2002 *Sacrifices* (*Ṣundūq al-Dunyā*) (Chapter 2) but here, too, Mohammed seeks to understand the meaning of life in all its messiness—beyond good and evil, violence and love. His own ambivalence about the condition of exile is poetically addressed to the undecidability of being caught in between in the time of the Syria War: "I want to go back, but I don't go back."

It is through his encounter with Simav (which means "silvered water" in Kurdish), however, that Mohammed develops his most grounded sense of orientation toward his distant homeland. In an exemplary instance of the *mitsprechen* practiced by the literary witness-narrators discussed earlier, Mohammed calls on his local interlocutor on the ground to help him tell the story. "Simav, I'm thinking of making a film about this homeland of ours. I want it to be yours and mine. What do you say?" In the series of exchanges that follow, the nondiegetic tapping on a keyboard communicates to the viewer that the voiceover dialogue is mostly online. If Rima's virtual encounter with Yūsuf in *Drums of Love* is exhilarating, even romantic, prefiguring her adventurous journey through the Syrian revolution, the stakes here seem higher, the violence more palpable and destructive. "The camera is a criminal weapon [*silāḥ jarīma*]," Simav says, sardonically dismissing regime discourse, which is why she has had to smuggle a camera into her native city of Homs. In a conversation about the relationship between being inside and being outside the events of the war, Simav asks Mohammed,

> "Where are you?"
> "I'm here in Paris."
> "If your camera were here in Homs, what would you have shot?"
> "Everything."

When their conversation is interrupted for technical reasons, Mohammed wonders whether something has happened to Simav. Because of his inability to

FIGURE 36. Ossama Mohammed and Wiam Simav Bedirxan, *Mā' al-Fiḍḍa* (*Silvered Water, Syria Self-Portrait*) (Les Films d'ici, Proaction Film, 2014)

physically search for her, he must search digitally in the archive of images, what he calls again "the cinema of the perpetrator" and "the cinema of the victim." But in this section the difference between the murderer and the victim is effaced, rebels and soldiers become interchangeable, increasingly difficult to differentiate. A soldier in uniform spins on a swivel chair in a moment of unrestrained glee and is labeled a murderer (Figure 36), while another soldier—who might be a rebel or might be a regime fighter—falls asleep in a jeep and is labeled a victim.

Simav asks Mohammed whether he believes words still have any meaning; she has come to believe that words are dead. But they do mean something for Mohammed: "image" and "spirit," he says. Many images speak more loudly than words in the film, rendering the question moot: a dead dog in the street being slowly devoured by a mangy cat; a doll and a kitten lying in ashes; a wounded cat with only three legs boldly pressing its way through the city streets; another cat, scorched beyond recognition, resembles a fantastical monster, hauntingly mewling at the camera. Simav promises to leave all of her footage behind for Mohammed if she does not make it out alive, despairing over the prospect of finding herself homeless, without a family. Even though he admits to experiencing his own version of despair and uncertainty, Mohammed insists that survival is always the better choice. "Since I left Syria, I've become a coward," he says, as silvered water fills the frame. In the closing sequence, "The Thousandth Night," Simav says she is scared, that she has had to hide in a closet, under siege, that she misses her mother, her father, Syria itself. Mohammed then imagines and narrates a dream she might have had, one in which Simav was walking through bombed-out Homs, found a baby on the hood of a car, and carried the child in search of its parents.

Toward the end of the film, questions become more probing, existential. "What is Cinema? What is Beauty?" In a haunting sideways shot of a corpse hanging from a bridge on the outskirts of the city (Figure 37), Mohammed asks about his own experience in the time of the Syria War, the inevitability of exile, and the impossibility of return. The image bears an air of irreality and communicates the disorientation of the viewer as well as of the person behind the camera. The unnervingly dark beauty of such an image raises questions at the core of aesthetic theory. If there is a politics of outrage or opposition in the film, does this shot aestheticize that politics? Or, if the regime's aesthetic ideology in the time of the Syria War is to monopolize the visual representation of death and dying, is an image such as this an instance of resignified and politicized aesthetics? There are no easy answers here, and there has been substantial criticism of Mohammed for his use of graphic images such as these in the film.[71] "I search for my time in time," Mohammed plaintively states. "Who am I?" he asks. "Who is he, time?"[72] Meanwhile, Simav has encountered an intrepid orphan boy who brings the viewer along as he discovers unexpected moments of beauty and joy in the bombed-out streets: a flower, a cat, an unfamiliar sound. This surprising appearance of innocent joy jolts the viewer out of the numbing flow of violent imagery and suggests a different take on the time and experience of the Syria War, both in image and spirit.

Much like Rima in *Drums of Love* and the unnamed author-narrator in *Barbarians' Paradise*, Ossama Mohammed himself would seem to rank as a slow witness, a witness-narrator. Even the pace of his speech is markedly slow. Here is a different way of trying to understand *Silvered Water*, one that opens up a discussion with critical scholarship on death and dying in war cinema, a theme that is the primary focus of the coming and final chapter. There are those who question the decision to include graphic footage of torture and death in *Silvered Water*. But an important distinction can be made between the discourse of witnessing and the discourse of death. As Sue Tait argues, "the discourses of

FIGURE 37. Ossama Mohammed and Wiam Simav Bedirxan, *Māʾ al-Fiḍḍa* (*Silvered Water, Syria Self-Portrait*) (Les Films d'ici, Proaction Film, 2014)

witnessing are always in competition with discourses naming imagery of death and body horror 'pornography.'" In war journalism and war photography, the discourses of witnessing are abrogated: "Our obligations to treat the dead with dignity and respect are displaced by the corpse's evidentiary role."[73] Perhaps it is the preponderance of evidence that Mohammed and Bedirxan present in *Silvered Water* that makes the film such a stimulating but also discomfiting experience for the viewer. The tension between the slow witness and the pornographic gaze in the time of the Syria War cuts across the genres of literature and film. The same dichotomy is likely to continue to shape the encounter with war at multiple distances and at varying speeds well beyond the Syrian context.

THE SPEED OF THE SYRIA WAR

In an August 2012 interview with the now defunct Beirut daily newspaper *al-Safīr*, Nihad Sirees, who had fled his hometown of Aleppo and moved to Germany, said:

> Creative writing is stalled today. Not just for me, but for many other writers. The imagination withdraws to an interest in tangible reality. The superstars of writing today are those who write articles about "the events in Syria" or "the

> Syrian crisis" and, finally, "the Syrian revolution." People have come to prefer reading Facebook posts, the latest breaking news, or even a rumor to reading a story, even if its subject matter is the revolution. People are nervous about the country, about reality itself. . . . The best thing one can do is to be brief, to cast some light on what is happening . . . .my mind is now consumed by the latest news story, by trying to understand what is happening, by predicting what is going to happen . . . more than literary or artistic creation.[74]

In terms of the anxieties that confronted Syrian writers, Sirees's words would ring true, prescient, and perhaps essential even as the Syrian civil war appears to be grinding to a halt in the early 2020s. Sirees presents a binary opposition between understanding and empirical truth on the one hand and "literary or artistic creation" on the other. Given the defiant voices on display in his 2004 novel *The Silence and the Roar* (Chapter 4), this tonal shift to a greater degree of hesitation and uncertainty is striking. Such neat generic categories may not be helpful in the study of literature and other forms of cultural production. Syrian writers in the time of revolution and war struggle to establish their own faculty of understanding and relationship to empirical truth through the very process of literary or artistic creation. In a time of uncertainty, disinformation, and humanitarian catastrophe, the conditions and consequences of the Syria War made matters even more complicated for writers, journalists, and observers.[75]

"*Learn to think with pain*," Maurice Blanchot wrote in his scathing evaluation of the possibility for critical thought after Auschwitz.[76] Syrian writers and filmmakers have been learning to think with pain on the fly in the time of the Syria War. In order to make sense of this phenomenon, critics and historians need to return to first principles regarding the study of writing in war and other disasters. It is worth asking what the responsibility of the writer is—as an intellectual, a citizen, a journalist, a human being—in the face of mass atrocity and planetary crisis. What kind of literature—what forms, genres, styles, and conventions—emerged amid the surreal, saturated media environment that produced and framed the Syrian uprising, the militarized conflict, international war, humanitarian catastrophe, and refugee crisis that ensued in its wake? Such timeless and (un)timely questions can be apprehended in universal terms to be sure, but they also hold particular resonance for post-2011 Syria. This line of questioning is not purely academic for historians, for literature scholars and film critics, for readers and spectators; it flummoxes cultural critics, military strategists, politicians, and engaged citizens around the world. Most important, though, it challenges and provokes Syrian writers and ordinary people who hope to see a peaceful political solution to the Syria War and a return to some semblance of normalcy in the country.

Sirees's understandable concerns about the conditions of possibility for cultural production in the time of the Syria War notwithstanding, one of the most fascinating developments in the Syrian intellectual sphere since 2011 has been, in fact, an unprecedented flurry of what he refers to as literary or artistic creation. Beyond the blogs, Facebook posts, and skirmishes on social media to which Sirees refers, during the first few years of the Syrian revolution-cum-civil war a spate of memoirs and diaries were published that attempted to chronicle life under conditions of war, displacement, and vast human suffering. A simultaneous and unexpected efflorescence of Syrian novels bloomed as well. Whether or not Syrians preferred to read stories about such matters, as Sirees phrases it, and whether or not one might experience war fatigue from and through those narratives are open questions. In 2014 literary critic and novelist Nabil Sulayman identified a "sudden outburst" and "boiling-over" of the novel since the start of the Syrian uprising.[77] But what is the significance and impact of such an antiquated cultural form in relation to real-time journalism, human rights reporting, and social media activism? Furthermore, what criteria of judgment—what aesthetics, ethics, and politics—are adequate to writing and reading novels in light of human tragedy as immense as the Syria War? If the first casualty of war is truth—and it always needs to be stressed that this loss pales in comparison with more than half a million human deaths and that number many times over injured and displaced—the Syria War marked a turning point toward a new kind of anxiety about the verifiability of the most basic contours of reality, a widely shared problem in the age of post-truth.[78]

"War is a pulsation of violence, variable in strength and therefore variable in the speed with which it explodes and discharges its energy," wrote Clausewitz.

> War moves on its goal with varying speeds; but it always lasts long enough for influence to be exerted on the goal and for its own course to be changed in one way or another—long enough, in other words, to remain subject to the action of a superior intelligence.[79]

Clausewitz provoked the warrior and military strategist to think through the vectors of movement and speed while waging war on the battlefield. In concluding this chapter, I return to the broad problem of whether witnessing and representing war in literature are also governed by speed. In his illuminating reading of military theory and nineteenth-century European literature in the production of a new discourse on war spectatorship, Jan Mieszkowski observes:

> To be under fire is to experience the loss of control of one's own signifying practices. As much as a battle overwhelms soldiers with physical threats, it also crushes them with an onslaught of performative logics that leaves them with the sense that only overplaying or underplaying their hand will give them any hope of reasserting control over the apparent meaningfulness of their actions.[80]

This sentiment can be expanded and applied to soldiers and civilians who experience the "physical threats" of endless war even as they attempt to assert control over their own "signifying practices." It is worth clarifying that I do not present an argument about physical speed in the time of the Syria War—the battlefield operations of rebels or Islamists or the regime itself, or the velocity of regime barrel bombs dropped on civilian neighborhoods in Aleppo, or the flyovers and bombardment of strategic regime locations by Israeli warplanes, or the pace at which neurotoxins or other chemical weapons kill their unsuspecting victims, or how quickly Russian or Iranian or American-sourced reinforcements arrive in the country.[81]

Instead, I wish to draw attention to the imaginative horizons of speed and experience in the cultural production of the Syria Warscape. How is speed thinkable in the first place in the imagination of Syria War literature and film? Amid the surge in writing and filmmaking about the war, simple interpretative defiance in the face of linguistic or semantic breakdown, a response to quotidian catastrophe, to hell on earth, may be both a plausible explanation and a tangible consequence. "In a system based on the maximal reproduction and diffusion of images," to return to Susan Sontag, "witnessing requires the creation of star witnesses, renowned for their bravery and zeal."[82] There are star witnesses to be sure, although the galaxy of the Syrian civil war is filled with stars and they are of different sorts: shooting stars but also slow-moving objects that are less easy to identify or characterize. These slow-moving objects may not attract widespread attention, but their deliberate movement across the landscape of human experience offers literary critics and readers the opportunity to consider literature itself—the politics and practice of writing and reading—as a slow witness in a time of seemingly limitless human suffering and cataclysmic violence. Perhaps this is one moment in which writers, filmmakers, intellectuals, and citizens of all stripes can reclaim what Allen Feldman calls "the capacity to speak truth to war."[83] The instantiation of literature in public culture, the act of writing in a time of war and dislocation, no matter how frenzied, no matter how harried, may advance slow witnessing as an aesthetic possibility as well as an ethical path.

The temporality of the novel is governed not only by periodization but also by speed, the very notion of speed or velocity as a measure of the passage of time, which means that the speed of the plot may not always or necessarily be what is at stake in the aesthetic power embodied by the slow witness. In other words, the slow witness—as a character in narrative and as a characteristic of certain forms of narration itself—is not entirely defined by the pace at which characters and plot travel. In *Drums of War*, for example, Rima traverses the country at a breakneck pace, in a matter of days, quickly absorbing a panoramic view of the conflict. By contrast, in *Barbarians' Paradise* the Syria War is experienced at a more measured, grinding pace over the course of nearly three years. But whether a Syrian war novel is reduced to a single moment—approximating a war photograph—or attempts to keep pace with the revolution and the civil war itself—manic, frenzied, uncritical—one aesthetic implication of inscribing the Syria War in literature in real time is a commitment to challenging—or at least problematizing—the hegemony of speed. Literature offers the prospect of interrogating the politics and pitfalls of perpetual immediacy and instant transmissibility. Words and images cannot travel quickly enough, cannot speak loudly enough, even amid the *Drums of Love* (a title that riffs on the noise of the "drums of war") for Rima Khuri, who is split between a novelist and a "war reporter." Nor can they for the narrator in *Barbarians' Paradise*, torn between historian and sociologist. Here is one of several striking resemblances of the two novels. A similar dynamic is at play in *Silvered Water*, as Ossama Mohammed is also split into filmmaker and witness-narrator.

The punctuated, episodic nature of the writing and filmmaking discussed in this chapter suggests some important points about the nature of time in relation to the Syria War. In his work on the theory of the novel, Lukács pointed out the important relationship between time and narrative, namely that "the entire inner action of the novel is nothing but a struggle against the power of time," which he finds in the novel to be "real time—Bergson's *durée*—among its constitutive principles."[84] "Temporality," David Couzens Hoy says, "is a basic feature of interpretations of the world. An interpretation of the world will always have a temporal dimension, and if that temporality change[s], the interpretation will change as well."[85] But Pheng Cheah reminds us that the world itself is not always what it appears to be, and the world of the Syria War is an even more complicated place. Narrative is imbricated in the making of time and the remaking of temporality, as Cheah intriguingly views it: "'Narrative' in this sense is not derived from and opposed to reality. It neither presents nor represents the world but is a catachresis for the fabulous process of the opening of a world by the gift of time."[86] Putting the point slightly differently, he says, "In its very being, narrative is a simulacrum of temporalization."[87] But as readers and spectators of the crisis and catastrophe in Syria, what matters to us is not only that the time is very much out of joint but that words may fail us.

With circumstances sliding from bad worse, critical interpretation struggled to keep pace with the time of the Syria War, to find an adequate language that would analyze but also appreciate cultural production during this fraught period. In his reading of literature in the nuclear age, Derrida identified a "speed race" (*course de vitesse*) that ultimately reaches an "aporia of speed." In the midst of "a new experience of speed," there are "qualitative mutations" that also emerge alongside the "quantitative" acceleration of time in our age.[88] With respect to the challenge of thinking about literature and other matters in the nuclear age, Derrida may be right to conclude that "the critical slowdown may thus be as critical as the critical acceleration."[89] What if the witness-narrator as author and filmmaker is simply too slow to respond to an emergency, though? If slow witnessing is the deferral of death, what happens when witnesses, author-narrators, and fictional characters die? What if, in the end, literary and cinematic witnessing takes too much time? What are the aesthetic and political consequences of narration that takes temporality seriously without managing to contain the ravages of time itself? Tragically, this in all likelihood will lead to death and dying in the ruins of the Syrian revolution, producing what I introduce in Chapter 6 as the necroaesthetics of the Syria War: literature, film, and other forms of cultural production that reflect and wrestle with the scale of the war's death and devastation. The final chapter of *Revolutions Aesthetic* will analyze how Syrian writers and filmmakers have directly addressed "the end" in cultural production of the Syria War with depictions of and meditations on death, dying, and dead bodies. Even with the turn to such morbid affairs in Syrian literature and film, the agonistic dialectic between the aesthetics of power and the aesthetics of solidarity (as opposed to but sometimes in alignment with an aesthetics of resistance) continue to generate important creative differences, which speak to the conditions of possibility for altogether new aesthetics and politics in the time of the Syria War and in the postwar period to come. There may be no better way to end this modest literary-critical and scholarly "attempt" to make sense of disarticulated language and human disorientation in the face of the Syria catastrophe—even without any expectation of comfort or redemption—than by returning to Dante's *Inferno*:

> Who could find words, even in free-running prose,
> For the blood and wounds I saw, in all their horror—
> Telling it over as often as you choose
>
> It's certain no human tongue could take the measure
> Of those enormities. Our speech and mind,
> Straining to comprehend them, flail, and falter.[90]

Chapter 6

FACES OF DEATH

They said: the monuments of history have been leveled;
They said: ruin and burning struck them.
. . .
Through whatever path they sought safety,
Paths of death came in its stead.

— Ahmad Shawqi, "The Catastrophe of Damascus"[1]

As long as humans can remember, death has been the point at which all the lines of every real story converge.

— Václav Havel, "Stories and Totalitarianism"[2]

Though the universe of art is permeated with death, art spurns the temptation to give death a meaning. For art, death is a constant hazard, misfortune, a constant threat even in moments of happiness, triumph, fulfillment.

— Herbert Marcuse, *The Aesthetic Dimension*[3]

THE EGYPTIAN NEOCLASSICAL POET AHMAD SHAWQI (1870–1932) WAS stirred to pen his monumental verse "The Catastrophe of Damascus" (*Nakbat Dimashq*) as a modest protest against the bombardments of Damascus and other Syrian cities that were part of the brutal French colonial response to the Great Syrian Revolt of 1925–1927. The work is structured as an elegy for cities (*rithāʾ al-mudun*), a genre of classical Arabic poetry. Meanwhile, it salutes the suffering of the Syrian people as they struggled against foreign domination while also expressing an incipient Arab solidarity. The violence of colonialism was met not only with armed resistance but also with what Hussein N. Kadhim calls a "poetics of anti-colonialism." With respect to "The Catastrophe of Damascus" in particular, Kadhim writes, "The achievement of Shawqī lies fundamentally in his evolving a poetics that has creative recourse to tradition as it seeks to advance an anti-colonial agenda, to articulate a vision of a decolonized Arab subjectivity."[4] Comparable forms of solidarity have accompanied the struggle for life, liberty, and justice in Syria from the emergence of the uprising in early 2011. If not from the beginning, then from very early on, the Syrian revolution devolved from a political struggle into a military conflict soaked in blood. Syrian writers, artists, filmmakers, and others have raised their voices through creative expression and cultural production that directly tackles contemporary wartime horrors on a staggeringly gruesome scale, one that might seem familiar to those who lived through the atrocities of French colonial domination and that rivals Shawqi's "paths of death." The slow witness to the catastrophe of the Syria War—the complex interdependence of witnesses, witness-narrators, and witnesses to the witnessing discussed in Chapter 5—helps to create but also struggles against the distance between their own subject position and the suffering on display in their art. In a sense, this proximity of suffering is rendered material through the physical and imaginative destruction of individual human lives, laid bare and placed on display in writing and visual culture. "The impact of seeing what was once alive and human," it might be argued in this connection, "is the very thing that distances you from it" but also "enacts an inhuman death, a copy of death, a death less *event* than it is *thing*."[5]

The primary focus of this chapter is the immediacy of macabre sights and graphic depictions of revolution, war, and violence in text and image, part of what is perhaps an unsurprising spike in literary and cinematic engagements with the themes of death, dying, and dead bodies. Meanwhile, the struggle around aesthetic ideology in the face of an enduring state policy aiming to capture the cultural and intellectual fields by controlling the narrative of "authentic" creative expression and truly "revolutionary" discourse continues to shape the conditions of cultural production in wartime Syria. As with other moments in modern and contemporary Syrian history, the agonistic interplay among the aesthetics of power, the aesthetics of solidarity, and the aesthetics of resistance gives structure to this struggle over and across the cultural field. Recent novels and films from and about Syria constitute a kind of literary-cultural morgue, a textual and visual apparatus that has "produced" the dead bodies and the experiences of death and dying that suffuse the Syria Warscape. This chapter attempts to make sense of this mortifying dimension of contemporary Syrian cultural politics—the irruption of visceral experience and representation in art, politics, and everyday life. Bodies and gore are spattered all over the cultural consciousness of the Syrian revolution, which is comprehensible, at one level, in terms of the harrowing mortality statistics, unofficial as they may be given that there are no reliable numbers: more than half a million dead, well over a dozen million displaced internally and forced into foreign exile or refugee status of some kind. The depiction of death and dying in cultural production during the Syria War is occurring alongside—and in some kind of dialogue with—works produced in the shadow of the Arab uprisings. The works under consideration in this chapter struggle to adequately respond to the violence with which the Syrian revolution has been met—to depict the corporeal qualities of its devastation. To do justice to what Adorno calls "reality at its most extreme and grim" in the time of the Syria War, "artworks that do not want to sell themselves as consolation must equate themselves with that reality."[6]

Human carnage, body parts, and suffering are on wide display, often circulating online, sometimes in graphic and gory detail, other times through symbolic or elliptical aesthetic references. And yet the question of representation persists. Syria War writing is not unlike literary attempts in the time of the Yugoslav Wars (1991–2001), one instructive comparative example that Dragana Obradović describes as "this time of insecurity—the parentheses of war—[that] reveals literature as the foothold on which the crisis is endured, even if it is endured in pain, in indignation, and in defeat."[7] On the other hand, there is both potential and risk in such attempts at comparison when it comes to reading and interpreting literature and cultural production in wartime. "War," writes Frederic Jameson, "offers the paradigm of the nominalist dilemma: the abstraction from totality or the here and now of sensory immediacy and confusion."[8] This perspective sensibly addresses the matter of form and conceptual framing in cultural production, indicating that the representation of loss, suffering, and annihilation can lead to the dulling of human senses and the evisceration of meaning and pain in these historical contexts. In the same move, however, Jameson seems to almost denigrate "war culture" tout court, arguing that "one often has the feeling that all war novels (and war films) are pretty much the same and have few enough surprises for us, even though their situations may vary."[9] It is unclear whether this is true of every genre of writing and art or whether there is something specific about war that flattens the creativity, solidarity, and experimentation on display in such work. The notion that the commonalities of war culture across historical contexts should negate the significance of representation and creative expression in a time of extreme violence is difficult to accept.

Whatever the case, it bears remembering that literature, cinema, and other forms of cultural production in the time of the Syria War did not emerge ex nihilo. Political, aesthetic, and social struggles that determined the character of Syrian artistic creation during the preceding five decades of Baʿthist rule were not simply absented with the 2011 uprising and the consequent civil war. Chapter 4 focused on representations of visual and auditory aspects of surveillance in early 2000s cultural production, the embodied and affective experience of the security state in Syrian literature and film. Chapter 5 explored how this visual culture was transformed in the time of the Syria War, a moment characterized by a highly political aesthetics of witnessing as well as engagement—however tentative, however powerless—with epistemological uncertainty. And if that chapter demonstrated how Syrian writers contributed to an unprecedented efflorescence of the novel form in ways that reflect the specific conditions of suffering and displacement in wartime, authors and filmmakers also grappled with the emotional, psychological, and cultural dimensions of death in the imaginative spaces of fiction and film. Through the discussion of Ossama Mohammed and Wiam Simav Bedirxan's *Silvered Water, Syria Self-Portrait* (*Mā' al-Fiḍḍa*), we saw how an in-depth encounter with the bodies destroyed in the Syria War need not result in voyeuristic fixation on the corporeality of wartime devastation; despite the potshots taken against Mohammed and Bedirxan for their ostensible glorification of violence, only a few minutes of *Silvered Water* linger on dead or dying bodies. We also saw how fiction writing in and about Syria has been indelibly marked by experiences of destabilization, displacement, and disbelief. Journalistic and testimonial witnessing, both fast and slow, demonstrate how the 24/7 news cycle and the compression of time/space have fundamentally transformed the relationship between Syrian writers and filmmakers—of both fiction and nonfiction, narrative and documentary—and narration itself.

In this chapter, I argue that the conditions of possibility for Syrian writers and filmmakers to continue creating compelling and mimetically plausible imaginative worlds have been determined, in part, by the deathly reality they must confront on a regular basis. If the grisly sight of dead bodies runs the risk of becoming banal for its ubiquity, narratives of destruction and loss are essential to constructing a vision of Syrian displacement and misery that can be translated into technical and political languages. For the most part, however, scholarly and popular discussions about the Syria War continue to center on grand strategy, military dynamics, humanitarian intervention (in its nonviolent and violent forms), and the persistent failure to find a diplomatic solution. How has the Syrian subject been transformed in the midst of these hellish and unstable forms of reality, though?[10] How are intimate relationships influenced by everyday death, dying, and mourning? What does grief look, sound, and feel like in the context of this devastation? Can literary and visual representation ever be adequate to such visceral shock and abject carnage? Is the juggernaut of the Syria War reducible to quotidian matters like burial rites and final resting places? Is there, in the end, a plausible place for the dead—or the living for that matter—to rest? What might the imagination and representations of the dead in literature and cinema tell us about the cultural politics of the Syria War? In what ways is the dead body itself—in pieces, decomposing, haunting—capable of wielding influence? What is the relationship between death in its literary and aesthetic registers and the politics of death, or the necropolitical?

In recent Syrian War literature, corpses can be found—as individual subjects and collective actors—weighing like a nightmare on the living. Fictionalized war landscapes are apocalyptic, populated with ground flesh, severed limbs, disappearances, and bodies demanding identification, transportation, and even communal reconciliation. The dead are physically—that is to say, not just emotionally, psychologically or spiritually—a burden on the living.[11] Beyond the necropolitical conditions that characterize how a state or other authority attempts to exercise control over living and dying, there is a necropolitical dimension to the imaginative landscape of Syrian cultural production. This calls for an adequate theoretical language to distinguish the aesthetic from the necropolitical—"contemporary forms of subjugation of life to the power of death" in Achille Mbembe's formulation[12]—which I refer to as the *necroaesthetics* of the Syria War: the assemblage of literary, cinematic, artistic, and performative discourses oriented around representation of various dimensions of death, dying, and dead bodies.

Abir Hamdar rightly draws attention to "the necropolitical dimension of the Syrian conflict,"[13] but veers off in a reading of film and art that represents "the Syrian corpse" as "the paradoxical agent of what we might call *post-mortem resistance*,"[14] part and parcel of "a new politics of resistance which seeks to affirm [its] dignity."[15] I have no a priori objection to the notion that the Syrian corpse can "have" dignity, can speak, and can even (re)join the revolution. I find it more interesting, though, to explore how it functions as a vehicle for the transmission of different kinds of meaning, desire, and politics. Agency is a thorny question in this regard and cannot be so easily dispatched by summarily assigning political or ethical intention to inanimate objects or through recourse to uncomplicated symbolic and allegorical interpretation of the dead and the dying in literary fiction and other cultural production. Must the cultural production of/in the revolution—its "documentary imperative"—always and by definition be about "struggle" and adhere to the doggedly optimistic or romantic conventions of "the revolution"?

It is difficult to ignore the fact that such analytical categories are restatements or perhaps (re)appropriations of the wooden language of the Asadist-Baʿthist cultural revolution itself. Bearing in mind the discussion of time, temporality, and witnessing in the cultural politics of the Syrian revolution in Chapter 5, what would an aesthetics of revolution capable of both resisting and transcending the logic of state-defined aesthetic ideology in Baʿthist Syria look like? In broader philosophical terms, is it vulgar, as some might argue, to make art under such circumstances? Does the creative blockage described by Nihad Sirees in Chapter 5 signify a fundamental lack of political commitment? Or is it, as novelist Khaled Khalifa has argued, vulgar to remain silent?[16] What are the ethics of creating literature and film in the age of the Syria War? To be clear, I am not challenging the assertion that the politics of dignity so central to the Syrian revolution may be recuperated and articulated in aesthetic terms about and even through the dead. Perhaps most important, it is not the place of a metropolitan, non-Syrian scholar such as me to dictate to Syrian revolutionaries, intellectuals, and scholars how they ought to understand this history of revolution and war. What the work discussed in this chapter suggests, however, is that dignity and redemption are not the only or always the most appropriate mode through which to engage with aesthetic representations of death in the time of the Syria War, the necroaesthetics of its culture. Historians and critics need to remain attentive, as Sue Tait puts it, to the way in which "graphicness is used to encode realism; the way the deployment of new reality effects within the aesthetics of ultraviolence are used as signifiers of plausibility and veracity."[17]

It is no easy feat to derive a critical-aesthetic vocabulary adequate to the violence and destruction in the literature and film of the Syria War without turning gratuitous, vulgar, or romantic. To be sure, the aesthetics of resistance needs to be taken seriously, but, as I have argued throughout *Revolutions Aesthetic*, the Syrian cultural field can be better understood as having been shaped by an agonistic dialectic between the aesthetics of power and the aesthetics of solidarity. In Chapter 5, I argued that novels and films were one means by which Syrian writers and filmmakers grasped epistemological certainty in the time of the Syria War, finding in the former a ground on which aesthetics and politics could be established and debated. This chapter explores how death in the literature and film of the war became a thematic venue for consideration of identity, community, and politics. Death is everywhere and nowhere at once, eternal yet extremely specific to a particular moment. The localization of death talk on the corpse, a lifeless and motionless character in some recent Syrian fiction and film, sheds light on how writers and filmmakers have attempted to imbue the banality of dying in a situation of mass death not just with dignity but with meaning, to ventriloquize suffering beyond mortality. The containment of the horror of mass death in the individual dead body is an act of artistic control. But how effectively do representations of death, dying, and/or the dead body communicate suffering and struggle to the reader of fiction or the viewer of cinema? Furthermore, what might be the ethical, emotional, and political consequences of such messaging?

"Death, whether faced in actual dying or in the inner awareness of one's own mortality, is perhaps the most antipolitical experience there is," Hannah Arendt observed in *On Violence*.

> It signifies that we shall disappear from the world of appearances and shall leave the company of our fellow-men, which are the conditions of all politics. As far as human experience is concerned, death indicates an extreme of loneliness and impotence.[18]

Such an understanding of death as it pertains to the conditions of possibility for social solidarity and political action needs to be situated in relation to Arendt's conception of instrumental violence. The meaning of the political remains particularly tangled and therefore continues to represent one site of discursive struggle. Critical theorists and postcolonial intellectuals from Walter Benjamin (on transcendental or redemptive violence) to Frantz Fanon (on revolutionary violence) and Achille Mbembe (on necropolitics) have contested and complicated Arendt's formulation. As Judith Butler elegantly explains,

> [Arendt] seeks to base democratic law on a conception of power that makes it distinct from violence and coercion. . . . In her political lexicon, violence is defined as coercion, and power is defined as nonviolent, specifically, as the exercise of collective freedom. Indeed, [Arendt] holds that if law were based in violence, it would therefore be illegitimate, and she disputes the contention that law can be said to be instated or preserved by violence.[19]

The banality of such violence amid conditions of war, displacement, and social trauma contributes to the possibility of finding in death other kinds of power—emotional, symbolic, political, *and* aesthetic. The representation of death in much Syria War literature and culture portrays the dead and the dying in unsentimental terms, as bodies and remains that must simply be dealt with. In other words, there are both symbolic and political forces at work in this field of necroaesthetics.

Politics in Syria War literature is not the exclusive purview of the living; the dead also contribute to the making of social and political space. "The institution of war represents—for soldiers and civilians alike, for everyone—the right to a specific form of death," writes literature scholar Steven Miller.[20] If this is the case, though, is this form universal? The symbolic valences of death in battle may become scrambled in the context of civil war and its literary monuments. Are there specific *forms* of death that occur in different times and places? What is the temporality of this "right to a specific form of death"? Is it a right that must be articulated and exercised in the present? In the moment of death itself? Or, perhaps, is "the right to a specific form of death" restricted to the experience of the living, tended by those who wish to ensure the dignity of the dead and the dying? As we saw with Hanna Mina's *Death of a Brave Man* in Chapter 2, Mufid set the time and place of his own death by suicide, in a moment that would generally not be construed as wartime. For Miller and others interested in the monumental memorialization of war death, of *war beyond death*, as he calls it, the continued demands and agency of the dead fall away. But literary critics deal with a different set of concerns, namely the extent to which tropologies of death—the symbolic and aesthetic universes within which cultural production enables, defines, and considers the consequences of death and dying—inform the politics of the possible in the present as well as in the future. In this sense, the causes and consequences but also the modalities of death and dying in the Syria War cannot be so easily determined by authors and protagonists of Syria War literature. On the contrary, the problem of the dead body—its form and its fate, its political value, means of disposal, and appropriate interpretation—remains stubbornly rooted in the text, grounded in lived and imagined corporeal experience, but it also stretches the limits of mortality itself through the continuing animation of the dead beyond the grave.

Dead bodies figure in distinct yet interrelated ways in the wartime culture discussed in this chapter: the novels *al-Mawt 'Amal Shāq* (*Death is Hard Work*) by Khaled Khalifa (2016), *Qamīs al-Layl* (*Night Shirt*) by Sawsan Jamil Hasan (2014), *al-Gharānīq* (*The Cranes*) by Mazin 'Arafa (2017), and the film *Yawm Aḍ'atu Ẓillī* (*The Day I Lost My Shadow*) by Soudade Kaadan (2018). Death and dying are the impetus for an estranged trio of siblings to both come together and fall apart in *Dying is Hard Work* as they drag their father's lifeless body across the treacherous territory of the Syria War. In *Night Shirt*, the overdetermined meaning of an abandoned corpse functions as the fulcrum of a mystery, becoming the site of anxiety and preoccupation for an entire neighborhood as it struggles to define the body's identity, culture, and future. *The Cranes* draws our attention to the masculinist violence of dictatorship, patriarchy, and war as nightmarish fantasies torture the living and the dead alike. In all of these novels, a collective subject must reckon with the emotional and political significance of death and dying. The chapter concludes with a discussion of the debut feature film by French-Syrian director Soudade Kaadan, *The Day I Lost My Shadow*, in which anxieties over death are represented by fungible human bodies, as shadows disappear in a manner that illustrates life's fragility in times of war, dislocation, and loss.

AS I LAY DYING IN THE SYRIA WAR: KHALED KHALIFA'S *DYING IS HARD WORK* (*AL-MAWT 'AMAL SHĀQ*)

Khaled Khalifa was born in Aleppo in 1964 and is one of the best-known Syrian novelists and screenwriters. His novels *In Praise of Hatred* (*Madīḥ al-Karāhiyya*) (2006) and *No Knives in the Kitchen of This City* (*Lā Sakākīn fī Maṭābikh hadhihi al-Madīna*) (2013) received widespread critical acclaim and have been translated into English, among other languages.[21] In *Dying Is Hard Work* (*al-Mawt 'Amal Shāq*), the corpse of 'Abd al-Latif al-Salim is a cipher harboring contradictions to his three children—Bulbul (Nabil), Husayn, and Fatima—who hardly knew their father while he was alive.[22] As in William Faulkner's *As I Lay Dying*, which I briefly re-hearse here, the death of a senior family figure—in this case the matriarch, Addie Bundgren—turns out to be less disruptive for its emotional pain than the burden of disposing a loved one's worldly remains. The Bundgren family struggles against economic hardship and natural obstacles in their quest to provide Addie, mother of five, a dignified burial in her hometown of Jefferson, Mississippi. Along the way, the family endures internecine bickering, physical danger from the elements, moral scandal, and bad luck. Although the Bundgrens eventually succeed in transporting Addie to her final resting place, they are left broken physically, psychologically, and morally. Death, for Faulkner—as for Khalifa—is hard work indeed.[23]

Dr. Peabody, who helps the Bundgren family with Addie's transport and burial, meditates on his own relationship to death and dying: "I can remember how when I was young"

> I believed death to be a phenomenon of the body; now I know if to be merely a function of the mind—that of the minds of the ones who suffer the bereavement. The nihilists say it is the end; the fundamentalists, the beginning; when in reality it is no more than a single tenant or family moving out of a tenement or a town.[24]

At a key moment in the journey to Addie's ancestral home, Samson and his wife Rachel offer shelter to the travelers. "Because I got just as much respect of the dead as ere a man," Samson says, "but you've got to respect the dead themselves, and woman that's been dead in a box four days, the best way to respect her is to get her into the ground as quick as you can. But they wouldn't do it."[25] As in

Dying Is Hard Work, the Bundgren family's quixotic journey to bury a loved one amid dire circumstances—poverty and natural disaster in Faulkner; war and displacement in Khalifa—is perceived by people met along the way as a fool's errand or a morally objectionable luxury. Unlike the dead body in *Dying Is Hard Work* but like the corpse in *Night Shirt* (discussed later), however, Addie is able to speak for herself in a chapter told entirely from her perspective.[26] In fiction the dead may be subaltern, but in some cases they may be endowed with the capacity to speak and to stand for something.

It is the desire of the corpse in both *As I Lay Dying* and *Dying Is Hard Work* to have their loved ones inter their remains in their hometowns—Jefferson, Mississippi, for Addie; for ʿAbd al-Latif the fictional village of al-ʿAnnabiyya, located in rebel-held territory outside of Aleppo, not far from Idlib, which happens to be Khaled Khalifa's home region. Bulbul (who insists on not being called by his proper name, Nabil) has been estranged for years from his two younger siblings, Husayn and Fatima. Husayn is the prodigal son who disappointed his parents' expectations by having a relationship with an older woman and doing jail time for drug-related offenses. Bulbul, meanwhile, remains the responsible one. After a divorce from his wife Hiyam, Nabil had returned to Damascus in order to live with his father, who was battling the terminal illness that eventually took his life. Four years of grinding civil conflict had eroded the political optimism and will to live of all three children. Bulbul manages to convince his brother and sister to accompany him on a journey from Damascus to northern Syria to bury their father. From the start, the trip is beset by frustrating difficulties and absurd mishaps. If the Bundgren family—Pa and his five children—face economic hardship and natural instability in their attempt to give Addie a suitable burial, the three children in *Dying Is Hard Work* are up against even more unpredictable and dangerous elements: the shifting currents of the Syria War. The trio must navigate checkpoints manned by the Syrian regime, the Free Syrian Army, and Islamist-jihadist elements across the country, as well as confront the general state of political collapse and human carnage that litters the landscape. Over the course of a drive north in a jalopy of a minibus which should take hours but ends up consuming days, the third-person narrator describes the trip, the interior states and memories of all three living characters, and the life experiences of their deceased father. The hellish narrative is punctuated by moments of boredom, despair, and detached reminiscing about the children's experiences with their father.

ʿAbd al-Latif had died peacefully in his bed in Damascus, after confiding in Bulbul his dying wish to be buried in the cemetery in his ancestral village alongside family members including his sister Layla, who had committed suicide rather than submit to an arranged marriage. Bulbul's willingness to accept this charge is a "rare moment of courage."[27] But he feels remorse for not telling his father how difficult this work will likely wind up being: "There were mass graves everywhere filled with casualties who'd never even been identified. No *ʿaza* lasted more than a few hours now, even for the rich: death was no longer a carnival people threw in order to demonstrate their wealth and prestige."[28] For Bulbul, this was a profound change in the culture. "For the first time, everyone was truly equal in death. The poor and the rich, officers and infantry in the regime's army, armed squadron commanders, regular soldiers, random passersby, and those who would remain forever anonymous."[29] Husayn is dispatched to rent a minibus for which they will improvise an ambulance sign. Bulbul, Husayn, and Fatima find the morgue overflowing when they go to pick up their father's body. If they pay the ten thousand lira required to expedite the corpse's release, they cannot bribe their way through traffic. "Husayn recalled how funeral processions used to be respected back in peacetime—cars would pull over, passersby would stop and cast you genuinely sympathetic looks."[30] The English-language edition of the novel lacks the following sentence: "But in wartime the passing of a funeral was a banal event that didn't inspire anything but the envy of the living," who were consigned to "painfully waiting for death."[31] As they slog through central Damascus, Husayn is insulted by passing cars and thinks about the popular expression "The living endure beyond the dead"; years of the Syria War had taught him that this was not true and that the dead outlast the living.

> Death is a solitary experience, of course, but nevertheless it lays heavy obligations on the living. There's a big difference between an old man who dies in his village, surrounded by family and close to the cemetery, and one who dies hundreds of kilometers away from them all.[32]

After being waved through the last checkpoint in Damascus, the trio believe they can make it to ʿAnnabiyya by the middle of the night, that the body might not rot beside them. But when they are stopped at a checkpoint just before the international road, their journey is imperiled because they have no identification for the corpse. When a soldier pulls them aside, Husayn whispers to Bulbul, "They're going to arrest the body" because ʿAbd al-Latif had been wanted by the *mukhābarāt* at one point.[33] Bulbul protests that "he himself support[s] the current regime—he and his father had been estranged!"[34] Nevertheless, the officer explains that according to their records their "father was still alive and still wanted. It didn't matter if he had in the meantime turned into a cadaver."[35] It ceases to be clear "whether the state regarded a person as being merely a collection of documents or rather an entity of flesh, blood, and soul."[36]

Bulbul flashes back to the night before when he sat with his father just before he died, finding it hard to fathom how anyone can die a "natural" death anymore.

> In recent months, when people died, no one bothered asking after the hows and the whys. They already knew the answers all too well: bombings, torture during detention, kidnappings, a sniper's bullet, a battle. As for dying of grief, for example, or being let down by your body, deaths like that were rare—and no one lamented a death that didn't have any outrage attached to it.[37]

Reflecting on what it would take for him to fulfill his father's final wish—even with the assistance of his siblings—Bulbul concludes that it is all too much: "Death had become hard work. Just as hard as living."[38]

Bulbul and his siblings start to wonder what their father's corpse means, what it is worth, whether it merits all the trouble to which they are subjecting themselves to make this journey. Although they pose a literal question—"What did his father's body mean?"[39]— it is just as interesting to consider *how* as well as *what* corpses mean in Syria War novels. What kind of necroaesthetics is becoming visible in the novels of the Syrian revolution? How does one approximate the omnipresence of death for Syrians inside and outside the country? After finding a place to stay the night in Homs, they store the corpse in the local morgue thanks to Lamya and Zuhayr: Lamya is a friend of Bulbul's ex-wife Hiyam, and she and her husband Zuhayr have turned their home into a field hospital and safe house for displaced people. Bulbul remembers all he had done to help secure Zuhayr's release from prison many years before. Lamya used to visit him in Damascus until she moved back to her native village and married Zuhayr. Nevertheless, he "often thought that the true meaning of love was what we had never experienced and what was now lost to him."[40] When they have to quickly make space for dead soldiers at the morgue, they notice that their father's body "... had begun to swell; its skin was turning blue and a shade of green that looked almost moldy."[41]

Bulbul had divorced his wife Hiyam and moved home to live with his father, who was remarried to a woman named Nifin, making Bulbul the closest of all three children to their father. Although Bulbul and ʿAbd al-Latif had disagreed about politics and the war, they could commiserate over romantic disappointment. ʿAbd al-Latif had been tenaciously opposed to the regime and unwilling to leave his house even as the country disintegrated. "What do the martyrs need?" ʿAbd al-Latif muses:

> Nothing, was his reply, and he went on: Even if they were alive, nothing. He liked the idea of renunciation and asceticism in these times, the same way he liked seeing himself as a living martyr seeking death at every moment, a man who had truly destroyed the walls of fear by reviving a cherished notion: that of the brave man who couldn't have cared less about that cruelest of all humanity's fears: death.[42]

As we saw in Chapter 2, the aesthetic ideology of heroic masculinity in Asadist-Baʿthist Syria was predicated on strength and decisiveness. Here is a different kind of antihero from the male protagonists of earlier Syrian novels and films. In the time of the Syria War and in the shadow of decades-old authoritarian rule, the hallmarks of bravery now include "renunciation and asceticism" as well as fearlessness in the face of cruel fate, an elegiac mood shot through with melancholy and loss. When the siege of the city had finally drawn to an end, ʿAbd al-Latif visited the local cemetery and planted flowers on the graves of the martyrs, recorded the names of the dead and the dates of their deaths. He thought about the fact that nobody would be left to care for the dead one day but that those who remained would still want to know where their loved ones were buried. "He didn't know why people would want to know this, as such, but considered running the graveyard a sacred duty just the same; the living looked after themselves well enough."[43] Nifin, meanwhile, had became more cynical, craving revenge for the death of her son, who had been dragged through the streets, but also feeling that nothing could avenge her loss:

> A person becomes little more than another corpse abandoned by the roadside, one that should really be buried. She knew that she was already just such a body,

> but she still needed to die before she could find peace under the earth. And, for her, dying was the hardest work of all.[44]

Bulbul has a different vision of death: "The corpse swaying to and fro in the minibus was the only truth he had left. He still thought of it as a real person, a collection of tangible, worldly sensations: it could do things; it wasn't just a gelatinous lump,"[45] perhaps his only locus of potential reconnection with his siblings. While he acknowledges the cynicism of Husayn, Nifin, and others about the value of a single corpse, he tries to keep this thought at bay, preferring to believe that one "could make do with a torn shirt or a severed leg wrapped in a shroud inside a closed coffin . . . Many families had buried their loved ones without once laying eyes on the horrifying sight of their dismembered corpses."[46] The hard labor—an alternative translation of the novel's title—of caring for the dead requires a commitment to the departed under circumstances that are not chosen by the living.

It takes the group four hours to travel fifty kilometers. The prospect of reaching 'Annabiyya by sundown is looking dim. Meanwhile, each sibling's interior state is consumed with anxiety about what is going to happen to their relationships once their task is complete. Things seem clear to Bulbul:

> If this nightmare ended and they made it to 'Annabiyya, he would wash his hands of the past entirely. He no longer had a father or a mother, and all links to his siblings would be severed for good. He would insist that his own son bury him in the nearest possible graveyard. He didn't want anyone to read the Fatiha over his grave; what good did that do the dead? . . . Few would have objected if the three siblings had tossed their father's body into a ditch.[47]

But moving the van forward is complicated further by military personnel who get in their way, seemingly unfazed by the decomposing body:

> The corpse had become an object of revulsion without an identity; it wasn't merchandise and it wasn't a person. After death a person becomes a third sort of thing, neither animal nor mineral. Records are closed on their account; they are struck out of the family ledgers with a red line; their belongings are thrown into garbage bags or picked over by scavengers from near and far.[48]

The officers express the same bureaucratic rationality that had already rendered their adventure absurd: "Life and a death are only a matter of official documents."[49] After traversing this final regime checkpoint with a timely fax from the hospital attesting to the identity of the dead body, they enter the territory of the Free Syrian Army; even though their experience at this checkpoint is smooth, the siblings are in an increasing state of distress.

> The calmest of the four was the corpse, of course, which knew no fear or worry; blue tinged, it swelled with perfect equanimity and didn't care that it might explode at any moment. When it vanished, at last, it would do so willingly, unconcerned with wars, soldiers, or checkpoints.[50]

The three travelers come upon a checkpoint manned by foreign Islamist fighters even as Fatima points out that the body has begun to split open in its advanced state of decomposition. Stray dogs attracted by the stench trail their vehicle. "No one wanted to look at the corpse. It had become a plague upon them, nothing less."[51] The siblings start to bicker: Husayn loses his composure, threatens to toss the body from the minibus, then shoves Fatima out into the mud. In response Bulbul lunges at Husayn and they fight. Everyone winds up exhausted and in tears, covered in mud and rain, the corpse on the verge of falling out of the minibus. They are taken in by a family in a small village, Husayn with a black eye and Bulbul scratched up. Meanwhile, as they dress their wounds, Fatima washes the corpse.

By the time they leave the village and make their last push to al-ʿAnnabiyya, ʿAbd al-Latif's corpse is disintegrating, flesh sliding off bone. They can hardly muster any emotional commitment to their cause. "The grave, to be completed, needed a body."[52] The mood among the siblings has turned starkly practical, cynical even: "They had lost their awe of death, and the body no longer meant anything to them—this morning they could have offered it to that pack of hungry dogs without a second thought."[53] Bulbul becomes more agitated the closer they get to their destination, then returns to thinking about the body itself. "Putrefaction is the real insult to the body, not death." It is here that Bulbul finally understands "why bodies are shrouded before burial. It is the last moment of dignity, the last image the deceased's loved ones should preserve before the body disappears from their eyes forever."[54] At the final checkpoint they are questioned by local Islamists in an improvised religious court: the history of their father's political commitments is put on trial, all three are questioned about their beliefs, and Bulbul is thrown into the local jail. Husayn and Fatima are permitted to go, finally, and they are now assisted by their cousin Qasim.

But time and biology continue to eat away at their father. "The corpse was unbearable . . . The body had turned into a putrid mass, no longer appropriate for a dignified farewell. It would be enough to recite a quick prayer over it and to throw a handful of earth into the grave and run."[55] After spending the night in jail, Bulbul's release is accomplished by the intercession of his Uncle Nayef, who takes him to be with his siblings. At this point, Bulbul decides he is no longer going to use that nickname. Fatima greets him warmly, in tears, but Husayn remains aloof. Although they have ostensibly made their father's wish come true, ʿAbd al-Latif is haphazardly buried far from the family plot, alongside dozens of freshly arrived dead scattered about the cemetery. Bulbul is furious that they are unable to bury his father next to his sister or near his mother or grandmother.

As they leave al-ʿAnnabiyya, their mission complete, Bulbul momentarily considers fleeing across the border into Turkey but rejects the idea. They pass the outskirts of Aleppo before turning back toward Damascus. The return trip takes far less time than their journey north, and they arrive home that same evening. Fatima has gone mute, no longer capable of expressing herself through speech. Husayn cannot show his siblings any compassion, falling into his own silence with a seemingly insurmountable grudge against Bulbul and the family. Bulbul enters his house at about nine in the evening. He vows to go by his given name, Nabil, from now on. In the closing scene, settling in for the night, he undergoes a strange transformation, a Kafkaesque metamorphosis, the complete dissolution of self, family, and community. The death of his father has turned Bulbul back into Nabil, re-creating him as a dead body consigned to decay in his father's bed. Here, then, is Bulbul's end:

> He, too, was now just a cadaver. He got up and put his head under the hot-water tap. He wanted his features to melt and disappear. His silence would last all night. He walked to his bedroom, slipped into bed, and felt like a large rat returning to its cold burrow: a superfluous being, easily discarded.[56]

Tragically, Bulbul's struggle to secure his father's dying wish has led to Nabil's disintegration, reducing him to a living-dead hybrid. Whereas his siblings have lost their speech and their faculties of emotional experience, Bulbul loses the very capacity to remain himself, to stay human. There seems to be no escape from all-consuming death in wartime Syria. Dying is not an individual experience, and the collective process of accommodating the surplus of death in the time of the Syria War results in physical faltering, communitarian fracturing, and, ultimately, collapse. In *Dying Is Hard Work*, just as Erin E. Edwards notes about *As I Lay Dying*, death "is not so much a discernible moment as a liminal and unpredictable domain."[57]

Aestheticizing decay runs the risk of doing violence against the dead. "Just as the corpse, particularly the corpse rendered monstrous by violence, may provoke disgust rather than empathy," Sue Tait warns us, "the mortification of the body may repulse, titillate and fascinate."[58] In discourse on human rights—including critical scholarship on forensics—bodies and fragments are exhumed, dragged out of the ground in order to unearth and unsettle conceptions of war, violence, justice, and memory.[59] In these literary depictions of death and dying in wartime Syria, bodies are in motion, unearthed in the sense of remaining suspended between ontological conditions, being not yet buried, not quite dead. The dead—more precisely those who are *not* undead—exist among the Syrian people, making death and dying more mysterious and more terrifying. But the decomposition of ʿAbd al-Latif's body is compensated for or at least mirrored in other breakdowns: the dissolution of family bonds; the collapse of Nabil's body as he decompensates in his father's bed; Fatima's lost speech; the erosion of social cohesion and national coherence. Redemption is fugitive, as these three siblings fail to remain morally bound to one another in the wake of their father's death. In this sense, *Dying Is Hard Work* affords the reader an opportunity to witness a fictional yet specific representation of Syria in its most desperate moments of generalized disorder and interrupted interment. As opposed to the revolutionary optimism on display in *Drums of Love* (Chapter 5), *Dying Is Hard Work* offers neither palliatives nor bromides to those who yearn for hope or reconciliation in the midst of the Syrian apocalypse. Furthermore, if the inclusion of corpses and dead bodies in fiction is one way to meditate on the relationship between the living and the dead, the dead (and even the dying) may seem better off—or at a minimum no worse—than the living. "All wrongs committed against the dead are committed against their ante-mortem selves," George Pitcher claims.[60] However, some forms of mortal insult, Khaled Khalifa insists, can be added even to fatal injury.

REVOLUTION BEYOND DEATH: SAWSAN JAMIL HASAN'S *NIGHT SHIRT* (*QAMĪṢ AL-LAYL*)

The problems of managing death with grace are brought to the forefront in *Dying Is Hard Work.* Individual family members struggle to maintain fraying bonds even as they work hard to keep the dangers of life in wartime at bay. On the other hand, the labor (*al-ʿamal*) of dying requires a collective effort. In Sawsan Jamil Hasan's 2014 novel *Night Shirt* (*Qāmīṣ al-Layl*), the hard work of dying falls on the community at large in its obligation to identify and dispose of a body, its coming to terms with the significance and consequences of death, and its contemplation of the possibility of renewal or rebirth in the time of the Syria War.[61] Hasan was born in Latakia, studied to become a medical doctor, and worked with the Syrian Ministry of Health before turning to fiction writing, having published nearly half a dozen novels.[62] She now lives in Germany. *Night Shirt* is set in Latakia, on the northwestern coast, where the author-narrator Haya and her entire city are shaken by the mysterious death of Jigha, a mentally unstable man from the al-Khurnuba (Carob) neighborhood. Al-Kharnuba is in the old city of Latakia, where Haya, a writer and journalist from the same neighborhood, is collecting stories about the revolution and its aftermath. In a sense, Haya is a witness-narrator akin to the slow witnesses discussed in Chapter 5. She is concerned for the safety and well-being of her son Nawwar, who is studying in Aleppo, even as her relationships with friends and relatives are strained by differences of opinion concerning the war, sectarianism, and other political matters. A drifter with no family to claim his dead body, whom everyone seems to recognize but nobody knows well, Jigha had existed in perpetual breakdown, drunk and indigent after being wounded in the 1967 War. His corpse rots in the morgue until the very end of the novel, when the *mukhtar* is finally compelled to ask the community to participate in his burial. Consequently, major unrest breaks out and the novel reaches a supernatural ending, to which we will return.

The novel takes place over the course of a single day, the gap between Jigha's death and his burial. Narrative perspective swerves from third-person omniscient to various first-person perspectives, often without warning, as in other Syria War novels discussed in this book. *Night Shirt* centers the story of Haya and her relationships as the community is forced to grapple with the death of a single, relatively unknown individual. In a sense, the death of Jigha throws into relief the fragility of human life while also calling into question an individual's worth. If the corpse in *Dying Is Hard Work* demands the immediate attention of his family in order to expedite his burial, Jigha's body lingers, nags at the novel's characters, and tears at the social fabric, eventually threatening to inflame sectarian hatred, unearth personal trauma, and send the city into the abyss of inconsolable sorrow.

Latakia is in the throes of the war—"the events" (*al-aḥdāth*)—as pro- and antiregime elements battle for influence across the urban landscape. But the al-Khurnuba neighborhood is distinguished for its sectarian diversity and tolerance.[63] Jigha would often be there, usually drunk. The news of his death "hit the neighborhood like a lightning bolt, spread at the speed of sound." Nobody knows who found him dead, but rumors soon begin to fly: he had been face down in a puddle of arak; his shirt had been torn off, shredded by whipping; he had been stabbed as revenge for being an informant with the *mukhābarāt*; someone from the regime's *shabbīḥa* had turned on him. Regardless of the true circumstances, the people of the neighborhood now wonder why they had never seemed to notice him living in their midst. Why had they never interacted with him, asked about his religious background and sectarian identity, inquired who he truly was? "In reality, nobody knew where Jigha was from, or to which sect or religion he belonged. Jigha belonged to the bottle of *arak* first and foremost."[64] It is thus unclear where he ought to be buried. "Syria had become a country of martyrs and conflicted martyrdom."[65]

The pressures of the ongoing conflict and escalating sectarian tensions are taking a toll on the people of Latakia. Haya has to navigate a perilous matrix of sectarian identity and religious difference after having disrupted the insularity of her own ʿAlawī community by marrying a leftist Sunni man named Nizar. Haya and her sister-in-law Widad (who is Sunni) become embroiled in a discussion about the revolution. As they argue over who has sacrificed sufficiently for the cause of the nation, talk shifts toward the ʿAlawī community in Latakia and whether enough people had stood up against regime atrocities in Hama during the 1980s and during the Syria War elsewhere around the country. Jigha's death has opened up a more profound communal meditation on the meaning(s) of death, dying, and dead bodies in the history of the Syrian nation. Unlike the body of the patriarch in *Dying Is Hard Work*, the symbolic value of the dead in *Night Shirt* is more explosive, intersecting with long-standing struggles over national identity and sectarian particularism.[66]

Haya thinks television is a dangerous element because it "doesn't show us the world the way that it is in fact, but instead presents us with images that distort reality."[67] Her cousin Nawras has become a paranoid shut-in, convinced he is under constant surveillance. This leads Haya to muse expansively:

> I don't know why Jigha occupies this existential status but I can feel it. He is present, like a symbol that unifies the entire neighborhood, but what does he symbolize exactly? Did Jigha enjoy such importance that his death could be this loud? Or does his death have this violent resonance in our time, in particular? We have been living on the edge of death for many months now, living between its claws, its fangs. Why should the death of a man who doesn't have any place in our social fabric, whose presence and absence are no different because of the tense and cautious and frightened and confused situation? Who is going to announce Jigha's death? And who would be the decisive authority in certifying his death?[68]

The uncertainty that shrouds Jigha—his biography, mortal remains, and symbolism—disrupts other characters' sense of self. "I'm afflicted by a state of lethal nihilism," says Haya.

> A state of meaninglessness, pointlessness. I live at the mercy of fear and sorrow, scenes of murder, dismembered bodies and body parts hoisted up in front of the salivating cameras. . . . Images that colorize death. Death is the one and only master, Syrian death. . . . Has there ever been a people who innovated new forms of death?

Haya goes out to buy cigarettes and gets to thinking about Syrian social diversity. When her reverie is interrupted by sudden bombardment, she wonders, "Oh God. How long is this reality going to besiege me? Doesn't death ever get tired?"[69] Haya has been connecting with many different women by helping to spread their stories, including one woman whose twenty-four-year-old son left university one Friday to go out and demonstrate and never returned. His parents had spent weeks trying to locate him, until the father was summoned to one of the security agencies in Damascus to identify his corpse "on a screen," wondering whether this would ever bring them any certainty: "Yes, he would have to look, how could he not look when the screen in front of him is his only certainty?" Still he is left with lingering questions about what he was actually seeing: "His son's face or the face of a corpse? What does a corpse mean in the dictionary of life? Not only a corpse but the image of a corpse? Is this his son?"[70] If the only possibility of closure for families of the disappeared and the deceased is to physically identify their bodies, corpses seem to appear only as ciphers, mediated references to the departed. Characters in *Night Shirt* struggle to find and identify corpses but then founder on whether they can comprehend what a corpse is in the first place.

Meanwhile, Haya gets to know a young woman named Hind, nicknamed Henouda, who, it turns out, had known Jigha. She had met him on the street and shared her story with him: she had been on the run, fleeing from the Baba ʿAmro neighborhood of Homs to Latakia, shuttling from place to place as the enthusiasm of the Syrian uprising gave way to a noxious civil war. Hind describes leaving Homs under extreme duress after her mother was killed and a soldier tried to rape her:

> In a war of this kind death has phases and passions, in a war that flops around like a blind beast stomping on anything that crosses its path. New forms of suffering are created: a father kills himself after seeing his mother and his father and his brother and his wife murdered. He kills himself and leaves behind an apology to his only son. Another father tears up the family album because he no longer needs it, as everyone who fills up its pages has been taken by cruel death [*al-mawt al-ghāshim*]."[71]

Midway through the novel, Jigha himself appears as an already dead narrator recounting his experience as a drunk man on the street before dying. As he recalls it, "inside of me there was a man who was dying and another who was rising and the two of them were struggling over my being [*kiyān*]. It felt like this city was turning into one giant grave that still wasn't big enough to hold me."[72] "Syrian death" is constituted by scales—a forgotten corpse lying in the street, an individual grave in a cemetery, the city as a collective tomb, perhaps the entire country as one mass grave. The more despondent Jigha had become, the more he took to drink. He claims to have once held the patriotic and nationalist values of his generation, having fought in the 1967 war, but bitterly losing hope in the cause of Arab unity. So he had cared only about the bottle of arak he carried with him. Now Jigha is cognizant, even in the depths of his despair, of having functioned as a witness before his death: "I was neither human nor devil: I was a ball of fire, a giant eye devouring images, sights, sounds, and movements, chewing them up and spitting out their pulp in order to smooth out my insides."[73] Jigha had begun to wish for death so that he "wouldn't be the only witness [*al-shāhid al-waḥīd*]."[74] Jigha's debilitating loneliness in life—abandoned by the Arab nationalist cause, disappointed by the Syrian national leadership that had failed to take up the charge in the aftermath of the Six-Day War, and his utter alienation from his community and society—is tethered to his sense of bearing witness as a solitary individual. If witnessing is among the ethical responsibilities with which the living are saddled in the time of the Syria War (Chapter 5), then death might be a reprieve from that onerous task. From the unlikely vantage point of death itself, though, Jigha can offer such comfort neither to the reader nor to himself. Be that as it may, his deathly condition opens up the space for a different kind of commentary on the state of the nation.

> But today I am in greater pain, possibly because the wound is fresh and the bleeding hasn't stopped, the wound of Syria, the wound of our people being evicted from their homes, fleeing death as it rains down on them from the sky, buffeting them as the wind whips from every direction. When the pain is palpable, when we can identify with our own eyes and ears and nerves, when we can smell death as it devours our organs bit by bit, it's different than the pain coming from history, which books teach us about or folk wisdom mentions. This is death pulsing with life, we hear it panting like a predator stalking its prey.[75]

The Syrian people find no escape from their suffering, not even in death. The very concepts of life and death—as separable and opposing states—are at risk of losing all meaning for Jigha. The country itself is transmogrified into a "wound," absorbed into the surreally hybrid phenomenon of "death pulsing with life." Death is the grounds for interpretation and the horizon of narration in *Night Shirt*. The possibility of "greater pain" in the afterlife than in this world bespeaks a kind of literary terror that suffuses the aesthetic ideology of Syrian writers stuck between the hopes of the revolution and the violence of the war.

In "the time of Syrian death" (*zaman al-mawt al-sūrī*), death presents itself as a powerful actor on the historical stage, a danger but perhaps also a clarifying force. "Syrian death is only read about anymore in one particular variety: killing."[76]

> In Syria there is mass death, collective massacres. . . . Two murderers in one, twins, both belong to the same soil but the two of them have destroyed this earth, brothers have become enemies. And if identity persists even after death, then every side's writing of murder in Syria insists on delivering the message, not only the message of force and the desire for hegemony but also the message directed to the family of the dead, to his identity, which in Syria still doesn't accept any classification other than sectarian [*madhhabī*]: a minoritarian system. A revolutionary majority. Even Syrian death led the revolution off track.[77]

The fate of Jigha's mortal remains is explosively contested. The *mukhtar* has brought Jigha's corpse from the morgue and placed it under the mulberry tree in the center of town so people can congregate and discuss what should be done. "Mukhtar!" someone shouts. "Who's going to wash him and pray for him? We don't even know his religion or his sect!"[78] Accusations are hurled about his sectarian identity being the reason for his drinking problem. Tension leads to brawling, chairs thrown in anger, and eventually someone opening fire. Suddenly Hind appears, leaps up onto the coffin and tries to climb inside with Jigha, begging him not to abandon her, at which point she starts to metamorphose into some kind of otherworldly creature.[79] When another gun goes off, Hind suddenly bursts into flames and, as the flames consume her, a voice rings out:

> Uncle Jigha bears all of your sins, scatter our ashes in the garden of the abandoned house, don't bicker about his burial for he died according to the religion of humanity, died with God in his heart. Don't disagree with one another after today about anything at all. Our ashes will sprout flowers of affection. . . . [Mohamed] Bouazizi immolated himself in order to set fire to the [Tunisian] regime. I am lighting myself on fire so that you may see the way forward.[80]

Hind is transformed into a *jinniyya*, a female djinn, and because genies are made of oil, the reader learns, she ignites into a roaring inferno in the midst of the gathered crowd. As Haya bears witness to these unimaginable developments, she remembers something she believes she had read by the French philosopher Gilles Deleuze: "The failure of revolutions inspires a new situation, ignites the spark of revolutionary-becoming anew. The situation of people living under tyranny and repression truly heads towards revolutionary-becoming because there is no other solution." The novel ends with Haya stumbling away from the scene of immolation, muttering under her breath, "The revolution lives on."[81]

It is important to recall that the epigraph at the start of *Night Shirt* on the "revolutionary-becoming" (*ṣayrūra thawriyya*) that emerges out of political failure is drawn from Deleuze. How are we to interpret these references, though? While neither the opening passage nor the dialogue at the end of the novel appears to be a direct quotation, there is a logic to this citation of "revolutionary-becoming." The Deleuzian concept of *devenir-révolutionnaire* might be a plausible philosophical explanation of the antihero at the center of literature and film in the time of the Syrian revolution and the Syria War (and not only in *Night Shirt*). This figure can be understood as a counterpoint to the "hero" of the Asadist-Baʿthist cultural revolution during the late twentieth century (Chapter 1). According to Deleuze, "revolutionary-becoming . . . is not the same as the future of the revolution" because the revolution itself "does not necessarily happen through the militants."[82] In other words, the ordinary folk, a vagabond like Jigha, say, might provide a beacon of hope in dark times, catalyze revolutionary action or consciousness in a way that proves that the vanguard of the Asadist-Baʿthist cultural revolution—whether the leader or the party—cannot monopolize the virtues undergirding heroism and historical transformation. But becoming is a difficult concept to unravel insofar as it flies in the face of history itself, since an "event's becoming is beyond the scope of history," as Deleuze puts it.[83] If revolutionary-becoming disrupts the futurity of revolutionary ideology by grounding the revolutionary subject in its present-tense subjectivation, then this figure may also be capable of escaping the clutches of history itself. The novel is bookended by two iterations of death: Jigha's leads to his incomplete or failed burial, suggesting that his own purgatory in the time of the novel is also the space for his postmortem "becoming-corpse," as Erin E. Edwards says, a process that "outlives the moment of death."[84] But Hind's self-immolation is a second death, which appears to salvage a version of death that is neither meaningless nor unjust but voluntary and possibly redemptive. All of a sudden, Haya's resolve is stiffened when she realizes that the revolution may live on in its revolutionary-becoming, which transcends the paired deaths of Jigha and Hind. In this regard, the event of *Night Shirt*—the founding moment at which the subject of the Syrian revolution comes into view, however fleetingly— not only may be the death of Jigha, with all its thorny implications of sectarian difference and (pan-Arab) national unity in post-1967 Syria, but may also be the doubled sacrifice of Hind dying alongside (already dead) Jigha, an event that restokes the flagging resolve of ordinary Syrian witnesses, intellectuals, and activists. Haya's response may seem emotionless as she appears nonplussed by the supernatural course of events occurring right before her eyes. Even if the revolution cannot be said definitively to have failed, the tragedy of *Night Shirt* is its invocation of loss—the fullest expression of self-sacrifice in Hind's case—at the limit point of revolutionary-becoming.

Hasan's characters take comfort in what might be termed the aesthetic power of revolutionary failure. The momentary foreclosure of political possibility—the death of the post-1967 Syrian subject (call him Jigha) and the subject of the Syrian uprising (call her Hind)—opens up new avenues for an unpredictable, and possibly unprecedented revolutionary process, in what might be read as the novel's aesthetics of solidarity. The revolutionary martyr is denuded of religious content and yet retains an aura of sacralized violence, hinting at the possibility of redemption if not salvation. By the same token, the prosaic politics of witnessing in *Night Shirt* is embodied in the autonomic functioning of the human senses, an affect theory of revolution perhaps, which would not be limited to narrative, witnessing that transcends representation and opens up the pores of literary sensibility such that one feels the revolution in order to see; here is a kind of synesthesia that differs from the one we saw in Rosa Yaseen Hasan's *Rough Draft* (Chapter 4), where the auditory technique of surveillance allows a different kind of "seeing" (like a security state). The name Jigha is a strange sort of totem, an unfamiliar (perhaps unique) name, though it is distinguished for its homophony with *jīfa*, a synonym for corpse. While *Dying Is Hard Work* highlights the burden on individuals and families in the face of death and dying in the time of the Syria War, *Night Shirt* reveals the social webs that radiate from and bunch together around the dead body, beyond individual, family, and community. The dead bodies at the center of *Night Shirt* belong to the entire city of Latakia somehow, and, by extension, to the Syrian nation.

The crux of the novel is the collective inability to identify Jigha's sectarian identity, but it is also the unwillingness of its characters to ignore the problem of sectarian identity altogether, suggesting that death cannot fully contain the mounting tension between tribalism and pluralism among the Syrian people. By no means should this be misunderstood as an argument that the Syria War is simply a conflict over sectarian identity or sectarian difference. But the centrality of (mis)identifying the sectarian identity of Jigha's *jīfa* (corpse) indicates not only that dying is difficult but that old habits die hard and that undoing sectarianism in the time of the Syria War is hard as well. Revolutionary becoming is not impossible in the universe of *Night Shirt*, as the displaced activist Hind finds a kindred spirit in the outcast Jigha. Hind's spectacular sacrifice, her quasi-mystical immolation unmistakably evokes the self-immolations that kicked off the Arab uprisings in the first place and opens up the possibility of secular revolutionary martyrdom in the Syria War. The witnessing undertaken by Haya, Nawras, and other characters (to say nothing of the reader) become a banner, a badge, or an article of clothing worn by the living as a testament to the sacrifice and struggle of the dead regardless of their political affiliation or sectarian identity. It would be risky to reduce the novel to allegory: sectarian, national, or revolutionary. The ties of family, community, and nation are solid enough throughout *Night Shirt* for one to believe that these bonds might survive the horrors of the war and allow reconstruction of another kind to emerge in its aftermath. If liberal platitudes such as tolerance and unity are obliterated in Jigha's untimely death, Hind's voluntary annihilation leaves behind legacies and ashes that might serve as raw material for new kinds of politics, an altogether novel community to come.

WE HAVE MET THE DICTATOR AND HE IS US: MAZIN ʿARAFA'S *THE CRANES (AL-GHARĀNĪQ)*

The potential redemption of Syrian life through individual and collective sacrifice portrayed in *Dying Is Hard Work* and *Night Shirt* can be suppressed and even reversed through the cruel inertia of the status quo in the time of the Syria War. In the fifteen years since Nihad Sirees published *The Silence and the Roar* (Chapter 4), writers and artists have confronted the challenges of reformism from above even as more dangerous circumstances emerge. The character, concept, and culture of the leader—the embodiment of regime power in the logic of heroism essential to Asadist-Baʿthist cultural revolution—remains central to the Syrian literary imaginary. In his 2017 novel *The Cranes* (*al-Gharānīq*), Mazin ʿArafa presents a dizzying take on "the dictator novel."[85] Unspooling the fractured mind of the author-narrator, the hallucinatory qualities of this narrative resemble a hall of mirrors more than a monument to ideological conformity. In a sense, this bildungsroman tracks the history of Syria through times of dictatorship, revolution, and war through the eyes and experience of a protagonist who considers himself a leader in his own right. The author-narrator confabulates, dreams, and occasionally inhabits worlds where the line between an ordinary citizen and a powerful dictator is permeable, where sexual desire, material self-interest, and certifiable madness are the core of political power, a universe that transcends but also eerily reflects our own. If *The Silence and the Roar* presents a literary perspective on the psychology of ordinary people and bureaucratic officials living under authoritarian dictatorship, *The Cranes* is a gonzo deep dive into the psychosis of the leader figure, a tour of the myriad pathologies that sprout from persistent authoritarian domination. As the delirium of omnipotence envelops numerous characters, the maniacal qualities associated with a tyrannical dictator turn out to be latent inside each and every one of us. The novel thereby wrestles with moral questions about human nature in a manner reminiscent of Ossama Mohammed's 2002 *Sacrifices* (*Ṣundūq al-Dunyā*) (Chapter 2).

Mazin ʿArafa was born in 1955, received a bachelor's degree in French literature at Damascus University, and then earned his doctorate at Marie Curie University in Lublin, Poland, before settling in Germany. His first novel, *Waṣāyā al-Ghubār* (*Legacies of Dust*), was published in 2011, and his most recent novel, *Sarīr ʿalā al-Jabha* (*A Bed on the Front*) was published in 2019.[86] In *The Cranes*, an unnamed protagonist occupies the space between the state and the people, the dictator and the citizen, the secular revolutionary nationalist and the religious fundamentalist. The setting is never clearly defined and there are enough gestures toward universal themes that one might conceivably—though implausibly—argue that the novel is *not* set in Syria. Whatever the case, the plot establishes the fluid political and social landscape of a country under authoritarian dictatorship that has descended into the surreality of civil war. The title of the novel may be a reference to what is referred to as "the story of the cranes" (*al-gharānīq al-ūlā*), also known as "the satanic verses." Satan is reputed to have whispered into the Prophet Muhammad's ears two lines of praise for the pagan goddesses worshipped by the Quraysh which were erroneously included in the memorized version of the oral Qur'an.[87] If one wishes to accept this interpretation as the intended reference in the title, then the evil at work in the novel may also relate to the usurpation of political authority by an unjust ruler, the whisper of authoritarianism supplanting the evildoing of a satanic force. Such mistaking of idols for gods harbors another, perhaps even deeper significance in relation to the "deifying" (*ta'līh*) of the leader in Syrian political culture as a false idol, one yet to fall (Chapter 1).

The Cranes is written entirely in the first-person voice of an author-narrator who also serves as what I call a witness-narrator, an omniscient character who is at once chronicler of events and conscience of the novel—in other words, a figure who has both a functional and an ethical role to play. Divided into four parts—"Sorrow," "Sadism," "Intifada," "Madness"—this quartet is performed as a kind of dirge for contemporary Syrian history. In "Sorrow" (*kaʾāba*), the author-narrator describes the bleak life of a government bureaucrat who works in the registry office of a small town that stands in as a microcosm of life in the capital, where statues of the leader are erected all over the place and his portraits adorn the walls of people's houses. Wartime circumstances guide the author-narrator's thoughts, fantasies, and life experiences toward the macabre. The cost of erecting a statue honoring the General-Leader (*al-zaʿīm al-jinarāl*) had come at the expense of providing the people with electricity, justified by the "calling for the illumination of their reactionary darkness with the light of revolutionary ideas."[88] The protagonist keeps a "sacred photograph" of the General-Leader in his office, dozes off under its watchful gaze, reads the state newspaper, watches state television, and makes every effort "to display . . . affection and respect for the dignified General-Leader." He hallucinates that it is he on screen as the General-Leader: "I felt extremely nervous about the danger of what I was seeing."[89] Coffeehouses (and brothels) are the main sites of sociability in this country, not only where the desires of the masses can be satiated but also where the energy of popular opinion can be expended on petty matters and weightier themes. His friends are also government employees: Abu Khalid, the mailman; Abu Samir, the garbage truck driver; one-eyed Abu Sulayman, the nurse; and Abu Yasin, an employee at the morgue who had been mauled in a horse cart accident when he was little.

The author-narrator is frustrated with his marital life, and while his wife sleeps with him, she has begun to raise his suspicions about what she does outside the house without him or at home when he is not there. He becomes fixated on the fact that he has been losing weight, on his wife who appears to be gaining weight, on the broken mirror that has been placed at the entrance to their house, and on the alluring mustache of the General-Leader. When his sexual potency starts to flag, he laments his performance as a communal embarrassment with the leader's portrait hanging above him.

> I thought about the national disappointment my penis caused in front of her, it had started to contract and shrink in historically embarrassing moments over the course of our physical relationship, in the shadow of distortion and instability caused by the adversarial gaze of the General Leader in his portrait that was upside-down above the bed.[90]

This is not unlike the libidinal politics on display in *The Silence and the Roar* (Chapter 3). When sex with his wife becomes unbearable, the author-narrator begins to drift off into another world. He notices that his wife only climaxes when she looks "with affection and kindness" at the portrait of the General-Leader, which leads his relationship with the leader "to become more complicated, as it started to oscillate between my affection for him as symbol of the nation [*al-waṭan*] during the daytime and my hatred of him as the thief of my wife in the evening."[91]

In response, he begins to fantasize about a young woman called Marila, who also betrays him with the General-Leader, which starts keeping him up at night. When the security agent at his office, Abu al-ʿAynayn, hears that the author-narrator can find nothing good on television to keep him company, he offers him a magical device that will allow him to watch films nobody else can see. Mysteriously, the first film he watches opens on a shot of the brothel in their town with the following title: "Marila: A Dream from the North Country." Marila materializes exactly as he has dreamed about her, and the video turns into a pornographic film as a group of men show up and start having sex with her. "I feel as though I had reached the edge of madness watching the film," the author-narrator confesses.[92] Then, impossibly, Marila turns toward the camera to address him directly:

> Come and see me early in the evening, before your General-Leader shows up with his medals and patriotic patches that pierce my soft body and irritate me with their agitated scratching . . . how much longer will this situation persist? When will you become a General-Leader so that we can be free to do as we please?[93]

In a follow-up conversation with Abu ʿAynayn, he confirms his allegiance to the regime and takes home another film, "Ultimate Justice Against the Gangs of Darkness: Concept by the Commander General-Leader, the Genius

Revolutionary Struggler; Directed by the Bureau of Ideological and Revolutionary Propaganda in the Security Services."[94] This training video about a group of elite fighters in the Soldiers of the Revolution (*Junūd al-Thawra*) turns out to be raw footage of a massacre carried out by regime forces. After viewing it, the author-narrator hallucinates about becoming the General-Leader because people call him "Leader" and make offerings of corpses and body parts to him. Now installed in the role of General-Leader, he begins devouring human flesh. "I eat it with great gusto," the author-narrator raves. "It's so delicious, I wipe my blood-stained hands on my medals and my patriotic patches . . . I become smarter, braver, hornier."[95] When he wakes up in the morning from this gory dream and walks past the mirror on his way to work, the hallucination seems not to have ended: "I walk past the mirror, I can't see my face, I no longer have a face."[96] There is a tortured relationship between corporeal experience and the dissolution of the self under the sway of dictatorial power, grotesque entanglements of sex and death. This regimented introduction of approved films into the visual landscape of the author-narrator also presents a literary reflection of images and cinema in the construction of state ideology in Asadist-Baʿthist Syria.

On the heels of this disturbing experience, the author-narrator starts having nightmares about dead bodies.

> Shredded mutilated corpses, strewn all over the empty town . . . in the empty squares, on the roads at frightening interchanges, on the smashed pavement. . . . Corpses hang from dry tree branches, dilapidated mud rooftops, and darkened electricity poles. Corpses everywhere that nobody picks up.[97]

Suddenly the corpses begin rising up into the air, spinning, moaning and weeping, pawing at him. Startled awake by the dream, his wife tells him to shut up, to go sleep in the kitchen if he cannot keep still, and to call his girlfriend Marila if he needs help. He takes a walk to the graveyard, where he hears the same noises from his dream. His friend Abu Yasin tells him those are the sounds of "the living dead." Later he comes across two women in the road, a mother and daughter, who claim they have just crawled out of a hole, possibly a mass grave. "We are the dead who were buried in the pit by evildoers," the daughter tells him, "we come out of there at night to have some fun, to breathe the fresh air, to plant and water roses, to drink tea, and to sing mournful songs."[98] The mother tells him they were having dinner at home while their husbands were out demonstrating when a shell crashed into the building and killed them. While there is not enough space here for a comparative reading of zombies and the undead, it is worth noting that the presence and reanimation of living-dead figures resonates beyond the literary fiction of Asadist-Baʿthist Syria. The ritual practices of the living dead in the novel indicate that even the dead try to have a bit of fun in the time of the Syria War. Their simple pleasures, what perhaps should be called *everyday deathlife* or *everyday afterlife*, represent a point of stability and solace in a world altogether thrown out of kilter.

When he returns home, the author-narrator is told by the women at his house that he has been away for fifteen days—even though he had experienced only a surreal, late night stroll—and that Abu ʿAynayn had come around looking for him. Abu Yasin had also been to see him and then left with his wife. Now facing the loss of both his wife and his girlfriend, he starts to go mad, stabbing at the portraits of the General-Leader but, shockingly, new portraits magically appear, "elegant and radiant, covering the entire length and breadth of the walls with hypnotic and symmetrical regularity. They are portraits of me. That's right. I'm the new General Leader."[99] Discovering that his wife and Abu Yasin have taken down the portrait of the leader over the bed, he slips inside the frame. " . . . and become a more radiant and more glamorous portrait than the one that was in there previously . . . I'm so proud of myself, I have succeeded in my own revolutionary movement."[100] Here the achievement of revolutionary victory is made possible for a single individual through the removal of the leader, whether by force of will or by supernatural powers. Now *his* minions begin to arrive—humans and statues proceeding in rows as military marches blare in accompaniment. A counter-coup has already broken out in an attempt to overthrow him, but it is suppressed; then another revolutionary movement calling for "Bread, Dignity, Freedom" arises briefly before everyone is blown to bits, at which point he awakens, alone in his room, the walls clean and freshly painted. This hallucinatory unraveling suggests the inexorable return of revolutionary transformation, a recursive history in which one dictator is swapped for another even as renegade military elements and a discontented populace struggle to reclaim control over their country.

Part two, "Sadism," contains some striking resonance with Ossama Mohammed's *Sacrifices* (*Ṣundūq al-Dunyā*) (Chapter 2) in its exploration of the psychology of a "dictator character" or personality type. The author-narrator's grandmother sparks the action with a prophecy that is misunderstood from the start. When she says, "Even if you become Leader . . . " the people in the village take this to mean "*When* you become Leader . . ." As a boy he had had a youthful romantic dream of becoming a leader, but his confusion sets in early when he imaginatively transforms his father's lighter into a toy bus and "drives" or "leads" it, failing to understand until he gets older that there is a difference between what the General-Leader does when he "leads" (*qiyāda*) the people and when the boy "drives" (*qiyāda*) the lighter-bus.[101] The family is subjected to media propaganda announcing that a revolution has taken place in the country, with Communiqué No. 1 blasted over the radio declaring that the "national armed forces" have seized not only the cinema houses, the media outlets, and so forth, but also "children's arcades, doves' and birds' nests, the centers of dreams in the minds of [the] citizens . . . and every place that can be touched by conspiracies and treacherous actions against the patriotic leadership of the army." The people have been warned: "Be advised. Nighttime curfew in all dream regions until further notice."[102] If this oversharing of intentions to control minds and win hearts is clumsy coup-making, the leadership now stumbles over its words in earnest, releasing dozens of communiqués and proceeding to get lost in the conflicting details. When the neighborhood gets together to watch the events unfolding on television, the audience expresses its true desires. "We the simple masses ask for them to leave us in peace, we want to watch comedy serials on television instead of this, 'Hammam al-Hina' with Ghawar al-Tushi and Kibrit bi-Midfa with Mahmud Jabr."[103] Interestingly, in this counterfactual history of dictatorship, the popular comedy of Durayd Lahham (Chapter 3) is portrayed as having staunchly oppositional politics. The boy's transformation into a dictator continues as he sits under an olive tree, is bitten by a red ant, and proceeds to go berserk. "I imagined myself a commanding General Leader, and I began to carry out a real massacre, as I killed the savage ants, ten, a hundred, two hundred, a thousand." From here, he thinks about killing more insects, other creatures; if he cannot kill all the ants, then he will kill snakes, animals, people, whatever it takes "to reach the mindset of a brutal Leader who is sure of himself."[104] There is an echo here, too, of the self-confident masculinity venerated in socialist-realist discourse of committed writers such as Hanna Mina (Chapter 2). More important, though, is the moral that becoming a real man requires the experiences of pain and impotence as well as the embrace of unbridled, even sadistic violence.

The political sadism surging up in this dictator in training is matched by what he calls sexual sadism, both of which are seen as "important qualifications for success" as a leader.[105] His youthful crushes on neighborhood girls are dashed when every last one of them spurns him. Instead of retreating inside himself or finding other outlets like a good young leader, though, the boy exacts horrifying revenge. When he becomes deliriously jealous of his twelve-year-old cousin Nadya, who has fallen in love with a boy called Yasin, the author-narrator takes his revenge by cutting off the boy's penis and slicing off his cousin's breasts. When a boy goes out with another girl that he has feelings for, the author-narrator stabs him and throws him in front of a car.[106] His coming-of-age experience, from childhood to adolescence, is stained with blood and his deviant sexual maturation is bound up with violence. He becomes conscious of what is happening to his body, to the connection between "blood and savage instinctive tendencies . . . a simultaneously bloody and sexual pleasure."[107]

The country approaches the brink of destruction as the author-narrator is now caught between his fantasies of being a powerful General-Leader and the countervailing demands of everyday life. In the third part of the novel, "Intifada," he finds it increasingly difficult to differentiate between what is real and what is not. "My wife thinks I've gone mad, especially when I rave in my sleep, saying that I'm the General-Leader." But it turns out that this is not her biggest complaint. "What seems to really annoy my wife is my desire for her to scratch my back constantly, in the middle, a little bit to the right, in a place I can't reach," especially because he often asks her to do this while they are having sex and she is trying to climax.[108] The unpredictable consequences of an itchy back will return in the tragic ending of the novel. Despite the author-narrator's protestations that he is not going mad, his wife leaves him. Later, at an antiregime demonstration, he is shot in the shoulder even though he insists he had never been against the regime, that he is just out to observe what was happening.

The author-narrator bears witness to this version of history from the balcony of a presidential palace in a section entitled, "I am the General Leader and I Live and I Die": "I open my eyes on an amazing sight, waves of surging masses calling for my life, I, the struggling General-Leader, the unique one, the genius, with a hundred and twenty sacred and glorious attributes."[109] The crowd is diverse: men, women, and children; bearded and clean-shaven men; veiled and unveiled women; "even dead people, too, took a break from their graves, some of them came in shrouds, and others came as skeletons," all kinds of animals—donkeys, bulls, dogs, cows, chickens, rabbits—and even "foreign delegations from Mars . . . I didn't realize that I was loved by my people to this extent."[110] As he struggles to scratch the perennially itchy spot on his back, the crowd mistakes his awkward movement for waving and they erupt in applause, which immediately gives the author-narrator an erection that pokes through his military uniform. In an unlikely sequence of events, his concubine Marila is brought over so that he can have sex with her from behind while gazing out at the masses from the balcony, one hand conducting the crowd like an orchestra, the other holding onto Marila's waist: "At that moment Marila and the great masses became one, and I felt as though I was embracing them both at the same time, penetrating both of them at the same time with my dick that was hard for glory [*ʿuḍwī al-nāhiḍ naḥwa al-majd*]." His megalomania escalates as he feels himself surging with virility and power.

> I'm the General-Leader, my hard cock is brilliant and my hands are illuminated like purple fire. Marila is smoldering like an active volcano. . . . I am Hitler the Leader, I am Mussolini the Leader, I am France the Leader, I am Comrade Stalin, Comrade Mao Tse-Tung, Comrade Kim Il-Sung, Comrade Castro, I'm Churchill the Democrat, De Gaulle the Liberator, I'm the illiterate hero Guevara, I'm Abdel Nasser, Servant of the Masses, I'm the highest one in the sky and in the land of peace I am the eternal universe. I am absolute truth.[111]

The satirical depiction of a monomaniacal dictator with aspirations for world domination converges with blasphemous talk that transcends human power and reaches for something more cosmic, even divine. Now the critique of dictatorship through the language of idolatry—the Islamic parable of *The Cranes*—becomes salient. If the chaos and madness swirling around the fevered mind of the author-narrator acquires carnivalesque qualities, the power of dictatorship is inextricably bound up with carnal pleasures and temptations of the flesh. This deepening relationship between political power and sexuality is confirmed when everyone in the crowd begins having sex: men and women and children, the living and the dead, earthlings and Martians—"a single gelatinous mass."[112] The sexual rapaciousness of the leader has infected the society, exploding in an orgiastic fervor that might be read as its slavish emulation of the new General-Leader.

When he discovers that Marila has been sleeping with one of his personal secretaries, the author-narrator-cum-General-Leader snaps, harking back to the sadistic revenge he took in his boyhood. He threatens to torture the two of them in unspeakable ways before killing them, but his adviser Abu ʿAdnan comes rushing in, first cursing Marila and the secretary for insolence toward the General-Leader but then whispering, "General-Leader, Sir, I'm sorry to disturb your fit of sacred anger, but I need to inform you that there are gangs of the rabble outside that might be approaching the outer palace walls." Unsure of what to do when the General-Leader barks at him to attack the square, Abu ʿAdnan retorts that it's full of protestors as well as loyal soldiers. The leader shoots him point blank in the head. Turning to his other advisers and asking if there are any other issues, they rush off to carry out his orders. "Do you know how to scratch my back?" he asks another aide, Abu ʿAli al-Hut. "Of course, General-Leader, Sir," he replies. "I'm the best back scratcher, especially in times of national crisis and popular unrest."[113] But the General-Leader is not placated, hauling in the traitorous secretary who begs for mercy, blubbering that Marila had seduced him. The Leader is unconvinced. Carrying on about how hard he remains and how his sexual power combined with political savvy will ensure the defeat of the opposition, he proceeds to sodomize the secretary.

> I continue stabbing my prey violently, as the sound of explosions increases all around me, dead bodies are scattered in all directions. I feel pleasure when I smell the beautiful stench of blood and death, which only increases my lust so I thrust even harder... bloody body parts, bursts of gunfire. Beautiful terror. I'm Nero, I'm Genghis Khan and Timurlane. I'm al-Hajjaj and Abu Jaʿfar al-Mansur the Butcher, I'm Hitler and Stalin and Pinochet. I am all of those heroes.

Here the line between hero and villain is effaced altogether as the murderous monsters of world history are elevated to the status of role models. At this point, the author-narrator has Abu ʿAli al-Hut cut off the secretary's penis as the General-Leader shoots the man in the arm, which only causes the Leader to become more fully erect as he spirals into a frenzied rage: "I am the King of Death, I'm the Emperor of Hell, I'm the Lord Satan. I am Universal Evil.[114] After finally putting the man out of his misery by shooting him in the head, he declares that he has defeated "the rabble." When the General-Leader wakes up from this fever dream, it turns out that he has been on the balcony watching people protest the whole time.

The country goes up in flames and the author-narrator descends into his final unraveling in a time of all-out war. The merging of the author-narrator and the General-Leader is fully accomplished in Part 4, "Madness," as his mind is racked by repetitive thoughts. "I am 'the Commander of the Intifada' intellectual, I am 'Bassem al-Sama'' the jihadi youth, I am the 'General-Leader.'"[115] Given that everyone is implicated in the violence of the war, there can no longer be much difference between the General-Leader and "the revolutionary intellectual." The author-narrator feels split between these two figures and the tension between them drives him past mental imbalance and toward self-destruction.

> I am the echo of both of you idiots.
> Rather, I am the echo of the two of you who are obsessed with violence.
> Rather, I am the echo of the two of you who are drunk with power.
> But the "intifada" has caused you to shoot at your own head in your recurring nightmares, whether you're awake or asleep.

To the extent that the author-narrator's interior psychological state is overrun with the nightmarish phantasmagoria of authoritarian dictatorship, the circumstances of his death are distinct from those of Mufid in *End of a Brave Man* (Chapter 2). Lifting the gun to his temple, the author-narrator continues his ravings:

> I do not die, though, the country dies. My hand holds the same silver gun, and I aim it at my temple, my finger on the trigger, and at that moment my back itches like crazy in the area where my hand can't reach, and the derangement rises up in my head to the highest level and frequency in that moment, and my finger confidently squeezes the trigger without hesitation, and the bullet shoots out. . . . I do not die, though, the country dies.[116]

As in literary writing from Latin America, *The Cranes* "demonstrates in its very structure that in reality dictators are not powerful telluric forces, but ideological diversions, phantoms cast by the true powers in today's world."[117] The seeming omnipresence of the state and the ostensible omnipotence of the autocrat in *The Cranes*—as well as other "dictator novels" from Syria—might be understood in terms of Achille Mbembe's claim that "power in the postcolony can be said to be a construction of a particular type: hallucinatory."[118] One also finds here a resemblance to what Haytham Bahoora calls "the aesthetics of horror" in post-2003 Iraqi fiction:

> Nightmare scenarios . . . rely on a literary experimentalism that departs from narrative realism by constructing fantastic narratives of horror that abandon any pretense of representing reality in favor of the intangible, suggesting the impossibility of realistically rendering the experience of such brutality and implying that Iraqi reality is itself monstrous and irrational.[119]

These "nightmare scenarios" are on display in a wide range of Iraqi novels, most notably those of Sinan Antoon, Hassan Blasim, and Ahmed Saadawi.[120] Although there are meaningful differences between the faces of death in Iraqi and Syrian war literature, Bahoora's description fits well with the surreality of war, dictatorship, and monstrosity in *The Cranes*.

In "Madness," the concluding section of the novel, the author-narrator is simultaneously "the intellectual," "the jihadi," and "the Leader-General." In this sense, the "resistance" to power exercised and embodied by Fathi Sheen in *The Silence and the Roar* (Chapter 4) is irrelevant to the author-narrator of *The Cranes*, who is both ideologically attached to the dictator and psychologically indistinguishable from the leader, even surpassing the latter's cruel violence. The dictator exists inside every character in this novel, whether living or dead or somewhere in between. One cannot ignore the novel's dark comedy, too. It is worth asking whether *The Cranes* qualifies as a comic novel. To the extent that it is satire, it lampoons the leader as a fungible character in Syrian life and literature but also sends up the dictator genre itself. One can identify in *The Cranes* something of what Agnes Heller calls the "drifting of reality":

> The transition between possible and impossible hovers . . . there is no reality; nor is there truth beyond doubt. There can be, in the comic novel, no final solution. Paradoxes, games, plays, puzzles, and mysteries fill the pages of the comic novels and need not be entirely resolved.[121]

At the same time, the characters in comic novels are overdetermined. "It is their philosophy, their logic, the logic of their dreams (phantasmagoria and illusions included), which lends them complexity."[122] As the terrorism of dictatorship impinges upon the everyday lives of the author-narrator, other characters, and the reader, it remains unclear whether *The Cranes* is capable of escaping the regime's ideological universe, and that truly is no laughing matter.

DEATHLY ATTACHMENTS: SOUDADE KAADAN'S *THE DAY I LOST MY SHADOW* (*YAWM AḌAʿTU ẒILLĪ*)

Across the three novels discussed in this chapter, the surreality of the Syria War results in different kinds of reckoning with the work of the dead. From the labor of depositing mortal remains to the political danger of evaluating and dispensing with a human life, the inability to properly master, inhabit, or comprehend the condition of nonlife creates anxious prose. The otherworldliness of an unreliable narrator (or narrators) is relevant to the discussion that follows of a film, to stay with Agnes Heller, not set "in a pragmatic world" but rather one full of surreal happenings and hallucinatory confusion.[123] In both literature and film, death, the dying, and the (un)dead are material manifestations of loss and danger as well as screens for psychological, cultural, and political anxiety about the ubiquitous immediacy of human finitude. This concluding section looks at a recent feature film by French-Syrian director Soudade Kaadan that is set in the time of the Syria War and engages directly with the simultaneous horror of and fascination with death, dying, and the dead body. In Kaadan's *The Day I Lost My Shadow* (*Yawm Aḍaʿtu Ẓillī*) (2018), the everyday experience of death lays the foundation for a meditation on the mysterious nature of human embodiment. Kaadan was born in Paris in 1979, and her first two films—*Aziza*, a short, and *Shadow*, a narrative feature—were warmly received at international film festivals. She studied theater criticism at the Higher Institute of Dramatic Arts in Syria and graduated from the Université Saint-Joseph's Institut des Études Scénique, Audiovisuelles et Cinématographiques (IESAV) in Beirut. Before directing her first films she produced and made documentaries for NGOs and satellite television networks.

The opening title informs the viewer that *The Day I Lost My Shadow* is set in 2012 Damascus, as shadows are abandoning their bodies all over town. Sana and her son Khalil return home to their middle-class apartment, brushing past armed men who stand guard outside their building. Because there happens to be running water at that moment, she tries to do laundry for the first time in a while. When the electricity cuts out and she cannot open the washing machine, she snaps. "When will I die and finish this fucking life!" she shouts with her son standing there wearing his father's oversized sweater because he has no clean clothes. Sana drops Khalil at his grandfather's so that she can get to her job at the pharmacy. One morning she is lined up to have her gas canister refilled at the rationing station when the army arrives to announce that provisioning has ended for the day, before she and another dozen or so people can get their share. She watches a woman named Reem trying to calm her brother Jalal as he complains that he will not go home without gas for his family. Sana strikes up a conversation with Reem and Jalal, and the three decide to share a taxi to another part of town to find gas. As they approach a military checkpoint, the driver reveals that he has a camera in the glove box with footage of protests and interviews with activists. This would put him at serious risk, so he instinctively zooms through the checkpoint. They are chased and shot at until the driver eventually lets them out to wander into the agricultural land of the Ghouta, outside the urban center.

As the three walk through the rural landscape, Sana notices that Jalal has no shadow. They manage to convince a man to let them borrow his car, at which point Reem and Jalal get into an argument about how he needs to calm down because she does not want their mother to lose another son. Their brother Mazen had disappeared recently. Sana's husband, meanwhile, has been working in Saudi Arabia, reminding the viewer that loved ones go missing for a variety of reasons, not only because of regime repression and the war. Jalal had been imprisoned for 180 days, and his brother Mazen had, too. Jalal heard his brother being tortured, then his voice disappeared, then he lost his shadow, possibly. As they talk over a campfire in the wilderness, Jalal asks Sana whether she realizes that what is going on in Damascus is the opposite of what had taken place in Hiroshima: people woke up the day after the bombings in Japan to find nothing but shadows. Kadaan apparently had gotten the idea about shadows after watching Alain Resnais's *Hiroshima Mon Amour*.

> When you die, the world ends. And while you're alive you can't change anything in war. That's the way I felt. Those images in *Hiroshima* brought me to this emotional position I'm expressing. Maybe it isn't logical but people here live without shadows.[124]

In the morning, Sana and Reem discover that Jalal is gone, and they flag down a man in a truck who agrees to give them a ride. After failing to find Jalal, Reem

FIGURE 38. Soudade Kaadan, *Yawm Aḍaʿtu Ẓillī* (*The Day I Lost My Shadow*) (KAF Production, Acrobates Film, Metaphora Production, 2018)

decides to go with the pious Muslim driver to Friday prayer in Douma, which is also the site of an antiregime demonstration. Sana stays back with the women in the driver's family home until she is taken along with them for what they call "digging time."

In this macabre scene, Sana finds herself co-constructing an improvised graveyard. In addition to an aerial shot of veiled women hard at work digging pits, there is a remarkable sequence in which the camera is placed in the ground looking up at Sana's face as she furiously rips away dirt and digs a deeper hole. The view from below, from the perspective of the not-yet-dead-and-buried subject, communicates Sana's growing distress, anxiety, and fear but also obscures her face in shadow in a way that inverts the shadow-as-life metaphor that explains the film's title (Figure 38). Formally speaking, Sana might be acquiring a shadow through this morbid labor. The shadows here are "naturally" deathly. After tending to injured demonstrators who have just come back with Reem, Sana heads out into the woods and stumbles across Jalal's corpse, which she drags with her. She is accosted by a soldier who points his rifle at her and insists that he take the body with him because the corpse will have to be exchanged for a soldier in the regime's army. When Sana makes it clear that she is not going to allow him to leave with Jalal's body, the soldier shoots Jalal in the stomach, perhaps not just to make sure that he is dead but also to imply that the dead in the time of the Syria War may die multiple deaths. Sana drags Jalal's corpse down a dirt road, though now she is starting to lose her shadow, too (Figure 39). Finally, returning home with her gas canister, Sana is reunited with Khalil, taking pleasure in the mundane routine of doing laundry, bathing, and making dinner. When armed men show up at the house, Sana loses her shadow altogether while sitting in the kitchen with Khalil. "Don't be scared," she tells the boy as they look towards the door expectantly.

The atmosphere of the film is thick with death, fear, and dread. The disappearing shadows suggests small deaths that occur on a regular basis. Jalal's corpse is a constant companion, not unlike ʿAbd al-Latif in *Dying Is Hard Work*, one to be protected rather than feared or mourned. Sana seems less troubled by Jalal's dead body than she is by Reem's loss of her shadow. Given that Reem has just returned from the exhilarating experience of demonstrating against the regime for the first time, this sense of loss is all the more poignant. Interestingly, though, as opposed to much contemporary visual culture about and around Syria, *The Day I Lost My Shadow* is aesthetically clean, free of gore and chaos. The pacing is patient, the mood somber, the danger always on the doorstep but the action stays elsewhere, off screen. In a sense, one can find an aesthetic kinship with the work of Riyad Shayya and his film *Al-Lajāt* (1995), which articulates an aesthetic power and cinematic language with relative speechlessness (Chapter 2). In fact, in an interview with Nadim Jarjura, Kadaan said something

FIGURE 39. Soudade Kaadan, *Yawm Aḍaʿtu Ẓillī* (*The Day I Lost My Shadow*) (KAF Production, Acrobates Film, Metaphora Production, 2018)

reminiscent of Shayya's work: "The important thing to me in *The Day I Lost My Shadow* is that the story should not arrive with words. There are no discussions that express anything fundamental." This chasm between speech and image is so profound that it might be thought of as a kind of "dissociation," one that accepts the caesura between visual and verbal language and allows for a different aesthetics of solidarity to emerge. Words get in the way of the intimate experience of living with the dead. It is as if the audience has been enlisted to help Sana carry Jalal's shadowless dead body. This investment in the power of the image and visual language, as opposed to dialogue or words, also reflects Kadaan's relationship to genre, which is brought out in that same interview.

> In Syria, I had the feeling that I would not be able to make any films as a documentary filmmaker. I was convinced that the image cannot communicate reality. This is not philosophizing. How can my camera record these things? I used to ask myself: Is cinema capable of representing war? . . . The ugliness of war is larger than the image.[125]

Perhaps death can be more real, more tactile, and more comforting than disappearance; perhaps death's materiality—the stuff of the corpse—can be a foundation of solace for the bereaved.

SYRIA WAR NECROAESTHETIC

Representations of death have been analyzed by scholars of literature, film, and culture from myriad perspectives.[126] In his cultural history of the dead body, Thomas Laqueur argues that the dead have historically constituted a repository for human desires, anxieties, and imagination. Laqueur asserts that "we" are a singular, modern human community that stands united with a disposition toward death that "matters, everywhere and across time, as well as in particular times and particular places."[127] Whatever cultural differences may appear in the specific iterations of a relationship to the dead and to the dead body, culture (as opposed to nature) guides the fundamental stance of the living against or in relation to the dead. For Laqueur,

> there seems to be a universally shared feeling not only that there is something deeply wrong about not caring for the dead body in some fashion, but also that the uncared-for body, no matter the cultural norms, is unbearable. The corpse

> demands attention of the living, however that attention is paid. We have a gut aversion to the bare, bereft dead body.[128]

Interested in what he calls, somewhat ambiguously, "'corpses without consciousness,' bereft, vulnerable, abject,"[129] Laqueur also notes that "death and the dead may not have a history in the usual sense but only more and more iterations, endless and infinitely varied, that we shape into an engagement with the past and the present."[130]

It is worth returning now to the broader philosophical considerations of struggles around aesthetic theory in contemporary cultural criticism that were briefly discussed in the Introduction. Take, for example, the critique of idealist, materialist, and dialectical aesthetics by Allen Feldman, who argues that

> cultural anesthesia, political intangibility, and the inheritance of the uninheritable correspond to political aesthesis as marginalized, disqualified, deferred, or expelled sensory experience engendering a politics of disincarnation—the denudation of an embodied, situated, and common sensorium with the capacity to speak truth to war.[131]

Such a "politics of disincarnation" in the necroaesthetics of the Syria War creates the possibility of "speak[ing] truth to war" through *dis*embodied, *un*situated, and altogether alienated sensoria, whether through the spectral voice of Jigha in *Night Shirt* or the eerie physical disappearance of shadows in *The Day I Lost My Shadow*. More prosaically, a historical understanding of political aesthetics need not be limited to what Jacques Rancière describes as "the distribution of the sensible" but can also be understood as an attempt to build, make sense of, and even deconstruct what Allen Feldman calls "archives of the insensible."[132] The aesthetics of solidarity on display in the literature and film examined throughout *Revolutions Aesthetic* represents one way in which writers, filmmakers, and artists are able to "speak truth to war" while also reminding us that *speaking-with* (*mitsprechen*) is a viable alternative to the aesthetics of power promulgated by the regime and its supporters.

The politics and aesthetics of death in contemporary Syrian cultural production recalls to us the all too human dilemma of whether or not to look away from atrocity. [133] The politics of witness in the construction of a political and ethical subject in the time of the Syria War (Chapter 5) is linked in complicated ways to the necroaesthetics of Syria War culture. Death is a constant companion in the novels and film discussed in this chapter: they are all concerned with the simultaneous singularity and banality of death, the individual and communal experiences of dying, the various (after)lives of the dead. At the same time, they demonstrate how death in the time of the Syria War can be generative of new modes of creative expression. The stubborn, disruptive power of the corpse at the center of *Dying Is Hard Work*; the indeterminate status of the dead body in *Night Shirt*; the surreal fantasia of death beyond material existence in *The Cranes*; and the "becoming-corpse" that survives even as human shadows fade in *The Day I Lost My Shadow*: there is no such thing as *the* Syrian corpse but rather a multiplicity of representations of Syrian corpses imbued with different meanings that are subject to debate and resignification.

Demands for life, liberty, and dignity surged into public view in the early days of the Syrian revolution. The haltingly militarized conflict metastasized into an incipient civil war. In time the situation devolved into an international war layered with proxy conflicts, at once fueling but increasingly overshadowed by a humanitarian crisis that rocked the Middle East, Europe, and beyond. The planetary scale of refugee flows and interminable human suffering both stuns and eludes international attention. But a crucial yet strangely fugitive experience at the heart of the Syria War is the unending scourge of premature death and senseless dying. Syrian literature and film during this period have not shied away from these matters. Politics is no longer biopolitical in terms of who possesses the sovereign power to determine who lives and who dies, but it has given way to a struggle around the very possibility of deciding (and narrating) *how* Syrians die and what their (too) many deaths mean.

Syrian cultural production has come full circle in the time of the Syria War. The "commitment literature" and socialist realism of the 1960s and 1970s made it morally and ideologically incumbent on writers to wrestle with the political and social impact of their characters, plots, narrative, and meaning making generally. The aesthetic ideology of Asadist-Baʿthist cultural revolution prioritized commitment and heroism in an idiom that was shot through with the concerns of a country under authoritarian rule in the midst of political-economic and ideological transformation. Writers and filmmakers working against the backdrop of an unspooling humanitarian catastrophe in the more recent time of the Syria War have stumbled into a different mode of critique: direct engagement with the aesthetics and politics of death. This necroaesthetics is a novel development in Syrian cultural production that should be understood in relation to the agonistic struggle over aesthetic ideology that has characterized an important but underappreciated dimension of Syrian history discussed throughout *Revolutions Aesthetic*. The question of what kind of responsibility is owed to the dead—to say nothing of what is owed to the living, the not-yet dead, those in existential limbo—is addressed through attempts to inter the present, bury the past, and unearth a different horizon of possibility for the future. It is not only the memory of dead generations that burden the living in contemporary Syria. The dying, the undead, and dead bodies increasingly populate material reality, circumscribing the imagination of other futures to come. In none of these macabre artworks of the Syria War—not in *Dying Is Hard Work*, *Night Shirt*, *The Cranes*, or *The Day I Lost My Shadow*—do living Syrians seem to exercise much power over matters of life and death. One might then be tempted to conclude with Hannah Arendt that fixation on death in the Syrian fictional imaginary is bound up with the antipolitics of the Syria War. But perhaps these myriad representations of death in contemporary Syrian cultural production will inspire other and even more creative views toward the coming—imminently, one can only hope—postwar Syria.

Conclusion

THE ART OF THE REAL

A revolution in the cultural sphere would run the risk of remaining superstructural or ideological if it were simply a case of artists and intellectuals proclaiming their solidarity with the great proletarian revolution; things take on a different quality if the sphere of cultural production is itself seen as a site rife with antagonism.

—Sven Lütticken, "Cultural Revolution"[1]

It is never easy to distinguish an appeal to taste and sentiment which offers an alternative to autocracy from one which allows such power to ground itself all the more securely in the living sensibilities of its subjects.

—Terry Eagleton, *The Ideology of the Aesthetic*[2]

Fundamentally the Baath is more than a party. It is a state of mind, an atmosphere, a faith, a doctrine, a culture, a civilisation with its own intrinsic worth.

—Salah al-Din al-Bitar, "The Rise and Decline of the Baath"[3]

THE SYRIAN NATIONAL FILM ORGANIZATION (AL-MU'ASSASA al-ʿĀmma li-l-Sīnamā, NFO) rarely produces documentaries anymore. While it may never have been the preferred genre of this leading state cultural institution, the shift away from documentary is particularly striking in light of the unprecedented success of privately produced and internationally supported documentary films that have been made about Syria by both Syrians and non-Syrians over the past several years. One crucial development concerning cultural production in the time of the Syria War is the growing power and influence of capital and intellectual input from the Gulf States as well as European and US-based filmmakers and culture-funding agencies.[4] For the most part, NFO-produced films were deemed consonant with the aesthetic ideology of Asadist-Baʿthist cultural revolution. As I have argued throughout this book, however, not all of the films released by the NFO fulfilled such ideological strictures. In 1974, for example, the NFO funded one of the most scathingly critical films ever made about the Baʿthist regime, one that was never legally screened in Syria. Conceived through a collaboration between the acclaimed playwright Saʿdallah Wannous and filmmaker Omar Amiralay, *Everyday Life in a Syrian Village* (*al-Ḥayā al-Yawmiyya fī Qarya Sūriyya*; 1974) was shot in 1971–1972 and—alongside Amiralay's *The Chickens* (*al-Dajāj*; 1977) and *A Flood in Baath Country* (*Ṭūfān fī Bilād al-Baʿth*; 2003)—it remains one of the most unflinching works ever made about government policies in Syria. Nearly ten years into the "socialist transformation" launched in the Syrian countryside after the Baʿth Party seized power in 1963 through which a primarily pastoralist and agricultural society was slated for accelerated development, the effects of that social and political project were hardly felt in the provinces. Even as an increasing number of people were either leaving behind or being pushed off their land, the lives of displaced peasants, town dwellers, and nomads remained mostly unaffected by this suite of modernizing reforms. Whereas about half of "the country's labor force was engaged in agriculture" in 1970, this figure would drop dramatically to 31.8 percent by 1979, indicating a mixed record of success in ameliorating living conditions in the countryside.[5]

Everyday Life counterposes scenes of extreme poverty, overcrowded schools, heated arguments around the administration of justice, and impassioned demands for adequate health care against subdued interviews with unbothered government bureaucrats who have been dispatched to the country's periphery to promote the agenda of the Baʿth Party and the Syrian government. The juxtaposition of such markedly divergent realities produces a cinematic effect of profound irony and biting satire. During the late 1960s, Amiralay studied film at the Institut des hautes études cinématographiques (IDHEC) in Paris, a lively institution for cinéastes and film students from around the world; lived through the May 1968 uprising; and was influenced by the nouvelle vague among other currents in mid-twentieth-century Western European cinema. In this regard, he stands out among his Syrian contemporaries, many though not all of whom were trained in the Soviet Union at the All-Union State Institute of Cinematography in Moscow (VGIK). In an interview with *Cahiers du cinéma* in 1978, Amiralay expressed his conviction that "[documentary] cinema must move toward reality, tell the truth with the least number of intermediaries." The kind of filmmaker who pursued this set of goals would contribute to what he termed "an austere cinema," one that did not require "intermediaries" to interpret the story being visually represented. It could be argued that this is precisely what made Amiralay's early work in *Everyday Life* and *The Chickens* not only successful political criticism but also a mesmerizing aesthetic experiment.[6]

One of the most arresting scenes in *Everyday Life* takes place when a representative of the Ministry of Culture traveling through the northeastern frontier town of Dayr al-Zur supervises a free public film screening, introducing the film with platitudes about the uplifting value of cinema in developed and civilized societies (Figure 40). The film being shown is *Beautiful Shots of the Syrian Arab Homeland* (*al-Waṭan al-ʿArabī al-Sūrī fī Laqaṭāt Jayyida*). After the bureaucrat has finished droning on about the patriotic virtues embedded in cinema itself—a cultural form that, he makes sure to remind them, is utterly foreign to Syrians—the ragtag assortment of peasants and pastoralists who have been rounded up to watch are subjected to incongruous images of scantily clad beachgoers who might be Syrians or Lebanese or dwellers of another Mediterranean country in a movie set to the music of a modern jazz ensemble. The people on screen lounge on the beach, swing in hammocks, frolic with their pet dogs, and insouciantly smoke hookahs as children scamper about making sandcastles and diving into the surf. The tone deafness of a film like this being shown to the inhabitants of such a poor, rural, and traditional community raises important questions for a historian of aesthetics, politics, and cultural production in Asadist-Baʿthist Syria. Amiralay is clear that the selection of titles for the Ministry of Culture's ambulatory film units was concluded with little regard for the cultural or moral standards of the audience. In the 1978 *Cahiers du cinéma* interview, he said that the Ministry of Culture would show films, for example, about dairy production in Normandy or rockets being launched into space or Indira Gandhi's coming to power in India: the cultivation of a modern sensibility through cinema was deemed more important for the Asadist-Baʿthist cultural revolution than ensuring that the content of those films had any connection to the everyday life of ordinary Syrians. Amiralay found this unfortunate and risible:

> It would have been better they be absent than to play this role of creating complexes among the peasants. Imagine a peasant who lives on the edge of the desert in a lamentable situation, to whom you show Normandy, Normandy cows with huge teats that are emptied into buckets of milk. . . . It makes one want to commit suicide when one is confronted with daily reality after seeing this film. That's the dangerous side of these movies.[7]

Amiralay cautiously treads a fine line between his personal wish to show respect for the power and pedagogical value of cinema and calling into the question the brute force employed in this modernizationist agenda. There is a tension here, too, between the aesthetics of power in the Asadist-Baʿthist cultural revolution—the prevailing aesthetic ideology deployed by the Syrian state starting in the early 1970s—and the aesthetics of solidarity I have identified throughout this book as a critical alternative to the ideological strictures of state culture that is distinct from the blunt aesthetics of resistance, an aesthetics of solidarity shaped by state ideology but not entirely beholden to its political and aesthetic agenda. It is not so easy to separate Asadist-Baʿthist cultural revolution (from above) from its aesthetics of power, which relies on a discourse of *speaking-to* or *speaking-for* and oppositional forms of expression that include *speaking-with* and *speaking-against*, which I have described in terms of

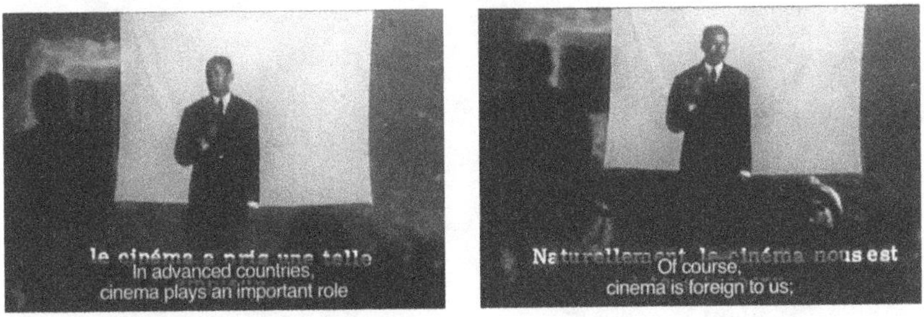

FIGURE 40. Omar Amiralay, *al-Ḥayā al-Yawmiyya fī Qarya Sūriyya* (*Everyday Life in a Syrian Village*) (National Film Organization, 1974)

an aesthetics of solidarity and an aesthetics of resistance. To be sure, this is a heuristic typology of aesthetic ideologies in Baʿthist Syria; they may overlap in both formal and substantive ways, as in the overdetermined style of Amiralay's documentary, caught between his commitment to objective documentation and the surprisingly subjective irruption of ideology toward the end of the film.

Amiralay brings to light important ideological ramifications of the visual collision between bourgeois leisure activities on the Mediterranean coast and the activities of the deprived lives of the vast majority of rural Syrians during the 1960s and 1970s. There is a relentless critique of state power in these incongruous depictions. The conclusion of the film amplifies that critical tone, ending with an impassioned speech by an elderly man who rails against the regime for failing to provide basic services and infrastructure for the provinces. This man has appeared throughout the film as a punctuating marker, much like the irregularly recurring shots of piston engines chugging along in the provinces in support of infrastructural development projects. A similar technique of syncopated images can be seen in *The Chickens*. In some sense, this interruption functions as a pointed reminder of the hegemonic narrative used by the state on ongoing modernization projects. Although edited into the film narrative with enough time to allow the viewer to apprehend the experience of disruption, the intervening shots are rapid enough to put the viewer in mind of subliminal messages that smuggle in suggestive themes beyond conscious comprehension. This subtle subversion of propaganda is paired with a much more withering treatment of unsophisticated sloganeering. "We're hungry and dying!" the old man screams as he tears his shirt off, exposing his chest to the viewer in dramatic fashion in the final moment. A freeze frame of this act of defiance dissolves into bold slogans that appear starkly on screen:

WE MUST ALL
GET INVOLVED IN THE STRUGGLE
FOR OUR COMMON SALVATION
THERE ARE NO CLEAN HANDS
THERE ARE NO INNOCENTS
THERE ARE NO SPECTATORS
WE MUST ALL
PLUNGE OUR HANDS

INTO THE MUD OF OUR SOIL
AND EVERY SPECTATOR
IS A COWARD
OR A TRAITOR

At a formal level, such rousing political language at the end is noteworthy, and Amiralay has left us some clues as to how best to make sense of this choice. "We did not want to make an ideological intervention with comments or section headings [*intertitres*]," Amiralay explained to *Cahiers du cinéma*: "We had only one ideological intervention at the end of the film, and I don't know how much we needed it—the line from Frantz Fanon who says that any spectator is a traitor or a coward."[8] By repurposing the revolutionary language of Fanon, which resonates quite interestingly with some key words in the Baʿthist lexicon—terms and concepts that are decidedly debased by Asadist-Baʿthist rule—Amiralay draws the viewer's attention to the power of cinema to mobilize public opinion and inspire committed political action. Here the viewer is confronted by a puzzling statement about the intersection of ideology, spectatorship, and cultural production. Is the spectator who views the films screened by the state depicted in *Everyday Life in a Syrian Village* a coward and a traitor? Or are viewers of Amiralay's film itself being labeled cowards and a traitors if they simply remain passive bystanders, if they do not take up the "struggle for our common salvation"?[9] And which struggle is being invoked here? The Arab nationalist struggle against Zionism and imperialism waged by the Syrian state—the vanguard of the revolution, the Hanoi of the Arab world? Or the struggle for justice waged by ordinary people—the secular left to the Islamist right—in a country buffeted by military coups and decades of postcolonial disorder? The struggle against military dictatorship or the struggle *of* the military dictatorship and its devotees against both internal dissension and external threats? And, most challenging, who is the we indexed by our common salvation? Who is the collective subject interpellated by the ideology of this set of claims? Is it the Syrian people? The Syrian nation? The global community of cinephiles who might see Amiralay's film? These questions may be unanswerable or at least require further debate, but the potential richness of this discussion speaks to the enduring significance of the film as well as the continuing challenges of an adequate historical assessment of aesthetics and politics in postcolonial Syria. Perhaps one of the most subversive aspects of this concluding move—the invocation of Fanon—has to do with the fact that Amiralay has slyly managed to emblazon a revolutionary slogan not derived from the heroic deeds and words of the leader himself on a film produced by the state-administered NFO. At the same time, the way these words flash across the screen points up the emptiness and the distraction of regime discourse; the formal resemblance of such a slogan to the hollow platitudes plastered on posters and walls, shouted at rallies and marches all over the country, subtly sidelines demands for conformity and social compliance made by the regime's ideological cult.

Although *Everyday Life* was banned in Syria, it remains a cultural touchstone for successive generations of Syrians, especially those who are critical of the regime. There may be a plausible explanation of why the film passed muster with Syrian censors in the first place. In his early documentaries, Amiralay adheres to an aesthetics of resistance—against economic underdevelopment, against imperialism, against political apathy—that morphologically approximates the state-sanctioned aesthetics of power. As Shareah Taleghani points out, "Amiralay uses the combination of visual and verbal irony to disrupt the official progress narrative of the Baʿthist regime."[10] But he also claims to embrace a pragmatic or nonideological approach to filmmaking, a perfectly realistic documentary style that requires no political statement whatsoever; he wishes to be forgiven for his indulgence of one "ideological intervention," which he now regrets. Amiralay would likely agree that the key aesthetic struggle in Syria concerned "the language of truth," the site of the country's "battle in one of its most dangerous domains." He also might be disconcerted to find how different his own interpretation of these terms was from the presumed intention of Hafiz al-Asad when he used such language.[11] Ironically, the attempt by Syrian state institutions to monopolize truth, in part through cultural production, drove Syrian filmmakers, writers, artists, and public intellectuals away from a quest for what Amiralay called reality in this specific instance, and toward direct mimetic engagement with a political and social context that could not be so easily challenged or controlled; it proved similarly challenging to represent such matters in literature and film without raising the ire of an intolerant and capricious dictatorial regime.

This jagged disjuncture between the aesthetic ideology of state institutions and the cultural orientations of Syrian writers, filmmakers, artists, and many others must be placed in historical perspective. The periodization employed throughout this book is a conventional one: 1963—1966—1967—1970—1973—1982—2000—2011—? These dates mark salient turning points in modern Syrian history, but it bears remembering that they are markers of political change: coups, wars, presidential transition, revolutionary uprising. Since the advent of what I have been calling Asadist-Baʿthist cultural revolution, launched during the 1970s under the auspices of Hafiz al-Asad's corrective movement, Syrian literature and film have been characterized by competing artistic trends comprehensible in terms of what I have called throughout this book the aesthetics of power, the aesthetics of solidarity, and the aesthetics of resistance. These aesthetic categories change over time, occasionally overlapping and even indistinguishable—and bear in mind that these are hardly the only aesthetic categories in modern and contemporary Syrian cultural production worthy of scholarly attention. Still, their broad outlines have endured, differentiating the aesthetic ideology of cultural production over the course of five decades of modern Syrian history. If the Asadist-Baʿthist cultural revolution inaugurated a new era in Syrian cultural and intellectual history, other punctuating events would bring the struggle over aesthetic ideology more clearly into view. The defeat (*al-hazīma*) of the Arab armies by Israel during the Six-Day War of June 1967 and the so-called victory (*al-intiṣār*) of the Arab world in the October War of 1973 had lasting effects in the Syrian cultural field; and although the consequences of defeat have been occasionally discussed in this book, there is much more to be said about the reflections of war across late-twentieth century Syrian literary and visual culture generally. Moreover, embedded in the rather conventional chronology tracked throughout *Revolutions Aesthetic* is a transformative period in the history of the country that cannot be easily reconstructed through documentary and literary evidence, namely the domestic armed conflict in Syria (1979–1982) that culminated in the 1982 massacres at Hama. Fueled in large part by Islamist movements but also by social forces inimical to the regime, this insurrection against the Baʿthist dictatorship left a blind spot in the cultural historical record. Massive disinformation coupled with widespread secrecy and silence about events ensured that the cultural memory of the period would remain muffled. The erasure of the Hama massacre and that era of national turmoil is a historical phenomenon that awaits more careful political, social, intellectual, and cultural reconstruction.[12]

One of the most significant ruptures in modern Syrian history that has occasioned a bit more historical reflection opened up around the time of Hafiz al-Asad's death in 2000. By no means was this seismic event received by everyone inside and outside Syria with the same sense of loss, but whatever the response, al-Asad's passing occasioned myriad demands for national reckoning, catalyzing a number of political and structural reforms, however cosmetic in nature, which in turn made it possible to imagine new kinds of cultural liberalization. If the death of Hafiz al-Asad and the reformism from above, as I have characterized it, of Bashar al-Asad during the first decade of the twentieth-first century saw a subtle transformation in the country's cultural politics, with greater opportunities for creative expression and collaboration with artistic trends across the region and around the world, the cultural politics of the Syrian revolution and subsequent war and humanitarian catastrophe revolved around struggles over truth and the very constitution and (re)definition of reality. The contested relationship between aesthetics and politics has been at the heart of Syria's ideological, political, and social transformation over the course of the twentieth and early twenty-first centuries; the cultural schisms attending the Syrian revolution and the Syria War are therefore comprehensible in light of that history. The "emergency cinema" of the Abounaddara collective, for example, is not only a response to wartime conditions and the "right to the image" but also a political and philosophical cry for a return to a visual language committed to documenting reality. This orientation is not the only indication of an unmistakable kinship between Abounaddara and Omar Amiralay, a sign of continuity in the cultural politics of documentary in modern Syria.[13]

In February 2011, just as the popular uprising was starting to coalesce, another kind of activism was under way in the Syrian cultural sphere. Following the untimely death of Omar Amiralay on February 5, over 300 Syrians branding themselves "People Concerned with Matters of Syrian Cinema" criticized the director of the NFO, Muhammad al-Ahmad (b. 1961), for what they deemed insensitive, irresponsible, and politically untenable remarks that he had made in an appearance on Syrian state television. Al-Ahmad identified a "fundamental problem" in the work of Amiralay which his fans seemed unacceptably inattentive to, namely, that "he was a person lost between a political [activist] [*al-siyāsī*] and a documentary filmmaker." Of course, the implication was that a real artist would not tarnish his craft with a political brush. In the immediate aftermath of Amiralay's death, and some forty years after the release of *Everyday Life*, al-Ahmad was using his vaunted position and influential voice to criticize the passing of a Syrian artistic icon even as he was being collectively mourned. In their statement of protest, the concerned group argued that what al-Ahmad said had exceeded "the limits of cinematic artistic criticism." In a press conference the following week, al-Ahmad defended his commitment to upholding the importance of cinema in Syrian public life. He was appointed director of the NFO in January 2000 and served until July 2016. In this role, he was responsible for overseeing the production, release, and screening of films in both the public and private sector, which made him the highest authority supervising the Damascus International Film Festival. It is noteworthy that al-Ahmad was tapped to become minister of culture in July 2016, earning him even more prestige and authority in the state cultural apparatus, not only because his ascension demonstrated the government's specific acknowledgment of his loyalty and reliability but also because of the regime's recognition of the significance of cinema.[14] This was, after all, a moment in which the ubiquity of images, the power of screens, and the need to communicate political messages through visual culture demanded that the regime step up its media capabilities.[15]

With the participation and acclaim of such venerable filmmakers as ʿAbd al-Latif ʿAbd al-Hamid, the Ministry of Culture, the NFO, and al-Ahmad supported a new generation of filmmakers who continued to promote the aesthetic ideology of state culture. To be sure, the content and form of this cultural production changed dramatically. During the first decade of the twenty-first century, as the regime embarked on its project of neoliberal reforms and cultural opening, reflections of the evolving state ideology's conception of the good life and responsible governance could be seen in such NFO productions as the 2009 film *Marra Ukhrā* (*Once Again*) by Joud Said (b. 1980) and in privately funded television serials such as *Buqʿat Ḍawʾ* (*Spotlight*) and *Fawq al-Saqf* (*Above the Ceiling*).[16] The regime promoted its own vision of wartime cultural production, including cinema, in response to the effervescent oppositional visual culture associated with the Syrian uprising. Said's 2017 film *Maṭar Ḥimṣ* (*Homs Rain*) was among the most controversial in this regard. Said's cinematic output hardly slowed in the time of the Syria War because he enjoyed the stalwart support of the NFO thanks in part to close personal relationships with Muhammad al-Ahmad and ʿAbd al-Latif ʿAbd al-Hamid. His films included *Ṣadīqī al-Akhīr* (*My Last Friend*) (2013) and *Bi-Intiẓār al-Kharīf* (*Waiting for Autumn*) (2015). Shot in wartime Homs with the cooperation and protection of the army and the regime itself after the vast majority of the city's residents had been displaced, *Homs Rain* has four chapters, each one corresponding to a month during February–May 2014: "The Rain of Madness," "The Rain of the Heart," "The Rain of Hope," and the "Rain of Darkness." The evolving symbolism of rain over the course of the film—from ominous threat to morbid sadness and, eventually, sustenance in a time of siege and uncertainty—encodes the natural resilience of the place to accompany but also survive the unnatural destruction of human creation. In the opening shot, Said announces, "We are not in the business of documentation or reproduction [of reality], but rather [of telling] a fictional story with imaginary characters based upon true events . . . *Homs Rain* is a testimony [*shahāda*] made out of blood and love."

The viewer first encounters an uncontextualized shot of an abandoned, bombarded street, followed by a slow advance through other sections of the decimated city, immediately raising the question of representation, specifically of atrocity and ruination, in the real time of war. The film opens with a shot of the main characters huddled together toward the end of their story, with Yousef (Muhammad al-Ahmad, not to be confused with the minister of culture), a veteran and self-avowed patriot, and Yara (Lama al-Khatib), an aid worker who has smuggled herself into the city to search for her brother who had gone missing in action while serving in the Syrian army. The pair flank two young children, an orphan boy named Jad and a little girl named Sarah. Yara is writing in her journal—a habit of Yousef's as well—while melodramatic music swells and a voiceover begins the narrative: "We died. Of love." The camera pans upward, through the ground and we discover the foursome hiding out in a tomb. A dead man lies on the ground of a cemetery, a grave with a prominent cross visible in the background. An attempt is made to rescue civilians from the old city in a deal negotiated between the regime and jihadi fighters commanded by Abu ʿAbdallah, played by Joud Said himself. The coordinated evacuation goes haywire just as the last civilians are crossing the square and the jihadi fighters open fire. Escaping the melee, Yousef and Jad wind up inside a church with Ilya (Husayn ʿAbbas), the only priest to remain at his post, cementing the centrality of Christianity to this story of steadfastness and survival against Islamist invaders, effectively hammering home the message that the preservation of Syrian Christianity depends on regime power.

Eventually the five cross paths on the street and together move into an abandoned house where the political and sexual tension is thick between Yousef, the veteran of the Syrian army, and Yara, the activist with the Syrian revolution. When he challenges her by demanding to know who she truly is, she retorts, "I am the voice of every person you oppress." Yousef replies that he is humiliated and oppressed because he is responsible for fighting to allow people like her to walk around safely (Figure 41, top left). At first Yousef accuses Yara—and, by extension, the Syrian revolution—of being in league with the jihadists, but their budding romantic relationship ultimately creates a narrative in which the regime and the revolution are one, united in their patriotism and opposition to radical jihadism. No matter what disagreements there may have been between the protestors and ordinary people unhappy with authoritarian rule in the country, they are now united, essentially whitewashing the regime's violent repression of the revolution and sidelining the demands of the revolutionaries themselves. Yara is wounded in a shelling and Yousef falls deeply in love with her as he nurses her back to health. Later on, as Yara and Yousef sit atop a battered Ferris wheel, Yousef tells her that the smell of destruction reminds him of his childhood in Lebanon during the civil war. "At a certain moment," he tells Yara, "you feel like you need to search for a country." This saccharine love story unspools against the backdrop of fictional and all too real atrocities, adding to the sense that politics is being aestheticized in a troublingly vulgar way.

Suddenly the band of five is kidnapped by the armed daughters of "The General," a former air force pilot who is in control of the neighborhood. The General interrogates them one by one in order to identify them and their political commitments. Yara confesses to being part of the revolution while also insisting that she is a loyal patriot searching for her soldier brother. The General announces that he was a pilot during the October 1973 War, referencing his patriotism as well as his participation in the country's national "victory" (*al-intiṣār*), a founding moment of national honor and heroism celebrated by the regime of Hafiz al-Asad, prominently memorialized, for example, at the October War Panorama in Damascus (the mural at the beginning of Chapter 1). Yousef is questioned about his loyalties: "Are you a foreign or local militant? Answer me in Arabic." After responding that he "support[s] the Karameh football club and speak[s] Arabic fluently," he rattles off a litany of simple Arabic sentences out of which he constructs an allegory of civil war as petty conflicts between brothers. “I'm in the army just like you,” he says. The General decides to send them all to his field prison, where they encounter about a dozen people, all of them secularists who introduce themselves with a healthy dose of national pride and then reveal their estimable education, showcasing the intellectual firepower and cosmopolitanism of the Syrian people.

The climactic scenes revolve around a new agreement that will facilitate the peaceful evacuation of jihadists from Homs. When Yousef confronts Abu ʿAbdallah and his fighters in the street, the latter demands that Rima be handed over to him in exchange for everyone else's safe passage, claiming that she has information about the killing of his father. The two men snarl competing claims to Syria at one another—Abu ʿAbdallah in God's name and Yousef in the name of his ancestors and his children. Yousef refuses to agree to the terms and fighting breaks out between the jihadists and the remnants of the Syrian army that have been protecting the group. As the final battle rages at the Christian cemetery outside Father Ilya's church, Yara encounters a soldier who has news of her missing brother, informing her that he is dead but that his body has never been found. When one of the general's daughters shoots at the jihadists, Ilya is stabbed in the back by a jihadi fighter and then shot in the front by Abu ʿAbdallah. His dying words are that people like these fundamentalists come and go but the land will remain, along with those who live and die for it. Here patriotism is articulated through a Christian voice, cementing not only the union of “the revolution” with the regime but also the multisectarian harmony of Syria under regime control. One of the General's daughters is captured and brought into a car to speak with Abu ʿAbdallah, who believes this might be Rima, the one who knows who killed his father, and she says, raving, that this is from *my* father, as she detonates a grenade that blows them all to bits. The young daughters fighting as part of the General's militia reflect the gendered ideological discourse of the regime, which claims to protect minorities and, in particular, women. Moreover, the inversion of a stereotype about Islamist politics here leads to the jihadi commander being killed in a secular nationalist suicide bombing.

In an eerie image, a hand surges up through the soil of the cemetery just behind Ilya's corpse, as if the dead are now rising from the grave, an act with both secular and religious connotations (Figure 41, top right). This scene can be apprehended in terms of the survival of everyday life and quotidian forms of resistance beyond death, not unlike the reading of death, dying, and the (un)dead in Syria War culture discussed in Chapter 6. *Homs Rain* ends where it began. The final shot is of Yousef, Yara, Jad, and Sarah at the top of the Ferris Wheel overlooking destroyed Homs. Mulling over what to do next, they shout toward the horizon, "We shall go back home, Homs." The irony is that they are technically already "home" in Homs, even if they are not *at home* as the city they once knew has been destroyed and now exists only in imagination and ruination (Figure 41, bottom row). The idea is thus subtly put forward that the city has been taken from them by foreigners and infiltrators and so they must collectively struggle to reclaim and remake it. Writing in the daily newspaper *al-Akhbār*, Syrian novelist and critic Khalil Suwaylih (whose 2014 novel *Barbarians' Paradise* [*Jannat al-Barābira*] was discussed in Chapter 5), praised *Homs Rain*, comparing it to the work of the Sarajevo-born filmmaker and controversial public figure Emir Kusturica (b. 1954) because of its playful deployment of fantasy (*fāntāziyā*) even in a time of extreme suffering and mass death.[17] One noteworthy similarity between the two filmmakers is their decision to shoot in the midst of armed conflict, in the case of *Homs Rain* a city that had been "cleared" by the Syrian Arab Army for the express purpose of making this film. Suwaylih credulously assessed the movie's emotional and political premise without considering its context, the material conditions of its production, or the ethical questions raised by such an unusual filmmaking practice.[18] Some described the film as cinematic propaganda, exhorting "pro-revolution production companies" to "produce revolutionary films close to the truth, and immortalize the stories of the revolution, its massacres and the destruction." Otherwise "the only image the world will see after a while will be the ones the regime produced through its tools."[19]

A worthwhile comparison can be drawn between *Homs Rain* and *Return to Homs* (*'Ā'id ilā Ḥims*), which presents an altogether different perspective on living in the ruins of a brutal civil war. In this 2013 documentary by Talal Derki, the homecoming of Syrian soccer star Abdul Basset al-Saroot guides viewers through the war-torn urban landscape by introducing them to protestors who improvise armed resistance and techniques of survival in the face of a rapidly escalating civil war. Mainly shot on a handheld digital camera, *Return to Homs* was awarded the World Cinema Grand Jury Prize for documentary at the 2014 Sundance Film Festival. It is arguable, following media scholar Katarzyna Ruchel-Stockmans, that the film "demonstrates how . . . reality is an intrinsically staged event that also simultaneously stages itself. Reality and fiction merge, and become indistinguishable, forming a novel world, one that is always already mediated."[20] By contrast, the politics of *Homs Rain* is beholden to the regime ideology of antijihadism and the platitudinous standpoint of calling for tolerance, for everyone in the country to *just get along*—an ostensibly nonpolitical or antipolitical position. It is difficult to discern an ethical position for viewers to take other than gratitude and obligation toward the guardians of Syrian patriotism, namely the regime itself. In other words, the "staging" of reality and fiction in both documentary and narrative film is shot through with aesthetic ideology in ways that must be carefully disentangled. In a thoroughly different cinematic idiom than that articulated as "alternative cinema" in the era of Asadist-Ba'thist cultural revolution, *Homs Rain* revels in the aestheticization of war, ruination, and suffering, its aesthetics of power now cloaked in a melodramatic mood.[21] Melodrama, it turns out, is no longer an enemy of the state.

FIGURE 41. Joud Said, *Maṭar Ḥimṣ* (*Homs Rain*) (National Film Organization, 2017)

In defense of his characterization of Amiralay as too political in his early 1970s documentaries, culture minister Muhammad al-Ahmad attempted to distinguish between his personal opinion as a longtime film critic and his official opinion as a representative of the Syrian government. It is precisely the distinction between government spokesperson and critical intellectual—between the aesthetics of power and the aesthetics of solidarity or the aesthetics of resistance—that has been stubbornly difficult to see and fully police in Asadist-Baʿthist Syria. The famed *Struggle for Syria* that emerged in the mid-twentieth century, which served as shorthand for the regional and international geopolitics of the Middle East, placed Syria at the center of the most important power struggles of the era and continues to fascinate political scientists and historians. *Revolutions Aesthetic* establishes the importance of our historical reckoning with a related and comparable struggle around aesthetic ideology in Syria, one which shaped the production of literature and film as well as other kinds of art during the late-twentieth and early twenty-first centuries. This tension between an aesthetics of power—Asadist-Baʿthist cultural revolution—and the alternative—an aesthetics of solidarity and an aesthetics of resistance—continues to shape the cultural field in contemporary Syria. Further research might bear out this argument for other forms of cultural production beyond cinema and literature.

One year after the dustup over Amiralay's legacy, a coalition of disaffected writers and intellectuals founded the Syrian Writers' Association (Rābiṭat al-Kuttāb al-Sūriyyīn, SWA), an organization self-consciously established as an alternative to the state-managed Arab Writers' Union (Ittiḥād al-Kuttāb al-ʿArab, AWU). The members of this new association lambasted Husayn Jumʿa, then head of the AWU, for his unstinting support of the regime during the first year of its repressive and violent reprisals against protestors and oppositionists. In her analysis of the SWA and its publication, *Awrāq*, which was launched a year after the association's founding, Alexa Firat locates the significance of the group in its challenge to the legitimacy of the Syrian regime and the cultural institutions it supports.[22] Persistent taboos that had long constrained the Syrian literary imagination—most notably writing about the domestic armed conflict in Syria (1979–1982) and the destruction of Hama in 1982 that led to the death of at least 20,000 people—were shattered as the country was torn apart by civil strife and as many writers and intellectuals went into exile in the Arab world,

Europe, and elsewhere.[23] The emergence of a constellation of literary voices in Syria with the courage to confront controversial matters in literature was a reason to be optimistic about potential creative futures. "This discourse was not possible in the Syrian cultural field before 2011," Firat concludes, "because of the highly structured, censored, and oppressive architecture of the field of power."[24]

One of the most remarkable literary achievements in this regard is Fawwaz Haddad's monumental 2014 novel *al-Sūriyyūn al-Aʿdāʾ* (*Enemy Syrians*).[25] While there is not space here for its full consideration, I will briefly discuss *Enemy Syrians* and its reception in order to bring my discussion of the evolving agonistic struggle over aesthetic ideology in contemporary Syria to a close. Fawwaz Haddad was born in Damascus in 1947 and studied law at Damascus University before going to work in the private sector. Although he maintained a personal interest in fiction writing, for a long time he had no public profile and he did not publish his first novel until 1991. His early works were primarily historical novels, evoking exceptionally rich Damascene urban detail. More recently, a number of his works have been nominated for the International Prize for Arabic Fiction (IPAF), otherwise known as "the Arabic Booker." Whether historical or contemporary, Haddad's novels are exemplary instances of realist prose, and his command of sentence, style, and structure are among the defining qualities of his literary craft. Haddad's protagonists, almost entirely male, are swept up in unexpected plots of confusion, intrigue, and deception, often in relation to powerful local, national, or international institutions.[26]

Enemy Syrians is a wartime realist tragedy through which Haddad addresses the contemporary moment of Syrian catastrophe but also reconsiders the problems of truth, historical justice, and collective memory with respect to the events of the domestic armed conflict in Syria (1979–1982). The novel is split into two temporalities, with three distinct stories, or threads, running through both. The first is set in and around February 1982, during the siege and murderous destruction of Hama. In response to "terrorist" attacks on government installations, including more than one attempt on the life of Hafiz al-Asad, the Syrian regime sent in its army and security forces, including the defense companies led by al-Asad's brother Rifʿat, to "cleanse" the city of Muslim Brotherhood activists and their families. The city was razed to the ground, and some estimate that as many as 20,000 people may have been killed. As we have seen, Hama long constituted a "blind spot" in Syrian cultural and public memory.

In her enduringly relevant 2001 essay "The Silences of Contemporary Syrian Literature," Mohja Kahf argued that

> the ultimate silence of contemporary Syrian literature is its collective silence about the Hama massacre of 1982. . . . That a trauma of the magnitude of the Hama massacre is nowhere to be found in contemporary Syrian literature is stunning and, of course, impossible; Hama, being nowhere in Syrian literature, can be read in it everywhere.[27]

A great deal has changed over the past twenty years, and a number of Syrian novelists have now begun to reckon seriously with the pulverization of Hama and other cities in 1982.[28] Images of urban devastation on display in *Homs Rain* must cruelly remind some viewers of a besieged Hama from thirty years before. It is a painful irony that "a trauma of the magnitude of the Hama massacre" only resurfaced in everyday talk and cultural production, though, alongside the dizzying scale of violence and destruction in the time of the ongoing Syria War. It also helps to explain Haddad's decision to juxtapose those two moments in his novel.

Enemy Syrians opens with the unexpected arrival of an infant on the Damascus doorstep of a judge at the Court of Cassation (*Maḥkamat al-Naqḍ*), Salim al-Raji. The child—Hazim—turns out to be the orphaned son of Salim's brother ʿAdnan, a doctor who disappeared and whose family—his father, wife, and other children—were murdered in broad daylight in their Hama neighborhood in 1982. Salim and his colleagues believe in the possibility of transitional justice in Asadist-Baʿthist Syria, convinced that reform may transform the nature of political rule and state-society relations. Such an investigation requires clear-eyed analysis of what actually took place—a difficult prospect with such strong restrictions on speech around certain sensitive matters. In a wide-ranging discussion of the challenges confronting any institutional consideration during the time of "the events" in 1982, when legal observers and others were struggling to collect information and testimonies about what was taking place in Hama, Salim's friend, mentor, and law professor Rushdi denies the technique of accounting.

> The issue isn't who made more mistakes. . . . Unfortunately, the country's national army behaved like barbarian invaders. . . . I wouldn't only say there was

a total absence of law, but very little mercy as well. But let's hold off on talking about assigning responsibility until we have more information.[29]

The country and the international community ultimately held off "assigning responsibility" or pursuing justice indefinitely.

The second thread in the novel is the story of the army captain Sulayman, who is also known as "the Engineer," ironically, it turns out, owing to the fact that he was a failed engineering student and also because he went on to become close to the president, tasked with engineering commemorations of regime forces who cleansed the city of Hama, in a ceremony meant to rival and outshine any commemoration of the dead and disappeared organized by victims and their families. The third main thread of the novel concerns the disappeared ʿAdnan, Salim's brother, who had been spared summary execution by a sympathetic officer but nonetheless wound up with thousands of other political prisoners in Tadmor (Palmyra) Prison. The middle section of the novel follows ʿAdnan's unraveling in Tadmor, where he languishes for thirty years and where he is tortured, loses his mind, and helplessly watches as his identity is shattered into fragments. The narrative alternates between the first-person voice of Salim al-Raji in some chapters and third-person omniscient with free indirect discourse in others. Part 1 is entitled "The Land of Eternity and Death" (*Bilād al-Khulūd wa-l-Mawt*), which is a play on the concept of eternity (*khulūd* and *abad*) that has been bound up with regime discourse in Asadist Syria, with Hafiz al-Asad referred to in some venues as "The Leader for all Eternity" (*al-qāʾid ilā al-abad*). This part returns directly to the individual stories and broader political context of the domestic armed conflict in Syria (1979–1982) and the atrocities committed in Hama in February 1982. Part 2 of the novel, "A New World" (*ʿĀlam Jadīd*), is much shorter, set in the spring of 2011. The story lines converge in this part, thirty years after the massacres at Hama, amid the emerging revolutionary uprising. ʿAdnan, who miraculously has survived his time in prison, where the same Defense Brigades responsible for razing Hama have also slaughtered hundreds and possibly thousands of prisoners, returns to Damascus, like a man "walking out of the grave." ʿAdnan is shocked to learn from his brother Salim that his son Hazim has survived. ʿAdnan communicates how damaged he has been by his time in prison, how he has become a different person, two people, even three, attempting to rationally explain how he can see clearly those others who have become part of his self-conception. As ʿAdnan and Hazim try to relate to one another upon being reunited after all these years, they walk silently around the streets of Damascus, gazing in wonder and terror at ubiquitous posters of Bashar al-Asad, which have replaced the once familiar images of al-Asad père that ʿAdnan knew all too well. In this regard, father and son seem to mirror and be mirrored by *the* father and *the* son of the ruling family and the nation.

In addition to sorting through specific family histories between the horrific events of 1982 and the unsettling uncertainty of 2011, the novel shifts in order to engage with questions of forgiveness and reconciliation, memory, and justice. Salim—a sincere, stalwart reformist exemplifying the period of Bashar al-Asad's first decade of reformism from above—explains to ʿAdnan how the 1980s "was a black period in the history of the country and that many things have changed." ʿAdnan retorts, "Nothing at all [has] changed," asking, "who could give back life to the dead who were unjustly murdered or compensate those who rotted in prison and suffered irreparable damage"?[30] Sulayman the Engineer, for his part, is well aware that ʿAdnan has been freed and wishes to see him. Salim naively persists in thinking that Sulayman and ʿAdnan might be able to meet one another on civil terms, to find a way to recognize each other's common humanity. The Engineer is unrepentant, though, and ʿAdnan—hearing of an encounter that Salim had with the Engineer previously—spends the next two days in total silence before packing a bag and disappearing. One night the Engineer comes home to find ʿAdnan waiting for him in his living room, brandishing a gun in his face. With a little help from his friends from Hama, ʿAdnan had broken into Sulayman's posh villa, a material perk for those who strictly adhere to regime loyalty for long periods of time. ʿAdnan engages in imaginative fantasy, a kind of revenge therapy, visualizing different ways he can murder Sulayman right then: one bullet at a time, tying him up and leaving him to rot, or cutting off one limb after another. Sensing the danger, Sulayman breaks down and begs for forgiveness, pleading that he was only following orders back then. "Justice is not vengeance or revenge," ʿAdnan proposes, aiming his criticism at both the regime and the president as well as his regnant successor under whom he has long suffered. Rather,

> it is the destruction of this unjust state . . . which must be obliterated. That would be justice, for the torture that afflicted hundreds of thousands of people, for a country that has been drowned under the flow [*dabīb*] of death and fear.[31]

In one of the final meditations on the part of Sulayman the Engineer, avatar of the Syrian "deep state," it might be said, he bemoans that nobody has any pity for the country, that everything is going to be destroyed. Sulayman is double-crossed in the end, receiving the same fate as anyone who dares to show the slightest disloyalty toward the regime. He sees clearly what lies ahead, not just for him but for the entire country: "thousands of dead and wounded and disappeared and suffering masses. Don't worry, though, this is the country of eternity and death, glory and fear." But Sulayman himself had neither "suffered from fear" nor "reveled in glory. Eternity [is] for someone else. Death [is] for him."[32] Sulayman, and other representatives of the regime brought into these conversations toward the end of the novel, play with this conceptual opposition between the eternity of the ruling clique—the al-Asads and their closest allies—and the death that awaits everyone else, whether regime supporters or members of the opposition.

In this moving work of literary fiction Haddad addresses some of the most challenging and painful aspects of contemporary Syrian history. Salma Salim says that *Enemy Syrians* functions as a trial (*muḥākama*) of an entire era. The novel deserves attention and close reading, Salim continues, beyond the headlines and hot takes. "It is a novel about dictatorship in the stage of society's slow destruction, its transformation into fragments, and the transformations of the soul of humanity in the crucible of eternal despotism [*bawtaqat al-tasalluṭiyya al-mu'abbada*]."[33] Not all readers of *Enemy Syrians* have been so sanguine. Haddad's regular presence on the list of nominees for the Arabic Booker has led some critics to belittle his literary achievements as political brownie points. Writing in the Beirut daily newspaper *al-Akhbār*, Yazan al-Haj argues that it is not possible to "separate the change in Fawwaz Haddad's novelistic style from his fame after the shortlist of the 2009 Booker Prize." Whereas Haddad was once "a calm writer, far removed from the cliquishness [*shalaliyya*] of the Syrian cultural scene," his newfound shot at celebrity has led him astray. In language that is strikingly reminiscent of Muhammad al-Ahmad's lambasting of Omar Amiralay, al-Haj accuses Haddad of writing in such a way that blurs the line between political activist and artist: "In most of the novel's pages, the reader can barely determine whether he is reading a political book or a work of art." The lurid and ideological dimensions of *Enemy Syrians*, he claims, do not even raise the novel to the level of "yellow journalism." Al-Haj's primary criticism of the book, it seems, derives from its offensive collapse of art into politics, a politics steeped in stereotypes—especially sectarian ones—that uncritically mimic the discourse of Syrian revolutionaries.

> Society is divided into two parts: one part that is an ʿAlawī or ʿAlawi-tized [*mutaʿalwan*] military; the other part civilian, brutalized, Sunni, of course. We do not find any other shades throughout this hellish labyrinth in which the writer places us.

Whereas al-Haj praises Haddad for his earlier historical fiction that dealt with the period of French Mandate rule or the mid-twentieth-century heyday of Arab nationalism, he chastises him for playing sectarian politics in *Enemy Syrians* by reconstructing the violence of the early 1980s and having the temerity to tie it directly to the ongoing crisis. "Art had a presence" in Haddad's earlier work. "But now politics has swallowed up meaning and presence and everything has dried up."[34] Al-Haj sensibly notes that there is something inherently political about approaching one of the black holes of Syrian cultural memory. There is something more complicated albeit no less political about Haddad's going a step further in attempting to connect the ethics of historical reconstruction with respect to the massacres at Hama in 1982 and the surrounding domestic armed conflict in Syria (1979–1982) to the ongoing struggle for life, liberty, and dignity in contemporary Syria.

No doubt, the thorny and even explosive issues of sectarianism in Syrian society and history must be considered in any reassessment of the events of 1982. The nature of the conflict between the regime—dominated but not monopolized at the highest ranks of the government, security apparatus, and army by ʿAlawī individuals, especially those related or close to the al-Asad family—and its heavily although by no means exclusively Islamist opposition cannot be understood without attending to the problem of sectarianism.[35] In one of the most inflammatory moments of *Enemy Syrians*—one that no doubt enraged many readers and critics—an intellectual supportive of the regime named ʿArif gets into a conversation with Sulayman the Engineer about what will happen if the protests become stronger and more widespread. His prediction is based on the presumed ʿAlawī sectarian character of the regime itself and the regime's inextricability with the president.

> The president won't be able to overthrow the regime. The president and the regime are one and the same thing that cannot be taken apart. . . . If one of them falls then so does the other. The [ʿAlawī] sect can't do anything . . . its hands are tied [*murghama*]. It will stand with the president, not by choice. The young men of the sect are in the army, the *mukhābarāt*, and the *shabbīḥa*.[36]

Here ʿArif appears to be providing a diagnostic opinion, but he also offers his personal interpretation:

> I don't want for this regime to change. I can't imagine any other. Do you know why? Because I'm sectarian. I'll admit that. I used to think I was immune to those feelings, but the issue is more important than feelings. I won't ever accept us not being in power. This is our state . . . we seized power, what justification is there for us to give it up to anyone else.[37]

The venerable literary critic and novelist Nabil Sulayman concurs with much of the criticism of *Enemy Syrians*, and not only on ideological grounds. Initially taking potshots at internal inconsistencies of characterization and even grammatical mistakes, Sulayman ultimately returns to the same fundamental disapproval of the novel on the grounds that it trucks in dangerous sectarian stereotypes, specifically about the ʿAlawī character of the regime and the portrayal of ʿAlawīs generally as backward, uncouth, and servile. He equates *Enemy Syrians* with "a political report" and "a military report" that lead Haddad to "bid farewell to the novelistic art altogether." However convincing one finds his criticism of the novel, Sulayman leaves us with one of the questions that has governed the agonistic struggle around aesthetic ideology in Syria since the 1970s: "Isn't this novel definitive proof of the tyranny of the political over art?"[38]

Throughout *Revolutions Aesthetic*, I have argued that the struggle around aesthetic ideology in the time of Asadist-Baʿthist cultural revolution from 1970 to the present has resulted in an uneven and incomplete attempt by the state to structure, censor, and dominate the literary and cinematic fields. As we saw in the political thought of Tayyib Tizini and other intellectuals supportive of this project of cultural revolution, for example, "art for art's sake" could not be endorsed because the pursuit of revolutionary culture would be part and parcel of the new regime's aesthetic orientation. Film critic Muhammad Shahin and others lambasted melodrama (especially in the Egyptian studio system) as reactionary and risible. In the 2010s, by contrast, one finds the significance of art and politics to be scrambled in sometimes surprising ways. Omar Amiralay was a political filmmaker and not an artistic one because he directly tackled the contradictions and even failures of Baʿthist modernization projects in the Syrian countryside during the 1970s. Meanwhile, Joud Said is celebrated as a cinematic wunderkind for working hand in glove with the Syrian armed forces in order to produce a romantic melodrama of "wartime Syria" against the backdrop of the devastated old city of Homs and in the shadow of displaced communities. Conversely, Fawwaz Haddad, a writer who only occasionally aligns himself with the Syrian revolution (or the regime for that matter), is maligned as a "political" writer and insufficiently literary not only because he has decided to write about the Syrian uprising as it unfolds but because he dares to comment on the relationship between current affairs and the history of violence in Baʿthist Syria.

One of the more striking aspects of the founding of the SWA itself in 2012 is that it was announced from Abu Dhabi. It might be argued that in the time of the Syria War, the scale of the struggle over aesthetic ideology has irrevocably transcended the confines of the national space and the nationalist imaginary, in part because of the dislocation of an overwhelming number of Syrian citizens into exile. With the arrival of hundreds of thousands of Syrian refugees in Europe—Germany in particular—the parameters and the stakes of the struggle over aesthetic ideology in Syria and in Syrian culture have become more complex. More impactful is the role that the Gulf States have increasingly played in shaping Syrian cultural production during the 2000s and 2010s, whether in funding and producing television serials, sponsoring film production, or drawing attention to Syrian and other Arab writers through the creation of a generously endowed suite of literary prizes. These developments should not obscure the fact that Syrian cultural politics were never entirely isolated from global trends during the pre-2011 or pre-2000 periods. Anthropologist and music critic Jonathan Shannon correctly points out that in the mid-2000s "Syrian artists *as well as* state agents [drew] on globally circulating ideologies of authenticity in order to promote—in contradictory ways—a modern Syrian national culture."[39] Throughout the twentieth and early twenty-first centuries, Syrian cultural production was fundamentally shaped and reshaped by regional as well as international trends, but it was not truly globalized, tragically, until the time of the Syria War. A macabre interest on the part of major publishing houses in New York and London in Syrian writing during the time of the Syria War has contributed to an unprecedented (yet still regrettably modest) boom in translation (into English) of works from Syria.[40]

Revolutions Aesthetic points up the need to understand the relationship between aesthetic ideology and cultural production in Baʿthist Syria historically. Certain aspects of that dynamic—the agonistic dialectic between an aesthetics of power and its others, primarily—have been characterized by continuity. In other ways, this politico-aesthetic formation could be said to have evolved substantially over the past fifty years, as "political art" escaped the guarded purview of the Asadist-Baʿthist cultural revolution only to become an aspersion cast on writers, filmmakers, and other artists who do not toe the line of regime diktat, now reduced to being merely political. Social realism, political commitment, and other aesthetic forms common to mid-twentieth-century cultural production (Chapters 2 and 3) were challenged in important ways by new kinds of literature, film, and intellectual debate during the 1990s and early 2000s. Artistic experimentation during the late twentieth and early twenty-first centuries contributed to the opening of new spaces for difference and disagreement in the Syrian cultural field (Chapter 4). Bashar al-Asad's first decade in power, a period of reformism from above, initially appeared to be a potential moment of transition. Literary, cinematic, and artistic experimentation expanded in some instances even as certain aspects of Asadist-Baʿthist aesthetic ideology were reinscribed in cultural production. Challenges to the state monopoly over culture exemplified by the rise of television and film privately funded in many cases by Gulf capital were accompanied by renewed attempts by Syrian state cultural institutions to sponsor and promote the regime's own aesthetic ideology. Films by a new generation of filmmakers produced by the NFO—such as Joud Said (as we have seen) and Basil al-Khatib—were more technologically enhanced and enjoyed a wider audience than those by earlier generations of Syrian filmmakers, partly through the flows of regional and global circuits that structure cinematic production, circulation, and reception. In the literary sphere, the "commitment" and avant-gardism of Asadist-Baʿthist cultural revolution softened in response to clamoring demands from intellectuals, artists, and ordinary people for greater rights and representation in this period of uncertainty following the death of Hafiz al-Asad. Liberal platitudes about tolerance, deliberation, and caution seemed to replace vociferous calls for literary experimentation or for steadfast adherence to aesthetic norms of nationalism and anti-imperialism.

In the editorial opening the July 2001 issue of *al-Mawqif al-Adabī*, at the peak of the "Damascus Spring," editor-in-chief Walid Mushawwah insisted that "the Arab nation" still needed "the struggling, revolutionary, and leaderly [*al-qā'id*] intellectual," one who would be "steadfast in the face of ongoing nationalist breakdowns." Here, the language of Asadist-Ba'thist cultural revolution survived in its more or less prototypical form. Mushawwah pivoted to argue that intellectuals need not be so concerned with opposing "political power" as achieving "the acceptance of the other," respecting the other's "right to disagreement without that being grounds to accuse him, or to judge him for treason, disloyalty, and collusion."[41] It was truly a fantastic work of aesthetic-ideological refashioning for this state-administered cultural publication: not only to no longer champion long-standing keywords of Asadist-Ba'thist cultural revolution—struggle, resistance, commitment, conscience—but instead to articulate a full-throated defense of (neo)liberalism, to attempt to replace the language of agonistic struggle with the bland tones of tolerance, sympathy, and civility. The fracturing of Syrian cultural politics and aesthetic ideology during the post-2011 period can be understood in terms of the tension between what I have called Ba'thist cultural revolution under Hafiz al-Asad—the state's attempt to monopolize the discourse of revolution itself—and the contentious reclamatory politics of revolutionary cultural production during the Syrian uprising and after (Chapters 5 and 6). Although I sympathize with Salwa Ismail's attempt to name an "aesthetics of Revolution" that is expressive of "the edifying force of the initial quest for affirming one's humanity and aspiration to live a life worth living," the aesthetics of cultural production in the time of the revolution and the Syria War needs to be understood historically, which requires attention to the articulation and the fate of other kinds of "revolutionary" aesthetics or, at least, recognition that the lexicon of "revolution" has been heavily contested in contemporary Syria.[42]

Some might insist that Ba'thism—as an ideological system, a political party, a motive force in the shaping of Syrian life—has been moribund for some time, extinct even, and that the sweeping claims about cultural revolution made in this book are therefore overblown. It would not be unreasonable to argue that what remains of Baʿthism in Syria, whether in the world of ideas or in the material world of institutions and everyday life, has been whittled down to a skeleton, the bones of a creature that may have always been more myth than flesh anyhow. But contrary to the expectations of military and political "experts" such as Amos Perlmutter, who argued in 1969 that "The burden of Baʿth ideology is too heavy for a country as poor and divided as Syria," the Asadist-Baʿthist cultural revolution has played a key role in structuring the conditions of possibility for creative expression in Syria for more than fifty years. It is identifiable through attempts by the state and nonstate actors to promote an aesthetics of power committed to specific visions of heroism, masculinity, virtuous leadership, pan-Arab unity, state sovereignty, cultural patriotism, and political commitment that accord with the doxa of Asadist-Baʿthist rule, with political Asadism. This is meant neither as a normative statement that approves of the cultural politics of the Syrian regime and its institutional representatives nor as a call for axiomatic support of the revolutionary cultural activities of those committed to reforming the system or bringing it down. The more modest ambition of this book has been to historicize a different struggle for Syria that has been right under the nose of historians, literature scholars, film critics, and students of politics: a struggle over the very conditions of possibility for cultural production and aesthetic experience, a set of battles that has ebbed and flowed in relation to evolving political and social conditions yet has remained stubbornly focused on the ideological parameters within which creative expression and meaning making can be articulated. Cultural forms in addition to the novel and feature film—short stories, documentaries, visual arts, poetry, drama, and so forth—would make worthy objects of further critical-historical analysis, which might bolster or complicate the arguments made throughout this book. Such scholarship could also augment or at least throw new light on the dominant scholarly fields of political, military, and social history.

As the Syria War approaches some kind of a denouement or status quo post bellum, what rises from the ashes may certainly wind up being a retrenchment of neoliberal autocracy or perhaps an even fiercer, more emboldened form of authoritarian rule in the wake of what will surely be spun by the regime as a victory. Whereas earlier struggles over aesthetic ideology in Syria focused on matters of national and regional significance, the present struggle for Syria has taken on international and even planetary significance. Scholars and political analysts identified Syria as an arena for Cold War conflict during the mid-twentieth century. The now decade-long Syria War has also been marked in blood by geopolitics: Russian, US, and European intervention has intersected with regional struggles for hegemony that pit a strategic axis including Israel, Saudi Arabia, and most of the Gulf States against Iran, Hizballah, and the Syrian government and its allies. Even if and when a just and stable peace is achieved through diplomatic negotiation, Syria will still have to face complex political and security considerations as the country embarks on the arduous process of reconstruction and, one hopes, the return, no matter how difficult, of whatever proportion of its displaced and refugee populations wishes to go home. But the end of the Syrian nightmare can also be viewed more hopefully: to welcome the dawn of new imaginative horizons that might eventually rescue the country from the limited perspective of the nation while also celebrating the accomplishments of the country's multisectarian nationhood; to free it from the dogmatism of ideology and leader worship while honoring the traditions of thought and political engagement that also defined the country; to pull it out of relative isolation but also protect and preserve its identity, dignity, rights and sovereignty; and, finally, just possibly, to point toward a future in which aesthetics in the Syrian context can return to some of that term's most basic and appealing meanings: the cognitive and sensuous appreciation of beauty in the world, a great deal of which can be found in Syria and will no doubt be enjoyed there once again by Syrians and non-Syrians alike.

Acknowledgments

This book has taken me a long time to finish, for reasons that are both personal and circumstantial. The last time I was able to visit Syria was in summer 2011. I had managed to secure a tourist visa that spring, even as the uprising was beginning to take shape. News of what was going on inside the country was sketchy, at best, even from the perspective of neighboring Lebanon, where I was spending most of that summer, surrounded by anxious gossip about what was happening just on the other side of the mountains. Some friends advised me not to make the trip; others encouraged me not to let that visa go unused: one day I decided to take a shared taxi from Beirut's Charles Helou Terminal. While I did not venture outside of Damascus during my visit, I witnessed chilling harbingers of the chaos, violence, and destruction yet to come, even if I had no idea about that at the time. It turned out I was the only person sleeping in the dormitory at the French Institute (L'Institut Français du Proche-Orient, IFPO) in Abou Rummaneh, which would have been an unusual enough experience without the eerie mood then pervading the city, which was noticeably on edge. It was very late one night when, from the rooftop of the IFPO, I heard the slogan "The People Want the Fall of the Regime! (al-Shaʿb Yurīd Isqāṭ al-Niẓām!)" for the first time. Another evening, as I was strolling through the old city, I heard the chants again and saw with my own eyes a small "flying demonstration" (*muẓāhara ṭayyāra*), or flash mob, which I must admit was a real thrill. I visited friends in Barzeh, Jaramana, the Palestinian refugee camp of Yarmouk, and elsewhere. In Yarmouk I attended a party where I encountered a young activist from Homs who had fled the city and told a rapt group harrowing stories about the organizing that was happening there and the unimaginable repression being unleashed on protestors. This was my first direct encounter with personal testimony about the Syrian uprising and the looming Syria War. One other detail about the party I remember is the films being projected on the walls of the apartment, one of which was the animated short *Fallen Art* (2004) by the Polish artist Tomasz Bagiński, a haunting satire of aestheticized violence under authoritarian military circumstances. Every time I watch it, I get chills.

On another day, which happened to be a Friday, while cruising the outskirts of the city in a French academic friend's car, the two of us were stopped at a Syrian army checkpoint. My friend told the soldiers we were French and American, respectively, but pretended not to speak Arabic (even though both of us do) and claimed—sagely, I would add—that we had left our passports at home in order to avoid any bureaucratic entanglements. The officer waved us past, barking that we should go straight home. Making our meandering way back toward central Damascus, we passed through Douma. I saw lime-green buses parked up and down streets that were packed with listless soldiers sweltering in the heat, waiting for orders to crack down on the imminent demonstrations. Now this all seems like an ominous harbinger of the deadly forces that would conspire against the Syrian revolution. The seedlings of resistance that were breaking through during those early days would crash into political, ideological, and military obstacles that quashed most revolutionary aspirations in a bloodbath of historic proportions.

My scattered memories cast a grim shadow as I make the final revisions to this cultural and intellectual history of Syrian literature and film. I am mindful of the relative ease with which I was able to move into, around, and out of Syria as it teetered on the edge of an abyss. I had always been an outsider interested in Syrian history and culture: over the past decade, I have been a non-Syrian writing about Syria, but now I was no longer able to visit or spend time in the country. In a sense, literature and film—Syrian cultural production of different kinds—became lifelines to Syria throughout those tumultuous years. Whatever minor estrangement from the country I may have experienced during this time, though, pales in comparison with the suffering and struggles of the Syrian people, both inside and outside of Syria, in a time of revolution, war, and displacement.

Back in 2006, I attended "The Road to Damascus: Discovering Syrian Cinema" at the Pacific Film Archive in Berkeley, California. This touring edition of an ArteEast exhibition was an unusual opportunity for those living on the West Coast to learn about and celebrate Syrian cinema; it was also my first encounter with Ossama Mohammed's stunning film *Sacrifices* (*Ṣundūq al-Dunyā*, 2002). The atmosphere throughout the festival was electric. I can still remember walking out of the theater in a daze after viewing *Sacrifices* and a number of other films, with an inchoate appreciation of these powerful works of art that said something profound and essential in a language of cinema I could not fully comprehend. In the years that followed—before pirated films circulated freely around the internet—I struggled to track down hard copies of the films I saw there and others I learned about then. Since that time, I have done my best to educate myself in the history, sensibilities, and cultural effects of Syrian cinema and other artforms. Having the opportunity to get to know Ossama Mohammed and Noma Omran, in particular, has been one of the highlights of my journey of personal education and professional research.

My connection to Syria and the Arabic-speaking world has been profoundly enhanced by my relationships with novelists and novels. In fact, I first arrived at this project through reading literature and translating Arabic novels and nonfiction into English. Thus, I would like to express my deep respect for Syrian writers and their craft. My interactions with them have opened my eyes, my mind, and my heart, exposing me to contrasting interpretations of Syrian history, diverse views on contemporary politics and culture, and creatively imaginative visions for the future. Heartfelt thanks go out especially to Nihad Sirees, Rosa Yaseen Hasan, Samar Yazbek, Khaled Khalifa, Faysal Khartash, Mamdouh Azzam and Itab Azzam, and Fawwaz Haddad. I would also like to thank other Syrian friends anonymously for their kindness and hospitality during the times I was able to spend in the country prior to 2011. I look forward to the day when it becomes possible once again to appreciate the splendiferous beauty of Syria up close.

My field research on modern Syrian history began back in the early 2000s. Visits to the country prior to 2011 and the auxiliary research that followed were made possible by generous financial and logistical support from institutions that I acknowledge here: the Harvard Society of Fellows, the William F. Milton

Fund at Harvard University, the Princeton Institute for International and Regional Studies (PIIRS), the Princeton University Committee on Research in the Humanities and Social Sciences (UCRHSS), the Princeton Departments of History and Near Eastern Studies, the Elias Boudinot Bicentennial Preceptorship, the Carnegie Corporation's Andrew Carnegie Scholars Program, and the Europe in the Middle East/Middle East in Europe program at the Forum Transregionalen Studien, especially its director, Professor Georges Khalil, and the indefatigable staff at the Staatsbibliothek in Berlin as well as the Widener and Firestone libraries.

I have had numerous opportunities to present my work during the time of this research, and I am grateful to the organizers and administrators who made seminars and lectures possible at the following venues: University of California, Los Angeles, University of Chicago, University of California, Berkeley, Stanford University, George Washington University, Bard College, the Graduate Center at the City University of New York, Yale University, Barnard College, Harvard University, the American University of Beirut, Lund University, the Institut d'études de l'Islam et des Sociétés du Monde Musulman (IISMM) at the École des Hautes Études en Sciences Sociales (EHESS), the Université du Québec à Montréal (UQAM), the Robert Schuman Centre for Advanced Studies at the European University Institute, Florence, the Program in Translation and Intercultural Communication at Princeton University, and, finally, annual meetings of the Middle East Studies Association and the American Comparative Literature Association

I am honored to now be officially part of the Stanford University Press family. It is universally agreed that publishing a book with Kate Wahl is a rare gift—now I know that to be true from firsthand experience: her professionalism, enthusiasm, and brilliance shone through all of my interactions with her. I also look forward to future conferences where I will not have to approach her sheepishly in order to update her as to how *the book* is (not) coming along. Thanks to Caroline McKusick for her no-nonsense yet cheerful editorial assistance. Dianne Wood was a fantastic and professional copyeditor. Charlie Clark and Gigi Mark smoothly guided me through the final stages of editing and indexing. Ruanne Abou-Rahme and Basel Abbas kindly offered artistic advice and technological guidance in order to improve the quality of those images that appear throughout this book. I also acknowledge the relevant publishers for permission to republish sections of the following: "Who Laughs Last: Literary

Transformations of Syrian Authoritarianism," in *Middle East Authoritarianisms: Governance, Contestation, and Regime Resilience in Syria and Iran*, eds. Steven Heydemann and Reinoud Leenders (Stanford, CA: Stanford University Press, 2013), 143–65; and "Sight, Sound, and Surveillance in Baʿthist Syria: The Fiction of Politics in Rūzā Yasīn Ḥasan's *Rough Draft* and Samar Yazbik's *In Her Mirrors*," *Journal of Arabic Literature* Vol. 48, No. 2 (BRILL, 2017): 211–44.

My dear friend Jon Levy cooked up the idea of inviting me to the University of Chicago for a book manuscript workshop in Fall 2019, which lit a fire underneath me to complete a draft of the book in advance of the spirited day and a half that was dedicated to thinking through the stakes and the argument of this project. The day before the workshop, I had the opportunity to give a public lecture on materials that are now part of Chapter 3. Ghenwa Hayek, Orit Bashkin, Lisa Wedeen, and Jon Levy all took this event extremely seriously, and I hope that evidence of their insightful suggestions appear all over this book. I remain flattered and touched by their brilliance and generosity, but of course any errors or infelicities are entirely due to my own shortcomings. My most sincere thanks to colleagues and friends who have offered moral support and intellectual guidance over the years: Joshua Guild, Elliot Colla, Ted Swedenburg, Emily Drumsta, Levi Thompson, Robyn Creswell, Saphe Shamoun, Charif Kiwan, Amir Moosavi, Aaron Jakes, Hal Foster, Eduardo Cadava, Fadi Bardawil, Margaret Litvin, Daniel Sheffield, Alexa Firat, Zaki Haidar, Beth Baron, Shareah Taleghani, Kevin Martin, Marina Rustow, Rob Karl, Dan-El Padilla Peralta, M'hamed Oualdi, Augustin Jomier, Bruno Carvalho, Sabrina Mervin, Randi Deguilhem, François Burgat, Catherine Mayeur-Jaouen, Rania Samara, Alex Zucker, Thaer Deeb, Janina Santer, Samer Frangieh, Mohammed Dagman, Anne-Marie McManus, Jon Levy, Chiara Cordelli, Stephen Kotkin, Nasser Abourahme, Toby Jones, Nancy Reynolds, Jennifer Derr, Shira Robinson, Michelle Campos, Kristen Alff, Basma Fahoum, Vladimir Hamed-Troyansky, Marwan Hanania, Brandon Wolfe-Hunnicutt, Joshua Landis, Seda Altuğ, Marilyn Booth, Moishe Postone, Fred Donner, Stefan Winter, Jens Hanssen, Joseph Ben Prestel, Rasha Salti, Tarek El-Ariss, Elizabeth Holt, Jason Frydman, Erol Ülker, Joel Beinin, Beshara Doumani, David Bellos, and Zia Mian. I would like to single out Karen Emmerich—friend, colleague, neighbor!—for knocking some sense into me in the latter days of revising. And a shoutout to the students in undergraduate and graduate seminars who helped me work through ideas: Murat Bozluolcay, Julian Weideman, Simon Conrad, Amina Elgamal, Chaya Holch, Dina Kuttab,

Zev Mishell, Samuel Prentice, Meghan Slattery, Daniel Yassky, Shazia Babul, Christian Bischoff, Carlos Giron, Joshua Judd Porter, Emma Pannullo, Seyitcan Ucin, Christopher Walton, Isaac Wolfe, Michael Battalia, Chen Gong, Janna Aladdin, Nina Youkhanna, Tim Louthan, Katy Montoya, Elizabeth Tsurkov, Ömer Topal, Spenser Rapone, and Cevat Dargin. I am particularly grateful to Janna and Michael for helping me prepare the index.

A world without music is not one in which I would be able to live, certainly not one where I would be able to complete a book. Bands and musicians I celebrate to along with this book: Bad Religion, The Barr Brothers, Baptists, Built to Spill, Converge, Dave Holland, David August, Every Time I Die, Full Cookie, Honey Dijon, Joe Claussell, Julian Lage, Lagwagon, Motor City Drum Ensemble, Phish, Propagandhi, Robert Schumann, The Slip, Stanton Moore, Trap Them. Special thanks to James "The Force" Forcinito, Tom "The Hotline" Monaghan, and the Sandwich King.

I finished the book manuscript in New Mexico toward the end of our first summer of coronavirus pandemic. I will be eternally grateful to Victoria Sojourn-Prince for putting up with me and welcoming me into her home.

Without the love, support, and encouragement of my friends and family I might not have made it to this point. These people have saved my life more than once. Words on a page in a book they will likely never read cannot fully plumb the depths of my love, respect, and gratitude. Benjamin, Gaën, Natasha, Irène, Keith, Stéphanie, Zoé, Émilie, Dave, Mila, Dr. Rosen, Marcy, Bill, Nasser, Spencer, Bike Josh, Jon, Chris, Martina, Landon, Sawyer, Kirk, MJ, August, Isi, Kev, Josh, Benjamin, Amara, Shirley, Brendan, Hilary, Adeline, Wesley, Emilia, Beth, Katy, Mike, Tom, Ollie, Sarah, Alex, Marcia, John Kerry, Elliot, John, Allen, Wendy, Micayla, Harrison, Victoria, Alexander, David, and Diane.

This book is dedicated to my parents, Allan and Geri Weiss, who selflessly laid down nonmaterial foundations of love and support that have given me the resilience and self-confidence to chase after my goals, headlong and unencumbered.

Notes

INTRODUCTION

1. Regional Congress of the Arab Baath Socialist Party, *Program of the March 8th Revolution* (Damascus: Ministry of Information, 1965), 140.

2. Reinhart Koselleck, "Historical Criteria of the Modern Concept of Revolution," in *Futures Past: On the Semantics of Historical Time*, trans. Keith Tribe (Cambridge, MA: MIT Press, 1985), 39–54, at 40.

3. Muhammad al-Maghut, "After Long Thinking," in *The Fan of Swords: Poems*, trans. May Jayyusi and Naomi Shihab Nye (Washington, DC: Three Continents Press, 1991), 41–42, at 41.

4. Sven Lütticken, "Cultural Revolution," *New Left Review* 87 (May/June 2014): 115–31, at 115.

5. Salaheddin Bitar [Salah al-Din al-Bitar], "The Rise and Decline of the Baath," *Middle East International* (June 1971): 12–15, at 13.

6. To be clear, this transition needs to be more carefully examined; I am *not* arguing, however, that the pre-1963 Baʿth Party was dominated or determined by Michel ʿAflaq or ʿAflaqist thinking. Instead, I wish to draw attention to the fact that splinter factions of the Baʿth Party in Syria have had political *as well as* ideological/intellectual dimensions. I thank Saphe Shamoun for encouraging me to clarify this point. On ʿAflaqism in modern intellectual history, see my "Genealogies of Baʿthism: Michel ʿAflaq Between Personalism and Arabic Nationalism," *Modern Intellectual History*

Vol. 16, No. 2 (December 2020): 1193–1224. The term "Asadism" (*al-asadiyya*) has long been used colloquially to refer to the system of rule in Syria. Scholarly evaluations of the term are less common. See, though, Najib Ghadbian, *al-Dawla al-Asadiyya al-Thāniyya: Bashshār al-Asad wa-l-Furaṣ al-Ḍā'i'a* ([S.l.]: Najīb al-Ghaḍbiān, 2006); Burhan Ghalioun, "'Al-Asadiyya' fī al-Siyāsa al-Sūriyya, aw, Dawr al-Siyāsa al-Iqlīmiyya fī Taḥqīq al-Sayṭara al-Dākhiliyya," in *Ma'rakat al-Iṣlāḥ fī Sūriyā*, ed. Radwan Ziadeh (Cairo: Markaz al-Qāhira li-Dirāsāt Huqūq al-Insān, 2006), 15–45; Rustum Mahmud, "Al-Asadiyya," *al-Jumhuriyya*, March 29, 2016. http://aljumhuriya.net/34745.

7. Koselleck, "Historical Criteria of the Modern Concept of Revolution." Among this vast literature, see, for example: Jack A. Goldstone, "Toward a Fourth Generation of Revolutionary Theory," *Annual Review of Political Science* Vol. 4 (2001): 139–87; Theda Skocpol, "Explaining Social Revolutions: Alternatives to Existing Theories," in *States and Social Revolutions: A Comparative Analysis of France, Russia and China* (Cambridge: Cambridge University Press, 1979), 3–43; 'Azmi Bishara, *Fī al-Thawra wa-l-Qābiliyya li-l-Thawra* (Doha: Arab Center for Research & Policy Studies, 2012); Fadi Bardawil, *Revolution and Disenchantment: Arab Marxism and the Binds of Emancipation* (Durham, NC: Duke University Press, 2020); Mona El-Ghobashy, "Reviving Revolution," *The Immanent Frame: Secularism, Religion, and the Public Sphere* (July 6, 2021). https://tif.ssrc.org/2021/07/06/reviving-revolution/

8. While it will only be discussed in passing at various points in this book (see the discussion of Samar Yazbek and Rosa Yaseen Hasan in Chapter 4 and Fawwaz Haddad in the Conclusion, for example), interrogating sectarianism is crucial to explicating political rule and cultural politics in Asadist-Ba'thist Syria. For a range of views on the subject, see Nikolaos Van Dam, *The Struggle for Power in Syria: Sectarianism, Regionalism, and Tribalism in Politics, 1961–1978* (London: Croom Helm, 1979); Elisabeth Picard, "Y-a-t-il un problème communautaire en Syrie?" *Maghreb-Machrek* 87 (janvier-mars 1980): 7–21; Fabrice Balanche, "Clientélisme, communautarisme et fragmentation territoriale en Syrie," *a contrario* 11 (mars 2009): 122–50; Max Weiss "Mosaic, Melting Pot, Pressure Cooker: The Religious, the Secular, and the Sectarian in Modern Syrian Social Thought," in *Arabic Thought Against the Authoritarian Age: Towards an Intellectual History of the Present*, ed. Jens Hanssen and Max Weiss (Cambridge, UK: Cambridge University Press, 2018), 181–202. Also, given the tendency of studies on sectarianism to lump in discussion of ethnic and tribal difference, it bears mentioning that this book does not engage with representations of and by Armenian, Kurdish, and tribal communities in contemporary Syria. Scholarly work on these topics, which would be

important contributions to Syrian studies, might well reinforce or complicate the arguments made throughout *Revolutions Aesthetic*.

9. Michael Walzer, "On 'Failed Totalitarianism,'" in *1984 Revisited: Totalitarianism in Our Century*, ed. Irving Howe (New York: Harper & Row, 1983), 103–21, at 121. Even less worthy of attention on this question than Walzer is Paul Berman. Whereas Walzer conflates authoritarianism and totalitarianism, Berman finds a way to collapse fascism and totalitarianism: "Etymologically speaking, the two words are practically the same," he writes, because they both emerged from a "Mussolinian" vernacular. Of course, Berman would also famously bring down the analytical, political, and logical walls separating Islam, Communism, and fascism. Paul Berman, *The Flight of the Intellectuals* (Brooklyn, NY: Melville House, 2010), 50. See, too, though, Sylvia Sasse and C. Schramm, "Totalitäre Literatur und Subversive Affirmation," *Die Welt der Slaven* LXII (1997): 306–27.

10. Slavoj Žižek, *Did Somebody Say Totalitarianism? Five Interventions in the (Mis) use of a Notion* (London: Verso, 2001), 3.

11. Hannah Arendt, *The Origins of Totalitarianism* (New York: Harcourt, Brace, 1951), 323.

12. Esther Meininghaus, *Creating Consent in Baʿthist Syria: Women and Welfare in a Totalitarian State* (New York: I. B. Tauris, 2016), 25; emphasis in the original.

13. Ibid., 14. In an even-handed commentary on Syrian political rule, Hassan Abbas criticizes the state media environment in Syria for aspiring to "the generalized totalitarianization of society." Abbas, "Censure et information," *Confluences Méditerranée* N° 44 (hiver 2002–2003): 39–46, at 41.

14. Anson Rabinbach, "Totalitarianism Revisited," *Dissent* Vol. 53, No. 3 (Summer 2006): 77–84, at 78.

15. Volker Perthes, "*Si Vis Stabilitatem, Para Bellum*: State Building, National Security, and War Preparation in Syria," in *War, Institutions, and Social Change in the Middle East*, ed. Steven Heydemann (Berkeley: University of California Press, 2000), 149–73, at 150.

16. Hanna Batatu, "Some Observations on the Social Roots of Syria's Ruling Military Group and the Causes for Its Dominance," *Middle East Journal* Vol. 35, No. 3 (1981): 331–44; Raymond Hinnebusch, "Syrian Under the Ba`th: State Formation in a Fragmented Society," *Arab Studies Quarterly* Vol. 4, No. 3 (Summer 1982): 177–99; Hinnebusch, *Authoritarian Power and State Formation in Baʿthist Syria: Army, Party, and Peasant* (Boulder, CO: Westview Press, 1990); Steven Heydemann, "The Political Logic

of Economic Rationality: Selective Stabilisation in Syria," in *The Politics of Economic Reform in the Middle East*, ed. Henri J. Barkey (New York: St. Martin's Press, 1992), 11–39; Eberhard Kienle, *Entre jama'a et classe: le pouvoir politique en Syrie* (Berlin: Das Arabische Buch, 1992); Hanna Batatu, *Syria's Peasantry, the Descendants of Its Lesser Rural Notables, and Their Politics* (Princeton, NJ: Princeton University Press, 1999); Heydemann, *Authoritarianism in Syria: Institutions and Social Conflict, 1946–1970* (Ithaca, NY: Cornell University Press, 1999); Bassam Haddad, "The Formation and Development of Economic Networks in Syria: Implications for Economic and Fiscal Reforms, 1986–2000," in *Networks of Privilege in the Middle East: The Politics of Economic Reform Revisited*, ed. Steven Heydemann (New York: Palgrave Macmillan, 2004), 37–66.

17. Joshua Stacher, "Reinterpreting Authoritarian Power: Syria's Hereditary Succession," *The Middle East Journal* Vol. 65, No. 2 (Spring 2011): 197–212, at 207.

18. Joshua Stacher, *Adaptable Autocrats: Regime Power in Egypt and Syria*. (Stanford, CA: Stanford University Press, 2012), 57.

19. Ibid., 20, 31–35 passim.

20. Louis Althusser, "Ideology and Ideological State Apparatuses (Notes Towards an Investigation)," in *Lenin and Philosophy, and Other Essays*, trans. Ben Brewster (London: New Left Books, 1971), 127–86, at 144.

21. Ibid., 160.

22. Ibid., 158.

23. Ibid., 159.

24. Russell A. Berman, "Aestheticization of Politics: Walter Benjamin on Fascism and the Avant-Garde," in *Modern Culture and Critical Theory* (Madison: University of Wisconsin Press, 1989), 27–41; Josef Chytry, *The Aesthetic State: A Quest in Modern German Thought* (Berkeley: University of California Press, 1989); Terry Eagleton, *The Ideology of the Aesthetic* (Cambridge, MA.: Basil Blackwell, 1990); Susan Buck-Morss, "Aesthetics and Anaesthetics: Walter Benjamin's Artwork Essay Reconsidered," *October* Vol. 62 (Fall 1992): 3–41; Martin Jay, "'The Aesthetic Ideology' as Ideology; or, What Does it Mean to Aestheticize Politics?" *Cultural Critique* No. 21 (Spring, 1992): 41–61; Paul De Man, *Aesthetic Ideology* (Minneapolis: University of Minnesota Press, 1996); Robert Kaufman, "Red Kant, or the Persistence of the Third *Critique* in Adorno and Jameson," *Critical Inquiry* Vol. 26, No. 4 (Summer 2000): 682–724; Mike Wayne, "Kant's Philosophy of the Aesthetic and the Philosophy of Praxis," *Rethinking Marxism* Vol. 24, No. 3 (July 2012): 386–402.

25. Omnia El Shakry, "'History Without Documents': The Vexed Archives of Decolonization in the Middle East," *American Historical Review* Vol. 120, No. 3 (June 2015): 920–34, at 934.

26. In a study of Cuban and Angolan literature and film during the post-1989 period, which resonates with the cultural consequences of the 1967 defeat in the Arabic-speaking world, Lanie Millar scrutinizes "narratives of disappointment [that] revisit the question of the radical future possibilities of revolution through techniques of citation and imitation such as allegory, satire, pastiche, and historical re-writings." Millar, *Forms of Disappointment: Cuban and Angolan Narrative After the Cold War* (Albany: State University of New York Press, 2019), xvi. Thanks to Karen Emmerich for this fascinating reference.

27. Anneka Lenssen's history of art and art criticism during the mid-twentieth century is a rare conjoining of deep research and broad imagination in refuting this perspective, setting the bar very high for those writing the cultural history of modern Syria. Lenssen, *Beautiful Agitation: Modern Painting and Politics in Syria* (Berkeley: University of California Press, 2020).

28. For a searing analysis of the political and cultural ramifications of this moment for Lebanese Marxist thought and its exponents, an only orthogonally comparative case, see Bardawil, *Revolution and Disenchantment*.

29. Andrew Hewitt, *Fascist Modernism: Aesthetics, Politics, and the Avant-Garde* (Stanford, CA: Stanford University Press, 1993), 57.

30. Peter E. Gordon, "What is Intellectual History? A Frankly Partisan Introduction to a Frequently Misunderstood Field." (Spring 2012). https://ces.fas.harvard.edu/uploads/files/Reports-Articles/What-is-Intellectual-History-Essay-by-Peter-Gordon.pdf

31. Zeina G. Halabi, *The Unmaking of the Arab Intellectual: Prophecy, Exile and the Nation* (Edinburgh: Edinburgh University Press, 2017), 28. See, too, Sabry Hafez, "The Transformation of Reality and the Arabic Novel's Aesthetic Response," *Bulletin of the School of Oriental and African Studies* Vol. 57, No. 1 (1994): 93–112.

32. Yasmeen Hanoosh, "Contempt: State Literati vs. Street Literati in Modern Iraq," *Journal of Arabic Literature* Vol. 43 (2012): 372–408, at 374.

33. Patricia A. Herminghouse, "Literature as 'Ersatzöffenlichkeit'? Censorship and the Displacement of Public Discourse in the GDR," *German Studies Review* Vol. 17 (Fall 1994): 85–99, at 87.

34. Jacques Rancière, "The Aesthetic Dimension: Aesthetics, Politics, Knowledge." *Critical Inquiry* Vol. 36, No. 1 (Fall 2009): 1–19; Sianne Ngai, *Ugly Feelings* (Cambridge, MA: Harvard University Press, 2005); Ngai, *Our Aesthetic Categories: Zany, Cute, Interesting* (Cambridge, MA: Harvard University Press, 2012). I will return to this point in Chapter 1, but it's worth noting here that foundational works in European aesthetic theory (those that had a noticeable influence on Syrian discussions of aesthetics and politics during this period and even those that did not) were not translated into Arabic until the late-twentieth century. Also, interestingly, some of those works were translated via bridge languages, as in the cases, for example, of Hegel (by Jurj Tarabishi from the French) and Schiller (by Wafa' Muhammad Ibrahim from the English). See, for example, Imanuyil Kant (Immanuel Kant), *Naqd Malakat al-Ḥukm*, trans. Sa'id Al-Ghanimi (Beirut: Manshūrāt al-Jamal, 2009); Fridrish Shillir, (Friedrich Schiller), *Fī al-Tarbiyya al-Jamāliyya li-l-Insān*, trans. Wafa' Muhammad Ibrahim (Cairo: al-Hay'a al-Miṣriyya al-'Āmma li-l-Kitāb, 1991); Hayghil (Georg Wilhelm Friedrich Hegel), *al-Madkhal ilā 'Ilm al-Jamāl: Fikrat al-Jamāl*, trans. Jurj Tarabishi (Beirut: Dār al-Ṭalī'a li-l-Ṭibā'a wa-l-Nashr, 1988 [2nd ed.]); Fridrik Hayghil, (Georg Wilhelm Friedrich Hegel), *Muḥāḍarāt 'an al-Fann al-Jamīl, al-Ḥalqa al-Ūlā: 'Ilm al-Jamāl wa-Falsafat al-Fann*, trans. Mujahid 'Abd Al-Mun'im Mujahid (Cairo: Maktabat Dār al-Kalema, 2010); Jurj Lukash (Georg Lukács), *al-Tārīkh wa-l-Wa'ī al-Ṭabaqī*, trans. Hanna al-Sha'er (Beirut: Dār al-Andalus, 1982 [2nd ed.]); Lukash (Georg Lukács), *Dirāsāt fī al-Wāqi'īyya*, trans. Nayif Ballur (Beirut: al-Mu'assasa al-Jāmi'iyya li-l-Dirāsāt wa-l-Nashr wa-l-Tawzī', 1985 [3rd ed.]); Tiyudur W. Adurnu (Theodor W. Adorno), *Naẓariyya Istiṭīqiyya*, trans. Naji al-'Awnali (Beirut; Baghdad: Manshūrāt al-Jamal, 2017).

35. Works I have found useful include: Jing Wang, *High Culture Fever: Politics, Aesthetics, and Ideology in Deng's China* (Berkeley: University of California Press, 1996); Ban Wang, *The Sublime Figure of History: Aesthetics and Politics in Twentieth-Century China* (Stanford, Calif.: Stanford University Press, 1997); Liu Kang, *Aesthetics and Marxism: Chinese Aesthetic Marxists and Their Western Contemporaries* (Durham, NC: Duke University Press, 2000); Cristina Vatulescu, *Police Aesthetics: Literature, Film, and the Secret Police in Soviet Times* (Stanford, Calif.: Stanford University Press, 2010); Katerina Clark, *Moscow, the Fourth Rome: Stalinism, Cosmopolitanism, and the Evolution of Soviet Culture, 1931–1941* (Cambridge, MA: Harvard University Press, 2011); Nadje al-Ali and Deborah Al-Najjar, eds. *We Are Iraqis: Aesthetics and Politics in a Time of War* (Syracuse, N.Y.: Syracuse University Press, 2013); Cécile Bishop, *Postcolonial Criticism and Representations of African Dictatorship: The Aesthetics of Tyranny* (London: Modern

Humanities Research Association and Maney Publishing, 2014); Nathaniel Greenberg, *The Aesthetic of Revolution in the Film and Literature of Naguib Mahfouz (1952–1967)* (Lanham, MD: Lexington Books, 2014); Ben Tran, *Post-Mandarin: Masculinity and Aesthetic Modernity in Colonial Vietnam* (New York: Fordham University Press, 2017)

36. Rancière, "The Aesthetic Dimension," 5.

37. Jacques Rancière, "The Aesthetic Revolution and Its Outcomes: Emplotments of Autonomy and Heteronomy," *New Left Review* 14 (March–April 2002): 133–51, at 137.

38. Georg Lukács, "Hegel's Aesthetics, trans. David Taffel," *Graduate Faculty Philosophy Journal* Vol. 23, No. 2 (2002): 87–124, at 97. See, too, Lydia L. Moland, *Hegel's Aesthetics: The Art of Idealism* (New York: Oxford University Press, 2019).

39. Terry Eagleton, "The Ideology of the Aesthetic," *Poetics Today* Vol. 9, No. 2 (1988): 327–38, at 330. See, too, Matthew Sharpe, "The Aesthetics of Ideology, or 'The Critique of Ideological Judgment' in Eagleton and Žižek," *Political Theory* Vol. 34, No. 1 (February 2006): 95–120.

40. Mike Wayne, "Kant's Philosophy of the Aesthetic and the Philosophy of Praxis," 399. Immanuel Kant, *Critique of Judgment*, trans. J. H. Bernard (New York: Hafner Press, 1951). Also see Michael Sprinker, *Imaginary Relations: Aesthetics and Ideology in the Theory of Historical Materialism* (London: Verso, 1987); Bart Vandenabeele, "Aesthetic Solidarity 'After' Kant and Lyotard," *The Journal of Aesthetic Education* Vol. 42, No. 4 (Winter 2008): 17–30.

41. In response to her own question, "What is the relevance of aesthetics in a time of violence?" miriam cooke writes, "The creative process allows us to process what seems to be beyond comprehension because it is beyond words until it is shaped into evocative images and stories." cooke, *Dancing in Damascus: Creativity, Resilience, and the Syrian Revolution* (New York: Routledge, 2017), 116.

42. Lisa Wedeen, *Ambiguities of Domination: Politics, Rhetoric, and Symbols in Contemporary Syria* (Chicago: University of Chicago Press, 1999), 131.

43. Yaseen Noorani, "Redefining Resistance: Counterhegemony, the Repressive Hypothesis and the Case of Arabic Modernism," in *Counterhegemony in the Colony and Postcolony*, ed. John T. Chalcraft and Yaseen Noorani (New York: Palgrave Macmillan, 2007), 75–99, at 93.

44. Lila Abu-Lughod, "The Romance of Resistance: Tracing Transformations of Power Through Bedouin Women." *American Ethnologist* Vol. 17, No. 1 (February 1990): 41–55; Lilie Chouliaraki, *The Ironic Spectator: Solidarity in the Age of Post-Humanitarianism* (Malden, MA: Polity, 2013).

45. Alexis Tadié, "La Culture et l'état au proche-orient," *Esprit* (juillet 2003): 98–110, at 105.

46. Walter Benjamin, "The Work of Art in the Age of Mechanical Reproduction," in *Illuminations*, trans. Harry Zohn (New York: Schocken, 1968), 217–51; Benjamin, "The Work of Art in the Age of Its Technological Reproducibility [First Version], trans. Michael W. Jennings," *Grey Room* 39 (Spring 2010): 11–37.

47. Buck-Morss, "Aesthetics and Anaesthetics," 38.

48. Ibid., 5.

49. Cécile Boëx, "Syrian Cinema: Autonomous Spaces," *Film Comment* Vol. 42, No. 3 (May–June 2006): 12–15, at 12.

50. Mary Beth Tierney-Tello, *Allegories of Transgression and Transformation: Experimental Fiction by Women Writing under Dictatorship* (Albany: State University of New York Press, 1996), 18.

51. This point is reminiscent of an important earlier debate in comparative literature about the relationship between "Third World" contexts and the overdetermined significance of national allegory. See Fredric Jameson, "Third-World Literature in the Era of Multinational Capitalism," *Social Text* No. 15 (Autumn, 1986): 65–88; Aijaz Ahmad, "Jameson's Rhetoric of Otherness and the 'National Allegory,'" *Social Text* No. 17 (Autumn, 1987): 3–25; Madhava Prasad, "On the Question of a Theory of (Third World) Literature," *Social Text*, No. 31/32 (1992): 57–83; Neil Lazarus, "Postcolonialism and the Dilemma of Nationalism: Aijaz Ahmad's Critique of Third-Worldism," *Diaspora: A Journal of Transnational Studies* Vol. 2, No. 3 (Winter 1993): 373–400; Julie McGonegal, "Postcolonial Metacritique: Jameson, Allegory and the Always-Already-Read Third World Text," *Interventions* Vol. 7, No. 2 (2005): 251–65.

52. Tierney-Tello, *Allegories of Transgression and Transformation*, 19–20. The short stories of Zakariya Tāmir, which are only briefly discussed in Chapter 2, could be explored further in this connection, for example.

53. Wedeen, *Ambiguities of Domination*. miriam cooke, by contrast, argues that cultural production in Syria can be understood in terms of a conscious project to shape public opinion, which she terms "commissioned criticism." cooke, *Dissident Syria: Making Oppositional Arts Official* (Durham, NC: Duke University Press, 2007).

54. Inke Arns and Sylvia Sasse, "Subversive Affirmation: On Mimesis as a Strategy of Resistance," in *East Art Map: Contemporary Art and Eastern Europe*, ed. IRWIN (London: Afterall, 2006), 444–55, at 445.

55. Ibid., 452.

56. Ami Ayalon, "From Fitna to Thawra," *Studia Islamica* No. 66 (1987): 145–74, at 146.

57. Ibid., 149–50.

58. Ibid., 155

59. Ibid., 158. Koselleck notes how the earliest uses of the term during the early modern period in "the West" were strongly influenced by the Copernican Revolution and revolved around the concepts of circulation, return, and restoration. Koselleck, "Historical Criteria of the Modern Concept of Revolution," 41–44.

60. Ayalon, "From Fitna to Thawra," 165. Michael Cook radicalizes this argument by arguing that Sunni Islamists and "Islamic fundamentalists" in the postwar period are by definition politically conservative, while the Iranian Revolution is an exceptional event that proves the rule about Shiʿi Islamist and "Islamic fundamentalist" conservatism as well. Sunni Islamism "can be socially subversive," Cook writes, but has never had "an articulate program of social revolution." Cook, *Ancient Religions, Modern Politics: The Islamic Case in Comparative Perspective* (Princeton, NJ: Princeton University Press, 2014), 182. Denigrating the lack of an Islamic tradition of politics akin to that of Hindu fundamentalist nationalism and Latin American Catholic liberation theology, Cook fails to present a definition of revolution against which the empirically dense comparison presented in this book might be measured. Furthermore, there seems to be little consideration in this work of the voluminous scholarly literature on secularism, secularity, and the secular modern, of how "religious" and "secular" revolutionary movements are not necessarily so easily separated. For a very different approach to this question, see Ellis Goldberg, "Smashing Idols and the State: The Protestant Ethic and Egyptian Sunni Radicalism," *Comparative Studies in Society and History* Vol. 33, No. 1 (January 1991): 3–35. Syrian philosopher Sadiq Jalal al-ʿAzm responds, albeit obliquely, to the same point by rejecting the notion that there is a contradiction between his critique of the religious (Sadiq Jalal al-ʿAzm, *Naqd al-Fikr al-Dīnī* [Beirut: Dar al-Ṭalīʿa, 1969]; al-ʿAzm, *Critique of Religious Thought,* trans. George Stergios and Mansour Ajami [Berlin: Gerlach Press, 2015]), on the one hand, and his support for both the Iranian Revolution and liberation theology in Latin America, on the other hand. "The contradiction here is not in my position," al-ʿAzm said in an interview, "but in the position of those who once stood in support of the revolution of the Iranian people or the Liberation Theologists and their churches or for movements of national liberation almost everywhere, yet refuse to support the revolution of the Syrian people under the pretext that its demonstrations and protests spring from the mosque

and not from the opera house or the national theatre." "Interview with Dr. Sadiq Jalal Al-Azm: The Syrian Revolution and the Role of the Intellectual," *al-Jumhuriyya* (January 10, 2013). http://therepublicgs.net/2013/04/27/interview-with-dr-sadiq/.

61. Hannah Arendt, *On Revolution* (New York: Penguin Books, 2006 [1963]).

62. David Scott, *Conscripts of Modernity: The Tragedy of Colonial Enlightenment* (Durham, NC: Duke University Press, 2004), 217–20; Elizabeth Frazer and Kimberly Hutchings, "On Politics and Violence: Arendt Contra Fanon," *Contemporary Political Theory* Vol. 7, No. 1 (February 2008): 90–108; Christopher J. Finlay, "Hannah Arendt's Critique of Violence," *Thesis Eleven* Vol. 97, No. 1 (2009): 26–45. On the politics of translating *On Revolution* into Arabic, see Jens Hanssen, "Translating Revolution: Hannah Arendt in Arab Political Culture," *Startseite* Bd. 7, Nr. 1 (November 2013): www.hannaharendt.net/index.php/han/article/view/301/437.

63. Ayalon, "From Fitna to Thawra," 169. Bernard Lewis famously asserted that *thawra* in the classical period meant the state of being "stirred or excited," referring to the rising up of a camel. Lewis, "Islamic Concepts of Revolution," in *Revolution in the Middle East, and Other Case Studies: [Proceedings of a Seminar]*, ed. P. J. Vatikiotis (London: Allen and Unwin, 1972), 30–40, at 37. See, too, Weiss, "Genealogies of Baʿthism," 1211n68.

64. Ayalon, "From Fitna to Thawra," 170–71. Bernard Lewis claimed that the use of the term *inqilāb* "in Arabic is rare, and when it occurs it is usually derogatory." Lewis, "Islamic Concepts of Revolution," 40. Ofra Bengio argues that it was not until 1958 when Michel ʿAflaq "stop[ped] using *inqilab* in favor of *thawra*, but he took pains to explain that the new expression stood in for the former." Bengio, *Saddam's Word: Political Discourse in Iraq* (New York: Oxford University Press, 1998), 22.

65. Weiss, "Genealogies of Baʿthism," esp. 1210–19.

66. Yusuf al-Hakim, *Sūriya wa-l-Intidāb al-Faransī* (Beirut: Dār al-Nahār li-l-Nashr, 1983); Philip S. Khoury, *Syria and the French Mandate: The Politics of Arab Nationalism, 1920–1945* (Princeton, NJ: Princeton University Press, 1987); Keith David Watenpaugh, *Being Modern in the Middle East: Revolution, Nationalism, Colonialism, and the Arab Middle Class* (Princeton, NJ: Princeton University Press, 2006); Joshua M. Landis, "Nationalism and the Politics of *Zaʿama*: The Collapse of Republican Syria, 1945–1949" (Ph.D. Diss., Princeton University, 1997); Elizabeth Thompson, *Colonial Citizens: Republican Rights, Paternal Privilege and Gender in French Syria and Lebanon* (New York: Columbia University Press, 2000); Jean-David Mizrahi, *Genèse de l'état mandataire: service des renseignements et bandes armées en Syrie et au Liban dans les années*

1920 (Paris: Publications de la Sorbonne, 2003); Muhammad Hawash, *Takawwun Jumhūriyya: Sūriya wa-l-Intidāb* (Tripoli, Lebanon: Maktabat al-Sā'iḥ, 2005); Michael Provence, *The Great Syrian Revolt and the Rise of Arab Nationalism* (Austin: University of Texas Press, 2005); Leyla Dakhli, "L'Expertise en terrain colonial: les orientalistes et le mandat français en Syrie et au Liban," *Matériaux pour l'histoire de notre temps* N° 99 (2010): 20–27.

67. Kevin W Martin, *Syria's Democratic Years: Citizens, Experts, and Media in the 1950s* (Bloomington: Indiana University Press, 2015).

68. Saïd M. Ajami, "La Démocratie parlementaire occidentale en Syrie et son échec," Thèse du doctorat en droit, Université de Paris—Faculté de Droit et des Sciences Économiques, 1965, III.

69. Christoph Schumann, "The Generation of Broad Expectations: Nationalism, Education, and Autobiography in Syria and Lebanon, 1930–1958," *Die Welt des Islams* Vol. 41, No. 2 (July 2001): 174–205.

70. James P. Jankowski, *Nasser's Egypt, Arab Nationalism, and the United Arab Republic* (Boulder, CO: Lynne Rienner Publishers, 2001).

71. Weiss, "Genealogies of Ba'thism." See, too, Spenser R. Rapone, "Michel 'Aflaq and Political Metaphysics: The Integral Experience of the Ba'th," M.A. Thesis, The New School for Social Research, 2020.

72. Jean Hannoyer and Michel Seurat, *Etat et secteur publique industriel en Syrie* (Lyon: Centre d'études et de recherches sur le Moyen-Orient contemporain; presses universitaires de Lyon, 1979); Yahya Sadowski, "Ba'thist Ethics and the Spirit of State Capitalism: Patronage and the Party in Contemporary Syria," in *Ideology and Power in the Middle East: Studies in Honor of George Lenczowski*, ed. Peter J. Chelkowski and Robert J. Pranger (Durham, NC: Duke University Press, 1988), 160–84; Hinnebusch, *Authoritarian Power and State Formation in Ba'thist Syria*; Volker Perthes, "The Syrian Private Industrial and Commercial Sectors and the State," *International Journal of Middle East Studies* Vol. 24, No. 2 (May 1992): 207–30; Heydemann, *Authoritarianism in Syria.*

73. Michel Seurat, "Etat et paysans en Syrie," *Revue de Géographie de Lyon* Vol. 54, No. 3 (1979): 257–70, at 260.

74. Ibid., 259.

75. Fred Lawson, "Social Bases for the Hamah Revolt," *MERIP Reports* No. 110 (1982): 24–28, at 25.

76. Salah al-Din al-Bitar, "The Major Deviation of the Ba'th Is Having Renounced Democracy," *MERIP Reports* No. 110 (Nov.–Dec., 1982): 21–23, at 22.

77. Hinnebusch, *Authoritarian Power and State Formation in Ba'thist Syria*; Nazih Ayubi, *Over-Stating the Arab State: Politics and Society in the Middle East* (London: I. B. Tauris, 1995), 449–50; Heydemann, *Authoritarianism in Syria.*

78. Thomas Mayer, "The Islamic Opposition in Syria, 1961–1982," *Orient* Vol. 24, No. 4 (December 1983): 588–609, at 606.

79. Ibid., 605.

80. Steven Heydemann, "Taxation Without Representation: Authoritarianism and Economic Liberalization in Syria," in *Rules and Rights in the Middle East: Democracy, Law, and Society*, eds. Ellis Goldberg, Reşat Kasaba, and Joel S. Migdal (Seattle: University of Washington Press, 1993), 69–101; Raymond A. Hinnebusch, "Syria: The Politics of Economic Liberalisation," *Third World Quarterly* Vol. 18, No. 2 (June 1997): 249–65, at 262.

81. Raymond A. Hinnebusch, "Liberalization Without Democratization in "Post-Populist" Authoritarian States: Evidence from Syria and Egypt," in *Citizenship and the State in the Middle East: Approaches and Applications*, eds. Nils A. Butenschøn, Uri Davis, and Manuel S. Hassassian (Syracuse, NY: Syracuse University Press, 2000), 123–45.

82. Haddad, "The Formation and Development of Economic Networks in Syria"; Haddad, *Business Networks in Syria: The Political Economy of Authoritarian Resilience* (Stanford, CA: Stanford University Press, 2012). See, too, Hans Hopfinger, "Capitalist Agro-Business in a Socialist Country? Syria's New Shareholding Corporations as an Example," *Bulletin (British Society for Middle Eastern Studies)* Vol. 17, No. 2 (1990): 162–70; Hans Hopfinger and Marc Boeckler, "Step by Step to an Open Economic System: Syria Sets Course for Liberalization," *British Journal of Middle Eastern Studies* Vol. 23, No. 2 (November 1996): 183–202.

83. As part of its crackdown on the domestic Sunni Islamist insurgency since the late 1970s, the regime used extraordinary powers such as Law 49 (1980), which made membership in the Muslim Brothers organization a capital crime punishable by death.

84. Stacher, *Adaptable Autocrats*, 111.

85. Haddad, "The Formation and Development of Economic Networks in Syria," 39.

86. Elizabeth Suzanne Kassab, *Enlightenment on the Eve of the Revolution: The Egyptian and Syrian Debates* (New York: Columbia University Press, 2019).

87. Najib Ghadbian, "The New Asad: Dynamics of Continuity and Change in Syria," *Middle East Journal* Vol. 55, No. 4 (Autumn 2001): 624–41; Carsten Wieland, *Syria*

At Bay: Secularism, Islamism, and "Pax Americana" (London: Hurst & Company, 2006); Angela Joya, "Syria's Transition, 1970–2005: From Centralization of the State to Market Economy," in *Transitions in Latin America and in Poland and Syria*, ed. Paul Zarembka (Bingley, UK: Emerald Group Publishing, 2007), 163–201. On the early years of Bashar's presidency, see, too, Perthes, *Syria Under Bashar al-Asad*; David W. Lesch, *The New Lion of Damascus: Bashar al-Asad and Modern Syria* (New Haven, CT: Yale University Press, 2005); Shmuel Bar, "Bashar's Syria: The Regime and Its Strategic Worldview," *Comparative Strategy* Vol. 25, No. 6 (2006): 353–455; Ghadbian, *al-Dawla al-Asadiyya al-Thāniyya*; Ghalioun, "'Al-Asadiyya' fī al-Siyāsa al-Sūriyya"; Eyal Zisser, *Commanding Syria: Bashar Al-Asad and the First Years in Power* (London: Tauris, 2007); Samer Abboud, "The Transition Paradigm and the Case of Syria," in *Syria's Economy and the Transition Paradigm*, ed. Samer Abboud and Ferdinand Arslanian (St. Andrews: University of St. Andrews Centre for Syrian Studies, 2009), 3–31; Carsten Wieland, *Syria—A Decade of Lost Chances: Repression and Revolution from Damascus Spring to Arab Spring* (Seattle: Cune Press, 2012); Raymond A Hinnebusch and Tina Zintl, eds. *Syria From Reform to Revolt, Volume 1: Political Economy and International Relations* (Syracuse, NY: Syracuse University Press, 2015); Christa Salamandra and Leif Stenberg, eds. *Syria from Reform to Revolt, Volume 2: Culture, Society, and Religion* (Syracuse, NY: Syracuse University Press, 2015).

88. Lisa Wedeen, "Ideology and Humor in Dark Times: Notes from Syria," *Critical Inquiry* 39 (Summer 2013): 841–73. See, too, Thomas Pierret and Kjetl Selvik, "Limits of "'Authoritarian Upgrading' in Syria: Private Welfare, Islamic Charities, and the Rise of the Zayd Movement," *International Journal of Middle East Studies* Vol. 41, No. 4 (November 2009): 595–614; Raymond Hinnebusch, "Syria: From 'Authoritarian Upgrading' to Revolution?" *International Affairs* Vol. 88, No. 1 (January 2012): 95–113; Steven Heydemann and Reinoud Leenders, "Authoritarian Governance in Syria and Iran: Challenged, Reconfiguring, and Resilient," in *Middle East Authoritarianisms: Governance, Contestation, and Regime Resilience in Syria and Iran*, eds. Steven Heydemann and Reinoud Leenders (Stanford, CA: Stanford University Press, 2013), 1–32, at 4–8; Caroline Donati, "The Economics of Authoritarian Upgrading in Syria: Liberalization and the Reconfiguration of Economic Networks," in Heydemann and Leenders, eds. *Middle East Authoritarianisms*, 35–60.

89. Volker Perthes, *Syria Under Bashar Al-Asad: Modernisation and the Limits of Change* (Oxford: Oxford University Press for the International Institute for Strategic Studies, 2004), 64.

90. "Interview with Syrian President Bashar al-Assad," *Wall Street Journal*, January 31, 2011.

91. Muhammad Abi Samra, *Mawt al-Abad al-Sūrī: Shahādāt Jīl al-Ṣamt wa-l-Thawra* (Beirut: Riyad el-Rayyis li-l-Kutub wa-l-Nashr, 2012); Samar Yazbek, *A Woman in the Crossfire: Diaries of the Syrian Revolution*, trans. Max Weiss (London: Haus Publishing, 2012); Yassin al-Haj Saleh, *The Impossible Revolution: Making Sense of the Syrian Tragedy* (London: Hurst, 2017).

92. Reinoud Leenders, "'Oh Buthaina, Oh Shaʿban—the Hawrani Is Not Hungry, We Want Freedom!' Revolutionary Framing and Mobilization at the Onset of the Syrian Uprising," in *Social Movements, Mobilization, and Contestation in the Middle East and North Africa, 2nd ed.*, eds. Joel Beinin and Frédéric Vairel (Stanford, CA: Stanford University Press, 2013), 246–61, at 256.

93. Marwa Daoudy, *The Origins of the Syrian Conflict: Climate Change and Human Security* (Cambridge: Cambridge University Press, 2020).

94. It is striking if not altogether surprising to observe how quickly the scholarly engagement with Syria since 2011 has developed, quickly outstripping the literature on any other period in the country's modern history: Fouad Ajami, *The Syrian Rebellion* (Stanford, CA: Hoover Institution Press, 2012); Hinnebusch, "Syria: From 'Authoritarian Upgrading' to Revolution?"; Reinoud Leenders, "Collective Action and Mobilization in Dar'a: An Anatomy of the Onset of Syria's Popular Uprising," *Mobilization: An International Journal* Vol. 17, No. 4 (2012): 419–34; Stephen Starr, *Revolt in Syria: Eye-Witness to the Uprising* (London: Hurst & Company, 2012); Leenders. "'Oh Buthaina, Oh Shaʿban—the Hawrani Is Not Hungry, We Want Freedom!"; Christopher Phillips, *The Battle for Syria: International Rivalry in the New Middle East* (New Haven, CT: Yale University Press, 2016); Robin Yassin-Kassab and Leila Al-Shami, *Burning Country: Syrians in Revolution and War* (London: Pluto Press, 2016); Nikolaos van Dam, *Destroying a Nation: The Civil War in Syria* (London: I. B. Tauris, 2017); Adam Baczko, Gilles Dorronsoro, and Arthur Quesnay, *Civil War in Syria: Mobilization and Competing Social Orders* (Cambridge: Cambridge University Press, 2018); Sam Dagher, *Assad or We Burn the Country: How One Family's Lust for Power Destroyed Syria* (New York: Little, Brown, 2019); Daoudy, *The Origins of the Syrian Conflict*; Raymond A. Hinnebusch and Adham Saouli, eds., *The War for Syria: Regional and International Dimensions of the Syrian Uprising* (London: Routledge, 2020); Yasser Munif, *The Syrian Revolution: Between the Politics of Life and the Geopolitics of Death* (London: Pluto Press, 2020); Kevin Mazur, *Revolution in Syria: Identity, Networks, and Repression* (Cambridge: Cambridge University

Press, 2021); Itamar Rabinovich and Carmit Valensi, *Syrian Requiem: The Civil War and Its Aftermath* (Princeton, NJ: Princeton University Press, 2021).

95. Salwa Ismail, "Syria's Cultural Revolution," *The Guardian*, June 21, 2011. https://www.theguardian.com/commentisfree/2011/jun/21/syria-cultural-revolution-art-comedy. See, too, cooke, *Dancing in Damascus*; Rosa Yaseen Hassan, "Where are the Intellectuals in the Syrian Revolution? trans. Max Weiss," in *Arabic Thought Against the Authoritarian Age*, ed. Jens Hanssen and Max Weiss, 370–73; Yassin al-Haj Saleh, "The Intellectuals and the Revolution in Syria, trans. Max Weiss," in *Arabic Thought Against the Authoritarian Age*, ed. Jens Hanssen and Max Weiss, 374–79.

CHAPTER 1

1. Hafiz al-Asad, *Kadhālika Qāla al-Asad*, ed. Mustafa Tlas (Damascus: Dār Ṭlās, 2001), 345.

2. Thomas Carlyle, *On Heroes, Hero-Worship, & the Heroic in History: Six Lectures; Reported, with Emendations and Additions* (London: Chapman and Hall, 1840), 234, emphasis in original.

3. Larry Hartwick, "On 'The Aesthetic Dimension': A Conversation with Herbert Marcuse," *Contemporary Literature* Vol. 22, No. 4 (Fall 1981): 416–24, at 420.

4. Maha Qannut, "Usrijū Khayla al-Sibāq li-l-Sibāq," *al-Maʿrifa* No. 442 (July 2000): 5–8, at 5. For a helpful primer on the Ministry of Culture, see Assad Al-Saleh, "The Ministry of Culture in Syria: History, Production and Restriction of Official Culture," *Journal for Cultural Research* Vol. 20, No. 2 (2016): 137–56. On the role of Buthaina Shabaan (b. 1953), another important figure who articulated the position of the regime in cultural and intellectual terms as political and media adviser to the president from the late 2000s, see Al-Saleh, "Failing the Masses: Buthaina Shabaan and the Public Intellectual Crisis," *Journal of International Women's Studies* Vol. 13, No. 5 (October 2012): 195–211.

5. Qannut, "Usrijū Khayla al-Sibāq li-l-Sibāq, 5–7.

6. Ibid., 6.

7. Ibid., 7.

8. These dispositions toward state power can be understood as pedagogical or bureaucratic expressions of the anthropological "acting 'as if'" identified by Lisa Wedeen in her foundational interpretation of state power and cultural manipulation in Baʿthist Syria. Wedeen, "Acting 'As If': Symbolic Politics and Social Control in Syria," *Comparative Studies in Society and History* Vol. 40, No. 3 (July 1998): 503–23; and

Wedeen, *Ambiguities of Domination: Politics, Rhetoric, and Symbols in Contemporary Syria* (Chicago: University of Chicago Press, 1999). This sort of fawning praise for the leader could profitably be read against the history of panegyric praise poetry (*madḥ*) in classical Arabic letters. See, for example, James T. Monroe, "The Underside of Arabic Panegyric: Ibn Quzmān's (Unfinished?) 'Zajal No. 84,'" *al-Qanṭara* Vol. 17, No. 1 (1996): 79–116; Suzanne Pinckney Stetkevych, *The Poetics of Islamic Legitimacy: Myth, Gender, and Ceremony in the Classical Arabic Ode* (Bloomington, IN: Indiana University Press, 2002), 80–109; Stetkevych, "Abbasid Panegyric: *Badīʿ* Poetry and the Invention of the Arab Golden Age," *British Journal of Middle Eastern Studies* Vol. 44, No. 1 (2017): 48–72. For a counterintuitive interpretation of premodern panegyric from a global perspective, see Rebecca Gould, "The Much-Maligned Panegyric: Toward a Political Poetics of Premodern Literary Form," *Comparative Literature Studies* Vol. 52, No. 2 (2015): 254–88. I thank one of the press's anonymous reviewers for insightfully encouraging me to consider this line of comparison.

9. See, for example, al-Asad, *Kadhālika Qāla al-Asad.*

10. ʿAbd al-Hamid Muhammad al-Tarazi, *Ḥāfiẓ: Anta al-Amal* (Damascus: al-Maktab al-Fannī al-Tijārī al-ʿArabī, 1976); *Ḥāfiẓ al-Asad wa-Qaḍāyā al-Kitāba wa-l-Kuttāb* (Damascus: Ittiḥād al-Kuttāb al-ʿArab, 1978); Safwan Qudsi, *al-Baṭal wa-l-Tārīkh: Qirāʾa fī Fikr Ḥāfiẓ al-Asad al-Siyāsī* (Damascus: Dār Ṭlās, 1984); Qudsi, *Ḥāfiẓ al-Asad: al-Taḥaddiyyāt al-Kubrā wa-l-Istijābāt al-ʿUẓmā* (self-pub., 2000).

11. Lisa Wedeen, *Authoritarian Apprehensions: Ideology, Judgment, and Mourning in Syria* (Chicago: University of Chicago Press, 2019), 148.

12. Late twentieth- and early twenty-first century writers, artists, and intellectuals would continue to debate the advantages, achievements, and limitations of the Nahda project in intellectual and cultural terms. See, for example, Elizabeth Suzanne Kassab, "Summoning the Spirit of Enlightenment: On the Nahda revival in *Qadaya wa-shahadat,*" in *Arabic Thought against the Authoritarian Age: Towards an Intellectual History of the Present*, ed. Jens Hanssen and Max Weiss (New York: Cambridge University Press, 2018), 311–35; Ahmad Agbaria, *The Politics of Arab Authenticity: Challenges to Postcolonial Thought* (New York: Columbia University Press, 2022), 183–208.

13. Volker Perthes, *The Political Economy of Syria under Asad* (New York: I. B. Tauris, 1995), 189.

14. See, for example, Najib Ghadbian, *al-Dawla al-Asadiyya al-Thāniyya: Bashshār al-Asad wa-l-Furaṣ al-Ḍāʾiʿa* ([S.l.]: Najīb al-Ghaḍbiān, 2006); Burhan Ghalioun, "'Al-Asadiyya' fī al-Siyāsa al-Sūriyya, aw, Dawr al-Siyāsa al-Iqlīmiyya fi Taḥqīq al-Sayṭara

al-Dākhiliyya," in *Maʿrakat al-Iṣlāḥ fī Sūriyā*, ed. Radwan Ziadeh (Cairo: Markaz al-Qāhira li-Dirāsāt Ḥuqūq al-Insān, 2006), 15–45; Rustum Mahmud, "Al-Asadiyya," *al-Jumhuriyya* (March 29, 2016). http://aljumhuriya.net/34745.

15. Wedeen, *Ambiguities of Domination*, 84.

16. Najah al-ʿAttar, "Dawr al-Thaqāfa fī Bināʾ al-Insān wa-l-Waṭan," *al-Maʿrifa*, No. 209 (July 1979), 7–20, at 20.

17. Patrick Seale, *Asad of Syria: The Struggle for the Middle East* (London: I. B. Taurus, 1988), 343.

18. Al-ʿAttar, "Dawr al-Thaqāfa fī Bināʾ al-Insān wa-l-Waṭan," 20. Carlyle's work was translated into Arabic by the Egyptian intellectual Muhammad al-Sibaʿi and published in installments in the Egyptian *al-Bayān* and in a full version in 1911. See Shaden M. Tageldin, "Secularizing Islam: Carlyle, al-Sibāʿī, and the Translations of 'Religion' in British Egypt," *PMLA* Vol. 126, No. 1 (January 2011): 123–39; Maya Kesrouany, *Prophetic Translation: The Making of Modern Egyptian Literature* (Edinburgh: Edinburgh University Press, 2019), 114–54. Both Tageldin and Kesrouany highlight the reference that late nineteenth- and early twentieth-century Egyptian intellectuals and scholars made to the Prophet Muhammad as they wrestled with Carlyle's theory of heroes and heroism.

19. "An important aspect of the sacralisation of politics in Syria was the deification of Hafez al-Asad as a figure of national salvation," writes Salwa Ismail. "Al-Asad's deification should not be understood as his being regarded as a deity in the conventional sense, though the language of divinity was used." Ismail, *The Rule of Violence: Subjectivity, Memory and Government in Syria* (New York: Cambridge University Press, 2018), 35.

20. Thomas Mayer, "The Islamic Opposition in Syria, 1961–1982," *Orient* Vol. 24, No. 4 (December 1983): 588–609, esp. 595–97. See, too, Raphaël Lefèvre, *Ashes of Hama: The Muslim Brotherhood in Syria* (New York: Oxford University Press, 2013), 86–96.

21. The second part of the article, which is less relevant to my purposes here, analyzes two novels: *al-Fahd* by Haydar Haydar (Damascus: Dār Ibn Rushd, 1977 [1968]) and *Shams fī Yawm Ghāʾim* by Hanna Mina (Damascus: Wizārat al-Thaqāfa, 1973) [Hanna Mina, *Sun on a Cloudy Day*, trans. Bassam Frangieh and Clementina Brown (Pueblo, CO: Passeggiata Press, 1997)].

22. Hanna ʿAbbud, "Ṣūrat al-Baṭal fī al-Riwāya al-Sūriyya," *al-Mawqif al-Adabī*, No. 129–130 (February 1982): 66–84, at 66.

23. Ibid., 66.

24. Ibid., 67.

25. Ibid.

26. Ibid., 68.

27. Ibid., 69.

28. Hannah Arendt, *The Origins of Totalitarianism* (New York: Harcourt, Brace, 1951), 374.

29. Steven Heydemann, *Authoritarianism in Syria: Institutions and Social Conflict, 1946–1970* (Ithaca, NY: Cornell University Press, 1999), 164.

30. Raymond A. Hinnebusch, "Syria Under the Ba'th: State Formation in a Fragmented Society," *Arab Studies Quarterly* Vol. 4, No. 3 (Summer 1982): 177–99; Hinnebusch, *Authoritarian Power and State Formation in Ba'thist Syria: Army, Party, and Peasant* (Boulder, CO: Westview Press, 1990).

31. According to Hinnebusch, military expenditures rose ninefold between 1945 and 1957. Hinnebusch, *Authoritarian Power*, 50.

32. Gérard Michaud (Michel Seurat) and Jim Paul, "The Importance of Bodyguards," *MERIP Reports* No. 110 (Nov.–Dec., 1982), 29–31, at 30.

33. Fadia Kiwan, "La tradition des coups d'état et la pérennisation d'une dictature," Thèse d'État, Paris 1, 1984, 248–49.

34. Naomi Joy Weinberger, *Syrian Intervention in Lebanon: The 1975–76 Civil War* (New York: Oxford University Press, 1986); Raymond A. Hinnebusch, "The Islamic Movement in Syria: Sectarian Conflict an Urban Rebellion in an Authoritarian-Populist Regime," in *Islamic Resurgence in the Arab World*, ed. Ali E. Hilal Dessouki (New York: Praeger, 1982), 138–69; Fred Lawson, *Why Syria Goes to War: Thirty Years of Confrontation* (Ithaca, NY: Cornell University Press, 1996).

35. Alasdair Drysdale, "Ethnicity in the Syrian Officer Corps: A Conceptualization," *Civilisations* Vol. 29 (1979): 359–74, at 369. On the significance of sectarianism and ethnicity in the formation of the Syrian armed forces, see Gordon H. Torrey, *Syrian Politics and the Military, 1945–1958* (Columbus: Ohio State University Press, 1964); Michael Van Dusen, "Intra-Generational and Inter-Generational Conflict in the Syrian Army" (Ph.D. Diss., Johns Hopkins University, 1971); Itamar Rabinovich, *Syria under the Ba'th, 1963–66: the Army Party Symbiosis* (Jerusalem: Israel Universities Press, 1972); Hanna Batatu, "Some Observations on the Social Roots of Syria's Ruling, Military Group and the Causes for Its Dominance, " *Middle East Journal* Vol. 35, No. 3 (Summer 1981): 331–44; N. E. Bou-Nacklie, "Les troupes spéciales: Religious and Ethnic Recruitment, 1916–46," *International Journal of Middle East Studies* Vol. 25, No. 4 (November 1993): 645–60; Mustafa Tlas, *Tārīkh al-Jaysh al-'Arabī al-Sūrī* (Damascus: Markaz al-Dirāsāt al-'Askariyya, 2000).

36. Raymond A. Hinnebusch, *Syria: Revolution from Above* (London: Routledge, 2001), 65.

37. Michel ʿAflaq, *Arab World* XIII, No. 3102 (February 25, 1966), 3, cited in Van Dusen, "Intra-Generational and Inter-Generational Conflict," 189.

38. Kiwan, "La tradition des coups d'état," 249.

39. Hizb al-Baʿth al-ʿArabī al-Ishtirākī, *Some Theoretical Principles: Approved by the Six[th] National Congress, October 1963* (Beirut: Dār al-Ṭalīʿa, 1974), 77.

40. Mustafa Tlas, "Thawrat Adhār wa-Binā' al-Jaysh al-ʿAqā'idī," *Jaysh al-Shaʿb* No. 1026/1027 (March 7, 1972): 10–11, at 10

41. Al-Asad, *Kadhālika Qāla al-Asad*, 148.

42. Tlas, "Thawrat Adhār," 10, emphasis mine.

43. Wedeen, "Acting 'As if.'"

44. Tlas, "Thawrat Adhār," 11.

45. Mustafa Tlas, "al-Waḥda al-ʿArabiyya Ḍarūra Istrātījiyya," *al-Maʿrifa* No. 127–128 (September–October 1972): 3–6, at 4.

46. Al-Asad, *Kadhālika Qāla al-Asad*, 131.

47. Amos Perlmutter, "From Obscurity to Rule: The Syrian Army and the Baʿth Party," *Western Political Quarterly* Vol 22, No. 4 (December 1969): 827–45, at 844.

48. Michel Seurat, "Les Populations, l'état et la société," in *La Syrie d'aujourd'hui*, ed. A. M. Bianquis, and André Raymond (Paris: Éditions du Centre national de la recherche scientifique, 1980), 87–141, at 136.

49. Ibid., 137.

50. Elisabeth Picard, "Espaces de référence et espace d'intervention du mouvement rectificatif au pouvoir en Syrie 1970–1982," Thèse de doctorat de 3e cycle, Institut d'études politiques de Paris, 1985, 272.

51. Yezid Sayigh, "Agencies of Coercion: Armies and Internal Security Forces," *International Journal of Middle East Studies* Vol. 43, No. 3 (August 2011): 403–5, at 403.

52. Salwa Ismail cogently identifies "the massacre," for example, as one instrument of Asadist-Baʿthist statecraft through violence. Ismail, *The Rule of Violence*, 54–63.

53. Seale, *Asad of Syria*, 169.

54. Picard, "Espaces de référence," 168.

55. For a clarifying discussion of this point in the Iraqi context, see Orit Bashkin, "Hybrid Nationalisms: *Waṭanī* and *Qawmī* Visions in Iraq under ʿAbd Al-Karim Qasim, 1958–1961," *International Journal of Middle East Studies* Vol. 43, No. 2 (May 2011): 293–312.

56. Elisabeth Picard, "Syria Returns to Democracy: The May 1973 Legislative Elections," in *Elections Without Choice*, ed. Guy Hermet, Richard Rose, and Alain Rouquié (London: Macmillan, 1978), 129–44, at 130.

57. Heydemann, *Authoritarianism in Syria*, 217.

58. *Ḥāfiẓ Al-Asad wa-Qaḍāyā al-Kitāba wa-l-Kuttāb* (Damascus: Ittiḥād al-Kuttāb al-ʿArab, 1978), 17.

59. Ibid., 44. Minister of culture Najah al-ʿAttar parroted this language about there being "no censorship of thought except for the censorship of conscience." See, for example, al-ʿAttar, "Dawr al-Thaqāfa fī Binā' al-Insān wa-l-Waṭan," 19.

60. Suzanne Kassab points out Tizini's uneasy position within the Syrian intellectual milieu early in the transition to Bashar al-Asad's rule. See Kassab, *Enlightenment on the Eve of the Revolution: The Egyptian and Syrian Debates* (New York: Columbia University Press, 2019), 144.

61. Tayyib Tizini, *Ḥawla Mushkilāt al-Thawra wa-l-Thaqāfa fī "al-ʿĀlam al-Thālith"* (Damascus: Dār Dimashq li-l-Ṭibāʿa wa-l-Nashr, 1971 [?]), 224–25.

62. Ibid., 252.

63. "Muqābala maʿa Zakarayā Tāmir,"*al-Maʿrifa* No. 126 (August 1972): 108–16, at 108–9.

64. Ibid., 112.

65. Ibid., 116.

66. Hal Foster, "For a Concept of the Political in Contemporary Art," in *Recodings: Art, Spectacle, Cultural Politics* (Port Townsend, WA.: Bay Press, 1985), 139–55, at 143.

67. miriam cooke makes a related point about the potential for adapting and resignifiying "regime art" in her study of theater and prose writing in late 1990s and early 2000s Syria. cooke, *Dissident Syria: Making Oppositional Arts Official.* (Durham, NC: Duke University Press, 2007). My point here is about the ideological and philosophical scaffolding established by regime-supporting intellectuals that was part of an attempt—a failed attempt, it could be argued—by the Asadist regime to capture the cultural field.

68. Al-Asad, *Kadhālika Qāla al-Asad*, 83.

69. I discuss the history of Michel ʿAflaq and ʿAflaqism—one variety of Baʿthist ideology—in Weiss, "Genealogies of Baʿthism: Michel ʿAflaq between Personalism and Arabic Nationalism," *Modern Intellectual History* Vol. 16, No. 4 (December 2020): 1193–1224.

70. Naomi Saqr, *Walls of Silence: Media and Censorship in Syria* (London: Article 19, 1998), 17.

71. Muhammad al-Maghut, "After Long Thinking," in *The Fan of Swords: Poems*, trans. May Jayyusi and Naomi Shihab Nye (Washington, DC: Three Continents Press, 1991), 41–42.

72. Michaud (Seurat) and Paul, "The Importance of Bodyguards," 29.

73. Al-Asad, *Kadhālika Qāla al-Asad*, 329.

74. Shihada Khuri, *al-Adab fī al-Maydān* (Damascus: Maṭbaʿat Dimashq, 1950). See, too, Verena Klemm, "Different Notions of Commitment (*Iltizām*) and Committed Literature (*Al-Adab Al-Multazim*) in the Literary Circles of the Mashriq," *Arabic and Middle Eastern Literatures* Vol. 3, No. 1 (2000): 51–62, at 53; Yoav Di-Capua, *No Exit: Arab Existentialism, Jean-Paul Sartre, and Decolonization* (Chicago: University of Chicago Press, 2018), 91–92.

75. Hani al-Rahib, "Min al-Sayḥān ilā Ittiḥād al-Kuttāb," *Jaysh al-Shaʿb* (March 14, 1967): 20–21, at 20.

76. For example, Article 1 of Syria's General Law of Printed Matter dates from 1949 and remains in force. Under this clause, "presses, bookshops and publications of all kinds are free and nothing limits their freedom except this law." Saqr, *Walls of Silence*, 17.

77. Fadiyya al-Mulayyih Halawani, *al-Riwāya wa-l-Aydiyūlūjīyā fī Sūriya, 1958–1990* (Damascus: al-Ahālī, 1998); Muhammad Riyad Wattar, *Shakhṣiyyat al-Muthaqqaf fī al-Riwāya al-ʿArabiyya al-Sūriyya: Dirāsa* (Damascus: Ittiḥād al-Kuttāb al-ʿArab, 2000); Jamal Chehayed and Heidi Toelle, *al-Riwāya al-Sūriyya al-Muʿāṣira: al-Judhūr al-Thaqāfiyya wa-l-Tiqnīyāt al-Riwāʾiyya al-Jadīda: Aʿmāl al-Nadwa al-Munʿaqida fī 26 wa-27 Ayār 2000* (Damascus: al-Maʿhad al-Faransī li-l-Dirāsāt al-ʿArabiyya, 2001); Stefan G. Meyer, *The Experimental Arabic Novel: Postcolonial Literary Modernism in the Levant* (Albany: State University of New York Press, 2001); Elisabeth Vauthier, *La Création romanesque contemporaine en Syrie de 1967 à nos jours* (Damascus: IFPO, 2007); Alexa Firat, "Post-67 Discourse and the Syrian Novel: The Construction of an Autonomous Literary Field" (Ph.D. Diss., University of Pennsylvania, 2010); Firat, "Cultural Battles on the Literary Field: From the Syrian Writers' Collective to the Last Days of Socialist Realism in Syria," *Middle Eastern Literatures* Vol. 18, No. 2 (2015): 153–76. Richard Jacquemond tells a comparable story, rooted in Bourdieu's sociology of literature, culture, and taste, about writers and literature in Egypt. Jacquemond, *Entre scribes et écrivains: le champ littéraire dans l'Egypte contemporaine* (Paris: Sindbad Actes Sud, 2003).

78. Shakib al-Jabiri, *al-Aʿmāl al-Riwāʾiyya: Naham, Qadar Yalhū, Qaws Quzaḥ, Wadāʿan Ya Afāmiyā* (Damascus: Wizārat al-Thaqāfa, 2009). More research needs to be done on the history of literary culture in modern Syria, especially on the history of the novel.

79. Nabil Sulayman and Bu ʿAli Yasin, *al-Aydiyūlūjīyā wa-l-Adab fi Sūriya, 1967–1973* (Beirut: Dār Ibn Khaldūn, 1974).

80. ʿAdnan Bin Dhurayl, "al-Riwāya al-Sūriyya al-Muʿāṣira," *al-Maʿrifa* No. 146 (April 1974): 23–49, at 23. The cultural consequences of the 1967 defeat for Arabic intellectual culture have been amply described and analyzed. The defining work on the subject is Elizabeth Suzanne Kassab, *Contemporary Arab Thought: Cultural Critique in Comparative Perspective* (New York: Columbia University Press, 2010).

81. Sulayman and and Yasin returned to the subject a few years later in *Maʿārik Thaqāfiyya fī Sūriya, 1975–1977* (Beirut: Dār Ibn Rushd, 1980). See, too, Firat, "Cultural Battles on the Literary Field."

82. Hassan Abbas, "La Littérature en Syrie dans la seconde moitié du XXe siècle," *Europe*, No. 870 (octobre 2001): 171–97, at 181.

83. "Naḥwa Baʿth Thaqāfī ʿArabī," *al-Maʿrifa*, No. 150 (August 1974): 5–6.

84. Ibid., 5.

85. Ibid., 6.

86. Ibid., 6.

87. As the director of the Vanguard Theater (*Masraḥ al-Ṭalāʾiʿ*) at the Regional (Syrian) Seventh Vanguard Dayr al-Zur cultural festival said to anthropologist Evelyn Early in 1982: "Those who oppose the study of popular culture hate colloquial dialects. The Arab Writers' Union does not even recognize colloquial dialects; writers who write in the colloquial have been forced to write some of their works in classical Arabic so that they will be respected." Early, "Poetry and Pageants: Growing Up in the Syrian Vanguard," in *Children in the Muslim Middle East*, ed. Elizabeth Warnock Fernea (Austin: University of Texas Press, 1995), 410–19, at 412.

88. "Hadhihi al-Majalla," *al-Mawqif al-Adabī*, No. 1 (May 1971[?]): 3–4, at 3.

89. Ibid.

90. Ibid., 4.

91. Sidqi Ismaʿil, "al-Ḥiss al-Jamāhīrī wa-Riyāʾ al-Naqd al-Adabī," *al-Mawqif al-Adabī*, No. 1 (May 1971[?]): 5–16.

92. Sulayman and Yasin, *al-Aydiyūlūjīyā wa-l-Adab fī Sūriyā*, 178.

93. Ismaʿil, "al-Ḥiss al-Jamāhīrī," 6.

94. Ibid., 7.

95. Ibid., 8.

96. Sidqi Isma'il, "Ḥawla Mā Huwa Ṭalī'ī fī al-Adab," *al-Mawqif al-Adabī*, No. 5/6 (September 1971): 3–8, at 5.

97. Ibid., 6.

98. Ibid., 8.

99. Peter Bürger, *Theory of the Avant-Garde*, trans. Michael Shaw (Minneapolis: University of Minnesota Press, 1984), 91.

100. Husam al-Khatib, "al-Naqd al-Adabī: Fa'āliyya Mustaqilla am Tābi'a?" *al-Ma'rifa* No. 126 (August 1972): 61–69, at 65.

101. Ibid., 67.

102. Fredric Jameson, *Marxism and Form: Twentieth-Century Dialectical Theories of Literature* (Princeton, NJ: Princeton University Press, 1971), 172.

103. Ibid., 191, emphasis in the original.

104. 'Ali Najib Ibrahim, *Jamāliyyāt al-Riwāya: Dirāsa fī al-Riwāya al-Wāqi'iyya al-Sūriyya al-Mu'āṣira* (Damascus: Dār al-Yanābī', 1994).

105. Ibid., 25.

106. Georg Lukács, *The Theory of the Novel: A Historico-Philosophical Essay on the Forms of Great Epic Literature*, trans. Anna Bostock (Cambridge, MA: MIT Press, 1971), 17.

107. Robert B. Campbell, "Literary Criticism in Syria," *CEMAM Reports (Center for the Study of the Arab World)* Vol. 5 (1977): 223–52, at 247.

108. Firat, "Post-67 Discourse and the Syrian Novel," 66.

109. Viola Shafik notes that the French Mandate authorities hindered the completion of Syrian-made films during the colonial period. Shafik, *Arab Cinema: History and Cultural Identity* (Cairo: American University in Cairo Press, 2007 [1998]), 15. On the importance of gender in the French colonial administration of cinema under the Mandate in Syria, see Elizabeth Thompson, "Sex and Cinema in Damascus: The Gendered Politics of Public Space in a Colonial City," in *Middle Eastern Cities 1900–1950: Public Places and Public Spheres in Transformation*, ed. Hans Christian Korsholm Nielsen and Jakob Skovgaard-Petersen (Aarhus, Denmark: Aarhus University Press, 2001), 89–111.

110. Subhi al-Shaykh, "al-Mu'assasa al-'Āmma li-l-Sīnamā fī al-Quṭr al-'Arabī al-Sūrī Yaqūm bi-Wājibihā Kāmilan," *al-Jundī*, No. 785 (February 14, 1967): 16–17. The most important works on the history of cinema in Syria are Salah Duhni, *Sīnamā—Sīnamā* (Damascus: Ittiḥād al-Kuttāb al-'Arab, 1979); Mounir Zamni, "Le cinéma syrien au

passé et au présent," in *La Semaine du cinéma arabe: du 14 au 21 décembre 1987* (Paris: Institut du monde arabe, 1987), 67–71; Diana Jabbour, "Syrian Cinema: Culture and Ideology," in *Screens of Life: Critical Film Writing from the Arab World, Vol. 1*, ed. Alia Arasoughly (Quebec: World Heritage Press, 1996), 40–62; Cécile Boëx, "Syrian Cinema: Autonomous Spaces," *Film Comment* Vol. 42, No. 3 (2006): 12–15; Rasha Salti, "Critical Nationals: The Paradoxes of Syrian Cinema," in *Insights into Syrian Cinema: Essays and Conversations With Contemporary Filmmakers*, ed. Rasha Salti (New York: Rattapallax Press, 2006), 21–44; Mayyar Al-Roumi and Dorothée Schmid, "Le cinéma syrien: du militantisme au mutisme," in *Cinéma et monde musulman: cultures et interdits*, ed. Madkour Thabet, Mayyar Al-Roumi, and Dorothée Schmid (Paris: L'Harmattan, 2009), 4–26; Boëx, *Cinéma et politique en Syrie: écritures cinématographiques de la contestation en régime autoritaire, 1970–2010* (Paris: L'Harmattan, 2014).

111. "Durayd Laḥḥām: al-Sīnamā Wasīla li-l-Taʿbīr ʿan Fikra, Muqābala maʿa ʿAmmār Maṣāriʿ," *al-Ḥayā al-Sīnamāʾiyya*, No. 22 (Summer 1984): 12–17, at 17.

112. Margaret Litvin, "Translator's Introduction to 'Portrait of a Friend: Sonallah Ibrahim' by Mohamad Malas," *Alif: Journal of Comparative Poetics* No. 36 (2016): 201–25; Litvin, "Fellow Travelers? Two Arab Study Abroad Narratives of Moscow," in *Illusions and Disillusionment: Travel Writing in the Modern Age*, ed. Roberta Micallef (Boston: ILEX/Harvard University Press, 2018), 96–118. See, too, Gabrielle Chomentowski, "Filmmakers from Africa and the Middle East at VGIK During the Cold War," *Studies in Russian and Soviet Cinema* Vol. 13, No. 2 (2019): 189–98.

113. The same metaphor is invoked in publicity for a Syrian film festival that was held in Berlin in 2011: "A Silent Cinema—Highlights of Syrian Cinema." https://www.arsenal-berlin.de/en/arsenal-cinema/past-programs/single/article/1697/2804/archive/2009/october.html

114. *al-Ḥayā al-Sīnamāʾiyya*, editorial, No. 1 (Fall 1978): 3.

115. Najah al-ʿAttar, "Majalla Jadīda, Mutakhaṣṣiṣa Naṣdar al-Yawm," *al-Ḥayā al-Sīnamāʾiyya*, No. 1 (Fall 1978): 4–5.

116. Ibid., 4.

117. Ibid., 5.

118. *al-Ḥayā al-Sīnamāʾiyya*, editorial, No. 3 (July 1979): 30.

119. Muhammad Shahin, "Li-Mādha Mahrajān Dimashq al-Sīnamāʾī?" *al-Ḥayā al-Sīnamāʾiyya*, No. 4 (October 1979): 4–5.

120. Not to be confused with the 1972 Tewfik Saleh adaptation *The Dupes* (*al-Makhdūʿūn*), also produced by the NFO.

121. Neil Levi, "'Judge for Yourselves!'—The *Degenerate Art* Exhibition as Political Spectacle," *October* Vol. 85 (Summer 1998): 41–64. See, too, Jeff O'Brien, "'The Taste of Sand in the Mouth': 1939 and 'Degenerate' Egyptian Art," *Critical Interventions: Journal of African Art History and Visual Culture* Vol. 9, No. 1 (2015): 22–34.

122. Muhammad Shahin, "al-Fīlm . . . Mas'ūliyya Qawmiyya," *al-Ḥayā al-Sīnamā'iyya*, No. 2 (March 1979): 4–5, at 4.

123. Ibid., 5. Syrian alternative cinema is discussed briefly in Shafik, *Arab Cinema*, 154–58.

124. Muhammad Shahin, "al-Sīnamā al-latī Nurīd," *al-Ḥayā al-Sīnamā'iyya*, No. 5 (Winter 1980): 4–5.

125. Ibid., 4.

126. Ibid., 5.

127. In his study of the films of Moroccan director Moumen Smihi, Peter Limbrick argues that film scholars can do more to break down the binary opposition between "commercial, popular" cinema and "smaller, national cinemas on an art cinema model." Limbrick, *Arab Modernism as World Cinema: The Films of Moumen Smihi* (Berkeley: University of California Press, 2020), 12.

128. Shahin, "al-Sīnamā al-latī Nurīd," 5.

129. Nabil Maleh, "al-Sīnamā . . . Lughat al-ʿAṣr," *al-Maʿrifa*, No. 131 (January 1973): 7–21, at 20.

130. Najah al-ʿAttar, "Hānūyī al-ʿArab!" in *Min Mufakkirat al-Ayyām: Maqālāt wa-Dhikrayāt* (Damascus: Wizārat al-Thaqāfa wa-l-Irshād al-Qawmī, 1982), 303–7, at 305.

131. Fatima Mohsen, "Cultural Totalitarianism," in *Iraq Since the Gulf War: Prospects for Democracy*, ed. Fran Hazelton (London: Zed Books, 1994), 7–19, at 11.

132. Liu Kang, "Hegemony and Cultural Revolution," *New Literary History* Vol. 28, No. 1 (Winter 1997): 69–86. See, too, Yaseen Noorani, *Culture and Hegemony in the Colonial Middle East* (New York: Palgrave Macmillan, 2010); Brecht De Smet, *Gramsci on Tahrir: Revolution and Counter-Revolution in Egypt* (London: Pluto Press, 2016).

133. Antonio Gramsci, *Selections from the Prison Notebooks of Antonio Gramsci*, ed. and trans. Quintin Hoare and Geoffrey Nowell Smith (New York: International Publishers, 1971), 149.

134. Katerina Clark, *Moscow, the Fourth Rome: Stalinism, Cosmopolitanism, and the Evolution of Soviet Culture, 1931–1941* (Cambridge, MA: Harvard University Press, 2011), 113.

135. Al-Qudsī, *al-Baṭal wa-l-Tārīkh*, 15.

136. Ibid., 18, emphasis added.

CHAPTER 2

1. Zakariya Tamir, "Rijāl" in *al-Ḥiṣrim: Qiṣaṣ* (Beirut: Riyad el-Rayyes, 2000), 31.

2. John Berger, *Ways of Seeing* (London: Penguin, 1972), 64.

3. Kaja Silverman, *Male Subjectivity at the Margins* (London: Routledge, 1992), 47.

4. Others have offered accounts of the gender politics and gendered symbolism of Syrian literature and film. Further research can be done on the ideological and iconography of gender as it pertains to women and femininity, a topic I do not engage with here for reasons of space, not because it does not deserve attention. In the sparse extant scholarship on modern and contemporary Syrian cultural production and gender, the focus tends to be on women, with some important exceptions. See Samira Aghacy, *Masculine Identity in the Fiction of the Arab East Since 1967* (Syracuse, NY: Syracuse University Press, 2009); Rebecca Joubin, *The Politics of Love: Sexuality, Gender, and Marriage in Syrian Television Drama* (Lanham, MD: Lexington Books, 2013).

5. Zeina G. Halabi, *The Unmaking of the Arab Intellectual: Prophecy, Exile and the Nation* (Edinburgh: Edinburgh University Press, 2017).

6. Standout examples of Middle East masculinity studies that deal with culture—broadly construed—include Mai Ghoussoub and Emma Sinclair-Webb, eds., *Imagined Masculinities: Male Identity and Culture in the Modern Middle East* (London: Saqi, 2000); Elizabeth F. Thompson, "Soldiers, Patriarchs, and Bureaucrats: Paternal Republicanism in French Syria and Lebanon," in *Representing Masculinity: Male Citizenship in Modern Western Culture*, ed. Stefan Dudink, Karen Hagemann, and Anna Clark (New York: Palgrave Macmillan , 2007), 213–33; Nouri Gana, "Bourguiba's Sons: Melancholy Manhood in Modern Tunisian Cinema," *Journal of North African Studies* Vol. 15, No. 1 (March 2010): 105–26; Paul Amar, "Middle East Masculinity Studies: Discourses of 'Men in Crisis,' Industries of Gender in Revolution," *Journal of Middle East Women's Studies* Vol. 7, No. 3 (Fall 2011): 36–70; Wilson Chacko Jacob, *Working Out Egypt: Effendi Masculinity and Subject Formation in Colonial Modernity, 1870–1940* (Durham, NC: Duke University Press, 2011); Sune Haugbolle, "The (Little) Militia Man: Memory and Militarized Masculinity in Lebanon," *Journal of Middle East Women's Studies* Vol. 8, No. 1 (Winter 2012): 115–39; Alessandro Columbu, "*Hadatha*, Dissent and Hegemonic Masculinity in the Short Stories of Zakariyya Tamir," in *Generations of Dissent: Intellectuals, Cultural Production, and the State in the Middle East and North Africa*, ed. Alexa Firat and R. Shareah Taleghani (Syracuse, NY: Syracuse University Press, 2020), 52–79.

7. Aghacy, *Masculine Identity*, 17.

8. Alexa Firat, "Post-67 Discourse and the Syrian Novel: The Construction of an Autonomous Literary Field" (Ph.D. Diss., University of Pennsylvania, 2010); Firat, "Cultural Battles on the Literary Field: From the Syrian Writers' Collective to the Last Days of Socialist Realism in Syria," *Middle Eastern Literatures* Vol. 18, No. 2 (2015): 153–76.

9. Hanna Mina, *al-Maṣābīḥ al-Zurq* (Beirut: Dār al-Ādāb, 1954).

10. Firat, "Post-67 Discourse and the Syrian Novel, 40. See, too, Muhammad Rajab Baridi, *Ḥannā Mīna: Kātib al-Kifāḥ wa-l-Faraḥ* (Beirut: Dār al-Ādāb, 1993). In his own words, see Hanna Mina, *Baqāyā Ṣuwar: Riwāya* (Damascus: Manshūrāt Wizārat al-Thaqāfa wa-l-Irshād al-Qawmī, 1975), translated as *Fragments of Memory: A Story of a Syrian Family,* trans. Olive E. Kenny and Lorne Kenny (Austin: Center for Middle Eastern Studies, University of Texas, 1993); and Hanna Mina, *Kayfa Ḥamaltu al-Qalam* (Beirut: Dār al-Ādāb, 1986).

11. Hanna Mina, "Līnīn . . . wa-l-Adāb," *al-Ṭarīq* No. 4–5 (April–May 1970): 186–97, at 187.

12. Hanna Mina and Najah al-ʿAttar, *Adab al-Ḥarb* (Beirut: Dār al-Ādāb, 1979), 19. A somewhat more nuanced appraisal of ideological diversity in the Syrian cultural field during that period can be found in Nabil Sulayman and Bu ʿAli Yasin, *al-Aydiyūlūjīyā wa-l-Adab fī Sūriya, 1967–1973* (Beirut: Dār Ibn Khaldūn, 1974).

13. Hanna Mina, *Nihāyat Rajul Shujāʿ: Riwāya* (Beirut: Dār al-Ādāb, 1989), 17.

14. Ibid., 59.

15. Ibid., 62.

16. Ibid., 67.

17. Ibid., 71.

18. There is a meaningful difference between representations of prison and those of imprisonment, though, and the genre of "prison literature." The best work on the subject is Shareah Taleghani, *Readings in Syrian Prison Literature: The Poetics of Human Rights* (Syracuse, NY: Syracuse University Press, 2021).

19. Mina, *Nihāyat Rajul Shujāʿ*, 89.

20. Aghacy, *Masculine Identity*, 35.

21. Ibid., 36.

22. Mina, *Nihāyat Rajul Shujāʿ*, 106.

23. Ibid., 104. There is an uncanny (and almost surely coincidental) similarity here to the (imaginary) irruption of horns from the head of the protagonist in Faysal Khartash, *Roundabout of Death*, trans. Max Weiss (New York: New Vessel Press, 2021), 13: "My head had always been round, but now it appeared to have become egg-shaped.

At least that's the way it seemed as I looked at myself in the bathroom mirror; all of a sudden it was elongated, and it seemed as if there were two tiny bumps bulging out in arousal, making me look like some kind of sexual deviant, so I quickly smoothed down my hair to cover them. There might have been something wrong with the mirror, or maybe something wrong with me."

24. Mina, *Nihāyat Rajul Shujā'*, 211–12.

25. Ibid., 228.

26. Ibid., 243.

27. Ibid., 301–2.

28. Ibid., 367.

29. Ibid., 378.

30. Ibid., 406.

31. Ibid., 407.

32. Christa Salamandra, "Consuming Damascus: Public Culture and the Construction of Social Identity," in *Mass Mediations: New Approaches to Popular Culture in the Middle East and Beyond*, ed. Walter Armbrust (Berkeley: University of California Press, 2000), 182–202.

33. Christa Salamandra, *A New Old Damascus: Authenticity and Distinction in Urban Syria* (Bloomington: Indiana University Press, 2004), 122.

34. Joubin, *The Politics of Love*, 163–71.

35. Ibid., 164.

36. Ibid., 164.

37. Ibid., 166–67.

38. Ibid., 171.

39. Mamdouh Azzam, *Mi'rāj al-Mawt: Riwāya* (Suwayda, Syria: Dār Samarqand li-l-Thaqāfa wa-l-Nashr, 2009 [1988]); Mamdouh Azzam, *Ascension to Death*, trans. Max Weiss (London: Haus, 2018). My references to the novel are from the English-language edition.

40. While Azzam has continued writing throughout the time of the Syria War, his best received works, after *Mi'rāj al-Mawt*, are *Qasr al-Maṭar: Riwāya* (Damascus: Wizārat al-Thaqāfa, 1998) and *Arḍ al-Kalām: Riwāya* (Damascus: Dār al-Madā, 2005).

41. Azzam, *Ascension to Death*, 86.

42. Ibid., 87.

43. Ibid., 88.

44. Ibid., 99.

45. Ibid., 112.

46. Ibid., 113.

47. Ibid., 11.

48. Ibid., 45.

49. Ibid., 47.

50. Ibid., 49.

51. Ibid., 55.

52. Ibid., 58.

53. Ibid., 52.

54. Ibid., 65.

55. Ibid., 67–68.

56. Ibid., 117.

57. ʿAli al-ʿAqabani, "Raḥīl al-Mukhrij Riyāḍ Shayyā," *al-Ḥayā*, June 16, 2016.

58. I remain extremely grateful to Irène Labeyrie for sharing a digital copy of *Al-Lajāt* with me, and one hopes that the resources will be found to properly restore the remaining extant copies of the film.

59. Emre Çaglayan, "The Aesthetics of Boredom: Slow Cinema and the Virtues of the Long Take in *Once Upon a Time in Anatolia*," *Projections* Vol. 10, No. 1 (Summer 2016): 63–85, at 64. See, too, Matthew Flanagan, "Towards an Aesthetic of Slow in Contemporary Cinema," *16:9* Vol. 29, No. 6 (November 2008). http://www.16-9.dk/2008-11/side1 1_inenglish.htm; Jonathan Romney, "In Search of Lost Time," *Sight & Sound* Vol. 20, No. 2 (February 2010): 43–44; Manohla Dargis and A. O. Scott, "In Defense of the Slow and the Boring," *New York Times*, June 5, 2011. https://www.nytimes.com/2011/06/05/movies/films-in-defense-of-slow-and-boring.html; Emre Çaglayan, "Screening Boredom: The History and Aesthetics of Slow Cinema" (Ph.D. Diss., University of Kent, 2014).

60. Khalil Suwaylih, "*al-Fīlm* Al-Lajāt *li-l-Mukhrij Riyāḍ Shayyā: Arāʾ wa-Shahādat*," *al-Ḥayā al-Sīnamāʾiyya* No. 46 (Autumn 1996): 116–20, at 117.

61. In Chapter 4 I return to the trope of mirrors and the politics of vision in my discussion of Samar Yazbek's 2010 novel *In Her Mirrors* (*Lahā Marāyā*).

62. Ibid., 116.

63. André Bazin, *What Is Cinema? Vol. 1*, trans. Hugh Gray (Berkeley: University of California Press, 2005), 10.

64. Suwaylih, "*al-Fīlm* Al-Lajāt," 117.

65. Diana Jabbour, "Syrian Cinema: Culture and Ideology," in *Screens of Life: Critical Film Writing from the Arab World, Volume 1*, ed. Alia Arasoughly (Quebec: World Heritage Press, 1996), 40–62, at 50.

66. Mayyar Al-Roumi and Dorothée Schmid, "Le cinéma syrien: du militantisme au mutisme," in *Cinéma et monde musulman: cultures et interdits*, ed. Madkour Thabet, Mayyar Al-Roumi, and Dorothée Schmid (Paris: L'Harmattan, 2009), 4–26, at 18–19.

67. Riyad Shayya in conversation with Salwa Na'imi in *Barīd al-Janūb*, cited in Suwaylih, "*al-Fīlm* Al-Lajāt," 120.

68. Historian Robert Blecher stakes out this position in his interpretation of *Al-Lajāt*. "The de-emphasis of dialogue, however, comes at a price: while the film's scenes are beautifully shot," Blecher writes, "the connections between them are often unclear. Drifting, the viewer sometimes feels like a lost tourist, impressed with the scenery but not really sure where s/he is going." Blecher, "History as Social Critique in Syrian Film," *Middle East Report* 204 (Jul.–Sep., 1997): 44–45, at 45.

69. Christa Salamandra, "Nabil Maleh: Syria's Leopard (Syria)," in *Ten Arab Filmmakers: Political Dissent and Social Critique*, ed. Josef Gugler (Bloomington: Indiana University Press, 2015), 17–33, at 20.

70. Suwaylih, "*al-Fīlm* Al-Lajāt," 118.

71. Rebecca Joubin, "Syrian Drama and the Politics of Dignity," *Middle East Report* 268 (Fall 2013): 26–29, at 26.

72. Jabbour, "Syrian Cinema," 42–43.

73. "Layālī Ibn Āwā: An Takūn Lidayka Afkār wa-fī Qalamika Ḥibr," *al-Ḥayā al-Sīnamā'iyya* No. 35–36 (Spring–Summer 1989): 5–7, at 5.

74. Ibid.

75. Muhammad Ahmad Salih, "Nujūm al-Nahār: Wilādat Fīlm Jadīd," *al-Ḥayā al-Sīnamā'iyya* Vol. 33–34 (Summer 1988): 4–10, at 5.

76. Ibid.

77. Bandar 'Abd al-Hamid, "Liqā' ma'a Usāma Muḥammad," *al-Ḥayā al-Sīnamā'iyya* No. 37 (Spring 1990): 11–17, at 15.

78. Cécile Boëx. "Syrian Cinema: Autonomous Spaces," *Film Comment* Vol. 42, No. 3 (2006): 12–15, at 14.

79. Viola Shafik, *Arab Cinema: History and Cultural Identity* (Cairo: American University in Cairo Press, 2007 [1998]), 245–46.

80. Rasha Salti, "Nujum Al-Nahar: Stars in Broad Daylight," in *The Cinema of North Africa and the Middle East*, ed. Gönül Dönmez-Colin (London: Wallflower Press, 2007), 101–11, at 110.

81. Shafik, *Arab Cinema*, 67.

82. Sadiq Jalal al-ʿAzm, *al-Naqd al-Dhātī baʿda al-Ḥazīma* (Beirut: Dār al-Ṭalīʿa, 1968); al-ʿAzm, *Self-Criticism After the Defeat*, trans. George Stergios (London: Saqi, 2011).

83. Al-ʿAzm addressed the problem of religious intolerance in the Arab world in another work, *Naqd al-Fikr al-Dīnī* (Beirut: Dār al-Ṭalīʿa, 1969); al-ʿAzm, *Critique of Religious Thought*, trans. George Stergios and Mansour Ajami (Berlin: Gerlach Press, 2015). See, too, Max Weiss, "True Believers in the Modern Middle East," in *Formations of Belief: Historical Approaches to Religion and the Secular*, ed. Philip Nord, Katja Guenther, and Max Weiss (Princeton, NJ: Princeton University Press, 2019), 150–62.

84. Elizabeth Suzanne Kassab, *Contemporary Arab Thought: Cultural Critique in Comparative Perspective* (New York: Columbia University Press, 2010).

85. One exemplary exception is Aghacy, *Masculine Identity*.

86. David Scott, "The Dialectic of Defeat: An Interview with Rupert Lewis," *Small Axe* Vol. 5, No. 2 (September 2001): 85–177, at 86.

87. Columbu, "*Hadatha*, Dissent and Hegemonic Masculinity," 78. On the very short story in Arabic, see Ibrahim Taha, "The Modern Arabic Very Short Story: A Generic Approach," *Journal of Arabic Literature* Vol. 31, No. 1 (2000): 59–84.

88. Tamir, "Intiẓār Imrāʾa," in *al-Ḥiṣrim: Qiṣaṣ*, 155.

89. R. W. Connell and James W. Messerschmidt, "Hegemonic Masculinity: Rethinking the Concept," *Gender & Society* Vol. 19, No. 6 (December 2005): 829–59, at 832.

90. Joubin, *The Politics of Love*, 118.

CHAPTER 3

1. Durayd Lahham, quoted in Riad Ismat, "The Arab World's Comic Gadfly: Syria's Duraid Lahham," *The Middle East* (March 1980): 52–54, at 53, cited in Evelyn A. Early, "Darid Laham: Political Satirist as Modern Storyteller," in *Everyday Life in the Muslim Middle East*, ed. Donna Lee Bowen and Evelyn A. Early (Bloomington, IN: Indiana University Press, 1993), 264–70, at 269.

2. Durayd Lahham, quoted in Michael Slackman, "An Arab Artist Says All the World Really Isn't a Stage," *New York Times*, August 19, 2006.

3. Theodor W. Adorno, *Minima Moralia: Reflections from Damaged Life* (London: New Left Books, 1974), 210.

4. James Bennet, "The Enigma of Damascus," *New York Times*, July 10, 2005; Joan Juliet Buck, "Asma al-Assad: A Rose in the Desert," *Vogue*, March 2011; Lisa Wedeen,

Authoritarian Apprehensions: Ideology, Judgment, and Mourning in Syria (Chicago: University of Chicago Press, 2019), esp. 27–29.

5. Khaled Khalifa garnered noteworthy attention around this time, for example, appearing on the world literary stage for his warmly received third novel, *In Praise of Hatred* (*Madīḥ al-Karāhiyya*). Robert F. Worth, "A Bloody Era of Syria's History Informs a Writer's Banned Novel," *New York Times*, April 12, 2008. See Khaled Khalifa, *Madīḥ al-Karāhiyya: Riwāya* (Beirut: Dār al-Ādāb, 2008) [Khaled Khalifa, *In Praise of Hatred*, trans. Leri Price (London: Doubleday, 2012)]. Khalifa's 2016 novel *Dying Is Hard Work* is discussed in Chapter 6.

6. Slackman, "An Arab Artist Says All the World Really Isn't a Stage."

7. Riad Ismat, "The Arab World's Comic Gadfly: Syria's Duraid Lahham," *The Middle East* (March 1980): 52–54, at 53.

8. Lisa Wedeen, *Ambiguities of Domination: Politics, Rhetoric, and Symbols in Contemporary Syria* (Chicago: University of Chicago Press, 1999), 88–92. Wedeen deepens her critique (and our understanding) of political power in Syrian cultural production in "Ideology and Humor in Dark Times: Notes from Syria," *Critical Inquiry* Vol. 39 (Summer 2013): 841–73; and *Authoritarian Apprehensions: Ideology, Judgment, and Mourning in Syria* (Chicago: University of Chicago Press, 2019).

9. Among many other facets of cultural production, Boëx has studied "commodification" and "popularization" of cinema in the Syrian space. Her massive bibliography includes "Syrian Cinema: Autonomous Spaces," *Film Comment* Vol. 42, No. 3 (2006): 12–16; "*Tahiyā as-Sīnamā!* Produire du sens: les enjeux politiques de l'expression dans l'espace public," *Revue des mondes musulmans et de la Méditerranée* 115–116 (2006): 231–48; "Être cinéaste syrien. Expériences et trajectoires multiples de la création sous contrainte," in *Itinéraires esthétiques et scènes culturelles au proche-orient*, eds. Nicolas Puig and Franck Mermier (Beirut: Institut français du Proche-Orient, 2007), 175–201; "La Contestation médiatisée par le monde de l'art en contexte autoritaire: l'expérience cinématographique en Syrie au sein de l'organisme général du cinéma 1964–2010" (Ph.D. Diss., Université Paul Cézanne-Aix Marseille III, 2011); "The End of the State Monopoly over Culture: Toward the Commodification of Cultural and Artistic Production," *Middle East Critique* Vol. 20, No. 2 (Summer 2011): 139–55; "La Grammaire iconographique de la révolte en Syrie: usages, techniques et supports," *Cultures Conflicts* No. 91/92 (automne/hiver 2013): 65–80; *Cinéma et politique en Syrie: écritures cinématographiques de la contestation en régime autoritaire: 1970–2010* (Paris: L'Harmattan, 2014); "La Vidéo comme outil de l'action collective et de la lutte armée," in *Pas de printemps pour la*

Syrie: les clés pour comprendre les acteurs et les défis de la crise (2011–2013), ed. François Burgat and Bruno Paoli (Paris: La Découverte, 2013), 173–84.

10. For a brilliant example of this kind of analysis, see Wayne Koestenbaum, *The Anatomy of Harpo Marx* (Berkeley: University of California Press, 2012). I return to this point about the cultural politics of comedy—laughter and the carnivalesque—in the 1993 film *The Extras (al-Kūmbārs)* by Nabil Maleh and the 2004 novel *The Silence and the Roar (al-Ṣamt wa-l-Ṣakhab)* by Nihad Sirees (Chapter 4); and in the 2017 novel *The Cranes (al-Gharānīq)* by Mazin ʿArafa (Chapter 6).

11. Masʿud Hamdan, "The Carnivalesque Satires of Muhammad Al-Maghut and Durayd Lahham: A Modern Layer of Comic Folk Drama in Arab Tradition," *Journal of Dramatic Theory and Criticism* Vol. 18, No. 2 (Spring 2004): 137–48. See, too, Hamdan, *Poetics, Politics and Protest in Arab Theatre: The Bitter Cup and the Holy Rain* (Sussex, UK: Sussex Academic Press, 2005).

12. Norman Manea, "On Clowns: The Dictator and the Artist," *Literary Review* Vol. 35, No. 1 (Fall 1991): 5–25; Paul Bouissac, *The Semiotics of Clowns and Clowning: Rituals of Transgression and the Theory of Laughter* (London: Bloomsbury Academic, 2015).

13. Film historian Viola Shafik notes that Lahham's films "have been well received by Egyptian audiences" in part because they rely upon "the same mixture of social criticism, verbal comedy, musical inserts, and theatrical performances as many Egyptian feature films." Shafik, *Arab Cinema: History and Cultural Identity* (Cairo: American University in Cairo Press, 2007 [1998]), 27.

14. Faruq al-Jammal, *Durayd Laḥḥām: Mishwār al-ʿUmr* (Beirut: Sharikat al-Maṭbūʿāt, 2002), 25–39.

15. On *October Village*, see Edward Ziter, *Political Performance in Syria: From the Six-Day War to the Syrian Uprising* (New York: Palgrave Macmillan, 2015), 96–102; Wedeen, *Ambiguities of Domination*, 93–95. On *Cheers Oh Homeland*, see Ziter, *Political Performance in Syria*, 210–12; Wedeen, *Ambiguities of Domination*, 95–97.

16. W.J.T. Mitchell, *What Do Pictures Want? The Lives and Loves of Images* (Chicago: University of Chicago Press, 2005), 25.

17. Ismat, "The Arab World's Comic Gadfly," 54.

18. Sune Haugbolle, "The (Little) Militia Man: Memory and Militarized Masculinity in Lebanon," *Journal of Middle East Women's Studies* Vol. 8, No. 1 (Winter 2012): 115–39; Rebecca Joubin, "The Politics of the *Qabaday* (Tough Man) and the Changing Father Figure in Syrian Television Drama," *Journal of Middle East Women's Studies* Vol. 12, No. 1 (2016): 50–67.

19. Hafiz al-Asad, *Kadhālika Qāla al-Asad*, ed. Mustafa Tlas (Damascus: Dār Ṭlās, 2001), 79.

20. Hannah Arendt, *On Violence* (New York: Harcourt, Brace & Company, 1970), 45.

21. Adorno, *Minima Moralia*, 210.

22. Georges Bataille, "Un-Knowing: Laughter and Tears, trans. Annette Michelson," *October* Vol. 36 (Spring 1986): 89–102, at 97.

23. Rebecca Joubin, *The Politics of Love: Sexuality, Gender, and Marriage in Syrian Television Drama* (Lanham, MD: Lexington Books, 2013), 116.

24. Alasdair Drysdale, "The Asad Regime and Its Troubles," *MERIP Reports* Vol. 12 (Nov.–Dec., 1982): 3–11, at 7. See, too, for example, Omar Ilsley, "Syria: Hama Massacre," in *Hushed Voices: Unacknowledged Atrocities of the 20th Century*, ed. Heribert Adam (Highclere, UK: Berkshire Academic Press, 2011), 125–37.

25. Noël Carroll, *Theorizing the Moving Image* (New York: Cambridge University Press, 1996), 150. See, too, Donald Crafton, "Pie and Chase: Gag, Spectacle and Narrative in Slapstick Comedy," in *Classical Hollywood Comedy*, ed. Kristine Brunovska Karnick and Henry Jenkins (New York: Routledge, 1995), 106–19.

26. Ziter, *Political Performance in Syria*, 100.

27. "Durayd Laḥḥām: al-Sīnamā Wasīla li-l-Taʿbīr ʿan Fikra, Muqābala maʿa ʿAmmār Muṣāriʿ," *al-Ḥayā al-Sīnamāʾiyya*, No. 22 (Summer 1984): 12–17, at 16, emphasis added.

28. Andrew Hewitt, *Fascist Modernism: Aesthetics, Politics, and the Avant-Garde* (Stanford, CA: Stanford University Press, 1993), 169.

29. André Bazin, *What is Cinema? Vol. 1*, trans. Hugh Gray (Berkeley: University of California Press, 2005), 145.

30. Patrick Seale, *Asad of Syria: The Struggle for the Middle East* (London: I. B. Taurus, 1988), 174.

31. Wedeen, *Ambiguities of Domination*, 98.

32. Shafik, *Arab Cinema*, 36. The same is true of a dream sequence that skewers authoritarian power in Samir Zikra's 1986 film *Events of the Coming Year* (*Waqāʾiʿ al-ʿĀmm al-Muqbil*). See Wedeen, *Ambiguities of Domination*, 117–20.

33. Wedeen, *Ambiguities of Domination*, 99.

34. Robert B. Pippin, *Filmed Thought: Cinema as Reflective Form* (Chicago: University of Chicago Press, 2020), 107. See, too, Carl Plantinga, "Art Moods and Human Moods in Narrative Cinema," *New Literary History* Vol. 43, No. 3 (Summer 2012): 455–75.

35. Pippin, *Filmed Thought*, 107.

36. miriam cooke, *Dissident Syria: Making Oppositional Arts Official* (Durham NC: Duke University Press, 2007).

37. Marilyn Booth, "Oppositional Arts in Syria," *Review of Middle East Studies* Vol. 43, No. 1 (Summer 2009): 48–51, at 50.

38. Lisa Wedeen, "Tolerated Parodies of Politics in Syrian Cinema," in *Film in the Middle East and North Africa: Creative Dissidence*, ed. Joseph Gugler (Austin: University of Texas Press, 2011), 104–12. See, too, Gayatri Devi and Najat Rahman, eds., *Humor in Middle Eastern Cinema* (Detroit: Wayne State University Press, 2014).

39. "Durayd Laḥḥām: al-Sīnamā Wasīla li-l-Taʿbīr ʿan Fikra," 14.

40. Slavoj Žižek, *Did Somebody Say Totalitarianism? Five Interventions in the (Mis) use of a Notion* (London: Verso, 2001), 85.

41. "Durayd Laḥḥām: al-Sīnamā Wasīla li-l-Taʿbīr ʿan Fikra," 16.

42. In addition to Nihad Qalʿi and Muhammad al-Maghut, cultural icons with substantial fan bases inside and outside of Syria can be profitably compared with Lahham, among them Humam Hut (Homam Hout). Edward Ziter refers to Hout as a" vaudeville star" who "had previously bent over backwards to demonstrate his loyalty to the Assad regime. However, he publicly endorsed the resistance after fighting spread to his home town of Aleppo." Ziter, *Political Performance in Syria*, 10. See, too, George Baghdadi. "Political Satire Rocks the Boat in Syria," *CBS News*, April 30,2010. https://www.cbsnews.com/news/political-satire-rocks-the-boat-in-syria/. Thanks to Saphe Shamoun for reminding me of this connection.

43. Ibrahim al-Jaradi, "Mīlūdrāmā, hadhā al-Fann al-Mu'aththir wa-l-Bā'isa," *al-Ḥayā al-Sīnamā'iyya*, Vol. 6 (Spring 1980): 65–71.

44. Peter Brooks, *The Melodramatic Imagination: Balzac, Henry James, Melodrama, and the Mode of Excess* (New Haven: Yale University Press, 1976), 205, my emphasis. On melodrama outside the canon of European literature, see, for example, Joel Gordon, *Revolutionary Melodrama: Popular Film and Civic Identity in Nasser's Egypt* (Chicago: Middle East Documentation Center, 2002); Lila Abu-Lughod, *Dramas of Nationhood: The Politics of Television in Egypt* (Chicago: University of Chicago Press, 2005); Ravi Vasudevan, *The Melodramatic Public: Film Form and Spectatorship in Indian Cinema* (Raniket: Permanent Black, 2010).

45. Georg Lukács, *The Theory of the Novel: A Historico-Philosophical Essay on the Forms of Great Epic Literature*, trans. Anna Bostock (Cambridge, MA: MIT Press, 1971), 35.

46. Gilles Deleuze, *Cinema 1: The Movement-Image*, trans. Hugh Tomlinson and Barbara Habberjam (Minneapolis: University of Minnesota Press, 1989), x. See, too, Pippin, *Filmed Thought*.

47. Hewitt, *Fascist Modernism*, 169.

48. Slackman, "An Arab Artist Says All the World Really Isn't a Stage."

CHAPTER 4

Note: Portions of this chapter were published previously in different form in "Who Laughs Last: Literary Transformations of Syrian Authoritarianism," in *Middle East Authoritarianisms: Governance, Contestation, and Regime Resilience in Syria and Iran*, ed. Steven Heydemann and Reinoud Leenders (Stanford, CA: Stanford University Press, 2013), 143–65; and "Sight, Sound, and Surveillance in Baʿthist Syria: The Fiction of Politics in Rūzā Yasīn Ḥasan's *Rough Draft* and Samar Yazbik's *In Her Mirrors*," *Journal of Arabic Literature* Vol. 48, No. 2 (November 2017): 211–44.

1. Muhammad al-Maghut, "The Tattoo," in *The Fan of Swords: Poems*, trans. May Jayyusi and Naomi Shihab Nye (Washington, D.C.: Three Continents Press, 1991), 21–22, at 21.

2. Hannah Arendt, *The Origins of Totalitarianism* (New York: Harcourt, Brace, 1951), 431.

3. Wai Chee Dimock, "A Theory of Resonance," *PMLA* Vol. 112, No. 5 (October 1997): 1060–71, at 1066.

4. Nabil Maleh had first-hand experience with film comedy, having directed Durayd Lahham in *Ghawār James Bond* (1974). For more on Maleh and *The Extras*, see Josef Gugler, "*The Extras* (Nabil Maleh): Lovers Suffer the Twin Repressions of Patriarchal Cuture and a Police State," in *Film in the Middle East and North Africa: Creative Dissidence*, ed. Josef Gugler (Austin: University of Texas Press, 2011), 125–33; Christa Salamandra, "Nabil Maleh: Syria's Leopard (Syria)" in *Ten Arab Filmmakers: Political Dissent and Social Critique*, ed. Josef Gugler (Bloomington: Indiana University Press, 2015), 17–33.

5. Lisa Wedeen, *Ambiguities of Domination: Politics, Rhetoric, and Symbols in Contemporary Syria* (Chicago: University of Chicago Press, 1999), 117.

6. I borrow this use of *mitsprechen*—"voices speaking with and through one another, *at the same time*"—as a cultural manifestation of speaking in a collective voice from Michael G. Levine, *The Belated Witness: Literature, Testimony, and the Question of Holocaust Survival* (Stanford, CA: Stanford University Press, 2006), 4. I will elaborate

on the point in Chapter 5 in order to show how witnessing in literature and film converged with a broader collective attempt at speaking-with, or *mitsprechen*, in the time of the Syria War.

7. Lisa Wedeen, "Acting 'As If': Symbolic Politics and Social Control in Syria," *Comparative Studies in Society and History* Vol. 40, No. 3 (July 1998): 503–23.

8. Oussama Mohammad, "Tea is Coffee, Coffee is Tea: Freedom in a Closed Room," in *Insights into Syrian Cinema: Essays and Conversations with Contemporary Filmmakers*, ed. Rasha Salti (New York: Rattapallax Press, 2006), 149–63, at 162.

9. ʿAbbas Beydoun, "Riwāyat 'al-Mukhābarāt,'" *al-Safīr*, August 12, 2009.

10. Ibid. The *mukhābarāt* novel can be situated in relation to a slightly different style of fiction writing, namely the "dictator novel," which is on display in *The Silence and the Roar* (discussed in this chapter) and recurs in my discussion of the 2017 Mazin ʿArafa novel, *The Cranes* (*al-Gharānīq*) (Chapter 6). ʿAbbas Beydoun, "'Dīktātūr' al-Riwāya al-ʿArabiyya," *al-Safīr*, October 15, 2010. The dictator novel is typically associated with Eastern Europe, South America, and sub-Saharan Africa. Mario Vargas Llosa and Gabriel García Márquez, among others, explore the psychology of the dictator in order to shed light on the pathologies and corruption of modern Latin American societies. Gabriel García Márquez, *The Autumn of the Patriarch*, trans. Gregory Rabassa (New York: Harper & Row, 1976); García Márquez, *The General in His Labyrinth*, trans. Edith Grossman (New York: A. A. Knopf, 1990); Mario Vargas Llosa, *The Feast of the Goat*, trans. Edith Grossman (New York: Farrar, Straus, and Giroux, 2001). See, too, Roberto González Echevarría, "The Dictatorship of Rhetoric/the Rhetoric of Dictatorship: Carpentier, García Márquez and Roa Bastos," *Latin American Research Review* Vol. 15, No. 3 (1980): 205–28; Gerald M. Martin, "On Dictatorship and Rhetoric in Latin American Writing: A Counter-Proposal," *Latin American Research Review* Vol. 17, No. 3 (1982): 207–27; Hosam Aboul-Ela, "Imagining more Autumns for North Africa's Patriarchs: The Dictator Novel in Egypt," *Words Without Borders*, February 11, 2011. https://www.wordswithoutborders.org/dispatches/article/imagining-more-autumns-for-north-africas-patriarchs-the-dictator-novel-in-e; Magalí Armillas-Tiseyra, *The Dictator Novel: Writers and Politics in the Global South* (Evanston, IL: Northwestern University Press, 2019).

11. Gamal al-Ghitani, *Waqāʾiʿ Ḥārat al-Zaʿfarānī* (Cairo: Maṭbaʿat Madbūlī, 1976) [Gamal al-Ghitani, *The Zafarani Files* trans. Farouk Abdel Wahab (Cairo: American University in Cairo Press, 2009)]; al-Ghitani, *al-Zaynī Barakāt: Riwāya* (Cairo:

Maktabat Madbūlī, 1975) [al-Ghitani, *Zayni Barakat* trans. Farouk Abdel Wahab (Cairo: The American University in Cairo Press, 2004)].

12. Sonallah Ibrahim, *Tilka al-Rā'iḥa* (Cairo, 1966) [Ibrahim, *That Smell: &, Notes from Prison*, trans. Robyn Creswell (New York: New Directions, 2013)]; Ibrahim, *al-Lajna: Riwāya* (Cairo, 1981) [Ibrahim, *The Committee: A Novel*, trans. Mary S. St. Germain and Charlene Constable (Cairo: The American University in Cairo Press, 2002)]; and Ibrahim, *al-Talaṣṣuṣ: Riwāya* (Cairo: Dār al-Mustaqbal al-ʿArabī, 2007) [Ibrahim, *Stealth*, trans. Hosam Aboul-Ela (New York: New Directions, 2014)]. See, too, Christopher Stone, "Georg Lukács and the Improbable Realism of Ṣunʿ Allah Ibrāhīm's *The Committee*," *Journal of Arabic Literature* Vol. 41, No. 1 (2010): 136–47. It would be instructive to also compare the ways in which affect—sight and sound and embodied experience—has been articulated in nonfiction, for example, in the case of Mustafa Khalifa's prison narrative, *al-Qawqaʿa: Yawmiyyāt Mutalaṣṣiṣ* (Beirut: Dār al-Ādāb, 2008) [Khalifa, *The Shell: Memoirs of a Hidden Observer*, trans. Paul Starkey (Northampton, MA: Interlink, 2016)].

13. Sinan Antoon, *Iʿjām: Riwāya* (Beirut: Dār al-Ādāb, 2004) [Sinan Antoon, *I'jaam: An Iraqi Rhapsody*, trans. Sinan Antoon and Rebecca C. Johnson (San Francisco: City Lights, 2007)].

14. Friederike Pannewick, "Dancing Letters: The Art of Subversion in Sinān Anṭūn's Novel *Iʿjām*," in *Conflicting Narratives: War, Trauma and Memory in Iraqi Culture*, ed. Stephan Milich, Friederike Pannewick, and Leslie Tramontini (Wiesbaden: Reichert Verlag, 2012), 65–74.

15. Nabil Sulayman and Bu ʿAli Yasin, *al-Aydiyūlūjīyā wa-l-Adab fī Sūriyā, 1967–1973* (Beirut: Dār Ibn Khaldūn, 1974); Samar Ruhi Faysal, *al-Ittijāh al-Wāqʿī fī al-Riwāya al-ʿArabīyya al-Sūrīyya: Dirāsa* (Damascus: Ittiḥād al-Kuttāb al-ʿArab, 1987); Muhammad Kamil al-Khatib, Nabil Sulayman, and Bu ʿAli Yasin, *Maʿārik Thaqāfiyya fī Sūriya, 1975–1977* (Beirut: Dār Ibn Rushd, 1980); Jean Fontaine, "Prose syrienne contemporaine," *IBLA* Vol. 55, No. 169 (1992): 89–110; Fadiya al-Mulayyih Halawani, *al-Riwāya wa-l-Aydiyūlūjīyā fī Sūriyya, 1958–1990* (Damascus: al-Ahālī, 1998); Jamal Chehayed and Heidi Toelle, eds., *al-Riwāya al-Sūrīyya al-Muʿāṣira: al-Judhūr al-Thaqāfiyya wa-l-Tiqnīyāt al-Riwā'īyya al-Jadīda: Aʿmāl al-Nadwa al-Munʿaqida fī 26 wa-27 Ayār 2000* (Damascus: al-Maʿhad al-Faransī li-l-Dirāsāt al-ʿArabīyya, 2001); Mohja Kahf, "The Silences of Contemporary Syrian Literature," *World Literature Today* Vol. 75, No. 2 (Spring 2001): 224–36; Elisabeth Vauthier, *La création romanesque contemporaine en Syrie de 1967 à nos jours* (Damascus: IFPO, 2007); Alexa Firat, "Post-67 Discourse and the Syrian Novel:

The Construction of an Autonomous Literary Field" (Ph.D. Diss., University of Pennsylvania, 2010); Firat, "Cultural Battles on the Literary Field: From the Syrian Writers' Collective to the Last Days of Socialist Realism in Syria," *Middle Eastern Literatures* Vol. 18, No. 2 (2015): 153–76.

16. R. Shareah Taleghani, "The Cocoons of Language, the Betrayals of Silence: Contemporary Syrian Prison Literature, Human Rights Discourse, and Literary Experimentalism" (Ph.D. Diss., New York University, 2009); Taleghani, "Vulnerability and Recognition in Syrian Prison Literature," *International Journal of Middle East Studies* Vol. 49, No. 1 (February 2017): 91–109. One example of the intimate or affective politics of surveillance can be found in the gripping paranoia depicted in the short story "The Smell of Heavy Footsteps" (1987) by Ibrahim Samu'il. See Samu'il, "Rā'iḥat al-Khaṭw al-Thaqīl" in *Rā'iḥat al-Khaṭw al-Thaqīl: Qiṣaṣ* (Damascus: Dār al-Jundī li-l-Nashr wa-l-Tawzī', 1988), 41–48. I thank an anonymous reviewer for the press for this reference.

17. For a comprehensive history of the 'Alawīs in Greater Syria and Anatolia, see Stefan Winter, *A Secular History of the 'Alawīs: From Medieval Aleppo to the Turkish Republic* (Princeton, NJ: Princeton University Press, 2016). On 'Alawī doctrine and religious practice, see Yaron Friedman, *The Nuṣayrī-'Alawīs: An Introduction to the Religion, History, and Identity of the Leading Minority in Syria* (Leiden: Brill, 2010).

18. The term "uncivil society" is borrowed from Stephen Kotkin and Jan Gross, who dissect and diagnose the bureaucratic and military cadres that once populated and administered the Communist regimes in Eastern Europe. Kotkin and Gross, *Uncivil Society: 1989 and the Implosion of the Communist Establishment* (New York: Modern Library, 2009).

19. Kahf, "The Silences of Contemporary Syrian Literature," 235.

20. Weiss, "Who Laughs Last." See, too, Christa Salamandra, "Prelude to an Uprising: Syrian Fictional Television and Socio-Political Critique," *Jadaliyya*, May 17, 2012. https://www.jadaliyya.com/Details/25966; Lisa Wedeen, "Ideology and Humor in Dark Times: Notes From Syria," *Critical Inquiry* 39 (Summer 2013): 841–73; Cécile Boëx, *Cinéma et politique en Syrie: écritures cinématographiques de la contestation en régime autoritaire: 1970–2010* (Paris: L'Harmattan, 2014).

21. While I do not discuss the increasing frequency with which Syrian writers, intellectuals, and ordinary people engage with memories and legacies of the Hama massacres (1982) and the domestic armed conflict in Syria (1979–1982) in this chapter, I will return to address this topic briefly in the Conclusion.

22. Walter Benjamin, "The Author as Producer, trans. John Heckman," *New Left Review* 62 (July–August 1970): 83–96, at 95.

23. Of course, there is a range of humorous cultural production in Syria that engages with different forms of comedy. See, for example, the satirical cartoons of 'Ali Farzat that were published in the state newspaper *Tishrīn* and, later, a satirical journal *al-Dūmarī* (on which see Wedeen, *Ambiguities of Domination*, 107–12) as well as the work of writers like Khatib Badla, a figure who has not received nearly enough scholarly attention. See, for example, his single-authored collections: *Ḥakā lī al-Akhras: Sukhriyyat Ṣaghīra* (Damascus: Dār al-Ahālī, 1987); *Imrā'a Taksir al-Ẓahr* (Damascus: Dār al-Yanābī', 1994); *Waqt li-Ṭalāq al-Zawja* (Damascus: Wizārat al-Thaqāfa fī al-Jumhūriyya al-'Arabiyya al-Sūriyya, 1998). Badla also edited several collections of satirical writing, including *Qiṣaṣ wa-Ḥikāyāt wa-Ṭarā'if min 'Asr al-Dīktatūriyya fi Sūriya* (Ra's al-Khayma: Dār Nūn li-l-Nashr, 2014), and *Ḥikāyāt Sūriyya lahā 'Alāqa bi-l-Istibdād* (Ra's al-Khayma: Dār Nūn li-l-Nashr, 2015).

24. Nihad Sirees, *al-Kūmidīyyā al-Fallāḥiyya* (Damascus: Maṭābi' Alif Bā' - al-Adīb, 1996 [1990]). *The Peasant Comedy* is discussed briefly in Stefan G. Meyer, *The Experimental Arabic Novel: Postcolonial Literary Modernism in the Levant* (Albany: State University of New York Press, 2001), 99–100; and cited in Jonathan Holt Shannon, *Among the Jasmine Trees: Music and Modernity in Contemporary Syria* (Middletown, CT.: Wesleyan University Press, 2006), 213n6. See, too, Sirees, *Hālat Shaghaf: Riwāya* (Dbiyeh, Lebanon: Dār 'Aṭiyya, 1998) [Sirees, *States of Passion*, trans. Max Weiss (London: Pushkin Press, 2018)].

25. Nihad Sirees, *al-Ṣamt wa-l-Ṣakhab* (Beirut: Dār al-Ādāb, 2004); Sirees, *The Silence and the Roar*, trans. Max Weiss (New York: Other Press, 2013). References are to the English-language edition. *The Silence and the Roar* is critically analyzed in Samira Aghacy, *Masculine Identity in the Fiction of the Arab East Since 1967* (Syracuse, NY: Syracuse University Press, 2009), 123–29.

26. *The Silence and the Roar*, 124.

27. Ibid., 124–26.

28. Fawwaz Haddad, *al-Mutarjim al-Khā'in: Riwāya* (Beirut: Riyad el-Rayyes li-l-Kutub wa-l-Nashr, 2008), 41.

29. *The Silence and the Roar*, 11–12.

30. Relatedly, see Robyn Creswell, "Poets in Prose: Genre & History in the Arabic Novel," *Daedalus* Vol. 150, No. 1 (Winter 2021): 147–59.

31. *The Silence and the Roar*, 119.

32. Ibid., 62.

33. Ibid., 134.

34. See, for example, Taleghani, "The Cocoons of Language"; Taleghani, "Vulnerability and Recognition in Syrian Prison Literature"; miriam cooke, "The Cell Story: Syrian Prison Stories after Hafiz Asad," *Middle East Critique* Vol. 20, No. 2 (Summer 2011): 169–87.

35. *The Silence and the Roar*, 61.

36. Agnes Heller, *Immortal Comedy: The Comic Phenomenon in Art, Literature, and Life* (Lanham, UK: Lexington Books, 2005), 78.

37. Slavoj Žižek, *The Sublime Object of Ideology* (London: Verso, 1989), 28.

38. Theodor W. Adorno, *Minima Moralia; Reflections from Damaged Life* (London: New Left Books, 1974), 210.

39. Jerry Palmer, *The Logic of the Absurd: On Film and Television Comedy* (London: BFI, 1987), 213.

40. Achille Mbembe, *On the Postcolony* (Berkeley: University of California Press, 2001), 155; Cécile Bishop, *Postcolonial Criticism and Representations of African Dictatorship: The Aesthetics of Tyranny* (London: Modern Humanities Research Association and Maney Publishing, 2014).

41. Ann Elizabeth Gaylin, *Eavesdropping in the Novel from Austen to Proust* (Cambridge: Cambridge University Press, 2002), 7–8.

42. Rosa Yaseen Hasan, *Samāʾ Mulawwatha bi-l-Ḍawʾ: Qiṣaṣ* (Beirut: Dār al-Kunūz al-Adabīyya, 2000); also by Hasan: *Abnūs: Riwāya* (Damascus: Manshūrāt Wizārat al-Thaqāfa fī al-Jumhūrīyya al-ʿArabīyya al-Sūrīyya, 2004); *Nīghātīf min Dhākirat al-Muʿtaqalāt al-Siyāsiyya: Riwāya Tawthīqīyya* (Cairo: Markaz al-Qāhira li-Dirāsāt Ḥuqūq al-Insān, 2008); *Ḥurrās al-Hawāʾ: Riwāya* (Beirut: Riyad el-Rayyes li-l-Kutub wa-l-Nashr, 2009); and *Al-Ladhīna Masaḥahum al-Siḥr: Min Shaẓāyā al-Ḥikāyāt* (Cologne: Dār al-Jamal, 2016). Very little has been written about Hasan. Shareah Taleghani discusses *Nīghātīf* in *Readings in Syrian Prison Literature: The Poetics of Human Rights* (Syracuse, NY: Syracuse University Press, 2021), 25–26, 37–40. See, too, Martina Censi, "Rappresentazioni Del Corpo Nel Romanzo Delle Scrittrici Siriane Contemporanee," Università Ca' Foscari Venezia, 2013; Censi, "Capitolo terzo: *Ḥurrās al-hawāʾ* di Rūzā Yāsīn Ḥasan: corpo e attesa o nell'attesa del corpo," 67–91; and Censi, "Rewriting the Body in the Novels of Contemporary Syrian Women Writers," in *Gender and Sexuality in Muslim Cultures*, ed. Gul Ozyegin (Burlington, VT: Ashgate, 2015), 297–315. In "Rewriting the Body," Censi discusses Samar Yazbek's *Rāʾiḥat al-Qirfa*, Rosa Yaseen Hasan's *Ḥurrās*

al-Hawā', and Hayfa' Bitar's, *Imrā'a min Hadhā al-'Asr*. None of Hasan's full-length works have yet to be translated into English.

43. "On Cultural Production and the Syrian Revolution: Part 3 of an Interview with Rosa Yaseen Hassan," *Jadaliyya*, July 4, 2011. http://www.jadaliyya.com/pages/index/2046/on-cultural-production-and-the-syrian-revolution_a; Hassan, "Where are the Intellectuals in the Syrian Revolution? trans. Max Weiss," in *Arabic Thought Against the Authoritarian Age: Towards an Intellectual History of the Present*, ed. Jens Hanssen and Max Weiss (Cambridge: Cambridge University Press, 2018), 370–73.

44. Rosa Yaseen Hasan, *Brūfā: Riwāya* (Beirut: Riyad el-Rayyes li-l-Kutub wa-l-Nashr, 2011).

45. While the title term *brūfā*—an Arabic transliteration of the Italian *prova*—might arguably be translated as "experiment" or "rehearsal," the performative aspect of the term is less germane than the textual and even legalistic, in the sense of "proof" or "evidence." Hence the novel is typically referred to by its Arabic title *Brūfā*, although there are points at which the textual significance of the term justifies the use of this slightly unorthodox translation, "rough draft." The "performance" of writing the rough draft—and thinking about it out loud in the narrative itself—might merit further consideration.

46. In this respect, *Brūfā* has something in common with postmodern narrative in that it draws attention to the constructedness of the text, not only the draft of the *mukhābarātī* here but also the novel itself.

47. Hasan, *Brūfā*, 12.

48. Ibid., 13.

49. Ibid., 15.

50. It is worth noting the similarities between *Brūfā* and Dima Wannous's 2009 novel *Kursī* (*Chair*): Wannous, *Kursī: Riwāya* (Beirut: Dār al-Ādāb, 2009). *Kursī* is discussed briefly in Salwa Ismail, *The Rule of Violence: Subjectivity, Memory and Government in Syria* (New York: Cambridge University Press, 2018), 79–80. There is also resonance here with the shadowy Stasi agent protagonist at the heart of East German writer Wolfgang Hilbig's psychological novel *Ich*: *'I'* trans. Isabel Fargo Cole (London: Seagull Books, 2015). See, too, Tyler Curtis, "Writing Under Surveillance: The Subversive Fiction of Wolfgang Hilbig," *Boston Review*, March 15, 2016: http://bostonreview.net/books-ideas/tyler-curtis-wolfgang-hilbig-sleep-righteous.

51. Hasan, *Brūfā*, 113.

52. Ibid., 115.

53. Nikolaos van Dam, "Middle Eastern Political Clichés: 'Takriti' and 'Sunni' Rule in Iraq; 'Alawi' Rule in Syria, a Critical Appraisal," *Orient* Vol. 21, No. 1 (January 1980): 42–57; Fabrice Balanche, *La région alaouite et le pouvoir syrien* (Paris: Karthala, 2006); Balanche, "Clientélisme, communautarisme et fragmentation territoriale en Syrie," *a contrario* No. 11 (March 2009): 122–50.

54. Eberhard Kienle, *Entre jamaʿa et classe: le pouvoir politique en Syrie* (Berlin: Das Arabische Buch, 1992), 14. See, too, my "Mosaic, Melting Pot, Pressure Cooker: The Religious, the Secular, and the Sectarian in Modern Syrian Social Thought," in *Arabic Thought Against the Authoritarian Age: Towards an Intellectual History of the Present*, ed. Jens Hanssen and Max Weiss (Cambridge: Cambridge University Press, 2018), 181–202. I return to this theme in the Conclusion through a discussion of Fawwaz Haddad's novel *al-Sūriyyūn al-Aʿdāʾ* (*Enemy Syrians*) (Beirut: Riyad el-Rayyes li-l-Kutub wa-l-Nashr, 2014).

55. Hasan, *Brūfā*, 115.

56. Ibid., 118.

57. Ibid., 113.

58. It may not mean much that the more archaic term *ṭughyān* is used here rather than *istibdād* to index tyranny. One interpretation of this choice might be an attempt to distance the *mukhābarātī*'s conception of tyranny from the liberal critique of unjust rule, as it has been articulated and inspired by the late nineteenth-century Aleppo-born lawyer and intellectual 'Abd al-Rahman al-Kawakibi in his *Ṭabāʾiʿ al-Istibdād wa-Maṣāriʿ al-Istiʿbād*. See *al-Aʿmāl al-Kāmila li-ʿAbd al-Raḥmān al-Kawākibī, maʿa Dirāsa ʿan Ḥayātihi wa-Athārihi*, ed. Muhammad ʿImara (Cairo: al-Hay'a al-Miṣriyya al-ʿĀmma li-l-Ta'līf wa-l-Nashr, 1970), 328–438. Alternatively, in his discussion of the political theology of Egyptian Islamist Sayyid Qutb, Ellis Goldberg notes that *ṭughyān* "has to do with overstepping boundaries (including "going beyond in disbelief")," which might go some way towards explaining the strange effects of sensory experience and individual submission to power in the case of this security agent in *Rough Draft*. Goldberg, "Smashing Idols and the State: The Protestant Ethic and Egyptian Sunni Radicalism," *Comparative Studies in Society and History* Vol. 33, No. 1 (Jan., 1991): 3–35, at 15.

59. Hasan, *Brūfā*, 179–85.

60. Ibid., 23.

61. Ibid., 90.

62. Ibid., 41–48, 121–29.

63. Ibid., 225–26.

64. Ibid., 38–39.

65. Ibid., 75n30.

66. Ibid., 23.

67. Ibid., 53.

68. Ibid., 60n23.

69. Ibid., 129.

70. Ibid., 232.

71. Ibid., 233.

72. Ibid., 234.

73. There is an analogous plot point in the 2011 television drama serial (*musalsal*) *al-Wilāda min al-Khāṣira* (*Born from the Loins*), when a screenwriter character becomes frustrated after an encounter with a government censor and throws her script out the window in anger, taking an altogether different position on the possibility of writing in the shadow of the Baʿthist Syrian surveillance state. See Rebecca Joubin, *Mediating the Uprising: Narratives of Gender and Marriage in Syrian Television Drama* (New Brunswick, NJ: Rutgers University Press, 2020), 210–11.

74. Stephen Brockmann, *Literature and German Reunification* (Cambridge: Cambridge University Press, 1999), 89.

75. Dima Wannous, "'Brūfā': Riwāyat Rūzā Yāsīn Ḥasan: Riwāyat al-Talaṣṣuṣ," *al-Safīr*, October 22, 2011. http://alawan.org/article10568.html; Khalil Suwaylih, "Rūzā Yāsīn Ḥasan: Marathīyya li-Jīl al-Khayba," *al-Akhbār*, July 26, 2011. https://www.al-akhbar.com/node/17449. Lanie Millar reminds us that representations of disappointment in literary and cinematic narrative can be understood as "a fundamentally collective feeling." Millar, *Forms of Disappointment: Cuban and Angolan Narrative After the Cold War* (Albany: State University of New York Press, 2019), xvi.

76. Nabil Sulayman, "Rūzā Yāsīn Ḥasan Tafḍaḥ Laʿbat al-Ṣawt wa-l-Tanaṣṣut al-Istikhbārātī," *al-Ḥayā*, August 10, 2011.

77. Meyer, *The Experimental Arabic Novel*, 38.

78. Volker Braun, *Hinze-Kunze-Roman* (Frankfurt am Main: Suhrkamp, 1985), on which see http://www.complete-review.com/reviews/braunv/hkroman.htm; Christa Wolf, "What Remains," in *What Remains and Other Stories*, trans. Heike Schwarzbauer and Rick Takvorian (New York: Farrar, Straus, and Giroux, 1993), 231–95.

79. Cheryl Dueck, "The Humanization of the Stasi in 'Das Leben der Anderen,'" *German Studies Review* Vol. 31, No. 3 (October 2008): 599–609; John Griffith Urang, *Legal Tender: Love and Legitimacy in the East German Cultural Imagination* (Ithaca, NY:

Cornell University Press, 2010), 186–92; Flagg Taylor, "Post-Totalitarianism in *The Lives of Others*," *Perspectives on Political Science* Vol. 40, No. 2 (2011): 61–67; John T. Hamilton, "Conspiracy, Security, and Human Care in Donnersmarck's *Leben Der Anderen*," *Historical Social Research / Historische Sozialforschung*, Vol. 38, No. 1 (2014): 129–41.

80. Urang, *Legal Tender*, esp. Chapter 5, "Eye Contact: Surveillance, Perversion, and the Last Days of the GDR," 164–92. For a comparable perspective on the poetics of the Securitate in Communist Romania, see Cristina Vatulescu, *Police Aesthetics: Literature, Film, and the Secret Police in Soviet Times* (Stanford, CA: Stanford University Press, 2010).

81. Urang, *Legal Tender*, 171–72.

82. Alfred Tennyson, "The Lady of Shalott," in *The Poetical Works of Alfred Tennyson* (Boston: James R. Osgood, 1878), 12–14, at 13.

83. Umberto Eco, "Mirrors," in *Semiotics and the Philosophy of Language* (Bloomington: Indiana University Press, 1984), 202–26, at 208.

84. Samar Yazbek, *Taqāṭuʿ Nīrān: Min Yawmiyyāt al-Intifāḍa al-Sūriyya* (Beirut: Dār al-Ādāb, 2012) [Yazbek, *A Woman in the Crossfire: Diaries of the Syrian Revolution*, trans. Max Weiss (London: Haus Publishing, 2012)]; Idem., *Bawwābāt Arḍ al-ʿAdam* (Beirut: Dār al-Ādāb, 2015) [Samar Yazbek, *The Crossing: My Journey to the Shattered Heart of Syria*, trans. Nashwa Gowanlock and Ruth Ahmedzai Kemp (London: Rider Books, 2015)]; Idem. *Al-Mashāʾa: Riwāya* (Beirut: Dār al-Ādāb, 2017).

85. Samar Yazbek, *Mufradāt Imrāʾa: Qiṣaṣ* (Beirut: Dār al-Kunūz al-Adabīyya, 2001); Yazbek, *Ṭiflat al-Samāʾ: Riwāya* (Beirut: Dār al-Kunūz al-Adabīyya, 2002); Yazbek, *Ṣalṣāl: Riwāya* (Beirut: Dār al-Kunūz al-Adabīyya, 2005); Yazbek, *Jabal al-Zanābiq: Ḥaky Manāmāt* (Damascus: Dār al-Madā li-l-Thaqāfa wa-l-Nashr, 2008); Yazbek, *Rāʾiḥat al-Qirfa: Riwāya* (Beirut: Dār al-Ādāb, 2008).

86. Samar Yazbek, *Lahā Marāya: Riwāya* (Beirut: Dār al-Ādāb, 2010).

87. Ibid., 13.

88. Ibid., 67.

89. Ibid., 163.

90. Ibid., 24.

91. Ibid., 26.

92. Ibid., 29–33.

93. Historians debate the significance and symbolism of the Shaykh Salih al-ʿAli revolt in terms of the relationship between ʿAlawī particularism and Syrian nationalism, but mention is often made of him to gesture toward his anticolonial nationalist

credentials, which are precisely what is at stake in this struggle over family history and memory in the novel. See ʿAbd al-Latif al-Yunus, *Thawrat al-Shaykh Ṣāliḥ al-ʿAlī* ([Damascus]: Dār al-Yaqẓa al-ʿArabiyya, 1961 [1947]); Hamid Hasan, *Ṣāliḥ al-ʿAlī Thāʾiran wa-Shāʿiran* (Damascus: Manshūrat Dār Majallāt al-Thaqāfa, 1973); Ayman Ahmad Shaʿban, *Ṣāliḥ al-ʿAlī Thawra wa-ʿAqīda* (Damascus: A. A. Shaʿbān, 1989); Joshua M. Landis, "Nationalism and the Politics of *Zaʿama*: The Collapse of Republican Syria, 1945–1949" (Ph.D. Diss., Princeton University, 1997), 150–58; Qays Ibrahim ʿAbbas, *al-Shaykh Ṣāliḥ al-ʿAlī: Awrāq wa-Shahādāt* (Damascus: al-Takwīn, 2005); ʿIsa Abu ʿAllush, *Ṣafaḥāt Majhūla min Thawrat al-Shaykh Ṣāliḥ al-ʿAlī* (Latakia: Dār Dhū al-Fiqār li-l-Ṭibāʿa wa-l-Nashr wa-l-Tawzīʿ, 2007); Mahmud ʿAbd al-Rahman Al ʿAbbas Salman, *Imām al-Mujāhidīn wa-Shaykh al-Thuwwār al-Shaykh Ṣāliḥ al-ʿAlī: Qāʾid wa-Qaḍiyya* (Tartus: Maktabat Shāsh, 2009). On French discursive constructions of the ʿAlawī community under the Mandate, see Max Weiss, "Community, Sect, Nation: Colonial and Social Scientific Discourses on the ʿAlawīs in Syria during the French Mandate and Early Independence Periods," in *The ʿAlawīs of Syria: War, Faith and Politics in the Levant*, ed. Michael Kerr and Craig Larkin (New York: Oxford University Press, 2015), 63–75.

94. Yazbek, *Lahā Marāya*, 148–49.

95. Urang, *Legal Tender*, 171–72.

96. Yazbek, *Lahā Marāya*, 150.

97. Ibid., 151–52.

98. Ibid., 153.

99. Ibid., 154.

100. Ibid., 155.

101. Ibid., 203.

102. Ibid., 206.

103. Ibid., 207.

104. Ibid., 209.

105. Jacques Lacan, "The Mirror Stage as Formative of the Function of the I as Revealed in Psychoanalytic Experience," in *Écrits: A Selection*, trans. Alan Sheridan (New York: Norton, 1977), 1–7, at 6. On the development of Lacan's thinking about the mirror stage as well as his often overlooked debt to the French psychologist Henri Wallon (1879–1962), see Jane Gallop, "Lacan's 'Mirror State': Where to Begin," *SubStance: A Review of Theory and Literary Criticism* 37/38 (1983): 118–28; Martin Jay, *Downcast Eyes:*

The Denigration of Vision in Twentieth-Century French Thought (Berkeley: University of California Press, 1993), 339–52; Elisabeth Roudinesco, "The Mirror Stage: An Obliterated Archive, trans. Barbara Bray," in *The Cambridge Companion to Lacan*, ed. Jean-Michel Rabaté (Cambridge: Cambridge University Press, 2003), 25–34.

106. Michel Foucault, "Des espaces autres" in *Dits et écrits 1984* (conférence au Cercle d'études architecturales, March 14, 1967)," in *Architecture, Mouvement, Continuité* 5 (October 1984): 46–49; all references are to the expanded and "corrected" text published in Foucault, *Le corps utopique: suivi de Les hétérotopies* (Paris: Lignes, 2009).

107. Jameson, "The Politics of Utopia," *New Left Review* 25 (January/February 2004): 35–54, at 54.

108. Foucault, *Le corps utopique*, 25.

109. Carolyn Burke, "Irigaray Through the Looking Glass," *Feminist Studies* Vol. 7 (Summer 1981): 288–306, at 296. Thanks to Elliott Colla for this reminder.

110. In her critical evaluation of Joud Said's 2009 film *Once Again* (*Marra Ukhrā*), Wedeen highlights the conspicuous consumption on display in the film—including the personal use of surveillance devices—as an index of the rising neoliberal fetishization of the good life in 2000s Syria. "Public surveillance in the film has become privatized in typical neoliberal fashion." Wedeen, "Ideology and Humor in Dark Times," 859. *Stars in Broad Daylight* points up how the boundary between "public" and "private" modes of surveillance was never so neatly defined during Hafiz al-Asad's rule. "One of the recurrent motifs in remembrances of life under Hafez al-Asad," according to Salwa Ismail, "was the sense of being the object of the security gaze—that of the security services or of a vast network of watchers in schools, at work and at home." Ismail, *The Rule of Violence: Subjectivity, Memory and Government in Syria* (New York: Cambridge University Press, 2018), 196.

111. Thomas Y. Levin, "Rhetoric of the Temporal Index: Surveillant Narration and the Cinema of 'Real Time,'" in *Ctrl (Space): Rhetorics of Surveillance from Bentham to Big Brother*, ed. Thomas Y. Levin, Ursula Frohne, and Peter Weibel (Cambridge, MA: MIT Press, 2002), 578–93, at 582.

112. Robert B. Pippin, *Filmed Thought: Cinema as Reflective Form* (Chicago: University of Chicago Press, 2020), 131.

113. Yazbek, *Lahā Marāya*, 119–20.

114. Ibid., 117.

115. Ibid., 241.

116. Ibid., 244.

117. Ibid., 251.

118. Ibid., 252–53.

119. Sharika Thiranagama and Tobias Kelly, "Introduction: Specters of Treason," in *Traitors: Suspicion, Intimacy, and the Ethics of State-Building*, ed. Thiranagama and Kelly (Philadelphia: University of Pennsylvania Press, 2010), 1–23, at 9.

120. Yazbek, *Lahā Marāya*, 39.

121. Ibid., 39.

122. Ibid., 170–89.

123. Stefan Winter points out that "there are no good sources, other than hearsay, family lore or [Muhammad Ghalib] Al-Ṭawīl (which is basically the same thing)" on the Ottoman siege of Aleppo—a.k.a. the "Aleppo massacre." "There is nothing at all in the Arabic chronicles of the period that I have seen," Winter continues, "and I can promise you there is nothing in the Ottoman chronicles. I think everyone is simply extrapolating from Selim's massacres (probably exaggerated too, but that's another story) of the Kizilbas, but the fact of the matter is there were probably very few Shiites, and no Alawis, living in Aleppo at the time. What there is in Ottoman tax documents of the time are a few tantalizing clues of bloodshed and rebellion in the mountains at the time of the Ottoman conquest. But if anything people then fled the mountains for Hama and Aleppo, rather than the other way around." (Email communication, August 21, 2013). Winter is referring to Muhammad Amin Ghalib al-Tawil, *Tārīkh al-ʿAlawīyyīn* (Beirut: Dār al-Andalus li-l-Ṭibāʿa wa-l-Nashr, 1966 [1924]).

124. Yazbek, *Lahā Marāyā*, 255.

125. Ibid., 270.

126. Ibid., 279–82.

127. Ibid., 286.

128. Ibid., 287–88.

129. Nabil Sulayman, "Samar Yazbik Tabḥath ʿammā Warāʾ al-Marʾā," *al-Ḥayā*, September 1, 2010.

130. Muhammad Barrada, "Sijāl ḥawla Riwāyat Samar Yazbik "'Lahā Marāyā': al-Wāqiʿ al-Sūrī bi-Wijhi al-Usṭūrī," *al-Ḥayā*, September 15, 2010.

131. Rasim al- Madhun, "'Lahā Marāyā": Riwāyat al-Sūriyya Samar Yazbik: al-Siyāsa Tandamaj fī al-Ḥayā wa-la Tuhaymin ʿalayhā,'" *al-Ḥayā*, December 17, 2010.

132. Peter Sloterdijk, *Critique of Cynical Reason*, trans. Michael Eldred (Minneapolis: University of Minnesota Press, 1987), 145.

133. Zakariya Tamir, "Mulakhkhaṣ mā Jarā li-Muḥammad al-Maḥmūdī," in *al-Numūr fī al-Yawm al-ʿĀshir: Qiṣaṣ* (Beirut: Dār al-Ādāb, 1978), 83–86.

134. Susan Buck-Morss, "Aesthetics and Anaesthetics: Walter Benjamin's Artwork Essay Reconsidered," *October* Vol. 62 (Autumn 1992): 3–41, at 6.

135. Jill E. Twark, *Humor, Satire, and Identity: Eastern German Literature in the 1990s* (Berlin: Walter de Gruyter, 2007), 75.

136. David Lyon, *The Electronic Eye: The Rise of Surveillance Society* (Minneapolis: University of Minneapolis Press, 1994); Lyon, *Surveillance Studies: An Overview*. (Cambridge, UK: Polity, 2007); Zygmunt Bauman and David Lyon, *Liquid Surveillance: A Conversation* (Cambridge, UK: Polity Press, 2013).

137. Mike Nellis, "Since *Nineteen Eighty Four*: Representations of Surveillance in Literary Fiction," in *New Directions in Surveillance and Privacy*, ed. B. J. Goold, and Daniel Neyland (Cullompton, UK: Willan Pub, 2009), 178–204, at 200n1.

138. Wedeen, "Acting 'As If,'" 523.

139. Kahf, "The Silences of Contemporary Syrian Literature," 232–33.

CHAPTER 5

1. Tzvetan Todorov, "Narrative-Men," in *The Arabian Nights Reader*, ed. Ulrich Marzolph (Detroit, MI: Wayne State University Press, 2006), 226–38, at 238.

2. Bart Verschaffel, "The Depiction of the Worst Thing: On the Meaning and Use of Images of the Terrible, trans. Gregory Ball," *Image & Narrative* Vol. 14, No. 3 (2013): 5–18, at 8.

3. Paul Virilio, *Speed and Politics*, trans. Mark Polizzotti (Los Angeles: Semiotext(e), 2006), 78.

4. Samar Yazbek, *A Woman in the Crossfire: Diaries of the Syrian Revolution*, trans. Max Weiss (London: Haus, 2012), 50 [See, too, the original Arabic version: *Taqāṭuʿ Nīrān: Min Yawmiyyāt al-Intifāḍa al-Sūriyya* (Beirut: Dār al-Ādāb, 2012)].

5. Ibid., 78.

6. Samuel Weber, *Targets of Opportunity: On the Militarization of Thinking* (New York: Fordham University Press, 2005), 18

7. The best book on the subject is Kamran Rastegar, *Surviving Images: Cinema, War, and Cultural Memory in the Middle East* (New York: Oxford University Press, 2015). See, too, Lina Khatib, "Lebanese Cinema and the Representation of War," in *Film in the Middle East and North Africa: Creative Dissidence*, ed. Josef Gugler (Austin: University of Texas Press, 2011), 134–45.

8. miriam cooke, *War's Other Voices: Women Writers on the Lebanese Civil War* (New York: Cambridge University Press, 1987); cooke, *Women and the War Story* (Berkeley: University of California Press, 1996); Ikram Masmoudi, *War and Occupation in Iraqi Fiction* (Edinburgh: Edinburgh University Press, 2015). See, too, Dragana Obradović, *Writing the Yugoslav Wars: Literature, Postmodernism, and the Ethics of Representation* (Toronto, ON: University of Toronto Press, 2016).

9. Emily Drumsta, "Chronicles of Disappearance: The Novel of Investigation in the Arab World, 1975–1985" (Ph.D. Diss., University of California, Berkeley, 2016), 51.

10. Barbara Foley, *Telling the Truth: The Theory and Practice of Documentary Fiction* (Ithaca, NY: Cornell University Press, 1986), 41.

11. Pace Laura U. Marks, who argues that "glitch aesthetics" are reflections of "an everyday problem in countries with poor infrastructure, including most of the Arabic-speaking world." Laura U. Marks, *Hanan Al-Cinema: Affections for the Moving Image* (Cambridge, MA: MIT Press, 2015), 250. I do not find the varied aesthetics of emergency video uploads to be emblematic of anything specific to Syria or even the Syria War itself. It is, rather, a hallmark of the contemporary global media moment, in which interrupted transmissions and incomplete circulation constitute a specific modality of uncertainty, precarity, and danger. See, too, Kari Andén-Papadopoulos, "Media Witnessing and the 'Crowd-Sourced Video Revolution,'" *Visual Communication* Vol. 12, No. 3 (2013): 341–57. I would emphatically differentiate this phenomenon, however, from the *purposive and consciously named* emergency cinema of Abounaddara and other revolutionary filmmakers.

12. Donatella Della Ratta, "The Unbearable Lightness of the Image: Unfinished Thoughts on Filming in Contemporary Syria," *Middle East Journal of Culture and Communication*, Vol. 10, No. 2–3 (2017): 109–32; Della Ratta, *Shooting a Revolution: Visual Media and Warfare in Syria* (London: Pluto Press, 2018). See, too, Josepha Ivanka Wessels, *Documenting Syria: Film-Making, Video Activism and Revolution* (London: I. B. Tauris, 2019).

13. Rob Nixon, *Slow Violence and the Environmentalism of the Poor* (Cambridge, MA: Harvard University Press, 2011), 275. Nixon (and my own argument here) echoes a global discourse about slowness, one that has been extended to food, reading, and other everyday life practices. For a popular survey, see Carl Honoré, *In Praise of Slow: How a Worldwide Movement is Challenging the Cult of Speed* (San Francisco: HarperSanFrancisco, 2004). On the relationship between speed and violence in Western imperialism, see Virilio, *Speed and Politics*; Virilio, *Vitesse et politique: essai de dromologie* (Paris: Galilée, 1977).

14. Lisa Wedeen, *Authoritarian Apprehensions: Ideology, Judgment, and Mourning in Syria* (Chicago: University of Chicago Press, 2019), 105.

15. Michael G. Levine, *The Belated Witness: Literature, Testimony, and the Question of Holocaust Survival* (Stanford, CA: Stanford University Press, 2006), 10, emphasis in original.

16. Given the presence of writers and other "real-world" characters in these works, there may be value in exploring the relationship between these works and the genre of metafiction, although space prevents me from taking up that question here.

17. Susan Sontag, *Regarding the Pain of Others* (New York: Farrar, Straus and Giroux, 2003), 108.

18. Jan Mieszkowski, *Watching War* (Stanford, CA: Stanford University Press, 2012), 4.

19. Maha Hasan, *Ṭubūl al-Ḥubb: Riwāya* (Beirut: Riyad el-Rayyes li-l-Kutub wa-l-Nashr, 2013).

20. Ibid., 31.

21. Ibid., 163–65.

22. Ibid., 126.

23. Ibid., 130.

24. Ibid., 186.

25. Ibid., 133.

26. Ibid., 178–79.

27. Ibid., 185–87.

28. Ibid., 187.

29. Ibid., 168.

30. Hisham al-Wawi, "'al-Mawt 'Amal Shāq' li-Khālid Khalīfa: Riḥlat al-'Awda ilā al-Qabr," *al-Nahār*, February 17, 2016.

31. Hasan, *Ṭubūl al-Ḥubb*, 55.

32. Dominick LaCapra, "Toward a Critique of Violence," in *The Modernist Imagination: Intellectual History and Critical Theory: Essays in Honor of Martin Jay*, ed. Warren Breckman, Peter E. Gordon, A. Dirk Moses, Samuel Moyn, and Elliot Neaman (New York: Berghahn Books, 2009), 210–41, at 212.

33. Khalil Suwaylih, *Jannat al-Barābira: Riwāya* (Cairo: Dār al-'Ayn li-l-Nashr, 2014).

34. Ibid., 166.

35. Robert Pinsky, trans, *The Inferno of Dante: A New Verse Translation* (New York: Farrar, Straus and Giroux, 1994), 7.

36. Ibid., 19.

37. Hasan, *Ṭubūl al-Ḥubb*, 181.

38. Suwaylih, *Jannat al-Barābira*, 9.

39. Ibid., 89.

40. Ibid., 7–8.

41. Ibid., 35. A word is in order on this unorthodox translation of *al-balāgha.* I do not believe that the narrator is referring to "eloquence" or "rhetoric"—more conventional translations of the term—so much as the very conditions of possibility for communication, for "language" as such.

42. Ibid., 43–44.

43. Ibid., 43.

44. Ibid., 90.

45. Reinhart Koselleck, "Does History Accelerate?" trans. Sean Franzel and Stefan-Ludwig Hoffman, in *Sediments of Time: On Possible Histories* (Stanford, CA: Stanford University Press, 2018), 79–99.

46. Suwaylih, *Jannat al-Barābira*, 38.

47. Ibid., 89.

48. Ibid., 89.

49. Ibid., 138.

50. Ibid., 39.

51. Ibid., 40.

52. Ibid., 52.

53. Ibid., 72.

54. Ibid., 85.

55. Ibid.

56. Ibid., 86.

57. Ibid.

58. Ibid., 87.

59. Ibid., 124.

60. Ibid., 119–20.

61. Ibid., 158.

62. Ibid., 164.

63. Sayyid Mahmud, "Khalīl Ṣuwayliḥ: Ḥāwaltu Tawthīq Alf Yawm min al-Jahīm al-Sūrī," *al-Ḥayā*, July 8, 2014.

64. Suwaylih, *Jannat al-Barābira*, 165.

65. Ibid., 166.

66. Shohini Chaudhuri, "The Alterity of the Image: The Distant Spectator and Films About the Syrian Revolution and War," *Transnational Cinemas* Vol. 9, No. 1 (2018): 31–46, at 37.

67. Especially in light of some criticism Mohammed's film has received for claiming to speak *on behalf of* or even *speaking-to* Syrians inside of Syria, mine is a slightly different argument from the one Lisa Wedeen presents in her interpretation of *Silvered Water* as "a collective enterprise." Wedeen, *Authoritarian Apprehensions*, 134. See, too, miriam cooke, *Dancing in Damascus: Creativity, Resilience, and the Syrian Revolution* (New York: Routledge, 2017), 68–70; Chad Elias, "Emergency Cinema and the Dignified Image: Cell Phone Activism and Filmmaking in Syria," *Film Quarterly* Vol. 71, No. 1 (Fall 2017): 18–31, esp. 22–26; Della Ratta, *Shooting a Revolution*, 138–43; Wessels, *Documenting Syria*, 52–54.

68. Matthew Flanagan, "Towards an Aesthetic of Slow in Contemporary Cinema," *16:9* Vol. 29, No. 6 (November 2008). http://www.16-9.dk/2008-11/side11_inenglish.htm.

69. Allen Feldman, *Archives of the Insensible: Of War, Photopolitics, and Dead Memory* (Chicago: The University of Chicago Press, 2015), 94.

70. Ibid., 108. My argument here differs from the aesthetics and politics of "the imperfect image" discussed in Katarzyna Ruchel-Stockmans, "Towards a Poor Cinema: The Performativity of Mobile Cameras in New Image Wars," in *Visualizing War: Emotions, Technologies, Communities*, ed. Anders Engberg-Pedersen and Kathrin Maurer (New York: Routledge, 2018), 110–29.

71. Wedeen, *Authoritarian Apprehensions*, 130.

72. Compare Paul Virilio, *War and Cinema: The Logistics of Perception* (London: Verso, 1989).

73. Sue Tait, "Visualising Technologies and the Ethics and Aesthetics of Screening Death," *Science as Culture*, Vol. 18, No. 3 (September 2009): 333–53, at 336. Other critical accounts of documentary in relation to the politics of humanitarianism include Leshu Torchin, *Creating the Witness: Documenting Genocide on Film, Video, and the Internet* (Minneapolis: University of Minnesota Press, 2012); Pooja Rangan, *Immediations: The Humanitarian Impulse in Documentary* (Durham, NC: Duke University Press, 2017). For a more optimistic interpretation of engagement and empathy through film from a distance, see Sarah Kozloff, "Empathy and the Cinema of Engagement: Reevaluating the Politics of Film," *Projections* Vol. 7, No. 2 (Winter 2013): 1–40; Carl Plantinga, *Screen Stories: Emotion and the Ethics of Engagement* (New York: Oxford University Press, 2018).

74. Yusuf ʿAkkawi, "Writing, Revolution, and Change in Syria: An Interview With Nihad Sirees, trans. Max Weiss," *Jadaliyya*, August 23, 2012. https://www.jadaliyya.com/Details/26935/Writing,-Revolution,-and-Change-in-Syria-An-Interview-with-Nihad-Sirees

75. Yazbek, *A Woman in the Crossfire*; Muhammad Abi Samra, *Mawt al-Abad al-Sūrī: Shahādāt Jīl al-Ṣamt wa-l-Thawra* (Beirut: Riyad el-Rayyes li-l-Kutub wa-l-Nashr, 2012); Jonathan Littell, *Carnets de Homs: 16 Janvier-2 Février 2012* (Paris: Gallimard, 2012).

76. Maurice Blanchot, *L'Écriture du désastre* (Paris: Gallimard, 1980), 219, italics in original.

77. Nabil Sulayman, "Fawra Riwā'iyya Sūriyya wa-Asmā' Tatanaffas ʿala Sard al-Ma'sā bi-Judhūrihā wa-Tafāṣīlihā," *al-Hayā*, December 24, 2014.

78. On the politics of performance and (post-)truth in the social-mediatized landscape of the Syria War, see Matt Jones, "Sarin Gas Heartbreak: Theatre and Post-Truth Warfare in Syria," *Theatre Journal* Vol. 72, No. 1 (March 2020): 61–79.

79. Carl von Clausewitz, *On War*, trans. Michael Howard and Peter Paret (Oxford: Oxford University Press, 2007), 28.

80. Mieszkowski, *Watching War*, 73.

81. More than ten years since the Syrian uprising and the disinformation campaigns that swirled around it, legal challenges to the impunity of the early phases of the Syria War have begun to emerge. In both Germany and France, there are now attempts to prosecute affiliates of the Syrian regime for war crimes related to the use of chemical weapons in late 2013. See Marlise Simons, "Criminal Inquiries Loom Over al-Assad's Use of Chemical Arms in Syria," *New York Times*, March 2, 2021. https://www.nytimes.com/2021/03/02/world/europe/syria-chemical-weapons-assad.html; Wedeen, *Authoritarian Apprehensions*, 87–95.

82. Sontag, *Regarding the Pain of Others*, 33.

83. Feldman, *Archives of the Insensible*, 9.

84. Georg Lukács, *The Theory of the Novel: A Historico-Philosophical Essay on the Forms of Great Epic Literature*, trans. Anna Bostock (Cambridge, MA: MIT Press, 1971), 121.

85. David Couzens Hoy, *The Time of Our Lives: A Critical History of Temporality* (Cambridge, MA: MIT Press, 2009), 93.

86. Pheng Cheah, *What Is a World? On Postcolonial Literature as World Literature* (Durham, NC: Duke University Press, 2016), 184.

87. Ibid., 312.

88. Jacques Derrida, "No Apocalypse, Not Now (Full Speed Ahead, Seven Missiles, Seven Missives), trans. Catherine Porter and Phillip Lewis," *Diacritics* Vol. 14, No. 2 (Summer 1984): 20–31, at 20.

89. Ibid., 21.

90. Pinksy, *Inferno of Dante* , 237.

CHAPTER 6

1. Ahmad Shawqi, "Nakbat Dimashq," in *Dīwān al-Nahḍa* (Beirut: Dār al-ʿIlm li-l-Malāyīn, 1982), 162–66, at 164; this translation comes from Hussein N. Kadhim, *The Poetics of Anti-Colonialism in the Arabic Qaṣīdah* (Leiden: Brill, 2004), 45.

2. Václav Havel, "Stories and Totalitarianism, trans. Paul Wilson," *Index on Censorship* Vol. 17, No. 3 (1988): 14–21, at 14.

3. Herbert Marcuse, *The Aesthetic Dimension: Toward a Critique of Marxist Aesthetics*, trans. Herbert Marcuse and Erica Sherover (Boston: Beacon Press, 1978), 68.

4. Kadhim, *The Poetics of Anti-Colonialism*, 44.

5. Gary J. Shipley, *Stratagem of the Corpse: Dying with Baudrillard, a Study of Sickness and Simulacra* (London: Anthem Press, 2020), 22.

6. Theodor W. Adorno, *Aesthetic Theory*, ed. Gretel Adorno and Rolf Tiedemann, trans. Robert Hullot-Kentor (Minneapolis: University of Minnesota Press, 1997), 39.

7. Dragana Obradović, *Writing the Yugoslav Wars: Literature, Postmodernism, and the Ethics of Representation* (Toronto: University of Toronto Press, 2016), 160.

8. Fredric Jameson, "War and Representation," *PMLA* Vol. 124, No. 5 (October 2009): 1532–47, at 1532.

9. Ibid., 1533.

10. Salwa Ismail discusses the role of individual and collective memories of state violence under Hafiz al-Asad in the construction of Syrian subjectivity during the twenty-first century. "In Syria," Ismail writes, "violence constitutes a modality of government." Ismail, *The Rule of Violence: Subjectivity, Memory and Government in Syria* (New York: Cambridge University Press, 2018), 194.

11. Literature and culture from Lebanon and Iraq in wartime are instructive comparative cases. See, for example, miriam cooke, *War's Other Voices: Women Writers on the Lebanese Civil War* (Cambridge: Cambridge University Press, 1987); Ken Seigneurie, *Standing By the Ruins: Elegiac Humanism in Wartime and Postwar Lebanon* (New York: Fordham University Press, 2011); Haytham Bahoora, "Writing the Dismembered Nation: The Aesthetics of Horror in Iraqi Narratives of War," *Arab Studies Journal* Vol. 23,

No. 1 (Fall 2015): 184–208; Ikram Masmoudi, *War and Occupation in Iraqi Fiction* (Edinburgh: Edinburgh University Press, 2015); Kamran Rastegar, *Surviving Images: Cinema, War, and Cultural Memory in the Middle East* (New York: Oxford University Press, 2015), esp. 155–84.

12. Mbembe, "Necropolitics, trans. Libby Meintjes," *Public Culture* Vol. 15, No. 1 (Winter 2003): 11–40, at 39.

13. Abir Hamdar, "The Syrian Corpse: The Politics of Dignity in Visual and Media Representations of the Syrian Revolution," *Journal for Cultural Research* Vol. 22, No. 1 (2018): 73–89, at 77.

14. Hamdar, "The Syrian Corpse," 74.

15. Ibid., 86. miriam cooke makes a similar move by assimilating critical cultural production during the Syrian revolution or the time of the Syria War to the work of the "artist-activist," a figure that can be (read as being) as restrictive as it may be expressive. cooke, *Dancing in Damascus: Creativity, Resilience, and the Syrian Revolution* (New York: Routledge, 2017), 1–2.

16. Soraya Morayef, "Khaled Khalifa: 'Revolutions Can't be Reversed,'" *Jadaliyya*, July 8, 2014. http://www.jadaliyya.com/pages/index/18435/khaled-khalifa_revolutions-cant-be-reversed; Khaled Khalifa and Rachael Daum, "Syrian Novelist Khaled Khalifa: 'I Have Always Wondered About the Ability of Some Writers to Remain Silent,'" *Arabic Literature (in English) Blog*, April 11, 2016. https://arablit.org/2016/04/11/syrian-novelist-khaled-khalifa-i-have-always-wondered-about-the-ability-of-some-writers-to-remain-silent/.

17. Sue Tait, "Visualising Technologies and the Ethics and Aesthetics of Screening Death," *Science as Culture* Vol. 18, No. 3 (September 2009): 333–53, at 336.

18. Hannah Arendt, *On Violence* (New York: Harcourt, Brace & Company, 1970), 67–68.

19. Judith Butler, "Critique, Coercion, and Sacred Life in Benjamin's 'Critique of Violence,'" in *Political Theologies: Public Religions in a Post-Secular World*, ed. Hent de Vries and Lawrence Eugene Sullivan (New York: Fordham University Press, 2006), 201–19, at 207.

20. Steven Miller, *War After Death: On Violence and Its Limits* (New York: Fordham University Press, 2014), 4.

21. Khalid Khalifa, *Madīḥ al-Karāhiyya: Riwāya* (Beirut: Dār al-Ādāb, 2008 [2006]) [Khaled Khalifa, *In Praise of Hatred*, trans. Leri Price (London: Doubleday, 2012)]; Khalid Khalifa, *Lā Sakākīn fī Maṭābikh hadhihi al-Madīna: Riwāya* (Beirut: Dār al-Ādāb,

2013) [Khaled Khalifa, *No Knives in the Kitchens of This City*, trans. Leri Price (Cairo: Hoopoe, 2016)].

22. Khaled Khalifa, *Al-Mawt 'Amal Shāq: Riwāya* (Cairo: Dār al-'Ayn li-l-Nashr, 2016). While I cite Leri Price's English-language translation, *Death Is Hard Work* (New York: Farrar, Straus and Giroux, 2018), throughout, I refer to the novel as *Dying Is Hard Work*, a title I prefer for its resonance with Faulkner's *As I Lay Dying*. Also, this research was concluded before the appearance of the English-language edition.

23. For the influence of Faulkner on generations of Arab writers in modern and contemporary literary history, see Tawfiq Yousef, "The Reception of William Faulkner in the Arab World," *American Studies International* No. 33, No. 2 (1995): 41–48; Hosam Aboul-Ela, *Other South: Faulkner, Coloniality, and the Mariátegui Tradition* (Pittsburgh, PA: University of Pittsburgh Press, 2007), 130–35.

24. William Faulkner, *As I Lay Dying* (New York: Vintage, 1964), 42–43.

25. Ibid., 110.

26. Ibid., 161–68.

27. Khalifa, *al-Mawt*, 5; *Death*, 4.

28. Khalifa, *al-Mawt*, 6; *Death*, 4–5.

29. Khalifa, *al-Mawt*, 6; *Death*, 5.

30. Khalifa, *al-Mawt*, 11; *Death*, 11.

31. Khalifa, *al-Mawt*, 11.

32. Khalifa, *al-Mawt*, 15; *Death*, 16.

33. Khalifa, *al-Mawt*, 25; *Death*, 28.

34. Khalifa, *al-Mawt*, 27; *Death*, 31.

35. Khalifa, *al-Mawt*, 28; *Death*, 31.

36. Khalifa, *al-Mawt*, 28; *Death*, 32.

37. Khalifa, *al-Mawt*, 35; *Death*, 40.

38. Khalifa, *al-Mawt*, 35; *Death*, 41. While I have opted to rely on the published English-language version of the novel, my preference for "dying" over "death" reflects the novel's depiction of human finitude as a complex and contingent process that defines the struggles of these three characters and everyone they encounter along the way.

39. Khalifa, *al-Mawt*, 43; *Death*, 51.

40. Khalifa, *al-Mawt*, 58–59; *Death*, 70.

41. Khalifa, *al-Mawt*, 51; *Death*, 61.

42. Khalifa, *al-Mawt*, 74; *Death*, 87–88.

43. Khalifa, *al-Mawt*, 77; *Death*, 92.

44. Khalifa, *al-Mawt*, 79; *Death*, 94.

45. Khalifa, *al-Mawt*, 80; *Death*, 96.

46. Khalifa, *al-Mawt*, 82; *Death*, 98.

47. Khalifa, *al-Mawt*, 95; *Death*, 112–13.

48. Khalifa, *al-Mawt*, 99; *Death*, 117.

49. Khalifa, *al-Mawt*, 99; *Death*, 118.

50. Khalifa, *al-Mawt*, 106; *Death*, 126.

51. Khalifa, *al-Mawt*, 114; *Death*, 136.

52. Khalifa, *al-Mawt*, 129; *Death*, 154.

53. Khalifa, *al-Mawt*, 130; *Death*, 154.

54. Khalifa, *al-Mawt*, 135; *Death*, 160–61.

55. Khalifa, *al-Mawt*, 138; *Death*, 164.

56. Khalifa, *al-Mawt*, 151; *Death*, 180.

57. Erin E. Edwards, *The Modernist Corpse: Posthumanism and the Posthumous* (Minneapolis: University of Minnesota Press, 2018), 42.

58. Tait, "Visualising Technologies," 335.

59. See, for example, Thomas Keenan and Eyal Weizman, *Mengele's Skull: The Advent of a Forensic Aesthetics* (Berlin: Sternberg Press, 2012).

60. George Pitcher, "The Misfortunes of the Dead," *American Philosophical Quarterly* Vol. 21, No. 2 (April 1984): 183–88, at 184.

61. Sawsan Jamil Hasan, *Qamīṣ al-Layl: Riwāya* (Amman: Dār Nūn, 2014).

62. Sawsan Jamil Hasan, *Ḥarīr al-Ẓalām: Riwāya* (Latakia: Dār al-Ḥiwār li-l-Nashr wa-l-Tawzīʿ, 2009); Hasan, *Alf Layla fī Layla: Riwāya* (Beirut: al-Dār al-ʿArabiyya li-l-ʿUlūm Nāshirūn, 2010); Hasan, *al-Nabbāshūn: Riwāya* (Beirut: Dār al-Ādāb, 2012); Hasan, *Khānāt al-Rīḥ: Riwāya* (Cairo: al-Hayʾa al-Miṣriyya al-ʿĀmma li-l-Kitāb, 2017).

63. Hasan, *Qamīṣ al-Layl*, 7

64. Ibid., 9.

65. Ibid., 12

66. Nabil Sulayman considers the significance of sectarianism in *Night Shirt* and the Syria War novel in "Sardīyya Sūrīyya Jadīda li-l-Ṭāʾifīyya," *al-Ittiḥād*, August 7, 2014. https://www.alittihad.ae//article/68406/2014. For a broader discussion of representations of the sectarian in contemporary Arabic literature, see Sulayman, *Akhyūlāt Riwāʾiyya li-l-Qamʿ wa-l-Ṭāʾifiyya* (Beirut: Dār al-Tanwīr li-l-Ṭibāʿa wa-l-Nashr, 2015).

67. Hasan, *Qamīṣ al-Layl*, 13.

68. Ibid., 37–38.

69. Ibid., 120.

70. Ibid., 124.

71. Ibid., 140.

72. Ibid., 165.

73. Ibid., 167.

74. Ibid., 168.

75. Ibid., 179.

76. Ibid., 195.

77. Ibid., 195.

78. Ibid., 198.

79. Ibid., 203–4.

80. Ibid., 204.

81. Ibid., 205.

82. Gilles Deleuze and Claire Parnet, *Dialogues,* trans. Hugh Tomlinson and Barbara Habberjam (New York: Columbia University Press, 1987), 2.

83. Gilles Deleuze, "Control and Becoming (Conversation with Toni Negri)," *Futur Antérieur* 1 (Spring 1990)," in *Negotiations, 1972–1990*, trans. Martin Joughin (New York: Columbia University Press, 1995), 169–76, at 170.

84. Edwards, *The Modernist Corpse*, 60.

85. Mazin ʿArafa, *al-Gharānīq: Riwāya* (Beirut: Nawfal, 2017). See, too, Magalí Armillas-Tiseyra, *The Dictator Novel: Writers and Politics in the Global South* (Evanston, IL: Northwestern University Press, 2019).

86. Mazin ʿArafa, *Waṣāyā al-Ghubār: Riwāya* (Damascus: Dār al-Takwīn, 2011); ʿArafa, *Sarīr ʿalā al-Jabha: Riwāya* (Beirut: Hachette Antoine, 2019).

87. Shahab Ahmed, "Ibn Taymiyyah and the Satanic Verses," *Studia Islamica* 87 (1998): 67–124; and Ahmed, *Before Orthodoxy: The Satanic Verses Incident in Early Islam* (Cambridge, MA: Harvard University Press, 2017).

88. ʿArafa, *al-Gharānīq*, 10.

89. Ibid., 19–20.

90. Ibid., 44.

91. Ibid., 49.

92. Ibid., 57.

93. Ibid., 58.

94. Ibid., 59.

95. Ibid., 65.

96. Ibid., 66.

97. Ibid., 68.

98. Ibid., 84.

99. Ibid., 95.

100. Ibid., 95

101. Ibid., 112.

102. Ibid., 115.

103. Ibid., 118.

104. Ibid., 119.

105. Ibid., 129.

106. Ibid., 142–44.

107. Ibid., 145.

108. Ibid., 161.

109. Ibid., 190.

110. Ibid., 191.

111. Ibid., 194.

112. Ibid., 195.

113. Ibid., 207–9.

114. Ibid., 209–11.

115. Ibid., 355

116. Ibid., 356.

117. Roberto González Echevarría, "The Dictatorship of Rhetoric/the Rhetoric of Dictatorship: Carpentier, García Márquez and Roa Bastos," *Latin American Research Review* Vol. 15, No. 3 (1980): 205–28, at 221.

118. Achille Mbembe, *On the Postcolony* (Berkeley: University of California Press, 2001), 165. See, too, Cécile Bishop, *Postcolonial Criticism and Representations of African Dictatorship: The Aesthetics of Tyranny* (London: Modern Humanities Research Association and Maney Publishing, 2014).

119. Bahoora, "Writing the Dismembered Nation," 188.

120. Sinan Antoon, *The Corpse Washer*, trans. Sinan Antoon (New Haven,CT: Yale University Press, 2013); Hassan Blasim, *The Corpse Exhibition and Other Stories of Iraq*, trans. Jonathan Wright (New York: Penguin Books, 2014); Ahmed Saadawi, *Frankenstein in Baghdad*, trans. Jonathan Wright (New York: Penguin Books, 2017).

121. Agnes Heller, *Immortal Comedy: The Comic Phenomenon in Art, Literature, and Life* (Lanham: Lexington Books, 2005), 78.

122. Ibid., 82.

123. Ibid., 78.

124. Nadim Jarjura, "Su'dad Ka'dān li-l-'Arabī al-Jadīd: Al-Nās hunā Ya'īshūn min Dūn Ẓalāl," *al-'Arabī al-Jadīd*, October 22, 2018.

125. Ibid. See, too, Dellair Youssef, "Su'dad Ka'dān: al-Wāqi'iyya al-Siḥriyya Tatasallal ilā Kull Aflāmī: Ḥiwār ma'a al-Mukhrija al-Sīnamā'iyya Su'dad Ka'dān," *Ḥikāya mā inḥakat/Syria Untold*, July 15, 2021. https://syriauntold.com/2021/07/15/.

126. The overdetermined meanings of death, dying, and dead bodies across different literary contexts constitute such a vast subject that this chapter can only present a partial reconstruction and analysis of this phenomenon. See, for example, Alan Warren Friedman. *Fictional Death and the Modernist Enterprise* (Cambridge, UK: Cambridge University Press, 1995); Robert H. Moser, *The Carnivalesque Defunto: Death and the Dead in Modern Brazilian Literature* (Athens: Ohio University Press, 2008); David Sherman, *In a Strange Room: Modernism's Corpses and Mortal Obligation* (New York: Oxford University Press, 2014); Thomas W. Laqueur, *The Work of the Dead: A Cultural History of Mortal Remains* (Princeton, NJ: Princeton University Press, 2015); Edwards, *The Modernist Corpse*; Jacqueline Elam and Chase Pielak, *Corpse Encounters: An Aesthetics of Death* (Lanham, UK: Lexington Books, 2018).

127. Laqueur, *The Work of the Dead*, 1.

128. Ibid., 8

129. Ibid., 1.

130. Ibid., 11–12.

131. Allen Feldman, *Archives of the Insensible: Of War, Photopolitics, and Dead Memory* (Chicago: The University of Chicago Press, 2015), 9.

132. Jacques Rancière, "The Aesthetic Dimension: Aesthetics, Politics, Knowledge," *Critical Inquiry* Vol. 36, No. 1 (2009): 1–19, at 5; Feldman, *Archives of the Insensible*.

133. For a searching discussion of this question, see Yassin al-Haj Saleh, *al-Faẓī' wa-l-Tamthīl: Mudāwalāt fī Shakl Sūriyā al-Mukharrab wa-Tashakkulihā al-'Asīr* (Beirut: Mu'assasat Dār al-Jadīd, 2021).

CONCLUSION

1. Sven Lütticken, "Cultural Revolution," *New Left Review* 87 (May/June 2014): 115–31, at 117.

2. Terry Eagleton, *The Ideology of the Aesthetic* (Malden, MA: Blackwell, 1990), 27.

3. Salaheddin Bitar [Salah al-Din al-Bitar], "The Rise and Decline of the Baath," *Middle East International* (June 1971): 12–15, at 12.

4. *City of Ghosts* (Matthew Heineman, 2017); *Our Terrible Country* (Muhammad Ali Atassi, 2014); *Return to Homs* (Talal Derki, 2013); *Of Fathers and Sons* (Talal Derki, 2017); *Cries from Syria* (Evgeny Afineevsky, 2017); *For Sama* (Waad al-Kateab, 2019); *Last Men in Aleppo* (Feras Fayyad, 2017); *The Cave* (Feras Fayyad, 2019). See, too, Wasim al-Sharqi, "al-Wathā'iqī al-Sūrī wa-Jumhūruhu: Bayna Bunyat al-Sūq wa-Falsafat al-Ikhrāj," *Ḥikāya mā inḥakat/Syria Untold*, December 18, 2019. https://syriauntold.com/2019/12/18/. One noteworthy feature of this documentary filmmaking fascination with the Syrian case is its co-implication with global discourses of humanitarianism. For a critique of the "humanitarian" practices of documentary films in relation to contemporary atrocity, see Pooja Rangan, *Immediations: The Humanitarian Impulse in Documentary* (Durham, NC: Duke University Press, 2017); relatedly, on the "irony" of what she calls posthumanitarian expressions of solidarity in global culture, see Lilie Chouliaraki, *The Ironic Spectator: Solidarity in the Age of Post-Humanitarianism* (Cambridge, UK: Polity, 2013).

5. Fred Lawson, "Social Bases for the Hamah Revolt," *MERIP* No. 110 (1982): 24–28, at 25. See, too, Raymond A. "Hinnebusch, "Rural Politics in Baʿthist Syria: A Case Study in the Role of the Countryside in the Political Development of Arab Societies," *Review of Politics* Vol. 44, No. 1 (January 1982): 110–30; Hanna Batatu, *Syria's Peasantry, the Descendants of Its Lesser Rural Notables, and Their Politics* (Princeton, NJ: Princeton University Press, 1999).

6. Jean-Louis Comolli and Serge Daney, "Entretien avec Omar Amiralay," *Cahiers du cinéma* No. 290–291 (juillet-août 1978): 79–89, at 79.

7. Ibid., 82.

8. Ibid., 81.

9. Along these lines, one might also think about the viewpoint of Amiralay's comrade in arms Saʿdallah Wannous, the playwright who called for a "theater of politicization" (*masraḥ al-tasyīs*) that would call into presence its own engaged audience. See Edward Ziter, *Political Performance in Syria: From the Six-Day War to the Syrian Uprising* (New York: Palgrave Macmillan, 2015); Robert Myers and Nada Saab, eds., *Sentence to Hope: A Saʿdallah Wannous Reader* (New Haven, CT: Yale University Press, 2019); Sonja Mejcher-Atassi and Robert Myers, eds., *The Theatre of Saʿdallah Wannous: A Critical Study of the Syrian Playwright and Public Intellectual* (Cambridge, UK: Cambridge

University Press, 2021). Amiralay also made a documentary about Wannous on the eve of his untimely death from cancer: Amiralay, "*. . . wa-Hunāk Ashyā' Kathīra Kāna Yumkin an Yataḥaddath 'anhā al-Mar'* (France-Syria: ARTE France–Grains de Sable, 1997).

10. R. Shareah Taleghani, "Docu-Ironies and Visions of Dissent in the Films of Omar Amiralay," in *Generations of Dissent: Intellectuals, Cultural Production, and the State in the Middle East and North Africa*, ed. Alexa Firat and R. Shareah Taleghani (Syracuse, NY: Syracuse University Press, 2020), 239–55, at 251. See, too, Hala Alabdallah's recent documentary about Amiralay: *Omar Amiralay: Sorrow, Time, Silence* (France-Syria: moderato, 2021).

11. This is drawn from the passage cited in the epigraph to Chapter 1. Hafiz al-Asad, *Kadhālika Qāla al-Asad*, ed. Mustafa Tlas (Damascus: Dār Ṭlās, 2001), 345.

12. Mohja Kahf, "The Silences of Contemporary Syrian Literature," *World Literature Today* Vol. 75, No. 2 (Spring 2001): 224–36; Omar Ilsley, "Syria: Hama Massacre," in *Hushed Voices: Unacknowledged Atrocities of the 20th Century*, ed. Heribert Adam (Berkshire, UK: Berskhire Academic Press, 2011), 125–37; Raphaël Lefèvre, *Ashes of Hama: The Muslim Brotherhood in Syria* (New York: Oxford University Press, 2013); Dara Conduit, "The Syrian Muslim Brotherhood and the Spectacle of Hama," *Middle East Journal* Vol. 70, No. 2 (Spring 2016): 211–26; Salwa Ismail, *The Rule of Violence: Subjectivity, Memory and Government in Syria* (New York: Cambridge University Press, 2018), esp. 131–58.

13. Ziter, *Political Performance in Syria*, 38–44; Robyn Creswell, "Syria's Lost Spring," *NYR Blog*, February 16, 2015. http://www.nybooks.com/daily/2015/02/16/syria-lost-spring/; Creswell, "Voices from a Different Syria." *NYR Blog*, March 21, 2016. http://www.nybooks.com/daily/2016/03/21/voices-from-different-syria-abounaddara-films/; Donatella Della Ratta, *Shooting a Revolution: Visual Media and Warfare in Syria* (London: Pluto Press, 2018); Lisa Wedeen, *Authoritarian Apprehensions: Ideology, Judgment, and Mourning in Syria* (Chicago: University of Chicago Press, 2019); Josepha Ivanka Wessels, *Documenting Syria: Film-Making, Video Activism and Revolution* (London: I. B. Tauris, 2019), 174–75. It may be too soon to definitively identify a distinct aesthetic that is both in and of the effervescent Syrian diaspora—as artists and communities in Germany, France, Lebanon, and elsewhere reshape what it means to be Syrian—since the emergence of the uprising in 2011. For a fascinating examination of the language of dissent in the time of the Syrian Revolution, see Ilaf Badr al-Din, *'Indamā Hatafū "li-l-Abad": Lughat al-Thawra al-Sūriyya* (Damascus: Dār Mamdūḥ 'Udwān li-l-Nashr wa-l-Tawzī', 2018).

14. Whereas Hafiz al-Asad ruled the country for thirty years with the same culture minister, Najah al-'Attar, it is striking that there have been no less than eight ministers during the Bashar al-Asad presidency: Maha Qannut (2000–2001), Najwa Qassab Hasan (2001–2003), Mahmud al-Sayyid (2003–2006), Riyad Na'san Agha (2006–2010), Riyad 'Ismat (2010–2012), Lubana Mshaweh (2012–2014), 'Isam Khalil (2014–2016), and Muhammad al-Ahmad (2016–).

15. For more on this contretemps, see Bashar Dreib, "Muḥammad al-Aḥmad Yarud 'alā al-Mudāfi'īn 'an 'Umar Amīrālāy...wa-Yakshif 'an Khāriṭat Mahrajān al-Sīnamā," *DP-News*, February 16, 2011. http://www.dp-news.com/pages/detail.aspx?articleid=74571; Ossama Mohammed, "al-Tamthīl bi-Amīrālāy," *al-Safīr*, February 25, 2011. https://assafir.com/Article/229597.

16. Donatella Della Ratta, "Dramas of the Authoritarian State," *Middle East Report Online: Interventions*, February 2012. http://www.merip.org/mero/interventions/dramas-authoritarian-state; Rebecca Joubin, "Resistance amid Regime Co-Optation on the Syrian television series *Buq'at Daw'*, 2001–2012," *Middle East Journal* Vol. 68, No. 1 (Winter 2014): 9–32.; Lisa Wedeen, "Ideology and Humor in Dark Times: Notes from Syria," *Critical Inquiry* 39 (Summer 2013): 841–73; Rebecca Joubin, *Mediating the Uprising: Narratives of Gender and Marriage in Syrian Television Drama* (New Brunswick, NJ: Rutgers University Press, 2020), 63–75.

17. Kusturica's sprawling historical epic *Underground* (*Podzemlje*) (1995), which is likely the film Suwaylih has in mind here (although Suwaylih incorrectly refers to Kusturica as Bosnian), is a manic and masterful achievement of world cinema awarded the Palme d'Or at the Cannes film festival. It has come under critical fire for its perceived pro-Serbian bias, both in its depictions of the Balkans during World War II and its slant on Yugoslav history in the decades that followed. Kusturica himself—in a fascinating parallel with respect to Said's politics that Suwaylih likely overlooked—has been accused of overemphasizing the historical suffering of Serbs and, relatedly, of being an apologist for the brutal rule of Slobodan Milošević.

18. Khalil Suwaylih, "Jūd Sa'īd: Dhāt Marra, Kānat Hunak . . . Ḥimṣ!," *al-Akhbār*, June 13, 2016. https://al-akhbar.com/Literature_Arts/215189/.

19. Zaman al-Wasl, "'Rain of Homs': Propaganda Film Whitewashes Assad's Crimes in Besieged City," *Syrian Observer*, October 25, 2017. https://syrianobserver.com/EN/features/21998/rain_homs_propaganda_film_whitewashes_assad_crimes_besieged_city.html. See, too, Enab Baladi, "Syrian Cinema in the Service of the Dictator, Concealing His Crimes," *Enab Baladi*, November 4, 2018. https://english.enabbaladi.net/archives/2018/11/syrian-cinema-in-the-service-of-the-dictator-concealing-his-crimes/.

20. Katarzyna Ruchel-Stockmans, "Towards a Poor Cinema: The Performativity of Mobile Cameras in New Image Wars," in *Visualizing War: Emotions, Technologies, Communities*, ed. Anders Engberg-Pedersen and Kathrin Maurer (New York: Routledge, 2018), 110–29, at 118.

21. My discussion of ruins and ruination here must remain cursory. For serious engagement with these questions, see Yael Navaro-Yashin, "Affective Spaces, Melancholic Objects: Ruination and the Production of Anthropological Knowledge," *Journal of the Royal Anthropological Institute* Vol. 15, No. 1 (March 2009): 1–18; Ken Seigneurie, *Standing by the Ruins: Elegiac Humanism in Wartime and Postwar Lebanon* (New York: Fordham University Press, 2011); Ann Laura Stoler, "'The Rot Remains': From Ruins to Ruination," in *Imperial Debris: On Ruins and Ruination*, ed. Ann Laura Stoler (Durham, NC: Duke University Press, 2013), 1–36; Andrew Scheinman, "Palmyra, or the Construction of Ruin," *Thresholds* 48 (Spring 2020): 62–72; Anne-Marie McManus, "On the Ruins of What's to Come, I Stand: Time and Devastation in Syrian Cultural Production Since 2011," *Critical Inquiry* Vol. 48, No. 1 (Autumn 2021): 45–67.

22. Alexa Firat, "Re-Formed Discourse: *Awrāq, Journal of the Syrian Writers' Association*," *Alif: Journal of Comparative Poetics* 37 (2017): 262–87, at 265.

23. Kahf, "Silences of Contemporary Syrian Literature." It bears emphasizing that a trickle of literature began to deal with Hama and its consequences during the early 2000s. For example, Manhal al-Sarraj, *Kamā Yanbaghī li-Nahr: Riwāya* (Sharjah: Dā'irat al-Thaqāfa wa-l-'Ilām, 2003); Khaled Khalifa, *Madīḥ al-Karāhiyya: Riwāya* (Beirut: Dār al-Ādāb, 2008) [Khaled Khalifa, *In Praise of Hatred*, trans. Leri Price (London: Doubleday, 2012)]. That trickle became a river following the 2011 uprising, as more recent work turned back to "the events" of 1982 amid fresh collective trauma: Manhal al-Sarraj. *'Āṣī al-Damm: Riwāya* (Beirut: Dār al-Ādāb, 2012); Khaled Khalifa, *Lā Sakākīn fī Maṭābikh hādhihi al-Madīna: Riwāya* (Beirut: Dār al-Ādāb, 2013) [Khaled Khalifa, *No Knives in the Kitchen of This City*, trans. Leri Price (Cairo: Hoopoe, 2014)]).

24. Firat, "Re-Formed Discourse," 279.

25. Fawwaz Haddad, *al-Sūriyyūn al-A'dā': Riwāya* (Beirut: Riyad el-Rayyes li-l-Kutub wa-l-Nashr, 2014).

26. Unfortunately, very little has been written about Haddad's oeuvre and not a single book-length work of his has appeared in English translation. See, though, Max Weiss, "Prelude to Solo Piano Music, *Vice Magazine*, December 3, 2012. https://www.vice.com/en/article/mvpngn/prelude-to-solo-piano-music-0004567-v19n11; Weiss, "Who Laughs Last: Literary Transformations of Syrian Authoritarianism," in *Middle East Authoritarianisms: Governance, Contestation, and Regime Resilience in*

Syria and Iran, ed. Steven Heydemann and Reinoud Leenders (Stanford, CA: Stanford University Press, 2013), 143–65, esp. 151–55.

27. Kahf, "Silences of Contemporary Syrian Literature," 235.

28. Most notably, the writer Manhal al-Sarraj, who now resides in Sweden. See al-Sarraj, *Kamā Yanbaghī li-Nahr*; Sarrāj, *'Āṣī al-Damm*. See, too, Astrid Ottosson al-Bitar, "Giving Voice to Silenced Stories in the Novel *Kamā Yanbaghī Li-Nahr* [*As Is Appropriate for a River*]," *Orientalia Suecana* 59 (2010): 73–84; Ismail, *Rule of Violence*, esp. 131–58.

29. Haddad, *al-Sūriyyūn al-A'dā'*, 51.

30. Ibid., 399.

31. Ibid., 434.

32. Ibid., 472.

33. Salma Salim, "Fawwāz Ḥaddād fī 'al-Sūriyyūn al-A'dā": Taḥawwulāt al-Bashar fī Bawtaqat 'al-Abad,'" *Bidāyāt* Vol. 10 (Winter 2015): 135–38, at 138.

34. Yazan El-Haj, "Fawwāz Ḥaddād Asīr La'nat al-Shuhra," *al-Akhbar*, October 3, 2014. https://al-akhbar.com/Kalimat/39000.

35. Such claims must be tempered by level-headed and sensible approaches to the problem of sectarianism in modern Syrian history. See, for example, Nikolaos van Dam, "Middle Eastern Political Clichés: 'Takriti' and 'Sunni' Rule in Iraq; 'Alawi' Rule in Syria, a Critical Appraisal," *Orient* Vol. 21, No. 1 (January 1980): 42–57; Christa Salamandra, "Sectarianism in Syria: Anthropological Reflections," *Middle East Critique* Vol. 22, No. 3 (2013): 303–6; Christopher Phillips, "Sectarianism and Conflict in Syria," *Third World Quarterly* Vol. 36, No. 2 (2015): 357–76; Max Weiss, "Mosaic, Melting Pot, Pressure Cooker: The Religious, the Secular, and the Sectarian in Modern Syrian Social Thought," in *Arabic Thought Against the Authoritarian Age: Towards an Intellectual History of the Present*, ed. Jens Hanssen and Max Weiss (Cambridge, UK: Cambridge University Press, 2018), 181–202.

36. Haddad, *al-Sūriyyūn al-A'dā'*, 446.

37. Ibid., 445.

38. Nabil Sulayman, "al-Ḥafr al-Siyāsī Ḥajar 'Athra fī Riwāyat Fawwāz Ḥaddād," *al-Ḥayā*, October 31, 2014.

39. Jonathan Shannon, "Metonyms of Modernity in Contemporary Syrian Music and Painting," *Ethnos: Journal of Anthropology* Vol. 70, No. 3 (September 2005): 361–86, at 362, emphasis added. Pace miriam cooke's argument that during the late twentieth and early twenty-first centuries, Syrian cultural production "did not leave the country;

[it was] absorbed," in *Dissident Syria: Making Oppositional Arts Official* (Durham, NC: Duke University Press, 2007), 68. This cultural isolation has also been described in terms of ignorance, whether unintentional or not, on the part of people outside of Syria: according to cooke, "Even specialists of Arabic literature did not know much about the cultural scene inside Hafiz [al-]Asad's Syria of the 1990s." "No Such Thing as Women's Literature," *Journal of Middle East Women's Studies* Vol. 1, No. 2 (Spring 2005): 25–54, at 25.

40. Anne-Marie McManus, "The Contemporary Syrian Novel in Translation," *Arab Studies Journal* Vol. 22, No. 1 (Spring 2014): 322–33. Syrian Arabic writing has been translated more often into French, German, and other European languages, but this has as much to do with the political economy of publishing Arabic literature generally as it does with Syrian writing per se. See Edward Said, "Embargoed Literature," *The Nation*, September 17, 1990, 278–79; Hosam Aboul-Ela, "Challenging the Embargo: Arabic Literature in the US Market," *Middle East Report*, No. 219 (Summer 2001): 42–44; Sherif H. Ismail, "Arabic Literature into English: The (Im)possibility of Understanding," *interventions* Vol. 17, No. 6 (2015): 916–31; Robyn Creswell, "Is Arabic Untranslatable?" *Public Culture* Vol. 28, No. 3 (September 2016): 447–56; Lina Mounzer, "War in Translation: Giving Voice to the Women of Syria," *Literary Hub*, October 6, 2016. https://lithub.com/war-in-translation-giving-voice-to-the-women-of-syria/.

41. Walid Mushawwah, "al-Muthaqqaf wa-Sulṭat al-Ḥiwār," *al-Mawqif al-Adabī*, No. 362 (July 2001): 5–7, at 6.

42. Ismail, *Rule of Violence*, 204.

Index

1967 War, 10–11, 30, 63–64, 86, 114, 116, 130, 139, 286, 290, 321, 353n26, 370n80

1973 War, 10, 41, 89, 321, 325

ʻAbd al-Hamid, ʻAbd al-Latif, 11, 33, 89, 98, 102, 104, 113–19, 132, 175, 177, 215–16, 229, 253, 323–24. See also *Nights of the Jackal* (*Layālī Ibn Awā*) (ʻAbd al-Hamid); *Stars in Broad Daylight* (*Nujūm al-Nahār*) (Mohammed)

ʻAbd al-Hamid, Bandar, 73, 122–24, 378n76

Abounaddara film collective, 137, 322, 398n11

Abu Sufyan, 55

"acting 'as if'" (Wedeen), 23, 55, 183, 363–64n8. *See also* Wedeen, Lisa

Adab al-Ḥarb (Mina and al-ʻAttar). See *War Literature*

Adonis (ʻAli Saʻid Ahmad Esber), 11, 137

Adorno, Theodor Wiesengrund, 16, 134, 153, 197, 270, 354n34, 379n3, 382n21, 389n38, 403n6; translation into Arabic, 354n34. *See also* Frankfurt school

aesthetic ideology, 2–3, 11–24, 32, 34, 39, 44–51, 57–59, 61, 69–71, 74–76, 78–83, 85–88, 98, 113, 131–32, 138–40, 155–56, 163, 173–75, 182–83, 194, 223, 230–31, 256–57, 260, 269, 273, 312–13, 317, 320–21, 329, 336–41

aesthetic theory, 15–18, 80–81, 260, 311, 354n34

aesthetics: dark, 105–6, 112, 260; and politics, 2–3, 20–23, 63–64, 82–83, 232, 267, 274, 312–13, 319–20, 322, 354n34; of power, 2–4, 14, 17–18, 32, 81–88, 98, 112, 119, 138, 148, 152–56, 161, 175–77, 186–87, 230, 311, 317, 320, 328, 340, 363–64n8; of resistance, 14, 17–18, 37–38, 98, 186, 254, 274, 317, 320; necroaesthetics, 38, 266–67, 272–76, 280, 310–13; of slowness, 37, 105, 235–37, 246–47, 255–56, 260–69, 398n13; of solidarity, 2, 14, 17–19, 37–38, 111–12, 183, 186–87, 195, 230–33, 254, 293, 310–11, 317–18.

affect, 54, 108, 185–87, 224, 271, 293, 386n12, 387n16. *See also* sensory experience; surveillance

ʿAflaq, Michel, 3–4, 27, 44, 52–53, 55, 56, 349–50n6, 358n64, 368n69

ʿAflaqism, 4, 62, 349n6, 368n69. *See also* ʿAflaq, Michel

agonistic struggle, 2–3, 15, 17–18, 20–21, 43, 81, 87–88, 184, 267, 269, 274, 313, 336–39 passim

Ahmad, Muhammad al-, 322–24, 329, 334–35. *See also* Amiralay, Omar; Syria: Ministry of Culture and National Guidance; National Film Organization; Said, Joud

ʿĀʾid ilā Ḥimṣ (Derki). See *Return to Homs*

Ajami, Saïd, M., 27

ʿAkkawi, Marwan, 144. See also *The Empire of Ghawar* (*Imbrāṭūriyyat Ghawār*)

ʿAlawīs, 5, 32, 52, 97, 118, 119, 188, 200–1, 203–4, 208–11, 220–22, 287, 334–36, 387n17, 393–94n93

Aleppo, 26, 31, 34, 67, 92, 190–91, 221, 237–41, 261–62, 264, 277–78, 284, 286, 383n42, 391n58, 396n123

Alexandria film festival, 110

Al-Lajāt (Shayya), 104–13, 119, 131–32, 216, 235–36, 309–10, 377n58, 378n67. See also *Ascension to Death* (*Miʿrāj al-Mawt*) (Azzam); Azzam, Mamdouh; masculinity; patriarchy; Shayya, Riyad; slow cinema

Al-Roumi, Mayyar, 74, 111

allegory, 22–23, 55, 103, 113, 129, 144, 148, 157, 172, 190, 294, 325–26, 356n51

Allen, Woody, 138, 176

All-Union State Institute of Cinematography in Moscow (VGIK), 74, 104, 253, 316, 372n112

alternative cinema (*al-sīnamā al-badīl*), 71–80, 119, 132, 139, 175, 328, 373n123. *See also* cinema; filmmaking; melodrama; Shahin, Muhammad

Althusser, Louis, 8–9, 16

American Revolution, 25–26

Amiralay, Omar, 33, 74, 244, 315–20, 322–23, 329, 337, 410n9. *See also* documentary film; *Everyday Life in a Syrian Village* (*al-Ḥayā al-Yawmiyya fī Qarya Sūriyya*)

Anderson, Wes, 121

animality, 92–96 passim, 112

animals, 106, 127, 163, 213, 282, 300–2

anti-imperialism, 1, 3, 21–22, 27, 34, 40, 46, 60–65, 76, 85–86, 160–61, 167, 319–20, 339

Anzur, Najdat Ismaʿil, 97

As I Lay Dying (Faulkner), 277–78

Antoon, Sinan, 187, 305, 386n13, 408n120

Arab-Israeli conflict, 10, 27–28, 34, 89, 264. *See also* Israel

Arab nationalism, 2–4, 8–9, 28–30, 34, 41, 46, 55, 58–60, 62–65, 68, 74–77, 80–81, 88–89, 130, 138, 156–63, 167–68, 173–75, 209, 217, 290, 292, 319, 339–40. *See also* Baʿthism; Nasserism

Arab Writers' Union (Ittiḥād al-Kuttāb al-'Arab), 4, 20, 47, 63–67, 88, 329, 370n87. *See also* literature; *al-Mawqif al-Adabī*; politics of literature
Arabic Booker (International Prize for Arabic Fiction), 330, 334
Arabic (language), 24–26, 45, 58, 65, 81, 325–26, 370n87, 390n45
'Arafa, Mazin, 48, 197–98, 294–306, 385n10. See also *al-Ghārānīq* (*The Cranes*)
Arendt, Hannah: 6, 25–26, 49–51, 181, 274–75, 313: on laughter, 153. *See also* laughter; *On Violence*; totalitarianism
Arsuzi, Zaki al-, 44
art, 1, 11–13, 16–17, 20–21, 71, 77, 79, 118–19, 137, 166, 178, 229, 268, 273, 334–38, 353n27, 368n67; art for art's sake, 11–12, 60–68, 71, 79, 336–37. *See also* aesthetics; avant-gardism
Asad, Bashar al-, 3, 9, 15, 19–20, 32–36, 136–37, 178–89, 202, 226–30, 238, 322, 333, 338, 368n60, 411n14; and reformism from above, 15, 19, 33–36, 136–37, 180, 230, 322, 333, 338
Asad, Basil al-, 32
Asad, Hafiz al-, 2–3, 6, 8–9, 19, 23, 29–34, 40–64, 80–83, 97, 119, 131, 135–36, 149, 167, 178–80, 186–89, 202–3, 209, 219, 229–30, 320–22, 325, 330, 332, 339, 395n110, 403n10, 411n14, 414n38; and revolution from above, 15, 19, 28, 30, 32, 34–35, 54, 317. *See also* Corrective Movement (*al-Ḥaraka al-Taṣḥīḥiyya*); cultural Asadism; Leader-worship
Asad, Rif'at al-, 31, 153–54, 330–31. *See also* Hama: 1982 massacres; Defense Brigades (Sarāyā al-Difā')
Asadism, 9, 44–46, 349–50n6, 364–65n14; cultural, 21, 32, 43–59, 82; political, 9, 44–46, 340
Asadist-Ba'thist cultural revolution, 1–5, 9–10, 13–24, 32, 34–35, 39, 40–83 passim, 86–92, 98, 111, 113, 130–33, 139–40, 155, 175, 186, 189, 197–98, 230–31, 256, 273–74, 292, 294, 312–17, 321, 328, 329, 336–40. *See also* aesthetics; Asad, Hafiz al-; Asadism; Ba'th Party; Ba'thism
Ascension to Death (*Mi'rāj al-Mawt*) (Azzam), 11, 99–104, 107, 112, 119, 132. See also *Al-Lajāt*; Azzam, Mamdouh; masculinity; patriarchy; Shayya, Riyad
'Attar, Isam al-, 30–31. *See also* Muslim Brothers (*al-Ikhwān al-Muslimūn*); political Islam
'Attar, Najah al-, 21, 45–49, 61, 74–76, 81, 89, 368n59, 411n14. *See also* Syria: Ministry of Culture and National Guidance; *War Literature* (*Adab al-Ḥarb*), (Mina and al-'Attar)
aura, 156, 178, 257. *See also* Benjamin, Walter
authoritarianism, 3, 5–7, 33–36, 187–98, 207–8, 210–11, 215–29 passim, 240, 254, 281, 295–306 passim, 312, 340–41, 351n9, 382n32; authoritarian upgrading, 34–36. *See also* totalitarianism

avant-gardism, 65–69, 76–79. *See also* art; Asadist-Ba'thist cultural revolution; commitment; *iltizām*; vanguardism
Ayalon, Ami, 24–26
Ayubi, Nazih, 30
'Azm, Sadiq Jalal al-, 11, 130, 357–58n60, 379n82
Azzam, Mamdouh, 11, 33, 87, 99–104, 229, 376n40. See also *Ascension to Death* (*Mi'rāj al-Mawt*); *Al-Lajāt*; masculinity; patriarchy; Shayya, Riyad

Badla, Khatib, 388n23
Bahoora, Haytham, 304–5
Bakhtin, Mikhail, 141
Banyas, 90–91
Barbarians' Paradise (*Jannat al-Barābira*) (Suwaylih), 240, 243–52, 327. *See also* the slow witness (slow witnessing); Suwaylih, Khalil; Syrian Revolution (2011–); Syria War
Barthes, Roland, 244–45
Bataille, Georges, 153
Ba'th Party, 1, 3–4, 24, 27–32, 43, 51–59, 187–89, 203–4, 314–20, 349–50n6; neo-Ba'th, 3–4, 28–30, 43, 51–59 passim. *See also* Ba'thism
Ba'thism, 3–4, 7–10, 28–30, 32, 43–44, 46, 54–55, 57, 60–62, 80–83, 135–38, 147–49, 161, 163, 182–83, 186–87, 194, 196, 209, 219, 239–40, 292, 314, 319, 339–40, 349n6, 368n69. *See also* 'Aflaq, Michel; Ba'th Party; Bitar, Salah al-Din; ideology
Bazin, André, 110–11, 156
Bedirxan, Wiam Simav, 38, 253–54, 271. *See also* Homs; Mohammed, Ossama; politics of witness; *Silvered Water, Syria Self-Portrait* (*Mā' al-Fiḍḍa*) (Mohammed and Bedirxan); the slow witness (slow witnessing)
Bengio, Ofra, 358n64
Benjamin, Walter, 16, 20, 178, 189, 275. *See also* aura
Berger, John, 84, 86
Bergson, Henri, 265–66
Beydoun, 'Abbas, 185–86. See also *mukhābarāt* novel
Bitar, Salah al-Din al-, 3–4, 27, 29, 30, 44, 314.
Blanchot, Maurice, 262
Blecher, Robert, 378n67
Boëx, Cécile, 21, 128, 140–41, 356n49, 378n77, 380n9
Border, The (*al-Ḥudūd*) (Lahham), 73, 143, 156–63, 174–76. *See also* comedy; Lahham, Durayd; Maghut, Muhammad al-; satire
Brooks, Peter, 177–78
Brūfā (Rosa Yaseen Hasan). See *Rough Draft*
Buck-Morss, Susan, 20, 224
Bürger, Peter, 69
Burke, Carolyn, 215
Burke, Edmund, 15
Butler, Judith, 275

Cahiers du cinéma, 316–19
Campbell, Robert, 71
Cannes film festival, 252

Carlyle, Thomas, 40, 46, 363n2, 365n18. *See also* heroism
carnivalesque (Bakhtin), 141–42, 152, 302, 381n10
Carroll, Noël, 154, 156
Chaplin, Charlie, 73; and Durayd Lahham, 138, 143–44, 154–56, 176. *See also* comedy
Cheah, Pheng, 266
Christianity, 222, 324–27
cinema, 1, 65, 71–80, 105–22, 128–29, 132–80, 182, 185, 216–19, 252–61, 309–10, 315–28, 338–39, 371–72nn109, 110, 373nn123, 127, 380n9, 381n13, 398n11, 412n16; alternative cinema (*al-sīnamā al-badīl*), 71–80, 119, 132, 139, 175, 328, 373n123; realist cinema (Mohammed), 256–57; slow cinema, 105–6, 235–36; surrealist cinema (Mohammed), 256–57. *See also* All-Union State Institute of Cinematography in Moscow (VGIK); filmmaking; Syria: National Film Organization; politics of film
Cinema Life (*al-Ḥayā al-Sīnamā'iyya*), 43–44, 73–80, 110, 118–24, 132, 155, 176–77. *See also* alternative cinema; filmmaking; Shahin, Muhammad; Syria: Ministry of Culture and National Guidance; Syria: National Film Organization; politics of film
Clark, Katerina, 82–83
Clausewitz, Carl von, 263–64. *See also* war
clowning, 137–38, 141–44, 150, 156. *See also* comedy; Lahham, Durayd; satire
Cold War, 27, 340–41
Columbu, Alessandro, 130–31
Colvin, Marie, 238
comedy, 79, 114–15, 117–19, 120, 124–25, 133, 183–84, 189–98, 300, 305–6, 381n10, 384n4, 388n23; politics of, 134–80. *See also* clowning; Ghawar; Lahham, Durayd; laughter; satire
commitment, 21–22, 59, 79, 80–83, 85–86, 88, 338–39; and film, 76–77, 79, 137–38; and literature, 21–22, 42, 63–71 passim, 88–89, 91, 189, 300, 312. See also *iltizām*; politics of literature; socialist realism
communism, 28–30, 81, 351n9, 387n18, 393n80
concept-history (*Begriffsgeschichte*), 4–5. *See also* Koselleck, Reinhart
Cook, Michael, 357n60
cooke, miriam, 175, 368n67, 404n15, 414n38
corpses, 260–61, 273–94 passim, 308–13 passim. *See also* death; dying; necroaesthetics; necropolitics
Corrective Movement (*al-Ḥaraka al-Taṣḥīḥiyya*), 2, 3–4, 7, 21, 29–30, 42–44, 51–60, 64, 81, 188, 321
corruption, 33, 36, 134, 153, 163–74, 204
coup-proofing, 57–58
coups, 24–27 passim, 52–54, 320–21; February 23, 1966 (neo-Ba'th coup), 28, 43, 55; March 8, 1963 (Ba'th coup), 28–29, 43, 46, 64, 71. *See also* Corrective Movement (*al-Ḥaraka al-Taṣḥīḥiyya*)

Cranes, The (*al-Gharānīq*) (ʿArafa), 294–306. *See also* ʿArafa, Mazin; the satanic verses
Cultural Battles in Syria, 1975–1977 (*Maʿārik Thaqāfiyya fī Sūriya, 1975–1977*) (Sulayman and Yasin), 370n81. See also *Ideology and Literature in Syria*; politics of literature; Sulayman, Nabil; Yasin, Bu ʿAli
cultural history, 8, 11–15, 21, 24–25, 31, 54, 139, 178, 224, 230–31, 321, 353n27. *See also* intellectual history
cultural liberalization: under Bashar al-Asad, 32–36, 136–37, 185, 230, 322; under Hafiz al-Asad, 61–62. *See also* economic liberalization; political liberalization; reformism from above
cultural memory, 31, 73–74, 210, 220, 246, 321, 330–31, 335
cultural revolution, 68, 314. *See also* Asadist-Baʿthist cultural revolution

Damascus, 26–28, 36, 59, 88–89, 142, 182, 217, 243–51 passim, 268–69, 306–7, 325
Damascus Declaration, 189
Damascus international film festival, 73–76, 109, 323
Damascus Spring, 33–36, 188–89, 339
Dante Alighieri: *Inferno, The*, 243–44, 267
Darʿa, 36–37, 254
Day I Lost My Shadow, The (*Yawm Aḍʿatu Ẓillī*) (Kaadan), 276, 306–10, 312. *See also* death; dying; Kaadan, Soudade; necroaesthetics; necropolitics; slow cinema
Dayr al-Zur, 316, 370n87
death, 12, 38, 86, 93, 96–97, 103–4, 221–23, 236, 238–52 passim, 255, 260–61, 266–313, 326–27, 333–34, 405nn22, 38, 409n126. *See also* dying; necroaesthetics; necropolitics; politics of death
Defense Brigades (Sarāyā al-Difāʿ), 31, 153–54, 332. *See also* Hama: 1982 massacres; Rifʿat al-Asad
degenerate art, 77
Deleuze, Gilles, 178, 291–94
Derki, Talal, 327–28
Derrida, Jacques, 266
dictator novel, 294–95, 304–5, 385n10
dictatorship, 6, 18, 22, 24, 32–33, 49–51, 54–55, 131–32, 152–53, 156, 178, 184–91, 200, 206, 210–11, 215, 217–19, 222–26, 276, 294–306, 319–21, 334, 385n10. *See also* authoritarianism; dictator novel; totalitarianism
dissident art, 14, 19–20
documentary film, 178, 246, 252–61, 271, 309–10, 314–23, 327–28, 401–2n73, 410nn4, 9. *See also* Amiralay, Omar; Bedirxan, Wiam Simav; Mohammed, Ossama
documentary imperative, 37–38, 234–38 passim, 242, 246–47, 273
documentary novel, 198, 233. *See also* the novel
Drums of Love (*Ṭubūl al-Ḥubb*) (Maha Hasan), 231, 237–42. *See also* Hasan, Maha

Drumsta, Emily, 232–33
Dūmarī, al-, 388n23
Dying is Hard Work (Khalifa), 242, 276-85, 293-4, 309, 312-13, 405nn 22, 38. *See also* Khalifa, Khaled

Eagleton, Terry, 16–17, 314. *See also* aesthetics; ideology
Early, Evelyn, 370n87
eavesdropping, 198–208 passim. *See also* listening; *mukhābarāt*; *mukhābarāt* novel; surveillance
economic liberalization: under Bashar al-Asad, 32–36, 188–89, 230; under Hafiz al-Asad, 31–32, 58. *See also* cultural liberalization; political liberalization; reformism from above
Edwards, Erin E., 285, 292
eggs, 124, 126–27, 254, 258. *See also* Mohammed, Ossama; *Sacrifices* (*Ṣundūq al-Dunyā*) (Mohammed); *Silvered Water, Syria Self-Portrait* (*Māʾ al-Fiḍḍa*) (Mohammed and Bedirxan)
Egypt, 22, 28–29, 58, 76–77, 132, 144, 337, 365n18, 369n77, 381n13
El Shakry, Omnia, 10
Empire of Ghawar, The (*Imbrāṭūriyyat Ghawār*) (ʿAkkawi), 79, 144–57, 163–64, 174, 176–77. *See also* Lahham, Durayd
End of a Brave Man (*Nihāyat Rajul Shujāʿ*) (Mina), 88–99; television adaptation, 97–98. *See also* Mina, Hanna
Enemy Syrians (*al-Sūriyyūn al-Aʿdāʾ*) (Haddad), 330–37. *See also* Haddad, Fawwaz
environment, 37, 106–10 passim, 191–92, 234–35
epistemological uncertainty, 20–21, 37, 228–34, 247–48, 252, 271, 274. *See also* phenomenological politics; seeing; politics of vision
Esprit, 19
eternity, 8–9, 32, 42, 49, 59, 98, 209, 239–40, 244, 256, 332, 334. *See also* temporality; time
Everyday Life in a Syrian Village (*al-Ḥayā al-Yawmiyya fī Qarya Sūriyya*) (Amiralay), 315–20, 322–23. *See also* Amiralay, Omar
existentialism, 49, 96
Extras, The (*al-Kūmbārs*) (Maleh), 181–86, 195. *See also* Maleh, Nabil

Fanon, Frantz, 68, 275, 319–20
Farzat, ʿAli, 388n23
fascism, 20–21, 46–51 passim, 351n9. *See also* authoritarianism; dictatorship; totalitarianism
Faulkner, William, 277–78, 405nn22, 23. See also *As I Lay Dying*
Feldman, Allen, 256–57, 265, 311
femininity, 84, 87, 92–106, 112, 119–21, 124, 130–32, 153, 181–84, 214–16, 227–29, 242, 374n4. *See also* gender; masculinity; patriarchy; sex: sexual violence; sex: sexuality
Fikr al-ʿAskarī, al- (*Military Thought*), 43–44, 62–63
film. *See* cinema

filmmaking, 71–80, 107, 118–19, 128–29, 139–42, 177, 183, 217–18, 236–37, 253–56, 265–66, 310, 315–16, 320–23, 327, 337–38, 398n11, 410n4; documentary, 178, 246, 252–61, 271, 309–10, 314–23, 327–28, 401–2n73, 410n4, 410–11n9, 411n10; politics of, 71–80, 315–20, 322–29, 337. *See also* All-Union State Institute of Cinematography in Moscow (VGIK); alternative cinema (*al-sīnamā al-badīl*); cinema; *Cinema Life* (*al-Ḥayā al-Sīnamā'iyya*); realist cinema; slow cinema; surrealist cinema; Syria: National Film Organization
Firat, Alexa, 63, 71, 88, 329–30
Foucault, Michel, 214–15
France, 237, 253, 402n81, 411n13
Frankfurt school, 16, 178. *See also* Adorno, Theodor Wiesengrund; Benjamin, Walter; Marcuse, Herbert
free indirect discourse, 91, 200, 212, 332
freedom, 1, 25–26, 61–67, 75–76, 148–49, 185
Free Syrian Army, 278, 283
French Mandate, 24, 26–27, 91–93, 144, 335, 371n109, 393–94n93
French Revolution, 25–26

García Márquez, Gabriel, 385n10
gender, 84–133, 153, 214–15, 326, 371n109, 374n4. *See also* femininity; masculinity; patriarchy; *qabaḍāy*; sex: sexual violence; sex: sexuality
German Democratic Republic, 14–15, 60, 120, 206–8, 224, 390n50, 402n81, 411n13. *See also The Lives of Others* (*Das Leben der Anderen*) (von Donnersmarck); Stasi (Ministerium für Staatsicherheit)
Germany, 46, 198, 261, 286, 295, 337
Gharānīq, al- ('Arafa). See *The Cranes*
Ghawar, 79, 98, 134–80, 300, 384n4. *See also* Durayd Lahham
Gordon, Peter, 12, 353n30
Gramsci, Antonio, 82, 373n133

Haddad, Bassam, 33
Haddad, Fawwaz, 192–93, 330–37, 413n25. *See also Enemy Syrians* (*al-Sūriyyūn al-A'dā'*); *The Treasonous Translator* (*al-Mutarjim al-Khā'in*)
Hafiz, Amin al-, 29, 55
Hafiz, Yasin al-, 11
Halabi, Zeina, 13, 354n31
Hama, 26, 28–31, 238, 248; 1982 massacres, 31, 153–54, 203, 321, 329–35, 387n21, 413n22
Hanoosh, Yasmeen, 14, 353n32
Ḥaraka al-Taṣḥīḥiyya, al-. *See* Corrective Movement
Hasan, Maha, 231–32, 237–42, 245. See also *Drums of Love* (*Ṭubūl al-Ḥubb*)
Hasan, Rosa Yaseen, 187–88, 198–208, 224–25, 229, 389n42. See also *Rough Draft* (*Brūfā*)
Hasan, Sawsan Jamil, 286–94, 406n62. See also *Night Shirt* (*Qamīṣ al-Layl*)
Hawrani, Akram al-, 28

Hawwa, Sa'id, 31, 46
Ḥayā al-Sīnamā'iyya, al- (*Cinema Life*), 43–44, 73–80, 110, 118–19, 121, 122–24, 132, 155, 176–77. *See also* Shahin, Muhammad; Syria: Ministry of Culture and National Guidance; Syria: National Film Organization
Ḥayā al-Yawmiyya fī Qarya Sūriyya, al- (Amiralay). See *Everyday Life in a Syrian Village*
Haydar, Haydar, 11, 66, 73, 365n21
Hegel, Georg Wilhelm Friedrich, 8: and aesthetics, 16–17, 355n38; Georg Lukács on, 16–17; translation into Arabic, 354n34
hegemonic masculinity, 117, 131–32
hegemony, 14, 18
Herminghouse, Patricia A., 14–15
heroism, 3–4, 40–51, 69–70, 78–86, 96–98, 102, 131–33, 147–48, 155–56, 172, 175, 182–83, 240, 256, 292, 294, 303, 312, 319–20, 365n18. *See also* Carlyle, Thomas
heterotopia, 214–15, 225. *See also* Foucault, Michel; mirrors
Hewitt, Andrew, 11, 156, 178, 353n29, 382n28, 384n47
Heydemann, Steven, 30–32, 51, 59, 346, 366n29, 368n57
Hilbig, Wolfgang, 390n50
Hinnebusch, Raymond, 30–32, 34, 54
Hiroshima Mon Amour (Resnais), 307
Hizballah, 34, 341
Homs, 238, 241–42, 258, 289, 323–31, 337. See also *Homs Rain* (*Maṭar Ḥimṣ*) (Said); *Return to Homs* (*'Ā'id ilā Ḥimṣ*) (Derki)
Homs Rain (*Maṭar Ḥimṣ*) (Said), 323–28. *See also* Homs; ruination; Said, Joud; Syria War
Hoy, David Couzens, 266
Ḥudūd, al- (Lahham). See *The Border*
humor. *See* comedy
Hut, Humam, 383n42. *See also* comedy; politics of comedy; satire

Ibrahim, 'Ali Najib, 70–71, 371nn104, 105
ideological state apparatuses (ISAs), 8–9; *See also* Althusser, Louis
ideology, 7–10, 11–12, 16–18, 22, 44–51, 54–57, 62, 86, 129–30, 137, 141, 148–49, 154, 190, 214–15, 292, 314, 317–20, 328, 339, 368n67, 374n4. *See also* aesthetic ideology; Althusser, Louis
Ideology and Literature in Syria, 1967–1973 (*al-Aydiyūlūjīyā wa-l-Adab fī Sūriya, 1967–1973*) (Sulayman and Yasin), 63–64, 375n12. *See also* Sulayman, Nabil; Yasin, Bu 'Ali
iltizām, 68, 80–81. *See also* commitment and literature
Imbrāṭūriyyat Ghawār. See *Empire of Ghawar, The*
In Her Mirrors (*Lahā Marāyā*) (Yazbek), 186, 201, 204, 208–22. *See also* Yazbek, Samar
Inferno, The (Dante Alghieri), 243–44, 267
L'Institut des hautes études cinématographiques (IDHEC), 315

intellectual history, 4–5, 8, 10–17, 28–31, 51–59, 64, 142, 349–50n6
intellectuals, 12, 14, 19–20, 33–34, 42–47, 59–64, 68–69, 130, 137, 156, 193–94, 229, 275, 304, 314, 329, 336–37, 339, 363n4, 364n12, 368n67; and the Syria War, 37–38, 239–40, 245. *See also* intellectual history
International Prize for Arabic Fiction (Arabic Booker), 330, 334
intimacy, 107, 125, 182–84, 206–8, 387n16
Iran, 34, 264
Iranian Revolution, 357–58n60
Iraq: Baʿthism in, 28–29, 55; literature and culture of, 81–82, 187, 304–35
Irigaray, Luce, 215
Ismail, Salwa, 339, 365n19, 367n52, 395n109, 403n10
Ismaʿil, Sidqi, 65–69, 77
Israel, 10, 27–28, 34, 52, 89, 116, 139, 162–63, 170, 264, 321, 341. *See also* Arab-Israeli conflict
Ittiḥād al-Kuttāb al-ʿArab. *See* Arab Writers' Union

Jabbour, Diana, 111, 117–18
Jacquemond, Richard, 369n77
Jadid, Salah, 29
Jameson, Frederic, 69–70, 270–71
Jannat al-Barābira (Suwaylih). See *Barbarians' Paradise*
Jaradi, Ibrahim al-, 177–78, 383n43
Jaysh al-Shaʿb (*The People's Army*), 50, 54, 62–63. *See also* Rahib, Hani al-; Syria: armed forces; Tlas, Mustafa
Joubin, Rebecca, 97–98, 117, 132, 153
Jundī, al- (*The Soldier*), 62–63, 73
June War (1967), 10–11, 30, 63–64, 86, 114, 116, 130, 139, 286, 290, 321, 353n26, 370n80

Kaadan, Soudade, 276, 306–10. See also *The Day I Lost My Shadow* (*Yawm Aḍʿatu Ẓillī*)
Kadhim, Hussein N., 269
Kahf, Mohja, 188–89, 226, 330–31, 387n19, 397n139, 411n12, 413nn22, 26
Kant, Immanuel: and aesthetic criticism, 15–17, 352n24, 355n40; *Critique of Judgment*, translation into Arabic, 354n34
Kassab, Suzanne, 33, 130, 360n86, 364n12, 368n60, 370n80, 379n83
Khaddam, ʿAbd al-Halim, 97
Khalifa, Khalid, 242, 273, 277–85, 380n5
Khalifa, Mustafa, 386n12
Khatib, Hamza al-, 36
Khatib, Husam al-, 69–70, 371nn100, 101
Khoury, Colette, 66
Khoury, Elias, 232
Khuri, Shihada, 62
Kiwan, Fadia, 52–54, 366n33, 367n38
Koselleck, Reinhart, 1, 4–5, 349n2, 350n7, 357n59, 400n45
Kūmbārs, al- (Maleh). See *The Extras*
Kusturica, Emir, 327, 412n16

Lacan, Jacques, 394–95n105; on the mirror stage, 214–15
LaCapra, Dominic, 242

Lahā Marāyā (Yazbek). See *In Her Mirrors*
Lahham, Durayd, 73, 79, 98, 134–80, 300, 381n13, 383n42, 384n4; comparison with Charlie Chaplin, 138, 143–44, 154–56, 176. *See also* Ghawar
language, 40, 67–68, 77, 82, 128–29, 235–36, 244–46, 266–67, 318–20, 339, 400n41
laqṭa, al- ("the shot"): 105, 216–19, 255–56. *See also* filmmaking; Mohammed, Ossama; politics of film; Shayya, Riyad
Latakia, 31, 88, 91–97 passim, 107, 114–15, 120–21, 198, 202–3, 215–16, 253, 286–93 passim
Latin America, 304, 357–58n60; literature of dictatorship in, 385n10
laughter, 118–19, 134, 150, 153, 181–92, 194–98, 224–25, 381n10. *See also* comedy; politics of comedy; satire
Lawson, Fred, 30, 359n75
Layālī Ibn Awā ('Abd al-Hamid). See *Nights of the Jackal*
Leader-worship, 41–42, 45–47. *See also* Asad, Hafiz al-; heroism
Lebanon, 26, 46, 81, 166–67, 170, 411n13; civil war literature, 232–33, 403–4n11; Syrian intervention in, 34, 52, 325
Leenders, Reinoud, 37, 346, 362n92
Lenssen, Anneka, 353n27
Levine, Michael G., 236, 384–5n6
Lewis, Bernard, 358nn63, 64
liberalism, 5, 62, 151, 294, 339, 391n58
liberalization. *See* cultural liberalization, economic liberalization, political liberalization
Limbrick, Peter, 373n127
listening, 23, 187, 198–202, 204–5, 207–8, 222–26. *See also* sensory experience; surveillance
literary criticism, 60–71, 79, 206–7, 224–25
literature, 22, 40, 47–51, 59–71, 88–89, 177–78, 187–89, 192–93, 196–97, 224–26, 232–33, 240, 242, 251, 262–67, 270, 272–73, 275–76, 305, 329–31, 356n51, 369n77, 403n11, 406n66, 413n22; *mukhābarāt* novel, 185–90, 198–208, 221–22, 224–26, 385n10, 390n46; politics of, 59–71, 329–36, 337–38; prison literature, 63, 187, 375n18, 386n12; world literature, 22–23, 178, 356n51, 380n5. *See also* the novel
Littell, Jonathan, 238
Lives of Others, The (*Das Leben der Anderen*) (Florian Henckel von Donnersmarck), 207, 392–93n79
love, 99–103 passim, 125, 182, 202, 205, 208–9, 216, 222, 242, 280–81, 324–25
Lukács, Georg, 16, 68–71, 178, 355n38, 371n106, 383n45, 402n84; importance for Syrian intellectuals, 16, 68–71; *The Theory of the Novel*, 69–70, 265–66; translation into Arabic, 354n34. *See also* ideology; the novel; realism
Lütticken, Sven, 314, 349n4, 409n1

Mā' al-Fiḍḍa (Mohammed and Bedirxan). See *Silvered Water, Syria Self-Portrait*
Ma'ārik Thaqāfiyya fī Sūriya, 1975–1977 (Sulayman and Yasin). See *Cultural Battles in Syria, 1975–1977*

Maghut, Muhammad al-, 138–42; collaboration with Durayd Lahham, 138–42, 153, 156–57, 163–64; 175, 383n42; poetry, 1, 62, 181, 183
Malas, Muhammad, 74, 114, 243
Maleh, Nabil, 73–74, 80, 139, 181–86, 195, 384n4. See also *The Extras (al-Kūmbārs)*
Maqdisi, Antun, 66
Marcuse, Herbert, 16, 40, 268
Maʿrifa, al- (Knowledge), 41–46, 48, 61, 64–71, 74–76, 80, 83
Marks, Laura U., 398n11
Marra Ukhrā (Said). See *Once Again*
Martin, Kevin, 27
Marx, Harpo, 138, 381n10
Marx Brothers, 143–44
masculinity, 27, 45–51, 84–133, 144–56 passim, 170, 181–84, 215–16, 276, 281, 294–306 passim, 340, 374n6; hegemonic masculinity, 117, 131–32. *See also* femininity; gender; patriarchy; *qabaḍāy*
masochism, 47–48
Maṭar Ḥimṣ (Said). See *Homs Rain*
Mawqif al-Adabī, al- (Literary Standpoint), 43–44, 46–51, 65–71, 339
Mawt ʿAmal Shāq, al- (Khalifa). See *Dying is Hard Work*
Mayer, Thomas, 31, 46
Mbembe, Achille, 197, 272–73, 275, 304–5
melodrama, 21–24, 77, 133, 174, 177–78, 328, 337. *See also* Brooks, Peter
"Men" ("*Rijāl*") (Tamir), 84. *See also* Tamir, Zakariya.
metempsychosis (transmigration of souls), 203–4, 209, 220–21. *See also* ʿAlawīs
Mieszkowski, Jan, 237, 264
Millar, Lanie, 353n26
Miller, Steven, 275–76
Mina, Hanna, 11, 61, 66, 70, 87–99, 229, 300, 375n12; literary prize, 198. See also *End of a Brave Man (Nihāyat Rajul Shujāʿ)*; *War Literature (Adab al-Ḥarb)*, (Mina and al-ʿAttar)
Miʿrāj al-Mawt (Azzam). See *Ascension to Death*
mirror stage, the, 214–15, 394–95n105. *See also* Lacan, Jacques
mirrors, 70–71, 106–7, 109, 119, 127–28, 183–84, 208–23, 225, 296, 298
Mitchell, W.J.T., 142–43
mitsprechen (speaking-with), 37–38, 183, 228–33, 236, 246, 253–54, 258, 311, 384–85n6
Mohammed, Ossama, 22–23, 33, 38, 87, 98, 102, 104–9 passim, 114, 118, 119–29, 132, 139, 175, 185–86, 215–19, 232–33, 252–61, 265, 271, 295, 299, 345, 401n67. See also *Sacrifices (Ṣundūq al-Dunyā)*; *Silvered Water, Syria Self-Portrait (Māʾ al-Fiḍḍa)*; *Stars in Broad Daylight (Nujūm al-Nahār)*
Mohsen, Fatima, 81–82
mukhābarāt, 35, 185–93, 198–208, 206–8, 224–26, 280, 287, 335–36. See also *mukhābarāt* novel; *shabbīḥa*, surveillance

mukhābarāt novel, 185–90, 198–208, 221–22, 224–26, 385n10, 390n46. *See also* the novel
Muslim Brothers (*al-Ikhwān al-Muslimūn*), 27, 30–32, 46, 330–36 passim, 360n83. *See also* political Islam
Mutarjim al-Khā'in, al- (Haddad). See *The Treasonous Translator*

Nahda, 67–69, 364n12
narrative, 13, 37–38, 49, 77–78, 97, 105–6, 112, 119, 124–25, 127, 175–76, 187, 199–200, 207, 211–12, 215, 217, 226–27, 232–33, 236–37, 246–47, 255–56, 265–66, 271, 286, 293, 390nn45, 46, 392n75
Nasser, Gamal Abdel, 28, 46, 302
Nasserism, 28
National Bloc (*al-Kutla al-Wataniyya*), 26
National Film Organization (al-Mu'assasa al-'Āmma li-l-Sīnamā, l'Organisme général du cinéma), 4, 14, 20, 71–79, 104–5, 112, 114, 119, 121–22, 132, 140, 144, 186, 314–15, 319–20, 322–24, 338, 372n120. See also *Cinema Life* (*al-Ḥayā al-Sīnamā'iyya*); documentary film; filmmaking; Syria: Ministry of Culture and National Guidance
nationalism. *See* Arab nationalism; Nasserism; Syria: nationalism; Syria: patriotism
Nayrabia, Muwwaffaq, 33
necroaesthetics, 38, 266–67, 272–76, 280, 310–13
necropolitics, 272–73
neo-Ba'th, 3–4, 28–30, 43, 51–59 passim
neoinstitutionalism, 7–8
NFO. *See* National Film Organization
Ngai, Sianne, 15
Night Shirt (*Qamīṣ al-Layl*) (Sawsan Jamil Hasan), 286–94. *See also* death; dying; Hasan, Sawsan Jamil; necro-aesthetics; necropolitics; politics of death; revolution: revolutionary-becoming (*devenir-révolutionnaire*) (Deleuze); sectarianism
Nights of the Jackal (*Layālī Ibn Awā*) ('Abd al-Hamid), 87, 113–19. *See also* 'Abd al-Hamid, 'Abd al-Latif; masculinity; patriarchy
Nihāyat Rajul Shujā' (Mina). See *End of a Brave Man*
Noorani, Yaseen, 18, 355n43
novel, the, 47, 63, 68–71, 86, 178, 185–87, 189–90, 207–8, 222–26, 230, 233–35, 261–71, 280, 370n78, 385n10; dictator novel, 294–95, 304–5, 385n10; documentary novel, 198, 233; *mukhābarāt* novel, 185–90, 198–208, 221–22, 224–26, 385n10, 390n46. *See also* literature; politics of literature; *The Theory of the Novel* (Lukács)
Nujūm al-Nahār (Mohammed). See *Stars in Broad Daylight*

Obradović, Dragana, 270
October War (1973), 10, 41, 89, 321, 325
October War Panorama (Damascus), 41, 325

On Violence (Arendt), 274–75. *See also* Arendt, Hannah
Once Again (*Marra Ukhrā*) (Said), 395n110. *See also* Said, Joud
Ottoman Empire, 24, 26, 210, 221, 396n123

Palmer, Jerry, 197, 389n39
Palmyra (Tadmor), 31, 332
Pan-Arabism. *See* Arab nationalism
patriarchy, 47–51, 85–88, 99–121 passim, 129–33, 152, 208–22 passim, 276. *See also* femininity; gender; heroism; masculinity; sex: sexual violence; sex: sexuality
patriotism, 4, 55–56, 60, 62–63, 85–86, 138–39, 168, 199–200, 219–20, 289, 316, 340; and *Homs Rain* (*Maṭar Ḥimṣ*) (Said), 323–28. *See also* politics of film; ruination; Said, Joud; Syria: National Film Organization; Syria: patriotism; Syrian Revolution (2011–); Syria War
People's Party (*Ḥizb al-Sha'b*), 26
performance, 116–17, 128–29, 141–42, 173, 390, 402n78
Perlmutter, Amos, 56, 340
Perthes, Volker, 7, 35, 44–45, 351n15
phenomenological politics, 229–31. *See also* sensory experience
Picard, Elisabeth, 57–58, 367n50, 367n54, 368n56
pleasure, 15–17, 78–79, 181–84, 196, 198, 224
poetry, 1, 11, 62, 66–68, 192–94, 217, 245–46, 268–69; praise poetry (*madḥ*), 363–64n8
political Islam, 24–25, 27–28, 30–32, 37, 46, 52, 55, 188, 202–3, 222, 248, 264, 278, 283, 302, 304–5, 319, 321, 324–26, 330–36 passim, 351n9, 357–58n60, 360n83, 391n58. *See also* Muslim Brothers (*al-Ikhwān al-Muslimūn*)
political liberalization, under Bashar al-Asad, 32–36, 136, 188–89, 230. *See also* cultural liberalization; economic liberalization
politics, 24, 26–39, 45–59, 320–21, 338–41; aesthetics and, 2–3, 20–21, 23, 63–64, 82–83, 232, 267, 274, 312–13, 319–20, 322, 354n34; of comedy, 134–80; of death, 268–313; of film, 71–80, 315–20, 322–29, 337; of literature, 59–71, 329–38; of masculinity, 84–133; of the senses, 181–226; of silence, 61, 74, 111–12, 183, 188, 190–92, 196, 330–31; of sound, 111, 114, 181, 187–92, 196–97, 199–201, 216–17, 246–47, 272, 386n12; of surveillance, 181–226; of vision, 84, 105–6, 122–23, 128–29, 137, 187, 201–2, 210, 216–19, 222–24, 230, 246, 249, 255–56, 269, 293, 386n12; of witness, 227–67. *See also* aesthetics and politics; authoritarianism; necropolitics; phenomenological politics; totalitarianism
prison literature, 63, 187, 375n18, 386n12
Progressive National Front, 30, 51
psychology, 35, 40, 48, 111, 139–40, 193–94, 201, 213–21 passim, 295, 299–306 passim, 385n10

qabaḍāy (strong man), 97–98, 145–48 passim. *See also* masculinity; violence

Qal'i, Nihad, 139–40, 142, 144, 153, 383n42. *See also* comedy; Lahham, Durayd

Qamīṣ al-Layl (Sawsan Jamil Hasan). See *Night Shirt*

Qannut, Maha, 41–42, 45

Qashush, Ibrahim, 238, 248

Qudsi, Safwan, 42, 83

Raghda: in *The Border* (*al-Ḥudūd*) (Lahham), 157; in *The Report* (*al-Taqrīr*) (Lahham), 164

Rahib, Hani al-, 63, 70

Rancière, Jacques, 15–16, 311, 354n34, 355nn36, 37. 409n132

rape. *See* sex: sexual violence

realism: 47–48, 64, 69–71, 79, 86, 96–97, 117–19, 236–37, 300; realist cinema (Mohammed), 256–57. *See also* politics of literature; socialist realism

reality, 70–71, 190, 213, 219, 228, 261–63, 266, 270, 274, 305–6, 317, 320, 322, 328

reformism from above, 15, 19, 33–36, 136–37, 180, 230, 322, 333, 338. *See also* cultural liberalization; economic liberalization; political liberalization

Report, The (*al-Taqrīr*) (Lahham), 143, 153, 157, 163–74. *See also* Lahham, Durayd; Maghut, Muhammad al-

representation, 22–23, 61, 128–29, 232–33, 256–57, 270–72, 293, 324

resistance, 11, 18–19, 21, 26, 141, 182–83, 273, 305, 327, 339. *See also* aesthetics of power; aesthetics of resistance; aesthetics of solidarity

Return to Homs (*'Ā'id ilā Ḥimṣ*) (Derki), 327–28. *See also* documentary film; Homs; *Homs Rain* (*Maṭar Ḥimṣ*)

revolution, 1–5, 9–10, 22, 24–26, 43, 48, 57, 60–61, 71, 74–79, 81–83, 130–31, 147–48, 230–31, 239, 269, 299, 319–20, 339, 353nn26, 28, 357–58n60, 358nn63, 64; concept-history of (Koselleck), 1, 4–5, 357n59; revolution from above, 15, 19, 28, 30, 32, 34–35, 54; revolutionary-becoming (*devenir-révolutionnaire*) (Deleuze) 291–94; revolutionizing culture (Tizini), 60–61, 89, 336–37. See also *inqilāb*; *On Revolution* (Arendt); Syrian Revolution (2011–); *thawra*

revolution from above, 15, 19, 28, 30, 32, 34–35, 54, 317. *See also* Asad, Hafiz al-; Asadism; revolution

Rough Draft (*Brūfā*) (Rosa Yaseen Hasan), 198–208. *See also* Hasan, Rosa Yaseen

ruination, 182, 324, 327–28, 412–13n20

Sa'ada, Antun, 27

Sacrifices (*Ṣundūq al-Dunyā*) (Mohammed), 119–29. *See also* masculinity; Mohammed, Ossama; violence

Sa'd al-Din, 'Adnan, 30–31, 46. *See also* political Islam

sadism, 47–48, 125–27, 221–22, 299–305. *See also* violence
Said, Joud, 323–28, 337–38, 395n110. See also *Homs Rain* (*Maṭar Ḥimṣ*); *Once Again* (*Marra Ukhrā*); ruination
Salamandra, Christa, 97–98, 112
Salti, Rasha, 128
Ṣamt wa-l-Ṣakhab, al- (Sirees). See *The Silence and the Roar*
Sarāyā al-Difāʿ (Defense Brigades), 31, 153–54, 332. *See also* Hama: 1982 massacres; Rifʿat al-Asad
Sarraj, ʿAbd al-Hamid al-, 28
Sarraj, Manhal al-, 413nn22, 27
satanic verses, the, 295, 302. *See also* ʿArafa, Mazin; *The Cranes* (*al-Gharānīq*)
satire, 22–23, 130–31, 133, 139–42, 151, 153, 160, 190, 197, 223, 240, 305, 315, 353n26, 383n42, 388n23. *See also* comedy; politics of comedy
Saudi Arabia, 341
Sayigh, Yezid, 57–58
Schiller, Friedrich: translation into Arabic, 354n34. *See also* aesthetics; translation
Schmid, Dorothée, 111
Scott, David, 130
Seale, Patrick, 45–46, 58, 167
sectarianism, 4–7 passim, 29, 31, 52, 118, 167, 187–88, 350–51n8, 366n35, 391n54, 414n34; Durayd Lahham on, 134–36; in *Enemy Syrians* (Haddad), 334–36, 414n34; in *In Her Mirrors* (Yazbek), 208, 210–13, 220–22; in *Night Shirt* (Sawsan Jamil Hasan), 286–87, 290–94, 406n66; in *Rough Draft* (Rosa Yaseen Hasan), 203–4. *See also* ʿAlawīs
secularism, 46, 135–37, 194, 294, 295, 319, 326–27
Sednaya prison, 31
seeing, 84, 184–89, 201, 209–10, 216–17, 222–24, 229–30, 249, 269, 293, 386n12. *See also* politics of the senses; sensory experience; the slow witness (slow witnessing); vision
Selim I, 221, 396n123. *See also* Ottoman Empire
sensory experience, 179–80, 184–89, 199–201, 224, 230, 247–49, 270–71, 293, 311, 391n58; *See also* listening; phenomenological politics; politics of the senses; seeing; sound; vision
Seurat, Michel, 29, 52, 56–57, 62, 359nn73, 74, 366n32, 367nn48, 49, 369n72
sex: sexual violence, 87, 113, 131, 215; sexuality, 84–113 passim, 116–17, 125, 182, 196, 202–3, 206, 225, 294–96, 302, 375–76n23; in *Ascension to Death* (*Miʿrāj al-Mawt*) (Azzam), 99, 101–5 passim; in The *Cranes* (*al-Gharānīq*) (ʿArafa), 276, 301–3; in *In Her Mirrors* (*Lahā Marāyā*) (Yazbek), 210, 221–22, 224; in *Nights of the Jackal* (*Layālī Ibn Awā*) (ʿAbd al-Hamid), 114, 117, 215–16; in *Sacrifices* (*Ṣundūq al-Dunyā*) (Mohammed), 124, 126–27, 129; in *Stars in Broad Daylight* (*Nujūm al-Nahār*)

(Mohammed), 130–31, 217. *See also* femininity; gender; masculinity; patriarchy
Shabaan, Buthaina, 263n4
shabbīḥa, 136, 170, 248, 287, 336. *See also* surveillance
Shafik, Viola, 128–29, 170, 371n109, 373n123, 381n13
Shahin, Muhammad, 73, 76–80, 89, 119, 132, 139, 337. *See also* alternative cinema (*al-sīnamā al-badīl*); *Cinema Life* (*al-Ḥayā al-Sīnamā'iyya*); Syria: National Film Organization
Shannon, Jonathan, 337
Shawqi, Ahmad, 268–69
Shaykh Salih al-ʿAli revolt, 210, 393–94n93
Shayya, Riyad, 11, 74, 104–14, 132, 139, 175, 216, 229–30, 236, 255, 309–10. See also *Al-Lajāt*; *al-laqṭa* ("the shot"); Mohammed, Ossama
Shīʿism, 187–88, 357–58n60, 396n123
Shishakli, Adib al-, 27
"shot, the," (*al-laqṭa*), 105, 216–19, 255–56. *See also* Mohammed, Ossama; Shayya, Riyad.
silence, 191–92. *See also* politics of silence
Silence and the Roar, The (*al-Ṣamt wa-l-Ṣakhab*) (Sirees), 48, 111, 153, 189–98, 221, 224–25, 262, 294–95, 297, 305, 385n10, 388n25. See also *mukhābarāt* novel; Sirees, Nihad
Silvered Water, Syria Self-Portrait (*Mā' al-Fiḍḍa*) (Mohammed and Bedirxan), 232, 252–61, 271. *See also* Bedirxan, Wiam Simav; Mohammed, Ossama
sīnamā al-badīl, al–. *See* alternative cinema
Sirees, Nihad, 111, 153, 180, 189–98, 224–25, 261–63, 273, 388nn24, 25. See also *The Silence and the Roar* (*al-Ṣamt wa-l-Ṣakhab*)
Six Day-War (1967), 10–11, 30, 63–64, 86, 114, 116, 130, 139, 286, 290, 321, 353n26, 370n80. *See also* Arab-Israeli conflict
Sloterdijk, Peter, 222–24
slow cinema, 105–6, 235–36. See also *Al-Lajāt*; cinema; Kadaan, Soudade; Shayya, Riyad
slow witness, the, (slow witnessing), 37–38, 232, 235–51, 260–67, 269, 271, 286. *See also* seeing; sensory experience; politics of witness
Social Market Economy, 33–34
socialism, 21, 29, 60–61, 147–48, 224, 315
socialist realism, 21–22, 63–64, 68–69, 79, 82–83, 86, 88, 96–97, 178, 189, 300, 312. See also *iltizām*; politics of literature; realism
solidarity, 2, 14, 17–19, 161, 163, 183, 186, 195, 201, 211–12, 230–33 passim, 254, 268–69, 293, 310–11, 314, 317, 410n4. *See also* aesthetics of solidarity; speaking-with (*mitsprechen*)
Sontag, Susan, 236, 264

sound, 111, 184–92, 196–97, 199–201, 216–17, 246–47, 272, 386n12. *See also* eavesdropping; listening; politics of sound; sensory experience; silence

Soviet Union, 74, 82–83, 88–89, 207, 316

speaking-for, 2, 14, 17–18, 317

speaking-to, 2, 14, 17–18, 186, 317, 401n67

speaking-with (*mitsprechen*), 37–38, 183, 228, 232–33, 236, 246, 253–54, 258, 311, 384–85n6

spectatorship, 84, 86, 105–6, 117, 128–29, 142–43, 217, 236–37, 253–54, 264, 318–20. *See also* cinema; documentary film; filmmaking

speed, 227, 231–36, 241–42, 248, 249, 252, 261–67, 398n13. *See also* the slow witness (slow witnessing); Wedeen, Lisa: on high-speed eventfulness

Stacher, Joshua, 7, 33, 352nn17, 18, 19, 361n84

Stars in Broad Daylight (*Nujūm al-Nahār*) (Mohammed), 107–8, 119–24, 127, 129, 186, 215–19, 252, 395n110. *See also* Mohammed, Ossama

Stasi (Ministerium für Staatsicherheit), 185, 207–8, 390n50. *See also* German Democratic Republic; *The Lives of Others* (*Das Leben der Anderen*) (von Donnersmarck); surveillance

state, the, 1–2, 7, 11, 14, 18–21, 35–37, 44, 54, 59–62, 76, 81, 87–88, 152, 163, 168–69, 184–85, 199, 201, 203, 224–26, 304–5, 328, 336, 339, 363–64n8; Syria as a Bonapartist state, 28, 30; Syria as a corporatist state, 4, 6, 30, 33, 51, 62; Syria as a fierce state, 30. *See also* ideological state apparatuses (ISAs) (Althusser)

state security services. See *mukhābarāt*; *shabbīḥa*; surveillance

Statement of 99 (2000), 33, 188–89

suffering: representation of, 235–36, 269, 270–71, 274, 328

suicide: in *End of a Brave Man* (*Nihāyat Rajul Shujāʿ*) (Mina) 96–99, 276–77; in *In Her Mirrors* (*Lahā Marāyā*) (Yazbek), 219–21

Sulayman, Nabil, 63–64, 336, 206, 222, 263, 406n66: and Bu ʿAli Yasin on Syrian literature, 63–64, 370n81, 375n12; on *Enemy Syrians* (*al-Sūriyyūn al-Aʿdāʾ*) (Haddad), 336; on *In Her Mirrors* (*Lahā Marāyā*) (Yazbek), 222; on *Rough Draft* (*Brūfā*) (Rosa Yaseen Hasan), 206; on sectarianism, 336, 406n66. See also *Ideology and Literature in Syria, 1967–1973* (*al-Aydiyūlūjīyā wa-l-Adab fī Sūriya, 1967–1973*) (Sulayman and Yasin); *Cultural Battles in Syria, 1975–1977* (*Maʿārik Thaqāfiyya fī Sūriya, 1975–1977*) (Sulayman and Yasin)

Suleiman, Elia, 138

"A Summary of What Happened to Muhammad al-Mahmudi" ("Mulakhkhaṣ mā Jāra li-Muḥammad al-Maḥmūdī") (Tamir), 223. *See also* Tamir, Zakariya

Sundance Film Festival, 328

Ṣundūq al-Dunyā (Mohammed). See *Sacrifices*
Sūriyyūn al-Aʿdā', al- (Haddad). See *Enemy Syrians*
surrealist cinema (Mohammed), 256–57
surveillance, 35, 171, 181, 184–89, 223–26, 230, 252, 387n16, 390n50, 392n73, 395n110; in *The Extras* (*al-Kūmbārs*) (Maleh), 181–84; in *In Her Mirrors* (*Lahā Marāyā*) (Yazbek), 208, 210–12, 222; in *Rough Draft* (*Brūfā*) (Rosa Yaseen Hasan), 198–208; in *Stars in Broad Daylight* (*Nujūm al-Nahār*) (Mohammed), 214–19. *See also* eavesdropping; listening; politics of surveillance
Suwayda, 99, 104
Suwaylih, Khalil, 107, 110–13, 206, 327, 412n16. See also *Barbarians' Paradise* (*Jannat al-Barābira*)
synesthesia, 199–200, 293
Syria: armed forces, 30, 40, 51–59, 62–63, 116–17, 125–27, 152, 167, 194, 200–3, 263–64, 324–27, 337, 366nn31, 35; Ministry of Culture and National Guidance, 19, 64, 73–76, 121–22, 316, 323, 363n4; National Film Organization (al-Mu'assasa al-ʿĀmma li-l-Sīnamā, l'Organisme général du cinéma), 4, 14, 20, 71–79, 104–5, 112, 114, 119, 121–22, 132, 140, 144, 186, 314–15, 319–20, 322–24, 338, 372n120; nationalism, 3, 7, 10, 21–22, 26–30, 34–35, 43, 54–56, 58, 62, 64, 74–76, 81, 143, 163, 210, 339, 393–94n93; patriotism, 55–56, 60, 62, 76, 85–86, 114, 138, 168, 199, 220, 316, 325–26, 328; political prisoners, 184, 198, 256, 332–33
Syria War, 37, 38–39, 134–37, 223, 227–67 passim, 269–94 passim, 299, 305–13 passim, 314–15, 322, 323–28, 337–41 passim
Syrian Revolution (2011–), 37–39, 135–37, 182, 186–87, 227–70, 273, 280, 292–93, 312, 322, 325, 335, 337, 404n15
Syrian Social Nationalist Party (SSNP), 27
Syrian Writers' Association (Rābiṭat al-Kuttāb al-Sūriyyīn), 329, 337
Syrian Writers' Collective (Rābiṭāt al-Kuttāb al-Sūriyyīn), 88

Tadié, Alexis, 19–20
Tadmor (Palmyra) prison, 31, 332
Tait, Sue, 260–61, 274, 285
Taleghani, Shareah, 320, 375n18, 387n16, 389n42, 411n10
Tamir, Zakariya, 61, 65, 66, 68, 84, 89, 130–31, 144, 189, 223, 357n52, 368n63, 374n1, 379n87, 397n133. See also *Empire of Ghawar*; "Men"; "A Summary of What Happened to Muhammad al-Mahmudi"; "Waiting for a Woman"
Taqrīr, al- (Lahham). See *The Report*
temporality, 124–25, 220, 228–32, 235, 252, 255, 265–66, 273, 275–76. *See also* speed; time
testimony, 183, 227–28, 235–36, 246–47, 252, 271, 324. *See also* politics of witness; the slow witness (slow witnessing)

Theory of the Novel, The (Lukács), 69–70, 265–66. *See also* ideology; Lukács, Georg; the novel; politics of literature
Third Worldism, 2, 22–23, 27, 43, 60, 76–77, 85–86, 356n51
Tierney-Tello, Mary Beth, 22–23
time, 37–38, 124–27, 159, 197, 227, 229, 230–37 passim, 247, 255, 260, 263–66, 271, 273, 292, 307–8. *See also* eternity; speed; temporality
Tishrīn, 243, 388n23
Tizini, Tayyib, 33, 60, 89, 336–37, 368nn60, 61, 62
Tlas, Mustafa, 42, 54–57, 59, 62
torture, 117, 172, 184, 189–90, 210–13 passim, 224, 248, 250, 252, 260, 280, 303, 307, 332–34
totalitarianism, 5–8, 20, 80, 181, 185, 187–89, 229–30, 351nn9, 13. *See also* Arendt, Hannah; authoritarianism
tragedy, 177–78, 242, 293, 330
translation, 80, 192–93, 277, 354n34, 365n18, 389n42, 390n45, 400n41, 405n38, 414–15n39
transmigration of souls (metempsychosis), 203–4, 209, 220–21. *See also* ʿAlawīs
trauma, 242, 251–52, 330–31
Treasonous Translator, The (*al-Mutarjim al-Khāʾin*) (Haddad), 192–93. *See also* Haddad, Fawwaz
Ṭubūl al-Ḥubb (Maha Hasan). See *Drums of Love*
tyranny, 41–42, 180, 201, 336, 391n58

ʿUjayli, ʿAbd al-Salam al-, 63, 70
Union of Soviet Socialist Republics (USSR), 74, 82–83, 88–89, 207, 316
United Arab Republic, 28, 30, 58
United States: invasion of Iraq, 34
Urang, John Griffith, 207–8, 211

vanguardism, 3–4, 45, 55–56, 58–59, 60–61, 65–68, 76–79, 88–89, 131, 292, 318–20. *See also* Asadist-Baʿthist cultural revolution; avant-gardism; commitment; *iltizām*
Vargas Llosa, Mario, 385n10
violence, 253, 355n41, 367n52, 403n10; aestheticization of, 248, 271, 285; Ghawar and, 142, 147–48, 150–51, 153–54; Hannah Arendt on, 274–75; and masculinity, 99–104 passim, 114, 116–17, 119–29, 276; sacralized, 293; sexual, 87, 94, 113, 120–21, 131, 215, 221–22, 224; and representation, 20–21, 38, 184–89, 223–25, 236–37, 248, 260–61, 268–313 passim, 323–38, 355n41, 409n133. *See also* masculinity; *On Violence* (Arendt); patriarchy
Virilio, Paul, 227, 398n13
vision, 119, 187, 210, 217–19, 222–26, 249, 394–95n105. *See also* mirrors; politics of vision; seeing; sensory experience; the slow witness (slow witnessing)

"Waiting for a Woman" ("Intiẓār Imra'a") (Tamir), 131. *See also* Tamir, Zakariya
Wallon, Henri, 394–95n105
Walzer, Michael, 5–6, 351n9
Wannous, Dima, 206, 390n50, 392n75
Wannous, Sa'dallah, 11, 66, 189, 315. See also *Everyday Life in a Syrian Village*
war, 45, 89, 125–27, 167, 236–37; Cold War, 27, 340–41; Lebanese Civil War (1975–1990), 232–33; October War (1973), 10, 41, 89, 321, 325; Six-Day War (1967), 10–11, 30, 63–64, 86, 114, 116, 130, 139, 286, 290, 321, 353n26, 370n80; Syria War, 37, 38–39, 134–37, 223, 227–67 passim, 269–94 passim, 299, 305–13 passim, 314–15, 322, 323–28, 337–41 passim; U.S. invasion of Iraq (2003), 34; World War I, 210; World War II, 10, 94, 412n16.
War Literature (*Adab al-Ḥarb*) (Mina and al-'Attar), 61, 89, 375n12. *See also* al-'Attar, Najah; Mina, Hanna; politics of literature
Wayne, Mike, 17
Wedeen, Lisa, 18, 23, 43, 45, 225, 230, 380n8; on "acting 'as if,'" 23, 55, 183, 363–64n8; on *The Extras* (*al-Kūmbārs*), 182–83; on high-speed eventfulness, 235–36; on neoliberal autocracy, 34; on *Once Again* (*Marra Ukhrā*) (Said), 395n110; on *The Report* (*al-Taqrīr*) (Lahham) 170, 173; on *Silvered Water, Syria Self-Portrait* (*Mā' al-Fiḍḍa*) (Mohammad and Bedirxan) 401n67; on tolerated parodies, 140–41, 175
witness-narrator, 236, 245–46, 252–58 passim, 260, 265–66, 286, 296
witnessing, 37–38, 237, 240–47 passim, 260–61, 264–66, 269, 286, 289–90, 292–93, 296, 311–12. *See also* politics of witness; the slow witness (slow witnessing)
A Woman in the Crossfire: Diaries of the Syrian Revolution (*Taqāṭu' Nīrān*) (Yazbek), 227–29, 252. *See also* Yazbek, Samar
world literature, 22–23, 178, 356n51, 380n5
writing, 46–51, 63–71, 81, 89, 91, 187–90, 206–7, 222, 224–26, 228, 232–37, 238–39, 261–65, 270–72, 329–30, 337–38, 369n77, 385n10, 390n45, 392n73, 399n16, 405n23. *See also* commitment and literature; *iltizām*; literature; the novel; politics of literature

Yasin, Bu 'Ali, 63–64, 370n81, 375n12. See also *Ideology and Literature in Syria, 1967–1973* (*al-Aydiyūlūjīyā wa-l-Adab fī Sūriya, 1967–1973*) (Sulayman and Yasin); *Cultural Battles in Syria, 1975–1977* (*Ma'ārik Thaqāfiyya fī Sūriya, 1975–1977*) (Sulayman and Yasin)

Yawm Aḍ'atu Ẓillī (Kaadan). See *The Day I Lost My Shadow*
Yazbek, Samar, 35, 180, 188, 208, 224, 227–29, 393nn84, 85. *See also* 'Alawīs; gender; heterotopia; *In Her Mirrors* (*Lahā Marāyā*); mirrors; surveillance; *A Woman in the Crossfire* (*Taqāṭu' Nīrān*)
Yom Kippur War (1973), 10, 41, 89, 321, 325
Yugoslav Wars, 270, 412n16

Za'im, Husni al-, 27
Zarzur, Faris, 63, 70
Ziter, Edward, 154, 383n42
Žižek, Slavoj, 5–6, 176, 197, 351n10, 383n40, 389n37

Stanford Studies in Middle Eastern and Islamic Societies and Cultures

Joel Beinin and Laleh Khalili, editors

Street-Level Governing: Negotiating the State in Urban Turkey 2022
ELISE MASSICARD

Protesting Jordan: Geographies of Power and Dissent 2022
JILLIAN SCHWEDLER

Media of the Masses: Cassette Culture in Modern Egypt 2022
ANDREW SIMON

States of Subsistence: The Politics of Bread in Contemporary Jordan 2022
JOSÉ CIRO MARTÍNEZ

Between Dreams and Ghosts: Indian Migration and Middle Eastern Oil 2021
ANDREA WRIGHT

Bread and Freedom: Egypt's Revolutionary Situation 2021
MONA EL-GHOBASHY

Paradoxes of Care: Children and Global Medical Aid in Egypt 2021
RANIA KASSAB SWEIS

The Politics of Art: Dissent and Cultural Diplomacy in Lebanon, Palestine, and Jordan 2021
HANAN TOUKAN

The Paranoid Style in American Diplomacy: Oil and Arab Nationalism in Iraq 2021
BRANDON WOLFE-HUNNICUTT

Screen Shots: State Violence on Camera in Israel and Palestine 2021
REBECCA L. STEIN

Dear Palestine: A Social History of the 1948 War 2021
SHAY HAZKANI

A Critical Political Economy of the Middle East and North Africa 2020
JOEL BEININ, BASSAM HADDAD, AND SHERENE SEIKALY, EDITORS

Showpiece City: How Architecture Made Dubai 2020
TODD REISZ

Archive Wars: The Politics of History in Saudi Arabia 2020
ROSIE BSHEER

Between Muslims: Religious Difference in Iraqi Kurdistan 2020
J. ANDREW BUSH

The Optimist: A Social Biography of Tawfiq Zayyad 2020
TAMIR SOREK

Graveyard of Clerics: Everyday Activism in Saudi Arabia 2020
PASCAL MENORET

Cleft Capitalism: The Social Origins of Failed Market Making in Egypt 2020
AMR ADLY

The Universal Enemy: Jihad, Empire, and the Challenge of Solidarity 2019
DARRYL LI

Waste Siege: The Life of Infrastructure in Palestine 2019
SOPHIA STAMATOPOULOU-ROBBINS

Heritage and the Cultural Struggle for Palestine 2019
CHIARA DE CESARI

Iran Reframed: Anxieties of Power in the Islamic Republic 2019
NARGES BAJOGHLI

Banking on the State: The Financial Foundations of Lebanon 2019
HICHAM SAFIEDDINE